PORTRAIT OF THE FREE STATE

A History of Maryland

PORTRAIT

OF

THE FREE STATE

A History of Maryland

By

DONALD MARQUAND DOZER

*Sometime Lecturer on
The History of Maryland, University of Maryland;
Professor of History, University of California, Santa Barbara*

TIDEWATER PUBLISHERS
CAMBRIDGE, MARYLAND
1976

Copyright © 1976, by Tidewater Publishers

All Rights Reserved

No part of this book may be used or reproduced in any manner whatsoever without written permission except in the case of brief quotations embodied in critical articles and reviews. For information address Tidewater Publishers, Cambridge, Maryland 21613

Library of Congress Cataloging in Publication Data

Dozer, Donald Marquand.
    Portrait of the Free State.

    Includes bibliographies and index.
    1. Maryland--History. I. Title.
F181.D65   975.2   76—47023
ISBN 0—87033—226-0

Shown on title page is the official symbol of the Maryland Bicentennial Commission, sponsor of the writing of this book.

Title page designed by G. William Kirschenhofer; printed and bound in the United States of America by Universal Lithographers, Inc., Cockeysville, Maryland and Optic Bindery, Glen Burnie, Maryland.

CONTENTS

Chapter		Page
	Foreword	ix
	Preface	xi
I	Where and Who?	1
II	Preparation for a New Colony	20
III	The Founding	33
IV	Challenges	50
V	Impact of the English Civil War	74
VI	Maryland Under the Commonwealth	94
VII	Domestic Problems and Boundary Controversies	110
VIII	A New Proprietor	129
IX	A Royal Province	142
X	Political Crosscurrents	168
XI	Tidewater and Westward Expansion	193
XII	An Uncooperative Colony	212
XIII	War for Independence	235
XIV	Maryland Under the Articles of Confederation	262
XV	A State in the New Union	290
XVI	Religious and Cultural Happenings	302
XVII	A Star-Spangled War	319
XVIII	Jacksonian Democracy in Maryland	341
XIX	New Ventures in Transportation	362
XX	Financial and Constitutional Crises	389
XXI	Prelude to Civil Conflict	415
XXII	The Brothers' War	435
XXIII	A Painful Reconciliation	466
XXIV	Economic Growth	493
XXV	The Seesaw of Politics	514
XXVI	Education and Recreation	542
XXVII	Maryland in World War II	561
XXVIII	The Free State in the Bicentennial Year	573
XXIX	Trends into the Future	590

Appendices
  Names and Origins of Counties 608
  Proprietors and Governors of Maryland 609
  Sites of Major Presidential Nominating Conventions . 613
  Maryland, My Maryland! 614
  Check List of Maryland County Histories 615
Index 617

Dedicated to our children
Charles Scott, Jane Blythe, and Hilary Marquand
Children of Old Maryland

FOREWORD

As one of the Thirteen Original Colonies, Maryland has a unique heritage and tradition that stretches back to its founding in 1634.

During the Bicentennial Era, the Maryland Bicentennial Commission has helped sponsor and encourage the development of historic works which would contribute to people's basic knowledge of our founding documents and historic events. The Commission regarded this as a singularly important educational goal for the benefit of future generations.

Dr. Donald Marquand Dozer has written such a history. He has developed the fullest possible portrait about our heritage—its cultural, political, economic, social and intellectual dynamics. He has drawn upon every practicable source of Marylandia, oral and written. He has utilized information from the archives and historical records.

As a consequence, his history contains a most comprehensive, readable record of the State's progress through the centuries. Students of all ages and all walks of life can learn from it, and they can draw strength and inspiration towards better understanding the need for working together to preserve our Freedoms.

The Maryland Bicentennial Commission is privileged indeed to have assisted in the final preparations of this modern record about "America in Miniature"—Maryland.

MARYLAND BICENTENNIAL COMMISSION

PREFACE

This book is the life history of a state, the state of Maryland, not the largest nor yet the smallest in the United States but one which presents a unique biography. Because of the territorial expansion of the United States, Maryland is no longer one-thirteenth of the whole as it was at the time of the adoption of the Articles of Confederation in 1781, nor is it one-thirty-sixth as it was at the end of the Civil War in 1865, but it is now only one out of fifty or two percent of the numerical total of the states of the federal union.

This history begins with the first founding of an English colony in America in the early seventeenth century. In the procession of the seasons almost three and a half hundred years have passed since Lord Baltimore's first colonists arrived in Maryland and two hundred years since the colony of Maryland became a state in the American Union.

Maryland's history has been called "a maze of contradictions," but what honest history is not just that, dealing as it must with people and with their complicated human nature? The experience of Maryland, first as a colony and then as a state in the American Union, reveals distinctions which differentiate it from all other states and which make its story well worth telling and retelling. Intermingling high purpose, bitter rivalry, sectional discord, political manipulation, class violence, story and legend, and withal much constructive effort, this record helps to explain Maryland's present position in the nation and the world, the attitudes of its people, and many of the problems that currently face them in this twentieth century.

Maryland suggests a panorama of Chesapeake Bay with its oystering and its water sports, of famous old eighteenth-century manor houses, of the busy port of Baltimore, of the lush wheat fields and orchards of the Piedmont Plateau, of the picturesque "Narrows" at Cumberland, and of the mountaintop vistas seen from Negro Mountain and Savage Mountain overlooking the valleys of western Maryland. Beginning at sandy beaches laved by the waters of the Atlantic Ocean, Maryland stretches inland to the high peaks of the Alleghenies, and is separated from Pennsylvania on the north by the famous Mason-Dixon line and from Virginia and West Virginia on the south by the Potomac River for its entire length. Within those bounds dwells the Maryland spirit, which is characterized by tolerance, facility in compromise, self-assurance, and a humorous appreciation of life.

Do state boundaries still have any significance in the general pattern of the history of the United States? The historian's task, it is claimed, is no longer to "glorify the fictitious distinctions" between one state and another but rather to "explain the natural inter-relationships and acculturation between places and peoples." In response, it may be pointed out that the persistence and indeed the proliferation of state and local historical societies attest the continuing concern of our people with the history of their own localities. Interest in local history has seemingly not abated despite the increasing attention that is being given to the outreaching actions of the United States beyond its own borders. Almost every town and hamlet has its local antiquarian, who in some cases may be only a "memory" man cherishing and recording local legend or in others may be accumulating and preserving data indispensable to an ultimate estimate of the American mind, for the American life-style can be known in its fullest sense only through a study of the way it has expressed itself in the daily living of the people. In their behavior at the local level will be found the essence of our national history, imparting to it the fundamental quality of American life.

More often than not, people live primarily in and for their locality rather than in a generalized regional cultural milieu or as members of an international community. Without discounting the influences that cross state boundaries, due allowance must be made for the fact that in the neighborhood citizens still find their most abundant opportunities for enjoying the durable satisfactions of individual and family living. This is particularly true of Maryland, an area rich in tradition and in local self-consciousness, which now, however, is threatened with absorption into a gigantic modern megalopolis.

The writer of local history must know how to integrate the specific history of the local area into the broader history of the times and of the nation and to preserve the local character in its relative setting without reducing the locality to an amorphous entity in a regional or national complex. In telling the story of Maryland I have sought to strike an optimum balance between the two, for though Maryland has been in and of the nation, it has been sadly torn between conflicting elements in the nation and has cherished throughout its history a tenacious regard for its rights as a separate entity. Here, in other words, is a state that displays character in its own right.

This is a history, not an encyclopedia. It aims not at the presentation of all the facts and names in Maryland's past but at the telling of a story so balanced that no one facet is given undue primacy over other facets and no single individual is accorded more than his due share of space,

Preface

praise, or censure. For this reason it has been necessary to omit mention of many community celebrities in Maryland's past who, though they may have become a part of local fame and legend, cannot be said to loom large in the broader perspective of the state.

Nor is this an official history despite its sponsorship by the Maryland Bicentennial Commission on the American Revolution. An official history of a free society can never be written, for in such a society the facts are open to anyone and everyone and are susceptible of widely varying interpretations. In a free society history cannot be frozen as bureaucratic truth.

My own family roots are deeply sunk in the Free State of Maryland, originating in a John Adams who came from England and settled in Charles County in 1700. Both my maternal and my paternal ancestors had many connections with Maryland, as well as with Virginia, before establishing my own branch of the family in southeastern Ohio in the early nineteenth century. By a happy chance I was later enabled to offer courses in the history of Maryland at the University of Maryland. For this encouragement to delve more deeply into this field of history I offer appreciative acknowledgment to the late Professors Hayes Baker-Crothers and Wesley M. Gewehr of the Department of History, University of Maryland, and, for generous and invaluable assistance in the delving, to the late Mr. James W. Foster, head of the Maryland Department of the Enoch Pratt Free Library in Baltimore and later Director of the Maryland Historical Society. To the present head of the Maryland Department in the Enoch Pratt Free Library, Dr. Morgan H. Pritchett and his staff, particularly Mrs. Marjorie B. Jones, Miss Mary C. Kennedy, and Miss Ann M. Peters, all of whom served as willing and patient quasi-collaborators in the final preparation of this book, I owe an unpayable debt of gratitude. The Maryland Department's incomparable collection of Marylandiana was indispensable, and the reference assistance of that Department as well as of the entire Library staff under its Director, Mr. Ernest Siegel, has shown a higher and better-informed sense of public service than this author has found in any other library.

I am profoundly grateful for the interest and the support given to this *Portrait of The Free State* by the Honorable Louise Gore, chairman, and by all the other members of the Maryland Bicentennial Commission on the American Revolution, especially the members of its Heritage Committee, Dr. Raymond O. McCullough, Dr. Isaiah A. Woodward, and Mrs. Eleanora Lynn, and the Executive Director of the Commission, General Clair C. Hutchin, Jr., U.S. Army, ret. Their constructive leadership in the celebration of the two-hundredth birthday of both the United States and Maryland, deserves the commendation of every Marylander.

For help in the preparation of the later chapters of this book, grateful mention should be made of officials of the Baltimore Chamber of Commerce, the Maryland Port Administration, the Greater Baltimore Committee, the Charles Center-Inner Harbor Management, Inc., the Baltimore Department of Housing and Community Development, the Maryland State Department of Transportation, the Maryland State Department of Employment and Social Services, the Baltimore Regional Planning Council, and the Maryland State Department of Economic and Community Development.

My especial thanks are due to Mrs. Isabella Hayes, of the Maryland Room, McKeldin Library, University of Maryland, for her assistance in locating and supplying essential research materials, and to my typist, Mrs. Pauline Mills, who prepared the manuscript in final form for publication. My gratitude to my wife, Alice Scott Dozer, for her support has already been expressed at other times and in other ways. Our daughter, Jane, has been most helpful with her advice on precise phraseology. For us and our family this book represents a true labor of love, reflecting our gratitude for long years of happy living in the Free State of Maryland and our affection for it.

DONALD MARQUAND DOZER

PORTRAIT OF THE FREE STATE

A History of Maryland

CHAPTER I
WHERE AND WHO?

Maryland is often called America in miniature. Its history broadly parallels the entire national experience, and it has fully shared the problems and the joys of that experience.

Situated midway along the Atlantic coastal area of the United States, Maryland is a middle-border state. Its northern boundary—the famous Mason-Dixon line—divided the free states of the North from the slave states of the South in the slavery controversy. Today it separates the Middle Atlantic states from the South Atlantic states. To this latter group of nine states, including the District of Columbia and extending southward to the Gulf of Mexico, Maryland belongs. Among those states, barring the District of Columbia, Maryland ranks seventh in area and fifth in population, according to the census of 1970. Though among all the states in the Union it stands forty-second in area, it is nevertheless larger than any one of the New England states except Maine.

The present eastern boundary of Maryland runs from a point on Chincoteague Bay slightly north of the 38th parallel of latitude along the Atlantic Ocean to the southern border of Delaware at 38 degrees and 27 minutes, thence west to the meridian of longitude 75 degrees and 42 minutes, and thence north following the western edge of Delaware to the parallel 39 degrees and 44 minutes, which forms the southern boundary of Pennsylvania. Along this parallel—the Mason-Dixon line—the entire northern boundary of Maryland runs. At the meridian of longitude 79 degrees and 30 minutes the western boundary of Maryland begins and runs directly southward to the headwaters of the northern branch of the Potomac River. The southern boundary of the state follows the southern bank of the Potomac River east to Smith's Point on Chesapeake Bay, crosses the Bay through Tangier Sound and the estuary of the Pocomoke River, and meets the Atlantic Ocean on Chincoteague Bay near the 38th parallel.

Of Maryland's 12,303 square miles almost one-fifth is water—a higher ratio of water to land than that of almost any other state. This is one of the determining factors in Maryland's history and helps to explain the long-continued maritime activity of her people. Chesapeake Bay with a water area of 1,726 square miles is the largest inlet on the Atlantic coast of the United States and measures 185 miles in length and from three to thirty miles in width. Over its broad surface, sometimes roughened by seasonal storms, ply ore boats from Venezuela, ocean liners bound for ports in England and the Mediterranean, and unnumbered skiffs, shallops, schooners, sloops, bugeyes, and dories. The Bay and the Atlantic Ocean account for the equable climate of eastern Maryland which in general is free from great extremes of heat and cold.

The variety of Maryland's surface features and the location of its bodies of water account for the fact that spring comes to the eastern part of the state about a month earlier than it comes to the western part. As a result the growing season for many crops varies from 230 days in the eastern to only 130 days in the western part of the state. Maryland's geographical position in the direct route of storms coming from both the southeast and the Great Lakes region gives it a rainfall which is quite adequate to the needs of agriculture and commerce. The annual precipitation in the state varies, according to localities, from 25 to 55 inches, with an annual average of 40.9 inches. The prevailing winds in Maryland blow from the west, but in summer they often come from the south.[1]

In diversity of climate and in topography the state reproduces on a small scale the characteristics of the nation. It rises from the sandbars along the Atlantic Ocean and the low-lying plains of the Eastern Shore to the high western mountains, which reach an elevation of 3,340 feet above the sea at the summit of Backbone Mountain. The surface of Maryland is divided into three distinct physiographic areas: (1) the Coastal Plain of southern and eastern Maryland, which is low and level, (2) the Piedmont Plateau which extends from the fall line of the rivers into north central Maryland and which is a rolling, hilly terrain, and (3) the Appalachian region of western Maryland, which is mountainous. Each of these regions has its own physiographic characteristics influencing the social habits, the economic activities, and the general complexion of the life of the people dwelling there.

The Coastal Plain comprises the region that extends from the Delaware Bay and the Atlantic Ocean westward to the fall line of the rivers and southward to the mouths of the Potomac and Pocomoke Rivers. It is the largest of the three great physiographic divisions, including over half the land area of the state. The surface of this region is a broad, low, nearly level plain inclined slightly toward the ocean. Its eastern edge, the Atlantic shoreline, consists of barrier beaches which have been thrown up by the ocean waves and enclose behind them lagoons, such as Chincoteague Bay and Assawoman Bay. This Coastal Plain is divided by the Chesapeake Bay into two separate regions—the Eastern Shore and the more elevated western region, which is known as Southern Maryland. This Bay, stretching almost entirely across the state from north to south is a "drowned" river bed representing a continuation of the Susquehanna River, which now empties into the head of the Bay. The river originally extended south to Cape Henry, but as the entire Coastal Plain sank the river bed itself was submerged. Similarly, other rivers including the Potomac, Patuxent, Patapsco, Severn, Gunpowder, Elk, and Choptank, which were formerly branches of the Susquehanna, were "drowned" and as they drowned formed the present wide estuaries at their mouths. The numerous bays and estuaries in Maryland's saltwater system make its coastline one of the longest of any state in the Union.

The principal occupations of the people of the Coastal Plain are agriculture, canning, fishing, and food preparation. The Eastern Shore, an area of sandy loam, has an equable climate, abundant rainfall, and a long growing season extending from early April to the end of October. It is one of the most productive farming sections in the United States for small fruits and vegetables. In the early years of tobacco culture the Eastern Shore specialized in this crop, but its tobacco production gradually declined and disappeared entirely because of soil exhaustion, poor marketing conditions, and the priorities given to fruit and truck crops. These latter agricultural specialties of the Eastern Shore include strawberries, peaches, pears, asparagus, corn, cucumbers, watermelons, cantaloupes, peas, beans, white and sweet potatoes, wheat, and tomatoes. Here the canning and freezing of these crops is a main industry. Dairying and poultry farming are also big business on the Eastern Shore, and the cutting of timber, particularly pine, and the manufacture of forest products provide a livelihood for many residents of the lower Eastern Shore counties. Near Preston in Caroline County the Linchester grist mill, which was originally built in 1681, still grinds the grain from neighboring farms with water power from Hunting Creek and is credited with being the oldest continuously operated industry in the entire nation.

Crabs and lobsters, as well as various varieties of fish, are important commercial and sport resources of Eastern Maryland. Hard-shell clams are found in the lower part of the Chesapeake Bay but are more abundant in Chincoteague and Sinepuxent Bays along the Atlantic shores than in the Chesapeake. Soft-shell clams (mananose) are found throughout the Chesapeake waters but have been commercially exploited only since 1951 when the invention of a hydraulic escalator dredge made it possible to harvest them economically. The Chesapeake Bay watermen make their living from the waters of the Bay, by clamming, which is done year-round, crabbing from April to December, oystering, which has a legal season from September through March, commercial fishing in the winter and spring, and sport-fishing with vacation parties from July to September. But in all these employments their fortunes depend upon the vicissitudes of the weather, the demands of the market, and the whims of vacationers. Virtually living on the water in times of full employment the Eastern Shore fishermen disdain to "go up through land," as they say, to get a different kind of job. Their faces reddened and the hairs on their muscular arms bleached white by the sun, they still represent the independent Maryland way of life.

Some of Maryland's eastern oyster towns have changed little in a century and a half. The Eastern Shore gives the impression of another day and another age. Though it is flanked on the north and west by industrial metropolises it has retained its rural and maritime character. There is a way of life here that is not centered around money, social classes, or education. Rather it emphasizes independence, relaxed living, and helpful concern for one's neighbors. The population of its largest city, Salisbury, numbered only a little more than 15,000 in 1970. But Cambridge, the county seat of Dorchester County, has dredged its harbor to accommodate large ocean vessels and has become the largest deepwater seaport on the Delmarva Peninsula (Delaware, Maryland, Virginia) and Maryland's second most important cargo seaport after Baltimore.

The vast majority of Eastern Shoremen still draw their living from the fields and waters. A favorite song of the fishermen as they unload their catch ends with the haunting refrain sung in a minor key:

Oh, a hundred years
Ain't a very long time
On the Eastern Sho!

Here the traces of early English settlement have lingered longest. Chestertown, perhaps the most traditionalist of the Eastern Shore settlements, still reflects an English atmosphere. The older residents adhere to the habit of the afternoon tea, and they still speak of the custom house "green" and the court house "green." As late as 1910 ninety-two percent of the 200,000 white inhabitants of the Eastern Shore were native born, of native parents, and in most cases came of old English stock.

Eastern Shoremen are culturally unique, independent, and clannish. "Everybody on the Shore," they explain, "is everybody else's tenth cousin." Their colloquial expressions include "It certainly is a pretty day, certain." They refer to the equinoctial season with its heavy rainfall and colder weather as "Sarvis Winter," because then the wild sarvis bush generally blossoms. They call the local cuckoo a "rain crow." Some call the muskrat a "mushrat," others a "marshrabbit." A stream or creek is called a "branch." People are referred to by their first names, Mis' Mary and Mis' Betty, Mister Tommy and Mister Joe—never Mrs. Smith and Mr. Nichols. In a usage long antedating the modern insistence upon Ms, both married and unmarried women are called Mis' Myrtle and Mis' Ruth even though they may have been married for a quarter century.

Here the pace of life is unhurried and peaceful. The towns have a sleepy look, particularly on Sundays and on weekdays after eight o'clock in the evening. The natives are genial, good-humored, and easygoing. They refer to those who are reared elsewhere as "outlanders." Outlanders are usually made welcome, but they never feel admitted into the "clan" nor are they ever accepted as "kinfolk." The women have a way of cooking all their own. Their specialties include peas served in their own soup with dumplings, fried chicken, oyster fritters, terrapin and crab dishes, Maryland beaten biscuits, and corn bread which is "better than wedding cake." The men regardless of occupation are passionately fond of sports, particularly fishing, hunting, and "ducking." Men and women are neighborly but curious about strangers and neighborhood doings; but after they have helped gossip to run its course they accept the offender again in the same stratum of society as before. A common saying is "Use what you have 'round about, make it do or do without." Sometimes it takes a bit of doing to "make it do." Eastern Shoremen guide their lives by superstition, which is, however, often based on common sense. In their planting they follow the phases of the moon. They do not plant corn until the leaves of the oak tree are as large as squirrel ears. They hesitate to start a new venture on Friday. A common saying is that if you start a new dress on Friday you will not live to wear it out. The same is deemed to apply to other undertakings, such as starting a paint job or moving to a new location. The Eastern Shore is a truly distinctive part of Maryland, but it is being hastened into modernity by the increasing traffic over the Chesapeake Bay Bridge connecting Annapolis with Kent Island and by the opening of the Chesapeake Bay Bridge-Tunnel in 1964 connecting the capes of the Chesapeake Bay. This latter bridge-tunnel complex, 17.65 miles in length, eliminated the last water barrier on the Ocean Hiway between New York and Florida and has put the entire Delmarva Peninsula on this main north-south highway route.

On the Coastal Plain of the Western Shore and in Southern Maryland, the climate and soils are similar to those on the Eastern Shore. The same crops are raised, but in Southern Maryland the principal crop is tobacco. It has formed the staple agricultural product of this area since early colonial times. After the fully grown tobacco plants are harvested in early fall they are air-dried in partially open tobacco sheds for from five to eight weeks and are then auctioned off to the highest bidders, mostly for the manufacture of cigarettes.

The importance of Southern Maryland in relation to other sections has declined since Lord Baltimore's colony began there in 1634. Comprising St. Mary's, Charles, Calvert, Prince George's and Anne Arundel Counties it shows the effects of three centuries of soil attrition caused by intensive cultivation of tobacco and by water run-off. These five counties produce practically all the tobacco crop of the state and constitute the Tobacco Belt of Maryland. Interspersed among the patches of growing tobacco and the unpainted tobacco sheds are fields of stunted corn and wheat and rows of ancient cedars serving as windbreaks. Fields long since abandoned have grown up with groves of willow oak, sycamore, pine, mulberry, and sassafras, enmeshed in an underbrush of sumac, dogwood, redbud, and colorful trumpet vines. Old plantation homes fronting on the rivers maintain themselves in decayed grandeur as survivals of an earlier age. Their Georgian lines and the large size of the slow-growing holly trees on their sloping lawns denote their antiquity. Much of the farm labor is supplied by Negroes living in what may be called rural slums, but here and there an immigrant family has established itself, has built up the impoverished soil, and makes an industrious living. A note of agricultural progress has been added to the farm area around Leonardtown, county seat of St. Mary's County, by Amish families who entered Maryland from Pennsylvania before World War II, attracted by the more liberal religious laws of Maryland.

In Southern Maryland the tradition of farm living persists, and the towns are small. Here survive only the wraiths of once flourishing settlements. St. Mary's City, where Lord Baltimore's colonists established their first settlement, is now an almost deserted village. Maryland, beyond reconstructing the old colonial State House at St. Mary's City, has not exploited the tourist possibilities of its early settlement, as have Virginia and Massachusetts. Of Port Tobacco, once an important river port situated at a bend in the Potomac River at the southern end of Charles County, only a few houses remain. With the decline of shipping and the coming of the railroad Port Tobacco lost the importance which it had long enjoyed, and finally in 1895 when its court house burned down it yielded to nearby La Plata its distinction as county seat of Charles County.

In these and other ghost towns of Southern Maryland it seems always to be a lazy Sunday afternoon. Along the ridges of the once flourishing La Plata-Port Tobacco area in Charles County can still be seen the distinguished homes of long ago, including Charleston owned by Daniel of St. Thomas Jenifer, Mulberry Grove where John Hanson lived, Rose Hill, the home of Dr. Gustavus Brown, one of George Washington's physicians, and, nearby, Habre de Venture, built by Thomas Stone, a signer of the Declaration of Independence.

In Southern Maryland the jousting tournament, which was one of the chivalric sports of the later Middle Ages, has been popular since the 1840's. The contestants vie with each other in turn in running a lance or spear through a small suspended metal ring while riding on horseback at full speed. This joust of the ring was regularly practiced in the Spain of Don Quixote and in Spain's colonies in America, where it was called the *juego de sortija,* but it appears to have been introduced into Maryland from Virginia in the early 1840's in imitation of the Scotch tournaments and in tribute to the popularity of Sir Walter Scott's Waverly novels, especially *Ivanhoe.*

At the instigation of State Senator Henry Fowler, the Maryland legislature made jousting the official sport of the state by law in 1962 and Maryland thus became the first state in the nation to have an official sport.[2] This "running at the rings" is often used to raise money for churches and charitable causes. Its popularity has extended beyond Southern Maryland to other counties of the state and has been taken over by some Negro groups. In recent times women also are participating as riders in the sport.[3]

Southern Maryland is being forced into modernity by the impact of the expanding national government in Washington and by the pressure for industrialization. The population of the three southernmost counties of Southern Maryland has doubled every 20 years since 1940 and is expected to double again by 1990 thus advancing from its present 115,000 (1974), to between 200,000 and 250,000. Of the present population 26 percent is non-white. The sources of income for residents of Southern Maryland are also changing as agriculture, the seafood industry, and forestry are supplanted by government services, wholesale-retail trade, and the construction industry.

Residents of the Coastal Plain on the Western Shore, like their neighbors on the Eastern Shore, also "farm the sea." Among the industries of this region the fishing industry, including both the oyster and clam fisheries, stands next in importance to agriculture. From the waters and marshes of Chesapeake Bay come many of the foods which have made the Maryland cuisine distinctive. These include not only oysters, clams, and many varieties of fish but also the canvasback duck and the terrapin, a water turtle of delicate flavor which formerly enjoyed high popularity. Lumbering is carried on in many of the remaining pine woodlots of Southern Maryland. Mining has less importance in the Coastal Plain than in any other region of the state, but it nevertheless constitutes an economic factor of some importance in the life of this area, utilizing the valuable clays, suitable for brick, tile, pottery, and sewer tile, which are found along the western edge of the region just east of the fall line. At several places in this region sand, which is useful for the manufacture of glass, is mined, and bog iron or carbonate ore is dug out and manufactured into high-grade steel.

Chesapeake Bay and its drowned river tributaries account for most of Maryland's water commerce. Preeminent among the ports of the Coastal Region is Baltimore, whose size and prosperity are largely attributable to its excellent port facilities and its ocean traffic with all parts of the world. It is situated 150 miles inland from the Virginia Capes on the estuary of the Patapsco River where it empties into the Bay. Its principal port terminals are owned by the Baltimore and Ohio Railroad, the Western Maryland Railroad, and the Pennsylvania Railroad, and they provide easy loading and unloading facilities for ships and direct rail transportation from shipside to all parts of the nation. Into Baltimore harbor come the iron ore and manganese that are used in the manufacture of steel, raw sugar to be refined, molasses to be transformed into commercial alcohol, petroleum to be cracked and distributed, and hundreds of other raw materials from abroad. And out of the port move cargoes of coal, wheat, iron and steel manufactures, fertilizers, copper work, canned fruits and vegetables, seafoods, and many other products of America's farms and factories.

Baltimore's harbor rumbles with the commerce of faraway places. Here cargoes from Liverpool, São Paulo, Yokohama, and Calcutta are unloaded from vessels with exotic names and crewmen who speak most of the languages of the earth. The port equipment includes gigantic dumpers which turn coal cars upside down and deposit their contents in the holds of ships, 15-story-high container cranes that can hoist truck trailers, that are single-unit containers, from shipside to deck, ore cranes which can unload 2,000 tons of ore an hour, and conveyor belts which transfer grain from huge tubular elevators into ships at the rate of 2,500 bushels a minute. The railroad wharves ringing the harbor form the medium for a continuous commerce and there the hinterland of Maryland and the foreign world commingle to the raucous noise of clanging freight cars, steamship whistles, and the clatter of loading apparatus.

From sea level on the east and southeast the Coastal Plain rises to an elevation of about 300 feet or more at the fall line of the rivers, which separates it from the Piedmont Plateau. The fall line runs in an irregular course from Elkton on the north by way of Baltimore and Laurel to the Great Falls of the Potomac. It marks the edge of the area of hard rocks where falls and rapids occur in the streams as they descend into the softer rocks of the Coastal Plain. The Piedmont Plateau of Maryland is a part of the larger plateau of the same name that stretches northward into Pennsylvania and southward into Virginia. In Maryland it extends westward from the fall line of the rivers to the eastern slope of Catoctin Mountain. Comprising Montgomery, Howard, Baltimore, Harford, Carroll, and Frederick Counties and parts of Cecil and Prince George's it includes about one-fourth of the land area of the state.

The Piedmont Plateau is an area of low, undulating hills which become higher toward the west, rising from a height of 300 feet above sea level at the fall line to about 800 feet in the central part of the region at Parr's Ridge and then sloping gradually to the Monocacy River. The rocks of the Piedmont Plateau are very ancient and very hard, and through them the streams have cut deep, narrow gorges. The chief streams of this region are the Monocacy, Patuxent, Patapsco, Gunpowder, and Susquehanna; and after they cross the fall line all of them except the Monocacy emerge into the Coastal Plain and become broad estuaries before they join the salt waters of Chesapeake Bay. The divide between the streams which flow into the Potomac and those which flow directly into the Chesapeake passes along Parr's Ridge from Manchester to Mount Airy, then to Sandy Spring, Laurel, and Bowie, and down the main peninsula of Southern Maryland to Point Lookout.

Manufacturing has developed as the leading industry in the Piedmont Plateau of Maryland, as also in the Piedmont Plateau of all the other states from Maine to Georgia. When factories were dependent upon water power many of them were built at the fall line of the rivers. Flour mills, which were favorably situated on this fall line in Maryland and which made Baltimore at one time one of the leading flour-milling centers in the country, have gradually disappeared under pressure from western competition. Their place has been taken by cotton mills which

Washington Monument, erected by the citizens of Boonsboro in July 1827. The first monument to George Washington ever to be completed in the nation. Photo by M.E. Warren

have sprung up in response to the southward trend of cotton manufacturing. The natural market and outlet for the products of Maryland's Piedmont region is Baltimore. Its principal manufactures include airplanes, steel, clothing, chemicals, and spices.

In the Piedmont region of Maryland agriculture ranks scarcely second to manufacturing, for this region contains some of the most fertile and best cultivated farmlands in the state. Many of the valleys have a limestone soil which yields heavy crops of hay, wheat, corn, oats, potatoes, and tomatoes and is well adapted to grazing. In the nearby populous centers of Baltimore and Washington the dairy and truck farming products of this region find ready markets. Of mineral resources this region possesses clay, limestone, granite, marble, slate, and sandstone. The limestone, which is quarried principally in Frederick and Baltimore Counties, is crushed and used in road building, is manufactured into cement, and is burnt for lime. Granite and marble from this region, quarried at Port Deposit in Cecil County, at Woodstock in Baltimore County, and at Ellicott City in Howard County, were used in the construction of the Capitol, the Washington Monument, and the Library of Congress in Washington and the Naval Academy at Annapolis. They have also helped to give Baltimore its reputation both as "The Monumental City" and as a city of white doorsteps. The red sandstone found near Rockville and at other places in Montgomery County, particularly near the mouth of Seneca Creek, was used in the construction of the Smithsonian Institution in Washington. In the Piedmont Region copper ore was found and mined in early colonial times, and it continued to be one of the most important mineral products of Maryland until the great copper mines of the Lake Superior region were opened up.

The third and westernmost physiographic region in Maryland is the Appalachian, which extends from the Catoctin Mountain in Frederick County to the western border and includes a part of Frederick County and all of Washington, Allegany, and Garrett Counties. This is the mountainous portion of the state. Its surface consists of ridges that run from the northeast to the southwest and alternate with deep and usually narrow valleys. The ridges are generally level and parallel and are broken only where the larger streams have cut deep gorges across them. Some of the ridges extend across the state, and others are ends of ridges that have their chief development in Pennsylvania, Virginia, or West Virginia. In early geological ages when the earth's crust was cooling the Appalachian region of Maryland was an area of great upheaval. The rugged mountain peaks which were thrown up at that time perhaps resembled the present, much younger Rocky Mountains but were subsequently worn down by rain, heat, and frost, operating slowly over thousands of years, to a high plateau from which the present valleys were later carved leaving the harder rocks as intervening ridges.

The eastern escarpment of the Appalachian region is formed by the Catoctin Mountain. Parallel to it to the west and separated from it by the narrow and beautiful Middletown Valley lies the Blue Ridge. This is higher than Catoctin having an average elevation of about 2,000 feet but rising to about 2,400 feet at Pen Mar, which straddles the Maryland-Pennsylvania line. The only gaps through it have been worn at the Pennsylvania line at Pen Mar and at the West Virginia line at Weverton. It continues south into Virginia where it forms one of the principal mountain ranges in the Shenandoah Valley.

West of the Blue Ridge lies the Hagerstown Valley, the largest valley in the Appalachian Region of Maryland. It is the Maryland portion of the Great Valley which extends north into Pennsylvania as the Cumberland Valley and into Virginia as the Shenandoah Valley. A broad plain over twenty miles wide, it has a rolling floor composed of limestone soil and is a region of high fertility. Beyond North Mountain, which forms the western boundary of the Hagerstown Valley, one enters a very rugged region crossed by ridges which here attain an elevation of some 1,800 feet and are cut by deep narrow valleys. Among the chief ridges are North Mountain, Tonoloway Ridge, and Sideling Hill in Washington County, and Town Hill, Green Mountain, Warrior Mountain, Collier Mountain, Martin Mountain, and Wills Mountain in Allegany County.

Going westward into Garrett County, the westernmost county of the state, one enters a section which is less rugged but higher than the Allegheny ridges. The mountains here rise from an elevated tableland known as the Allegheny Plateau, which is part of the plateau of the same name extending both north and south of the borders of Maryland. Its average altitude is about 2,500 feet, and above the plateau some of the ridges rise to more than 3,000 feet. Some of them have picturesque names. Dans Mountain was named for an early settler, Daniel Cresap, Big Savage Mountain for the pioneer surveyor, John Savage, and Negro Mountain for a Negro member of Colonel Thomas Cresap's command in the French and Indian War who lost his life in a foray against a band of Indians and who was buried on this mountain. Other high ridges in this region include Great Backbone Mountain, Meadow Mountain, and Laurel Hill. On the more level portions of the plateau the drainage is often so imperfect that it has created swamp areas which are known as "glades."

Where and Who?

In this Appalachian Region the largest watercourses are the Potomac, the Youghiogheny, the Casselman, the Savage, George's Creek, Wills Creek, Sideling Creek, Antietam Creek, and Catoctin Creek. The watershed between the streams flowing into the Youghiogheny, which eventually sends its waters into the Mississippi River, and those flowing into the Potomac, which empties its waters into Chesapeake Bay and the Atlantic Ocean, passes along the ridge of Backbone Mountain to Eagle Rock east of Deer Park, then shifts to Altamont and follows along the summit of Meadow Mountain and thence northward beyond the Pennsylvania line.

Along the southern border of Maryland throughout the entire extent of the Appalachian region flows the Potomac River. Its northern branch forms the southern boundary of western Maryland, and there it has cut many deep gorges which have been useful as gateways to the west for railroads and canals. Such a gorge it has cut through the Blue Ridge at Harper's Ferry, where its turbulent waters are joined by the waters of the Shenandoah River flowing northward from Virginia. The Youghiogheny is a rapid stream which runs north into Pennsylvania and there unites with the Monongahela at McKeesport to help form the Ohio River at Pittsburgh. George's Creek drains the coal region west of Cumberland and empties into the Potomac at Westernport. Wills Creek, which originates in Pennsylvania, enters the Potomac at Cumberland. It has carved several gorges through the ridges west of Cumberland, and in Wills Mountain at Cumberland has chiseled out a great gulch more than nine hundred feet deep which is called "The Narrows" and which is one of the most picturesque spots in Maryland.

The most important industry of the Appalachian region is mining. Here valuable deposits of coal, clay, and limestone have long been worked. In 1929 the bituminous coal industry accounted for 42.7 percent of the total value of Maryland's mineral products but thereafter entered into a serious decline. With the appearance of the energy crisis in the early 1970's and the resulting increase in the price of coal, however, many old mines have been reactivated and new ones opened to cause a modest mining boom. In 1972 the mineral production of the three western counties was valued at $25.3 million, representing about 22 percent of the value of the mineral production of the entire state.

In 1975 the Maryland Geological Survey estimated that Allegany and Garrett Counties contain 854.9 million tons of recoverable coal of which 354.1 million tons lie in the George's Creek Basin. This basin, situated west of Cumberland is underlaid by the famous "Big Vein" or "Fourteen-Foot" seam of coal, which continues north to the Pittsburgh coal region and south into West Virginia. In the Appalachian region of Maryland are also found deposits of "cement rock"—a cement which hardens under water—and fire clays which are used in the manufacture of fire brick. The iron ore which is also deposited in this mountain region has long since gone unworked because of competition from more abundant iron deposits elsewhere.

The second most important industry in the Appalachian region is lumbering. Approximately three-fifths of Allegany and Garrett Counties are covered with trees. Those of greatest value to the lumberman are white pine, hemlock, white oak, chestnut, beech, birch, and maple. All these are especially useful in making fine furniture, which is one of the chief manufactured products of this part of the state. In addition, the poplar or tulip trees are used in the manufacture of wood pulp, and the maple trees yield sap in the early spring which is boiled to form delectable syrup. Agriculture has relatively little importance in the Appalachian region except in the Hagerstown Valley. In this valley are raised large crops of wheat, corn, barley, oats, and hay, and large herds of cattle. But throughout the rest of the Appalachian region the mountainous character of the land and the thin and stony soils of the mountain ridges discourage agriculture. The soils are difficult to cultivate, and the valleys are narrow. The western slope of the Blue Ridge, however, in the vicinity of Pen Mar and Edgemont is well adapted to the growing of fine peaches, and Hancock is famous for its apples.

Manufacturing in the Appalachian region centers mainly in Cumberland and Hagerstown. Cumberland, the metropolis of western Maryland, became the state's second city in size in 1850 owing its growth to the coal resources of the George's Creek valley and its transportation outlets by way of the Baltimore and Ohio Railroad and the Chesapeake and Ohio Canal. Its economic growth in the twentieth century has been stimulated by the manufacture of lumber products, iron, glass, tires, and plastics. Hagerstown, which has the advantage of closer proximity to the markets of Baltimore and Washington, is noted for its furniture, leather, and aircraft industries.

Western Maryland is an area of smiling, fertile valleys, of tumbling mountain streams emptying into the broad Potomac, of isolated, mountain-bound homesteads, surrounded by narrow cornfields or precipitous apple and peach orchards, in rugged woodland settings. It is a region of small lumber and mining towns, each with its Main Street and its row of stores, including a bank, grocery stores, a moving-picture theater, a shoe shop, a poolroom and bowling center, beer parlors, beauty "salons," clothing stores, a drugstore, a barber shop, and the homes of its leading citizens set back from the street in spacious yards. The children attend a brick schoolhouse located on the outskirts of the town and surrounded by a well-worn playground. On Saturdays the Main Street throngs with hucksters, shoppers, and automobiles, for Saturday is market day, and into town come miners from the rich coal fields, lumberjacks, and farmers. Among them an easy congeniality prevails and social barriers do not exist. Each calls the other by his first name. They have a polyglot ancestry—Irish, German, Italian, Lebanese, Scotch, and many others. With the approach of Sunday the town takes on an air of quiet decorum, and the churches—Methodist, Baptist, Presbyterian, Lutheran, Catholic—fill to capacity with starched worshipers.

Though the original race that peopled Maryland has long since died out, Indian place names still linger on. These include the river names Potomac, Patuxent, Pocomoke, Susquehanna, Magothy, Monocacy, Patapsco, Nanticoke, Choptank, Anacostia, Catoctin, Conococheague, Nanjemoy, Piscataway, and Wicomico. The word Chesapeake is an English transliteration of an Indian word meaning Great Shellfish Bay. The land that is Maryland has been under two national flags—the flag of Great Britain and the flag of the United States. During the greater part of the almost century and a half of Maryland's colonial history, the British flag flew over the black and gold flag of the Baltimores, the proprietary family that governed the colony under the British crown. Many of Maryland's place names have an English origin as, for example, Cambridge, Dorchester, Kent, Prince George's, Queen Anne, Somerset, Worcester, Chester, Georgetown, Princess Anne, Prince Frederick, Marlboro, Harford, Westminster, Cumberland, and Salisbury.

But these unoriginal names, reflecting the nostalgia of the early colonists, are supplemented by many romantic and picturesque place names, some of which reveal real folk genius. Rising Sun took its name from a tavern whose shingle showed the sun peeping over the horizon. Silver Spring, which grew phenomenally to become the second city in size in the state between 1950 and 1960, took its name from the mica flakes that gleamed at the bottom of a spring there. Secretary was presumably named for Henry Sewall, who served as secretary of the province under the second Lord Baltimore. English Consul honors the British official, Will Dawson, who was British consul in Baltimore in 1816. T.B. was named for a boundary stone bearing the initials of the landowner, Thomas Brooke. Indian Head was the head of land where the white settlers found many Indian villages. Issue in Charles County was so named because the early colonists became involved in a controversy over several suggested names and finally settled the *issue* by a compromise. Fiddlesburg, according to tradition, commemorated a group of itinerant fiddlers. Accident was given to the name of the tract of land belonging to Brooks Beall which William Deakins marked off by "accident" in 1774. And the names of some of Maryland's early manors and plantations are redolent of legend and lore, as for example, Long Looked for Come at Last, My Lord's Gift, The Remains of My Lord's Gracious Grant, Well Meaning, Bachelor's Resolution, Bachelor's Hope, Duck Pye, Hen's Roost, Godsgrace, Dear Bought, Devil's Wood Yard, Come by Chance, What You Please, Do Better, His Lordship's Kindness, Altogether, The Garden of Eden, None So Good in Finland, Neighbor's Grudge, Plaindealing, Widow's Choice, Rest Content, Walker's Tooth, The Ending of Controversie, Hard Bargain, Cold Friday, and Cold Saturday. And many of the plantation homes still survive from colonial days serene amongst their groves of holly and oak and bathed on sultry summer days with the fragrance of their ancient boxwoods.

At the time of the census of 1970 Maryland had a total population of 3,922,399. Between 1940 and 1970 it rose from twenty-eighth to eighteenth among the states of the Union in number of people. In density of population in 1970 it stood fifth among the states, having 396.6 persons per square mile. In this respect it is outranked only by New Jersey, Rhode Island, Massachusetts, Connecticut, and New York. This high density is explained in part by Baltimore, which had a population of 905,759 in 1970 and the Baltimore metropolitan area 2,070,670. Between 1940 and 1950 Baltimore increased its population by more than ten percent and moved up from seventh to sixth place among all the cities of the nation, but by 1960 it had declined again to seventh place and remained there in 1970. The fact that Baltimore has long included almost half the people of the state has enabled it to play a dominant political role. Aside from Baltimore, the state has a dearth of large cities. Dundalk, in the Baltimore metropolitan area, which surpassed Silver Spring between 1960 and 1970 to become the second city in population in the state, numbered 85,377 inhabitants in 1970, and the third and fourth cities, Silver Spring and Bethesda, situated in the Washington metropolitan area, numbered respectively, 77,496 and 71,621 inhabitants in the same year. Between 1950 and 1970 the population of Annapolis, the capital, almost tripled, increasing from 10,047 to 29,592.

Maryland's population has grown more than twelve times since it was first officially counted in the census of 1790. Since 1900 its population has almost tripled. It has shown unusually large gains since 1920, increasing by 12.5 percent between 1920 and 1930, 11.6 percent between 1930 and 1940, 28.6 percent between 1940 and 1950, 32.3 percent between 1950 and 1960, and 26.5 percent between 1960 and 1970. During the last-named decade twenty of the twenty-three counties increased in population. In that period nearly three-fourths of the increase in the population of the state was accounted for by the counties of Baltimore, Prince George's, and Montgomery. Of these Prince George's County showed the largest percentage increase, 84.8 percent.

Since the first national census in 1790 Maryland has changed from a predominantly rural to a predominantly urban state. In the first census its urban population accounted for only 4.2 percent of the total, but it reached and passed the 50 percent mark during the decade between 1900 and 1910. According to the census of 1970, 76.6 percent of Maryland's people then lived in urban communities. Almost one-fifth— 17.9 percent—of the total population of the state is classified as Negro.

In general Maryland's population growth is confined to the Baltimore and Washington complexes, for, among the counties outside these two areas, as shown by the census of 1970, four contain no towns of 2,500 population and nine contain only one each. The bulk of the population growth is found in Baltimore County with 18 towns of more than 2,500 population, in Montgomery County with 21, and in Prince George's with 45.

The keynote of Maryland's history has generally been moderation dictated in part by the background and diversity of its people and in part by its position of geographical mediation between north and south. Maryland has been characterized both as "the gateway to the South" and as "a southern state looking North." Its commitment to tobacco-raising and horse-breeding emphasizes its southern viewpoint, but its industrial development definitely follows the pattern of northern industrial states. From the time of its emergence into statehood the political leaders of the state have, particularly during periods of national crisis, played or essayed to play a balancing role, acquiring in the attempt a deserved reputation as middlemen, conciliators, or perhaps, to state it more bluntly, opportunists.

These policies of equivocation, however, far from weakening the place of the state in history, have given it the status of a weathervane and have tended to range it on the side of national majorities. If Maryland's attitude of accommodation has seemed to stem more from political expediency than from principle it has nevertheless kept the state in the mainstream of American history. Maryland therefore has often appeared as a microcosm of what was happening in the nation as a whole.

Footnotes

[1] Maryland Department of Economic Development, *Maryland Economic Atlas,* Annapolis, Maryland, 1967, pp. 6, 7.

[2] Laws of Maryland, 1962, chapter 134.

[3] Mrs. Richard Robbins Kane, "Valiant Knights and Ladies Fair: A Story of the Jousting Tournament in Maryland," typescript in Maryland Department, Enoch Pratt Free Library, Baltimore; and G. Harrison Orians, "The Origin of the Ring Tournament in the United States," *Maryland Historical Magazine,* vol. XXXVI, No. 3, September 1941, pp. 263-277.

Sources and Additional Reading

Blood, Pearle, *Geography of Maryland,* Allyn and Bacon, Inc., Boston, 1967.

Carey, George, *A Faraway Time and Place: Lore of the Eastern Shore,* Robert B. Luce, Inc., Washington, New York, 1971.

——, *Maryland Folklore and Folklife,* Tidewater Publishers, Cambridge, Maryland, 1970.

——, *Maryland Folk Legends and Folk Songs,* Tidewater Publishers, Cambridge, Maryland, 1971.

Clark, Charles B., *The Eastern Shore of Maryland and Virginia,* 3 vols., Lewis Historical Publishing Co., Inc., New York, 1950.

Clark, William B., and Edward B. Matthews, "The Physical Features of Maryland . . . ," *Maryland Geological Survey, Reports,* VI (1906), [29]-92, The Johns Hopkins Press, Baltimore, 1906.

——, "The Geography of Maryland," *Maryland Geological Survey, Reports,* X (1918), [41]-160, The Johns Hopkins Press, Baltimore, 1918.

Earle, Swepson, *The Chesapeake Bay Country.* Fourth edition, revised 1934. Thomsen-Ellis Company, Baltimore, Md., 1934.

Footner, Hulbert, *Maryland Main and the Eastern Shore,* D. Appleton-Century Company, Inc., New York & London, 1942; reprint edition, Tradition Press, Hatboro, Pennsylvania, 1967.

Klingel, Gilbert C., *The Bay,* Dodd, Mead & Company, 1951; reprint edition, Tradition Press, Hatboro, Pennsylvania, 1967.

Lippson, Alice Jane, ed., *The Chesapeake Bay in Maryland: An Atlas of Natural Resources,* Johns Hopkins University Press, Baltimore & London, 1973.

Vokes, Harold E., *Geography and Geology of Maryland,* State of Maryland, Board of Natural Resources, Maryland, Geological Survey, Bulletin 19, Baltimore, 1957; revised and reprinted, 1968.

Wilstach, Paul, *Potomac Landings,* The Bobbs-Merrill Company, Indianapolis, 1932.

——, *Tidewater Maryland,* The Bobbs-Merrill Company, Indianapolis, 1931, and reprint edition, Tidewater Publishers, Cambridge, Maryland, 1969.

CHAPTER II
PREPARATION FOR A NEW COLONY

Before the coming of white men all the land that was to become Maryland, except tidal beaches, ocean sand reefs, and several enclaves of meadows or "barrens" in the eastern Piedmont region, was covered with native trees and dense undergrowth. The principal trees were oak, hickory, pine, poplar, maple, locust, chestnut, cypress, cedar, beech, wild cherry, sassafras, holly, and persimmon. The tangled growth under the trees was made up of vines of the wild grape, the Virginia creeper, dewberry, and morning-glory, and bushes of laurel, blackberry, raspberry, blueberry, huckleberry, cranberry, and many others. Through almost indistinguishable forest trails and along the water courses moved a primitive people who had lived there for many hundreds, perhaps even thousands, of years. Their origin is hidden in mystery.

All the native peoples living in the area between the Atlantic seacoast and the Mississippi River belonged to three great ethnological groups. (1) In the southeast lived the Appalachian or Muskogean group consisting principally of the tribes of the Creek, Choctaw, Chickasaw, Alabama, Apalachi, and Seminole. (2) In the territory that extended wedge-shaped from the Shenandoah Valley northward into the basin of the lower lakes and the upper St. Lawrence Valley lived the Iroquois group, whose principal tribes were the Cayuga, Cherokee, Conestoga, Erie, Mohawk, Neuter, Nottoway, Oneida, Onondaga, Seneca, Tuscarora, and Wyandot. Of this group the tribes that inhabited central New York state constituted the most powerful Indian confederacy in the territory now occupied by the United States. They claimed a suzerain authority over the other tribes of the group and were perennial foes to the tribes of the third group who surrounded them on all sides. (3) These were the Algonquian group who were spread over a wide area extending from the Atlantic seaboard west to the Mississippi River, south to Cape Hatteras and the Tennessee River, and north to the St. Lawrence River and Hudson Bay. To this Algonquian group the Maryland tribes belonged, numbering some seven or eight thousand. They included Accomacs (Accohanocs), Nanticokes, and Wicomicos on the Eastern Shore and the Susquehannocks, Yaocomicos, and Piscataways on the Western Shore.

Preparation for a New Colony

The Chesapeake Bay Indians lived in small huts built of saplings set firmly in the ground and bound together at the tops, forming a conical frame. On this they wove split poles and flexible branches and covered the whole structure with leaves, reeds, and bark. They usually located these so-called wigwams in groups or villages which they surrounded with a palisade of poles driven into the ground. During the hot summer months they abandoned these dwellings to live in temporary, more ramshackle structures.

These Indians, like their neighbors both to the north and to the south, roamed over an area which they generally claimed and defended as their own, though they neither practiced nor recognized any system of individual land ownership, as did contemporary Englishmen. In the early seventeenth century, when the English made their first successful efforts to establish colonies in North America, the Susquehannocks claimed all the country lying between the Potomac and Susquehanna Rivers. This was their hunting ground. The country south of the Potomac was recognized as falling under Powhatan's jurisdiction. In the Susquehannock country the local tribes who occupied the river valleys between the Potomac and the Susquehanna Rivers were considered subordinate to the ruling tribe whose headquarters were located on the shores of the Susquehanna. Subsequently, however, they transferred their council fires to the western shore of the Patuxent River in order to avoid the frequent attacks of the Iroquois from the north.

The Susquehannocks were visited by the doughty Captain John Smith when he explored and mapped the Chesapeake region in 1608. He described them as follows in his *General Historie of Virginia:*

... 60 of these Sasquesahanocks came to us with skins, bowes, arrows, targets, beads, swords, and tobacco pipes for presents. Such great and well-proportioned men are seldom seene, for they seemed like giants to the English, yea and to the neighbours, yet seemed of an honest and simple disposition, with much adoe restrained from adoring us as Gods. These are the strangest people of all these countries, both in language and attire; for their language it may well become their proportions, sounding from them as a voyce in a vault. Their attire is the skinnes of beares, and wolves, some have cassocks made of beares heads and skinnes, that a mans head goes through the skinnes neck, and the eares of the beare fastened to his shoulders, the nose and teeth hanging downe his breast, another beares face split behind him, and at the end of the nose hung a pawe, the halfe sleeves coming to the elbowes were the necks of beares, and the armes through the mouth with pawes hanging at their noses.

The main occupations of these Indians were hunting and fishing. Their country was covered with an immense mantle of forest and abounded in game. Bears were very numerous and formed a principal object of the Indian hunter's chase. Bear-hunting also became a favorite sport among Lord Baltimore's colonists in early Maryland. The early records show that bears were frequently encountered on the Patapsco near the present site of Baltimore, and the name survives in Bear Creek, one of the principal branches of that river. Bobcats or lynxes, which were usually called panthers or lions by the early colonists in Maryland who now saw these animals for the first time, were also plentiful but did little damage. The savage wolves were more destructive and ravaged the colonists' livestock to such an extent that the early governors of Maryland granted bounties of from one hundred to two hundred pounds of tobacco to anyone who killed a wolf. Herds of elk gathered at the salt licks—deposits of salt which they avidly licked from the ground—and buffalo roamed along the banks of the Potomac near the present site of Washington. Deer were so abundant in early Maryland that they ceased to be esteemed as food. George Alsop, whose "Character of the Province of Maryland," written in 1666, is one of our best accounts of the colony in the seventeenth century, wrote that in his own home there were

at one time ... fourscore Venisons ... so that this Venison ... so nauseated our appetites and stomachs, that plain bread was rather courted and desired than it.

Father Andrew White, a Roman Catholic priest and member of the Society of Jesus, who accompanied the first colonists to Maryland in 1634, wrote that deer were so plentiful "that they are rather an annoyance than an advantage."

Other Maryland animals that were hunted by both the natives and the English colonists included the beaver, otter, martin, mink, weasel, raccoon, opossum, hare, woodchuck, muskrat, skunk, and squirrel. Some of these provided fur which served as an important export commodity, and some were esteemed as food. The flying squirrel, in particular was viewed as a real curiosity. "When it flyes," wrote one of the early English chroniclers, "it extends all its feete which spread a part of thin skin which holds the wind butt cannot fly far."

Waterfowl were so abundant that they darkened the waters and even the sky, rising, as one of the colonists reported, "in millionous multitudes." As to ducks, "the water was so black with them that it seemed when you looked from the land below upon the water, as if it were a mass of filth or turf, and, when they flew up, there was a rushing and vibration of the air like a great storm coming through the trees, and even like the rumbling of distant thunder, while the sky over the whole creek was filled with them like a cloud." Wild turkeys grew so large in the Maryland woods as to be awkward and unwieldy. Some of them weighed as much as eighty-five pounds and could not fly but only fluttered over the ground. These turkeys, Father White wrote to his English friends, "are twice as large as our tame and domestic ones." They were so plentiful that their meat palled upon the appetites of the English newcomers. In addition, the Maryland woods were alive and colorful with partridges, woodcock, pheasants, wild pigeons, eagles, snipes, plovers, hawks, vultures, herons, orioles, blackbirds, mockingbirds, thrushes, and much other wildlife.

In this happy hunting ground of Maryland the Indians, though they were equipped with only spears and primitive bows and arrows before the coming of white men, displayed extraordinary skill in killing game. Usually operating in companies of two or three warriors and their families they established winter quarters in the best hunting areas or near the salt licks and there settled down for two or three months to lay in a supply of animal provisions. Sometimes companies of two hundred or three hundred Indians would set fire to the underbrush and drive the wild animals into narrow quarters where they could kill them with their bows and arrows. Or an individual hunter would disguise himself in a deerskin and stalk the grazing deer until he came close enough to use his bow and arrow. After the arrival of the white settlers the friendly Indians would sometimes agree to kill six or seven deer for any colonist who would repay them with a brilliantly colored blanket.

Fish teemed in the waters of early Maryland. Captain John Smith, while making his trip up Chesapeake Bay in the summer of 1608, noted the "aboundance of fish, lying so thicke with their heads above the water, as for want of nets, our barge driving amongst them, we attempted to catch them with a frying pan." Next trying the amusement of spearing the fish with their swords, Captain Smith and his men "tooke more in one houre than we could eate in a day." In the Potomac River near the present site of Washington "the Indians in one night commonly will catch thirty sturgeons in a place where the river is not above twelve fathom broad," reported a Virginia trader, Captain Henry Fleet, who traded with the Maryland Indians before the arrival of Lord Baltimore's colonists. The sealife in Maryland waters included the already mentioned sturgeon and, in addition, trout, shad, herring, skates, white salmon, perch, shrimp, rock, catfish, whales, grampuses, porpoises, mackerel, and crab. Sharks were also reported in Chesapeake Bay, and turtles were mentioned in the early chronicles. Oysters were plentiful and were highly esteemed as food by the Indians, but, like the terrapin, were not appreciated by the white settlers. When the Kent Islanders were reduced to eating oysters, they thought they were very close to starvation.

But the Indians of Maryland did not give all their time to hunting and fishing, for, like the neighboring tribes of both the Algonquian and Iroquois groups, they paid considerable attention to agriculture, raising maize, squash, and other vegetables, and tobacco. They highly esteemed tobacco for smoking. But they had done little to develop the land or utilize its rich resources. In the lush black topsoil of Maryland, which varied from four to six feet in depth, they could meet all their agricultural necessities with little work and primitive tools. They were living in the late Stone Age when they first encountered the white newcomers on the shores of the Chesapeake. They were not warlike or ferocious, and they showed neither fear nor resentment, little appreciating what effects the arrival of the white settlers would have upon their hunting grounds and their way of life.

The waters and shores of Chesapeake Bay were probably visited by dozens, perhaps hundreds, of French, Spanish, and English explorers before they were successfully colonized by the English in the early seventeenth century. The coasts of Maryland may have been skirted by Giovanni da. Verrazano, a Florentine navigator employed by King Francis I of France to make discoveries "in the northern parts" of America, on his second voyage in 1524. Two years later Chesapeake Bay was entered by a fleet of three large Spanish vessels carrying six hundred persons and headed by one of the high administrative officials of the Spanish island of Espanola, Lucas Vasquez de Ayllón. After leaving the Bay they sailed southward and founded a short-lived colony which they called San Miguel on the site where the English later founded Jamestown. Into Chesapeake Bay around 1570 came another company of Spaniards, led by Father Segura, Vice-Provincial of the Spanish Jesuits in Florida, with the object of converting the Indians to Roman Catholicism, only, instead, to be murdered by the Indians. By the end of the sixteenth century the land that was later to become Maryland had no white inhabitants and contained no surviving evidences of their earlier visits. It was a rich wilderness awaiting civilization.

Meanwhile the English were beginning to bestir themselves to serious effort at colonization in America, to which John Cabot's voyage a century earlier had given them a lawyer's claim. They were entering upon the imperialist phase of their history, that is, as their ambition to maintain control over their hereditaments on the continent had failed, they began the contest with their former rivals, France and Spain, to gain a command position over more primitive peoples and the resources of the American continents which those latter nations claimed. Under Queen Elizabeth they felt a new pride in their nationality as Englishmen and gloried in the exploits of their daring sea captains. Their country had been almost rent asunder by religious persecutions under Henry VIII, Edward VI, and Mary Tudor, and they now welcomed the middle way in religious matters which Queen Elizabeth followed. As English merchants and seamen shuttled back and forth between the ports of their home island and foreign lands they brought new wealth to Britain. This wealth was creating a new class of merchant capitalists and was making possible unprecedented displays of luxury in the castles and the town houses of the rich.

The maritime trade and the mercantile enterprise of the British combined to make capital abundant. New credit and banking systems were established, and usury, which had been condemned by the Christian Church before the Reformation as being an excessive charge upon the use of property, now was legalized. By these techniques of the new capitalism England was raising herself by her own bootstraps to a new national and even international preeminence. The rising bourgeois class was seeking new outlets for investment and finding some in manufacturing but more in commercial ventures to foreign countries. From Sir Francis Drake's voyage to America and thence around the world in 1580-1581, his English backers, who included Queen Elizabeth, drew profits of 4,600 percent. Behind the new merchant adventurers stood the power of a consolidated, strong, shrewd, and nationalistic monarchy bent on promoting and protecting their interests abroad. Capitalism in England was entering upon its heyday.

But while the rich were becoming richer in Elizabethan England the poor were becoming poorer. As the upper and middle classes increased in wealth and power the poor sank lower in the economic and social scale. Those who had little were losing even that little. Alongside the luxury and splendor of Elizabethan England stood rampant poverty and misery threatening the social order and possibly even the stability of the government. The expansion of capitalism, made possible in part by the enormous influx into Europe of gold and silver from Spain's colonies in America, was accompanied by serious social and economic dislocations. The resulting rise in prices had a disastrous effect upon the wage earners and the farmers of the nation.

In England was appearing an increasingly large class of underprivileged and dispossessed folk. The dissolution of the Catholic monasteries during the reign of Henry VIII had turned hundreds of monks and nuns out upon the streets. It had driven the tenants and laborers on the monastic properties to find living and employment elsewhere, and at the same time it had destroyed the institutions which had for centuries made it one of their principal objects to aid the poor. In the midland counties the change from farming to sheep-raising, which occurred as England turned increasingly to the manufacture and export of fine woolen fabrics, threw agricultural laborers out of work and created a class of floaters that would be called today the technologically unemployed. Vagabonds and "sturdy beggars" thronged the streets of London and other English towns, and those who refused to return to their home villages could be arrested, sent to the whipping post, bound out to a master, or thrown into the crowded prisons. England seemed to be overpopulated and to need foreign outlets for a surplus population. It was a nation which was ready not only for commercial expansion into new areas of the foreign world but also for actual colonization of her people abroad.

With the full knowledge and approval of the strong-minded Elizabeth, England's first overseas ventures in America took the form of buccaneering or piratical expeditions, such as those of Captain John Hawkins and Sir Francis Drake, directed against the swaggering power of Spain. From these England moved on to colonizing enterprises in America. In 1583 Sir Humphrey Gilbert, sailing under a letter patent from Queen Elizabeth, traversed the Atlantic Ocean to the west and took possession of Newfoundland for Elizabeth by right of the earlier discovery of John Cabot. He and all his expedition were drowned on the return trip and his voyage produced no tangible gain for England except this reassertion of Cabot's claim.

Gilbert's rights of exploration and colonization in America passed at his death to his half-brother, Sir Walter Raleigh, who sent out an exploring expedition of two vessels, commanded by Philip Amadas and Arthur Barlowe. They explored the coast of North Carolina and brought back such enthusiastic reports of the new land that Elizabeth permitted it to be named Virginia in her honor. In the spring of 1585 Raleigh dispatched another expedition, commanded by Ralph Lane, to begin a settlement, but Lane and his associates lacked the qualities essential for successful pioneering in the American wilderness. Their settlement, located on Roanoke Island in Pamlico Sound, did not prosper, and they finally abandoned it and returned to England.

Raleigh determined to try again. He now formed a company of "associates" composed of English capitalists who were willing to venture their money and others who were willing to venture their lives in Virginia, and with their cooperation he fitted out a new expedition of three vessels commanded by John White. Their intention was to settle in the Chesapeake Bay region, but when they stopped en route at Roanoke Island their pilot, a Portuguese named Simon Ferdinando, refused to transport them any farther and dropped them there. But this colony suffered an even more tragic fate than Raleigh's first colony. Because of the outbreak of war between England and Spain the Roanoke colony could receive neither supplies nor reinforcements from England for four years. Meanwhile the colony disappeared, possibly exterminated by the Indians.

During the closing years of Elizabeth's reign Englishmen, with the approval of the crown, continued their efforts to advance their knowledge of the western hemisphere and to make profits from overseas trade. As a means to these ends six English trading companies were formed, including the great East India Company, which was organized in 1600. These companies would serve as the effective instrumentalities of the exploring and colonizing zeal of Englishmen during the reign of Elizabeth's successor, James I. More than a century elapsed after Columbus' discovery of the western hemisphere before England was ready to make the serious effort required to establish a colonial foothold there.

England's new interest in Virginia, as the whole coast of North America claimed by England and lying north of Spanish Florida was called, was motivated in part by a desire to capitalize on the riches of the new world. Her appetite for colonies there was whetted by the incalculable wealth in gold and silver which her great rival, Spain, had been drawing from the Indies, particularly Mexico and Peru, for several decades. Virginia was pictured in Ben Jonson's *Eastward Hoe* as a country "where gold and silver is more plentiful than copper is with us." Englishmen then were attracted to Virginia by the lure of great wealth to be obtained there.

But if Englishmen could not find the precious metals there they might at least discover a northwest passage which would lead them through the North American land barrier to the Orient with its riches. In the 1570's and 1580's Martin Frobisher and John Davis had sailed for England into the northern waters west of Greenland discovering the bodies of water that still bear their names, but they had not penetrated to the waters of the South Sea, as the Pacific Ocean was then called.

English, French, and even Dutch navigators were inspired to explore the North American waters in search of a water passage to Cathay, trying successively the St. Lawrence and Hudson Rivers, and Chesapeake Bay.

But Englishmen had more soundly based reasons than these for their new interest in Virginia. Colonies there might help to drain off England's vagabonds and beggars and so relieve social pressures at home. Besides, colonies in America might be made profitable. They could provide the mother country with raw materials needed for England's nascent industry and with staple articles of trade, as the colonies of Spain and France in America were doing, thus contributing to the aggrandizement of the homeland or *entrepôt*. The soil of Virginia, Ralph Lane had reported, was the "goodliest under the cope of heaven" and was "very well peopled and towned." Even if the gold that the first explorers brought back with them proved on assay to be only iron pyrites or fool's gold, Virginia also had deposits of copper and iron. In addition the first explorers reported that the new lands were covered with seemingly limitless forests, which might, if exploited, free England from dependence upon the Scandinavian countries for lumber ranging from shingles for dwellings to masts for the royal navy. Virginia might also supply, according to current expectations, other commodities which the English at that time were compelled to buy from foreign nations, such as naval stores, glass, potash, drugs, flax, silk, pearls, dyes, and even sugar cane, oranges, lemons and other tropical fruits.

Besides the advantage of financial profit to be derived from colonies in America England might use colonies there to improve her balance-of-power position in relation to Spain whom she had just defeated. She could use them as a barrier in the west against the power of Spain. By her victories over Spain, which had begun with her defeat of the so-called Invincible Armada of Philip II in 1588, she was toppling Spain from her proud eminence and was exposing the hollowness of her imperial pretensions. When James I concluded a peace treaty with Spain in 1604 he left her so weakened that England no longer needed to fear Spanish reprisals for encroachments upon her domains in America. English sea captains and merchants could therefore challenge Spain's claims with impunity north of Florida and indeed in Florida itself and thus, freed from fear of the Spanish, could devote their attention to colonization. The international situation favored a great expansion of the British nation.

Accordingly in 1606 James I gave his official sanction to a new wave of colonization by issuing a patent under the great seal incorporating two companies, one consisting of "certain knights, gentlemen, merchants" in and about London, and the other of "sundry knights, gentlemen, merchants" in and about Plymouth. They were organized under distinguished auspices, the chief patron of the London Company being Sir Robert Cecil, the secretary of state, and the chief patron of the Plymouth Company being Sir John Popham, chief justice of the King's Bench. To those grantees whose headquarters were in London, the king gave the exclusive right to plant a settlement between 34 degrees and 38 degrees north latitude, and to those who lived in the west of England, he gave the exclusive right to plant a colony between 41 degrees and 45 degrees north latitude. He kept open to colonization by either company the intervening strip of territory extending from 38 degrees to 41 degrees and provided that the company which made the first settlement should have one-hundred miles of seacoast—fifty miles north to fifty miles south of the site of its first settlement.

By this charter England obviously claimed that the territorial limits of Virginia extended from the 34th parallel on the south, cutting through the mouth of the Cape Fear River, to the 45th parallel on the north, which forms the present dividing line between Vermont and Canada. The practical effect of the charter was to divide Virginia into three strips or zones. The southern zone extended from the Cape Fear River north to the mouth of the Potomac and was assigned to the London Company. The northern zone extended along the coast from the Bay of Fundy south to Long Island Sound and was assigned to the Plymouth Company. The middle zone, which comprised the territory between the mouth of the Hudson River and the mouth of the Potomac River, was left open to occupation by either company.

The London Company was the first of the two companies to win success. It fitted out three vessels which sailed from the Thames on December 20, 1606, and finally anchored in the James River. There on a low-lying, marshy, and disease-infested peninsula thirty-two miles from the river's mouth the colonists laid out a settlement which they called Jamestown. But they quarreled among themselves and showed such an aversion to physical labor and such a sad lack of ingenuity that they soon fell on the verge of starvation. Their ill-treatment of the Indian tribes who surrounded them—members of Powhatan's kingdom —threatened them with constant danger from that source. Whether or not Captain John Smith saved the colony, as he himself claimed, it is certain that after he became president of the council in 1608 the colony gained the strong leadership which it had formerly lacked. In the following year the company was granted a new charter which sought to remedy the defects of the earlier charter, increased the number of stockholders in the company, and enlarged the territorial bounds of the company to extend "from the point of land called Cape or Point Comfort, all along the sea-coast to the northward two hundred miles, and from the Point or Cape Comfort, all along the sea-coast to the southward two hundred miles" and "up into the land throughout, from sea to sea, west and northwest." Nevertheless in the "starving time" of 1608, while Smith was in England the colony almost perished. Surrounded by hostile Indians the settlers killed and ate dogs and horses; some even resorted to cannibalism. When they finally espied the relief vessels only sixty persons remained of the more than 500 who had been brought over from England. The Spanish ambassador in London, Gondomar, wrote to his sovereign, Philip III, "Here in London this colony Virginia is in such bad repute that not a human being can be found to go there in any way whatever."

At this juncture Virginia was redeemed from disaster by tobacco. "The stinking weed," as James I contemptuously called it, was first planted by John Rolfe in 1612, and by the spring of 1617 it was grown in the market place and even in the streets of Jamestown. By that year tobacco was a staple export of the colony and was bringing as much as twelve dollars a pound in London. In 1619 the tobacco exports of the colony amounted to 20,000 pounds; by 1620 they had increased to 40,000 pounds; and two years later they reached 60,000 pounds, in spite of the Indian massacre of that year which limited the area under cultivation. The enormous profitableness of tobacco as a crop defeated all the well meant attempts of the company in England to diversify the economic life of the colony by encouraging the production of silk, wine, and glass. Instead, the Virginia House of Burgesses, as the legislative assembly of the colony was called, undertook to stimulate the production of tobacco and to keep the price high by requiring the destruction of the lowest grade, stipulating the number of plants which each individual could raise, and limiting the number of utilizable leaves on each tobacco plant to nine. As a result of these crop-control methods the colony became so prosperous that, partly for this reason, it was taken over by James I in 1624 and was made a royal colony. In the following year Virginia tobacco was made a royal monopoly and at the same time the importation into England of competing tobacco from the Spanish colonies was prohibited.

By 1624 the colony of Virginia extended from the mouth of the James River up nearly as far as the site of Richmond; it spread out over the broad peninsula between the James River and the York River, then called the Charles; and it included a few settlements on the Accomac peninsula east of Chesapeake Bay. Its population, numbering about 4,000, lived either congregated in small settlements called boroughs or hundreds or in isolated plantations, bordering on the rivers. The colonists owned their own land, for in the administration of Sir Thomas Dale the early system of communal landholding and common storehouses was abolished and to the individual stockholders were assigned the common lands and other property of the company. The colonists also enjoyed representative government, for in 1619 while the London Company was under the leadership of Sir Edwin Sandys they were permitted to send representatives to a House of Burgesses meeting in the choir loft in Jamestown. Negro slaves had been introduced into the colony in 1619, but only 22 of them were living there in 1624. White servants, bound to service for terms of six or seven years, furnished the principal labor supply of the colony. As the plantations increased in size and number they constantly demanded larger supplies of cheap labor. Virginia was a primarily agricultural colony specializing in tobacco but also producing enough Indian corn or maize for home consumption and even some for export. In 1634 the colony sent more than 10,000 bushels to John Winthrop's Puritan colony at Boston.

By this latter year Virginia was no longer the only English colony along the Atlantic seacoast of North America, though she was unquestionably the most flourishing. In 1620 a gallant little band of English Separatists, harried out of England by the religious intolerance of James I and Archbishop William Laud, had found a haven on the shores of Massachusetts Bay on land, which, after the failure of the Plymouth Company, had been assigned to the newly formed Council for New England. Their original destination was the Chesapeake Bay region of Virginia, but they were carried by storms and a stubborn ship captain to the rocky coast of New England. By such accidents of fate the land that was to become Maryland failed to become the home of the Pilgrims. Nine years later on the shores of Massachusetts Bay north of Plymouth, English Puritans, driven from their homeland by both religious intolerance and economic pressures, began to settle in great numbers at Boston and nearby towns. South of these English colonies the Dutch had established themselves. There the Dutch West India Company claimed the whole region between the Mohawk Valley and Delaware Bay. Their principal settlement, New Amsterdam, located on the tip of Manhattan Island, soon became an *entrepôt* for the fur trade of the Connecticut, the Hudson, and the Delaware River valleys. Still nearer to Virginia on the shores of the Chesapeake Bay the colony of Maryland was being started.

Sources and Additional Reading

Andrews, Matthew Page, *Tercentenary History of Maryland*, 3 vols., vol. 1, S.J. Clarke Publishing Company, Chicago & Baltimore, 1925.

——, *History of Maryland: Province & State*, Doubleday, Doran & Company, Inc., Garden City, New York, 1929.

Bozman, John Leeds, *The History of Maryland from the First Settlement, in 1633 to the Restoration in 1660*, Baltimore, 1837.

McMahon, John Van Lear, *An Historical View of the Government of Maryland*, Baltimore, 1831.

McSherry, James, *History of Maryland from 1634 to 1848*, Baltimore, 1849.

Radoff, Morris Leon, *The Old Line State: A History of Maryland*, 3 vols., vol. 1, Baltimore, 1956.

Scharf, J. Thomas, *History of Maryland: From the Earliest Period to the Present Day*, 3 vols., Baltimore, 1879; reprint, 1967.

——, *History of Western Maryland*, 2 vols., Philadelphia, Pa., Louis H. Everts, 1882.

Walsh, Richard, & William Lloyd Fox, eds., *Maryland: A History 1632-1974*, Maryland Historical Society, Baltimore, 1974.

CHAPTER III
THE FOUNDING

The true founder of Maryland, the fourth successful English colony in America, was George Calvert, the first Baron Baltimore. He was born about 1580 at Kipling Manor in Yorkshire and was educated at Trinity College, Oxford. There he specialized in the civil law and in the modern languages, French, Italian, and Spanish, and after taking his bachelor's degree in 1597 entered the Inns of Court in London where he continued his study of the law for the next four years. In 1603 while taking the Grand Tour of Europe which educated young gentlemen of his day were expected to take, he made the acquaintance in Paris of Sir Robert Cecil, who was later to become chief patron of the London Company and through him may have become interested in colonization in America. When, after Elizabeth's death in 1603, Cecil became secretary of state under James I, Calvert was numbered among his friends. He thus acquired standing and influence at court. Soon afterward he married Anne Mynne, daughter of George Mynne of Bexler in Hertfordshire, who was described as belonging to the "lesser gentry" and possessing "few if any advantages of connexion, inherited wealth or formal education; he was probably first in trade as a woollen draper."[1] In 1606 their first son was born and was named Cecil for his patron.

George Calvert then served successively as Cecil's private secretary and clerk of the crown and of assize in County Clare, Ireland. He thus began his acquaintance with Ireland where he was later to hold large estates and to be listed on the roll of nobility. In 1609 he was elected member of Parliament from Bossiney in Cornwall. He received many honors from James I, even after Sir Robert Cecil's death in 1612. He was made clerk of the Privy Council and was appointed a member of two commissions that were sent to Ireland to report on the results of James' policy of bringing that country under the religion and law of England. While in Ireland, he acquired a strong dislike of the Jesuits and in his reports called attention to their harmful influence. In 1610 following the assassination of Henry IV of France he was chosen to represent England at the accession of the new French sovereign, Louis XIII. At the court in London he worked closely with James in formulating his policy on religious matters, and in 1617 was raised to the knighthood. In the following year he became the principal secretary of state, an office which corresponded to that of a modern prime minister.

In this office Calvert's caution, industry, integrity, and patriotism made him especially useful at a critical time in England's history, for England was becoming involved in the general European melee which later came to be called the Thirty Years' War. On the continent Bohemia, whose newly crowned King Frederick was James' son-in-law and which was a center of Protestantism, had already rebelled against the Habsburgs by the famous "defenestration" of Prague. England's friendship was being sought by both France and Spain, and both James and his principal adviser, Calvert, inclined toward an alliance with Spain. To this end, they determined to arrange a marriage between Prince Charles and the Infanta María, daughter of Philip III of Spain, though they must have known that in following this pro-Spanish policy they would encounter strong opposition both in Parliament and among the English people, to whom Spain was a traditional enemy. The experience of previous marriages of English sovereigns with Spanish spouses, as for example Henry VIII with Catherine of Aragon and Mary Tudor with Philip II, had not been happy for England. The Parliament which assembled in 1621 was determined to make the king throw off the influence of the Spanish Ambassador, Don Diego Sarmiento de Acuña, Count Gondomar, give up his scheme of the Spanish marriage, support his daughter, the wife of the deposed king of Bohemia, and throw England's influence behind the Protestant states of Europe. Over the protests of Calvert, who sat in this parliament as a member from Yorkshire and who chose to defend the king's pro-Spanish policy, Parliament agreed to grant money to James only on condition that he use it against Spain and marry the Prince of Wales to a Protestant wife.

But Calvert and the Marquis of Buckingham, who was James' other principal adviser, persisted in the policy of the Spanish marriage. They were convinced that England in her own national interest could not afford to antagonize Spain, which was still powerful enough to be a dangerous enemy. The stronger the Anglo-Spanish alliance, therefore, the better it would be for England, and nothing could cement such an alliance more firmly than the Spanish marriage.

Finally in 1623 Prince Charles obtained the king's consent to visit Spain in disguise with his most intimate friend, Buckingham, in order to complete the negotiations and bring the Infanta María back to England with him as his wife. But when they reached Spain, the prince was treated as a virtual hostage and was pressed by the Spanish authorities to comply with almost impossible conditions. Then too he could not win his way to the Infanta's heart, for she had been brought up in seclusion as a rigid Catholic. When the people of England learned that James, despite strong parliamentary opposition, was pushing ahead with his pro-Spanish policy they became furious. They now saw clearly that James, whose divine-right pretensions and unresponsiveness to popular pressures had already made him highly unpopular, was seriously contemplating the Spanish marriage and had even allowed the Prince of Wales to put himself in the power of Spain. Their pride as Englishmen was affronted by James' policy of subservience to Spain. Charles and Buckingham themselves soon felt the humiliation of their position and came home in disgust. Their return marked the end of good relations with the Habsburgs, and in 1624 Charles married Henrietta Maria, daughter of the assassinated Henry IV of France and sister of Louis XIII. For her Maryland would later be named.

As Calvert saw his policy of the Spanish marriage thus defeated and saw James, under the influence of the opportunistic Buckingham, now swing to a pro-French policy he knew that his political career was ended. He accordingly informed the king that he had become a convert to Catholicism and asked to be relieved of his duties as secretary of state. He had not been a brilliant statesman nor even a successful one. He has been described as "perhaps the most respectable and honest of the mediocre statesmen whom James, Charles, and Buckingham gathered about them." He was characterized by the French ambassador Tillières, writing at this time, as "an honorable, sensible, well-minded man, courteous toward strangers, respectful toward ambassadors, zealously intent upon the welfare of England." Unlike Buckingham, Calvert was distinguished for his wisdom, sincerity, and conscientiousness in the performance of his duties.

Calvert had been greatly honored by James with pensions and titles. In 1620 he had received a pension of £ 1,000 and a subsidy on imported raw silk which was later converted into a second pension of £ 1,000. At about the same time he had also received a manor of 2,300 acres in County Longford, Ireland. On James' insistence he continued, despite his conversion to Catholicism, to sit in the Privy Council, and in 1625 he was elevated to the Irish peerage as Baron Baltimore of Baltimore in the County of Longford. The original patent which he received from James read as follows:

We therefore, nearly considering in the person of our well-beloved and entirely faithful Councillor, George Calvert, Knight, gravity of manners, singular gifts of mind, candour, integrity, and prudence, as well as benignity and urbanity toward all men, and also reflecting in Our mind with how great fidelity, diligence, and alacrity he has served Us, both in Our kingdom of Ireland, whither not long ago, he was especially sent upon Our very weighty and most important business there, as also in this Our Kingdom of England, throughout many years, but especially since he was advanced near Our person to the place and honour of a Councillor and Our principal Secretary; and willing that some singular mark of Our royal favour may remain unto the aforesaid George and unto his posterity forever, by which not only he, but others also may perceive how highly We prize the fidelity and obedience of the said George, and how much We desire to reward his virtues and merits, We have decreed him to be inscribed among the number of the peers of Our said Kingdom of Ireland: Know Ye Therefore, that We, of Our especial grace, and of Our sure knowledge and mere motion, have exalted, preferred, and created the aforesaid George Calvert, Knight, unto the estate, degree, dignity, and honour of Baron Baltimore of Baltimore, within our Kingdom of Ireland.

When James died soon afterward, Calvert, now Lord Baltimore, declined to continue as a member of the Privy Council despite the solicitations of the new sovereign, King Charles, and retired to private life. He now turned his attention to the New World in which he had long been interested. As early as 1609 when he was only twenty-nine years of age he had served as a member of the East India Company and the second Virginia Company. After Virginia was made a royal colony in 1624 he became a member of the provisional council which managed the affairs of the colony under the crown. Two years earlier he had been made one of the eighteen councilors of the Council for New England. But he first directed his colonizing efforts toward the area north of New England. In the very year when the Pilgrims set out for the Chesapeake Bay, which they never reached, Baltimore purchased land in Newfoundland, which he named Avalon, and sent there a party of colonists under Captain Wynne. He was so encouraged by the glowing reports which reached him from his colonists and particularly by Captain Richard Whitbourne's "Westward Hoe for Avalon," published in 1622, that he applied to the king for a patent to this land. In the following year he received a grant of the southeastern peninsula of Newfoundland. By the royal charter which he received he was given a palatinate or quasi-royal authority over this province of Avalon—a name which the country around St. Johns, Newfoundland, bears to this day. Calvert thus introduced into America the palatinate form of government, which was incorporated later in the charter of Maryland. Though his powers under the charter of Avalon were almost absolute, he agreed that the laws of the colony should be made with the advice and consent of the freemen.

The Founding

The only condition of the grant was that he would give the king or his successor a white horse whenever he should visit the country.

After Baltimore laid down the responsibilities of public office, he visited Avalon in the summer of 1627, but he was disappointed in his province, which he found desolate and unpromising. In the following year he nevertheless came back, this time bringing with him Lady Baltimore, all his family except his eldest son, Cecil, and about forty colonists thus increasing the population of the little colony to about one hundred. When the French set upon some English fishing vessels in the harbors of Avalon, Baltimore furnished aid to his countrymen and so became involved in a petty warfare with the French. In these actions against the French the two vessels the *Ark* and the *Dove,* in which the first Maryland settlers later crossed the ocean, played a prominent part.

Toward the end of 1628 Baltimore first experienced the severities of a Newfoundland winter. He shiveringly wrote to King Charles that he had resolved "to quit my residence and to shift to some other [and] warmer climate of this new world, where the winters be shorter and less rigorous.... From the middle of October to the middle of May there is a sad fare of winter upon all this land; both sea and land so frozen for the greater part of the time, as they are not penetrable, no plant or vegetable thing appearing out of the earth until around the beginning of May, nor fish in the sea; beside the air so intolerable cold as it is hardly to be endured." Since he and many of his company had been sick during this arduous winter he determined "to commit this place to fishermen that are able to encounter storms and hard weather, and to remove myself with some forty persons to your Majesty's dominion Virginia." He besought Charles to grant him land there. His Newfoundland venture had cost him about £ 20,000, but Avalon would remain in the possession of the Baltimores until 1754.

Baltimore now proceeded to Virginia with some of his colonists to study the country and to select a site for a new settlement. But his reception in Virginia foreshadowed trouble between that colony and his future colony. His intentions were known to the Virginians and raised apprehensions in their minds that he might receive from the king a charter for the whole of their colony, which had been made a royal colony five years earlier. That he was rudely treated in Jamestown seems clear, for a Thomas Tindall there was later put in the pillory "for giving my Lord Baltimore the lie and threatening to knock him down." He was ordered by the Virginia officials to take the oath of supremacy which he as a loyal Catholic could not do, though he offered to take a modified form of it. Realizing that he could not establish among these people the sanctuary for persecuted Catholics which he envisaged, he determined to leave Virginia. But though thus severely rebuffed, he did not abandon his plan of establishing a colony in the New World.

Finally after returning to London Baltimore received from the king a grant of land between the James and Passamagnus (Chowan) Rivers, the latter crossing the northern border of present North Carolina. But almost immediately he encountered opposition from some of the members of the old Virginia Company who asserted that they themselves were preparing to settle colonists in that region. Baltimore then turned to the region north of Virginia, surrendered his grant of Carolana, as it was called, and received instead a grant of lands on both sides of Chesapeake Bay. A colony there would form a buffer between Virginia and the Dutch who had established themselves in the Hudson Valley. He is believed to have drawn up the Maryland grant himself. According to a later report, he left in it a blank for the name "which he designed should be Crescentia, or, the land of Crescence, but leaving it to his majesty to insert." Baltimore told Charles that he desired to name the province after him but could not do so because another American colony had already been named Carolina. He then accepted the king's proposal that the new colony be named in honor of the queen Henrietta Maria. So the name Maryland was adopted.[2] But Baltimore's health had been impaired by his arduous winter in Newfoundland, and on April 16, 1632 before his patent had passed the great seal he died at the age of 53 leaving his title and property to his eldest son, Cecil.

The Baltimore property included not only estates in England and Ireland but also the province of Avalon and the new grant of lands on Chesapeake Bay. The charter of Maryland, written in Latin, gave the new province a boundary line which ran "from the promontory, or head-land, called Watkin's Point" in Chesapeake Bay east to the Atlantic Ocean, then "into that part of the bay of Delaware on the north, which lyeth under the 40th degree of north latitude from the aequinoctial, where New England is terminated," thence along the fortieth parallel westward "unto the true meridian of the first fountain of the river of Pattowmack," thence southward to the southern bank of the Potomac and along the southern bank of that river to Chesapeake Bay, and "thence by the shortest line unto the aforesaid promontory, or place, called Watkin's Point." The charter granted to the proprietor perpetual possession of all lands and waters within these boundaries and all islands within ten marine leagues of the shore together with the mines and fisheries. It entrusted these large domains to him "in free and common soccage," that is by a feudal tenure held at a fixed symbolic rental of two Indian arrows, which were to be delivered at the castle of Windsor on Tuesday of Easter week every year, and an actual charge of one fifth of all the gold and silver found in the province.

Under the charter Lord Baltimore and his successors were given palatinate authority including all the rights and privileges which "any bishop of Durham, within the bishopric or county palatine of Durham, in our kingdom of England, ever heretofore hath had, held, used or enjoyed, or of right could, or ought to have, held [hold?] use or enjoy." The bishop of Durham had been assigned his fief in northern England as a military bulwark against the Scotch. Lord Baltimore's insistence upon including this clause in his charter suggested that he regarded his new province as a frontier outpost of empire and wished to govern it as a county palatine, subject only to the suzereignty of the king.[3]

In the charter he was given the right to make all laws for his colony, with the assent, however, of the freemen of the province, and ordinances not affecting life or property without their assent. He could make peace or war, put down insurrection, call out the militia and declare martial law, establish courts of justice and appoint all judges, magistrates, and civil officers, confer titles and dignities provided "they be not such as are now used in England," erect towns and cities, establish ports of entry and departure, erect and found churches and dedicate them "according to the ecclesiastical laws of our kingdom of England," sell or rent land, and levy duties on ships and merchandise. All laws made for the colony must be "consonant to reason and be not repugnant or contrary, but (so far as conveniently may be) agreeable to the laws, statutes, customs and rights of this our kingdom of England." The colonists in Maryland would remain English subjects and could trade freely in English ports paying only such "customs and impositions, subsidies and taxes, as our other subjects of the kingdom of England, for the time being, shall be bound to pay." They were to participate in making the laws and to be exempt from taxation by the crown. They were given the right to trade with friendly foreign ports—a right which Virginia did not enjoy. The charter concluded that if at any future time any doubt should arise as to the interpretation "of any word, clause, or sentence, contained in this our present charter," it should be given an interpretation that "shall be judged to be the more beneficial, profitable and favourable to the aforesaid now Baron Baltimore, his heirs and assigns."

This method of proprietary investiture was a method commonly used by national rulers of western Europe to promote the development of lands which they claimed in the Americas. It can be viewed as a transferral to the new continent of the practice of subinfeudation which was one of the features of the feudal system. By this method Charles I sought both to reward a faithful counselor by giving him the responsibility of colonizing and developing, for his own profit and for the profit of his heirs forever, the lands defined in the charter of Maryland. With this mandate from Charles I and under the guidance of the wise and astute Cecil Calvert, second Lord Baltimore, the way was now prepared for the settlement of Maryland.

The charter of Maryland which was issued to Cecil, Lord Baltimore, on June 20, 1632, almost immediately aroused opposition from the Virginians. They promptly sent a memorial to the king complaining that the generous privileges which he had given to the Marylanders would draw settlers away from other colonies. Besides, they said, the charter violated their own rights and land claims with which the crown had promised not to interfere when it made Virginia a royal colony. The land which the king had just granted to Baltimore was already settled by Virginians and the settlement of Maryland would deprive them of the profitable Indian trade in Chesapeake Bay which they had carried on for more than twenty-five years.

Virginia's most active trader in the Chesapeake Bay region was William Claiborne, a native of Kent, England, who had come to America as surveyor of the Virginia Company in 1621 at the age of twenty. A graduate of Cambridge University he accepted the position of surveyor under generous inducements from the company, including free transportation for three persons, a house and 200 acres of land, an annual salary of £ 30, an outright grant of £ 20 for books and instruments, and permission to make private surveys of land at a rate of six shillings a day. Four years after his arrival Claiborne was appointed secretary to the colony; by that time he had become one of its wealthiest and most influential members. In 1626 he was commissioned by Governor George Yeardley of Virginia to trade with the Indians of Chesapeake Bay, and his commission was renewed by Governor John Pott in the following year, authorizing him to lead an expedition against the Indians in Chesapeake Bay and to explore the waters and lands there between the thirty-fourth and forty-first degrees of latitude. So successful was he in his trade with the Indians of that region that he associated himself with a firm of London merchants, William Clobery and Company, who advanced capital to him for his business. He now undertook to establish a trading post on an island in Chesapeake Bay which Captain John Smith had called Winston's Island, and he, or rather Clobery and Company, obtained a commission from Charles I early in 1631 authorizing him and his associates to trade "for corne, furres or any other comodities in all parts of New England and Nova Scotia, where there is not already a patent granted, to others for sole trade" and directing the officers in Virginia to permit him and his companions to trade in "all aforesaid parts." This commission was of very definite and limited scope. It was neither a patent for land nor a grant of trade in Virginia.

Claiborne proceeded up Chesapeake Bay and built a trading post on the southern tip, Kent Point, of Winston's Island which he bought from the Indians and which he renamed Kent Island in memory of his home county in England. He did this on August 17, 1631, almost a year before the Maryland charter was granted to Baltimore. Here he established a plantation for himself which he called Crayford. He retained his Virginia residence, however, at Hampton and continued to sit in the Virginia Council. He sent Captain Nicholas Martin to the Virginia House of Burgesses in 1631-1632 as a representative of both Kent Island and the northern neck of Virginia. But his claims and the claims of Virginia to Kent Island were only squatter's rights. Based upon the commission issued by Charles I they were only rights to trade not to settle nor own land. His settlement there could not deny to the king of England the right to grant the lands of the Chesapeake to Lord Baltimore, as the king did in 1632.

The protest of the Virginians against Baltimore's patent was referred by the crown to the Lords Commissioners for Foreign Plantations, who after hearing the case urged a peaceful adjustment of the controversy. The king himself wrote to the Governor and Council of Virginia directing them to treat Lord Baltimore, who was planning to lead his colonists personally to America, "with that courtesie and respect that belong to a person of his rank and qualities and departed from hence in our very good grace and favour." The Privy Council in London ordered all officers of the crown to allow Baltimore's vessels to go to and return from Maryland "without any let or hindrance."

Meanwhile the proprietor of Maryland was preparing an expedition to occupy his new province. Profiting from the mistakes of his predecessors in colonization in America he laid his plans carefully with the primary aim of establishing a great family estate with lucrative commercial possibilities. To this end, he organized a joint stock company offering to adventurers who would help to finance the enterprise the opportunity for the first two years to share proportionately in the profits of the company. Each such adventurer would transport to the colony as many persons as possible and would settle them on lands granted to each investor in proportion to the number transported. The proprietor's policy for the settlement and development of his province was based upon individual initiative and freedom of enterprise.

In order to attract colonists Baltimore advertised the charms of Maryland and other inducements for settlement there in *A Declaration of the Lord Baltemore's Plantation in Maryland, nigh upon Virginia: manifesting the Nature, Quality, Condition and rich Utilities it contayneth,* which was probably written by Father Andrew White of the Society of Jesus. In particular he praised "The Ayre, serene and gentle, not so hot as Florida, and old Virginia, nor so cold as New England, but between them both, having the good of each, and the ill of neither." The Lord Baltimore, concluded the *Declaration,* sits in his office in Bloomsberry at the upper end of Holboyne in London and "hath good advantage to assist" prospective adventurers in "those things, by reason of the many Provisions hee maketh both for himself and others."

But before dispatching his colonists to Maryland, Lord Baltimore concluded that because of the campaign against his charter by the Virginia lobby at court he must remain behind in England, and he therefore reluctantly abandoned his intention of leading the first company to Maryland. He accordingly put his brother Leonard, then about twenty-eight years of age, in charge of the expedition that was to sail on the *Ark* and the *Dove* and sent also a younger brother, George. Leonard Calvert, who was thus chosen to guide the fortunes of Maryland in America and who served as lieutenant governor of the colony for the next twelve years, was able, judicious, and completely faithful to Lord Baltimore's interests. With him were associated Jerome Hawley, who was a brother to the governor of the British colony of Barbados, and Thomas Cornwaleys, a Protestant who became the military leader of the new settlement in Maryland. These three formed the nucleus of the Council. Like Leonard Calvert, Cornwaleys was a second son of a member of the English nobility. Thirteen other "gentlemen" are mentioned as being members of this first expedition, and Lord Baltimore wrote that it included in addition about three hundred laborers and handicraftsmen. The majority of the "gentlemen" were Roman Catholics, and probably most of the rest of the company were Protestants. One member of the first expedition was Mathias da Sousa, a "mulatto," who was probably purchased in Barbados before the expedition reached the shores of Maryland.

Lord Baltimore's instructions to his colonists, dated November 13, 1633, revealed his foresight and wisdom. Devout but not bigoted in his Catholicism, Cecil was undertaking to establish a colony for a nation and a king who had rejected Catholicism and were persecuting Catholics. He was proposing to establish an asylum for abused English Catholics but had no intention of founding a colony just for them—a colony which like Plymouth and Massachusetts Bay admitted only their co-religionists. The Puritans sought in their New England settlements freedom for Puritans to worship God according to Puritan ways, but Lord Baltimore had a higher revelation. He proposed to found a colony where all men could find religious freedom. His colony would not be straitlaced, as were the Puritan colonies in New England, nor would it, like them, be limited only to religious conformists.

In carrying out his plans, therefore, to found a colony which would yield him a financial profit, would serve as an asylum for Roman Catholics, and would attract other immigrants, Cecil, Lord Baltimore, refrained from uniting church and state. Religious liberty would exist in Maryland from the beginning. There Catholics and Protestants would mingle freely and live together in harmony for many years. At a time when religious bigotry and intolerance were rampant in Europe and the Thirty Years' War, largely fought over religious matters, was raging, Baltimore founded a colony in America which was based upon religious liberty. Here the principle of religious toleration was established and practiced two years before Roger Williams, the New England Baptist, made it a cardinal tenet of his new colony of Rhode Island and Providence Plantation and many years before any European prince adopted it. Tolerance, moderation, compromise—these would be the guiding principles of Maryland. For these qualities Maryland both as a colony of the Baltimores and later as a free state in the American Union would be distinguished.

Baltimore enjoined the Governor and Councilors of his colony that they "preserve unity and peace amongst all the passengers on Shippboard, and that they suffer no scandall nor offence to be given to any of the Protestants, whereby any just complaint may heereafter be made, by them, in Virginea or in England." They must see to it that the Catholics in the colony practiced their religion "as privately as may be" and remained "silent upon all occasions of discourse concerning matters of Religion." They were also to seek information "concerning the private plotts of his Lo[rdshi]pps adversaries in England" and to send such information "by some trusty messenger in the next shipps that returne for England." Baltimore commanded his colonists to preserve peace with the Virginians and on no account to go to Jamestown unless they were driven there "by some extremity of weather (w[hi]ch god forbidd)." For their first settlement he advised them to search out a place on Chesapeake Bay or the "Pattawomeck River" that is "probable to be healthfull and fruitfull," might be "easily fortified," and "may be convenient for trade both w[i]th the English and savages." He directed them to send a messenger, who "is conformable to the Church of England," to carry the king's instructions to Governor John Harvey of Virginia, to notify him of the arrival of the Marylanders, to assure him of their good disposition toward Virginia, and to present him with "a Butt of sacke." Baltimore also directed the Governor and Commissioners to notify Claiborne of their arrival and of their authority over the province and to invite him to confer with them. He was "willing to give him all the encouragement he cann to proceede" in his settlement on Kent Island and wished to assure him that he desired to do justice to everyone. If Claiborne refused to confer with the Governor and Commissioners, Baltimore instructed them to "lett him alone for the first yeare" meanwhile informing themselves of his strength and his connection with Virginia.

Before receiving these instructions the expedition had sailed down the Thames in two small vessels, the *Ark* of between 300 and 400 tons, which had already carried the first Lord Baltimore's colonists to Avalon, and the *Dove,* which was a pinnace of only 50 tons. They were soon overtaken, however, by crown officials, and all the passengers, 127 in number, were required to take the oath of allegiance, thus professing themselves Protestants. After all of them had complied with this request the vessels proceeded to the Isle of Wight where they took on two Jesuit priests, Fathers Andrew White and John Altham, and possibly others who had been unwilling to take the oath of allegiance or had only recently decided to go to Maryland. Leaving Cowes at ten in the morning on Friday, November 22, they soon encountered a severe storm, and the small *Dove* disappeared from the sight of the anxious watchers on the *Ark.* The *Ark* encountered another storm on November 30, so furious that the sailors themselves said "they had seene ships cast away with lesse violence of weather." Without sails the ship floated upon the water "like a dish," recorded Father White, but it successfully weathered the storm, and for the remaining three months of the trip "had not one howre of bad weather, but soe prosperous a navigation, as our mariners never saw so sweet a passage."

Taking the usual southern route by way of the West Indies which served as a halfway house between England and America, the *Ark* reached Barbados on January 3, 1634, and remained there until January 24 during which time, to the great amazement and joy of all the passengers on the *Ark,* they saw the *Dove* sail into the harbor. After reprovisioning their vessels in the West Indies, the expedition finally arrived in Virginia on February 24, 1634, and, disobeying their instructions, anchored at Point Comfort. There they were welcomed by Governor Harvey who promised to furnish them "with all manner of provisions, cattle, hogs, corn, poultry, and fruit trees, as well as bricks and tiles for the Lord Proprietary's seat though much against his council's will." They also met Claiborne who informed them that "the Indians were all in armes to resist us, having heard that 6 Spanish ships were a comeing to destroy them all." Father White, the chronicler of the expedition, suspected that "The rumour was most like to have begunne from himselfe."

On March 5 the *Ark* and the *Dove* entered the province of Maryland at the mouth of the Potomac River. They thought the Chesapeake Bay "the most delightfull water" they had ever seen, and Father White wrote that the Potomac was "the sweetest and greatest river I have seene, so that the Thames is but a little finger to it. There are noe marshes or swampes about it, but solid firme ground, with great variety of woode, not choaked up with undershrubs, but commonly so farre distant from each other as a coach and fower horses may travale without molestation." Sailing slowly up the Potomac River they finally landed on March 25, 1634 at St. Clement's, now Blackiston's Island, which then probably contained about 80 acres and was located at a place where the banks of the Potomac came close together. Making a cross out of a large tree they set it up, celebrated the mass, and "tooke possession of this Countrey for our Saviour, and for our Soveraigne Lord the King of England." This was the birthday of Maryland.

Leaving the *Ark* at St. Clement's Island, Leonard Calvert took the *Dove* and another pinnace, which had been hired in Virginia, and ascended the Potomac River to explore the country and to establish friendly contacts with the Indians. He took with him an interpreter, Captain Henry Fleet, who had lived as a captive among the Indians for several years and after his release had continued to trade with them. At "Patowmecke Towne," probably at or near Aquia Creek, they found an Indian tribe whose ruler or *werowance* was a child. They were welcomed by his uncle, Archihau, who was regent of the tribe, and Father Altham delivered to him a brief discourse "touching the errours of their religion." The visitors assured the Indians that they came not to make war but only to spread good will.

Leaving this friendly ruler, Calvert and his followers sailed twenty leagues farther up the river to Piscataway, the seat of the "emperor." There they found the Indians hostile, but Calvert mollified them with assurances of peace and persuaded their chief to confer with him in his ship. While several hundred suspicious savages milled about on the shore Calvert informed their chief that they came to teach the Indians a "divine doctrine" which would "lead them to heaven" and asked him whether he "would be content" that the English colonists should "set downe in his Countrey." To this question the werowance cryptically answered "that he would not bid him goe, neither would hee bid him stay, but that he might use his owne discretion."

Calvert and his party now returned to St. Clement's Island seeking, as they journeyed, a suitable site for a settlement. Perceiving the value of Fleet's services to the colonists Calvert offered him a share of the beaver trade of the new province and took his advice as to the best location for a settlement. In company with Fleet he journeyed in a barge up the St. George's River, now St. Mary's, which empties into the Potomac about fifteen miles from its mouth, to "a most convenient harbor and pleasant country lying on each side of it, with many large fields of excellent land, cleared from all wood." The site seemed admirably suited for a settlement, for the soil was good, the air clear, timber and fresh water abounded, the harbor could accommodate "ships of any burthen," and the place could easily be fortified. Here on this desirable site lived the Indian tribe of Yaocomico. Calvert went on shore and was welcomed by the werowance in a friendly manner that augured well for the future relations between the Marylanders and the Indians. After inspecting the country roundabout, he presented the chief and the elders of the tribe with axes, hoes, knives, and cloth, and thus wisely at the beginning established friendly relations with them.

The Indians in turn agreed to allow the newcomers to live in one part of their town and surrendered their wigwams and fields of corn. They also offered to turn the entire village over to Calvert's settlers at the end of the harvest. Their conduct was the more remarkable because in 1622, only twelve years before, the Indians in Virginia had almost obliterated the white settlements on the James River, and even "a few daies before" the Marylanders arrived, as Father White wrote, the Potomac River Indians had taken up arms against the English, but now they, "like lambes yeeld themselves, glad of our company, gieving us houses, land, and liveings for a trifle." The pious priest saw in it "the finger of God," but in fact the Yaocomicos had a practical reason for befriending the strongly armed newcomers. They were subject to devastating raids from the fierce Susquehannocks to the north and hoped to live under the protection of the whites. They now agreed with the Marylanders to live together peaceably and to pay damages for any injuries done. Relations between the two races in Maryland from the very beginning, therefore, were placed on a treaty basis, and the land on which the newcomers settled was freely turned over to them by the natives.

To this site, which they called St. Mary's, soon came the *Ark* and the pinnaces, and there within a four-sided palisade, 120 yards square, they established their first settlement fortifying it with "six murderers in posts most convenient," which, wrote Calvert, were "sufficient to defend against any such weak enemies as we have reason to expect here." From the *Ark* and the *Dove* they removed the slips of fruit trees which they had foresightedly brought with them and planted orchards. From the friendly Indians they either received as gifts or bought deer, partridges, squirrels, turkeys, and great quantities of fish, oysters, and maize. They allowed the squaws to move freely among them with their children, and the women of the colony learned from the Indian women how to prepare bread from the Indian corn. The two Jesuit priests converted one of the Indian wigwams into the first chapel in Maryland.

The friendly relations which were thus established between the Maryland settlers and the tribes of southern Maryland were never broken. The Indians accepted a dependent status under the Maryland government, which later made laws for their protection, and they submitted their choice of chiefs to the governor for ratification. In 1651 Lord Baltimore made an interesting proposal for dealing with the friendly Indian tribes of the "Mattapanians the Wicomocons the Patuxants, the Lamasconsons the Kighahnixons and the Chopticons." He directed that a tract of eight- or ten-thousand acres "in the head of Wicocomico River called Choptico" be created into a manor named Calverton for the benefit of these tribes. These Indians, he wrote in a letter to the Maryland governor, had probably been harassed by the Susquehannocks and now expressed a "desire to put themselves under our Protection and to have a Grant from us" of that land. The Proprietor stated that they had been "not only always well affected unto" the English settlers but also "willing to Submit themselves" to Baltimore's government, and he hoped that their settlement on this manor "may be a means not only to bring them to Civility but also to Christianity and may Consequently, be as well an Addition of Comfort and Strength to the English Inhabitants, as a safety and protection to those Indians." He appointed Robert Clarke, the Surveyor General, as steward of the manor, authorizing him to hold the manor courts and to grant fifty-acre tracts of land to the Indians subject to an annual rent of one shilling per fifty acres and certain services.[4]

The Lord Proprietor and the General Assembly had started the practice of reserving Indian lands for their occupants as early as 1650, and in 1669 they established an Indian reservation on the south bank of the Choptank River but without the forms of feudalism which the Proprietor had prescribed. Though the Maryland authorities endeavored sincerely to protect the Indians in the Province, they were unable to prevent encroachment on the lands by the whites and hostile action against them by northern tribes. Without this protection the population of the friendly Indian tribes of Maryland dwindled away. In 1670 when the Indians sent a deputation to the governor to renew their treaties with him they pathetically apologized for their weakness and for their inability to offer any presents worth accepting and asked only "that hereafter, when their nation may be reduced to nothing, they may not be scorned and chased out of our protection." To this plaint they received assurances from the governor that as long as they kept their promises under their league "we should not scorn or cast off the meanest of them." The Yaocomicos, Piscataways, Patuxents, and other Indian tribes of southern Maryland never wavered in their friendship for the Marylanders; only the fierce Susquehannocks and Nanticokes gave trouble to them, and their hostility was serious and long-continued.

Footnotes

[1] G.E. Aylmer, *The King's Servants: The Civil Service of Charles I*, Columbia University Press, New York, 1961, p. 117.

[2] Milton Rubincam, "Queen Henrietta Maria: Maryland's Royal Namesake," *Maryland Historical Magazine*, vol. 54, No. 2, June 1959, pp. 131-148.

[3] Thomas G. Lapsley, *The County Palatine of Durham*, New York, 1900.

[4] *Archives of Maryland*, vol. I, pp. 329-330.

Sources and Additional Reading

Andrews, Matthew Page, *The Founding of Maryland,* The Williams and Wilkins Company, Baltimore, and D. Appleton-Century Company, 1933.

Aylmer, G.E., *The King's Servants: The Civil Service of Charles I,* Columbia University Press, New York, 1961.

Brantly, William T., *The English in Maryland, 1632-1691,* in Justin Winsor, ed., *Narrative and Critical History of America,* 8 vols., vol. III, [517]-562 (Chapter XIII), Houghton Mifflin Company, 1884-1889.

The Founding

Browne, William Hand, *George Calvert and Cecilius Calvert, Barons Baltimore of Baltimore,* Dodd, Mead, and Company, 1890.

———, *Maryland: The History of a Palatinate,* Revised and Enlarged Edition, Houghton Mifflin Company, Boston and New York, 1912.

Calvert Papers, 3 vols., Fund Publications, nos. 28, 34, and 35, Maryland Historical Society, Baltimore, 1889-1899.

Forman, Henry Chandlee, *Jamestown and St. Mary's: Buried Cities of Romance,* Johns Hopkins Press, Baltimore, 1938.

Hall, Clayton Colman, *The Lords Baltimore and the Maryland Palatinate,* Baltimore, Nunn & Co., 1904.

———, ed., *Narratives of Early Maryland, 1633-1684,* Charles Scribner's Sons, New York, 1910; reprint 1959.

Ives, Joseph Moss, *The Ark and the Dove: The Beginning of Civil and Religious Liberties in America,* Longmans, Green & Co., London and New York, 1936; reprint 1969.

Lapsley, Thomas G., *The County Palatine of Durham,* New York, 1900.

Maryland Historical Society, *Archives of Maryland,* 72 vols., Baltimore, 1883-1970.

Mereness, Newton D., *Maryland as a Proprietary Province,* 1901; reprint 1968.

Neill, Edward D., *The Founders of Maryland as Portrayed in Manuscripts, Provincial Records and Early Documents,* J. Munsell, Albany, 1876.

———, *Thomas Cornwallis and Early Maryland Colonists,* David Clapp & Son, Boston, 1889.

Semmes, Raphael, *Captains and Mariners of Early Maryland,* Baltimore, Johns Hopkins Press, Baltimore, 1937.

Steiner, Bernard C., *The Beginnings of Maryland, 1631-1639,* Johns Hopkins University Studies in History and Political Science, Series 21, Johns Hopkins University Press, Baltimore, 1903.

———, "The First Lord Baltimore and His Colonial Projects," American Historical Association, *Annual Report for the Year 1905,* pp. 109-122, Washington, 1906.

White, Father Andrew, S.J., *Relatio Itineris in Marylandiam,* Fund Publication No. 7, Maryland Historical Society, Baltimore, 1907.

CHAPTER IV

CHALLENGES

In accordance with Lord Baltimore's instructions his colonists in Maryland surveyed the land in their new settlement and built their houses "near adjoining" each other on streets regularly laid out. They somewhat pretentiously incorporated their settlement as St. Mary's City. Each settler who had equipped and transported himself received 100 acres of land, his wife the same amount, each child over sixteen years of age 50 acres, each man servant between the ages of sixteen and fifty 100 acres, and each woman servant under forty years of age 50 acres. For each 50 acres the colonist was required to pay a quitrent of twelve pence in the commodities of the country. Each colonist who brought five men to Maryland received 1,000 acres and could erect his estate into an English manor, the owner or lord of which might "enjoy within the said Mannor a Court Leet and Court Baron, with all things thereunto belonging, according to the most usual forme and custome of England." During the first fifty years of the new colony, that is until 1684, when the proprietor ceased to create manors, sixty-two manors were thus patented to private "adventurers" by the Lord Proprietor.

So favorable were the beginnings of Maryland that when the Proprietor received his first news of the colony, he hastened to publish in 1634 the *Relation of Maryland,* based upon Father White's *Briefe Relation.* In it he spread the information that his colonists had already planted corn and had obtained hogs and cows from Accomac; that the rich soil produced an abundance of berries, sassafras, persimmons, acorns, walnuts, and chestnuts and was alive with animals and birds of all kinds. He invited others to transport themselves to his colony and in a later edition, 1635, informed them that suitable houses would be erected at St. Mary's for the entertainment and accommodation of newcomers.

Though Baltimore had directed his brother to start the manufacture of salt and to search out deposits of saltpeter, iron, and other minerals, the basis of the economic life of the colony was agriculture and the fur trade. So plentiful was corn in Maryland that in the summer of 1634 Leonard Calvert sent the *Dove* with a cargo of corn to

Boston. John Winthrop, the governor of the Massachusetts settlement, noted in his *Journal* the arrival of the *Dove* at Boston, but he was not favorably impressed by the Marylanders. He recorded that they cursed and swore "most horribly." The strait-laced magistrates of Boston finally requested the master of the *Dove* "to bring no more such disordered persons among us." But Thomas Weston, who had helped to finance the Pilgrim colony at Plymouth, left Puritan New England to become lord of Westbury Manor in Maryland.

Maryland's trade in furs gave rise to more serious difficulties, for Virginians had hitherto enjoyed a virtual monopoly of this business. Claiborne had established his fur-trading post on Kent Island and had already met Calvert in Virginia. Even before Calvert's arrival he had asked the Virginia Council how he should "demean himself in respect of the Lord Baltimore's patent and his deputies." The Council answered that "they wondered why there should be any such question made" and that they knew of no reason why they should render up the right of the Isle of Kent, more than any other formerly given to this colony." Until the validity of Baltimore's charter could be established in England the Virginians resolved to maintain all their rights and privileges and meanwhile to "observe all good correspondency" with the Marylanders. The cause of this friction between the two colonies was their common interest in the fur trade.

The principal champion of Virginia's claim to this trade was Claiborne. His little settlement on Kent Island had been almost wiped out by fire in 1631, but by 1633, acting as an agent for Clobery and Company, he was employing twenty-two persons to work on the company's stock and to trade with the Indians. Among these was the first African who appears on the records in Maryland, for in November 1633 Claiborne paid £1.5.0 "for a neger's service some months." The religious needs of the settlement were served by the Rev. Richard James, an Anglican, who was the first clergyman in Maryland and who received £60 a year as tithes for his services. The fur trade was the principal business of the settlement, but in 1634, Claiborne wrote, this was "mutch hindered and molested by the Indians falling out with us and killing our men and by the Marylanders hindring our trade." According to his account, the Marylanders closed his trade by proclamation on April 8, 1634, and surprised some of his boats, which were probably sailing somewhere in the neighborhood of Kent Island.

Claiborne's grievances against the Marylanders were entangled with Virginia politics, for he was one of the faction in the Virginia Council who bitterly opposed the Governor, Sir John Harvey, and determined to drive him from office. As a weapon against him they raised the cry that he was befriending the "Jesuitical papists" in Maryland. "Here" in Virginia, wrote one of the Virginia settlers, Captain Thomas Young, who was sympathetic to the Marylanders, "it is accounted a crime almost as heinous as treason to favor, nay, to speak well of that colony of my Lord's. And I have observed, myself, a palpable kind of strangeness and distance between those of the best sort in this country, which have formerly been very familiar and loving to one another, only because the one hath been suspected to have been a well wisher to the Plantation of Maryland." The presence of Lord Baltimore's colony in America therefore had disruptive effects upon politics in Virginia.

The Marylanders became convinced that Claiborne was inciting the Indians against them by spreading reports that they were Spaniards, and they presented this charge to the Virginia government. Accordingly, four of the members of the Virginia Council and Claiborne met with two Maryland representatives, George Calvert and Frederick Wintour, at Patuxent to question the Indian chiefs as to the origin of this rumor. The chiefs admitted that they thought Calvert's party were Spaniards but denied that Claiborne had told them so. According to Claiborne this investigation by official representatives of the two colonies cleared him of the accusation; but according to the Marylanders, Claiborne and his fellow councilor Mathews had "subtilely inveigled into their company two very young gentlemen," George Calvert and Wintour, and persuaded them to "accompany them to the examination of the Indians." In Claiborne's presence they had then asked the Indians only such questions as served their purpose and after reducing the examination to writing had induced George Calvert and Wintour to sign it. By this so-called investigation the friction between the two colonies, growing out of the struggle for the fur trade of the Chesapeake region, was intensified; and in September, 1634, Lord Baltimore directed his brother, the governor, to seize Claiborne, imprison him at St. Mary's, and take possession, if possible, of the Kent Island plantation. The rivalry between the two settlements in Maryland seemed headed for a showdown.

At this juncture Clobery and Company sent a petition to the king alleging that the Marylanders had already shot at their men and boats in Chesapeake Bay. In response the king sent a letter to the Governor and Council of Virginia prohibiting "Lord Baltimore, as all other pretenders, under him, or otherwise, to plantations in those parts" from doing violence to Clobery and Company and "from disturbing or hindering them in their honest proceedings and trade in the Kentish Island near to Virginia" which they had established "by our commission." This interposition by the king on behalf of the Company seemed to strengthen Claiborne's position, and he now sent out his pinnace, *Long Tayle*, commanded by Thomas Smith, to the Patuxent River in the very heart of the Maryland colony to trade for corn and furs with the Indians.

This was a flagrant act of defiance of Baltimore's authority in the territory assigned to him by the crown. Early in April 1635 when Captain Fleet and three other members of Calvert's group overtook Smith, they asked him by what right he traded there. Getting an unsatisfactory answer, they seized the vessel and took her to St. Mary's. There Governor Calvert upheld Fleet's action explaining that he had issued orders "to stop all vessels they should find trading in the Province." Accordingly he retained the vessel but allowed Smith and his men to depart with only one gun and no provisions.

The seizure of the *Long Tayle* led to the first naval engagement in American waters. Claiborne immediately sent out the *Cockatrice*, with thirteen armed men commanded by Lieutenant Ratcliffe Warren, to demand the return of the *Long Tayle* and to capture vessels belonging to the Marylanders. Calvert then fitted out two pinnaces, the *St. Margaret* and the *St. Helen,* and the hostile vessels met in the Pocomoke Sound on April 23, 1635. In the ensuing engagement one of the Marylanders was killed and of the Kent Islanders three men were killed and three wounded.

The news of this battle produced a great commotion in Virginia, for Governor Harvey had already defended the seizure of the *Long Tayle* by the Marylanders and, according to his enemies, had declined to carry out or even to read the king's orders relating to Clobery and Company. Accordingly, the Council arrested him for treason and sent him back to England offering as their chief allegation against him "that he was a Marylander, that is one that favored too much my Lord Baltimore's plantation to their prejudice." The newly elected governor of Virginia, Captain John West, then put Claiborne under bond to keep the peace and required similar bond of every Marylander who visited Virginia.

Now occurred a fortunate event which enabled Calvert eventually to gain possession of the Kent Island settlement. Clobery and Company sent over Captain George Evelin to supersede Claiborne as agent and commander at Kent while Claiborne returned to England. Though Evelin is reported to have spoken at first against the claims of Baltimore to Kent Island, he soon had an interview with Calvert either at St. Mary's or in Virginia at which he was thoroughly converted to the

Governor's views, and, according to Claiborne's subsequent charges, he proceeded to release the servants at Kent Island, to carry away the property of the plantation there, and to spend his time in constructing a manor, called Evelinton, at Piney Point on the Potomac which had been granted him by Calvert.

The Maryland governor was so encouraged by Evelin's actions and so emboldened by new instructions from his brother, the proprietor, that he now wrote to the Kent Islanders promising to pardon their past offences if they would submit to him and offering to appoint any person of their own choice as their commander. But this generous offer elicited no favorable response from the islanders, who, under the influence of John Butler, Claiborne's brother-in-law, and Thomas Smith, refused to submit. Baltimore therefore appointed Evelin commander of the island authorizing him to hold court, determine certain specified civil and criminal cases, and appoint necessary officers. Evelin, armed with this commission from Calvert, returned to Kent Island and tried to persuade the settlers there that they would fare better under the government of Maryland than under that of Virginia, for, said he, under Baltimore's government, "you might carry your commodities and your tobacco and pipestaves into what country you would, which the Virginians cannot. Claiborne's patent is of no effect, merely giving authority to trade in Nova Scotia and places near New England and not in the Bay of Virginia or Maryland." Even this argument, however, was unavailing, and warrants were issued for the arrest of three of the leaders of the opposition.

The islanders were not finally subdued until Calvert himself in February 1638 led against them a military expedition, which included 30 choice musketeers. His first issued a proclamation, signed by himself, Hawley, and John Lewger, charging the islanders with having committed "many piracies, mutinies, and contempts," having disobeyed warrants for the arrest of malefactors, and having conspired with the Susquehannocks and other Indians against the welfare and safety of the Province. He then conducted his armed followers to the island taking with him his loyal coadjutor Evelin. But no battle had to be fought, for the Marylanders, arriving at the settlement a little before sunrise, found it unguarded and surprised the inhabitants. They then gathered together as prisoners all who lived within the palisaded fort and marched to the plantations of Butler and Smith taking their prisoners with them. There Calvert found and arrested both of these men and then proclaimed a general pardon for all the other inhabitants of the island. The whole island submitted to him, and he informed them that Baltimore would always be ready "upon their deserts to condescend to anything for their goods."

Calvert then sent the prisoners, Butler and Smith, back to St. Mary's in his pinnace, assembled the inhabitants of Kent Island to choose representatives for the General Assembly, and promised to furnish them with patents from the Proprietor for their lands. He appointed conservators of peace and a sheriff for the island and later confiscated all the property on the island belonging to Clobery and Company and to Claiborne. He also sent a band of his armed followers with two small pieces of ordnance to reduce another trading post belonging to Claiborne which was situated on Palmer's Island at the mouth of the Susquehanna River. Claiborne had acquired this island from the Susquehannocks and, apparently erroneously believing it to be north of the 40th parallel, had established there in 1637 a settlement which included a trading house well supplied with Indian trading goods, four indentured servants, eight cows, and sixty hogs. Calvert's men now seized the fort, carried away the men and livestock, and brought the island and its Protestant settlers under the jurisdiction of Lord Baltimore.[1]

At St. Mary's the assembly passed a law attainting Claiborne of piracy and murder, confiscating all his personal and real property, and declaring that his "blood was corrupt" so that he could neither inherit nor transmit property nor further exercise his civil rights. They brought Thomas Smith to trial on an indictment for piracy and pronounced him guilty by a vote of 18 to 1. Calvert then sentenced him to death by hanging, declared all his property forfeited, and refused to accord him the right of benefit of clergy. Maryland put to death Smith and one of the other Kent Island "rebels," Edward Beckler, but, curiously enough, did not bring Butler to trial. Calvert hoped to win him over to his side and evidently did so, for he soon commissioned him Captain of the Kent Island militia and second only to the commander of the island. Evelin soon disappeared from the records, but he had played a very important part in extending Baltimore's control over the Eastern Shore.

Claiborne now filed a petition with the king asking for a confirmation, under the great seal, of the grant of Kent Island and offering to pay £ 50 per year for the island and the same sum "for the plantation in the Susquehannoughs country." This petition was referred to the Lords Commissioners for Plantations, a distinguished group of eleven men presided over by the Archbishop of Canterbury, and when they met to consider Claiborne's complaint on April 4, 1638, both Claiborne and Baltimore were present with their counsel. After hearing the case the Commissioners decided that Claiborne's license was a license to trade with the Indians where "the sole trade had not been formerly granted by his majesty to any other" and that it gave no title to settle or trade with the Indians on Kent Island or at any other place within Baltimore's grant. This decision, which thus removed Kent Island from the control of Virginia and recognized it as a part of Maryland, was accepted as conclusive by the Virginia Governor and Council who now issued a proclamation forbidding any Virginian to "use, exercise or entertain any trade or commerce for any kind of commodity whatsoever with any of the Indians or salvages" in Maryland or even to travel among them without license from Lord Baltimore. But the decision did not settle the question of Claiborne's property rights in Maryland. It was therefore not accepted as conclusive by the persistent Claiborne, who continued to assert his claim and to give Maryland much further trouble.

Meanwhile, how fared the little colony at St. Mary's? After the settlers had been there for nearly a year Governor Calvert called an assembly of the people to make certain laws and ordinances for the colony, but all the laws that they passed were disallowed by Lord Baltimore who claimed the right under his charter to take the initiative in legislation. In the following year the Proprietor authorized Governor Calvert to summon an assembly of the freemen or their deputies, to show them a draft of "laws and ordinances for the good government" of Maryland which he had prepared and to secure their assent to the enactment of these laws. Taking advantage of the latitude allowed in these orders, Cornwaleys and his followers discarded the system of allowing every freeman to sit in the legislature and changed the character of representation to the burgess system.

This second Assembly convened at St. Mary's on January 25, 1638, and included at various times sixty-four different persons representing Kent Island and the three hundreds into which St. Mary's had been divided.[2] They sat as one house with three councilors, Thomas Cornwaleys, Robert Wintour, and John Lewger in attendance and the Governor presiding over the body. Many of the members held proxies for freemen who were unable to attend, Calvert himself holding five, which was the largest number from the Western Shore. Freemen who were absent without proxies were subject to fines, but the three Jesuits —Copley, White, and Altham—who pled sickness, were excused as also were others who could not cross St. George's River. A freeman could always revoke his proxy by personally appearing in the Assembly. Of course indentured servants, who probably constituted a majority of the inhabitants, were not summoned and were not represented by proxies. But when such persons finished their periods of indenture and became freemen they were eligible for membership in the Assembly. Maryland's first mulatto, Mathias da Sousa, for example, became a freeman in that way in 1641 and as a freeman was a member of the Maryland Assembly in that year.[3]

The Assembly first adopted rules for its own procedure. It then took under consideration the draft of laws which had been prepared by the Proprietor and voted not to adopt them. By what laws then should the province be governed? Calvert explained that his commission gave him power to act under the laws of England in civil cases and in criminal cases not extending to life and limb, but the Assembly decided to be governed only by laws of its own choosing and finally selected a committee of five members, consisting of Calvert, Cornwaleys, Wintour, Evelin, and Justinian Snow, to draft a set of laws for adoption by the Assembly and presentation to the Proprietor. The Governor yielded with good grace to the Assembly's wishes, probably because he had already been specifically informed by his brother, the Proprietor, that the Assembly might "propound and prepare other wholesome laws" to be transmitted to Baltimore for his approval. He interpreted this instruction to mean that the Proprietor would not strenuously insist upon his right to the initiative in legislation. Thus, early in the history of the colony the Assembly, by reason of its own assertiveness and the wisdom of an indulgent proprietor, established itself as a true legislature with powers to initiate and enact laws.

The Committee accordingly formulated a series of laws, now regrettably lost, which were ratified by the Assembly and transmitted to the Proprietor for his approval. At the close of 1638 Leonard Calvert received a letter from his brother yielding his claim to the initiative in law-making and authorizing the Governor in every General Assembly "to give assent unto such laws as you shall think fit and necessary for the good government of Maryland," if such laws were approved by the majority of the freemen or their deputies. Thereafter the laws of the Province if they conformed to the laws of England and were approved by the Governor would remain in force until and unless they were vetoed by the Proprietor.

The Governor now summoned the third Assembly to meet at St. Mary's City on February 12, 1639, and in preparation for it he called the first general election in Maryland's history. Each hundred—now five in number including Kent Island—chose two burgesses with the exception of Mattapanient which, being small, chose only one. This third

Assembly when it met included Governor Calvert, Secretary Lewger, other members of the Council, and nine burgesses—sixteen members in all, and it sat as one house. Their first act was entitled "An Act for establishing the house of Assembly & the laws to be made therein." In this act the Maryland burgesses claimed to represent the freemen of the province "as do the Burgesses in the House of Commons" in England and declared that they constituted the House of Assembly. The Assembly not only considered legislative matters but, again like the parliament in London, sat as a court, heard trials, and meted out punishment to offenders.

With the exception of the act mentioned above this Assembly passed only one statute, but it was of a general all-inclusive nature—an omnibus law—and contained some highly interesting provisions. It declared first that "Holy Church within this Province shall have all her rights, liberties, and indemnities, safe, whole and inviolable in all things," thus enacting that all religious sects which were later defined as those "professing to believe in God the Father, Son and Holy Ghost," should be free from unlawful interference by the civil authorities. It required all inhabitants to take "an oath of allegiance to his majesty," and after the adjournment of the Assembly Calvert set a good example by having the secretary administer the oath to him, and then he himself administered it in turn to all the Council. The act also recited that the inhabitants should have all their "rights and liberties according to the great charter of England" thus reaffirming fully for Marylanders their rights as Englishmen. In accordance with Baltimore's instructions, the Assembly conferred upon the Governor jurisdiction in civil suits and upon the Governor and Council jurisdiction in criminal cases, but they stipulated that a jury trial must be held in cases involving the loss of life or limb. The act also dealt with the subject of officers' fees, which was to give rise to a long controversy in Maryland, by requiring that they be paid in accordance with an accompanying table of fees; and it provided that the debts of an insolvent debtor be paid in the following order, first, debts to the Lord Proprietor, second, fees to public officers, third, ordinary debts, and fourth, debts for "wine and hot waters"—an interesting enactment unfavorable to the liquor traffic. And finally the act required every tobacco grower to "plant and tend 2 acres of corn" so that the colony would not be dependent for corn upon outside sources of supply and authorized the Proprietor to collect an export duty of five percent upon all tobacco shipped to any place not in England, Ireland, or Virginia.

The procedure and the enactments of this and later assemblies throw interesting light upon the history of early Maryland. The records of all the assemblies after the second are fairly complete, except those for the years 1644-1645 and 1646. They show that the Assembly while it was in session usually convened twice a day—once at eight o'clock in the morning and again at two o'clock in the afternoon. But the Assembly of 1642 met an hour and a half after sunrise. During busy sessions they did not scruple to transact public business on Sundays. During the sessions the members of the Assembly enjoyed freedom of speech and freedom from arrest. Their sessions were presided over by the governor, who possessed the power either to adjourn or to dissolve the Assembly.

The system of sending elected representatives from the hundreds to the Assembly, which began with the third Assembly in 1639, was continued in the fourth Assembly. But in addition the Governor summoned to the Assembly men who were not elected by their hundreds. This two-fold method of choosing the burgesses was apparently based on the method used in England for summoning the Lords and the Commons. The governor of Maryland, like the king of England, issued special writs to the members of the Council and to some of the more influential planters, and he prescribed the methods to be used in choosing the elected delegates. But when the governor called the fifth Assembly in 1641, he abandoned this double method and instead reverted to the practice that he had originally followed. He simply summoned all freemen in the province to come to the Assembly either in person or by proxy.

This Assembly consisted of forty-one men, including six of the seven councilors. When the governor convoked later assemblies his practice varied between the two methods depending apparently upon his preference at the time, for it was not prescribed by law. When he summoned the Sixth Assembly, he again invited each of the hundreds to choose one or two burgesses as delegates and in addition issued personal writs to Cornwaleys, Giles Brent, William Blount, John Langford, Thomas Gerard, Robert Evelin, Cuthbert Fenwick, Robert Clerk, and William Britton. In summoning the Seventh Assembly Calvert reverted to the proxy system by inviting all the "freemen inhabiting the Province" to appear in person or to send "delegates sufficiently authorized." Among the delegates who met in this Assembly at St. Mary's on September 5, 1642, Giles Brent held seventy-three proxies, all from men of Kent. Its total membership included at one time or another twenty-three men, but they held proxies for one hundred and seventy-seven persons. The members who were personally summoned apparently received no pay, but each elected burgess who had attended the sixth Assembly received an allowance of forty pounds of tobacco for each day of service and those from Kent received an additional allowance, probably to cover their travel. The charges of the Assembly were apportioned among the hundreds, showing that in 1642 St. Mary's had twenty-nine taxpayers, St. George's thirty, St. Clement's twenty, St. Michaels forty-five, Mattapanient forty-five, and Kent County seventy-one.

The Maryland Assembly was originally a unicameral legislature. But in the session of 1642 one of the members asked that the burgesses might sit "by themselves and have a negative." This request was denied by Governor Calvert. Not, apparently, until 1646 was the Assembly divided into two houses. But this division was foreshadowed by the Assembly of 1642 which ruled that a bill could become law only by the favorable action of a majority both of those burgesses who were personally summoned and of those who were elected. This recognition of the principle of bicameralism on the model of the English parliament was the earliest recorded in the colonies, and although Maryland's legislature was not the first actually to divide into two houses—the Massachusetts legislature began to do so in 1644—no other colonial legislature after Maryland chose to follow this system until North Carolina did so in 1666.

At the Fourth Assembly an interesting proposal for "stinting the planting of tobacco" was made following the precedent already set by Virginia. It was a forerunner to tobacco legislation in Maryland's later history and of crop-control legislation of our own time, but it failed of passage in this Assembly. In its stead the House passed a bill for "destroying of unsound tobacco." This necessitated an inspection system, and the act therefore provided that no tobacco should be exported from the Province until it was sealed by a sworn viewer or inspector. It also set up a table of inspection fees, defined bad tobacco as that which "shall be judged ground leaves, second crops, leaves notably bruised or worm eaten, or leaves house burnt, sun burnt, frost bitten, weather beaten in the house, sooty, wet, or in to high case, so that the viewer on his conscience may reasonably think that it is not likely to last until mid-summer following." The act provided that such tobacco must be burned. Based on the Virginia inspection act of 1624 this law, like later laws of Maryland on the subject, undoubtedly was intended to raise the quality of Maryland tobacco and so to sustain the price of the product.

Like many of the other early laws of the Maryland Assembly this act was considered temporary; it was intended to continue in force for only two years. Among other temporary laws that were enacted was one compelling planters to fence cornfields against cattle, another forbidding the exportation of corn, another conferring control of marriage entirely upon the secular authorities, and another authorizing county courts to "moderate the bills, wages, and rates of artificers, laborers, and chirurgeons." An Act of the Assembly of 1641 prescribed the penalty of death and loss of goods or of seven years' servitude upon runaway apprentices. The Assembly of 1642 established a judicial system for the Province conferring jurisdiction upon county courts and a Provincial Court and declaring that cases must be adjudicated "according to the law, or most general usage of the Province," or, in default of these, "according to equity and good conscience, not neglecting (so far as the judge or judges shall be informed thereof and shall find no inconvenience in the application to this Province) the rules by which right and just useth and ought to be determined in England in the same or the like cases." The Maryland Assembly thus claimed the right to determine what laws of the mother country were applicable and should be used in the Province.

Maryland claimed the same discretionary power with reference to English law in setting up its system of punishments. The Assembly of 1642 stipulated that crimes should be punished according to the statutes of the Province and, in default of these, "according to the best discretion of the judge or judges, judging as near as conveniently may be to the laudable law or usage of England." Court proceedings also were to follow the laws of the province or, in default of those, the procedures used in England. This Assembly adopted a criminal code, which defined as capital offenses acts of treason, wilful murder, plotting the death of or violence to the Proprietary or the Governor, communicating with an enemy of the Province, and opposing the Lord Proprietary with armed force. The code defined "less capital offenses" as homicide, piracy, robbery, sacrilege, and polygamy, and made them punishable by death, branding in the hand, forfeiture of lands and goods, exile, or imprisonment, though a prison had not yet been built. It also prescribed punishments for less serious offenses fixing the fine for drunkenness, for example, at one hundred pounds of tobacco, which should be used for constructing a prison. The fine for profanity was set at five pounds of tobacco.

In general Maryland's penal legislation conformed to the standards of the time. Theft, bigamy, and witchcraft were punishable by death and perjury by nailing the culprit's ears to the pillory. Various crimes were punished by burning with branding irons with the letters H,R,M,T, and others, signifying the character of the crime.[4] Servants who stole from their masters were subjected to a public whipping of thirty stripes for the first offense and branded for the second. Those who ran away and were caught were punished by having their period of servitude doubled. These punishments were not imposed upon "gentlemen," however, and a convicted criminal could be excused from the death penalty if he could prove that he could read and was therefore entitled to "benefit of clergy," though he was still subject to branding and imprisonment.

Maryland was often aroused during these early years by Indian alarms but suffered no such serious warfare as did Virginia in the early 1620's or the New England colonies in the Pequot War of 1637. When Baltimore's colonists were troubled by the warlike Susquehannocks and some of the Eastern Shore tribes in 1639, Calvert and his councilors made plans for an expedition against them. The early colonial records reveal nothing further about this expedition nor of a second expedition which was planned in January 1640. But later in the same month Calvert proclaimed that as "we are in peace and amity" with the Patuxents "I have taken them into our protection and prohibit all Englishmen from offering injury" to them. The assembly had already agreed that trade with the Indians should be controlled entirely by the proprietor, and the governor had advised his brother in England that the trade would be spoiled if he permitted too many persons to engage in it. He accordingly issued licenses to only a few traders and forbade all the colonists to sell arms or ammunition to the Indians.

The governor went still further in the following year and, in an attempt to control the unfriendly Indians, forbade all persons in the Province to harbor or entertain any Indian and authorized the Kent Islanders to "shoot, wound, or kill any Indian coming" upon the island. In 1642, he reaffirmed these orders. In addition he required all householders to supply themselves with sufficient guns, powder, and shot for each able-bodied man and ordered that no man should discharge three shots in a quarter of an hour except to give an alarm. When such an alarm was given all inhabitants within earshot of it were to repeat it. Ablebodied men were forbidden to go to church or any considerable distance from home without arms.

But as the Indians became more menacing and killed five Virginians and eight Marylanders, Governor Calvert sent a letter to the governor of Virginia proposing "an expedition against the Indians, for the vindicating of the honor of our nation, and also to deter the like outrages for the future." The Maryland Assembly then authorized the Governor to prepare an expedition taking every third man who could bear arms and provisioning and arming him at the expense of the hundred. To protect the colony against further Indian attacks the Assembly authorized the Governor, whenever the safety of the Province was threatened by the assault or invasion of the Indians, to impress vessels, men, arms, and ammunition up to certain specified limits. They granted an allowance to the sergeants in each hundred for training the militia as train-bands and exempted the justices of the peace and the commanders of the counties from such service. They also provided that persons who were disabled in the defense of the colony would receive medical attention and their wives and children would be cared for at the expense of the Province or the county—an act which was the prototype of later pension legislation in Maryland.

On the day when the Assembly adjourned, September 13, 1642, Calvert proclaimed the Susquehannocks, Wicomeses (possibly an Iroquois tribe), and Nanticokes enemies of the Province and dispatched a small expedition to Kent Island, under the command of William Brainthwait, Commander of the island. Its purpose apparently was preventive rather than punitive, for it pushed no farther than Kent Island and returned after two days. The failure of the expedition to wage an aggressive campaign was charged to Giles Brent who was alleged to have opposed it because he had been superseded as Commander of Kent Island, but he was later cleared of this charge and was restored to his office. As the Indian alarm continued, Calvert warned the Indians in early 1643 not to come near the English, on peril of their lives, without bringing an Englishman with them or bearing a "flag or fane of white fustian with his Lordship's arms in wax, ensealed thereon"; any Indians who did not comply with these instructions might be killed with impunity. He also commissioned Cornwaleys to head an expedition against the Susquehannocks, with promise of a reward from the booty of the expedition, but the plan was abandoned—probably because the planters were unwilling to leave their fields during the season of spring plowing. Calvert then concluded a six-weeks' truce with the Nanticokes and exempted them from the warning of his earlier proclamation.

Calvert's policy was to deal firmly but also fairly with the Indians, as was shown during the trial of John Elkin. Elkin was summoned to explain why he shot and killed the chief of the Yaocomicos. He admitted the killing but received a verdict of *not guilty* from the jury on the ground that the Indian was a pagan and they had no precedent in the laws of Virginia to make the killing of a pagan Indian murder. Their verdict was highly displeasing to the Governor, who replied to the jury that the tribe to which the dead man belonged was at peace with the

Marylanders and that "they ought not to take notice of what other colonies did, but of the law of England." He therefore sent them back to "consider better" of their opinion. When the jury came out again, they reported a verdict of "murder in his own defence" and were again sent back by the Governor to reconsider their decision. Their third verdict likewise was unsatisfactory. Calvert then "willed" that the verdict be not entered and that a new jury be called. From this new jury he obtained a verdict of manslaughter which was satisfactory to him. One of the members of the first jury was then fined one thousand pounds of tobacco because he had remarked insolently: "If an Englishman had been killed by the Indians, there would not have been so many words made of it." Obviously the Governor, though he may have thus played fast and loose with English common law practices, was actuated by considerations of policy. If the verdicts of the first jury virtually exonerating Elkin had been allowed to stand, any trigger-happy colonist in a rash moment could have brought all the horrors of Indian warfare upon his peaceloving comrades.

The Marylanders did not abandon the plan of a retaliatory campaign against the Susquehannocks. After Leonard Calvert's return to England in April 1643, the acting governor, Giles Brent, appointed Cornwaleys "Commander of the County of St. Mary's for all military affairs" and authorized him to lead another expedition against "those barbarous and inhumane pagans." The acting governor sent ten men to build a fort—probably called Fort Conquest—on Palmer's Island in the Susquehanna, and Cornwaleys marched against the Indians. The expedition, however, was unsuccessful and lost two field pieces to the Indians as well as several guns and other goods. The failure may have been due to the help which the Indians received from the Swedish settlers on the Delaware. According to one contemporary account, the Swedes had "hired out 3 soldiers to the Susquehannocks who taught them the use of our arms." Clearly Maryland alone, through Calvert's restrictions upon the sale of arms and ammunition to the Indians, was not able to prevent them from procuring military equipment, for the Maryland Indians could obtain them not only from the Swedes but also from French, Dutch, and English traders. The failure of the expedition against the Susquehannocks may also have been due to the fact that the Marylanders waged only a half-hearted campaign against them. James Cauther, who commanded a company in Cornwaleys' expedition, was alleged to have brought his troops back too early and failed to perform his duty. As a result, the Susquehannocks continued troublesome to the colony until

1652 when Richard Bennett of Virginia, who, together with Claiborne, had seized control in Maryland and ousted Lord Baltimore's authority, concluded a treaty with them at the Severn River.

This treaty of the Severn was apparently solicited by the Susquehannocks. Five of the chieftains met with five Maryland commissioners headed by Bennett, to draw up its provisions. The fact that the treaty was witnessed by William Lawson and Jafer Peter for the governor of New Sweden indicates that the Susquehannocks were in alliance with the Swedes. The treaty recognized Maryland's claims to all land north of the Patuxent River, which was the southern boundary of the Susquehannock territory, and south of Palmer's Island, and the North East River, "excepting the ile of kent, and Palmers Islands, which belongs to Captaine Clayborne." It provided for reciprocal reparation for future damages, for reciprocal return of fugitives, and for twenty-days' warning by either side before beginning a war. The Indians agreed that on business expeditions to the Maryland settlements they would come by water and not by land and further agreed that they would not allow more than eight or ten of their people to come at any one time in order to avoid trouble. All former injuries, declared the treaty, being "buried and forgotten, from henceforward they doe promise and agree to walke together and Carry one towards another in all things as friends and to assist one another accordingly." [5]

The Marylanders thus settled their difficulties with the Susquehannocks, but they continued to have trouble with other Indian tribes. In mid-1652 the Maryland governor issued a proclamation against the Yaocomico and Matchoatick tribes who lived on the south side of the Potomac and who hunted in St. Mary's and Charles Counties. He warned them to stay out of Maryland and threatened to drive them out if they did not heed his warning. Marylanders on the Eastern Shore were also troubled by the Nanticokes and, in response to a petition from four of the Commissioners of Kent to relieve their "deplorable condition and take some speedy course for the suppressing of these heathens," the Maryland governor and his Council made elaborate preparations for a punitive expedition. But the expedition never set forth, for the Puritans of Anne Arundel refused to join it arguing that it would be "dangerous for their health." Moreover, as the plans for the expedition became known to the Indians, the Marylanders lost the advantage of a surprise attack. Three decades later, in 1686 they established an Indian reservation near Snow Hill on the Eastern Shore, for the Pocomoke, Annemessex, Manokin, Nassawatten, and other Indian tribes.

While the authorities in Maryland were thus defending the colony against its hostile neighbors, the Proprietor in England was having serious difficulties with the Jesuits in the Province, growing out of the somewhat pretentious claims of the Society in the matter of landholding and in the matter of exemption from the power of the civil authorities. During the early days of Maryland the Jesuits were obliged to hold the property of the church in their own names as gentlemen adventurers; they could then explain that the church as an organization held no property. Since the property was held by individual priests the church was thus able to take advantage of the Anglo-Saxon respect for private property.

In 1637 five Jesuits were carrying on their missionary labors at St. Mary's. Since they were forbidden by the rulers of the Province to dwell among the Indians, they worked chiefly among the settlers, converting many of them to the Catholic faith, performing the sacraments, preaching sermons, and taking care of the sick and dying. Of these Andrew White had accompanied the first colonists on the *Ark* and became the first superior in the colony, and John Altham, who likewise came in the *Ark,* preached at Kent Island. Apparently, these two brought in twenty-eight servants in 1634 and so were entitled to receive 6,000 acres of land, and another priest, Thomas Copley, alias Philip Fisher, S.J., who came to the Province in 1637 and conducted the secular affairs of the mission, brought in nineteen servants and claimed, according to one report, 4,000 acres, and according to another 285,000 acres, 8,000 of which he proposed to use for the Jesuits. These large landholdings were made possible by the new conditions of plantation which the Proprietor issued in 1636, giving 2,000 acres to a man who brought in ten persons in 1634 or 1635 and erecting all landholdings of 1,000 acres or a multiple of 1,000 into manors.

The demands of the Jesuits were first presented to Baltimore in a letter from the aggressive Thomas Copley in 1637. He complained that the rulers of the colony were not providing for the conversion of the Indians, were not showing any favor to ecclesiastical persons, and were not granting to the church "the immunity & privileges which she enjoys everywhere else." The Jesuits, he protested, were being required to furnish 1,500 pounds of tobacco for building a fort when they should be exempt from taxation. Father Copley therefore asked the Proprietor to issue a "private order that we may, while the Government is Catholic, enjoy these privileges: (1) That the church and our houses may be sanctuary," (2) that the Jesuits and their servants might be free from the public taxes and services, (3) that they should be exempt from the final authority of the civil courts, (4) that they might go and live among the Indians without first procuring a license from the Governor, (5) that they be permitted to trade with and buy corn from the Indians without asking permission from the authorities of the Province, and (6) that they themselves be permitted to determine what ecclesiastical privileges they would surrender to the government. On this letter the Lord Proprietor wrote: "Herein are demands of very extravagant privileges."

But the Jesuits must have been granted some of these demands, for by 1639 they were carrying on more active missionary work among the Indians. The saintly Father White, who showed none of Copley's bitterness or greed and who had acquired a true love for Maryland and its people, moved to the seat of the Patuxents, one hundred and twenty miles from St. Mary's, where he labored to convert the chief of the tribe. Despairing of his conversion, he moved to the wigwam of the Tayac or chief of the Piscataway tribe about fifteen miles south of the later District of Columbia and succeeded in converting the Tayac, his wife, and his daughter. He persuaded him to abandon his savage clothing for European garments, to try to learn English, and to put away his concubines in order to live, Father White reported, "content with one wife that he may the more freely (as he said) have leisure to pray to God." When the Tayac asked to be baptized, the Jesuits after due consideration agreed to perform the rite with an elaborate ceremony attended by the Governor and Secretary of the Province. Not only the Tayac but also his queen, his daughter, and some of the principal men of the tribe were baptized, and his name, Kittamaquund was changed to Charles and his wife's name to Mary. In the afternoon the king and queen were married in accordance with Christian rites and litanies were chanted in honor of the Virgin Mary. So laboriously did Father White work in these services that he contracted a fever which made him ill for the rest of the year. The work of the Jesuits was so highly esteemed by the Indians, not only for their missionary labors but also for their mercy in providing food during the drought of 1639, that the king of the Anacostans asked to live with them. They even conceived the idea of establishing a college and Father Brock secured the approval of the superior of the order in England for this project, but it was not carried out.

The conversion and baptism of the Tayac of the Piscataway tribe gave the Jesuits considerable advantage in the work of converting the Indians, and even after the death of the Tayac in 1641 their influence and work grew. Because Piscataway was near the hostile Susquehannocks the fathers moved their missionary station to Potopaco, a name later altered to Port Tobacco. There in the long evenings by the light of a candle Father White prepared a catechism, a grammar, and dictionary in the Indian language, the earliest work in English on Indian philology in the New World. But the Jesuits did not confine their work to one center, for, taking interpreters and servants with them, they rowed up and down the Patuxent and Potomac Rivers preaching to the natives and performing acts of mercy. Father White continued to preach occasionally at Piscataway, and Father Thomas Copley ministered to the English and the Indians at St. Mary's. In 1641 two other priests came to Maryland from England.

Cecil, Lord Baltimore, began his attack upon the Jesuits as early as 1638, probably because he learned at that time that they had secretly acquired lands from the Indians within the territory defined by his patent. He was therefore faced with the very problem with which Claiborne had confronted him: Could he permit lands in Maryland to be held by any other title than as grants from the Proprietary? And, in addition, he had now to decide whether he would allow great estates to grow up in his province, held in mortmain, always increasing and never reverting to secular hands. The Jesuits were becoming large landowners in Maryland and were acquiring great influence even in the secular life of the colony. They were helping to populate the province, for by 1638 they had brought over about sixty settlers and had become entitled to hold at least one manor. This they acquired as of right in accordance with the Proprietor's regulations, and they held it in addition to the lands which they had procured from the Indians. As owners of a manor they were required to equip and maintain fifteen men in battle (knight's service) and pay twenty shillings annually as quitrent on every 1,000 acres of land that they occupied. They were also subject to all the fines and punishments imposed by the Proprietor's government and were expected to attend the sessions of the Assembly, but they refused to accept these secular obligations.

To Lord Baltimore, therefore, was presented the question whether the Jesuits, the only ecclesiastics in Maryland, were to be subject to his authority or would be free to operate outside his authority under the jurisdiction only of their ecclesiastical superiors. Could there be two laws and two jurisdictions in Maryland? Were there to be courts there that neither administered his laws nor acknowledged his writs? Should lands in Maryland held solely for religious and educational purposes be exempt from taxation at the cost of a serious reduction in the Proprietor's revenue from the province? The astute Baltimore in his attitude and future actions toward the Jesuits in his colony may also have been influenced by the quite realistic expectation that as his colony grew, it would probably become increasingly Protestant in religious complexion. As the apprentices and indentured servants there became freemen, electors, and officeholders, the Assembly itself could be expected to become predominantly Protestant. The wisest course for the Catholic Proprietor, therefore, if he expected to continue to draw profits for his family from the colony, was to cooperate with the growingly powerful Protestant majority there.

Baltimore's opportunity to reassert his own sole jurisdiction over the colony and at the same time to appease the Protestant element came in 1641 when he issued new Conditions of Plantation. In these he offered a manor, now limited to 2,000 acres, to everyone who would bring twenty persons into the province in one year. The manor would be subject to an annual quitrent of 40 shillings "in the commodities of the country." Under these Conditions the Jesuits might still acquire large landholdings in Maryland, but to forestall this possibility the Proprietor, who was highly dissatisfied with their actions, took steps to remove them from the province. He therefore petitioned the Congregation for the Propagation of the Faith in Rome to appoint secular priests to take charge of the Maryland Mission. His petition was granted in August 1641, and Baltimore was authorized to remove the Jesuits from Maryland. Ecclesiastical authority there was conferred upon Dom Rossetti, Archbishop of Tarsus. Baltimore now sent two secular priests to Maryland and instructed his brother, the Governor, to give them proper accommodations. He incorporated in the new Conditions of Plantation a provision that "no corporation, society, fraternity, municipality, political body (whether it be ecclesiastical or temporal)" might possess lands in their own right without special license from the Proprietary and that all grants made to such bodies without license "shall be, by the very fact, void." He required all recipients of lands to take an oath acknowledging him to be "true and absolute Lord and Proprietary" and agreeing not to secure any lands by grant from the Indians nor from any other person who did not derive a title from a Proprietary grant.

Governor Calvert hesitated to publish these new Conditions of Plantation because he feared that he would be excommunicated under the papal bull *Coena domini,* which claimed for the Pope full supremacy over all powers and persons, forbade anyone to violate the ecclesiastical liberties and rights of the Catholic Church, and declared that ecclesiastics were exempt from the jurisdiction of secular courts. When Calvert, however, interpreted the conditions to apply only to future grants, he was assured by the Jesuits that he would not incur the penalty of excommunication. The Jesuits concluded, however, that if they consented to take the required oath both they and the governor would become subject to excommunication. Father White then formulated and sent to the Provincial of the Society in England, Henry More, no fewer than twenty queries as to the proper status of the Jesuits in the colony. He explained that in this "newly planted" country neither Provincial Synod nor spiritual courts had been created nor had the canon law been accepted because "three parts of the people of four (at least) are heretics," that is, Protestants. He asked specifically whether Catholic laymen could hold office, whether ecclesiastical courts could be set up under Baltimore's authority or only under special authority from the Pope, whether Catholic members of the legislature could consent to laws which were contrary to Catholic policy, and whether lands granted to religious persons were exempt from taxation. Thus the Maryland Jesuits referred the controversy directly to the consideration of the English Provincial of the Order.

Baltimore now tried to stiffen his brother's resistance to the Jesuits in the Province. In 1642, he furnished him with a new commission which gave him full authority to carry out all the powers granted to the Lord Proprietor in the Charter. In addition, he attempted to prevent the departure from England of two new Jesuits bound for Maryland, though the officials of the order in England appealed to him to give his consent. When one of the Jesuits nevertheless secretly boarded Captain Ingle's ship in the Downs bound for Maryland in November 1642, Baltimore became highly incensed describing the event in a letter to his brother "as a high affront unto me." Baltimore directed his brother to seize "the man" when he arrived in the Province, or, if he should escape into the Indian settlements, to seize Copley, the temporal coadjutor of the order, and send him back to England for failing to apprehend the newcomer. He thought his brother had been too lenient with the Jesuits and wrote "If you do not that right unto me, as I require from you in my instructions, . . . I shall have just cause to think that I have put my honor there in trust to ill hands, who betray me to all the infamous contempts that may be laid upon me."

Baltimore believed that the Jesuits in England "do design my destruction" and were trying to overthrow the government in Maryland. "Laymen would be the basest slaves and most wretched creatures upon the earth," he wrote to his brother, if all the acts of clergymen done under the "mask and vizard" of God's honor and the propagation of the Christian faith" should "be accounted just and to proceed from God. . . . If the greatest saint upon earth should intrude himself into my house against my will . . . with intention to save the souls of all my family, but withal gave me just cause to suspect that he likewise designs my temporal destruction, . . . although with all he do perhaps many spiritual goods, yet certainly I may and ought to preserve myself by the expulsion of such an enemy and by providing others to perform the spiritual good he did, who shall not have any intention of mischief towards me."

In this parable Baltimore based his actions against the Jesuits upon both the natural right of self-preservation and the English doctrine that a man's house is his castle. He obviously shared the generally prevailing English view, held by Catholics and Protestants alike, that the religious must be subordinate to the secular authority in temporal matters. He had heard, he continued in his letter to his brother, the governor of Maryland, that Father White had already received a grant of land directly from the Piscataways without obtaining his permission. He firmly directed his brother "not to suffer any grant of any lands for the future to pass my seal here to any member of the Hill [the Jesuits] there, nor to any other person in trust for them upon any pretence or claim whatsoever, without especial warrant under my hand and seal." But though the Proprietor was hostile to the Jesuits in the colony because of their land greediness and their temporal pretensions he was certainly not hostile to Catholic interests, as shown by the fact that he was sending over two Catholic secular priests and instructed the Governor to give them proper accommodations and support.

Father More, the English superior of the Jesuits, was more conciliatory than the Jesuits in Maryland. After sending a report of the whole controversy to the Congregation for the Propagation of the Faith in Rome, he settled it directly with Lord Baltimore. He assured him that his new Conditions of Plantation would not subject him or his governor to excommunication and released certain Jesuit lands in Maryland to the proprietor. Under his firm but pacific guidance the Jesuits in Maryland now signed an agreement, prepared by Baltimore, in which they abandoned their claim to receive lands from the Indians, admitted that they and all other ecclesiastics in Maryland were bound by the laws of the Province, and agreed that they could have no more rights in Maryland than they enjoyed in England. Since peace was thus reestablished in the colony between the Jesuits and the Proprietor on the Proprietor's own terms, he now recalled the secular priests from the Province and again recognized the work and activities of the Jesuits there.

Baltimore's struggle with the Jesuits prepared the way for and helps to explain Maryland's famous Act concerning Religion of 1649, and it has left its imprint on Maryland's history in other ways. Baltimore's insistence throughout that struggle upon the subordination of the Jesuits to the civil authorities early conditioned Marylanders to a belief in the separation of church and state, which took the form later of the exclusion of clergymen from membership in either house of the Assembly. Lord Baltimore's strong opposition to land monopoly by the Jesuits may be reflected also in that article of Maryland's Declaration of Rights, adopted in 1867, which declares that land in excess of five acres may not be held by any ecclesiastic or ecclesiastical body or for a religious use "without the prior or subsequent sanction of the Legislature." [7]

But because of the generally enlightened attitude of the Proprietor toward religious differences among his colonists, the careful advance planning which he devoted to his colonizing enterprise, and the auspicious factors of climate and environment in the Chesapeake setting of the new colony, the founding of Maryland was accompanied by few of the hardships which earlier English colonies in America had suffered. Of the English colonies already established there it was the first that was successful from the beginning. The troubles that would soon afflict the colony and even threaten Cecil Calvert's control over it would stem largely from collisions among political factions in the mother country eventuating in civil war.

Footnotes

[1] Erich Isaac, "Kent Island, Part I: The Period of Settlement," *Maryland Historical Magazine*, vol. 52, No. 2, June 1957, pp. 93-119. Part II, "Settlement and Land Holding under the Proprietary," *ibid.*, vol. 52, No. 3, September 1957, pp. 210-232.

[2] The hundred was a land unit which was carried over from England to Maryland as a subdivision of a county or shire. It probably meant originally an area of 100 *hides*, a hide being the unit of land required to support one peasant family. The hundred court exercised both civil and criminal jurisdiction in local matters.

[3] William H. Browne, editor, *Proceedings and Acts of the General Assembly of Maryland*, January 1637 to September 1664, Baltimore, 1883, IV, p. 120.

[4] Raphael Semmes, *Crime and Punishment in Early Maryland*, Johns Hopkins Press, Baltimore, 1938, 1966; reprint 1970, p. 35. Semmes speculates that the brand "H" signified hog stealers, "R" runaway servants, "M" murderers, and "T" thieves.

[5] *Archives of Maryland*, vol. III, 227-278.

[6] Henry Foley, S.J., *Records of the English Province of the Society of Jesus*, vol. III, pp. 372-379.

[7] Foley, *cit.sup.*, pp. 361-367.

Sources and Additional Reading

Claiborne, John Herbert, *William Claiborne of Virginia: With Some Account of his Pedigree,* G.P. Putnam's Sons, New York and London, 1917.

Dennis, Alfred Pearce, "Lord Baltimore's Struggle with the Jesuits, 1634-1649," *Annual Report of the American Historical Association,* 1900, I, 107-125, Washington, 1901.

Foley, Henry, S.J., *Records of the English Province of the Society of Jesus,* 7 vols., Burns and Oates, London, 1877-83, vol. III, London, 1875-1882.

Hale, Nathaniel Claiborne, *Virginia Venturer: A Historical Biography of William Claiborne, 1600-1677.* Richmond, 1951.

Johnson, John Hemsley, *Old Maryland Manors,* Johns Hopkins University Studies, Series 1, No. 7, Johns Hopkins University, Baltimore, 1883.

Latané, J.H., *The Early Relations between Maryland and Virginia,* Johns Hopkins University Studies, Series 13, Nos. 3, 4, Johns Hopkins Press, Baltimore, 1895.

McCormac, Eugene Irving, *White Servitude in Maryland, 1634-1820,* Johns Hopkins University Studies, Series 22, Nos. 3, 4, Johns Hopkins Press, Baltimore, 1904.

Petrie, George, *Church and State in Early Maryland,* Johns Hopkins University Studies, Series 10, No. 4, Johns Hopkins Press, Baltimore, 1892.

Semmes, Raphael, *Crime and Punishment in Early Maryland,* Johns Hopkins Press, Baltimore, 1938.

Smith, Charles Ernest, *Religion under the Barons of Baltimore,* E.A. Lycett Co., Baltimore, 1899.

Steiner, Bernard C., "Maryland's First Courts," American Historical Association, *Annual Report for the Year 1901,* vol. 1, pp. 211-229.

Wyckoff, Vertrees J., "Land Prices in Seventeenth-Century Maryland," *The American Economic Review, XXVII,* No. 1, pp. 82 ff. (March 1938).

CHAPTER V

IMPACT OF THE ENGLISH CIVIL WAR

By 1640 Lord Baltimore's settlements in Maryland formed one of nine English colonies scattered along the Atlantic seaboard of North America from Maine on the north to Virginia on the south. All of them, including even those that had a spontaneous origin in America, owed allegiance to the British crown and recognized its authority in varying degrees over them. Maryland, like her neighbors among the English colonies perched precariously as outposts of empire on the rim of the American wilderness, was dependent upon the mother country. The colony on the Chesapeake, the property of an English Catholic nobleman, would be seriously affected by the friction that was developing between crown and parliament in the mother country and that would eventuate in civil war in 1642.

Charles I, like his father, James I, claimed to rule by divine right. But, unlike his father, he was unable to play successfully his assumed role of God's vice-regent on earth. His inflexible commitment to the Anglican religious establishment made him unpopular with English Puritans, who migrated from England in large numbers during his reign. He and his advisers, Archbishop William Laud and Thomas Wentworth, Earl of Strafford, could not tolerate Puritanism nor countenance Puritan reforms of the Church of England. Nor could they espouse Catholicism. If Charles appeared at times to be less than militant in his attitude toward English Catholics, as, for example, in his support of Lord Baltimore's colonizing venture in America, he could not, as a matter of policy, openly make concessions to Rome. He was unable to accommodate himself to the rising popular ferment in England and instead aggravated it by his own pretensions to personal rule.

The Parliament which assembled in London in November 1640 and which came to be known as the Long Parliament attempted to bring Charles' personal rule to an end. It abolished both the Court of Star Chamber and the Court of High Commission and enacted bills of attainder against both Archbishop Laud and the Earl of Strafford. It virtually took control of the English government and in the "Grand Remonstrance" presented to the nation a list of grievances against the king and a defense of its actions. Thereupon five members of the parliament were seized by the king as traitors, and he saw virtually the whole of southern England turn against him. The king then proceeded to set up his royal standard at Nottingham in August 1642 and summoned all loyal subjects to rally to his support. Thus the English civil war began.

Would the colonies in America become involved in this war growing out of controversies over political and religious authoritarianism in England? Lord Baltimore's popularity in his American province on the eve of the English Civil War was attested by an action of the Maryland legislature in its session in early 1642. Desiring "to return his Lordship some testimony of their gratitude" for his "great charge & solicitude in meinteining the Govermt & protecting the Inhabitants in their persons rights and liberties and to contribute some support toward it so far as the young & poor estate of the Colony will yett beare," this assembly voluntarily and unanimously enacted that every inhabitant of the colony, both freemen and servants, over the age of twelve years, should contribute fifteen pounds of tobacco to the proprietor. Would his popularity survive the hard decisions that he would have to make as the political controversies in England sharpened into civil war and his colonists in America took sides in that war? His policy in general can be characterized only as one of canny opportunism, but it was a policy which enabled him to save his estates in America.

Lord Baltimore, whose wife, the Lady Anne Arundel, came of a strong royalist family, sought to remain neutral throughout the conflict, and this he was able to do with reasonable success. How he contrived to do so amidst the bitter struggles of the time, cannot now be clearly established. According to one report, Parliamentary leaders feared that he would flee England for Maryland, and in March 1642 they procured a writ of *ne exeat regno* (let him not leave the kingdom) requiring him to give bond that he would not leave England without the consent of Parliament. When the civil war soon afterward began Baltimore was among those who flocked to the king's standard.

When news of the outbreak of civil war arrived in Maryland, Governor Calvert prepared to depart for England. He turned over his authority in Maryland to Giles Brent appointing him "Lieutenant General, Chancellor, Admiral, Chief, Captain, Magistrate, and Commander, as well by sea as by land, of this Province of Maryland and of the islands to the same belonging" and authorizing him to exercise the full powers which he himself exercised under Lord Baltimore's commission. The governor then returned to England and arrived there just when the king was fixing his court at Oxford and Prince Rupert, commanding his field forces, was storming Bristol. In the king's camp Calvert found his brother, Lord Baltimore, and gave him the latest reports from Maryland. These apparently inspired the proprietor to make preparations to visit Maryland, for he now instructed the Council at St. Mary's, headed by Brent, to suspend grants of land in his province and to take no action on certain other problems until his arrival. But he was obliged to give up his plans to visit the colony, for Parliament in November 1643 appointed the Earl of Warwick governor over all the American colonies and authorized him not only to govern them and to advance the true Protestant religion there but also to appoint and remove colonial governors and other officers. Since Baltimore did not know whether Warwick and the council which was appointed to assist him would intervene in Maryland or not he decided to remain in England in order to look after his proprietary interests.

During Leonard Calvert's absence in England Richard Ingle, a blunt sea captain from London and a rabid champion of Parliament, entered Maryland and started trouble which resulted in two years of anarchy and confusion—the co-called "plundering time." According to the charges against him, he boasted that he had been a captain for Parliament against the King; at Accomac he had defied authorities acting in the King's name and, standing with his curtal-ax drawn, had said "I will cut off his head that comes aboard"; he had declared "Prince Rupert was a rogue or rascal. . . . If I had him aboard the ship I would whip him at the Capstan," and "The King is no King, nor will I acknowledge him for my King longer than he joins with the honorable his House of Parliament." These utterances threw the Maryland authorities into a quandary, for if they refused to punish him they would commit the province to the side of Parliament and if they arrested him as a traitor they would commit Maryland to the side of the King. Brent had him arrested and given into the custody of the sheriff, Parker, and put a guard of thirty men on board his vessel, the *Reformation*. But when Ingle was brought to trial four successive juries which were impanelled to consider the charges against him failed to reach a verdict, bringing in the sole reply "Ignoramus." Their action or rather non-action probably reflected the strength of the pro-Parliamentary sentiment in Maryland.

Responding to this sentiment the provincial authorities now moderated their hostility to Ingle and resorted to an ingenious device to get rid of him and at the same time to avoid the necessity of taking sides overtly in the Civil War. After nightfall Parker the sheriff, and Cornwaleys and Neale, both members of the Council, took Ingle on board his ship, discharged the guard with the remark "All is peace," and allowed Ingle to escape with his ship. They were later indicted for this "prison break, rescue, misdemeanor, and contempt" and were brought to trial before

Brent, who heard the case without a jury. Cornwaleys defended himself by saying that he considered the original charges against Ingle of no importance and that he supposed he was taking Ingle on board ship with the approval and consent of Brent and the Council. He was found guilty by Brent of being an accessory to Ingle's escape and was fined one thousand pounds of tobacco. His fine was then suspended. Parker had already been removed from his office as sheriff by Brent, but he was soon restored to it. In the trial of Neale, who had accompanied Ingle on board his ship, the charges against him were dismissed by Brent in default of proof, and he was reinstated in the Council.

Marylanders continued to trade with Ingle even after this affair. He was apparently allowed to linger in the waters of the Province after his "escape." After depositing a barrel of powder and four hundred pounds of shot as security for his return, he carried on his business freely in the Province. He even received freight of tobacco from Brent and finally departed peaceably, as he afterward said, "without any show of discontent or dislike at all." The authorities of Maryland could congratulate themselves that they had saved their faces, had rid themselves of Ingle, and had even used him to carry their cargoes to England.

When Leonard Calvert returned to Maryland in the early autumn of 1644 he brought with him a new commission which was different in certain respects from his earlier commissions. It specifically gave him the authority, which he had impliedly possessed before, to assent to laws which were enacted and which would, upon receiving his signature, remain in force until the Proprietor approved or disapproved them. But his new commission did not authorize him to assent to laws which were to continue in force for only a limited time as for a fixed number of years or only until the next assembly should meet. So began the dispute over the question of temporary and permanent laws which continued as long as Maryland remained a Province, for the Marylanders claimed the privilege of passing temporary laws of limited duration in order to check the Proprietary, to insure frequent summoning of the Assembly, and to preserve their rights, whereas the proprietor and his governor in the colony insisted upon statutes of longer duration which would require their approval. The question at issue here was whether the colony should govern itself on an *ad hoc* basis by means of flexible regulations of its own devising or whether its course should be charted over the years by the Proprietor in England through a fixed code of laws of indefinite duration.

Further provisions of the Governor's new commission related to land titles. Lord Baltimore was losing some of his rents because **squatters** were moving into Maryland and settling on his lands without troubling to secure grants or patents from him. In this way they were even rendering doubtful the titles of rightful landholders who held patents to their land under the proprietor's seal. To prevent this abuse of Baltimore's rights the governor had earlier issued orders requiring all occupants of lands to take out patents for them within twelve months. The proprietor now instructed him not only to require squatters to validate their claims in this way but also to take an oath of fidelity to him. The governor must also certify that land grants assigned to patentees in Maryland were duly surveyed and that they contained no more land than the patentees were entitled to.

In England Baltimore was clearly sympathetic with King Charles in his war against Parliament and was counting upon a royalist victory. When Governor Calvert set out from England to return to Maryland he therefore took with him a letter from the king authorizing him to seize any ship belonging to "any Londoner, or other persons in rebellion" that he might meet on his voyage to America. From the proceeds of the sale of such a captured ship Calvert should pay half to Lord Baltimore and should turn over the other half to the king. He apparently had no opportunity, however, on his voyage across the Atlantic to make use of this authority of marque and reprisal. In his letter from the king he was further directed to go to Virginia and there, with the aid of the staunchly royalist governor, Sir William Berkeley, to seize all ships and other property of "any Londoners whatsoever, or of any of our cities, towns, or places in actual rebellion against us." For, said the king in his letter, the London merchants "drive a great trade in the dominion and colony of Virginia, receiving daily great advantages from thence, which they impiously spend in vast contributions towards the maintenance of an unnatural war."

This commission from the king created division in Maryland between the governor and the assembly. It did not ostensibly apply to Maryland, which was therefore presumably considered by the king to be safely loyal to him. But the first assembly that met at St. Mary's after Calvert's arrival somewhat gratuitously declared, according to later testimony by Copley and Brent, "that they would have free trade with Londoners and others under the protection of Parliament and that they would not receive any commission to the contrary." Calvert thereupon immediately departed for Virginia where he probably tried to put into effect his commission from the king.

While Calvert was thus cooperating with Governor Berkeley at Jamestown in the king's interest both Claiborne and Ingle again entered Maryland's history. Claiborne had continued as a member of the Virginia Council and had been appointed by the king as treasurer of the Council for life. After he had received the adverse decision of the Lords Commissioners for Plantations in 1638 his remaining herd of livestock on Kent Island had been confiscated by Lord Baltimore's sheriff on the island on orders of Captain Brent. In the late autumn of 1644 Claiborne sailed up the Chesapeake with two vessels on what was apparently a punitive expedition to seize Brent. But when his men found out that he carried no authorization they deserted him. In this action, which thus proved abortive, Claiborne apparently did not try to take advantage of Calvert's pro-royalist actions but was merely seeking revenge against Brent and recovery of his personal property. But for his action he was declared by Governor Calvert to be an enemy of the Province of Maryland and all correspondence with him was forbidden. By this treatment Claiborne's bitterness against Maryland was only intensified and he actively cooperated with Ingle in undermining Baltimore's authority in his province.

As Calvert had been furnished a commission to defend the king's cause in Virginia, so Ingle arrived in Virginia in early 1645 on his ship, the *Reformation,* bearing letters of marque from Parliament. He was authorized by the Lord High Admiral, acting under orders from Parliament, to seize ships bound to or from any place in hostility to Parliament. When he learned from Claiborne that Calvert had received a commission from the King he seized upon it as justification for an attack upon Maryland. He now proposed to his men that they change their trading voyage to a "man of war cruize" against Maryland, since the Maryland authorities were obviously hostile to Parliament. Offering his men one-sixth of the proceeds of whatever they might seize in Maryland he proceeded north to St. George's River bent on plunder. His vessel mounted a white flag and first captured a Dutch vessel, the *Speagle,* which had been peacefully trading in Maryland for two months. Ingle, finding Giles Brent on board, made him prisoner. He and his men then plundered the Maryland settlements, seizing and destroying hogsheads of tobacco, confiscating jewelry, burning the barns and houses, and scattering the cattle. Ingle, professing to be a zealous Puritan, made Cornwaleys the especial object of his hatred, probably because Cornwaleys was an Anglican. Ignoring the aid that he had received from Cornwaleys only a year before in escaping from the province, he now pillaged Cornwaleys' manor, the Cross, seized his tobacco, carried away his silver, linen, bedding, brass, and pewter, killed or dispersed all his livestock, made his servants prisoners, and even took the locks from the doors and the glass from the windows. He next plundered the two houses of Thomas Copley, the temporal coadjutor of the Jesuits, and carried him, John Lewger, and Giles Brent prisoners to London taking with him at the same time the great seal of the province. Ingle probably took Father White and Father Fisher as prisoners to London at the same time, for they were taken to England as prisoners in that same year, 1645.

Ingle's outrageous actions, by which he involved Lord Baltimore's colony in the religious controversies of the English civil war, threw both the proprietor and the colony of Maryland on the defensive. As the opposition to Catholics was rampant in England it seemed improbable that they could obtain any reparation for Ingle's acts of vandalism, particularly since the forces of Parliament, under whose authority Ingle had acted, were obviously gaining the upper hand. Father White was confined in Newgate Prison for two years and was then released by the House of Commons on condition that he leave England within fifteen days. Brent, Copley, and Lewger brought suit for damages against Ingle, but the decisions in their cases have not been found. Ingle's suit to have the *Speagle* condemned as his prize, however, was decided against him probably because it involved England's relations with the Netherlands. It nevertheless furnished Parliament with a justification for passing soon afterward the first of the famous Navigation Acts intended to keep Dutch vessels from trading with England's colonies. Cornwaleys brought suit in England against Ingle for damages to his property in the amount of £3,000. To this suit Ingle filed a reply which revealed his religious animus. Attempting to justify his assault upon Cornwaleys and the Maryland colony generally, he declared that it had been his purpose to prevent Governor Calvert from executing "a tyrannical power against the Protestants, and such as adhered to the Parliament" and that he "did venture his life and fortune in landing his men and assisting the said well affected Protestants against the tyrannical government and Papists and malignants." Eventually he apparently compromised his differences with Cornwaleys.

Ingle's actions against Maryland both in the colony and in England coincided with a general attack upon Lord Baltimore's charter. Some of the inhabitants of Maryland submitted in November 1648 to the Committee of Lords and Commons for Foreign Plantations a petition, probably carried to England by Ingle, complaining against "the tyrannical government of that Province, ever since its first settling by recusants" and asking that Parliament take control of the colony. Another petition submitted by a widow, Mary Ford, "in behalf of the Protestant inhabitants in Virginia and Maryland," accused Cornwaleys of being "a great agent and factor for settling a Popish faction in Maryland" and of assisting Baltimore's "poisoned purposes" to "rob, murder, and destroy." At the same time Cloberry and seventeen other merchants trading to Virginia and Maryland also petitioned the Lords to take Maryland away from Baltimore because he and his agents "have acted horrid things in that Province as Papists and Rebels."

In reply to these charges Baltimore submitted a petition to the Lords explaining that he had "engaged the greatest part of his fortune" in Maryland and asking for time in which to prepare a defense of his charter. Moreover, as Oliver Cromwell and his New Model Army gained victories foreshadowing the triumph of the Parliamentary cause, Baltimore prudently began to swing over to the Parliamentary party. The charges against him were accordingly postponed from time to time until December 23, 1651, when the Council of State decided to permit Baltimore to "pursue his cause according to law."

Meanwhile conditions in Maryland had become chaotic. Governor Calvert was in Virginia, and the deputy governor Brent was a prisoner in London. In this crisis the Council, taking matters into its own hands and acting without Calvert's knowledge or approval, set up a provisional government and chose Captain Edward Hill as governor. The new governor's first task was to restore order and repair the damage done to the colony in the "plundering time." He then summoned an assembly, which was apparently composed of the anti-Baltimore party, for it was described by the Assembly of 1649 as consisting, with only two or three exceptions of the "rebelled party" and Calvert's "professed enemies." In a judiciary act which the Assembly of 1646 passed it omitted all reference to the laws of England, whether through negligence or by deliberate intent is not clear. All the enactments of this assembly were disallowed by the proprietor on the ground that some of them were "very prejudicial to our rights and royal jurisdictions" in Maryland and that the rest were "inconvenient for our people there." All the proceedings of this assembly have been lost.

The moves toward independent action in the colony unfavorable to the proprietor's interests were ended when Governor Calvert finally returned from Virginia with soldiers and reasserted his authority over the province. He received oaths of fealty from Lewger, Gerard, and Greene of the Council and from thirty-five or forty freemen. In an attempt apparently to check further disaffection and to discourage collusion between his enemies inside and outside the province, he forbade any person to leave St. Mary's or to receive anyone coming from outside St. Mary's or from Kent Island without his permission. As conditions on Kent Island continued unsettled he visited it in April 1647 and received oaths of fealty from fourteen freemen there. He directed his newly appointed officials on the island to seize the property of all who refused to take the oath or who had fled from the island. Just when he had succeeded in restoring order and reestablishing the authority of Lord Baltimore throughout the province, Leonard Calvert died on June 9, 1647. Near the site of his grave at St. Mary's the state of Maryland erected a monument in 1890 commemorating the "wisdom, justice, and fidelity" of Maryland's first governor.

Before his death Governor Calvert named Mistress Margaret Brent, spinster, as executrix of his estate and Thomas Greene, a Catholic and royalist, as governor. His only public instructions to Mistress Brent were "Take all and pay all." The administration of his estate presented his executrix with many difficulties. She was granted letters of administration by the new governor and prepared an inventory of Calvert's estate showing that he had possessed 24,404 pounds of tobacco, a large frame house and one hundred acres of town land, and another large house and three manors at Piney Neck. Among his personal effects were seven horses, furniture, arms, a few books, a bone cross, a gold reliquary case, a kneeling desk, and a "picture of Paul's." From the estate Mistress Brent took 5,432 pounds of tobacco for her own salary and paid 9,522 pounds to the soldiers. When she assessed Lord Baltimore 18,548 pounds of tobacco for his indebtedness to the estate he protested against her handling of his late brother's affairs. But she was warmly defended by the Assembly which declared that "it was better for the Collonys safety at that time in her hands, than in any mans else in the whole Province after your Brothers death for the Soldiers would never have treated any other with that Civility and respect and though they were even ready at times to run into mutiny yet she still pacified them." The strong-minded, intrepid Mistress Brent then asked that she be "declared Baltimore's attorney by an order of Court" and was given authority by the Provincial Court to act as such in matters relating to the settlement of the estate.

Thomas Greene now assumed executive authority over Maryland as governor by designation of Leonard Calvert, but his authority did not go unchallenged. Hill, who had acted as governor during the "plundering time" by election of the Council, brought action before the Provincial Court for half the proprietary's rents and half the customs receipts for the year 1646 when he had served as governor. He alleged that this income had been "covenanted unto him by Leonard Calvert,

Esq., for his service in the office of Governor." To that office, he insisted, he had been rightfully chosen during Calvert's absence. But he weakened his case by contending that Calvert had later unlawfully invaded the province and by demanding that he be recognized by the Council as governor in place of Greene. If the Council would not acknowledge him as governor he threatened cryptically that "others of humors different" from his who "embrace a parliamentary influence might prove fatal to the whole." With rival claimants for the governorship the colony seemed likely to fall into anarchy and the claims of Lord Baltimore to Maryland, which were already under assault in England, might be endangered.

Hill was able to secure the support of Governor Berkeley of Virginia, who wrote a letter on his behalf to Greene. In reply Greene upheld his own claims to the governorship explaining that it had come to him by Calvert's nomination and that he would loyally defend Baltimore's right and title to Maryland until the proprietor appointed a new governor. At the same time he asked Berkeley to "take some effectual course that Captain Hill may not by his evil designs and practices proceed to disturb" the peace of Maryland, as he had threatened to do by invading the province from Virginia. At the same time Greene took strong measures to punish Hill's sympathizers in the province. Continuing Calvert's policy he required all persons who were concerned in the Ingle rebellion to take an oath of fealty to the Lord Proprietary and the Governor and forbade them to have hearings in Court or to remain in the Province until they took the oath. Under these orders he received oaths of fealty from fourteen men in 1647, eleven in 1648, and four in 1649. In early 1648 he issued an amnesty proclamation pardoning all the inhabitants of the Province who had engaged in Ingle's rebellion three years before and who now yielded obedience to the proprietary government.

As a result of these and other similar measures Greene was able to overcome Hill's challenge to his authority and to establish his control over the province. This was particularly important, for Baltimore's authority was virtually in abeyance. The proprietor's interest there was now ably represented only by Governor Greene and Mistress Brent. Greene's first assembly met in Lewger's house in January 1647. It included all the freemen of the province represented either personally or by proxy and consisted of seventeen men holding 122 proxies. On the second day of the session Mistress Brent came before the Assembly and "requested to have vote in the howse for herselfe and voyce allso." She evidently made this request not for her own personal satisfaction but as Leonard Calvert's executrix and the proprietor's attorney. When the governor rejected her request she then "protested against all proceedings in this present Assembly, unless she may be present and have a vote."

In Maryland where women who were heads of families were granted lands on the same terms as men, established and managed plantations, and brought suits in the provincial court, "Mistresse Margarett Brent, Spinster," was one of the most original and capable representatives of her sex. In 1640 she adopted Mary, daughter of the Tayac of the Piscataway settlement and four years later this Mary, then eleven or twelve years of age, married Giles, Margaret's brother, who was at least thirty years her senior, in a marriage which has been called Maryland's counterpart of the Pocahontas-John Rolfe romance in early Virginia. Not only was Margaret Brent an outspoken champion of women's rights, but as "his Lordship's Attorney" she loyally and tirelessly defended the proprietor's interests in the province. She was a frequent litigant in court cases which she instituted on his behalf, and between 1642 and 1650 her name appears in the records of the Provincial Court of Maryland one hundred and thirty-four times. For example, as attorney for the Proprietor, she asked the House to try her case against Thomas Gerard for "violently and contemptuously" transporting out of the Province six hogsheads of tobacco without paying or giving security to pay the customs in violation of the provincial statute. This case was postponed and apparently received no further consideration. She brought suit against Edward Cummins for taking persons and goods out of the sheriff's hands and for "uttering words of great contempt" against the Governor and the "authority of the government." For this she succeeded in having him censured and fined by the court. She brought suit against one Knight of Kent Island and recovered a judgment against him. She instituted proceedings on behalf of the Proprietor asking that "stoppage be made of a cow and her increase now in possession of Thomas Copley and claimed by William Hardich [Hardwick] and intended to be transported out of the Province by him, as his Lordship has an interest in all uncertain titles." Toward the end of 1648 she induced the Court to rule that the property of rebels living on Leonard Calvert's manors should be forfeited to his estate in accordance with English law.

Governor Greene, too, ably and staunchly supported the Proprietor's interests. When the Assembly undertook to repeal the customs act of 1647 as "too burthensome and inconvenient" and to challenge the legality of all the acts of the Assembly of 1647 the Governor boldly declared: "In the face of this present assembly I shall, to the utmost of my power, by virtue of his Lordship's commission given to me in that behalf, see the due observance of the same throughout all the parts of the Province, until his Lordship's disassent thereto shall appear under his hand and seal." But Greene was a Catholic, and since Maryland continued to be subjected to much criticism as a popish province oppressing and terrorizing Protestants he was demoted by the Proprietor to the Council and was replaced as governor by a Protestant, William Stone, in August 1648. Perhaps Greene had incurred the proprietor's displeasure by his leniency toward the Jesuits, who were beginning to operate again in Maryland. Father Fisher had just been allowed to return from England and was reestablishing the Jesuit mission to the Indians at St. Inigoes. To his superior in the order he wrote immediately after his return to Maryland: "By the singular Providence of God, I found my flock collected together after they had been scattered for three long years; and they were really in more flourishing circumstances than those who had opposed and plundered them; with what joy they received me and with what delight I met them, it would be impossible to describe, but they received me as an angel of God." He recommended that Maryland and its neighboring colony to the south be united in one mission since "a road by land through the forest has just been opened from Maryland to Virginia; this will make it but a two days' journey and both countries can now be united in one mission."

The new governor, Stone, at the time of his appointment was forty-five years old and was serving as sheriff of Northampton County, Virginia. He had called himself to Baltimore's attention by offering "to procure 500 people of British or Irish descent to come from other places and plant and reside" in Maryland. Upon assuming the governorship he was given as much land in the province as he could ride around in a day and so acquired his manor, Avon, on the Nanjemoy River in an area that later became Charles County. In the commission which he received from the proprietor he was required to promise in his oath of office that he would not "molest or discountenance" for his religion any person "professing to believe in Jesus Christ and, in particular, no Roman Catholic" who was faithful to Baltimore and did not conspire against the civil government of Maryland. He was also required to promise that he would not discriminate against persons in conferring offices or favors because of their religion but would, on the contrary, advance "his Lordship's service here and the public unity and good of the Province without partiality," and that if any person in the Province should molest any Christian for his religion he would protect the person so molested and punish the offender. All the members of the new Governor's Council were Protestant with the exception of Thomas Greene and John Pile, and all of them, of course, were appointed and commissioned by the Proprietary, but the Governor was given the authority to add two or three "able and faithful" persons to the Council during the next twelve months. So Lord Baltimore accommodated himself to the new religious and political complexion of England where Cromwell and his army were rising to power.

As Ingle had carried off the Great Seal of Maryland Baltimore now repudiated any document sealed with it and sent over a new seal of massive silver. It was to be kept by Governor Stone and, except for the period between 1692 and 1715 when Maryland was a royal province, has served as the seal of Maryland from that time to the present. It bore the arms of George Calvert, the first Lord Baltimore, and of his mother Alice Crosland or Crossland, quarterly, surmounted by the cap or coronet of a count palatine and above this the Calvert crest. The supporters were a farmer and a fisherman symbolizing Lord Baltimore's two provinces of Maryland and Avalon. Beneath on a scroll was the Calvert motto, *Fatti Maschii Parole Femine,* which is translated "manly deeds, womanly words." Behind and forming a background for the whole is an ermine mantle, and surrounding all is the legend *Scuto Bonae Voluntatis Tuae Coronasti Nos* ("Thou hast crowned us with the shield of Thy good will," Ps. V, 12, Vulgate). On the obverse is the fugure of the proprietor on horseback and in full armor surrounded by his name and titles in Latin, *Cecilius Absolutus Dominus Terrae Mariae et Avaloniae, Baro de Baltimore,* which is translated "Cecil, absolute Lord of Maryland and Avalon, Baron of Baltimore."

With the new commission to Stone and the new seal the Proprietor sent over to Maryland in 1648 new "Conditions of Plantation," which were made applicable not only to the British and the Irish but also to settlers of French, Dutch, and Italian birth. They required that an oath of fidelity to Baltimore must be taken by every "adventurer" before receiving his grant and stipulated that none of Baltimore's manors could be granted without special warrant. The new "Conditions" perpetuated the provisions of the old "Conditions" of 1641 which forbade corporations, societies, fraternities, guilds, and bodies politic to hold land in their own name or that of any other person without special license. They also forbade the sale of land to anyone in trust for such a corporation or for uses forbidden by the statutes of mortmain without a similar special license "because all secret trusts are usually intended to deceive the government, or some other persons, and by experience are found to occasion many suits and dissentions." In this manner the Proprietary continued the safeguards against the Jesuits and against all other land or commercial monopolies within his province.

William Stone presided as Lieutenant Governor of the province over the assembly which convened on April 2, 1649 and which is justly judged the most famous of Maryland's colonial assemblies because it enacted into law the renowned "Act concerning Religion." The proceedings of all but the last day of this assembly are lost, and the only information about it has to be gleaned from the laws that it passed and from two letters, one of which was signed by all the Councillors and burgesses present on the last day of the session and sent by them to Lord Baltimore, and the other of which was sent by Baltimore to Governor Stone on August 26, 1649, some four months after the assembly had adjourned. These show that at the beginning of the session Thomas Hatton, the new secretary, on arriving from England, brought with him to Maryland sixteen measures which had been drafted by Lord Baltimore and which the proprietor intended should serve, when approved by the assembly, as a complete code of laws for the colony. If these draft laws were accepted by the assembly Baltimore offered to repeal all other laws of the colony except the acts condemning and attainting Claiborne. To the assembly Baltimore presented the laws as an "all or nothing" proposition; he directed Governor Stone not to approve any of them unless the assembly approved all sixteen of them without alteration.

This the assembly declined to do, and in their letter of explanation, sent on April 21, which was probably the closing day of the session, they showed a spirit of scarcely veiled defiance. In that letter the Councillors and burgesses described the miseries and calamities of the province which had occurred and continued since Ingle's "plundering time." Though they professed loyalty to the proprietor they complained of his heavy exactions from the province. They had found it impossible to accept his laws, they said, because they had found them "long and tedious," and they had therefore been obliged to modify them before they could pass upon them as permanent laws for the colony. They pointedly asked Baltimore to send "no more such Bodies of laws, which serve to little or no other end than to fill our heads with suspicions, jealousies, and dislikes of which verily we understand not. Rather, "they continued, "we shall desire your Lordship to send some short heads of what is desired." If he would do so in the future they promised to give him "all just satisfaction that can be thought reasonable by us." They considered that Baltimore's objectives in the colony were fourfold: (1) "That the country may be preserved with peace and governed with justice," (2) that it might furnish him "some competent support," (3) that a "stock of cattle may be raised again" for him, and (4) that all who had assisted in reestablishing his authority in Maryland should be given satisfaction. In pursuance of these assumed purposes they had therefore chosen from Baltimore's draft laws those which seemed "most conducing to confirm a long desired and settled peace among us" and to them added other laws of their own which they considered "most necessary and best suitable" to existing conditions in the colony.

This historic assembly passed twelve laws which they forwarded to Baltimore for his approval. Among those which the assembly itself probably initiated were two which were intended to put the colony in a more effective posture of defense against Indian attacks. The assembly also reaffirmed an earlier statute requiring every tobacco grower to plant two acres of corn in order to reduce the dependence of the colony upon imported foodstuffs. In another law they imposed penalties for the stealing of hogs. Among the laws which had probably been drafted by the proprietor was one which granted him for seven years a duty of ten shillings on every hogshead of tobacco carried from Maryland in any Dutch vessel to any non-English port. By this act the proprietor would derive an income from the non-English trade of the province which, along with the trade of the other English colonies in North America, was falling increasingly into the hands of ship captains from the Low Countries. But this act, so advantageous to the proprietor, was virtually nullified by a parliamentary enactment, one of the earliest of the so-called Navigation Acts, passed in the following year, which forbade foreign vessels to trade with the colonies except under license from Parliament or the Council of State. A parliamentary act of 1651 carried this policy of commercial exclusivism or imperial preference still further by requiring that goods imported from Asia, Africa, and America into Britain or the British colonies must be brought only in English ships.

The laws of the Maryland Assembly of 1649 included also an act assuring Baltimore that the colony would raise a bull and sixteen cows for him because his herd had been used up in defending the province; an act providing punishment for counterfeiting the proprietor's great seal; an act declaring void all purchases of lands from the Indians which were not confirmed by Baltimore; and another providing purnishment for seditious speeches and actions against the proprietor and his government. The origin of the three remaining acts is doubtful. One of these punished fugitive indentured servants and fugitive debtors, the second forbade the kidnapping and sale out of Maryland of any friendly Indian and the delivery of arms to any Indian without special license from the Governor, and the third is the famous "Act concerning Religion."

This act has probably given rise to more controversy than any other act of a colonial assembly in America. Was it proposed by the Proprietor, or did it originate in the Maryland Assembly? Who were the members of that Assembly, and what were their religious opinions? It has been described by the Maryland historian, John Van Lear McMahon, as "one of the proudest memorials of our colonial history" and by another student of Maryland history as "really a most disgraceful piece of intolerance."

From the first establishment of the colony Lord Baltimore had followed a policy of liberty of conscience and freedom of religion. He had instructed the Governor and Councillors who headed the first expedition of the *Ark* and the *Dove* to see that "no scandall nor offence be given to any of the Protestants" and that Roman Catholics should "be silent upon all occasions of discourse concerning matters of Religion." In the history of religious toleration Maryland, under Cecil Calvert's wise guidance, was, from the beginning, a real pioneer, comparable only to the Netherlands and certain Anabaptist communities in the Rhine Valley. Not until the colony of Rhode Island and Providence Plantation was founded by Roger Williams two years after Cecil Calvert's first colonists arrived at St. Mary's was Maryland's example of religious toleration duplicated in America.

On only two occasions prior to 1649 did Lord Baltimore's injunctions as to religious toleration appear to have been violated in Maryland. In both cases the offenders were Catholics and they were promptly punished for molesting Protestants upon religious matters. In 1638 William Lewis, a Catholic, who was employed by Thomas Cornwaleys came upon two servants of his master who were reading aloud a book of sermons by a Protestant minister. Lewis denounced the author and Protestant ministers in general and forbade the men to read the book. For this action he was tried before Governor Calvert, Secretary Lewger, and Cornwaleys and was sentenced to pay a fine of 500 pounds of tobacco and to give security for his good behavior in the future. The second case arose in 1641 when Dr. Thomas Gerard, also a Catholic, carried off some books and the key from the chapel of St. Mary's. The Protestants, who apparently used the chapel, complained to the assembly which ordered the restitution of the stolen articles and fined Gerard 500 pounds of tobacco to be applied "towds the maintenance of the first [Protestant] minister as should arrive" in the Province. Apparently, therefore, religious toleration was observed and enforced in Maryland from the beginning—long before the enactment of any statute upon the subject.

When, after the triumph of the Puritan Parliament in England, Baltimore deemed it wise to appoint a Protestant governor of Maryland he sought to secure for Roman Catholics in his American colony the same measure of toleration as he had granted to Protestants there from the beginning. For that reason he required the new governor to take an oath that he would protect Catholics in their rights and would not discriminate against them. Among the sixteen laws that Baltimore sent over for the Assembly's approval were probably included draft provisions of an act which provided the framework or nucleus of Maryland's Toleration Act of 1649. In this act the broad-minded and statesmanlike Baltimore showed that he was far in advance of his time. In the preceding year when the European nations made a general peace settlement in the Treaty of Westphalia ending the Thirty Years' War all that they could agree upon by way of a religious settlement was the principle of *cuius regio eius religio,* allowing each prince to determine the religion of his own subjects. When they finally, much later, accepted the principle of religious toleration they did so not by deliberate choice, as in Baltimore's case, but because their people had become indifferent toward religious matters.

What were the provisions of the Maryland "Act concerning Religion?" This act, which heads the list of laws passed by the Assembly of 1649, seems to be made up of two bills because a second preamble occurs in the middle of the act and the tone of the first part is far less liberal than the tone of the second part. The second part contains phrases which are identical with those of the Governor's oath. It seems certain therefore, that the Proprietor originated the act and wrote the draft provisions which have survived as the second part and that the Assembly before ratifying it added provisions of its own which form the first part.

The act begins negatively providing that whoever blasphemes God, denies that the Saviour Jesus Christ is the son of God, or denies the divinity of any person of the Holy Trinity shall be punished with death and confiscation of lands and goods; that whoever uses "reproachfull" words concerning "the blessed Virgin Mary the Mother of our Saviour or the holy Apostles or Evangelists" shall be punished for the first offense by a fine of £5, and in default of fine, by whipping and imprisonment, for the second offense by a £10 fine or whipping and imprisonment, and for the third offense by forfeiture of all property and perpetual banishment; that whoever calls anyone, either inhabitants or persons trading in the Province, a "heritick, Scismatick, Idolator, puritan, Independant, Prespiterian, popish priest, Jesuite, Jesuited papist, Lutheran, Calvenist, Anabaptist, Brownist, Antinomian, Barrowist, Roundhead, Sepa[ra]tist, or any other name or terme in a reproachfull manner relating to matter of Religion shall for every such Offence forfeit and loose the some of tenne shillings," half of which should go to the one taunted; that profaning the "Sabbath or Lords Day called Sunday by frequent swearing, drunkennes or by any uncivill or disorderly recreacōn, or by working on that day when absolute necessity doth not require it" shall be fined.[1]

These provisions, which undoubtedly originated with the Maryland assembly, seem severe today and inconsistent with religious liberty. But the first clause in the act, providing punishment for those who deny the divinity of any person of the Holy Trinity, set a standard which was quite high in the seventeenth century. It was never invoked at any time against any person in Maryland. The last clause which provided punishment for profanation of the Sabbath, using the Puritan word sabbath, was probably inserted in its entirety by the assembly. Lord Baltimore would hardly have used the word Sabbath as synonymous with Sunday, though the Puritans, with their fondness for Hebrew names, customarily used it in that sense.

The second part of the act begins with a preamble which declares that "whereas the inforceing of the conscience in matters of Religion hath frequently fallen out to be of dangerous Consequence in those commonwealthes where it hath been practised, And for the more quiett and peaceable government of this Province, and the better to p̄[re]serve mutuall Love and amity amongst the Inhabitants thereof ... noe person or p[er]sons whatsoever within this Province, ... professing to beleive in Jesus Christ, shall from henceforth bee any waies troubled, Molested or discontenanced for or in respect of his or her religion nor in the free exercise thereof ... nor any way compelled to the beleife or exercise of any other Religion against his or her consent, soe as they be not unfaithfull to the Lord Proprietary, or molest or conspire against the civill Governemt established or to bee established in this Province under him or his heires." The act further provided that any and every person who molested another Christian for his religion must pay him treble damages and forfeit 20 shillings for each offense or, in default of the fine, must be punished by public whipping and imprisonment during the pleasure of the proprietor.

This act, then, represented a compromise on the subject of religious toleration between the views of the colonists in Maryland on the one hand and of the Proprietor on the other. The second part of the act which proclaims the broad principle of religious liberty and the dangerous consequences of a contrary policy probably was a part of the draft prescribed by Lord Baltimore. The act as a whole when finally passed by the assembly almost certainly did not embody the Proprietor's original views, but it was wisely accepted by him and on August 6, 1650 was confirmed, along with several other acts, under his hand and seal.

The credit for Maryland's Toleration Act belongs to Cecil Calvert, Lord Baltimore. It was initiated by him, and though it failed to provide the broad religious liberty which he prescribed in the governor's oath it was finally approved by him. If it was in fact a defensive move on his part, designed to protect his coreligionists in Maryland at a time when Roman Catholics in his colony formed a minority and were threatened with persecution, the act nevertheless stands as a notable repudiation of religious bigotry and a landmark of enlightened statecraft. In it Maryland can find historical basis for its claim to the title "The Free State," for by this act it demonstrated its freedom from the religious intolerance which was still rampant in the mother country, on the continent of Europe, and even in several of her sister colonies in America. From the beginning Maryland was a place of free refuge to all immigrants who accepted the religious doctrine of the Trinity. To the principle of religious toleration the first Proprietor of Maryland strictly adhered. It was likewise enforced by his heirs and successors to the title—even by those who lacked his firmness and wisdom. Only during the period of Puritan dominance in Maryland from 1654 to 1658 was this principle repudiated. Throughout Maryland's colonial history no one was ever banished or put to death under her laws on account of his religious beliefs.

Footnotes

[1] *Archives of Maryland,* Assembly I, 244-245.

Sources and Additional Reading

Brown, Benjamin, F., *Early Religious History of Maryland: Maryland Not a Roman Catholic Colony,* Innes & Co., Baltimore, 1876, 34 p.

Byrns, R.K., "Religious Tolerance in Colonial Maryland," *Catholic World,* vol. 138, pp. 694-700, March 1934.

Davis, George Lynn-Lacklan, *The Day Star of American Freedom: or the Birth and Early Growth of Toleration in the Province of Maryland . . .,* J. Murphy & Co., Baltimore, 1855.

Gambrall, Theodore C., *Church Life in Colonial Maryland,* George Lycett, Baltimore, 1885.

Ingle, Edward, *Parish Institutions of Maryland,* Johns Hopkins University Studies, series 1, No. 6, Johns Hopkins University, Baltimore, 1883.

Johnson, Bradley T., *The Foundation of Maryland and the Origin of the Act Concerning Religion,* J. Murphy & Co., Baltimore, 1883.

Neill, Edward D., *Maryland Not a Roman Catholic Colony,* Johnson and Smith, Minneapolis, 1875.

——, *Terra Mariae; or Threads of Maryland Colonial History,* J.B. Lippincott & Co., Philadelphia, 1867.

Russell, William T., *Maryland; The Land of Sanctuary. A History of Religious Toleration in Maryland from the First Settlement until the American Revolution,* J.H. Furst Co., Baltimore, 1907.

Steiner, Bernard C., *Maryland During the English Civil Wars,* Part I, Johns Hopkins University Studies, Series 24, Nos. 11, 12. The Johns Hopkins Press, Baltimore, Maryland, November-December 1906.

——, *ibid.,* Part II. Johns Hopkins University Studies, Series 25, Nos. 4, 5. The Johns Hopkins University Press, Baltimore, Maryland, April-May 1907.

CHAPTER VI

MARYLAND UNDER THE COMMONWEALTH

Maryland, like England, began a new era in its history in 1649. The execution of Charles I removed the last obstacle to full control over England by the victorious Puritans under parliamentary leadership. In Maryland the Toleration Act of that year embodied in legislative enactment the religious policies which the Proprietor had introduced and followed in the colony from the beginning and encouraged the influx into the colony of new groups of religious dissenters. The Proprietor, in initiating the Toleration Act, may have been partly influenced by a desire to make his colony more attractive to immigrants and hence more profitable to himself. Maryland's resources could only be developed by additional manpower.

Maryland attracted English settlers partly because of the appeal of the sheer idea of religious freedom, from which the Toleration Act of 1649 was a retreat, but a retreat which was not serious enough to impede immigration. Tolerance of all religious creeds, of differing viewpoints, of human error and failure was the theme of Maryland from the beginning. Lord Baltimore and his colonists knew that in this life one must often show toleration toward others. "You have to bite your tongue plenty of times," say the folk in southern Maryland. But, however effective this principle of toleration may have been in attracting settlers to Lord Baltimore's colony, the appeal of Maryland as a place of settlement for Englishmen was primarily economic. It offered abundance of land, new means for making a livelihood, and opportunities for adventure and perhaps political prestige.

As early as 1643, during "the plundering time," Lord Baltimore had given Cuthbert Fenwick a letter to be carried to Boston inviting Massachusetts Puritans to migrate to Maryland. In this letter he offered land, "free liberty of religion and all the privileges which the place afforded" only requiring in return that the Puritans should pay "such annual rent as should be agreed upon." But he could induce none of the New England Puritans to move to his colony on the Chesapeake. Governor John Winthrop recorded acidly that none of his subjects had "temptation that way." Maryland did not become the objective of a Puritan migration until 1649, and the migration, when it began in that year, came not from New England but from Virginia, probably under the inspiration and leadership of Maryland's new Protestant governor, William Stone. As Puritan colonists began to move into Maryland they further reduced the influence of Lord Baltimore's Catholic followers, caused the formation of two new counties, and seriously complicated the politics of the Province. The Protestant governor, exercising control over many diverse religionists, was obliged to give satisfaction to both a Catholic Proprietor and a Puritan Parliament in England.

The Puritans who began to migrate to Maryland in 1649 were harried out of Virginia by the royalist governor, William Berkeley. There the Anglican church had been established since the beginning of the colony, but in 1642 a Congregational or Independent church was organized. In spite of the laws of that colony against dissenters, it grew until it numbered probably 118 members by 1648. But in that year the members began to be persecuted by a more rigid enforcement of the laws against dissenters and their church was broken up. They therefore responded eagerly to the solicitation of Maryland's Governor Stone inviting them to settle in Lord Baltimore's province. In 1649 these Virginia Puritans, numbering perhaps as many as 300 in all, established a settlement on the west side of the Chesapeake near the mouth of the Severn River and named it Providence. They were welcomed into the province and were given lands there in accordance with Baltimore's Conditions of Plantation.

The Proprietor himself meanwhile had taken action to attract immigrants from Virginia into Maryland. As an inducement to a Virginian, Robert Brooke, to move into his colony, he appointed him a member of the "Privy Council of State within our said Province of Maryland" because he "doth, this next summer's expedition, intend to transport himself, his family and a great number of other persons and good store of provision and ammunition" into Maryland and to settle there "a considerable plantation." He designated Brooke commander of a new county, to be "newly set out round about and next adjoining" his settlement and to contain as much area as was usually allotted to counties in Maryland and Virginia. When Brooke finally arrived, he brought with him his wife, ten children, twenty-one men servants, and seven women servants—forty persons in all—and the territory in which he settled south of the Patuxent River was erected in November 1650 into Charles County by action of the governor and council at St. Mary's. This county was short-lived, however, for the order by which it was created was revoked by the governor in July 1654.

Maryland had been fortunate, for thus far it had not been obliged to commit itself officially to either the royalist or the parliamentary cause.

Since it was a proprietary colony, writs there ran in the name of the Proprietor, not in the name of the king. Governor Stone, following the cautious policy of the Proprietor, wisely refused to take an official position in relation to the political controversy in England. But now the aftermath of the English Civil War between the king and Parliament began to echo ominously in the Chesapeake. While Stone was temporarily absent from the colony in November 1649, Acting Governor Thomas Greene committed the irreparable blunder of proclaiming the eldest son of the executed king as Charles II and announcing a general pardon to all the inhabitants of the province. This he did in defiance of a law of Parliament which explicitly declared that any person "who should presume to declare Charles Stuart, son of the late Charles" to be king, "should be deemed and adjudged a traitor." Officials in Scotland, Ireland, and Virginia who had violated this act by doing what Greene did in Maryland, had already been punished as traitors. Since Lord Baltimore's position was jeopardized and the attack upon him was renewed by his enemies as a result of Greene's ill-considered action, he hastened to disavow this as well as all other acts of Greene as acting governor and declared them null and void unless they should be confirmed by Governor Stone. He also removed Greene as a member of the "Council of State, Commissioner of our Treasury," and from all other offices in Maryland.

By his rejection of Greene and his support of Maryland's Protestant governor, Baltimore gave a new grievance to the royalist party. Already he had offended them by appointing Stone as governor, by allowing an influx of Puritans into his colony, by permitting the Puritans to acquire ascendancy there, and by accepting the Parliamentary victory in England. He was now threatened by the royalists with the loss of his colony and was repudiated by the young Stuart pretender to the throne, Prince Charles. Early in 1650 Charles, from his place of exile in Europe, issued a commission to Sir William Davenant, the poet and godson of Shakespeare, designating him Lieutenant Governor of Maryland, because, Prince Charles alleged, "the Lord Baltemore . . . doth visibly adhere to the Rebells of England, and admits all kinde of schismatics and sectaries and other ill-affected persons to the said Plantations." But Lord Baltimore was not deprived of his colony by Davenant, who, it appears, made no attempt to gain control in Maryland.

The new Puritan colony at Providence was represented for the first time in the Assembly which convened at St. Mary's in April 1650. This Assembly sat as two houses, the Upper House consisting of the Governor, Secretary, and members of the Council, and the Lower House consisting of fourteen burgesses elected from Providence, the Isle of Kent County, and the six hundreds of St. Mary's County, namely, St. Clement's, St. Mary's, St. George's, St. Inigoes, St. Michaels and Newtown Hundred. This Assembly formally adopted the bicameral system, and this division into two houses remained in force throughout the remaining time of the Proprietary government. Among the acts of this Assembly was an act erecting that "part of the Province over against the Isle of Kent, formerly called Providence by the inhabitants, into a shire or county, by the name of Anne Arundel," the Lord Proprietor's wife, who had died in 1649 at the age of thirty-four. Soon afterward Edward Lloyd was appointed Commander of the new county by Governor Stone. To the principal river in the county he gave the Welsh name, Severn.

In spite of Baltimore's wisdom and discretion, he encountered increasing opposition in Maryland after 1649, for he failed to give complete satisfaction to either the royalist or the Puritan factions. As a past recipient of a royal monopoly, he had become a symbol of authoritarian power conferred upon him by a Stuart king, and as an absentee landlord drawing profits from his colony in America, he was the target of an anti-monarchical movement which was triumphant in England and which was becoming popular in Maryland. His tenure of Maryland appeared to some of his colonists to be only a vestige of a discredited English monarchism which, like it, should be swept away. Accordingly, when Lord Baltimore included in the draft laws which he sent over to Maryland in 1649 a provision recognizing the charter of Maryland and prescribing an oath of fidelity to him as the Proprietor, the Maryland Assembly rejected it. They objected to the words "Absolute Lord and Proprietary" and "Royal Jurisdiction" which he used and contended that under this authority they could be enslaved by him.

Lord Baltimore, attempting to allay the suspicions of the Marylanders, explained in reply that his claim to be "Absolute Lord and Proprietary" was the exact title conferred upon him in the charter of Maryland, and he denied that he had any intention of enslaving them. As a result he was able to secure from the Assembly of 1650 a grudging act recognizing his "lawful and undoubted right of title" as "Absolute Lord and Proprietary." But the rest of this act was couched in language so fulsome as to be ominous. This predominantly Protestant Assembly promised to "maintain, uphold, and defend" Baltimore "for ever, until the last drop of our blood be spent, . . . in all the royal rights, jurisdictions, authorities, and preeminences" given him by the charter, so far as these did not "prejudice the just and lawful liberties, or privileges, of the free born subjects of the Kingdom of England." The Assembly pointed proudly to the "unspeakable benefits we have received by your Lordship's vigilancy" and the "inestimable blessings" which Baltimore "poured on this Province, in planting Christianity among a people that know not God." But when this Assembly finally passed Baltimore's draft of an "act for taking of an oath of fidelity to the Lord Proprietary," they omitted the word "Absolute" from the Proprietor's title and the word "Royal" before "Jurisdiction."

Meanwhile Oliver Cromwell, as the leader of the Parliamentary armies, determined to reduce to obedience the English colonies in America which remained loyal to the monarchical cause. Parliament, in October 1650, forbade all trade and intercourse with Virginia and the West Indies for their "divers acts of Rebellion" and authorized the Council of State "to send ships to any of the plantations aforesaid, and to grant commissions to such persons as they shall think fit, to enforce all such to obedience, as stand in opposition to the Parliament, and to grant pardons, and settle governors in the said islands, plantations and places, to preserve them in peace, until the Parliament take further notice." After Cromwell finally overthrew the royal party at the battle of Worcester in September 1651, the new Commonwealth government appointed a commission consisting of Captains Robert Dennis, Richard Bennett, Thomas Stagg, and Captain William Claiborne "for the reducing of Virginia and the inhabitants thereof to their due obedience to the Commonwealth of England." Though Parliament had not mentioned Maryland by name in the ordinance of 1650, the Council of State did not doubt that they had power to "enforce" Maryland also "to obedience" and instructed the commissioners that "upon your arrival at Virginia, you . . . shall use your best endeavors to reduce all the plantations within the Bay of Chesapeake to their due obedience to the Parliament." They authorized the commissioners further to pardon the inhabitants who should submit and to "use all acts of hostility that lies in your power" against those who refused to submit. When the colonists had yielded, the commissioners were required to administer an oath "to be true and faithful to the Commonwealth of England as it is now established" and "cause all writs, warrants, and other process whatsoever to be issued forth . . . in the name of the keepers of the Liberty of England by authority of Parliament."

When this commission, appointed to consolidate the control of Parliament over the American colonies, arrived in Virginia with some 700 troops, they established Bennett as Governor of the colony and Claiborne as Secretary. The irrepressible and ubiquitous Claiborne, now backed by Parliament, prepared once again to fish in the troubled political waters of

Maryland. He and Bennett proceeded to St. Mary's where they removed Governor Stone, Secretary Hatton, and all the members of the council from office and appointed a new Council with Robert Brooke as its chief. They also summoned a new assembly but authorized only those freemen who had taken an oath to support the Commonwealth to vote in the election of burgesses. The Puritan commissioners had first to overcome the scruples of Stone and Hatton, who insisted that Parliament had not intended to divest Baltimore of his rights in the province and that writs there should continue to run in his name. When they finally persuaded them to yield these points "until the pleasures of the State of England be further known," they restored Stone and Hatton to their former offices. By these actions they so undermined Lord Baltimore's authority in the province that the Puritans of Anne Arundel County refused to send delegates to the Assembly of 1651 because of "some reports in those parts of a dissolution or resignation" of Baltimore's patent, "which might perhaps make them doubtful what to do, till they had more certain intelligence" from England.

From the standpoint of the Parliamentary commissioners their restoration of Governor Stone to office was a mistake, as they later found out to their cost, for Stone was a man of courage, deep conviction, and steadfast loyalty to the Proprietor who had originally appointed him to his office. He was now seemingly caught in a vise between the orders of the Parliamentary commissioners and Lord Baltimore's interests. When the order of Cromwell's hand-picked Barebone's Parliament proclaiming Cromwell "lord protector of the Commonwealth of England, Scotland and Ireland and of the dominions and territories thereunto belonging" reached Maryland in the spring of 1654, Stone commanded all persons to submit to it. At the same time he took the fateful step of breaking away from the orders of the Parliamentary commissioners, who were then absent in Virginia, and decreed that writs should "run in the Proprietary's name as heretofore" inasmuch as this "cannot any ways derogate from our obedience" to the Commonwealth. In this action he professed complete loyalty to the Commonwealth but acknowledged Baltimore's powers as Lord Proprietor of the Province. Soon afterward in pursuance of the Proprietor's instructions, Stone punished Robert Brooke for his willingness to assist the Parliamentary commissioners by removing him from the command of Charles County, which had been established by ordinance of November 21, 1650. At the same time he erected the territory on both sides of the Patuxent River into Calvert County.

These actions of Stone antagonized the Puritan faction in Maryland. They immediately reported to Bennett and Claiborne what Stone had done and refused to take the oath to support the Proprietor. If they took the oath, they complained, they would be obliged to "maintain popery and a popish Anti-Christian Government, which we dare not do, unless we should be found traitors to our country, fighters against God, and covenant breakers." Bennett and Claiborne hastily returned to Maryland, though the Parliament from which they had derived their authority had expired over a year before. According to their report they "applied themselves" to Stone and his Council but received only "opprobrious and uncivil language." Suspecting, whether rightly or wrongly is not known, that Stone was mustering his men for an attack upon them, they joined the Puritans north of the Patuxent and from there issued a proclamation against Stone and threatened to call in aid from Virginia, of which Bennett was still governor.

At this juncture, Stone was stiffened in his resistance to the Puritans by a letter which he received from the proprietor instructing him either to take vigorous action against them or to turn over the Province to a new governor. At the same time, Stone received a letter from Cromwell commending a newcomer, Dr. Luke Barber, to him and addressed to "Capt. Stone, Governor of Maryland." Interpreting this letter as evidence of Cromwell's approval of his tenure as governor and encouraged by news that Cromwell had not deprived Baltimore of either his patent or his land, Stone prepared to drive the Puritans from power. He first sent a party of men to seize the Provincial records from Richard Preston, a new member of the Parliamentary commission. Not finding Preston at his home, the expedition not only seized the records but also ransacked his house. They also carried away the first known archivist of Maryland, John Sutton, who had been appointed by the Assembly "to attend the Records for any that should have occasion to use them, either for search or copy." Then, after rejecting the conciliatory offers of the Puritans in a brusque and offensive manner, Stone collected an expedition of between two hundred and two hundred and fifty men and proceeded north by land and by water toward the Puritan strongholds. As they went, they seized arms, ammunition, and provisions and intimidated hostile settlers.

At daybreak on the morning of Sunday, March 25, 1654, the twentieth anniversary of the landing of Lord Baltimore's first colonists in Maryland, Stone and all his men, drawn up in martial array and flying their black and yellow colors, marched against the Puritan forces. Probably at the present Horn Point on the Severn near Annapolis he met William Fuller and his Puritan army of more than a hundred men drawn up under the standard of the Commonwealth and engaged them in a battle. The Proprietary army was routed, over twenty of their men were slain, including Thomas Hatton the Secretary, and Stone himself was wounded.

With Governor Stone's defeat in this battle of the Severn, the power of Lord Baltimore in Maryland was temporarily ended. The Puritan forces, who had lost only three men killed on the field, attributed their victory to God and held a "religious, humble and holy rejoicing." Having taken practically the entire Proprietary force prisoner, they held a Council of War and condemned to death most of the members of the Maryland Council and several of the lesser men of Baltimore's party, but they actually executed only four, William Eltonhead, Captain William Lewis, John Leggat, and John Pedro. For the following three years the Puritans ruled Maryland.

The Parliamentary commissioners who took charge of Maryland after their victory at the Severn, purported to act as "Comissioners for his highness, to the reducing and settling the Plantations of Virginia and Maryland." They now deposed Stone and compelled him "to lay down his power lately assumed from the Lord Baltimore and to submit ... to such government as the commissioners should appoint." They then chose ten Puritans headed by Captain William Fuller as "Commissioners for the well Ordering, directing and Governing the affaires of Maryland" under the Protector, and arranged for the summoning of an Assembly elected only by those who had not "borne Armes in Warre against the Parliament or doe profess the Roman Catholick Religion." [1] This Assembly which met at the home of Richard Preston, one of the Commissioners, near Battletown on the Patuxent River in October 1654, passed forty-six brief laws. Among these was an act which recognized the conquest of the province by Bennett and Claiborne and repudiated the control of Baltimore and of every other power except that of the Commonwealth exercised by the Protector. This Assembly also repealed the act of 1649 concerning religion and passed in its stead a parody of that act.

This Puritan measure declared "That none who profess and Execise [sic] the Popish Religion Commonly known by the Name of the Roman Catholick Religion can be protected in this Province ... but are to be restrained from the Exercise thereof." The principle of religious toleration established in the earlier act was watered down to provide that "Such as profess faith in God by Jesus Christ (though Differing in Judgment from the Doctrine worship & Discipline publickly held forth shall not be restrained from but shall be protected in the profession of the faith) & Exercise of their Religion so as they abuse not this Liberty to the injury of others. The Disturbance of the publique peace on their part, Provided that this Liberty be not Extended to popery or prelacy nor to such as under the profession of Christ hold forth and practice Licentiousness." [2] By this act, the Puritans thus intolerantly denied religious liberty to Catholics, Episcopalians, and all other sects which in their judgment "hold forth and practice Licentiousness." As might have been expected, they also dealt severely with the Jesuits. After the battle of the Severn, the victorious Puritans plundered the homes of the Jesuits and drove them into Virginia.

The Puritans, now established in power in Maryland, thrust Lord Baltimore's authority into abeyance and compelled most of the Proprietary party to submit to them. The Puritan Assembly denied the Proprietor's right to issue patents to land and declared instead that "all those, that transport themselves or others into this Province have a right to land by virtue of their transportation" and might enter title for a particular tract of land at the county court. They changed the name of Anne Arundel County to Providence and created the territory between it and St. Mary's into Patuxent (later renamed Calvert) County. But their actions did not receive unqualified approval from Cromwell. Cromwell wrote to Bennett upbraiding him because he had "gone into" Maryland and "countenanced some people there in opposing the Lord Baltimore's officers; whereby and with other forces from Virginia" he had "much disturbed that Colony and people, to the endangering of tumults and much bloodshed there, if not timely prevented." He ordered Bennett and "all others deriving any authority from you" not to disturb "Baltimore, or his officers or people, in Maryland and to permit all things to remain as they were, before any disturbance or alteration made by you or by any other, upon pretence of authority from you." But Cromwell assured the Maryland commissioners that he did not intend to put a stop to their proceedings; he simply desired to "prevent and forbid any force or violence to be offered" by either Virginia or Maryland to the other.

Regardless of the outcome of the civil strife in Maryland, the controversy between the Proprietary party and the Puritan party would obviously be settled in England. Both sides, therefore, hastened to present their cases in writing. In 1653, the Proprietor's case was stated in an anonymous pamphlet "The Lord Baltemore's [sic] Case." Two years later the Puritan party replied to it in a similarly anonymous pamphlet entitled "Virginia and Maryland, or The Lord Baltamore's [sic] Printed Case Uncased and Answered." This pamphlet circulated the charges, among others, that Baltimore had made his Province a nursery for Jesuits, that he oppressed the Protestants or forced them to adopt Catholicism, and that he had permitted Dutch, French, and Italians to settle there and enjoy the same privileges as the English and Irish.[3] In the same year, the Puritans published two other pamphlets written to justify the men of Providence: (1) Captain Roger Heamans' "An Additional Brief Narrative of a late bloody design against the Protestants in Anne Arundel County," [4] and (2) "Babylon's Fall in Maryland," which was probably written by Leonard Strong.[5] To these Puritan publications Baltimore's champions responded with three pamphlets: (1) John Hammond's "Hammond vs. Heamans," [6] (2) John Langford's "A Just and Cleere Refutation of a false and Scandalous Pamphlet, Entituled Babylon's Fall in Maryland," [7] and (3) the vigorous and sprightly tract of John Hammond entitled "Leah and Rachel, or the Two Fruitful Sisters; Virginia and Mary-land." [8]

Baltimore was careful to keep his legal claims to Maryland clear and to seek to have them validated by the government of the Commonwealth. He complained to the Protector in 1655 that he "was interrupted in his rights and jurisdictions in Maryland." His complaint was referred by Cromwell to two agents, whose report was eventually referred to the Committee for Foreign Plantations, where it was given no attention. Nevertheless Baltimore proceeded to appoint Josias Fendall as governor of Maryland in place of Stone in July 1656. He may not perhaps have been entirely satisfied with Stone's loyalty to him and his interests, or he may have felt that Stone, by reason of past acts, had aroused so many animosities in Maryland that he would have to be replaced in the interest of harmony. Baltimore now instructed Governor Fendall to secure the peaceful submission of all who had opposed his government, to reestablish the act of 1649 concerning religion, and to resist Virginia's encroachments upon the Province. At the same time, he appointed a new council and sent over his younger brother Philip Calvert to serve as a Councillor and as Secretary of the Province.

But Governor Fendall and the new councillors could exercise only titular authority over the province of Maryland unless Lord Baltimore could reach an accommodation with the Puritan authorities who had seized control of the colony. Not until November 30, 1657, did Baltimore conclude articles of agreement with Samuel Matthews, representing "Bennett and other people in Maryland, now or late in opposition to his Lordship's government." Though, as the agreement declared, Baltimore had not yet been able to secure from Cromwell and the Privy Council in London a settlement of his claim "by reason of their great affairs," he was able to obtain from the Puritans in Maryland a complete recognition of his authority and submission to it. To him were now restored all the records of the Province and the great seal, and he in turn agreed that the Puritans might occupy the lands they had settled just as if no "plundering time" or battle of the Severn had occurred. But they must apply for patents to their lands within nine months, must take the oath of fidelity to the Proprietor, and must pay the usual quitrents. By these terms the Proprietor in effect granted a general amnesty to his enemies in the Province, but he agreed that any Puritans who wished to leave Maryland might do so freely within a year. His conviction of the wisdom of religious toleration, which would of course still redound mainly but not entirely to the advantage of the Roman Catholic minority in the Province, remained as strong as ever and he stipulated that he would never consent to the repeal of the act of 1649 concerning religion.

In pursuance of this understanding arrived at in England between Baltimore and Matthews, Fendall assumed executive authority over Maryland and published the articles of agreement which they had concluded. Desiring to confirm these arrangements with the Puritan authorities in the colony, he invited Fuller, Preston, and other members of the Puritan faction to meet with him, Philip Calvert, and Cornwaleys at "St. Leonard's Creek in Patusent River." There the representatives of the two parties drew up and signed, in March 1658, another agreement or treaty by which the Proprietor's representatives secured the submission of the Puritan faction on lenient terms. They also received the records and the great seal of the Province, and Fendall was publicly proclaimed governor. As Lord Baltimore thus again took over control of Maryland he treated as null and void all laws which had been passed by the assembly after the overthrow of his authority. Among the laws which he thus nullified was the Puritan act denying religious liberty to Catholics and to all other sects which "hold forth and practise Licentiousness." In its place the Proprietor now revived and substituted the act of 1649 "concerning Religion."

But Lord Baltimore's authority over the Province of Maryland, which had been formally recognized by the agreements, one concluded in England and the other in Maryland, and which was signalized by Fendall's assumption of the governorship, was not thus automatically restored. It continued to be jeopardized by disaffection within his colony, growing in part out of his claims for increased tax levies and in part out of the continuing resistance of the Puritan faction there to the restoration of Catholic rule. Fendall took advantage of these grievances, which were widespread among the Maryland colonists, to lead the resistance to the Proprietor and to betray Baltimore's interests.

When Baltimore issued Fendall his commission as governor of Maryland on July 10, 1656, he entrusted him with large powers which he may have considered necessary to enable Fendall to reduce the colony to subjection. But at the same time he imposed a check upon him by sending his own brother, Philip Calvert, to Maryland to act as both Secretary and Receiver General, ranking next to the governor in importance in the official hierarchy of the colony. While Philip Calvert upheld his brother's claims and interests in the colony, Fendall and Thomas Gerard, a member of the Council, disloyally launched a movement against him, which is usually called Fendall's rebellion. What their motives were cannot be clearly ascertained. Though both of them were Catholics, they may have hoped to ride a popular protest movement, which was predominantly Protestant, to personal popularity and financial profit. They assuredly could not have intended to advance Lord Baltimore's interests by their plot.

The Marylanders had, or felt they had, genuine economic grievances against the Proprietor. In 1647 the assembly had granted Baltimore a duty of ten shillings on every hogshead of tobacco exported from the Province on condition that he would bear the expenses of any war in which Maryland should become involved. After Fendall assumed the governorship in 1659, he was instructed by Baltimore to have this act repealed and to enact in its place a law which would authorize him to collect a duty of two shillings on every hogshead of tobacco exported to Great Britain or Ireland and ten shillings on every hogshead exported to any other country. The new law said nothing about the Proprietor's obligation to pay the expenses of the colony in war. This request of the Proprietor astonished and shocked the Marylanders, coming at a time when the Protectorate was crumbling to pieces in England, and it aroused strong opposition in the Province. The Marylanders believed that the duty act of 1647 had been repealed at the Proprietor's request in 1649, and they therefore regarded his instruction to Fendall as a new tax levy upon them, which they opposed.

Fendall now summoned an assembly to consider the Proprietor's request, inviting each of Maryland's counties to send four representatives. Charles and Baltimore Counties having just been established, Maryland's counties now numbered six—these two plus the older St. Mary's, Kent Island, Anne Arundel, and Calvert. But Anne Arundel County, the center of Puritanism, sent seven delegates in violation of the writs and gave the assembly a total membership of twenty-seven men. Of these at least twenty either were Puritans or had been connected with the former Puritan government of the colony. Only three members of the assembly were known to belong to the Proprietary party, but the majority of the members of the Council were loyal to him. Thus the stage was set for a conflict between the popular Lower House and the Proprietary Council over the question of taxation.

The assembly convened on February 28, 1660, in a spirit of defiance. Composed of a large majority hostile to the Proprietor, they first inquired as to the status of the export duty act of 1647 and found that it had not been repealed. But they took no action on the Proprietor's demand for a new export duty. Instead they adopted a declaration stating that "this Assembly of Burgesses judging themselves to be a lawfull Assembly without dependence on any other Power in the Province now in being is the highest court of Judicature." In this way they obviously intended to call attention to their own representative character as the popular body and invited a showdown with the Council representing the Proprietary party. By their action they not only in effect gave a negative answer to the Proprietor's request for the enactment of an export duty but they virtually challenged the authority of his agents in the colony. They seemed to be claiming for themselves authority as a complete legislature for the colony free to act without the governor and the members of the Upper House and independent of the Lord Proprietor.

When these large claims of the Assembly were challenged soon afterward at a conference between representatives of the two houses, Fendall, Gerard, and Utie declared in favor of the Lower House over the protests of Philip Calvert, Baker Brooke, and John Price. The Lower House then refused to allow the Upper House to sit as a separate body but invited its members to sit as individuals in the Lower House. Philip Calvert registered his protest against this action, calling it "a manifest breach of his l'ops Right Royall Jurisdiction and Seigniory" and asked to have his reasons entered on the journal of the Lower House. His request was refused by Governor Fendall, "Whereupon hee and Mr. Baker Brooke departed the howse (after leave asked) and given in these words or to this effect (vizt) you may if you please, wee shall not force you to goe or stay, uttered by the Governor."

The Lower House had thus virtually dissolved the Proprietary Council of the colony and now ruled supreme. It issued commissions to Fendall as Governor and to Gerard, Utie, and Slye as members of a new Council. Fendall and the Puritan Assembly controlled Maryland. But their control was short-lived, for Puritanism was waning in England and the Commonwealth was tottering to a fall. As the chaos that accompanied Richard Cromwell's poor, feeble reign had made possible Fendall's rebellion, so the restoration of the Stuarts under Charles II in 1660 foreshadowed Fendall's downfall. The restive stirrings of Marylanders for control of their own affairs were quieted by the reestablishment of stable government in England under a sovereign who would take pains not to upset the *status quo* nor to challenge the religious views of his subjects. The new king now ordered Virginia to aid Baltimore in regaining control of his Province, and Baltimore commissioned Philip Calvert as Governor. The new governor, who was the first Calvert to serve in that office since Leonard Calvert's death thirteen years before, immediately prepared to take vigorous measures against the rebels and collected an armed force to proceed against them. But he was not obliged to use it, for Fendall, seeing that resistance was useless, quietly surrendered.

The predominantly Puritan character of this abortive rebellion of 1659 was clearly revealed in Baltimore's instructions to Governor Calvert as to how to deal with Fendall. On no account was he to spare Fendall's life, wrote Lord Baltimore, "nor if you can doe it (without hazarding the regaineing of the Province) to pardon so much as for life any of those that sate in the Council of warr at Ann Arundel and concurred to the Sentence of death against Mr. [William] Eltonhead, or other of my friends then and there murthered, and have now againe engaged against me in this Second Rebellion, but to doe justice upon them and I shall iustify you in it." But this bloodthirsty order was not carried out. Fendall, Gerard, and Hatch were sentenced to banishment, and their estates were confiscated. But the sentences of Fendall and Gerard were remitted, and they were only debarred from holding office and voting. They were dealt with thus leniently probably because the Council was reluctant, in the unsettled state of the government, to irritate the Puritans further and because both Fendall and Gerard, being Catholics, had apparently been drawn into a Puritan plot. The leader of the Puritans, William Fuller, fled from the Province.

Governor Calvert did not propose to allow the opposition party to capture the Assembly again, and in issuing writs for the election of a new Assembly he directed the sheriffs, who were appointees of the governor in each county, to "cause to be elected such and so many discreete men as you shall thinke fitt to serve as Burgesses in the said Assembly." This Assembly passed several important acts—first of all, an act establishing a mint. Baltimore had urged this measure in 1659 and had actually coined some money, but the opposition questioned whether the Bishop of Durham, who was the prototype of Lord Baltimore's authority, had the power to coin money. After satisfying themselves on this point, the Assembly now passed the act providing in addition that counterfeiting of the Proprietor's coins should be punishable with death and that the Proprietor should accept this money for all debts due him by the Marylanders. This Assembly repealed the obnoxious act of 1647 providing for the collection of export duties on tobacco and imposed in its stead a tax of twelve pounds of tobacco on each taxable person in the Province to be paid to the Proprietor for the support of the government. Another act imposed a port and anchorage duty upon certain vessels trading to the Province but not owned in it. Not until 1671 did the Maryland Assembly pass an act which even approached the Proprietor's demand for an export duty on tobacco. To that extent the rebellion of 1659 was successful in lightening the taxation of the Marylanders.

With the collapse of Fendall's rebellion, Lord Baltimore, perhaps warned by that evidence of disaffection in his colony, more and more tended to treat Maryland as a family estate. From the death of Leonard Calvert in 1647, his interests in Maryland had not been adequately cared for, partly because of political complications in England but also partly because he had not had a member of the family representing him in the governorship. His appointment of Philip Calvert as Governor in 1660 after the suppression of Fendall's rebellion foreshadowed the policy of treating the government as a family affair. In Philip Calvert were centered all the chief offices of the colony, for he was designated not only Governor but also Chancellor, Secretary, and Treasurer. In 1661, Lord Baltimore sent over his son, Charles Calvert, with a commission as Governor, replacing Philip, who, however, remained Chancellor and Keeper of the Great Seal. At the same time, the Proprietor appointed Henry Sewall, an intimate friend of Charles Calvert, as Secretary of the Province. In 1664 the Calverts and their relatives dominated the Council. In the Upper House sat Charles Calvert, Philip Calvert, William Calvert, and Baker Brooke, who had married William Calvert's sister. Backed by the Proprietor, they were obviously able to control the decisions of the other four members, who included Jerome White, the Surveyor General, William Evans, commander of all the military forces of the Province, Henry Coursey, who was a close friend of Philip Calvert, and Thomas Trueman.

If Maryland was to be, as the Proprietor had intended from the beginning it should be, a colony tolerant of differing religious and political viewpoints, Baltimore must see to it that his own property interests there were not again jeopardized. To govern a colony of such diverse complexion without resorting to strong-arm methods required, as the events in Maryland during the period of the English Commonwealth showed, statesmanship of the highest order. As one means of carrying out this difficult task, the Proprietor, profiting from the error in judgment which he had made in selecting Fendall, now determined to keep the reins of authority in the hands of his family, without, however, limiting the powers of self-government which his colonists enjoyed both by charter and by prescriptive right. In this way, he could wisely administer his colony through trusted agents who had a shared common stake in it and who would help him to prevent his property in America from being despoiled.

Footnotes

[1] *Archives*, vol. III, p. 313.

[2] *Archives*, vol. 1, *Proceedings and Acts of the General Assembly of Maryland, 1637-1664*, pp. 340-341.

[3] These "Cases" are reprinted in Charles C. Hall, *Narratives of Early Maryland*, pp. 163-230.

[4] Reprinted in *Maryland Historical Magazine*, vol. IV, pp. 140-153 (1909).

[5] *Maryland Historical Magazine*, vol. III, pp. 228-240 (1908).

[6] Reprinted in *Maryland Historical Magazine*, vol. IV, pp. 236-251 (1909).

[7] Reprinted in Hall, *op. cit.*, pp. 247.

[8] Reprinted in Hall, *op. cit.*, pp. 277.

Sources and Additional Reading

Randall, D.R., *A Puritan Colony in Maryland*, Johns Hopkins University Studies in History and Political Science, Series 4, No. 6, Johns Hopkins University Press, Baltimore, 1886.

Steiner, Bernard C., *Maryland Under the Commonwealth: A Chronicle of the Years 1649-1658*, Johns Hopkins University Studies in History and Political Science, Series 29, No. 1, Johns Hopkins University Press, Baltimore, 1911.

CHAPTER VII

DOMESTIC PROBLEMS AND BOUNDARY CONTROVERSIES

Charles Calvert, the only son of Cecil, Lord Baltimore, who succeeded his uncle Philip Calvert as Governor of Maryland in 1661, held the office until the death of his father in 1675. The Province prospered under his rule. Roads and highways were constructed, ferries were established, harbors were improved, rules were adopted for the protection of orphans, and courthouses and jails were erected. For the support of Governor Calvert, the Assembly ordered a levy of twenty-five pounds of tobacco on every taxable inhabitant to be paid annually to him for his personal use, and in 1674 they ordered a duty of two shillings on every hogshead of exported tobacco to be paid to him for life.

During the prosperous times of the Stuart restoration after 1660, Maryland's population increased to an estimated 4,000; the expanding settlements spread out from St. Mary's, Kent Island, the Severn River, and the Annemessex and Manokin River settlements on the Eastern Shore, following the shores of the Bay and its navigable tributary streams. The land system ranged from individual small landholdings of a hundred acres to manors which varied in size from 1,000 to 16,000 acres and which formed self-sufficient communities with their own blacksmiths, carpenters, leatherworkers, and other artisans.

As a result of the growth of the Province, several new counties were organized after 1654 to supplement the four already in existence. In 1658, Lord Baltimore erected a new county which he named Charles in honor of his son Charles, who upon the death of his father later became the third Lord Baltimore. The Maryland Council had already established a county by the name of Charles in 1650 with Robert Brooke as Commander, but had repealed the order for its establishment in 1654 and had at that time erected the county of Patuxent in its stead. The bounds of the new Charles County were now fixed at "the river Wicomico to its head; and from the mouth of that river up the Potomac, as high as the settlements extend, and thence to the head of Wicomico." In 1695, the territory north of Mattawoman Creek was erected into Prince George's County. The limits of Charles County were then defined as the line of St. Mary's County on the east, Mattawoman Creek on the north, and "a straight line drawn thence to the head of Swanson's Creek, and with that creek to the Patuxent."

Domestic Problems and Boundary Controversies

Probably around 1659, Baltimore County was created out of territory north of Anne Arundel County. The order in council by which it was erected is lost, but the governor's proclamation of June 6, 1674, declared that "the southern bound of Baltimore county shall be the south side of Patapsco river." Talbot County was established in 1662, but, as with Baltimore County, the order by which it was created cannot be found. An act of Assembly of 1706 declared "that the bounds of Talbot County shall contain Sharp Island, Choptank Island, and all the land on the north side of the Great Choptank river; and extend itself up the said river to Tuckahoe bridge; and from thence, with a straight line, to the mill, commonly called and known by the name of Swetnam's Mill, and thence down the south side of Wye River to its mouth, and thence down the bay to the place of beginning, including Poplar and Bruff's Island." By order of Governor Calvert, Somerset County was established in 1666, bounded on the south by the southern boundary of the state on the Eastern Shore, on the west by Chesapeake Bay, on the north by Nanticoke River, and on the east by the ocean. Eight years later, Cecil County was created and named for the Lord Proprietor. During the Restoration period, therefore, Maryland grew to include nine counties, all of which, except one (Charles), fronted on Chesapeake Bay. Their names, with the approximate dates of organization, were as follows: St. Mary's (before 1637), Kent (1640), Anne Arundel (1650), Patuxent, later renamed Calvert (1654), Charles (1658), Baltimore (1659), Talbot (1662), Somerset (1666), and Cecil (1674).

Political power was centered in the Lord Proprietary and the General Assembly. Local government in Maryland was more nominal than real. In structure it followed the English pattern, operating through the institutions of the county, the hundred, the manor, the parish, and the town. Of these the county was the most important, but it provided no direct opportunities for the development of self-government. The county had no legislative body, and the county commissioners were appointed by the Proprietor upon the advice of the governor or the Assembly.

As soon as a county was officially created, it was divided by the county court into hundreds for administrative purposes. In this respect Maryland's system differed from the town system of New England, which was a product of Puritan Congregationalism. Because of the stronger centralization of authority in Maryland, the organization of towns was discouraged and towns were not given representation in the General Assembly.[1]

The Maryland counterpart of the New England town was the hundred which was the name given to the earliest civil divisions formed in the Province. These became effective agencies for expression of local opinion.

In addition, they maintained the polling places and the tax offices and provided the militia of the Province.[2] By 1775 most of the counties had from ten to fifteen hundreds; Frederick County had twenty-seven or possibly more.[3]

When in 1677, Maryland, along with England's other colonies in America, was asked by the Lords of the Committee of Trade and Plantations to answer certain queries as to conditions in the colony, one of Lord Baltimore's officials, probably the governor, sent the following report to London:

> The principall place or Towne is called St. Maryes where the Generall Assemblye and Provinciall Court are kept and whither all shipps Tradeing there doe in the first place Resort But it cann hardly be call'd a Towne It beeing in Length by the Water about five myles and in Breadth upwards towards the Land not above one myle in all which space excepting only my owne home and Buildings wherein the said Courts and Publique Offices are kept There are not above Thirty houses and those at considerable distances from each other and the buildings (as in all other parts of the provynce very meane and Little and Generally after the manner of the meanest farme houses in England Other places we have none That are called or cann be called Towns. The people there not affecting to build nere each other, but soe as to have their houses nere the Watters for conveniencye of trade and their Lands on each syde of and behynde Their houses by which it happens that in most places There are not fifty houses in the space of thirty myles And for this Reason it is that they have beene hitherto only able to divide This Provynce in Countyes without beeing able to make any subdivision Into Parishes or Precincts which is a Worke not to be affected untill it shall please God to encrease the number of the People and soe to alter their trade as to make it necessary to build more close and to Lyve in Townes.[4]

This report gave perhaps a too pessimistic picture of Maryland in the 1670's, but the colony was overshadowed both in population and influence by Virginia and was not as wealthy or strong as either its large neighbor or Massachusetts. Colonization there had proceeded in a kind of haphazard way and had taken the form of widely disparate settlements making for localism and decentralization of authority. The predominant activity in the colony was agriculture, which was carried on under a plantation economy on large manorial estates cultivated mainly by indentured white servants and a sprinkling of Negro slaves. Economic life was highly individualized and did not require towns. To Marylanders of the seventeenth century, city life offered few attractions. Their goal was to live on the land. For the further development of the resources of the colony, Maryland had an urgent need for increased population. To meet this need in part, Lord Baltimore in 1680 granted to Irish immigrants a vast tract of land one hundred miles long and eighty miles broad at the head of Chesapeake Bay, and four years later he named it the "County of New Ireland."

Domestic Problems and Boundary Controversies

Meanwhile Cecil Calvert, founder of Maryland and second Lord Baltimore, died at the age of 69 on November 30, 1675. He had never seen or visited Maryland, but from England he had governed his colony with firmness, justice, and moderation through the first forty-one years of its history. Administering the colony under a charter which embodied the absolutist governmental theories of the first two Stuart sovereigns, he wisely tempered its provisions in practice and thus, wiser than Charles I, succeeded in preserving both his domain and his life. During his proprietorship he received from the Maryland Assembly, as the legislative records of the colony show, many tributes to the wisdom and excellence of his administration and to his solicitude for his colony. As early as 1640, the Assembly declared their thankfulness "to almighty God for the benefits they had received since their colony was first brought here and planted at his lordship's great charge and expense and continued by his care and industry; and they desire that this may be preserved forever amongst their records as a memorial to all posterity of their thankfulness and fidelity." And as late as 1671, in an act granting him a tobacco duty, the two houses of Assembly explained that they passed it in "all Imaginable gratitude and thankfullnesse Reflecting uppon the great grace and favour Expressed by your Lordship to the people of this Province in the unwearied Care which your Lordship hath shewn and the vast Expences and Charge which your Lordship hath been putt unto from the tyme of their first seating in this your Lordships Province unto this instant, merely to preserve them in the Enjoyment of their lives, and liberties and the Increase and Improvements of their Estates and fortunes." [5]

These expressions by the Marylanders of their affection and esteem for a Proprietor whom few of them had seen have a sincere ring. Cecil Calvert had indeed frequently been put to great trouble and expense over his colony and, as concerns financial profits, had probably derived little net gain from it. He had had the responsibility of guiding the colony through an extraordinarily difficult period and ranks as one of the principal colony-builders of the English nation in America. Under his rule the little settlement of about 300 colonists at St. Mary's had increased to between 16,000 and 20,000 persons living in nine counties. Under his liberal policy of toleration, the Province had become a haven of refuge for many persecuted religious sects. When the first Assembly of Maryland met after his death, it passed an act enumerating all the laws which had been passed by previous assemblies and which still remained in force. Among them it included the act of 1649 "concerning Religion," which was Cecil Calvert's monument. Under his proprietorship controversies with the Virginians and with the Dutch had been satisfactorily smoothed out, as will be explained later.

At Cecil Calvert's death, his proprietorship passed to his only son, Charles, who had been Governor of Maryland since 1661 and who now became the third baron of Baltimore and the second Proprietor of the colony. He possessed his father's intelligence but, as events showed, lacked his prudence, foresight, and quiet tenacity of purpose. He immediately showed his intention of carrying out his father's policy of religious toleration, which, because of the Protestant preponderance in the colony, was especially necessary as a safeguard to Catholic interests there. The new Assembly which he convened, therefore, as aforementioned, confirmed the toleration act. He likewise made plain that, like his father, he accepted the principle of separation of church and state and would not consent to the setting up of an established church, whether Catholic or Protestant, in Maryland. This question was raised by a certain clergyman of the Church of England, the Reverend John Yeo, who wrote from Patuxent to the Archbishop of Canterbury complaining that there was no established ministry in Maryland. The Province of Maryland, he wrote, is in a "Deplorable estate & condition ... for want of an established Ministry there are in this Province tenn or twelve Countys [actually only nine] & in them at least twenty thousand Soules & but three Protestant ministers of us that are Conformable to the Doctrine & Discipline of the Church of England. ... the Popish Priests & Jesuits ... are incoraged & provided for & the Quaker takes care & provides for those th[a]t are Speakers in their conventicles, but no care is taken or Provision made for the building up Christians in the Protestant Religion. ... the lord's day is prophaned, Religion despised, & all notorious vices committed soe tht it is become a Sodom of uncleanness & a Pesthouse of iniquity." As the Lord Baltimore had recently gone to England, the Reverend Mr. Yeo begged the Archbishop to solicit from him support for a Protestant ministry.[6]

This letter, bewailing the low religious tone of Maryland and asking that funds of the colony be set aside for the support of the Anglican Church, was referred to the Committee on Trade and Plantations, which asked the new Proprietor for an explanation. In reply, Lord Baltimore explained that Maryland extended religious liberty to all forms of Christian faith and that each denomination supported its own ministers. He was unwilling to abandon this principle which had been followed in the colony from the beginning. Besides, he pointed out, thus perhaps adding confirmation to the Reverend Mr. Yeo's allegations, the Anglicans and Catholics in Maryland were outnumbered three to one by members of other sects. These latter nonconformists, he argued, should not and could not justly be required to support ministers who were not of their own faith. Thus the Proprietor preserved against attack the two basic principles which had guided the administration of the colony in religious matters throughout its history, namely, freedom of religion and separation of church and state. In these two principles Maryland's practice was at variance with that of the mother country as well as that of both Virginia and Massachusetts, which had their own established churches. Lord Baltimore here took a position to which the rest of the English-speaking world had not yet advanced.

Maryland as a land of religious freedom appealed to religious dissenters, in addition to Puritans, who were persecuted in other colonies. Under the influence of the religious intolerance that occurred during the period of Puritan supremacy, the Quakers in the colony were discriminated against for a brief time. While Fendall was governor he reorganized the militia system in order to improve the colony's defense against the Indians. By this reorganization he mustered for military service all the men in the Province between the ages of sixteen and sixty who were capable of bearing arms and enrolled the ablest in the train bands. This reorganization of the militia brought the government into conflict with the Quakers, many of whom had taken refuge in Maryland from the persecutions in New England and Virginia. In accordance with their religious principles, they refused to bear arms even in their own defense and sought to dissuade others from doing so. They also refused to take the juror's oath and the oath of fidelity on the ground that "they were to be governed by God's law and the light within them and not by man's law."

As a result of their disobedience of the colonial authorities, two active members and missionaries of the Quaker sect, who were not residents of Maryland, were arrested in 1658. One of them, Thomas Thurston, voluntarily offered to leave the Province. An order that all Quaker "vagabonds and idlers" should leave Maryland was now promulgated by the authorities. If they ventured to return, they would be whipped from constable to constable out of the Province. That order was directed, perhaps, primarily against the civil disobedience of the Quakers rather than their religious views, for, since they refused to swear oaths, they were liable to the imposition of certain political disabilities. Under this order Thurston was rearrested, but he pled on a technicality that the order did not apply to him since he had not been banished from the Province. He was accordingly released.[7] But both he and other Quakers were subjected to severe lashings by the Maryland authorities. Later, large numbers of Quakers settled in the Province, were unmolested, and prospered. Wenlocke Christison, for example, who was persecuted in England and scourged out of both Massachusetts and Rhode Island for his Quaker preaching, finally found sanctuary on a plantation in Talbot County appropriately named "The Ending of Controversie." [8] George Fox himself, the founder of the sect, visited Maryland in 1672 and held meetings, preaching on one occasion for five hours to a gathering of Indians, who gave him rapt attention to the end.[9]

Maryland's "open door" policy toward all religious sects had another consequence; it led to the definition of the boundary line between Maryland and Virginia on the Eastern Shore. When the Virginia Assembly passed an act in 1660 expelling the Quakers from that colony, those Quakers who lived on the Eastern Shore of Virginia petitioned Governor Philip Calvert to allow them to settle in Maryland. Their request was granted, and at the governor's orders they were assigned lands on the Eastern Shore of Maryland. They accordingly established settlements at Manokin and Annemessex and there concluded a treaty of amity with the Nanticoke Indians.

But Maryland's action in welcoming the Quakers was resented by the Virginians, who now tried to bring the emigrants back under their authority. Colonel Edmond Scarborough, who was appointed the agent of Virginia for this purpose, even invaded the Quaker settlements and tried to reestablish Virginia's control over them by force. For this action Governor Berkeley received a strong protest from Governor Calvert. Berkeley at once disclaimed Scarborough's attack as wholly unauthorized. The two governors now began negotiations to bring about an equitable and amicable adjustment of the boundary line between their colonies on the Eastern Shore, which had long been a source of controversy between them.

The southern boundary of Maryland, according to the charter of 1632 was to run "from the promontory or headland, called Watkin's Point, situate upon the bay aforesaid [Chesapeake Bay] near the river Wigh[comi]co on the West, unto the main ocean on the east; and between that boundary on the south, unto that part of the bay of Delaware on the north, which lyeth under the fortieth degree of north latitude from the aequinoctial, where New England is terminated." Because of the vagueness of this description and the uncertainty about the location of Watkin's Point, this boundary line had not been drawn. As a result of the dispute that had arisen between Maryland and Virginia over the Quaker settlements on the Eastern Shore, Philip Calvert and Edmond Scarborough were appointed commissioners of their respective colonies to determine the location of Watkin's Point and to mark the boundary line between the two colonies from that point to the ocean. They discharged this task in

Domestic Problems and Boundary Controversies 117

1668 and drew up an agreement fixing "the point of land made by the north side of Pocomoke Bay and the south side of Annamessex Bay . . . [as] Watkin's Point, from which said point, so called, we have run an east line agreeable with the extremest part of the westernmost angle of said Watkin's Point over Pocomoke river, to the land near Robt. Holston's, and there have marked certain trees, which are so continued by an east line, running over Swansecute's Creek, into the marsh of the seaside, with apparent marks and boundaries, which by our mutual agreement, according to the qualifications aforesaid, are to be received as the bounds of Virginia and Maryland on the Eastern Shore of Chesapeake Bay." So Maryland's southeastern boundary with Virginia was determined in its general features by friendly agreement between the two colonies.

Another interesting group of religious dissenters settled in Maryland. The Labadists were a sect of Quietists or Mystics founded by Jean de Labadie, a Frenchman, who had been educated as a Jesuit and later attacked both the Society of Jesus and the Catholic Church. After he was converted to Calvinism by reading *Calvin's Institutes,* he was ordained a Protestant minister and preached at Montauban, Orange, Geneva, and Utrecht. By some he was regarded as an irresponsible visionary and an arrogant egotist, but he was a brilliant theologian. Being a positive character of very strong views, he became embroiled in difficulties with both the ecclesiastical and the civil authorities and was formally deposed from the ministry. He then founded a church or communal society called the Evangelical, with Amsterdam in the Netherlands as its headquarters. His bold and fearless attacks upon the immorality and apathy of the church had a stimulating effect upon the established church in the Netherlands, which continued to feel his goad long after his death in 1674. At his death he was succeeded by Pierre Yvon as leader of the sect and the headquarters were removed from Amsterdam to Wieuwerd in Friesland, from which the church leaders exercised jurisdiction over all the branches of the sect. Later they transferred their headquarters to Bremen and still later to Altona, and as a result of their missionary activities, they set up several small communities in the Rhineland.

But the Labadists became interested in America, and in 1679 the organization at Wieuwerd sent out two missionaries, Peter Sluyter and Jasper Danckaerts, to look for a suitable location to establish a colony. These missionaries, after landing in New York, became acquainted with Ephraim Herrman, eldest son of Augustine, and converted him to their religion. The elder Herrman had been long connected with Maryland. He was born in Bohemia, probably in 1605, and during his adventurous early career learned surveying and became proficient in the French, Dutch,

German, and English tongues. As a soldier he saw active service under King Gustavus Adolphus of Sweden and then entered the employ of the Dutch West India Company at New Amsterdam. He became an important member of this Dutch colony at the mouth of the Hudson River and was appointed a member of the council of nine men formed by Governor Peter Stuyvesant in 1647.

In 1659 Augustine Herrman was sent by Governor Stuyvesant on a mission to Maryland and while there acquired a liking for the Province. He applied to Lord Baltimore for the grant of a manor, offering to make a map of Maryland in return for it. With Baltimore's permission he then took up some 4,000 acres on the Elk River in the region which he had traversed on his journey from New Amstel (New Castle) and named his grant Bohemia Manor. He also applied for and received letters of free denization entitling him to hold land, and in 1669 he and his family were naturalized by the first act of the kind passed in Maryland. He presented Baltimore with the map which he had promised and gradually increased his landholdings to 20,000 acres or possibly more, located in Cecil County in Lord Baltimore's Province, and in New Castle County, Delaware. There he established several manors which he nostalgically named Bohemia Manor, St. Augustine's Manor, Little Bohemia, and The Three Bohemian Sisters. In 1680 his son Ephraim, learning that the Labadist missionaries were seeking lands, brought them down to see his father at Bohemia Manor, for Maryland, like the Netherlands from which they came, was widely known for its hospitality to unorthodox religious sects. When the Labadist missionaries arrived in Maryland, they were received with kindness by the elder Herrman and were much impressed with the richness of the soil and the abundance of game in Maryland. They finally arranged to purchase a tract of some three or four thousand acres from the lord of Bohemia Manor, in what is now Cecil County, and then returned to Wieuwerd.

In 1683, the Labadist envoys came back with the nucleus of a colony and were given deeds to their land by Herrman. But by this time they had aroused his concern because of the large influence which they had contrived to gain over his son and because of their unusual religious practices. The leader of the Labadist colony, Sluyter, took for himself the whole title to the land and, making himself the despot of the little community, ruled it in an arbitrary fashion with the help of his wife. The colonists were industrious and frugal, but their eccentricities soon brought upon them the suspicion and dislike of their neighbors.

The Labadists, like the Quakers and the Mennonites to whom they were religiously related, stressed the personal relationship and the mystical communion of the individual with God. They laid great stress on the inner light and sought reform of life rather than doctrine. They accordingly rejected the sacrament of infant baptism and practiced the continuous sabbath. But they believed in the obligation of manual labor. Their system of church organization was one of communal ownership and responsibility like that of the early Christian church.

Each member of the Labadist community had his own special assignment of duties to perform. Some took charge of the laundry; others handled the cooking; and still others served as nurses. The families were given dwellings according to their needs, and those who joined the community deposited all their possessions in the common stock and wore uniform attire. Samuel Bownas, a minister of the Society of Friends, who visited the Labadist community in Maryland, wrote of them as follows:

> When supper came in, it was placed upon a large table in a large room, where, when all things were ready, came in at a call, twenty men or upwards, but no women. We all sat down, they placing me and my companion near the head of the table, and having passed a short space, one pulled off his hat, but not so the rest till a short space after, and then they, one after another, pulled all their hats off, and in that uncovered posture sat silent uttering no word that we could hear for nearly half a quarter of an hour, and as they did not uncover at once, neither did they cover themselves again at once, but as they put on their hats fell to eating not regarding those who were still uncovered, so that it might be ten minutes time or more between the first and last putting on of their hats. I afterwards queried with my companion as to their conduct, and he gave for an answer that they held it unlawful to pray till they felt some inward motion for the same, and that secret prayer was more acceptable than to utter words, and that it was most proper for every one to pray as moved thereto by the spirit in their own minds. I likewise queried if they had no women amongst them. He told me they had, but the women ate by themselves and the men by themselves, having all things in common respecting their household affairs, so that none could claim any more right than another to any part of their stock, whether in trade or husbandry; and if any one had a mind to join with them, whether rich or poor, they must put what they had in the common stock, and afterwards if they had a mind to leave the society they must likewise leave what they brought and go out empty-handed. They frequently expounded the Scriptures among themselves, and being a very large family, in all upwards of a hundred men, women and children, carried on something of the manufacture of linen and had a large plantation of corn, flax, and hemp, together with cattle of several kinds.

However strange these religious practices of the conscientious and serious-minded Labadist colonists seemed to their Maryland neighbors, they were carried on without molestation or interference by the Maryland authorities in accordance with the colony's policy of religious freedom. The Labadists may not have been cordially welcomed in Maryland, but they were at least tolerated. Finally in 1698 they abandoned their religious community living and divided their property among their members. Sluyter retained enough to become a wealthy man. At his death in 1722, the colony in Maryland came to an end, and at about the same time the parent community at Wieuwerd also went out of existence.

At the time when the Proprietor regained his authority over Maryland in 1658, his interests were being menaced in the northeast by the Dutch. Their claims to settlement rights in North America were based upon the voyages of Captain Henry Hudson to the Delaware Bay in 1609, as a result of which the Dutch West India Company, established in 1621, founded settlements or trading posts at Fort Orange on the Hudson River on the present site of Albany and Fort Nassau on the Delaware River, or South River, as it was then called, near the later town of Gloucester, New Jersey. In 1628 they decided to consolidate their interests in Manhattan Island and so abandoned Fort Nassau. In the following year, Samuel Godyn, a merchant of Amsterdam, and Samuel Bloemmaert obtained from the Dutch Assembly of Nineteen a charter and a grant of land on the west side of Delaware Bay extending northward thirty-two miles from Cape Henlopen to the mouth of the South (Delaware) River and inland for about two miles. Within this territory on the present Lewes Creek in Sussex County they established a Dutch settlement which they called Zwaanendael, or Valley of Swans, but it was wiped out by the Indians in 1631.

The Dutch therefore had no settlements upon the Delaware when Charles I granted to Lord Baltimore all the territory extending along the coast between Virginia and the 40th parallel of latitude. Within that area no permanent non-English settlements were established until the Swedes and Finns arrived in 1638. In that year, two Swedish vessels, *Kalmar Nyckel* and *Fogel Grip,* carrying some thirty soldiers and traders, sailed up the Delaware River and anchored at the later site of Wilmington. There the Swedes, Lutheran in religion, built a fort and trading post which they named Fort Christiana in honor of their twelve-year-old queen. Though Governor Wilhelm Kieft of New Amsterdam protested against this occupation of land claimed by the Dutch, he cooperated with the traders from Sweden-Finland in 1643 in driving away a colony of Englishmen from New Haven who had settled near the present town of Salem, New Jersey. But this harmonious relationship was later broken, and in 1655, after a series of disputes between them, the Dutch finally overthrew the Swedish power on the Delaware River, extended the boundaries of New Netherlands down to the Delaware, and divided the former Swedish territory into two Provinces, Altona (Wilmington) and New Amstel (New Castle).

The Swedish settlements south of the 40th parallel, which was the northern limit of Lord Baltimore's charter grant, had presented him with no formidable threat to his authority, for they never included more than

Domestic Problems and Boundary Controversies 121

400 men, women, and children living on some 700 acres of cleared land, which the New Sweden Company had purchased from the Indians.[10] But the Dutch were more powerful and aggressive. In 1659, therefore, Governor Fendall and his council, acting upon instructions from Baltimore, ordered Colonel Nathaniel Utie, who was one of the most adventurous pioneers in the colonization of the country around the head of the Chesapeake and a member of the Maryland council, to "repair to the pretended governor of a people seated in Delaware bay, within his lordship's province, without notice given to his lordship's lieutenant here, and to require them to depart the province." They shrewdly added, however, "that in case he find opportunity, he insinuate unto the people there seated, that in case they make their application to his lordship's governor here they shall find good conditions, according to the conditions of plantations, granted to all comers into this province, which shall be made good to them, and that they shall have protection in their lives, liberty, and estates which they shall bring with them."

With these instructions in his hand, Colonel Utie proceeded to New Amstel and performed his errand. He demanded of the Dutch that they either submit to Lord Baltimore or leave the Province and disclaimed all responsibility for the innocent blood that might be shed if they refused. His mission was unsuccessful, as he must have anticipated it would be. It was so offensive to crusty, one-legged Governor Stuyvesant at New Amsterdam that when he heard about it he immediately dispatched reinforcements of sixty soldiers to assist in protecting the Dutch settlements on the Delaware from invasion by Maryland and ordered Utie arrested as a spy. Utie, however, escaped, leaving behind the rumor that he would return with 500 men.

In a further attempt to defeat Utie's mission, Governor Stuyvesant protested directly to the Maryland authorities against their claims to lands belonging to New Netherlands. He sent Augustin Heerman (later changed to Augustine Herrman) and Resolved Waldron was envoys to complain to the Maryland government about Utie's conduct and to reaffirm the Dutch claim to the settlements on the Delaware. When they arrived in Maryland, they were informed by Governor Fendall and his council that Utie had acted upon instructions from them and from the Proprietor, that their settlements were within his jurisdiction, and that their "pretended title" to the Delaware region, which was derived from the States-General of the United Provinces, was "void and of no effect." The Dutch mission to Maryland, therefore, failed of its purpose, though it acquainted Heerman with the Province in which he later settled and became naturalized under the name of Herrman. The Dutch West India Company and its agent at

New Amsterdam, Governor Stuyvesant, now prepared to defend their settlements by force. In response to inquiries from Lord Baltimore's agent in Holland, Captain James Neale, the Council of Nineteen in Amsterdam informed him in September 1660 that they were "resolved to remain in possession and defend their rights" and that "if Lord Baltimore perseveres and resorts to violent measures they will use all the means God and nature have given to protect the inhabitants."

Lord Baltimore was also resolved to remain in possession and defend his rights to the colony assigned to him, and in July 1661 he applied for and secured from Charles II a confirmation of his patent. His complaints to the new Stuart sovereign about the Dutch on the Delaware must have reinforced the king's own bitterness toward the Dutch and gave international significance to the quarrel in which Maryland was involved. When the Dutch at New Netherlands began to encroach upon the English settlements in the Connecticut valley, Charles II granted to his brother James, Duke of York and Albany, on March 12, 1664, all the region extending from the western bank of the Connecticut River to the eastern shore of the Delaware River. The Duke of York promptly prepared a naval squadron of four vessels and 450 soldiers which he entrusted to Colonel Richard Nicolls with Sir Robert Carre, Colonel George Cartwright, and Samuel Meverick as associates. When this formidable expedition arrived in New Amsterdam, they received the surrender of the fort and colony without firing a shot and promptly changed its name to New York in honor of their patron. But they experienced more difficulty in reducing the Dutch settlements on the Delaware. When Sir Robert Carre appeared off New Amstel with two vessels and all the soldiers who could be spared from New York, he was obliged to storm and take the fort by force. New Amstel was now named New Castle and the river and bay were given their old English name, Delaware.

Charles II had meanwhile reaffirmed Baltimore's charter, but he apparently did not attach much importance to Baltimore's claim to the region east of the Delaware, for he included it in the grant which he made to the Duke of York in March 1664. Three months later and before the Duke of York actually received possession of the Dutch territory, he conveyed to Lord Berkeley and Sir George Carteret all the land between the Hudson River and the Delaware River extending as far south as Cape May and as far north "as the northernmost branch of said bay or river of Delaware, which is in 41° 40' of latitude, and worketh over thence in a straight line to Hudson's river." Lord Berkeley, in March 1674, conveyed his portion of New Jersey to John Fenwick in trust for Edward Byllinge, and from Byllinge William Penn later received a grant of a portion of this territory.

Domestic Problems and Boundary Controversies 123

Penn's interest in New Jersey, thus acquired, and his pecuniary claims against the English crown, based on services rendered by his father, inspired him with a desire to procure from Charles II a grant of land in America. He proposed to Charles in June 1680 that in lieu of the claims to which he was entitled for services, loans, and interest to the value of some £16,000 he be given lands west of the Delaware and north of Maryland. His petition was submitted to the privy council and copies were sent both to the secretary of the Duke of York and to Lord Baltimore's agents "to the end that they may report how far the pretensions of Mr. Penn may consist with the boundaries of Maryland, or the duke's propriety of New York, and his possessions in those parts." To this inquiry Lord Baltimore's agents replied "that if the grant pass unto Mr. Penn, of the lands petitioned for by him, in America, that it may be expressed to be land that shall be north of Susquehanna Fort, also north of all lands upon a direct line westward from said fort, for said fort is the boundary of Maryland northward."[11]

To this stipulation Penn agreed, and early in 1681 he received a grant of land in America from Charles II issued to him because of "the merits of the father, and the good purposes of the son." In it was assigned to him "all that tract or part of land in America, with the islands therein contained, as the same is bounded on the East by the Delaware River, from twelve miles distance northward of New Castle Towne, unto the three and fortieth degree of northern latitude, if the said river doth extend so far northward, but if the said river shall not extend so far northward, then by the said river so far as it doth extend; and from the head of the said river, the eastern bounds are to be determined by a meridian line, to be drawn from the head of the said river, unto the said forty-third degree. The said land to extend westward five degrees in longitude, to be computed from the said eastern bounds, and the said lands to be bounded on the north by the beginning of the three and fortieth degree of northern latitude, and on the south by a circle drawn at twelve miles distance from New Castle, northward and westward, unto the beginning of the fortieth degree of northern latitude, and then by a straight line westward to the limits of longitude above mentioned." Nothing was said about the Susquehanna fort.

This boundary clause gave rise to all the subsequent controversy between Penn and Baltimore over the limits of their two colonies. In other respects Penn's charter was copied almost directly from the charter of Maryland. It granted to Penn the free use of all ports, bays, rivers, and other waters of the Province, together with their produce and the produce of all mines, and the fee to the soil in soccage tenure, providing that Penn furnished the king with ten beaver skins annually and one-fifth of all the gold and silver discovered in his Province. Unlike the Maryland charter, however, it reserved to Parliament the right to levy taxes upon the inhabitants and required that all the laws of the colony must be approved by the privy council in England.

Penn immediately wrote a letter to Herrman and other Marylanders living at the head of Chesapeake Bay in which he invited them to acknowledge his government and advised them to pay no more taxes to Maryland. He then appointed William Markham to serve as deputy governor of his Province and instructed him to have an interview with Baltimore and to adjust their respective boundary claims, Markham, after providing himself with a sextant, found to his surprise that New Castle was twenty miles south of the 40th parallel and tried to avoid meeting Baltimore. But he was obliged to do so when Baltimore himself came to New Castle to confer with him at what proved to be an inconclusive meeting. Penn meanwhile was becoming eager to obtain a further grant from the Duke of York and at last was rewarded with a grant of New Castle, the territory twelve miles around it, and the land on the west shore of the Delaware south to Cape Henlopen, all of which had earlier been included in the Maryland charter.

In 1682, Penn himself arrived in the Delaware Bay with a group of colonists, took possession of his colony, and asked Baltimore for an interview. At the ensuing conference between the two proprietors in December 1682, Penn proposed that Baltimore accept, as an alternative to his northern boundary of the fortieth parallel, a new northern boundary which would be drawn east and west along a line two degrees north of the Capes which were "anciently reputed to lye within the latitude 37°5′[Capes Henry and Charles]." Penn thus suggested that Maryland extend its southern boundary thirty miles to the south at the expense of Virginia and give him a corresponding strip on the north. To this audacious proposal Baltimore firmly replied that his charter fixed his northern boundary at the fortieth parallel of latitude and that the most practicable and obvious solution of their problem was to take a good surveying instrument and fix the fortieth parallel at once. On this note the conference closed.

A second meeting between Penn and Baltimore occurred in May 1683, at which they retraced their old arguments. Penn, perhaps inadvertently, indicated that, not satisfied with his access to the sea through Delaware Bay, he desired in these boundary negotiations to get an outlet also through Chesapeake Bay. As this conference between two Proprietors, like the former one, ended inconclusively, Lord Baltimore

Domestic Problems and Boundary Controversies

resolved to go to England to press his claims there in person. Before departing, he convened the Maryland Assembly in April 1684 and explained to them that

> the great exigency of my affairs, not my own inclinations nor love for that place doth now draw me; it is to preserve my interest and settle my child in an undisturbed right before I die, that causeth me to resolve upon this voyage.
>
> ... having given you this assurance, I hope you will believe my stay there will be no longer than the procuring a decision of those matters you all know have been the subject of some differences between Mr. Penn and me. Those once happily ended, I shall soon return to this place, where it is my interest as also my inclination and delight to be.

After giving this explanation of the reasons for his departure, Charles Calvert, Lord Baltimore, appointed a council of regency, consisting of nine councillors, of whom William Joseph was president, to administer the Province under the nominal rule of his infant son, Benedict Leonard, and then sailed for England never to return.

Meanwhile Baltimore's case was injured and his standing at Court was imperiled by an unfortunate incident that occurred in Maryland. In 1680, Colonel George Talbot, an Irishman and a Catholic who was distantly related to Lord Baltimore's family, obtained a large grant of land on the Susquehanna, and in 1683 became Surveyor General of Maryland. After Baltimore's departure for England, this swashbuckler became the most influential member of the commission of deputy governors whom the Proprietor selected to govern the Province in his absence and during the minority of his son, Benedict Leonard. He built a fort near New Castle and ranged through the woods with his soldiers, terrorizing the Indians and bullying Penn's settlers. In 1684, he came into conflict with one of the most hated of the royal tax collectors, Christopher Rousby, who was a Protestant. Baltimore had already complained to the king of Rousby's arrogances, impertinences, extortions, and debaucheries but was confronted by a countercharge from Rousby before the Privy Council in England that Baltimore was obstructing him in the performance of his duties. Under this charge Baltimore received a rebuke from the king and a demand for damages of £2,500.

In 1684 while Rousby's ketch, belonging to the royal navy, was lying at St. Mary's, Talbot went on board the vessel and in the course of a violent quarrel with Rousby stabbed him through the heart. He was at once seized and, despite the protests of the Maryland Council, was carried off to Virginia for trial. In England the Proprietor immediately obtained an order from the Privy Council to have his kinsman sent to England for trial, but before the order reached Virginia, Talbot's wife and four friends released him from his prison near Gloucester on the

Rappahannock and took him back to his manor on the Chesapeake. According to a preposterous local tradition, Talbot hid himself in a cave along the Susquehanna and was fed by two tame hawks which brought him wildfowl. But he soon surrendered himself to the authorities and was delivered over to the Governor of Virginia, Lord Howard of Effingham. There he was brought to trial and convicted of the crime, but the Proprietor had meanwhile secured a pardon for him from the king.

Not only did this Talbot-Rousby affair aggravate Maryland's plight before the royal authorities, but the accession of the Duke of York to the English throne as James II in 1685 placed Baltimore at a further disadvantage in his negotiations with the importunate and influential Penn. The latter's case against Lord Baltimore in his claims to "the Three Lower Counties" of New Castle, Kent, and Sussex on the Delaware triumphed when the Lords of Trade and Plantations in London recommended to the new king in November 1685 that the "land lying between the River and Bay of Delaware and the Eastern Sea on the one side, and the Chesapeake Bay on the other be divided into two equal parts by a line from the latitude of Capte Hinlopen to the 40th degree northern latitude, and that one half thereof lying towards the Bay of Delaware and Eastern Sea be adjudged to belong to His Majesty and that the other half remain to the Lord Baltimore as comprised within his charter." They based their recommendation upon Penn's allegations that the Delaware lands had been settled by the Dutch and the Swedes before the date of the Maryland Charter, which assigned to Cecil Calvert, Lord Baltimore, only such lands within his charter limits as were "hitherto uncultivated and partly inhabited by savages." But, as noted above, this allegation upon which their Lordship's finding was based was erroneous, and Penn adduced no evidence to support it. Nevertheless, the recommendation of the Lords of Trade and Plantations dividing the disputed peninsula was accepted by the king and his Privy Council, and "the Three Lower Counties," thus taken away from Maryland, were then added by the king to Penn's Province in order to give it an outlet to the sea. But the injustice rankled in Maryland leading sometimes to border violence.

King James II became increasingly hostile to all the proprietary colonies in America and accelerated the previous Stuart policy of transforming them into royal provinces. In early 1687, he directed the attorney general, Sir Robert Sawyer, "to proceed in prosecution on the writ of *quo warranto* against the Lord Baltimore's and other proprietary charters." In reply, the Lord Baltimore pled "that the administration of his province had been at all times conducted conformably to his

Domestic Problems and Boundary Controversies 127

charter and to the laws of England; that he never was informed of the pleasure of his prince, but it was always obeyed, that neither he nor his father had done any act which could incur a forfeiture of a patent which they had dearly purchased in adding a considerable province to the empire." His plea would probably have been unavailing; but before judgment could be obtained on the writ of *quo warranto,* the king himself was driven from his throne and kingdom by the revolution of 1688. That revolution, called both the "Glorious Revolution" and the "Bloodless Revolution" in England, would bring serious problems to Lord Baltimore and his family and to the province which they governed in America.

Footnotes

[1] Lewis W. Wilhelm, *Local Institutions of Maryland,* The Johns Hopkins University Press, Baltimore, 1885.

[2] Wilhelm, *op. cit.,* 49-57.

[3] Newton D. Mereness, *Maryland As a Proprietary Province,* Macmillan, New York, 1901, 402.

[4] *Archives, Maryland,* V, 265.

[5] *Ibid.,* I, p. 284.

[6] *Archives,* vol. V, *Proceedings of the Council, 1667-1687,* 130-132.

[7] Kenneth L. Carroll, "Thomas Thurston, Renegade Maryland Quaker," *Maryland Historical Magazine,* vol. 62, No. 2, June 1967, pp. 170-192.

[8] Henry Chandlee Forman, "Wenlocke Christison's Plantation, 'The Ending of Controversie'," *Maryland Historical Magazine,* vol. XXXIV, No. 3, September 1939, pp. 223-227.

[9] Kenneth L. Carroll, "Talbot County Quakerism in the Colonial Period," *Maryland Historical Magazine,* vol. 53, No. 4, December 1958, pp. 326-370.

[10] The trading and colonizing activities of the Swedes and Finns on the Delaware are described in Benjamin Ferris, *A History of the Original Settlements on the Delaware* . . . Wilmington, 1846; Christopher Ward, *New Sweden on the Delaware,* Philadelphia, 1938; and John H. Wuorinen, *The Finns on the Delaware, 1638-1655,* New York, 1938.

[11] Alice L. L. Ferguson, "The Susquehannock Fort on Piscataway Creek," *Maryland Historical Magazine,* vol. XXXVI, No. 1, March 1941, pp. 1-9.

Sources and Additional Reading

Capek, Thomas, *Augustine Herrman of Bohemia Manor,* State Printing Office, Praha, Czechoslovakia, 1930.

Ferris, Benjamin, *A History of the Original Settlements on the Delaware, from Its Discovery by Hudson to the Colonization under*

William Penn. *To Which is Added an Account of the Ecclesiastical Affairs of the Swedish Settlers, and a History of Wilmington, from Its First Settlement to the Present Time,* Wilson & Heald, Wilmington, 1846.

Heck, Earl L. W., *Augustine Herrman, Beginner of the Virginia Tobacco Trade, Merchant of New Amsterdam, and First Lord of Bohemia Manor,* William Byrd Press, Richmond, Virginia, 1941.

James, Bartlett Burleigh, *The Labadist Colony in Maryland,* Johns Hopkins University Studies, Series 17, No. 6, Johns Hopkins Press, Baltimore, 1899.

Lunt, Dudley Cammett, *The Bounds of Delaware,* Star Publishing Company, Wilmington, Delaware, 1947.

Mathews, Edward B., *The Counties of Maryland: Their Origin, Boundaries, and Election Districts,* Maryland Geological Survey. Special Publication, Volume VI, Part V, Johns Hopkins Press, Baltimore, August 1907.

Mereness, N.D., *Maryland As a Proprietary Province,* The Macmillan Company, New York, 1901.

Tansill, Charles Callan, *The Pennsylvania-Maryland Boundary Controversy,* National Capital Press, Inc., Washington, D.C., [1915].

Thomas, Anne B., *The Story of the Baltimore Yearly Meeting, 1672-1938,* Baltimore, n.d.

Ward, Christopher, *The Dutch & Swedes on the Delaware, 1609-64,* University of Pennsylvania Press, Philadelphia, 1930.

Wilhelm, Lewis Webb, *Local Institutions of Maryland,* Johns Hopkins University Studies, series 3, Nos. 5-7, Johns Hopkins University, Baltimore, 1885.

Wuorinen, John H., *The Finns on the Delaware, 1638-1655: An Essay in American Colonial History,* Columbia University Press, New York, 1938.

CHAPTER VIII

A NEW PROPRIETOR

The turmoil of the Puritan period left in its wake a new spirit of independence, a disposition among the people to resist encroachments upon their liberties, and a favorable attitude toward religious dissent which encouraged the spread of Quakerism and the rise of organized Presbyterianism. Puritanism also had a leavening effect upon the practices of the Church of England in Maryland, for by reason of the distance from the mother country and the lack of Episcopal supervision, Anglicanism in Maryland lost much of its Catholic or "high church" character and became once more acceptable to Puritans. Puritanism in Maryland was never a separatist movement committed to withdrawal from the Established Church.

The acute factionalism in the colony which was engendered by Maryland's reaction to the English Civil War took the form of division not only along religious lines but also between the proprietary party and the popular party. Marylanders now began seriously to call in question the basic principle of the charter which had been granted to Cecil Calvert, the second Lord Baltimore, giving him and his heirs forever power over Maryland. They were growing increasingly restive under the taxing authority and the other limitations imposed upon them by the monopoly of the Baltimores and concluded that they as resident Marylanders were better qualified to develop the resources of their colony than was an anciently established proprietary family.

Opposition to proprietary rule flared up sporadically in Maryland and apparently with increasing intensity after 1660. When the Governor and Council championed a measure for the "cessation of Tobacco," which would have the effect of increasing the price of tobacco and hence the fees paid to officers of the Proprietor in Maryland, they encountered opposition from the Lower House representing the smaller planters and the popular cause. Several of the members of the Lower House who opposed this measure had been members of Fendall's Assembly in 1658-1659 and continued in the anti-proprietary party.[1]

The restiveness of the colony under authority from abroad caused a division between the two houses of the Assembly. The Lower House, representing the freemen of the colony, deplored that the Proprietor in England had the sole authority to confirm legislation which they passed in order to make it official and that in the exercise of his prerogative he could disallow colonial enactments. The members even allowed a clergyman, Charles Nicholett, to preach a sermon to them in which he urged them to keep before themselves the powers of the English House of Commons, to enact liberal legislation in accordance with the dictates of their consciences, and to do something about the heavy taxes of the preceding year. This sermon so offended the Upper House, which represented the proprietary party, that they summoned Nicholett before them, declared his sermon "seditious," fined him, and required him to ask the pardon of the Proprietor, Governor, and Assembly.

Successive assemblies repeatedly likened themselves to the House of Commons in England and claimed the privileges in Maryland that that body claimed in the government of England. The Maryland legislature passed an act in 1662 declaring that when the laws of the Province were silent, the laws and statutes of England would become applicable. Although this law remained in force for only a short time, it was in fact the first definite recognition in America of the power of the courts to apply the common law of England to colonial conditions. This position was accepted by the Proprietor who thus sanctioned the adoption of the common law. Much later controversy turned upon the question of conflict between the common law and the statute law of England.

Partly to counter the growing pretensions of the Assembly, the Proprietor and his party in Maryland began to limit the rights of freemen in the colony after 1670 and sought correspondingly to extend proprietary powers. In this respect they followed the example of Virginia which as a royal colony imposed new restrictions upon the franchise in 1670 in order allegedly to prevent disturbances at elections. Charles Calvert, as Governor and later as Proprietor of Maryland, showed little interest in the poorer classes of people in his colony and excluded them from representation in the Assembly which met in 1670. He now abandoned the practice of giving the vote to practically all the free male inhabitants which had been followed continuously since the founding of the colony. In issuing the call for the new Assembly, he instructed the sheriff of each county to summon only those freemen who had "within said County Visible seated Plantations of fifty acres of Land at the least or Visible personal Estates to the value of forty Pounds Sterling at the least" to the county court where they would elect delegates having similar property qualifications to represent them in the Assembly. Freemen of the colony who did not possess the requisite property qualifications were therefore now denied the privilege of voting for members of the Assembly and of serving in it. With the Assembly thus elected, the Governor had no serious difficulties, and he continued it by prorogation in office for six years. From 1670 to 1676, therefore, no new elections for members of the Assembly were called.

The machinations that Governor Charles Calvert used to outmaneuver the popular party were disclosed in a letter which he wrote to his brother, the Proprietor, in 1671 explaining how he had contrived to have two of the Proprietor's staunchest supporters, Thomas Notley and John Morecroft of St. Mary's, chosen as members of the Lower House, the former as speaker: "Mr. Notley is now Speaker of our Assembly; hee and Mr. John Morecroft being chosen Burgesses for the City of St. Maries, And by that Meanes I gott him into the Assembly. Though Doctor Wharton bee a good understandinge Man yett Dr. Morecroft is much more for our purpose, being the best Lawyer in the Country, and has always been (upon other Assemblies) a great Assertor of Yor. Lopps Charter and Privileges thereof, I durst not putt itt to an Election in the Countyes Butt tooke this way which I knew would certainly doe what I desired. And now I have gotten Mr. Notley into the Chaire, I have Assured him, that with yor. Lordships Leave, I am resolved to Keepe him there as longe as hee and I live together." [2]

It was this Assembly, thus rendered compliant by the Governor and dominated by the proprietary party, that passed the act authorizing the Proprietor to collect a tax of two shillings on each hogshead of tobacco exported from the colony, one half of which went to the Proprietor as a subsidy from his Province and the other half to the defense of the colony and the "necessary charges of the Government." In 1674, the Assembly extended the act of 1671 to grant a tax of two shillings on each hogshead of exported tobacco not only to the Proprietor during his life but also to Charles Calvert during his life. This same Assembly, upon demand of the Governor, agreed to build a brick house for him at public charge, and in the following year they granted him an expense allowance of 30,000 pounds of tobacco for entertaining the Council, nearly all of whom were members of the Calvert family. This Assembly in the last year of its existence—1676—extended the act of 1671 to make the two-shilling tax on every hogshead of exported tobacco continue not only throughout the life of the new Proprietor, Charles Calvert, third Lord Baltimore, but also throughout the life of his eldest son, Cecil Calvert, then only ten years old. They thus made the tax virtually hereditary.

This aristocratically inclined Assembly in 1674 confirmed Governor Calvert's policy of discriminating against non-property holders. It declared that members of county grand juries must pay their own expenses and explicitly forbade poor men to sit on them. It defined taxable persons very broadly to include all freemen above the age of sixteen, except ministers and priests, all imported male servants over ten years of age, and all slaves, both male and female, over ten years of age. Maryland, under the leadership of the Catholic proprietary party, was coming to be controlled by an elite class who were maintained in their specially privileged positions by the labor of all the freemen, servants, and slaves in the Province. The new class stratification, which was accompanied by discrimination against the unrepresented poorer classes, predisposed the latter to favor and cooperate with the Associators when they launched their rebellion against the government in 1689.

By this time the Council or Upper House of Maryland had become a virtual family monopoly of the Calverts. Every important office was given to some relative or special friend of the Proprietor. As a result, the members of the proprietary party were receiving a large proportion of the fees paid to the administrative officials of the Province. Baker Brooke, who had married the sister of William Calvert, was Surveyor-General as well as a member of the Council. His fees were increased by the Governor by a proclamation which was later ratified by the Assembly. William Talbot, a nephew of the Proprietor, was Secretary of the Province and was later succeeded in that position by William Calvert. Another relative of the Proprietor, Henry Darnall, was clerk of the Calvert County court, which was the most lucrative clerkship in Maryland because Calvert County now had the largest population of any county in the colony. Of the six members of Maryland's Upper House in 1676, five were members of the Calvert family and the sixth was a strong supporter of the Proprietor's party. To some of the members of the proprietary party, including Henry Courcy, the third Lord Baltimore made the so-called "Thumb Grant"—so called because it included all the land on the Eastern Shore that the king's thumb could cover on the map.

In the first year of Charles Calvert's proprietorship, his Province had difficulties with the Indians which produced serious consequences for both him and Virginia. After the treaty of the Severn, Maryland allowed the Susquehannocks, who had been decimated by smallpox and were being harried by their savage neighbors to the north, the Senecas and the Cayugas, to take refuge in the old lands of the Piscataways and to live there under a certain amount of protection from the English. In 1675, when several whites were murdered by Indians on both sides of the Potomac, the Marylanders and the Virginians sent a joint expedition against the Susquehannocks whom they suspected. Colonel John Washington of the Virginia forces and Major Thomas Trueman of the Maryland forces met with the Susquehannocks in a parley in which the

Indians solemnly denied any knowledge of the killings and laid the blame on the Senecas. Not satisfied with their explanation, Trueman ordered the chiefs of the Susquehannocks murdered. The combined military forces of Maryland and Virginia then laid siege to the Susquehannock fort but were unable to prevent the Susquehannocks from escaping into Virginia where they began to harry the frontier. There the frontiersmen were rallied to their defense by Nathaniel Bacon, who had lost an overseer in the Indian massacres. Eventually Bacon's forces turned against the government of the colony, which was still headed by the inept Sir William Berkeley, and which was charged with being indifferent to the welfare of the frontier.

At the same time Maryland, where popular grievances against the governing clique were widespread, experienced a rebellion which was similar to Bacon's rebellion in Virginia, though not so serious. Early in 1676 an anti-proprietary group in Maryland, undoubtedly influenced by the Bacon movement in Virginia, began a vigorous campaign against the proprietary party. In an anonymous pamphlet, probably written by Fendall, entitled "Complaint from Heaven with a Hue and Crye and a petition out of Virginia and Maryland," they protested against the heavy taxation, the Proprietor's nepotism, the monopoly of the government of the Province by Catholics, the unrepresentative character of the Assembly, and the requirement of an oath of allegiance to the Proprietor instead of to the king. They suggested that "a Vice Roye or Governor Generallissimo from his Majesty" be appointed over all the colonies in order to cope with the menace of the French and the Indians— one of the earliest known suggestions for the centralization of military authority in America. They also suggested (1) that the king take over the government of Maryland and appoint the governors, (2) that the king and parliament in England should decide all disputes between the Proprietor and the Marylanders, (3) that the tax of two shillings per hogshead of tobacco should be used only within the colony to support the Governor and to pay the public expenses, (4) that the Proprietor should not be allowed to oppress his tenants, (5) that Protestant ministers and free schools should be established in every county and maintained by the people, (6) that all the freemen regardless of their property holdings should be allowed to vote for delegates to the Assembly and that the delegates so chosen should be free from coercion, and (7) that the freemen of Maryland should have the right to appeal to the king for redress of grievances.[3]

These suggestions, in the nature of demands, were couched in anti-Catholic language and showed the sympathy of the unknown author or authors with the rebellion in Virginia. They were probably inspired by Fendall and members of his faction. So popular did they become among discontented groups in the Province that the Council feared that Bacon would invade Maryland and put himself at the head of the malcontents. The Governor therefore issued a proclamation against the fomenters of the revolutionary agitation, Davyes, Pate, and others, accusing them of circulating a seditious paper which threatened the subversion of the proprietary government and the Assembly and of gathering together sixty armed men in Calvert County to extort concessions from the Governor and Council. He ordered the mutineers to disperse, and, when they refused to do so, he had them arrested and Davyes and Pate hanged.

With the death of Bacon in the same year, the popular movement in both Virginia and Maryland collapsed. The resistance in Maryland had lacked a leader, for, as the Governor self-righteously reported to the Proprietor, "Never Body was more repleat with malignancy and frenzy then our people were about August last, and they wanted but a monstrous head to their monstrous body."[4] As a result of this threatened uprising, Lord Baltimore became more vigilant than before in his efforts to suppress all dissension that would disturb the prosperity of his Province. He exercised a stricter control over the Lower House, created new offices for his relatives and loyal friends, and made more diligent efforts to subdue rumors and resentments. To prevent Bacon's rebellion from spreading to Maryland after its collapse in Virginia, the Governor even went so far as to order the arrest of all Virginians fleeing into Maryland.

The Governor and Council, thrown on the defensive by the Davyes rebellion, which though minor in its immediate consequences, appeared to be symptomatic of deep underlying grievances, published a *Remonstrance and Explanation* in which they sought to justify their actions to the people of the Province. The heavy taxes, they said, were due to the Indian wars, the building of the State House at St. Mary's, and the expenses incurred in suppressing the insurrection of Davyes and his associates. As to the complaint that they had deprived freemen who had no property of the privilege of voting for delegates to the Assembly, they explained that they were simply following the practice in Virginia, the Barbados, and England; but they offered to petition the Proprietor to allow all freemen, regardless of their property holdings, to vote in the elections for the next Assembly. In the matter of the head tax or poll tax, under which, as the Maryland insurgents had protested, the poor were required to pay as much as the rich, the Governor and Council defended the system as the one that was used in Virginia and the British West Indies, and they did not offer to modify it. The poll tax therefore continued to rankle in the hearts of the poorer classes in Maryland, and it was cited by the Marylanders in their Bill of Rights one hundred years later as one of the offenses of the proprietary government which was "grievous and oppressive."

Despite this official *Remonstrance and Explanation,* the opponents of the Proprietor continued their agitation. They circulated the charge that the Catholics in the Province had formed an alliance with the Indians to exterminate the Protestants and that the Proprietor was furnishing them with shot and powder for this purpose. They became particularly assiduous in spreading these stories after the exposure of the Popish Plot in England in 1678 by the sensation-mongering Titus Oates. As a counterpart in Maryland, the anti-proprietary party spread the rumor that forty Irish families who were coming to the Province were really 40,000 Irish papists who were bent upon murdering the Protestants. So serious did these charges become that they led to several actual disturbances of the peace and impelled the proprietary party to take repressive action.

The leader of the opposition to the Proprietor appeared to be Fendall. Denounced as a "Rank Baconist" by the Proprietor, he had been elected to the Assembly in 1678 as a delegate from Charles County but was not permitted by the Acting Governor, Thomas Notley, to take his seat. In 1681 the Lord Baltimore finally undertook to enforce the provincial law against "divulgers of falce news" and had Fendall, Godfrey, and John Coode, an ex-clergyman, arrested on the charge that they were trying to stir up the inhabitants of Maryland and northern Virginia to mutiny. He then requested the Assembly to pass a more severe law against "those wicked and Malicious persons who spread lies and false stories to the disquiet of good people, and the disturbance of the Government." He also asked the Lower House not to allow Coode to sit as one of its members but met with an adamant refusal. Fendall was brought to trial on the charge of treason, was found guilty by a jury of speaking several seditious words, was fined 40,000 pounds of tobacco, and was banished forever from the Province. He went to Virginia and thus dropped out of Maryland's history. Godfrey's sentence of hanging was commuted to life imprisonment. Coode was also brought to trial, but was acquitted and was reelected to the Assembly in 1688.[5]

After the Davyes rebellion, disagreements between the Assembly of Maryland and the Proprietor, Charles Calvert, third Lord Baltimore, increased both in number and in acrimony. He vetoed many laws passed by the Assembly, among them an act reducing the severity of punishments in the Province, and disallowed all the laws, eighteen in number, passed by the Assembly of 1678. Quarrels arose also between the proprietary party and the popular party over the nature of the Proprietor's assent to laws. Measures enacted by the legislature were signed by the Governor with the words "The Proprietor willeth these to be laws." But this formula did not satisfy the legislature which contended that it was not the same as formal assent by the Proprietor and therefore left the laws in doubtful status, for the Proprietor could and did sometimes declare a law invalid several years afterward on the pretext that he had not assented to it. He preferred to leave some laws in a state of uncertainty so that if they proved damaging to his interest, he might later veto them. But this practice was resented by members of the legislature, particularly the Lower House, who sought to force him to express his approval or disapproval within a reasonable time. Since the Assembly could not be sure of the exact status of their enactments pending action on them by the Proprietor, they secured from him in 1681 a promise that in the future he would either approve or disallow their enactments within a period of eighteen months, but he refused to allow the Lower House to write this requirement into law in 1684.[6] When he reduced the number of delegates in the Assembly from each county from four to two in 1682, loftily claiming the authority to do so under "the Undoubted rights, Priviledges, and Powers of my Charter," the Assembly immediately protested, but they found Baltimore inflexible.

The Assembly discovered, however, a lever that they could use to move him. He desired above all, in the interest of his proprietary revenues, to secure from the legislature an act requiring that all ships trading in the Province unload, sell, and barter their imported goods at certain designated ports and obliging all tobacco producers to load their cargoes at these same ports. This requirement would favor not only the merchants of England who were pressing the Proprietor for the designation of such ports but also the large planters, members of the proprietary party, who were already favored with large land grants and offices, and at the same time it would impose a burdensome expense in time and transportation upon the small planters who were accustomed to trading with foreign ships directly at their own wharves.

In an effort to get such a law, the Proprietor summoned the members of the Lower House into the Upper House and harangued them with an angry speech. They responded by passing the law that he desired, but they passed it with the understanding that he and the Upper House would consent to a new election law restoring the representation in the Lower House from two to four delegates for each county. They were eventually defeated, however, for the Upper House, which was controlled by the Proprietor, faithlessly refused to honor their agreement. Not until after the overthrow of the proprietary government in 1690 did they find it possible to restore the old number of four delegates from each county.

After the Proprietor returned to England to defend his case against Penn, his relations with his colony in America went from bad to worse. At his departure, he designated his five-year-old son, Benedict Leonard, as Governor, but since the boy was too young to rule he left the government of the colony, as noted above, in the hands of a Council of State, which was composed of nine deputy governors. Of these, seven were relatives of the Proprietor. Working through them Baltimore, influenced undoubtedly by the pro-Catholic policy of the new Stuart sovereign of England, James II, and by the latter's attempts to introduce Catholicism into Virginia, now showed more open favors to the Catholic Church in Maryland. His encouragement of Catholicism there not only supported the religious policy of James II but coincided with the revocation of the Edict of Nantes in 1685 by Louis XIV of France with whom James was believed to be in league. At this juncture also the proprietary party, which controlled the Council, unwisely sought to require the colonists to pay their rents and fees in specie instead of in tobacco. For these reasons the Proprietor encountered increasing resistance from the members of the Maryland Assembly, who in 1686 and again in 1688 ominously refused his demand that they take an oath of fidelity to him.

Baltimore's position was not improved, either in England or in Maryland, by the overthrow of the Catholic James II in the revolution of 1688. He could hardly expect the new alien sovereigns of England, William of Orange and Mary, whose principal qualifications for the throne were their Protestantism and the hostility of the House of Orange to the Stuarts, to look with favor upon commitments made by an earlier Stuart predecessor to a Catholic nobleman. As the deposed King James fled to France and received aid there from Louis XIV, he prepared to fight to recover his throne using Ireland as a base of military operations against England. Since Baltimore was an Irish lord and a Catholic, his adherents in Maryland expected him to support the policies of James and Louis XIV. Indeed, the president of the Maryland

Council of State, William Joseph, indiscreetly and openly committed himself to the Jacobean cause and thus forfeited the good will of the Assembly and of the anti-proprietary group in the province.

These developments caused great excitement in Maryland. Might not the French attack all the English colonies by way of Canada? If they found allies in the Catholics and the Indians in Maryland they might destroy the Protestants. In March 1689, the rumor spread among the settlers at the mouth of the Patuxent River that the Catholics and Indians had already begun a massacre of settlers living at the head of the river. When they sent messengers off to the settlements at the head of the river to inquire into the rumor, they were told that the massacre had already begun among the settlements in southern Maryland. So rumor fed hysteria and created fears which had no basis in fact. The leading men of the colony who investigated the rumor reported that it was false and that it was "nothing but a sleeveless fear & Imagination fomented by the Artifice of some ill minded persons, who are studious to take all occasions of raising disturbances for their owne private & malitious interest." [7]

Lord Baltimore, however, had not committed himself to the lost cause of James Stuart. Immediately after the accession of William and Mary to the English throne, he sent orders to his officials in the colony to proclaim them sovereigns, but, unfortunately for him, his messenger died on the way to Maryland. He immediately despatched a second messenger with another proclamation, but already his enemies were pointing to Maryland's delay in recognizing the new sovereigns as intentional and as evidence of a popish plot.

This, combined with cumulative grievances going back for many years, served as a pretext for the overthrow of Lord Baltimore's rule in Maryland. As early as April 1689, "An Association in arms, for the defence of the Protestant religion, and for asserting the right of King William and Queen Mary to the Province of Maryland and all the English dominions" was formed with John Coode as its head. Four months later, this Association, encountering almost no resistance, took over the state house at St. Mary's and overthrew the proprietary government. They then issued "The Declaration Of the reason and motive for the pres[en]t appearing in arms of His Maj^{tys} Protestant Subjects in the Province of Maryland."

In this bill of particulars, they charged the Proprietor with reducing the number of delegates in the Assembly, disallowing laws of the Assembly, exacting excessive fees and imposing taxes that were illegal because levied without the consent of the freemen, allowing Protestants to be seized by armed Papists without warrants, commandeering men, houses, boats, and provisions in time of peace, mistreating the king's collectors of customs, disparaging allegiance to the crown in Maryland, favoring Catholics in the use of churches and chapels and in the appointment of officeholders, allowing the claims of William and Mary to the English throne to be ignored in Maryland, and threatening an alliance between the French, the Indians, and the Papists against the Protestants in Maryland. Their purpose, they said, was "to preserve, vindicate and assert the sovereign Dominion and right of King William and Queen Mary to this Province." [8]

This declaration was printed at St. Mary's by William Nuthead, the printer of the Province, and is the earliest known document with a Maryland imprint. Many of the allegations contained in it were justified, but some of them were not. The Associators now took the government of Maryland into their hands and sent a copy of their declaration to the king. Among those who supported it were some of the leading citizens of the Province including Henry Jowles, who held a high military command, Kenelm Cheseldyne, who was speaker of the Lower House, Nehemiah Blakiston, who was the king's collector of customs, and John Coode, who had been justice of St. Mary's and a delegate to the Assembly. The last three were sons-in-law of the Catholic Thomas Gerard who had participated in Fendall's rebellion against the Proprietor almost thirty years earlier.

From the number of signatures on the supporting petition it is clear that the Associators represented majority views in the colony. During their brief period of power they either arrested or dispersed their opponents in the Roman Catholic faction and summoned an Assembly which was more representative than any of Charles Calvert's assemblies had been. The memorials that were sent to the king attacking the declaration bore fewer signatures and came principally from officeholders and members of the Proprietor's party. These defenders of the Proprietor included Henry Darnall, who was a cousin of the Proprietor, Michael Taney, who had been sheriff of Calvert County since 1685, and Charles Carroll, a Catholic member of the proprietary group who had come from Ireland to Maryland in 1688 with a commission as Attorney General of the colony.

King William received the declaration from the Association and recognized that revolutionary body as the provincial government of Maryland. Needing no urging, he determined to take over the Province and make it a royal colony.[9] He may have been motivated by a desire to punish a conservative Catholic nobleman whose family had long maintained close relations with the Stuarts. Or he may have wanted to discipline Lord Baltimore for misgovernment of a colony of Englishmen. Perhaps, too, he saw merit in the previous Stuart policy of establishing a strong and direct royal relationship with the colonies in America and felt that it was all the more necessary now to consolidate the colonies in order to prepare them for united defense against the war with France—the beginning of the second Hundred Years' War—in which he was already involving his new kingdom.

Whatever the king's motives, he instructed his attorney-general in 1690 to proceed against Lord Baltimore's charter by a writ of *scire facias,* demanding that he show cause why his charter should not be annulled. But without waiting for this process, he asked Chief Justice Holt to rule that he might take the government of the Province into his own hands immediately. After getting a favorable decision, he declared Maryland a royal colony and appointed Sir Lionel Copley the first royal governor in August 1691. King William thus deprived Lord Baltimore of his proprietary rights in Maryland and reduced him from the virtually absolute sovereign of a princely domain to an absentee landlord. But he allowed him to retain his private rights in Maryland, to continue to collect his quitrents, and to keep his title to vacant lands. Over the protest of the Assembly, he also permitted Baltimore to retain his port duty of fourteen pence per ton on all foreign vessels trading with Maryland and one-half of the duty of two shillings on every hogshead of tobacco exported from the Province.[10]

So it was that revulsion against the Baltimores in Maryland, coinciding with constitutional reorganization in England and the overthrow of the Stuarts, terminated the political authority of the Proprietor in his American colony and transformed Maryland into a royal Province. Maryland was finally caught up in the centralizing colonial policy of England, which had been earlier applied by the Stuarts to other colonies in North America. But, somewhat curiously, the initiative for this action had come from the popular party in the colony, which was manifestly anti-proprietor and anti-Catholic, but obviously not anti-royalist. In the clash between the proprietary party, who based their case upon the Charter, and their adversaries, who stressed the precedents for freemen found in English history, was prefigured, at least to a limited degree, the later successful American struggle for independence from England growing fundamentally out of a similar clash between the theory of the royal prerogative on the one hand and the theory of natural rights of men on the other.

Footnotes

[1] *Archives*, vol. II, *Proceedings of the Assembly, 1666-1676*, 374; and *Archives*, vol. V, *Proceedings of the Council, 1667-1687*, 18.

[2] *Calvert Papers*, Maryland Historical Society Fund Publication, No. 28, 24.

[3] *Archives*, vol. V, *Proceedings of the Council, 1667-1687*, 134-139.

[4] *Archives*, vol. V, *ibid.*, 153.

[5] *Archives*, vol. V, *ibid.*, 311-334.

[6] *Archives*, vol. VII, *Proceedings of the Assembly, 1678-1683*, 182; and *Archives*, vol. XIII, *Proceedings of the Assembly, 1684-1692*, 37-39.

[7] J. Thomas Scharf, *History of Maryland*, I, 308-309.

[8] *Archives*, vol. VIII, *Proceedings of the Council, 1687-1693*, 101-102.

[9] *Archives*, vol. VIII, *ibid.*, 167-168.

[10] Michael G. Kammen, "The Causes of the Maryland Revolution of 1689," *Maryland Historical Magazine*, vol. 55, No. 4, December 1960, pp. 293-333; and Richard A. Gleissner, "Religious Causes of the Glorious Revolution in Maryland," *ibid.*, vol. 64, No. 4, pp. 327-341.

Sources and Additional Reading

Bond, Beverly W., "The Quit-Rent System in the American Colonies," *American Historical Review*, vol. XVII, pp. 496-516.

Carr, Lois Green, and David William Jordan, *Maryland's Revolution of Government, 1689-1692*, Cornell University Press, Ithaca and London, 1974.

Simpson, John Francis Minor, *Monocacy Valley, Maryland, Presbyterianism*, Great Southern Printing and Manufacturing Co., Frederick, Maryland, 1936.

Sparks, Francis Edgar, *The Causes of the Maryland Revolution of 1689*, Johns Hopkins University Studies, Series 14, The Johns Hopkins University Press, Baltimore, 1896.

Steiner, Bernard C., *The Protestant Revolution in Maryland*, American Historical Association, *Annual Report, for the year 1897*, pp. 279-353, Government Printing Office, Washington, D.C., 1898.

CHAPTER IX
A ROYAL PROVINCE

The new royal governor of Maryland, Sir Lionel Copley, passes briefly across the pages of Maryland's history. He owed his appointment to his success in bringing the port of Hull over to the side of Parliament and William of Orange after the overthrow of James II. Arriving at St. Mary's in 1692, he received the government from Coode and his fellow Associators and made it his policy from the beginning to work closely with the anti-proprietary and popular party in the Province, selecting Nehemiah Blakiston as president of the Upper House and Kenelm Cheseldyne as speaker of the Lower House.

The new Assembly which Governor Copley summoned to meet at St. Mary's first formally thanked William and Mary "for redeeming us from the arbitrary will and pleasure of a tyrannical Popish government, under which we have so long groaned" and then formally recognized the title of the new sovereigns to the English throne. In another act, entitled "For the Service of Almighty God and the Establishment of the Protestant Religion within This Province," this Assembly made the Church of England the established church, authorized the county authorities to divide the ten counties into parishes, and imposed an annual tax of forty pounds of tobacco upon each taxable person for the construction of churches and the support of the clergy.[1] In 1702 this law was modified to permit Protestant Dissenters and Quakers (the latter estimated to number about one-twelfth of the population of the colony) to maintain separate meeting houses provided they continued to pay their forty pounds per poll to support the established church. But the new government of Maryland refused to grant similar privileges to Catholics and instead sought to restrict the public religious exercises of Catholic priests and the civil liberties of Catholic laymen and to limit the further immigration of Irish Catholics. For a time they prohibited Catholic lawyers from practicing in the courts of Maryland. By 1708 Catholics formed only a little more than eight percent of the population of Maryland, numbering only 2,974 out of a total population of 33,833.

The establishment of the Church of England in Maryland resulted logically from the same causes as had led to the overthrow of the Proprietorship of Lord Baltimore, namely, fear of Roman Catholicism, antagonism to Lord Baltimore for his nepotism and administrative ineptitude, pressure from ambitious representatives of the people for increased political power, and desire to curry favor with the new Protestant sovereigns of England. But it did not follow immediately upon the enactment of the law of 1692, for opposition to the religious establishment from the Catholics and Quakers in Maryland succeeded in having that law, as well as similar laws of 1694 and 1696, disallowed by the Crown as violative of religious freedom in the Province. But this opposition was overcome by subterfuge in 1702 when a new act establishing the Anglican Church in Maryland was hastily and without notice signed by the new sovereign, Queen Anne.

The law of 1702 remained in force until the war for American Independence, but it did not redound immediately, nor perhaps even ultimately, to the advantage of the Anglican Church. Since the law did not specify the quality of the tobacco which was to be collected as a tax for the support of the church, the forty-pound payment was usually made in the worst "trash," and it furnished only inadequate provision for the clergymen in Maryland. Fortunately for the church, its affairs in the Province were entrusted by the Bishop of London, Henry Compton, to Dr. Thomas Bray, a church leader of great spirituality and administrative ability. When he arrived in Maryland in early 1700 as Commissary of the Church, he undertook to raise both the spiritual and financial level of the Anglican clergy. In his visitations at various places in the colony, he disciplined those clergymen who were guilty of scandalous conduct and greatly improved the moral tone of the church. He was the first advocate of the public library in America and was responsible for the establishment of libraries in most of the parishes of Maryland and in several of the other colonies. With a donation which he secured from Princess Anne, later Queen of England, he dedicated a library at Annapolis, called the Bibliotheca Annapolitina, which was the first lending library and contained the largest single collection of books in the British colonies.[2] Though he remained in Maryland less than six months, he left a deep impress upon its religious life, and he retained an abiding interest in it. So zealous was he for the work of the church that he became the founder of "The Society for Promoting Christian Knowledge," "The Society for the Propagation of the Gospel in Foreign Parts," and "Dr. Bray's Association for Founding Clerical Libraries and Supporting Negro Schools."

Throughout the colonial period, the Anglican Church in Maryland, as in all the rest of England's colonies in America, was regarded as lying within the diocese of the Bishop of London, probably because in the early days of colonization the Virginia Company had included the

Bishop of London among its members. But in fact the Anglican Church in the colonies was not legally subject to his ecclesiastical jurisdiction, for it continued to be a mission church and as such was the responsibility of the entire religious establishment in the mother country.[3]

The exact date when Presbyterianism first appeared in Maryland cannot be established, but members of that sect must have entered Maryland as early as 1649 because the famous "Act concerning Religion" of that year forbade the use of the word "Prespiterian" in a reproachful sense. The Presbyterians of Maryland do not seem to have organized a congregation until about 1657 when the first Presbyterian minister, The Reverend Francis Doughty, visited the Province. His arrival marks the beginning of organized Presbyterianism in Lord Baltimore's colony. Doughty had preached Presbyterian doctrines at Taunton, Massachusetts, as early as 1637 but had been expelled from his church there by the Independent ministers of Boston. He then migrated to New Amsterdam and later to Maryland, where he probably gathered a church about him at Nanjemoy in Charles County and from whence he also went to hold occasional services in Accomac County, Virginia. He was probably the first pastor of the first Presbyterian church in Maryland and found in that colony the liberty of conscience and religious freedom which he had elsewhere sought in vain.

Doughty's successor was the Reverend Matthew Hill, who came from England probably in 1669 and settled in Charles County. He had been driven from his chaplaincy in London for non-conformity, had lost all his possessions in the great fire of London in 1666, and arrived in Maryland with only a few clothes, a Bible, a concordance, and a small bundle of manuscripts. But he married the widow of one of the wealthiest planters of the Province, acquired an estate near Port Tobacco, and at his death in 1679, left considerable property including a library of seventy volumes. The efforts of Doughty, beginning as early as 1657, and of Hill after 1669 represent the first attempts to organize Presbyterianism in the American colonies.

After the death of Hill, the Presbyterian organization on the Western Shore was not served by any minister for many years, but it preserved its organization and was mainly held together by one of its elders, Ninian Beall, a well-known planter and one of Maryland's earliest pioneers in the manufacture of flour and iron. During that period, the center of Presbyterianism in Maryland and, indeed, in America, moved to the Eastern Shore. There it took on the character of a vigorous movement with the arrival in Somerset County in 1683 of the Reverend Francis Makemie and a group of other Scotch-Irish clergymen, in-

A Royal Province

cluding Traill, Wilson, and Davis. Though Makemie was not the first Presbyterian minister in America, as has sometimes been asserted, he soon became the most prominent clergyman of that sect in all the American colonies.

Makemie was a native of County Donegal, Ireland, and a former student at the University of Glasgow. He came to Somerset County, Maryland, in 1683 in response to a request from a "Collonell Stevens in Maryland beside Virginia" for a "godly minister," but he did not confine his ecclesiastical labors to that county nor even to Maryland. In his itinerant preaching he traveled as far south as Barbados and as far north as New England. In 1690, he settled on the Eastern Shore of Maryland and in the following year became pastor of the church in Rehoboth. He seems to have regarded himself as the organizer of the whole church and as a kind of Presbyterian bishop. He corresponded frequently with Increase Mather of Boston, and in 1704, he went abroad to obtain help from the Presbyterians of England and Scotland. Having secured the aid that he sought, he returned to Maryland, bringing with him two young clergymen, one an Irishman and the other a Scotchman. These men began to work in Somerset County, and in 1706, Makemie succeeded in persuading six other Presbyterian ministers to join with him in forming the Presbytery of Philadelphia, which thus became the first Presbytery of the American Presbyterian Church. Because he thus guided the movement to bind the scattered churches into a Presbytery, he may well be called the "Father of American Presbyterianism." Of the seven ministers who formed this Presbytery, five were then, or had been, working in Maryland. In 1710, the minutes of the Presbytery mention at least five congregations in Maryland—at Rehoboth, Snow Hill, Upper Marlboro, Manokin, and Wicomico. Except the church at Upper Marlboro, these were all located in Somerset County.

Presbyterianism was so strong in that county that in 1695 the Reverend James Buchan, a minister of the Established Church, complained that "the people will not pay him his dues, but will do so to the dissenting ministers," and as late as 1711 the Reverend Alexander Adams wrote to the Bishop of London that he was the only clergyman of the Church of England in Somerset County and was poorly paid, though the Presbyterian churches were well cared for. The Presbyterians were most numerous and powerful on the Eastern Shore, but their church at Upper Marlboro on the Patuxent was also large and flourishing. Its parish included all of Prince Georges County and part of Charles County, but was split in 1719 when the Presbyterian Church at Bladensburg was built. Another large group of Presbyterians settled in

Baltimore County, organized a church, and called a pastor. Cecil County also became a center of Presbyterianism, where the Ulster Presbyterians organized a number of churches, spreading over into adjoining parts of Pennsylvania and Delaware.[4]

These churches formed the largest group of Presbyterian churches in the American colonies and made Maryland a stronghold of Presbyterianism. But in the eighteenth century Maryland Presbyterianism did not fulfill its early promise. After the establishment of the Anglican Church in the colony, only excessively loyal Presbyterians could afford to contribute to the support of both their own church and the state church. Then, too, the Presbyterian Church demanded educated ministers, trained in Latin, Greek, and Hebrew, but it built no college in the colony to train such ministers and was obliged to draw its ministers from Glasgow and Edinburgh. The influence of Presbyterianism in Maryland may have been further reduced because its principal centers were on the Eastern Shore remote from the main settlements in the colony. In western Maryland Presbyterianism, which was associated with the Scotch-Irish settlers, made little headway against the Lutheranism and Moravianism of the German frontiersmen. It remained negligible there until 1753 when it appeared at Emmitsburg in the northern part of Monocacy valley.[5]

Governor Copley was ill during most of his brief term as Maryland's first royal governor. He died in September 1693 and was buried near the site of the first settlement at St. Mary's. He was succeeded by Francis Nicholson, who had been serving as lieutenant governor of Virginia since 1690. The appointment of Nicholson indicated that the Glorious Revolution of 1688 did not produce results as revolutionary as Parliament intended, for Nicholson, who had served in New York as lieutenant governor of the Dominion of New England until 1689, had been a loyal defender of the Stuarts. He was an army officer, tactless and hot-tempered.

A state house and prison had been built at St. Mary's at a cost of 330,000 pounds of tobacco, and the city had built there a residence for the governor at a cost of 100,000 pounds of tobacco. Nevertheless, the Assembly in 1694 voted to transfer the capital from St. Mary's to "Anne Arundell Towne," soon to be renamed Annapolis, on the ground that St. Mary's was not centrally located and that it was difficult to reach. They thus gave recognition to the shift in Maryland's population and the need for a more centrally located place of public business. But the move was also motivated in part by religious prejudice, for the majority of property owners in St. Mary's City were Catholic and belonged to the proprietary party. Against the removal of the capital, the people of St. Mary's protested in an "humble address" to the Assembly, but they received only a contemptuous answer from the Assembly. After the removal of the capital, real estate values in St. Mary's collapsed, and Maryland's first capital completely disappeared.[6]

In honor of Princess Anne who would soon become Queen of England, the second Assembly that met at "Anne-Arundell Towne" in 1695 ordered that that town should forever be "denominated, called and known by the Name and Port of Annapolis, and by no other Name or Distinction whatever." It also awarded contracts to Casper August Herrman, third son of Augustine Herrman of Bohemia Manor and a burgess from Cecil County, for the construction of a parish church, a schoolhouse, and a state house. Soon after the completion of the State House in 1697, Annapolis was described by a visitor as follows: "There are indeed [in Maryland] several Places alotted for Towns, but hitherto they are only titular ones, except Annapolis: where the Governour resides[.] Col. Nicholson has done his Endeavour to make a Town of that Place. There are about 40 Dwelling Houses in it, 7 or 8 of which can afford a good Lodging and Accomodations for Strangers. There are also a State-House, and a free School, built with Brick, which make a great Shew among a Parcel of Wooden Houses; and the Foundation of a Church is laid, the only Brick Church in Maryland. They have two Market Days in a Week; and had Governour Nicholson continu'd there a few Years longer, he had brought it to Perfection." [7]

The free school mentioned in this description had been provided for by the first Assembly that met at Anne Arundel Towne in 1694 and was the first one established in the Province. In 1622, many years before George Calvert began to plan for his colony in Maryland and fourteen years before John Harvard made his educational gift to Harvard College, Edward Palmer, a wealthy member of an old family in Warwickshire, England, and a graduate of Oxford, had acquired Palmers Island in the Susquehanna, situated a short distance below Port Deposit, with the intention of establishing there an institution of higher learning. In his will he stipulated that if his son and nephew had no direct heirs, the island should be used "for the founding and maintenance of a university and such schools in Virginia as shall be there erected and shall be called Academia Virginiensis Oxoniensis." But his proposal had produced no tangible results. The earliest effort to establish a public educational institution in Maryland was made in 1671, when the Upper House passed an act of this nature. But to this act the Lower House added an amendment that the schoolmasters must be either all of the

First Annapolis State House. Sketch by Elisabeth L. Ridout. Courtesy *Maryland Hall of Records Commission*

Established Church of England or alternatively one Catholic and the other Protestant. This proviso made the bill unacceptable to the Upper House, which was loyal to the Catholic interests of the Proprietor and which accordingly rejected the plan in its entirety. The only educational work in Maryland, therefore, was carried on by the parents of the children, by the parish ministers, and by occasional schoolmasters who came to the Province, usually as indentured servants.

As a British colony, Maryland had no educational institution of collegiate rank. The sons of planters who desired a classical education went abroad to study in the universities of Scotland and England or, in the case of Catholics, to universities in Belgium and France, or they enrolled at William and Mary College in Virginia. Members of the Maryland gentry in general appear to have shown less interest in bookish than in convivial recreations. They allowed learning and scholarship to be defended by professional men, specifically lawyers and clergymen, many of whom, however, proved derelict in this respect. Sons of the gentry were often educated at neighborhood schools taught by the local clergymen, and the daughters were seldom schooled even in the three R's. The education of girls was usually limited to needlework, deportment, and dancing.

To Governor Nicholson goes the credit for actually initiating the public educational system of Maryland. While lieutenant governor of Virginia, which had long been backward in educational matters, Nicholson had encouraged the establishment of the College of William and Mary in 1693. At that time Virginia called upon Maryland to support the new college with a penny tax on tobacco. This educational venture of Virginia may have stimulated Maryland to found a school of its own. Governor Nicholson submitted to the Assembly early in his administration, "a plan for building a free school, and the maintenance for a school master and usher and a writing master that can cast accounts." He himself offered to give £50 toward the building of the school and £25 a year toward the maintenance of the master. His generous offer inspired other persons to make contributions and in the following year prompted the Assembly to give public support to education. An act was passed which imposed certain specified duties upon furs and skins exported from the Province for the maintenance of free schools. Duties collected from these sources formed the school fund of Maryland for the next thirty years.[3]

In further planning for education in the Province, the Assembly of 1696 nominated the Archbishop of Canterbury with his consent as Chancellor of the new school, which was to be located in Annapolis and which in honor of the king would be named King William's School. They also drew up a list of visitors and trustees headed by Governor Nicholson and formulated a plan for the establishment of a similar school to be located at Oxford in Talbot County and of other schools to be located in every county in the Province. The first building of King William's School was built on a lot donated by Governor Nicholson on the south side of the State House and was completed in 1701. In 1696 Andrew Geddes was sent over by the Bishop of London to take charge of the school, but since it was unfinished, he was "placed out," according to the records of the Assembly, "as under master to the College School in Virginia, to save a present charge and to gain himself the more experience against the school is here built." This incident shows the close connection between the educational programs of Maryland and Virginia.

During the period when Maryland was a royal Province, it established its first regular postal service. In 1661 the Assembly had passed an act "for conveyance of letters concerning the State and public affairs" and thus provided for the first delivery of official mail. But not until 1695 was a postal service established for general mail delivery. Under this new arrangement John Perry was appointed post-rider at a salary of £50 per year and was required to cover his route eight times a year carrying messages and packages for the inhabitants of the Province. His route ran from Newton's Point on the Potomac to Benedict, Leonardtown, Annapolis, Kent, New Castle, and thence to Philadelphia. In 1710 Maryland's postal system was absorbed into the postal system which was established by Parliament in that year for all the English colonies in America.

During this period, Maryland's first printing press got under way. It was set up by William Nuthead, who thus became the first printer of Maryland. In 1682, forty-four years after the establishment of the first printing press in the English colonies at Cambridge, Massachusetts, Nuthead set up his press in Virginia. But so severe were the restrictions upon printing in that colony that sometime before 1686 he moved his equipment to Lord Baltimore's Province, the traditional place of refuge for oppressed Virginians. Maryland thus became the fourth English colony in America to support a printing press. Nuthead operated his press fairly regularly at St. Mary's City from 1686 to 1695. There he printed *The Declaration* of the Protestant Associators in 1689 and the legal and business forms that were in daily use in the Province. At his death his business was taken over by his wife, Dinah Nuthead, who removed the press to the new capital at Annapolis and received a commission from the Assembly "for the printing of blank bills bonds writts warrants of Attorney Letters of Admrcon [Administration] and other like blanks," but she soon remarried and abandoned the business. Being entirely uneducated and unable even to sign her own name, perhaps she had difficulty in securing a compositor or journeyman printer to operate the press. At least, no imprints bearing her name are known to be in existence; but she is the first woman in America who conducted or attempted to conduct a printing establishment.

The next printing press that was set up in Maryland was brought in by William Bladen in response to an authorization by the Assembly. He began to publish blank forms and legal papers, sermons, and the body of Maryland laws in 1700. At that time only twenty-seven years of age, he had already served as clerk of the Lower House and clerk of the Upper House and was later to become one of the most prominent members of the Province serving successively as Collector of the Port and District of Annapolis, Secretary of the Province, Attorney General, and architect of the State House. His son, Thomas Bladen, became governor of Maryland in 1742 and served in that office for five years. In May 1700, William Bladen proposed to the Assembly that he be authorized to print the Body of Laws of the Province, to supply each county with a copy, and to receive 2,000 pounds of tobacco for each such copy, and after receiving such authorization he published the first body of laws, the sole surviving copy of which later found its way to the Library of Congress. Being a planter, clerk, architect, and publisher, Bladen was not himself a printer, but his printing work was probably done by Thomas Reading. After he published the Body of Laws of 1700, he retired from the printing business and turned over the use of his press to Reading.

Following Reading's death in 1713, Maryland had no public printer for five years, and during that period the laws of the Assembly were copied by hand, distributed to the counties, and promulgated by the criers and the courts. In 1718, Evan Jones, who in the previous year had been employed by the Lower House to transcribe the records, asked permission of the Assembly to print the body of Maryland laws. In the same year he presented Maryland with a compilation of its laws which was printed on the press of Andrew Bradford in Philadelphia and which set forth the complete body of laws adopted in 1715. It constituted the earliest published body of permanent general law established in the Province. Jones later undertook to have other laws and addresses of the Assembly printed by Bradford at Philadelphia and thus treated Bradford, in the absence of a Maryland printer, as an unofficial printer for the Province.

In 1720, John Peter Zenger, who had come to America from the Rhenish Palatinate ten years before and had served an apprenticeship under the printer William Bradford in Philadelphia, came to Maryland, became naturalized, and was authorized to print the laws of the Province. He evidently complied with this authorization because the Assembly later allowed him "five hundred pounds of tobacco for the Printing the Laws for the Counties &ca. as [at] last Sessions," but no copies of his publications are extant. Two years later he removed to New York, set up a printing establishment there, and in 1733 became one of the principals in a trial for seditious libel which first established in the colonies the principle of freedom of the press. After Zenger's departure from Maryland, Andrew Bradford of Philadelphia continued to print a few official acts and debates of the Maryland Assembly. The office of public printer of Maryland assumed a new dignity with the arrival in Annapolis in 1727 of William Parks, who became one of the outstanding figures in the history of colonial printing.[9]

Throughout the period of royal government in Maryland, the Assembly was singularly tenacious in upholding its rights and privileges. Many instances of struggle occurred between the Lower House and the king's agents in which the representatives of the people challenged royal authority in an effort either to maintain political privileges which they had already won or to gain new ones. During the period of royal control, the breach between Maryland and the mother country began to widen. The colonists seemed to discover more grievances against the royal than against the proprietary government, possibly because, as they had developed their own habits of independent living in the New World, they were becoming increasingly distrustful of monarchy. They were beginning to question the exercise of any authority over them from abroad and feared that centralization of colonial affairs would destroy the self-government which they had enjoyed, in greater or less degree, from the very beginning of their settlement in America.

With the accession of Charles II, the English government had begun to amalgamate and consolidate its colonies in America. Under William and Mary this process was carried still further. In an attempt to improve colonial administration, William appointed eight Commissioners of Trade and Plantations in May 1696, including on it men who had long been interested in colonial affairs. To them he assigned the duties of studying ways by which England's trade with her colonies might be increased, providing general supervision over the government of the colonies, recommending approval or disapproval of colonial laws, receiving complaints from the colonies, and supervising the expenditures of public monies there. They were to serve as an advisory body to the king and the privy council in all matters relating to the colonies. Subject to final executive action by the king in council or by a secretary of state, these commissioners assumed authority over Maryland as well as all the other English colonies in America.

The consolidation of royal control over the colonies seemed to be necessitated and justified by the war with France—the second Hundred Years' War—which commenced in 1690. As the French began their military operations in America, they planned to invade Massachusetts and New York from Canada. Early in 1690, a war party of French and their Indian allies massacred the inhabitants of the frontier town of Schenectady. In this emergency the colonies summoned a Congress to meet at New York and "conclude on suitable methods for assisting each other for the safety of the whole." John Coode, the acting governor of Maryland, acknowledged the summons and sent two delegates to the Congress. There an agreement was reached among the six colonies represented in the Congress—New York, New Plymouth, Massachusetts, Connecticut, Virginia, and Maryland—to raise a force of 850 men for the defense of Albany, and of this number Maryland promised to contribute 100 soldiers. The Congress also planned an invasion of Canada and despatched an expedition which captured Port Royal and Acadia. The colonies petitioned England for troops to aid them against the French, but their request was turned down by the mother country, which was itself hard pressed by the war on the continent.

As the war with the French continued and became more desperate, Maryland was asked by the king in 1694 to raise supplies of money and men for the assistance of New York. The Assembly of Maryland, after first rejecting this request on the ground of expense, finally reconsidered it and resolved that they would, "according to their utmost abilities, at all times be ready to assist that government [New York] with such number of men and arms when need shall require and his excellency the governor shall intimate, the same as the strength and ability of this province will afford." They accordingly forwarded the money by Colonel Tasker and later sent their quota of men. Maryland thus responded favorably to the crown's first requisitions upon the colonies. But Maryland made little sacrifice in this war—the first of the four Anglo-French wars in which the American colonies became involved as parts of the British empire. This war of the League of Augsburg, or King William's War as it was called in America, ended in 1697 in a general peace settlement, the Treaty of Ryswick, which, however, proved to be only a truce, for England went to war again with France in 1702 in the War of the Spanish Succession to prevent Louis XIV from acquiring control over Spain.

Soon after the end of King William's War, Governor Nicholson was transferred to the governorship of Virginia, where, as in Maryland, he established a new capital—at Williamsburg. His successor, Nathaniel Blakiston, appointed in 1699, resigned in 1703 because of ill health and was succeeded by John Seymour. From these royal governors and from other sources the crown received numerous proposals for the consolidation of the English colonies in America into larger governing units. After Governor Nicholson's removal from Maryland to Virginia, he urged upon the crown the importance of bringing all the colonies under one head and maintaining a standing army, and he sought to impress the king with the growing spirit of independence in the colonies. The Board of Trade, however, pronounced the plan of consolidation impracticable at that time, though they recommended the appointment of a military commander-in-chief in the colonies.

The royal governors, who by appointment of the crown exercised executive authority over Maryland during the reign of King William, were different in many respects from their predecessors and were less familiar and less sympathetic with Maryland's problems. Some of them were contemptuous of the provincial Assembly, had a low opinion of colonists, and did not appreciate their developing spirit of independence and their cherished habits of self-government. When the first royal governor, Copley, for example, asked the Assembly to make its temporary laws perpetual, thus perhaps unwittingly reviving an issue that had formerly divided the Assembly and the Proprietor, the Assembly refused, explaining that they had "experienced the ill consequences of perpetual laws, so called, as to give them caution in being too forward of passing too many of that kind again." They took an even more positive stand when Copley's successor, Governor Nicholson, informed the Assembly that he had written to the Lords of Trade asking for a general pardon for the inhabitants of Maryland. The delegates stoutly answered that "they were not conscious that the Province labored under any guilt and therefore humbly conceived that they had no need of pardon." At this retort, which was indicative of a new spirit in the colony, Nicholson became angry and told the Assembly that they were the first body of people that ever refused their king's mercy. The tactless, authoritarian governor announced therefore that he would exact certain penalties of them which he had planned to remit, but despite this threat he was unable to persuade the Assembly to accept the proffered pardon.

Later, when Governor Blakiston, with equal lack of tact and no more provocation, asked the Assembly and people to give some signal proofs of their loyalty, thus impliedly suggesting their disloyalty, the Lower House replied with the following almost ominous answer: "You shall surely find his Majesty's subjects here of an ingenious, humble, obedient, and loyal disposition, and as sincerely endeavoring that nothing shall disconsonant the good harmony you wish to find . . . and although your Excellency, serving his Majesty in a higher station than any of us, may render your loyalty more perspicuous, yet we will contend that ours shall be uniform and proportionable; and as we never had any apprehension that his Majesty would retrench us of any of those rights and privileges here which we have in England, so will we always esteem his royal prerogative sacred, and hope we shall never see it misapplied to personal strife and contest, nor to justify any violent action."

What was Maryland's place as a royal Province within the British colonial system? Of her abundant resources and supplies, what did she contribute to the British mercantile system? From the beginning, except during a few good years, Maryland produced barely enough foodstuffs for her own needs, and frequently she was obliged to import supplies of food from New England. The reason for her indifference to the cultivation of grain, fruits, and vegetables was the profitableness of tobacco culture. This had been true from the beginning of her history and explains why as a royal Province she, along with Virginia, fitted so admirably into the British mercantile system. Tidewater Maryland, like tidewater Virginia, had a one-crop economy, and that crop was tobacco, which was grown for export. Because of its high yield per acre, its excellent keeping qualities, its light weight in shipment, and its value in the London market, it monopolized agricultural production to the virtual exclusion of all other major crops and forced an exhausting single-crop type of agriculture upon the soil. The cured leaves of the tobacco plant were packed into large hogsheads, which were either pushed by Negro slaves or pulled by horses over the "rolling roads" to the planters' wharves and there loaded on ships bound for England. By 1666, a special fleet of twenty English ships was required each year to transport Maryland tobacco.[10]

Following Virginia's example, Maryland made several attempts in the seventeenth century to regulate both the quality and the quantity of her tobacco, but the provincial authorities did not enforce these regulatory laws as successfully as did the Virginia authorities, with the result that the Maryland crop was regarded as inferior to that of Virginia. As the price of tobacco declined in England, both Maryland and Virginia were advised by the Privy Council to join in limiting production, but in Maryland this proposal became a subject of contention between the large planters of the Upper House, who could afford to cease planting for a year, and the small farmers of the Lower House, who could not afford to do so. When, however, they finally agreed with Virginia to limit production, Lord Baltimore, unwilling to suffer any curtailment of his revenues, refused to give his approval. By 1689, therefore, Maryland had no law limiting the amount of tobacco which the colonists could raise. Under the royal government the colonial officials made a somewhat greater effort to prevent further deterioration in Maryland's staple crop. Maryland, however, did not go so far as Virginia in regulatory legislation, and its tobacco continued inferior to that of Virginia.

Throughout the period of royal government, Maryland seemed far from prosperous, and many of the inhabitants were reduced to great poverty. Their plight was caused in part by the falling tobacco market in England and also by the depredations of French privateers. The Maryland Assembly reported in 1697 that tobacco was the only export of the colony to foreign countries, except for small quantities of furs and sassafras, and that Maryland's trade "ebbs and flowes according to the rise and fall of tob^o in the Market of England." The Assembly of 1714 complained about "ye lowness of y^t Ebb which this poor province in its Circumstances is reduced to." According to the Navigation Act of 1660, tobacco grown in the English colonies could be exported only to England or to the English plantations, and the figures for the period 1689-1714 indicate that Maryland's exports of tobacco to England averaged annually about 25,000 hogsheads or 10,000,000 pounds.

The Maryland planter sold his crop in one of two ways. Sometimes he shipped it at his own risk to a commission merchant in England who sold it for him and returned to him European goods to the value of the tobacco less his commission. If the English merchant was forced to sell at a loss or if he contracted a bad debt, the planter incurred the loss, became indebted to the merchant, and was obliged to continue sending his crops to the same merchant. Even in a favorable year, the planter received very small profits on his crop, for though a hogshead of tobacco sold for £21.10s in 1730, the duty amounted to £16, the freight to £4, and the merchant's commission to 15^s, leaving a net profit of only 15^s for the planter. The President of the Council of Maryland wrote to the Board of Trade in 1710, "The Generallity of the Planters, especially such as have shipped their Tobo's to their Correspondents in London are become Greatly Indebted to the Merchants, and very many of their

A Royal Province

Plantations and stocks are wholy mortgaged and forfeyted to them and others Dayly Desert their Abodes for feare of being imprisoned and repair to the southern Colonys, vizt south and north Carolina or Elsewhere to seeke new Settlem^{ts}."

A second method by which the Maryland planter disposed of his tobacco was to sell it from his plantation directly to the merchant's factor in Maryland or to the ship captains who carried it to England and sold it. This method had its drawbacks, for it did not enable the planter to take advantage of a rise of prices in England and placed him at the mercy of the ship captains. By whichever method he disposed of his crop, he secured only a small return even in the most favorable years. He usually attributed this low return to (1) the wars in which England became involved and which not only cut off the markets for Maryland tobacco on the continent of Europe but encouraged the nations of the continent to raise their own tobacco, (2) the high duty which the mother country levied on tobacco imported from the colonies, and (3) the fact that colonial tobacco was carried to England in small scattered vessels rather than in a single annual fleet and thus was not able to take advantage of a monopoly market. With the approach of peace with France in 1713 and the consequent removal of the danger from French ships, the price of Maryland tobacco rose and Maryland planters began to enjoy greater prosperity.[11]

After the restoration of the Stuarts in 1660 the British government steadily increased the duty on imported tobacco. In a law of 1660 Parliament levied a duty of a penny a pound on tobacco at entry and an additional penny a pound nine months after importation. In a law of 1685 it increased the duty to 3 pence a pound payable eighteen months after importation. In 1698 another act increased the rate another penny, and an act of 1703 raised the rate one-third of a penny higher, bringing the total duty up to 6-1/3 pence a pound on all tobacco imported into England. But Parliament stipulated that all these duties, with the exception of one-half penny per pound, would be refunded to the merchant who reexported within twelve months any tobacco that had paid the duties. Of the revenue which the British government received from this source, totaling probably £100,000, Maryland contributed about one-third. Naturally the home government sought to foster and encourage the tobacco industry in its American colonies.

Under the royal government, as previously under the proprietary government, Maryland tobacco also furnished a principal source of revenue for the support of English officials in the colony. These officials were paid from the revenues collected from the duty of two shillings on each hogshead of tobacco exported from the colony. During the proprietary period, one-half of this duty had been used for the support of the government and the other half had been paid to the Proprietor. When the Proprietor's claims to Maryland were forfeited to the crown, three-fourths of the government's share of the export duty on tobacco was paid to the royal governor and the other fourth was spent for the defense of the Province. A law of 1692 gave the governor an additional 3 pence per hogshead for his own use, and a subsequent law levied an additional duty of 3 pence per hogshead to defray the expenses of the Province. These three laws together made the duty on tobacco exported from the Province 2 shillings and 6 pence for each hogshead. Of the total duty collected, the governor received probably an annual average income of between £1,200 and £1,700 making him the highest paid of all the British colonial governors except the governor of Jamaica, who received £2,500 a year. Moreover, Maryland's governor was rendered independent of yearly appropriations by the legislature, and was, therefore, less subservient to the legislature than the governors of several of the other colonies, as, for example New York and Massachusetts, who were dependent for their salaries upon annual grants by the colonial legislatures. The royal governor of Maryland enjoyed this privileged position as the beneficiary of the earlier proprietary system.

The British government encouraged the production in Maryland of not only tobacco but also raw materials needed by the royal navy. For this purpose in 1664 the Lords of Trade removed the duties upon the importation from the colonies into England of hemp, pitch, and tar. As England's need for naval stores increased, particularly after the outbreak of the wars with France, the London authorities endeavored to stimulate the production of hemp, flax, tar, rosin, pitch, and naval timbers in Maryland. But they were not willing to develop this industry at the expense of tobacco and consequently allowed the economy of the Province to revolve almost entirely around tobacco. Maryland did little to meet the British need for naval stores. The colony exported no hemp or flax to England and prepared no large timber for the British navy. Her principal contribution was staves for barrels and casks, and even her exports of these materials were almost negligible. Even after the British government enacted a bounty law in 1705 to stimulate their production, Maryland's export of naval stores increased only slightly.

Nor did Maryland's other products bulk large in her export trade. Her fish and furs appear to have entered very little into her trade with foreign countries and with her sister colonies. Maryland exported very little, probably no, salted fish either to England or to the other American colonies and collected so small a duty each year on exported furs and skins as to prove that these exports were not an appreciable item in her trade. Since these duties were applied to the maintenance of the newly established King William's School, it is not strange that Governor John Hart, who became governor of Maryland in 1714, complained to the Assembly in the following year that "many young men of admirable natural parts grow up without the least improvement of art. [It is] more than time to repair that neglect that is shown to learning here." He advised the Assembly "to lay a foundation for sufficient schools that your sons may increase in knowledge as well as in wealth and honor."

Maryland's imports came largely from England and were obtained by the planters in return for the sale of their tobacco in England or were purchased from English ships trading with the colonies. Maryland, along with other English colonies in America which had formerly been valued by the mother country chiefly as sources of supply for raw materials, was now coming to be appreciated by England as an outlet or market for her industrial production. In both Maryland and Virginia manufacturing was negligible, and the colonists were obliged to depend upon England for many of their requirements for manufactured goods including shovels and other agricultural implements, wearing apparel such as hats and woolen clothing, soap, candles, and leather goods. Similarly they looked to the mother country for such products of non-English manufacture as linens, spices, fans, silks, wines, and drugs which were imported into the colonies through England from Europe and the Orient. Despite this dependence of Maryland and Virginia upon the mother country for their requirements of manufactured goods, they imported less from England than they exported to England. The colonists complained that they could not meet their requirements simply by importing from England and that they could not induce English merchants to send them adequate supplies of needed manufactured goods in a year of poor harvest.

This grievance of the Marylanders was set forth graphically in a letter which Governor Seymour sent to the Board of Trade. Since the Marylanders, he wrote, were "in debt to the Merchants Consignees in England [that is, the English Merchants] they send them little or no goods at all, most of the shipps comeing from London, upon freight, in their Ballast with their provisions only for the Voyage, So that many people here are almost starke naked, which has occasioned Some to turn their hands to manufacture of Lynnen and Woollen, and if your Lordships in your wisdome do not find out Some Expedient to have the Necessity of the Country relieved, by obliging the Merchants to

Send Supplys, it may be of ill Consequence to the Revenue arising on tobacco, which will be in greate measure layd aside by Such who find they can have nothing for it." To this veiled threat that the colony might engage in manufacturing to the disadvantage of tobacco production and the loss of royal revenue, crown officials responded by forbidding the colonies to develop manufacturing. But prohibitory legislation was hardly necessary for Maryland, for that colony was almost exclusively dedicated to agricultural production and would probably turn to manufacturing only in utter desperation. Even the bounties that were offered by the home government for the encouragement of linen and woolen manufactures produced almost negligible results. The little manufacturing that developed in Maryland was of the domestic sort, such as the spinning and weaving of wool, cotton, and flax in the home, and even this domestic form of manufacture was confined almost entirely to Somerset County on the Eastern Shore among the 600 or 700 Scotch and Irish who had settled there. During the period of royal government from 1690 to 1715, an authoritative study shows, "there is not a single record of the export from Maryland of articles of native manufacture."[1 2]

Through the many merchants and sea captains trading in the Province Marylanders found it profitable to import white servants, for though they were beginning to import Negro slaves in considerable numbers, they still depended upon white servants as the primary labor factor in plantation life throughout the period of royal government. Probably at this time they brought into the colony between 600 and 700 white servants annually. The Maryland legislature made some slight effort to regulate the quality and number of these servants, and in 1676 forbade the importation of English convicts as servants. This law was renewed in 1692 but was apparently ineffective because it ran counter to the interests of the home government. In the latter part of the 17th century Maryland received large numbers of convict laborers. In 1699 the colony laid a heavy duty upon the importation of Irish Catholic servants "to prevent too great a number of Irish Papists in the colony." But despite such restrictive legislation the importation of white men and women servants from the home country to Maryland continued throughout this period.

By the end of the seventeenth century Negro slaves were beginning to assume new importance as a factor in the labor system of the colony. Most of them were imported directly from the Guinea coast of Africa, although some came from the West Indies and from neighboring colonies. The annual number of Negro slaves imported into Maryland averaged between 300 and 600 at this time. Out of the entire population of the Province, numbering about 40,000, Negroes numbered 4,478 in 1704, but by 1720 they had increased to about 25,000 out of a total population of 80,000. This large gain was due, in considerable degree, to importation from abroad. It was stimulated after 1713 by the *Asiento* provision of the Treaty of Utrecht, which encouraged England's operations in the immensely profitable slave trade.

Marylanders imported almost nothing else of importance from foreign countries, except wines from Madeira and the Azores, and wine, rum, sugar, molasses, and salt from the Azores and the British West Indies. They also received these same products and dye woods and indigo from the English colony in Campeche in Central America. If they engaged in trade with other countries they violated the Navigation Acts, and this trade, being illicit, was not reported in the records of the colony. From New England, New York, and Pennsylvania, the tobacco colony of Maryland received supplies of foodstuffs, particularly beef, pork, peas, flour, butter, cheese, and even fish. When in 1704 the Assembly forbade the importation from Pennsylvania of certain specified commodities, namely bread, beer, flour, malt, wheat, grain, horses, and tobacco, it probably did so to encourage domestic production.

At the beginning of the eighteenth century as many as seventy vessels on an average came annually from England to Maryland to deliver supplies needed by the colonists and to carry away some 25,000 hogsheads of tobacco representing the annual production of that crop for export by the colony. Most of them discharged their cargoes from abroad and received Maryland's tobacco exports on the Western Shore, sending sloops up the creeks and rivers to private landing places of the planters and bringing back each planter's crop. In 1683 the Maryland legislature, upon demand by the Proprietor, had tried to change this individualistic system and to centralize the import-export trade of the colony by authorizing the creation of a certain number of towns to which all the tobacco must be brought for shipment, and later the royal officials attempted to have the law reenacted. But when the Maryland Assembly passed a bill in 1706 appointing certain towns where tobacco could be loaded on board ships, it was disapproved in England on the ground that the creation of towns would encourage the development of manufacturing in the colony. Shipmasters, therefore, were obliged to continue to get their cargoes from the private wharves of the planters along the Bay and along the banks of its tributary rivers.

During the Anglo-French wars, which were almost continuous after Maryland came under the direct control of the crown, English ships trading with the Province usually traveled in fleets or under the convoy of a British man-of-war. From the beginning of the war the British government permitted merchant vessels to leave the harbors of the home country only in fleets or under convoy and instructed the governors to prevent the sailing of single ships from their harbors because of the danger of seizure by the French. The British suspended these regulations during the short interval of peace from 1697 to 1702 but renewed them again when the War of the Spanish Succession broke out. During this period, Maryland ships usually sailed to England under convoy with the Virginia fleet. When they received the news up the Bay that the fleet was preparing to sail, the captains would bring their vessels to the mouths of the Patuxent and the Potomac Rivers and thence proceed to Point Comfort where they joined the Virginia fleet. In at least one instance, the Maryland vessels were ordered to join convoys in New York instead of in Virginia.

On reaching England, the tobacco of Maryland was delivered into the hands of wholesale merchants. Of these the merchants of London were the most influential because they owned most of the ships engaged in the trade and they fixed the freight rates and the price of the tobacco. They also influenced the policy of the government toward the trade and so contrived to bring the planters of Maryland under their control. By the heavy freight and commission charges which they imposed they allowed either only low profits or no profits at all to the tobacco planters and were largely responsible for their chronic indebtedness and the general poverty in the Province. In response to the pressure of the London merchants on the British government, Parliament, despite the protests of Maryland, passed an act in 1699 prohibiting the importation of tobacco in bulk into England. Later the British government disallowed acts of the Maryland Assembly which enlarged the size of the tobacco casks and penalized ship captains who "squeezed" them into their holds. In these and many other ways the London merchants exerted pressure on their government to adopt measures and follow courses of action which were contrary to the interests of the Maryland planters.

Maryland vessels carried on most of the waterborne commerce of the Province. In 1697, according to the best available figures, the colony had a total of 161 ships, sloops, and shallops built or building, some of which were as large as 400 tons. The Eastern Shore counties, which were less interested in raising tobacco than those on the Western Shore, specialized in shipbuilding and were encouraged by the royal government to develop this industry. Most of the trade routes of the Maryland

A Royal Province

vessels led directly to England—either to London or to the outports of western and southwestern England. On the way they often stopped at Madeira and the Azores for cargoes of wine to be carried back to Maryland. Some of them made frequent trips to Barbados, sometimes for the purpose of buying slaves. But most of the slaves imported into Maryland, after Negroes began to be imported into the Province in large numbers directly from the Guinea Coast, were brought in English ships and were exchanged in Virginia and Maryland for cargoes of tobacco.

Marylanders were just as prone to violate the Navigation Acts as were the residents of other British colonies. Those acts required that every vessel trading in the colony must have been constructed either in England or in the colonies, must be manned by an English crew, must import foreign commodities into the colony only through England, and must carry tobacco and other enumerated commodities only to England or to an English colony. According to a report submitted by Edward Randolph to the Commissioners of the Customs in 1686, these regulations were frequently broken in Maryland; tobacco was often exported from the colony on forged certificates or in vessels of New England and Scotland without being bonded for delivery in England, and quantities of foreign commodities were imported into Maryland illicitly through Scotland and Newfoundland. While Coode and his Associates were in control of the Province from 1689 to 1691, smuggling became more general, perpetrated largely by Scotch vessels. But their offenses were legalized in 1708 when Scotland was brought under the Acts of Trade. Under Governors Nicholson, Blakiston, and Seymour, smuggling became less prevalent, and the Acts of Trade were so strictly enforced that Marylanders complained about them. Under the Act of 1696, Governor Nicholson was commissioned a vice-admiral and was given authority to erect an admiralty court in Maryland to enforce the Navigation Acts. For his zeal in this cause he was highly commended by the royal officials. He and his successors also made vigorous and successful attempts to enforce the bonding requirements of the law and even maintained a small vessel in the Bay to detect illegal trading. As a result, during the rest of the period of royal control over the Province, breaches of the Navigation Acts were comparatively rare.

Upon the death of William III in 1702, the crown of England, in accordance with the Act of Settlement, descended to his wife's sister Anne, and her accession was proclaimed in all of England's colonies in America. Maryland alone passed an "Act of Recognition" of her title to the throne, which she rejected on the ground that it called in question her claim by authority of Parliament. In 1709, when Maryland's Governor Seymour died, the government of the colony was assumed by the President of the Council, Major-General Edward Lloyd, who served until the arrival of a new royal governor, Captain John Hart, in 1714.[13]

Meanwhile, for the previous quarter century, the Proprietor, Charles Calvert, had been making repeated efforts to regain control of the Province. During Maryland's history as a royal Province he kept an agent in the colony to attend to his private affairs and to protect his lands and revenues. His interests there were entrusted first to Henry Darnall, who was commissioned Agent and Receiver-General, and then after 1711 to Darnall's son-in-law, Charles Carroll, a wealthy and prominent Catholic. But during the period when the proprietary rights were in abeyance, the Proprietor's claims to continuing personal rights were repeatedly challenged. When, for example, his claim to strays, waifs, and other wild stock was questioned by the Maryland Council, it was assumed by the king by decision of His Majesty's solicitor-general on the ground that this claim did not rest upon any provision in the original charter grant to Lord Baltimore.[14]

The Proprietor became greatly distressed when his eldest son and heir, Benedict Leonard Calvert, "publicly renounced the Romish errors" and became a member of the Anglican Church—allegedly for mercenary motives. Lord Baltimore had given his son an allowance of £450 per year but withdrew it when he changed his faith. When he did so, Queen Anne, in the hope of gaining the support of Benedict Leonard and on the advice of her councillors, offered Benedict Leonard a pension of £300 per year during the life of his father and appointed one of his friends, Captain John Hart, as "captain-general and governor in chief of her Majesty's province of Maryland."

Hart was recommended for this office by Calvert himself because he promised to return to him £500 each year from the profits of the colony. When the new governor arrived in Maryland in May 1714, the colony had been virtually self-governing for the previous five years under Lloyd as interim governor. Hart's first Assembly granted him three pence on each hogshead of tobacco exported as long as he remained governor in order to compensate him for renting a dwelling because the colony had no governor's house. His salary was paid from one-half of the two-shilling duty on each hogshead of exported tobacco. When rumors of Queen Anne's death reached Maryland in 1714, Governor Hart traveled to Philadelphia, probably to ascertain whether or not the rumors were true, and after ascertaining that they were, proclaimed the new king, Prince George of Brunswick Lunenburg, as

A Royal Province

king. The governor and council took oaths to the new king, Governor Hart gave a "generous and splendid entertainment," and the provincial government instructed each county to proclaim the new king. Hart's actions evidently pleased Benedict Leonard Calvert, for he petitioned the new King George to continue Hart in office.

At this very time, Benedict Leonard's father, Charles Calvert, the third Lord Baltimore, died at the age of seventy-seven years. The death of this Catholic claimant to the proprietorship of Maryland prepared the way for the restoration of the colony of Maryland to the new Protestant Lord Baltimore. But in April 1715 Benedict Leonard Calvert, the fourth Lord Baltimore, himself died, passing on the title to his son Charles, then sixteen years of age, who became the fifth Lord Baltimore. His guardian, Francis Lord Guilford, immediately petitioned to have Maryland restored to Lord Baltimore's proprietorship. This petition was granted by the new king because, as he said, he wished "to give encouragement to the educating of the numerous issue of so noble a family in the Protestant religion." So Maryland, which had been a royal Province for a quarter of a century, became once more in 1715 a proprietary province, administered by Lord Guilford in the name of his ward, the fifth Lord Baltimore. Lord Guilford immediately issued a new commission to Governor Hart to continue as governor over the proprietary colony.

At the beginning of Maryland's history as a royal Province in 1689, Lord Baltimore's colonists had replaced proprietary misrule with direct rule by the king and Parliament. During the ensuing quarter century, their only relationship with the former proprietary family was financial in character and their political allegiance was rendered to the crown. As they, along with other American colonists of England, were thus drawn more closely into the imperial system, they benefited from the resulting expansion of their trade and commerce and developed increased contacts with the mercantile pattern and life style of the mother country. They thus entered the eighteenth century as members of an imperial complex which was emerging into a new position of international preeminence and holding out to them the promise of a brilliant future. For 25 years they remained free from the administrative authority of the proprietary family of the Baltimores although continuing financially tributary to it. With the restoration of proprietary control over them at the end of their experience as a royal Province, they found themselves once again subject to an administrative complex of King, Parliament, and Proprietor, which would come to be increasingly viewed as an alien overlordship.

Footnotes

[1] *Archives*, vol. XIII, *Proceedings of the Assembly, 1684-1692*, 425-430.

[2] Joseph Towne Wheeler, "Thomas Bray and the Maryland Parochial Libraries, *Maryland Historical Magazine*, vol. XXXIV, No. 3 (1939), pp. 246-265.

[3] Arthur Lyon Cross, *The Anglican Episcopate and the American Colonies*, Longmans, Green, and Company, London, 1902, pp. 1-24.

[4] Reverend L.P. Bowen, *The Days of Makemie, or, the Vine Planted, A.D., 1680-1708*, Presbyterian Board of Publication, Philadelphia, 1885. The early history of Presbyterianism in Maryland is summarized, with some inaccuracies, in Ernest Trice Thompson, *Presbyterians in the South*, 3 vols., John Knox Press, Richmond, Virginia, 1963-1973, vol. 1, 1607-1861, pp. 17-28.

[5] J.F. Minor Simpson, *Monocacy Valley Presbyterianism*, Frederick, Maryland, 1936, 3.

[6] Eugenia Calvert Holland, "Anne Arundel Takes Over from St. Mary's," *Maryland Historical Magazine*, vol. XLIV, No. 1, March 1949, pp. 42-51.

[7] J. Oldmixon, *The British Empire in America, Containing the History of the Discovery, Settlement, Progress, and Present State of all the British Colonies, on the Continent and Islands of America*, 2 vols., London, 1708, I, 195.

[8] Bernard C. Steiner, *History of Education in Maryland*, Government Printing Office, Washington, D.C., 1894, p. 19, and *Archives of Maryland*, vol. 19, pp. 276-279.

[9] Lawrence C. Wroth, "The St. Mary's City Press: A New Chronology of American Printing," *Maryland Historical Magazine*, vol. XXXI, No. 2, June 1936, pp. 91-111; and Elizabeth Christine Cook, *Literary Influences in Colonial Newspapers, 1704-1750*, Columbia University Press, New York, 1912. For *Maryland Gazette*, pp. 150-178.

[10] Alsop, *Character of Maryland*, in Hall, *Narratives*, 363.

[11] M.S. Morriss, *Colonial Trade of Maryland, 1689-1715*, Johns Hopkins University Press, Baltimore, 1914, *passim*.

[12] Morriss, *cit. sup.*, p. 73.

[13] Charles B. Clark, "The Career of John Seymour, Governor of Maryland, 1704-1709," *Maryland Historical Magazine*, vol. XLVIII, No. 2, June 1953, pp. 134-159.

[14] *Maryland Archives*, I, 418, 486; and VIII, 362, 393, and 423.

Sources and Additional Reading

Bowen, Rev. L.P., *The Days of Makemie, or, The Vine Planted, A.D., 1680-1708*, Presbyterian Board of Publication, Philadelphia, 1885.

Cook, Elizabeth Christine, *Literary Influences in Colonial Newspapers, 1704-1750*, Columbia University Press, New York, 1912.

Craven, Avery Odell, *Soil Exhaustion As a Factor in the Agricultural History of Virginia and Maryland, 1606-1860*, University of Illinois Studies in the Social Sciences, vol. XIII, Urbana, 1925.

Cross, Arthur Lyon, *The Anglican Episcopate and the American Colonies*, Harvard Historical Studies, vol. IX, Longmans, Green, and Co., London, 1902.

McIlvaine, James William, *Early Presbyterianism in Maryland*, Johns Hopkins University Studies, Series 8, Nos. 5, 6, Johns Hopkins University, Baltimore, 1890.

Middleton, Arthur Pierce, *Tobacco Coast: A Maritime History of Chesapeake Bay in the Colonial Era*, The Mariners Museum, Newport News, Virginia, 1953.

Morriss, Margaret Shove, *Colonial Trade of Maryland, 1689-1715*, Johns Hopkins University Studies, Series 32, The Johns Hopkins Press, Baltimore, 1914.

Norris, Walter Blake, *Annapolis: Its Colonial and Naval Story*, New York, Thomas Y. Crowell Company, 1925.

Page, Isaac Marshall, *The Life Story of Rev. Francis Makemie*, William B. Eerdmans Publishing Company, Grand Rapids, Michigan, 1938.

Pennington, Edgar Legare, *The Reverend Thomas Bray*, The Church Historical Society, Philadelphia, 1934.

Ridgely, David, ed., *Annals of Annapolis . . .*, Cushing and Brothers, Baltimore, 1841.

Riley, Elihu Samuel, *Annapolis, "Ye Antient Capital of Maryland," 1649-1901*, Annapolis, Annapolis Publishing Company, 1901.

Skirven, Percy Granger, *The First Parishes of the Province of Maryland*, The Norman, Rennington Co., Baltimore, 1923.

Steiner, Bernard C., "Rev. Thomas Bray and His American Libraries," *American Historical Review, II* (1896), pp. 59-75.

——, ed., *Rev. Thomas Bray: His Life and Selected Works Relating to Maryland*, Maryland Historical Society, Fund Publication No. 37, J. Murphy Co., Baltimore, 1901. Reprinted by Arno, 1972.

Thompson, Ernest Trice, *Presbyterians in the South*, 3 vols., John Knox Press, Richmond, Virginia, 1963-1973, vol. I, 1607-1861.

Wroth, Lawrence C., *The Colonial Printer*, 2d edn., Portland, Me., The Southwork-Anthoensen Press, 1938.

——, *A History of Printing in Colonial Maryland, 1686-1776*, Typothetae, Baltimore, 1922.

CHAPTER X

POLITICAL CROSSCURRENTS

The seeds of independence, which had been planted when Englishmen first began to establish colonies in America twenty-five hundred miles from their homeland, slowly germinated in the eighteenth century. Maryland's act of 1692 making the English church the established church in the colony contained a clause claiming for the colony all the privileges of Magna Carta and for that reason was rejected by the crown. A subsequent act of 1696 which declared that all the laws of England were in force in Maryland was similarly disallowed. The restoration of the proprietary government was made at the behest of the Proprietor's guardian—not at the behest of the people of the Province. The Proprietor himself was an unknown youth, who had had no contact with Maryland. Though he was a Protestant, he was regarded with suspicion by the Protestants of Maryland, who feared that he might seek to restore the Catholics to their former privileges. From this time onward, causes of friction between the Marylanders and their rulers in England seemed to multiply. But outwardly the restoration of Lord Baltimore's authority over the Province effected no considerable change in the life of the people and altered little the governmental system and the course of developments there.

The last Assembly that met under the royal government—the Assembly of 1715—passed forty-nine laws, which, according to John Van Lear McMahon, "for their comprehensiveness and arrangement are almost entitled to the name of a 'code.' They formed the *substratum* of the statute law of the province, even down to the revolution; and the subsequent legislation of the colony effected no very material alterations in the system of general law then established." [1] Probably a part of the credit for the excellence of the laws of this Assembly was due to the presence at the sessions of the distinguished Philadelphia lawyer, Andrew Hamilton, who was at that time a resident of Kent County, was elected a member of the Assembly, and served on its committee on laws. Many years later—in 1733—Hamilton would act as counsel for the young printer, John Peter Zenger, in his famous trial for libel in New York City. It is possible that he first became acquainted with Zenger in Maryland, for in 1720 Zenger settled in Kent County, was authorized to print the session laws for each county, and was naturalized by the Assembly as a citizen of Maryland.[2]

The Assembly of 1715 passed an act recognizing George I as king of England. It also enacted a law which formed the basis of Maryland's electoral system for over a century, authorizing the sheriff to conduct the elections in each county and continuing the limitation of the suffrage to forty-shilling freeholders. At the suggestion of the Upper House, this law included a clause penalizing qualified voters who did not exercise the franchise. Other laws of this session defined the duties of sheriffs, provided methods for the settlement of disputes between the whites and the Indians, banned the sale of liquor to Indians, forbade the kidnapping and sale of Indians out of the Province, prohibited the departure of persons from the Province without a pass, and imposed a heavy duty on the importation of rum, Negroes, and Irish servants, the purpose of the latter being "the prevention of importing too great number of Irish Papists." That Negro slaves were already becoming a problem in Maryland is shown by this Assembly's enactment of a new slave code regulating the conduct of masters toward their slaves. Other laws of this notable Assembly dealt with testamentary matters, the improvement of the quality of tobacco, the procedure of the courts, fees for the attorney general and for lawyers, the relief of poor debtors, immorality and drunkenness, wild horses in the woods, and importation of grain, bread, beer, and horses from Pennsylvania.

While this Assembly was in session, Governor Hart received from Lord Guilford his new commission as governor of the proprietary province. During the remainder of his administration, which continued until 1720, the history of the Province was marred by a series of quarrels between the governor and Assembly on the one hand and the Catholics on the other. The Maryland adherents to the cause of the Stuart pretender to the throne of England, encouraged by the insurrection which the Stuart faction in England had launched soon after the accession of George I, violated the peace and order of the Province by making a demonstration in Annapolis. While Hart was absent in Cecil County, "some wicked, disloyal and traitorous persons" loaded four of the great guns on the courthouse hill in Annapolis, and fired two of them on the anniversary of the Stuart pretender's birth, June 10, 1716. Hart hurried back, issued a proclamation offering a reward for the arrest of the guilty persons, and had them imprisoned and fined.

In addition, two other members of the Catholic royalist faction in the Province, Redmond and Coyle, the former a nephew of Charles Carroll, were arrested for "drinking the pretender's health and speaking contemptibly of the King." In the ensuing trial they were defended by Thomas MacNamara, a fiery and intemperate relative of Carroll's, who had been disbarred from practicing law in Pennsylvania and had migrated to Maryland. But his clients were convicted and heavily fined. This incident marks the beginning of the conflict between the Anglican and the Catholic parties in Maryland after the restoration of the proprietary government.

Soon after Charles, Lord Baltimore, received his charter from George I, Charles Carroll, who had served during the latter part of the period of royal control as the proprietary's personal agent in the Province, went to England and secured from Charles a commission as "chief agent, escheator, naval officer, and receiver-general of all rents, or arrears of rents, fines, forfeitures, tobaccos, or moneys for land warrants, of all ferries, waifs, strays, and deodands; of duties arising from or growing due upon exportation of tobacco aforesaid, tonnage of ships, and all other moneys, tobaccos, or other effects in any manner or ways now due, or hereafter to grow due, whether by protested bills of exchange or otherwise." Carroll claimed that this commission, which did indeed contain a grant of very extensive powers, conferred upon him certain public duties and rights, in particular the right to discharge Redmond and Coyle of their fines.

But Carroll's commission from the Proprietor was not construed by the governor to give the Proprietor's personal agent the large public powers which he claimed. To Hart the Proprietor's personal agent, though armed with a new commission, appeared to be merely a holdover from the regime of the last Catholic Proprietor. Hart told Carroll plainly that he would not regard him as a public officer, especially since Carroll declined to take the oath of abjuration required under the law of 1704; but Hart offered faithfully to assist him in the enforcement of any measures dealing with the Proprietor's "lands or other private matters." Hart had already advised the Proprietor "never to allow any papists in the public affairs of this province," and he now complained to the Assembly that the grant of such powers to another, "especially to a Papist," was such a lessening of his power and dishonor to his character that he desired to be recalled unless he could be restored to the full authority he held under the crown.

The governor was thrown on the defensive by Carroll's pretensions to the exercise of official powers, but in resisting those pretensions he was supported by both houses of the legislature. They prepared an address to the Proprietor praising Hart's "zeal" and "exact discharge of duty," and criticizing as unwise the Proprietor's decision to "lop off so many branches of Hart's power" and to give these "branches" to Papists. In the dispute between Hart as the representative of the crown and Carroll representing the Proprietor over the functions of the land office in the colony, the Maryland legislature recognized the rights of the Proprietor only as the chief landholder in the Province and insisted upon regarding the land office as a public agency.

But the legislature went still further. The Lower House presented an address to the king asking him to use his efforts to safeguard the Protestant religion in the Province. The Assembly also passed an act for the "better security of his Lordship's Government and the Protestant interest." This act, which remained in force during the remainder of the colonial period, required all officials in the Province to take the oath of allegiance to the Proprietor and abjuration of both Catholicism and the doctrine of transubstantiation, and it imposed a fine of £250 for violations of this requirement. Persons who took these oaths and later attended any papist assembly or joined in the "service at mass" were also made liable to the same penalty; but persons who were managing the private affairs of the Proprietor were exempted from the provisions of the act. By this anti-Catholic legislation, enacted at the instigation of Governor Hart, the Maryland legislature ensured that the government of the colony would remain in the hands of Protestants. Though it nominally did not apply to the Proprietor's personal agent in the colony it actually curtailed Carroll's political influence and rendered his office unimportant.

This legislation did not end Carroll's feud with Governor Hart and the Maryland legislature. Carroll questioned the validity of the laws passed by the Assembly of 1715, which formed the legal code of the Province, on the ground that the king had not given his sanction to the acts before the restoration of the proprietary authority, but he could not persuade the Assembly to give any weight to his arguments. Soon afterward, he wrote a letter to Hart warning him not to sign certain laws of the Assembly of 1716, particularly the revenue laws, and directing Hart to turn over to him all the revenue of the Province after deducting the governor's salary. This letter was delivered to Hart while he was suffering from a violent fever, and he immediately transmitted it to the Assembly. In reply, the Assembly advised the governor not to turn over the revenue to Carroll unless Carroll took the oaths. They deplored the threat contained in Carroll's letter, and they accused him of "using a very indecent way and freedom with Hart" in issuing such general directions to him. Following their advice Hart signed the bills and complained to the Assembly about the "insults in his sickness" and his inconsiderate treatment by Carroll. He publicly expressed the hope that the "gentlemen of the Romish communion will prudently consider their own interest and will content themselves with the lenity of the government they live under," and he advised the Protestants to show a "charitable demeanor toward their neighbors of another persuasion, since it is no longer in their power to do you any injury."

Of the acts which Carroll had warned the governor not to sign, the Proprietor and his guardian disallowed only one, though they insisted upon adding amendments to the bill which permitted the governor to take his salary directly from the revenues without transmitting it to the Proprietor. They promptly accepted the act which disqualified Catholics from holding office and reassured the Assembly that "your lord proprietary is not, as he has been maliciously suggested by some, a Papist in masquerade, but a true Protestant of the Church of England in which faith he is resolved to live and die." So strong was their endorsement of the anti-Catholic legislation that Carroll sent agents to England to work for the removal of Hart.

The Maryland assembly and council, thus confirmed in their policies for the Province, now acknowledged their loyalty to Lord Baltimore and expressed again their high opinion of Hart, declaring that the "largest opportunities we have had of demonstrating the esteem we have for your excellency have fallen so far short of amounting to a compliment that we are forced to acknowledge we have failed in doing justice to your merit. . . . Though we are limited in some other respects, we are not so in affection." Probably Hart enjoyed greater devotion and respect from the people of his Province than did any other governor of Maryland until Sir Robert Eden. His popularity with his own people was not exceeded by that of any other governor in England's colonies in America.

One of the significant innovations credited to Governor Hart was an act passed by the Assembly in 1716 to safeguard the records of the Province. Hart had secured an order that neither candles nor other fire should be allowed in the court house and that the clerk should see that the back door was locked every night and opened half an hour after sunrise every morning. At his suggestion the Assembly now appointed a committee to examine the records, and it reported that some had been lost and that many had been damaged in being moved from St. Mary's to Annapolis. The Assembly made provision for the repair of the old records and required all clerks in the future to give bond to deliver the records in good order to their successors.

Hart, like his predecessor Nicholson, was especially interested in advancing education in Maryland. The public revenues for the support of King William's School at Annapolis amounted to only about £20 a year, and the school was being supported mainly by contributions of charitable people of Annapolis. When Hart called the attention of the Assembly to this distressing condition, the Assembly complained that they were obliged to contribute too much to the support of the College of William and Mary in Virginia "by which never any one inhabitant of this [Province] have reaped the least advantage." They presented the same complaint to Baltimore and asked his help in getting the proceeds of Maryland's tax transferred to Maryland schools, instead of being applied "to a free school in Virginia, which by its remoteness from this province [is] wholly useless to any of its inhabitants." But this petition and a similar petition to Baltimore two years later, in 1719, met with no response, and since the Assembly was unwilling to impose an additional tax upon the Province, Maryland's one school struggled on as before.

Maryland's population in 1719, according to the report which Hart submitted to the Council of Trade and Plantations in the following year, consisted of 55,000 white inhabitants and 25,000 black, and he added, "The inhabitants are much increased of late years; by those born in the country; . . . by the great number of convicts; by the purchase of slaves and by many poor families, who transport themselves from Ireland." [3] This increase in population encouraged the governor to embark the colony upon an ambitious highway-improvement program. He urged upon the Assembly of 1719 the importance of good roads and asked them to enact new laws requiring the road overseers in each county to maintain the roads. He also asked them to provide for the construction of a public road through the Province. But these proposals were not acted upon favorably by the Assembly. The laws already enacted, they replied, were adequate to provide for road maintenance and needed only to be enforced. And they declined to undertake as a public responsibility the construction of a road through the heart of the Province, insisting that the construction of such a road was a responsibility of the several counties and not of the provincial government.

The status and activities of the Established Church in Maryland gave rise to many difficulties during this period of the colony's history. Despite the earlier efforts of the Reverend Thomas Bray on its behalf, the clergy in Maryland were poorly trained and so immoral as to have lost their influence with their parishioners.[4] On this subject Governor Hart reported to the Bishop of London that "there are some whose education and profession are a scandal to their profession" and he was amazed that "such illiterate men came to be in holy orders." So low had the influence and fortunes of the Anglican Church sunk that the clergy of the Eastern Shore complained to the Bishop of London: "It is a sad truth that we must declare that we have not one friend in the province, except our governor, to make our application to; nor any access to, nor place, nor employ in the government, nor friend in the world that we know of, but your lordship to stand by us." As members of a tax-supported institution, the Anglican Church, they felt neglected by the temporal authorities and were embittered by the denial of their petition for a bishop.[5]

After the Anglican Church was established in Maryland, it ceased to be controlled by the Society for the Propagation of the Gospel in Foreign Parts. It was no longer a mission, and the conduct of its affairs came nominally under the jurisdiction of the government. A commissary or representative of the Bishop of London could only "warn and rebuke"; he could not discipline the Anglican clergy or their parishioners in Maryland. Nevertheless, this office was revived in 1716, and, at the request of Governor Hart, two commissaries were sent to the Province, the Reverend Christopher Wilkinson for the Eastern Shore and the Reverend Jacob Henderson for the Western Shore.[6] Wilkinson, a man of piety and prudence, established and maintained harmony among the seven clergymen of the Eastern Shore. But in contrast to Wilkinson, Henderson, the commissary on the Western Shore, was officious and pugnacious and had difficulty with one of his clergymen, Henry Hall, who was a friend of Governor Hart.[7]

The governor himself now took a hand in the church problem. He convened all the Anglican clergymen of the Province, twenty in number, in the library at Annapolis and in an address urged them to preserve harmony and to present their grievances to the Assembly. The "Jesuits and other popish emissaries," he said, "are prevailing by the insinuating arts upon the weak and ignorant [and are] vigilant in gaining proselytes and seducing the unwary." The clergy in reply thanked him for his interest and, accepting his advice, soon presented a series of requests to the Assembly asking that the Assembly (1) recognize the authority of the Bishop of London over the ecclesiastical affairs of the Province, (2) pay the salary of a clerk to record the commissary's proceedings, (3) authorize the clergy to call upon the sheriffs to serve legal papers for them, (4) pay the traveling expenses of the church wardens, and (5) allow the commissaries and clergymen free use of the ferries in their travels. These requests seemed to many members of the legislature to aim at a too close identification of church and state, and though they were acceptable to the Upper House, they were rejected by the Lower. The principle of separation of church and state which had guided the policy of the first two Proprietors of Maryland obviously still had its adherents in the colony.

Hart's antagonism to the Catholics in Maryland continued down to the end of his administration as governor. He found it necessary to disbar the quarrelsome MacNamara from the practice of law and in this action was upheld by both the council and the Assembly of the Province. With Hart's approval they denounced the "restless spirits of a popish enterprising faction" in the Province and enacted a law, which continued in force throughout the rest of the colonial period, depriving Catholics of the franchise. For these actions Hart and the legislature were castigated by both MacNamara and Carroll for persecuting Catholics. Against this charge the Assembly defended Hart, explaining that the laws of Maryland imposed upon Catholics only the same legal and political disabilities as in England. When MacNamara proceeded to England and persuaded the Proprietor to disallow the law suspending him from the practice of law in Maryland, the Assembly in the Province found itself in an unpleasant dilemma. Hart explained to them that if they allowed MacNamara or any other person to insult and disrupt the courts, they would destroy their authority. But the Assembly was obliged to conform the law to Baltimore's wishes. Hart's difficulties with MacNamara continued until the latter's death in 1720.

Hart reviewed his policy toward the Catholics in his address to his last Assembly in 1720. The Catholics, he asserted, were in error in claiming that Maryland was established as an asylum for them, because the charter, under which alone they could live in Lord Baltimore's Province, did not specifically grant them the free exercise of their religion. And yet they freely practiced their religion and were still claiming the right to hold offices. If they could win control of the government of the Province, he predicted that they would destroy the Protestants; they would unite with the French Catholics, who were extending their boundaries southward from Canada and eastward from the Mississippi Valley. He proposed therefore that the Assembly summon some of the principal Catholics before it and interrogate them. If they refused to submit to public examination, they would be admitting guilt. He singled out for special condemnation Charles Carroll, who, he said, "by principle is an enemy of the Protestant constitution." With the consent of the legislature, therefore, he immediately summoned Charles and James Carroll, Henry Darnall, Benjamin Hall, Clement Hill, William Fitz Redmond, Henry Wharton, Charles Diggs, Peter Atwood (a priest), Major Nicholas Sewall, and Richard Bennett to appear before the Assembly. With them was probably associated Daniel Dulany, a Catholic lawyer, who now first appears in the records of Maryland, for in April 1720 Hart complained to the Upper House that Dulany had affronted Colonel Thomas Addison "by calling him a little Rascalous Fellow" whereas, declared Hart, "the sd Col. Addison is an honest Protestant and Lover of the King and Country, and . . . the sd Daniel Dulany is a noted favorer of the Papists."

Hart's summons was ignored by all the designated members of the Catholic party, although the legislature ascertained that the "most eminent of the Papists were in town at the time appointed to hear their pretensions." They thus scorned the attempt by the governor and legislature to examine their claims under the government of Maryland and to pry into their private affairs. The legislature concluded that the Catholics by their action "tacitly acknowledge that their pretensions are groundless and their exclamations most unreasonable."

Governor Hart had repeatedly received proof of the loyalty and support of the Maryland Assembly, and in 1719 he was given £200 currency by them as a partial reimbursement of the money which he had spent in the interest of the Province. But he did not evoke the same admiration from Baltimore and Guilford, and he was ordered by them to return to England in May 1720. The explicit reasons for Hart's recall were not given, but he had taken an intransigent position on the religious question in Maryland and had championed the cause of the popular party sometimes intemperately. After he arrived in London, he testified before the Board of Trade in such a way as to indicate that he still had the interest of Maryland close to his heart. In 1721 he was named by the king governor of the Leeward Islands in the West Indies, which included Antigua, St. Christophers, Nevis, Montserrat, and the Virgin Islands, and held this office until 1727. He had been described as "a strong, zealous, impetuous man, . . . a most devoted member of the Anglican Church and a faithful servant of the English Crown." He was probably overbearing and exacting and had many of the defects of his times and of his Irish blood, but, with it all, his conscientious devotion to duty, his single purpose to have his Province well governed, and his painstaking care of the details of administration made him a man who should not be forgotten. The code of laws which Maryland adopted under his influence remained his best monument and continued in force for more than half a century after his departure.

As Hart's successor in the governorship of Maryland the Proprietor petitioned the king to name his cousin, Charles Calvert. His request was granted, and Charles Calvert immediately left England for Maryland. He convened his first Assembly there in October 1720, notified them of his appointment, and expressed the hope that "old rancor and jealousy will now disappear."

Much of this "old rancor and jealousy" was a legacy of the period when Maryland was under the proprietorship of the second and third Lords Baltimore. The conflict then between the popular party and the proprietary party had become so acute that it had given the king a pretext for making Maryland a royal colony in 1690. During the next quarter century when Maryland was governed by the crown, the old antagonism continued, directed especially (as shown in the conduct of Governor Hart) against Lord Baltimore's private agent in the colony, Charles Carroll, and deeply infused with religious animus. When the colony was restored to Lord Baltimore in 1715, the old factionalism was intensified. It would evolve eventually into the independence movement of the 1770's. The traditional resentment against the pretensions of the proprietary party—a carry-over from the seventeenth century—was now aggravated by the worsening economic plight of the colony, by the increments of strength which came to the popular party through the opening up of new lands for settlement in the Piedmont section, and by the elements of class struggle which were introduced in the form of attacks by the agricultural population upon the professional classes.

The privileged status of the Proprietor's friends in the colony was evidenced by the lucrative fees which they received. Under the charter, the Proprietor enjoyed the right to constitute and appoint officers in the Province, and from this provision he deduced the right also to specify the fees for their support. The officers' fees were therefore fixed by him through the governor and council, but since they involved a financial outlay by the colonists they were regarded by the people, represented in the Assembly, as an infringement upon their power of the purse and of their right guaranteed in the charter to be free from any levy that would "oblige, bind, change or take away the Right or Interest of any person or persons, of or in Member, Life, Freehold, Goods or Chattels." The question of the officers' fees therefore became a source of bitter controversy between the proprietary party and the so-called "country" or popular party.

As early as 1676, the Lower House asked the Proprietor for a list of the fees so that they might incorporate it into law and so prevent the officers from charging higher fees.[8] When they obtained the list from the Proprietor, they wrote into the law the amounts to be paid to each officer and forbade the charging of rates in excess of those amounts. After Maryland was placed under royal government in 1690, the question of the officers' fees assumed a larger aspect and came to be viewed as an example of taxation without representation. The Lower House declared that "it was the undoubted right of the freemen of Maryland that no officers fees should be imposed upon them but by consent of their representatives in assembly, and that such liberty was established by several acts of parliament."[9] The Assembly accordingly incorporated the scale of officers' fees in an act which was to last for only three years. Subsequent assemblies reenacted the law from time to time with a few minor changes until 1719.

With the arrival of Hart's successor, Charles Calvert, the question of the officers' fees became more serious, involving, as it did, not only the salaries of all the principal officers of the Province but also the income of the Anglican clergymen, who were paid from the provincial treasury. And since all these fees were paid in tobacco, public officials were financially concerned with the quantity and quality of Maryland's tobacco crop. Thus were inextricably interconnected the problems of the applicability of English statutes to the American colonies, of the fees paid to the Proprietor's agents and the ministers of the Established Church in Maryland, and of the maintenance of the quality of Maryland's tobacco. These involved fundamental matters in the relationship between free Marylanders and a proprietary monopoly supported by the crown.

From an original haphazard arrangement in which many commodities, including beaver skins, grains, hides, powder and shot, had been used as media of exchange, Maryland, following Virginia's example, early adopted tobacco as the standard medium of exchange. In 1660 George Alsop reported "Tobacco is the current coyn of Maryland and will sooner purchase Commodities from the Merchant than money."[10] Tobacco and tobacco certificates passed current throughout the colony as the money of Maryland. In 1682 the Maryland Assembly sought to change this system by making corn, wheat, oats, barley, rye, peas, pork, beef, and bacon legal tender for all debts except the Proprietor's rents and the public taxes. But tobacco continued as the principal item of barter. Until 1715 the quitrents and alienation charges to the Proprietor were paid in tobacco. With the exception of customs duties, all dues and fees and the salaries of the Anglican clergy and colonial officeholders were paid in the same currency.

But the value of tobacco and with it the value of the negotiable paper based on tobacco fluctuated from year to year. When the supply exceeded the demand or when the quality was allowed to deteriorate, the price fell. And as Maryland's tobacco production increased enormously after 1700, tobacco became an inflated currency which constantly depreciated in value. Public officials in the Province whose incomes were dependent upon specific amounts of tobacco fixed by law therefore saw their incomes shrink.

During the seventeenth century three remedies had been proposed for improving the tobacco industry: (1) establishment of a limited number of ports where all tobacco intended for export must be inspected, (2) legal prohibition of adulteration—that is the mixing of "trash" or poor leaves with good—and (3) curtailment of tobacco production through a crop control system. These remedies had been enacted into law in both Virginia and Maryland and had proved quite effective in Virginia. But in Maryland they had aroused so much opposition, particularly from the smaller planters, that by 1689 all laws to control the production and export of tobacco had either expired or proved ineffective. After the restoration of the proprietary government in 1715, agitation began for reenactment of these measures of regulation and control. But they were now strenuously opposed by the large planters and by the professional classes in the colony, including salaried officials, the clergy, and the lawyers. Such measures, the professional men felt, might result in the lowering of their salaries. They were disinclined to accept legislation which would produce that assured result in the doubtful hope that eventually, as the price of tobacco increased, their incomes might again rise.

This question became involved in the rivalry between classes formed along social and economic lines. It gathered political importance in part because it was based upon genuine grievances, but it was susceptible of demogogic exploitation. Under the stress of deteriorating economic conditions the Lower House, representing the popular party, sought to limit the fixed fees paid to public officials, including the clergy, but, failing in that effort, they tried to force the officials to accept paper currency for their salaries. This experiment had already been tried in Massachusetts in 1690, but the value of that colony's paper money had quickly declined to one-third of its face value. When the attempt was later made in Maryland, starting in 1727, it was blocked by the Upper House which was dominated by the proprietary officials.

The problems of the fees of attorneys, public officers, and clergy seemed to arise and plague Maryland politics because the colony was on a tobacco barter basis. Those whose salaries were fixed in a definite amount of tobacco were unwilling to accept an equivalent for it in paper money upon the assumption that the value of the latter would remain constant. As tobacco was depreciating in value, colonial officials felt that their fees ought to be increased, not reduced. The popular party, on the other hand, desired both to reduce the officers' fees and to pass legislation that would cause Maryland's tobacco crop to rise in value, thus maintaining, as they asserted, the same relative level of officers' fees.

When the law fixing the fees expired in 1719, the fees question became a topic of lively controversy between the popular party and the proprietary party, aggravated by Maryland's economic plight. On this occasion Governor Hart urged the Assembly to extend the law until Lord Baltimore should come of age in 1720 or until he paid his promised visit to the Province. To this proposal the Lower House replied that the fees were oppressive to the people of the Province and ought to be discontinued altogether until the Proprietor's arrival. With the views of the Assembly the Upper House refused to concur, but a compromise law was agreed upon which effected a limited reduction in the fees of some of the officers of the Province. It remained in force for six years.

In 1724 the Assembly proposed to reduce the officers' fees by one-half.[11] Meeting opposition in the Upper House, they deferred action until the following year when they passed a law reducing the fees by one quarter. The Upper House followed the curious procedure of passing the bill and then petitioning the Proprietor to veto it. He accordingly did so, and, going further, enjoined the governor not to assent to any bill that reduced the officers' fees below the level established by the Act of 1719. By his veto he antagonized the popular party in Maryland. Thereafter, as the governor reported to the Proprietor, "Every insolent fellow thinks himself free to refuse paym't, and Brow beat, as it were, the Officers."[12]

Maryland, unlike the new England colonies, had made it possible for lawyers to occupy prominent positions in social and public affairs from the beginning. During the seventeenth century they exercised an influence in Maryland comparable to that of the clergy in Massachusetts. Because of their necessary involvement in matters affecting the interpretation of the land law, the legal relations between the Proprietor and his colonists, and the commercial activities of the colony, they enjoyed a privileged position. After the restoration of Lord Baltimore's authority over the Province, lawyers as a class therefore became a target of jealousy and criticism by the nonprofessional classes. In 1715 the Assembly passed an act "for rectifying the ill Practices of Attornies of this Province, and ascertaining fees to the Attorney General, Clerk of Indictments, Attorneys and Practitioners of the law in the courts of this province, and for levying the same by way of execution." By this act the Attorney General was forbidden in certain cases to collect any fees, and for actions in general lawyers were authorized to collect only fees in amounts specifically listed. In 1721 and 1722, the Assembly enacted additional legislation fixing legal fees, and in 1725 they passed an act to "restrain the ill practices of attorneys and to prevent their taking money fees," which was renewed in 1726 for three years and renewed again in 1729 for three years.

Meanwhile, in 1725, Daniel Dulany, Thomas Bordley, Joshua George, and Michael Howard, "late practitioners of the law in this Province," presented a memorial to the Upper House asserting that the fees bill was destructive of their privileges as British subjects and violated the provision of the royal charter which required that all laws enacted in the colony must be consonant to reason and not contrary to the laws of England. Failing in their purpose on this occasion, the memorialists renewed their complaints to the Proprietor in 1728 when the law came up for reconsideration in the Assembly. Dulany sponsored a bill to extend the English statutes to Maryland and supported his bill with a pamphlet published at Annapolis entitled "The Right of the Inhabitants of Maryland to the Benefit of the English Laws." But this bill, which in effect recognized the right of Parliament in London to legislate for the colony, was vetoed by the Proprietor.

But on the more limited question of the right of the Maryland Assembly to regulate legal fees, the Proprietor was finally persuaded to accept the views of the professional lawyers in the colony. When the Assembly reenacted the fees bill in 1729 and submitted it to the Proprietor in England, he disallowed it on the ground that it "was not agreeable to any known law here." But by his veto of this and several other laws, the Proprietor antagonized the Assembly, which now passed a sharply querulous resolution declaring that "This House having taken into consideration that the Right Honorable the Lord Proprietary hath frequently dissented to the Laws past in the Province by the Legislature thereof, which we conceived to be an Aggrievance to his Majesty's subjects therein and not warranted by the Charter, and as it is an Affair of the greatest importance to the people, to be at a certainty about their Laws, we desire your Honours to join with this House in applying to his Lordship, or in taking such other steps as may be necessary to settle a matter of such great Consequence."

By this complaint, which was concurred in by the Upper House, the Maryland legislature challenged the Proprietor's veto power over colonial legislation, but they secured no satisfaction from him. He continued to reduce their laws to ineffectiveness by his veto and did not curtail his exercise of the veto power until he had filled the Upper

House with members who were more favorable to his interest. Since he thus claimed the full measure of his proprietary prerogative, the Lower House, in order to check his pretensions, presented a proposal at this time that the colony support an agent in England to represent its interests before the British government. But this proposal was strongly opposed by the Proprietor and was rejected by the Upper House in 1729 and again in 1731.

In this controversy over the extension of the English statutes to Maryland, Daniel Dulany took the lead. He had migrated from Ireland to Maryland after a family quarrel and though he arrived penniless, contrived to become identified with some of the old landed families of Maryland and with the proprietary party. Under Charles Calvert's governorship he became Attorney General of the Province and served in that office for many years as chief prosecutor in criminal cases, representative of the Proprietor in all civil suits to which the Proprietor was a party, and legal adviser to the governor, council, and both houses of the legislature. He served for twenty years after 1722 as a representative of Annapolis in the Lower House and thereafter in the Upper House until his death. As chairman of the Committee of Laws of the Assembly, he carried on for ten years the controversy over the extension of the English statutes, in which he espoused the claims of the popular party against the Proprietor.

As the Assembly, representing the popular party in Maryland, sought to regulate the fees of lawyers, they sought also to control the salaries of the Anglican clergy. These salaries were fixed by an act of 1702, passed to complete the establishment of the Church of England in Maryland begun ten years before. Under this act every "poll" or taxable individual in the Province was required to pay forty pounds of tobacco annually to support the Anglican clergy. This "forty per poll tax," as it was called, aroused increasing opposition because of the inefficiency and immorality of the clergy and the inability of the legislature to remove or discipline them. It was especially irksome to the German settlers in the back country, who belonged to Lutheran and Reformed denominations and who were loath to support the established Anglican Church. Though the clergy were dependent upon the legislature for their salaries, they were independent of its control. A proposal was made in 1708 to subject the clergy to regulation by a Spiritual Court composed of the governor and three laymen, but it was vetoed by the governor. In 1725 it was revived and pushed by one of the prominent lawyers of the Province, Thomas Bordley, who was Dulany's chief rival for the leadership of the Maryland bar and who had just been defeated by him for the position of Attorney General. But it was vetoed again by the governor, the Bishop of London, and also the Proprietor.

Three years later the Assembly sought to reduce the salary of the clergy in a law "for improving the Staple of Tobacco."[13] The crop control clauses forbade an adult planter to cultivate more than 7,000 tobacco plants in any one year and a minor more than 3,500 plants, and these limitations were to be enforced by the vestry of each parish. Other clauses provided relief for debtors by permitting all levies and charges to be paid at the rate of ten shillings in current money or three-fourths of that amount in tobacco at the choice of the debtor. These would oblige the clergy therefore to accept thirty instead of forty pounds of tobacco per poll or a fixed rate of exchange between currency and tobacco, thus in either case reducing their salaries.

Against this law the clergy strongly protested. Meeting in secret, they appointed the Reverend Jacob Henderson, Commissary of the Western Shore, to present their complaints to the authorities in England. When Henderson arrived in England, he learned that Lord Baltimore was out of the country, but laid his case before the king, the Bishop of London, and the Society for the Propagation of the Gospel. As a result, the act was disallowed by the Proprietor on the ground, among others, that it bore with special hardship on the clergy. At Henderson's behest, he instructed the governor of Maryland "not to consent to any act the object of which was to diminish the revenues of the clergy." When Henderson returned to Maryland, he brought with him a commission from the Bishop of London designating him commissary of the entire Province, but his successful effort against the tobacco act was so bitterly resented by the Marylanders that he was threatened with physical violence.

In 1730 the Assembly passed another act which aroused the opposition of the clergy. It provided that in lieu of one-fourth of their stipend, the clergy should be paid in wheat, barley, corn, and oats, instead of tobacco, and it fixed the value of these alternative commodities in relation to tobacco. Though the act was opposed by the clergy, it was approved by both houses of the legislature and was sent to the Proprietor with an address from both houses in its favor. He accordingly allowed it to become law. When he visited his Province in 1733, he appointed two laymen, Daniel Dulany and Benjamin Tasker, as Commissaries-General to act as his agents in controlling the Anglican Church in Maryland. In the following year, he made Dulany the sole Commissary General and kept him in that office until his death. The question of the clergy's fees continued troublesome, and finally in 1747 the general tobacco control act passed in that year definitely reduced the annual tax for the support of the Anglican Church from forty to thirty pounds of tobacco per poll.

As long as Maryland made tobacco the basis of its currency, its economy operated essentially on a barter system. Tobacco and tobacco scrip may have well served the needs of a primitive economy, but as Maryland's foreign commerce expanded, the business interests there insisted upon developing a medium of exchange that would have international acceptance. Paper money seemed to offer the solution. The first circulating bank notes in Europe were issued by the Bank of England soon after its establishment in 1694, and this device appealed to England's colonists in America, who were otherwise dependent largely upon the illegal Spanish *reales* for metallic coins. Paper money of their own issue, they believed, would stimulate their trade both internal and external, would at the same time give them a stronger basis for credit transactions abroad, and would represent a gesture of economic independence.

The clamor for paper money which arose in Pennsylvania during the economic depression of 1722-1723 seemed to offer Maryland a solution to its problem of a circulating medium. Perhaps the problems that agitated Maryland's politics under the restored proprietorship could be solved if the tobacco certificates could be replaced by paper currency issued by the government. As trade between Maryland and England ran heavily against the colony, Maryland suffered a severe dearth of hard money, which was not compensated for by the small amounts of sterling that entered the colony with new immigrants from England or from harbor and pilotage fees or from the sale of tobacco certificates to merchants of Philadelphia to use in discharging their debts to London creditors. As tobacco certificates were not accepted as legal tender by British creditors, the debtor class in Maryland, which included some plantation owners, clamored for the issuance of paper currency, the usual expedient of debtors.

Responding to this demand for easy money, the *Maryland Gazette*, which had just begun publication in September 1727 under the direction of William Parks as the first newspaper south of Pennsylvania, reprinted in July 1729 Benjamin Franklin's "A Modest Enquiry into the Nature and Necessity of a Paper-Currency" which had been so effective in Pennsylvania that Franklin had been given the job of printing that colony's paper money. In late 1729, Governor Benedict Leonard Calvert, brother of the Proprietor, who had replaced Charles Calvert, explained the financial situation in Maryland to the Proprietor:

Money, or somewhat to answer its Current Effects in trade, is certainly much wanted here, wee may Barter Between one Another our Staple tobacco, but to Carry on and Inlarge our trade Abroad, & to Invite Artificiers [sic] Shipwrights, &c to settle amongst us, another species of Currency in payments, seems very desireable. New York, Pennsylvania &c are vastly improved in foreign Trade, as well as home Manufactures, by a Paper Currency it is that, in lieu of Specifick coin, which seems to give life, Expedition, and Ease to trade and Commerce. This has drawn them into Communitys or Towns; they are daily growing more and more populous, and are Supposed to Increase as proportionably in Credit and riches. In Virginia and Maryland the Case is Much otherwise; Tobacco is our Staple, is our All, and Indeed leaves no room for anything Else. It requires the Attendance of all our hands, and exacts their utmost labour, the whole year round; it requires us to Abhor Communitys or Townships, since a Planter cannot Carry on his Affairs, without Considerable Elbow room within his Plantation[.] When All is done, and our Tobacco sent home, it is perchance the most uncertain Commodity that comes to Market; and the management of it there is of such a nature and method, that it seems to be of all other, most lyable and Subject to frauds, in prejudice to the poor Planters. Tobacco Merchants, who deal in Consignments, get great estates, run no risque and Labour only with the pen; the Planter can scarce get a living, Runs all the risques attendant upon trade, both as to his negroes and Tobacco, and must work in variety of Labour. . . . An increasing Country and growing people, as this is, and a Staple, at best Uncertaine, but of late visibly declining in Value, as Tobacco is, wishes the people here to look about, and Enlarge their foundation in trade, to the which money or some Currency, which may answer the same uses, is necessary, and the Expedient to such End is a Paper Currency.[14]

This "Expedient" was strenuously resisted by the salaried class in the colony, including the Anglican clergy, but it was supported by the popular party. The agitation for paper money was reinforced by a humorous poem published at Annapolis in 1730 entitled "Sotweed Redivivus: Or the Planters Looking Glass. In Burlesque Verse. Calculated for the Meridian of Maryland." The author of this poem, E[benezer] C[ook], Gent, attributed the widespread poverty to Maryland's dependence upon tobacco. The people were

"Reduc'd to Penury indeed,
By feeding on this *Indian* Weed."[15]

Two years later the Assembly passed a bill to print £36,000 of paper money provided that the Proprietor approved. Since he did not give his consent, the bill never went into effect. But in that same year, 1732, the Proprietor himself visited Maryland, and while he was in the Province he approved an act of the legislature authorizing the issuance of paper currency in the amount of £90,000 to circulate for thirty-one years. This money was to be used in all future contracts and must be accepted as legal tender in the discharge of any money debt. All fees and levies, except those due to the clergy and to officers of state, and all securities and fines specified in tobacco in the existing laws of the Province could now be paid in paper money at the ratio of ten shillings per hundred pounds of tobacco. The exemption of the clergy and officers of state from the list of persons affected by the bill obviously explained why the bill was passed by the Upper House and was accepted by the Proprietor.[16] It was a compromise measure which satisfied the Lower House by authorizing the issuance of paper currency and the Upper House and the Proprietor by excluding the officers from the requirement of accepting their salaries in inflated money. At the same time the Proprietor issued a proclamation fixing the officers' fees at nearly the same level as stipulated in the Act of 1719. The Lower House, perhaps, intimidated by the presence of the Proprietor and gratified by the enactment of the currency measure, chose not to make an issue of it.

The method which the Maryland legislature adopted to put the new paper money into circulation was ingeniously contrived to solve also the tobacco problem of the colony. This had reached critical proportions, as set forth in a letter from the London Merchants who handled the tobacco crop of the Province. To a group of influential Marylanders the London Merchants reported that "the quantity imported into Great Britain, of late years, has really been more than all Europe doth consume within the year, which leaving every year a stock of old tobacco upon hand, has clogged the Markets in Europe, and that is another and indeed a grand cause of the lowness of the price." They considered three possible courses of action: (1) reduction of each annual crop, (2) destruction of all trash, that is, poor tobacco, and (3) abstention from planting every fourth or fifth year; and of these they recommended the first, which, they said, would have to be taken in cooperation with Virginia.

The Maryland legislature accepted this recommendation and incorporated it in the paper money act of 1733. They appointed three commissioners and a clerk, with headquarters at Annapolis, to issue the money. The Commissioners must issue to each head of a family thirty shillings in bills for each "taxable" and in return must see to it that each head of a family burned (in the presence of tobacco burners appointed by the act) 150 pounds of tobacco for each of his taxables in 1734 and the like amount in 1735. The rest of the paper money was to be put in circulation as follows: £3,000 were to be expended for a governor's residence, £500 were to be given to each county for jails, £500 were to be spent in repairs on the public buildings in Annapolis, and the remaining amounts were to be lent out on interest at four percent on either mortgage or personal security. For the redemption of the money, a sinking fund was to be established by a duty of one shilling, threepence upon each hogshead of tobacco exported from the colony. The management of this fund was placed in a board of trustees resident in London, which invested the duties in stock of the Bank of England. With these funds Maryland expected to retire all its paper currency at the end of thirty-one years.

When the Proprietor left Maryland to return to England in 1733, the era of good feeling between the proprietary and the popular parties which had existed during his visit ended and was succeeded by an era of bitter strife. The Proprietor himself had replaced Samuel Ogle as governor when he arrived in the Province, and before he left Maryland he turned the governorship over again to Ogle, who served in that position from 1733 to 1742. All of Ogle's skill as a compromiser was required to preserve peace between the conflicting political factions. In 1742 this experienced administrator turned over his office to Thomas Bladen, under whose governorship many of the colony's problems were put on the way to solution, particularly through the enactment of the tobacco inspection law of 1747. Perhaps Bladen's success was attributable to the fact that he was the only colonial governor of Maryland who was born in the colony. In 1747 he was replaced by Ogle who served as governor again for the next five years.

During the Proprietor's sojourn in Maryland in 1732-1733, he issued a proclamation fixing the officers' fees, as noted above, and in doing so set a precedent which would be followed later by Maryland's last royal governor, Sir Robert Eden, provoking a still more important controversy on this question in 1770-1773. In 1738, the Proprietor's action on this question was sharply challenged by the Assembly. Only the Assembly, they protested, had the right to fix these fees, and the Proprietor's "proclamations or orders of Council were invasions of the fundamental constitution of this province under the royal charter and against the lawful rights and liberties of his Majesty's liege subjects." The Assembly's protest produced a political crisis and a deadlock between the two houses of the legislature. As a result, the legislature was unable to pass a fee law for eight years, that is, until they could agree upon a general tobacco inspection law in 1747, in which they included a table of fees.

After the enactment of the paper currency act in 1733, hardly a year passed when persons were not prosecuted for refusing to destroy tobacco. The currency rapidly depreciated, going as low as half its par value. The deplorable state of the tobacco trade was set forth in early 1743 in an address which was written by Dulany and was presented by the governor and council to the Proprietor. Because of the poor quality of the colony's tobacco, it could not compete with Virginia's tobacco in trade transactions with English and French factors. Dulany attributed Maryland's difficulty to the unwillingness of the planters to submit to legislative controls intended to improve the quality of the crop. They still insisted upon exporting "trash," thus giving Maryland tobacco a bad name abroad. The superior quality of Virginia's staple export was due, the address explained, to that colony's inspection law which had originally been passed in 1730. The principal opponents of such a law in Maryland were the public officials, the lawyers, and the clergy, whose claims to fees specified in tobacco were fixed by law. If these tobacco payments were reduced and a stricter regulatory system for tobacco could be provided by law, the colony would prosper, it would attract needed immigrants, and it could dispose of the backlands to new settlers.

The agitation stimulated by this address and by the publicity given to it by the *Maryland Gazette* resulted in the enactment in 1747 of "An Act for amending the Staple of Tobacco, for preventing Frauds in his Majesty's Customs, and for the limitation of Officers' Fees." Originally enacted for five years, it continued in force until 1763. It represented an omnibus solution of the long controversies over the tobacco problem, the officers' fees, and the clergy's income. This act forbade that any tobacco be exported from the Province at any other place than from public warehouses after due inspection by officers appointed for that purpose. It designated eighty such warehouses and authorized the governor to appoint the inspectors for each from nominees chosen by the vestrymen and church wardens of each locality. The inspectors must open each hogshead and case of tobacco and test it as to weight and quality, and they were required to give to each person bringing tobacco promissory notes which would be valid throughout the county where the tobacco was inspected as payment for all debts and duties, parochial charges, and fees of officers and attorneys. The "forty per poll" tax for the clergy was now reduced to thirty pounds of tobacco. The act also established a table of officers' fees and contained provisions regulating the weights of tobacco casks, prescribing methods for nailing them, and fixing the requirements for inspectors. Of particular interest to debtors in the Province was a provision allowing one-fourth of a debt to be deducted if it was paid before May 16, 1747 in inspected tobacco.

This tobacco inspection act of 1747 successfully solved the old problems of declining tobacco prices, customs frauds, officers' fees, and the salary of the Anglican clergy. It did so by imposing an economy of scarcity and by limiting the freedom of Maryland's tobacco agriculturists. By establishing a stricter method of governmental control over Maryland's tobacco crop than had been provided in the paper money act of 1733, the inspection act produced a significant improvement in the quality of the tobacco exported from the Province and so acquired considerable popularity, though it continued to be an object of criticism by the clergy. As it tended to reduce the amount of tobacco raised in the Province, it encouraged the development of other branches of agriculture and gave the colony a more diversified and healthy economy. The clause which permitted debts to be scaled down if paid in inspected tobacco favored the debtor class and helped to reduce social discontent. The same could be said of the clause which provided for the issuance of tobacco notes, for these notes augmented the circulating medium in the colony and stimulated a new prosperity.

After the enactment of the inspection law of 1747, Maryland's experience with its paper currency, authorized by the act of 1733, became increasingly satisfactory. As that currency was gradually retired in accordance with the law, the value of the remainder of the currency in circulation rose rapidly and Maryland's currency was honored throughout the American colonies. There were some defects in Maryland's system, one of which was the scarcity of small bills which caused great inconvenience in making change. To remedy this defect, an ingenious Marylander, Stephen West, printed promissory notes of small denomination and circulated them for his own convenience. They were redeemable on demand at certain designated places including his own house in Upper Marlboro. He offered to call in his notes as soon as the legislature should issue a sufficient quantity of small notes to meet the needs of the Province. His notes circulated widely partly because they met a geniune need and could be redeemed in such small quantities that the users could not suffer great loss.[17]

When the accounts from the paper currency transaction were finally balanced in 1764, Maryland found that she had made a profit of £25,000 from the experiment. The law had been wisely administered, the amount of bills issued had been limited, they were regularly retired, and they rose in value after the inauguration of the tobacco inspection system.

In the short run, the political compromises which made possible the currency act of 1733 and the tobacco inspection act of 1747 resolved satisfactorily the major issues of the officers' fees and the quality of tobacco. However, at the same time, by highlighting more fundamental questions of the validity of English law and the role of proprietary and crown officials in the colony, they aggravated tensions, widened the developing chasm between the proprietary party and the popular party, and encouraged leaders of the popular faction to become increasingly assertive of colonial rights. But as yet the basic causes of friction between colony and mother country, involving the very rationale and substance of the imperial relationship, had been effectively glossed over.

Footnotes

[1] *An Historical View of the Government of Maryland from Its Colonization to the Present Day*, Baltimore, 1831, p. 282.

[2] Bernard C. Steiner, "Andrew Hamilton and John Peter Zenger," *Pennsylvania Magazine of History and Biography*, vol. XX, No. 3, pp. 405-408 (1896).

[3] *Maryland Historical Magazine*, vol. 29 (1934), 254.

[4] In an article in the *Maryland Historical Magazine*, vol. XLIV, No. 4 (December 1949), entitled "The Character of the Anglican Clergy of Colonial Maryland," the Reverend Nelson Waite Rightmyer attempted to exonerate the Maryland clergy of these charges.

[5] William Stevens Perry, ed., *Collections Relating to the American Colonial Church*, vol. IV (Maryland), pp. 89-91. See also Arthur Lyon Cross, *The Anglican Episcopate and the American Colonies*, pp. 39-42, 71-78.

[6] Newton D. Mereness, *Maryland As a Proprietary Province*, New York, 1901, 443.

[7] William Stevens Perry, ed., *Historical Collections Relating to the American Colonial Church*, vol. IV (Maryland), *passim*.

[8] Mereness, *Maryland*, 498, 499, 532.

[9] *Ibid.*, 375.

[10] Alsop, *A Character of Maryland*, Fund Publication No. 15, 68, Maryland Historical Society.

[11] *Maryland Archives*, vol. 35, 120.

[12] St. George L. Sioussat, *Economics and Politics in Maryland, 1720-1750*, The Johns Hopkins University Press, Baltimore, 1903. pp. 36-37.

[13] Thomas Bacon, *Laws of Maryland*, Annapolis, 1765, chapter 2.

[14] Calvert Papers, MMS. Letter No. 1087, also Fund Publication, No. 34, 68-81.

[15] "Sotweed Redivivus" was probably written by the Ebenezer Cooke, Gent., who wrote "The Sot-Weed Factor: Or, a Voyage to Maryland," published in London in 1708. It was highly critical of the tobacco industry in Maryland. See Bernard C. Steiner, *Early Maryland Poetry*, Fund Publication No. 36, Maryland Historical Society, Baltimore, 1900.

[16] *Maryland Archives*, vol. 39, 29-34, Upper House Journal, April 2, 1733, 273-280.

[17] *Maryland Gazette*, August 27, 1761.

Sources and Additional Reading

Alsop, George, *A Character of the Province of Maryland*, Fund Publication, No. 15, Maryland Historical Society, Baltimore, 1880.

Behrens, Kathryn L., *Paper Money in Maryland, 1727-1789*, Johns Hopkins University Studies, Series 41, No. 1, The Johns Hopkins Press, Baltimore, 1923.

Bridenbaugh, Carl, ed., *Gentleman's Progress: the Itinerarium of Dr. Alexander Hamilton, 1744*, University of North Carolina Press, Chapel Hill, 1948.

Christian, Charles M., and Thomas L. Christian, eds., *Two Hundred Years with the Maryland Gazette*, Annapolis, The Capital-Gazette Press, 1927.

Cooke, Ebenezer, *The Maryland Muse*, edited by Lawrence C. Wroth. Proceedings of the American Antiquarian Society, Worcester, Mass., 1935.

Gould, Clarence P., *Money and Transportation in Maryland, 1720-1765*, Johns Hopkins University Studies, Series 33, No. 1, Johns Hopkins Press, Baltimore, 1915.

Land, Aubrey C., *The Dulanys of Maryland: A Biographical Study of Daniel Dulany, the Elder (1685-1753) and Daniel Dulany, the Younger (1722-1797)*, Maryland Historical Society, Baltimore, 1955.

Perry, William Stevens, ed., *Historical Collections Relating to the American Colonial Church*, vol. IV, *Papers Relating to the History of the Church in Maryland*, published privately 1878.

Sioussat, St. George Leakin, *Economics and Politics in Maryland, 1720-1750, and the Public Services of Daniel Dulany the Elder*, Johns Hopkins University Studies, Series XXI, Nos. 6-7, The Johns Hopkins Press, Baltimore, 1903.

———, *The English Statutes in Maryland*, Johns Hopkins University Studies, Series 21, Nos. 11, 12, The Johns Hopkins Press, Baltimore, 1903.

Steiner, Bernard Christian, "Andrew Hamilton and John Peter Zenger," *Pennsylvania Magazine of History and Biography*, vol. XX, No. 3, pp. 405-408 (1896).

———, ed., *Early Maryland Poetry*, John Murphy Company, Baltimore, 1900.

———, "The Restoration of the Proprietary of Maryland and the Legislation against the Roman Catholics during the governorship of Capt.

John Hart, 1714-1720." In American Historical Association, *Annual Report . . . for the year 1899,* I, 229-307.

Werline, Albert Warwick, *Problems of Church and State in Maryland during the 17th and 18th Centuries,* The College Press, South Lancaster, Massachusetts, 1948.

Wyckoff, Vertrees J., *Tobacco Regulation in Colonial Maryland,* Johns Hopkins University Studies, Extra Volumes, New Series, No. 22, The Johns Hopkins Press, Baltimore, 1936.

CHAPTER XI

TIDEWATER AND WESTWARD EXPANSION

The principal areas of settlement in Maryland at the close of the seventeenth century were the shores of Chesapeake Bay and the valleys of the Potomac, Patuxent, and Patapsco Rivers as far inland as tidewater. The frontier line on the Western Shore corresponded roughly with the fall line running through the later sites of Washington and Baltimore. But already a few pioneers had pushed beyond that line into the Piedmont region following the north and south branches of the three main rivers and opening up a land area which would eventually form Carroll, Howard, and Montgomery Counties. There they encountered a stream of settlers moving southward from Pennsylvania. This westward shift of the population balance in Maryland was signaled by the removal of the capital from St. Mary's to Annapolis in 1695 and the founding of Baltimore in 1729.

By 1700 the primitive conditions of early frontier existence had been overcome. The standard of living rose rapidly throughout the eighteenth century, bringing new conditions of diffused comfort and even affluence. The planters of tidewater Maryland, with new wealth derived largely from land, tobacco, and the labor of Negro slaves, left behind the crudities and hardships of their frontier origin and developed a sophisticated social life modeled upon that of the mother country. As they increasingly emphasized the social amenities, they evolved the genial style of living that came to be associated with southern plantation life and that, in its distinctive Chesapeake Bay aspects, may be called the Maryland way. It was expressed in the simple elegance of plantation homes such as "Sweet Air" in Baltimore County, "Charles' Gift" on the Patuxent, "Whitehall" near Annapolis, and "Riversdale" and "His Lordship's Kindness" in Prince George's County.

The planters of the colony were fond of socializing. With their great houses, large families, abundant food, and many servants, they displayed a gracious hospitality. Their social life, dependent upon the plantation economy of the Chesapeake Bay region, centered in the clubs, "assemblies" or formal dances, and house parties of Annapolis, the "Paris of America," as Charles Carroll called it. There they participated in day-long fox hunts, sometimes commencing at one plantation and ending at another, and spending a large part of the night in drinking, dancing, and card-playing. Sufficiently affluent to afford leisure-time amusements, they acquired a wide reputation for conviviality and for interest in sports and games. Visitors commented on their fun-loving proclivities. "An universal Mirth and Glee reigns in Maryland amongst all Ranks of People, and at set times nothing but Jollity and Feasting goes forward," wrote the Reverend John Entick at the close of the colonial period. "You would think all care was then thrown aside, and that every Misfortune was buried in Oblivion." [1]

In many of these events alcoholic beverages were liberally inbibed, for drinking was a common practice among government officials high and low, the clergy, the planters, women, servants, seamen, and even Quakers. Among the favorite beverages, hard cider was the commonest being used by drinkers of all classes. Brandies were made from fruits growing in orchards and woods, including cherries, pears, peaches, elderberries, persimmons, and many others. Wine, beer, and ale were imported mainly from England, and the brewing industry did not become important in the colony until the Germans settled in Frederick County and raised barley, wheat, corn, rye, and oats in large quantities. Alcoholic liquors added zest to sports events and other diversions.

Among the latter, card-playing and dancing were favorites. On Chesapeake Bay and its tributaries Marylanders found inviting opportunities for the sports of fishing, boating, and skating in season. One of the earliest theaters in America was erected at Annapolis in 1752. Horse racing early became a popular pastime for members of the planter class, and Maryland races, held in the spring and fall, attracted wealthy planters and their blooded horses from other colonies. Annapolis possessed the best track for horse racing, and the first public races were held there in 1745. Other racetracks were laid out at Marlborough, Joppa, Chestertown, Elkridge, and Oxford, all situated in the tidewater region. The keen interest in this sport led "the principal gentlemen" to organize the Jockey Club of Annapolis in 1743 for the purpose of formulating rules and conducting the races as an orderly sport. It included among its members many officials of the Province and most of the landed gentry.

Some of Maryland's racing horses gained enduring fame. Spark, imported by Governor Samuel Ogle, had been given by the Prince of Wales to Lord Baltimore who in turn presented him to Governor Ogle. Selyma, the most famous mare of her day, was imported by Benjamin Tasker in Prince George's County, and she became the mother of the more famous Maryland-bred stallion, Selim, whose blood has flowed in the veins of many of the outstanding horses in United States racing history. The mother's fame is perpetuated into the twentieth century at the Laurel racetrack in the running of a race called the "Selima Stakes."

The Maryland way also found expression in the social and literary clubs which offered opportunities for their members to engage in lively discussion on current problems and cultural events. The South River Club of Anne Arundel County was probably founded as early as 1722, was granted land for a clubhouse in 1730, and is considered to be the oldest social club with a continuous existence in the United States. "The Ancient and Honorable Tuesday Club" was founded in Annapolis in 1745 at the home of Dr. Alexander Hamilton and included the leading wits and intellectuals of the capital.[2]

Class-conscious Marylanders of this dominant tidewater society were less innovative, less venturesome, less speculative than the Lees, Washingtons, and Fairfaxes of neighboring Virginia, and less inclined to mercantile pursuits than the colonists to the north. Accustomed to the amenities and conveniences of cultivated living, they could not appreciate the plight of the frontiersmen, living and fighting on the cutting edge of English civilization. For them the Maryland way was leisurely and complacent, but also individualistic, independent, and impatient of restraints. These latter traits found expression throughout the colonial period in the popular thrusts against the aristocratic pretensions as well as the financial levies of the Proprietor and the proprietary party. At levels below that of the proprietary party Maryland society was characterized by a high degree of mobility. Daniel Dulany, for example, who came to Maryland as an indentured servant, rose to become Attorney General of the Province, and others who made similar social ascents found in Maryland ample rewards for their industry, talents, and political perspicacity.

As the eighteenth century advanced, the economy of Maryland became increasingly dependent upon the labor of Negro slaves. The Negro had been introduced into Maryland at the time of the founding of the colony. Among the passengers on the *Ark* and the *Dove* who established the first settlement in Lord Baltimore's colony in 1634 was a mulatto, who probably was brought from Barbados. Eight years later Governor Leonard Calvert bargained with a shipmaster for the delivery of thirteen slaves, presumably Negroes, at St. Mary's.[3] The institution of slavery was recognized and regulated by law in the colony. Throughout the colonial period, or at least after 1692, any person coming as a resident into Maryland from any part of the king's dominions was allowed to bring his slaves free. As early as 1664, the Maryland Assembly passed an act obliging Negro slaves to serve for life, thus preventing them from suing for their freedom after they accepted Christianity. Seven years later the Assembly explicitly declared in "An Act for the Encourageing and Importation of Negros and Slaves into this Province" that neither slaves nor their progeny should be entitled to their freedom by reason of their conversion and baptism to Christianity.[4] This action was confirmed by the authorities in England in 1729, when, in response to an appeal from certain American colonists who were probably interested in promoting the Christianization of the blacks, the Crown Attorney and Solicitor General ruled that baptism did not change a slave's legal status. Slavery was therefore justified not as a penalty for heathenism but as a means of promoting the material prosperity of the colonies.

The union of slaves and free citizens presented many troublesome problems. As early as 1664 the Maryland Assembly declared that free English women who disgraced their nation by intermarrying with Negro slaves must serve as slaves as long as their husbands lived and that their children should serve as slaves until they were thirty years old. In 1715 the legislature forbade ministers and magistrates to marry any white to "any Negro whatsoever, or Mulatto Slave," and by an act of 1717 they excluded the testimony of any Indian or slave or free Negro or mulatto servant from all cases involving any Christian white person. By the beginning of the eighteenth century Maryland was receiving from 600 to 700 Negro slaves annually. A census list of the population of Maryland in 1712 shows that the Province contained 38,000 whites and over 8,000 Negroes and that in three of the southern counties the whites were greatly outnumbered by the blacks. By 1754 the whites numbered 107,963, the blacks 46,225. In the latter part of the eighteenth century shipments of slaves from Africa were not often advertised in the newspapers; most of the slaves offered for sale were born in Maryland and had acquired skills in a trade or a craft. Negro slavery supplied the major labor force of the colony and sustained its plantation economy.

The economy of Maryland, concentrating as did that of its sister colonies to the south upon the raising of tobacco, can be characterized as, predominantly, a system of commercial agriculture. But during the colonial period Maryland made some advances in manufacturing. By the operation of the Navigation Acts, designed to give the mother country a monopoly of the products of the colonies, Maryland, like England's other colonies in America, was encouraged to develop local industries. As these Acts were more strictly enforced and as the list of enumerated commodities that must be shipped to England was extended, the colonists gave increased attention to home industries. From other enactments of the British government, particularly the revenue laws, colonial industries also derived a certain amount of protection, and they were directly encouraged by the bounties sometimes offered by both the British government and the colonial governments for the purpose of discouraging imports from abroad. Such was the Maryland law of 1671 which granted a bounty of a pound of tobacco for every pound of hemp raised in the Province and two pounds of tobacco for every pound of flax in an attempt to restrict the importation of linen cloth.[5] In order to encourage the iron industry, Maryland exempted mechanics and other laborers employed in iron works from militia duty and the road tax, and during the War for American Independence extended the same privilege to employees of salt works and paper mills.[6]

But manufacturing was handicapped by Maryland's preoccupation with tobacco agriculture, by the lack of means for trading in a free world market, and by local impediments, among which may be mentioned the absence of towns, the lack of commercial information, and the difficulty of getting goods to market. Such conditions limited the possibility of developing centralized industries. But some of the larger plantations, operated by slave labor, provided a sufficiently large market for clothing, shoes, bedding, hardware, tools, and other implements as to constitute nascent manufacturing centers. In general, however, Marylanders preferred imported clothing for themselves and their slaves to the exclusion of home manufactures. Manufacturing in Maryland, over and above the rudimentary plantation industry, was largely instituted and financed by immigrants. The Principio Company, for example, was organized by British iron-masters who at first owned the entire stock but later admitted local Maryland and Virginia families to the enterprise.[7] It ultimately operated four furnaces and two forges and owned over 30,000 acres of land.[8]

By 1735 shipbuilding was fairly well established as an industry in Chesapeake Bay and its tributaries. Vessels of from 30 to 80 tons were being built at shipyards on the Choptank and the Nanticoke and at a shipyard at Fells Point which was operated by William Fell, the so-called "father of shipbuilding at Baltimore." For a time, Fells Point rivaled Baltimore, which had been authorized by the legislature on August 8, 1729, to be laid out on the north shore of the Patapsco River. But Fells Point was superior as a location for shipbuilding, shipping, and other marine activities. A report on colonial shipbuilding by Lord Sheffield in 1769 showed that out of 389 vessels built in all the colonies, 20 were built in Maryland, giving Maryland seventh place in the number of vessels built in the twelve shipbuilding colonies.

From the beginning of Maryland's history the Proprietor had derived his principal income from the exploitation of the land. He granted land originally to those who transported settlers into the colony, and he charged a perpetual quitrent on it. After 1683 the third Lord Baltimore added also a purchase price, called caution payment, of 200 pounds of tobacco per hundred acres. This price was steadily increased until 1717 when it was changed to money at 40 shillings sterling per hundred acres. In 1738 it was further increased from 40 shillings (£2) to £5 sterling per hundred acres, but there it remained until the War for American Independence. Frederick, the sixth Lord Baltimore, after succeeding his father, Charles, as Proprietor in 1751, determined to increase the revenue from his lands because he had extravagant tastes in horse racing and travel, because the population of his Province was rapidly increasing, and because the Penns were obtaining higher rates from their land. When he made an attempt to do so in 1753, however, he encountered such strong opposition from both Colonel Edward Lloyd, who was his agent in the colony, and from Governor Horatio Sharpe, that he abandoned the attempt. After the close of the French and Indian War he tried again to increase his revenues from Maryland's lands but was defeated by Daniel Dulany the younger.

Maryland offered special inducements to persons who would take up the backlands—particularly the lands along the disputed borders. Apparently as early as 1722 the colonial authorities began this policy of encouraging border settlements, but not until 1732 did the government offer special rates to settlers on the borderlands. It was encouraged to do so by the tide of German and other immigrants who were streaming from Pennsylvania across Maryland into the Valley of Virginia and whom Maryland wished to detain as settlers on her frontier lands. Accordingly, Maryland offered to any person with a family backlands of two hundred acres in the north and west between the Potomac and Susquehanna Rivers free of any purchase price and with a quitrent of only four shillings per hundred acres which would begin three years after settlement. The land became the property of the new owner in fee simple, that is to say, without any restrictions as to alienation of the property, but the quitrent must be paid in perpetuity. These inducements, which were later extended to the Eastern Shore, aided greatly in the settlement of the Province and ultimately increased the Proprietor's income. An example of the Proprietor's land-grant policy was the large tract on the upper Potomac which was patented to John Hawkins in 1753 and which was given the ornamental name Merry Peep o' Day. On it was later laid out a town which was originally called Berlin and was later renamed Brunswick.

The Proprietor organized a land office in 1681 to manage the sale of his lands and reorganized it in 1715, after he regained the government of the Province. The land office consisted of a judge and a keeper of the land records to grant warrants for taking up lands and to hear and decide disputes involving lands. All these officials, together with the surveyor-general, the examiner-general, their deputies and subordinates, received enormous fees, but because the land was looked upon as the private property of Baltimore and the land office was regarded as his personal agency, the Assembly was loath to reduce the fees of these officials. Even in the tobacco inspection bill of 1747 they did not reduce the land-office fees. In the later colonial period the fees of the land office were higher than those collected by any other branch of the government, and they constituted a severe burden on the settler. In 1764 Daniel Dulany estimated "that the Fees charged by the Judges or Registers of the Land-office, Surveyors, Examiner, Clerks, Chancellor, amount to an annual sum of at least, by the most moderate Computation, Half a Million of Tobacco."

The Proprietor of Maryland also claimed the money derived from the licensing of hawkers, peddlers, and keepers of ordinaries or taverns. For a considerable period of time, he collected the fees from this source and divided them among his secretaries, but in 1740 he was deprived of this revenue by the Assembly. The sixth Lord Baltimore revived his claim to these license fees as indemnity for alleged violations of his property rights but could not prevail upon the colonial legislators to divert these monies from a public use into his private treasury. Another source of revenue which the Proprietor sought to tap was the license fees for the operation of ferries in Maryland. The fifth Lord Baltimore instructed his agent Dulany to require ferry owners to secure licenses from him only. But his claims were blocked by the action of the County Court of Baltimore County, which asserted that the right to license ferries was theirs by custom, and by the Committee of Grievances of the Assembly, which pronounced Lord Baltimore's claim illegal. As a result the Proprietor surrendered his claim to these fees.

The chief purpose of the Proprietor's policy was to create a permanent revenue from the Province, and this he did by granting lands which were subject to the escheat, the alienation fine, and the quitrent. He received escheats of land when the owner failed of heirs or was subject to attainder of blood under the English law, and Baltimore extended the escheat to include forfeiture by suicide or treason and failure to conform to the conditions of the grant. Escheats must have returned a large revenue to the Proprietor, for many cases of this sort appear on the records. The Proprietor's extension of the English law of escheats did not arouse much opposition in the colony until 1760, but the Proprietor continued to profit from escheats down to the War for American Independence though he did so in the face of an ever-increasing opposition.

A second source of profit to the Proprietor was the alienation fine—a fine equal generally to one year's rent which was paid to the Proprietor on every alienation or transfer of land. But he was often bilked out of this fine by ingenious landowners who contrived to conceal their transfers of land. From this fine, therefore, the Proprietor received little profit. In 1754 Governor Sharpe suggested the novel scheme of a stamp tax as the only means of requiring all deeds to be registered; this should be imposed by Parliament, he declared, because the Maryland Assembly would never agree to it. His suggestion did not produce any results, and when the Proprietor later tried to secure a more rigorous enforcement of the alienation fines, he was blocked by his officers in the colony who were unwilling to carry out a policy which they knew would incur popular displeasure.

The heaviest burden on Maryland lands and the largest source of income to the Proprietor was the quitrent. This had been reserved to him from the beginning and was raised in successive "conditions of plantation" from twenty pounds of wheat to four shillings, and then to ten shillings for every hundred acres. In 1717 the Proprietor intimated that he would accept a duty of two shillings on every hogshead of exported tobacco as a full discharge of all quitrents and alienation fines, and at Governor Hart's suggestion this proposal was enacted into law. It relieved the Proprietor of the trouble and inconvenience of collecting quitrents from several thousand people scattered over the whole colony, and it increased his revenue from the Province. But it was viewed with increasing suspicion by the people of the Province as giving the Proprietor an undue profit. The Assembly nevertheless consented to renew it every year until 1733 when the delegates from the Western Shore defeated it. They felt that since the Eastern Shore was at this time turning from tobacco to grain, Western Shore tobacco producers ought not to be taxed on their tobacco exports to pay the commuted quitrents of the Eastern Shore grain growers.

Upon the termination of this commutation tax the Proprietor was once again obliged to collect his quitrents directly. He did so by farming them out to collectors of quitrents. The quitrent system, thus revived as a direct tax upon the lands in the Province, again became a cause of bitter complaint among the people. They were required to pay this tax in sterling coin, which was always scarce in colonial Maryland. Not until 1750 did the Proprietor agree to permit the quitrent to be paid in tobacco. But this concession gave relief only to the tobacco farmers of southern Maryland, not to the frontier farmers. The latter continued to protest that the Proprietor's rates were excessive and that his tax farmers were guilty of extortion.

To abate this latter criticism, the Proprietor's agent in 1754 required all the tax farmers and other receivers of quitrents to announce the rates in public notices posted in conspicuous places in order to eliminate fraud in the collection of the rents. But the total amount of revenue which the landowners in Maryland were required to pour into the coffers of the absentee Proprietor was considered a major grievance. The amount of the Proprietor's profits from the quitrents can be ascertained by Governor Bladen's statement to the Assembly in 1745 that the Proprietor had collected in that year £4,568,15s.4d, expected to collect £5,101,2s.2d in the following year, and would commute the quitrents for nothing less than £5,000 a year. Since these quitrents were regarded as oppressive, the Assembly sought to strike a new bargain with the Proprietor in order to commute the rents as before, but again tobacco growers of the Western Shore and grain growers of the Eastern Shore, who were almost evenly balanced in the Assembly, could not agree. They defeated a plan to tax nothing but tobacco, then failed to agree to a tax on grain, and finally dropped all export duties except those on tobacco and lumber. But this measure was rejected by Governor Bladen because it required the Proprietor to devote a part of his revenues to the defense of the Province.

With the accession of the spendthrift Frederick to the proprietary title, the new Proprietor made an effort to improve the system of collecting quitrents in order to gather increased revenues from his American Province. His uncle, Cecil Calvert, who became his secretary, worked out a scheme for compelling the sheriffs, as part of their duties, to collect the quitrents for a ten-percent commission, and he put this plan into practice in 1755. It lasted for twelve years but was never satisfactory. The avaricious Proprietor begrudged the ten percent for collection and tried to have it reduced to six percent, but could not persuade the sheriffs to accept this reduction. They found the work unprofitable even at ten percent and could carry it on only because they collected fees from the other duties of their offices. The sheriffs looked upon the collection of quitrents as a burden upon their offices;

at one time no one in Frederick County would accept the sheriff's commission, and it had to go to a man from Prince George's. Finally in 1767, the collection of quitrents was taken from the sheriffs and restored to private tax-farmers.

The Proprietor's receipts from manor rents, the ordinary sale of land, fees, and quitrents yielded him an enormous revenue, estimated in 1772 at £12,500 net a year. The quitrent in particular constituted a serious burden on the land of colonial Maryland and materially retarded the progress of the Province. Varying with the value of the land, it amounted to a property tax between one and twelve percent of the rental value of the land to be paid in perpetuity. Since the poll tax was collected for the support of the government, the quitrent was an additional charge collected for the sole profit of the Proprietor and not expended for governmental purposes. Moreover, it fell with equal weight upon the highly valuable land of Anne Arundel and Talbot Counties and the unimproved land of Dorchester and Frederick Counties. In comparison with the land values and taxes in Pennsylvania, Maryland's quitrents seemed unreasonably high, higher indeed than the land could bear. To the prospective settler, Maryland's heavily taxed land did not hold out attractive inducements and probably many settlers who were interested in Maryland turned off into other colonies. The Germans advancing into the great Appalachian Valleys at first avoided Lord Baltimore's colony for this reason; they and other immigrant families moved from Pennsylvania across Maryland into Virginia without taking up lands in his colony.[9]

Though Pennsylvania's quitrent was actually higher than Maryland's, its land was more valuable and was better improved by the industrious Germans; and Maryland's quitrent was twice as high as that of Virginia. The entire tax burden in Lord Baltimore's colony, including the poll tax, clergy's fees, fees to the land officials, and quitrents, was greater than in either of the neighboring colonies. But Maryland's system of quitrents produced the beneficial result of reducing the size of landholdings. When the quitrents were low, as in the early days of the colony, enormous tracts were taken up and erected into manors. The average land grant in Charles County before 1650 was nearly 1,200 acres. But this average fell as the quitrents advanced, and by 1735 the average size of the tracts warranted throughout the whole Province was only 158 acres. The quitrent, and to a lesser degree, the purchase price, tended to prevent a few individuals from monopolizing the land. In Virginia, where quitrents were lower, the landed estates were larger, population was even less dense than in Maryland, and fewer individuals possessed more wealth. In Pennsylvania, where quitrents were higher, landed estates were smaller, population was denser, and wealth was more equally distributed than in Maryland.

Maryland's unsettled boundary line with Pennsylvania was a source of continuing controversy between the Baltimores and the Penns until the last third of the eighteenth century. Lord Baltimore refused to relinquish his claims to the Delaware counties and in 1708 and 1709, at a time when he had been divested of his proprietary authority, he petitioned Queen Anne to set aside the order which King James II had issued in 1685, setting up a government for that colony, but his petitions were rejected. Charles Calvert, the fifth Lord Baltimore, finally agreed to a settlement with the sons of William Penn—John, Thomas, and Richard Penn—in 1732, renouncing his claims to the Three Lower Counties of New Castle, Kent, and Sussex and accepting the boundary line running west from Old Cape Henlopen to the middle of the peninsula and from the end of that line northwards up the peninsula to the western part of a circle with a twelve-mile radius drawn from the center of New Castle, then following that circle eastwardly to the Delaware River on the east. But as this agreement was not immediately put into effect, border incidents occurred between Marylanders and Pennsylvanians until Lord Chancellor Hardwicke in 1750 ordered Lord Baltimore to comply with the agreement. The Lord Chancellor's verdict was accepted as final by Frederick, the sixth Lord Baltimore, in 1760, and commissioners were appointed to run, mark, and lay out the boundary lines as provided in the agreement.

Meanwhile, the controversy between the Baltimores and the Penns over the disputed boundary between Maryland and Pennsylvania running west from the New Castle circle had broken out in border warfare in 1736 when Major Thomas Cresap, who lived on the Susquehanna River north of the present boundary line, was arrested by the sheriff of Lancaster County, Pennsylvania, and one of his men was killed in the skirmish. The governor of Maryland, Samuel Ogle, promptly dispatched Edmund Jennings, secretary of the Province, and Attorney General Daniel Dulany to Philadelphia to protest against the sheriff's action and to arrange "for effectually bringing to a just Punishment the inhuman Actors and Abettors of that savage Violence, as well as for restoring to Liberty and to a full Compensation for all their Hurts and Damages, the Persons of such who were hurried away into Confinement, and perhaps, may be still there detained by that Outrageous Multitude." But Jennings and Dulany accomplished nothing, for the

Pennsylvanians insisted that Cresap's house was located in their colony and that they therefore had exclusive jurisdiction over him.[10]

Even before the Pennsylvanians arrested Cresap, the Penns had instituted proceedings in chancery in 1735 to validate their boundary claims. After the border incident involving Cresap, the governors of both Pennsylvania and Maryland were enjoined by the King in Council to keep the peace. They accordingly agreed upon a temporary boundary line in 1739, which served until Penn's suit in chancery was settled in 1750 by Lord Chancellor Hardwicke. In accordance with his decision, both Proprietors soon afterward appointed commissioners to define the boundary between the two colonies, but their work was interrupted by the death of Charles, the fifth Lord Baltimore, in 1751 and the accession of a new Proprietor, Frederick, the sixth Lord Baltimore. The boundary then became involved again in litigation, which was terminated in 1760 by a new agreement between the Proprietors under which new commissioners were appointed. These commissioners, Charles Mason and Jeremiah Dixon, then began in 1763 to draw the boundary line in accordance with Chancellor Hardwicke's decision of 1750 and the subsequent agreement between the Proprietors, marking the boundaries and circle of Delaware and the line between Maryland and Pennsylvania. The so-called Mason-Dixon line, completed in 1767, followed the course mistakenly agreed upon by the fifth Lord Baltimore, and it made irrevocable Pennsylvania's acquisition of some two and a half million acres of Maryland's land situated south of the 40th parallel, which had been fixed as Maryland's northern border in its charter of 1632.[11]

In another boundary controversy, Maryland's claims to the territory lying between the north and south forks of the Potomac River were challenged by Virginia. According to Maryland's charter, its western boundary was to follow the meridian of the most western source of the "first fountain" of the Potomac. Maryland therefore claimed the south branch because it took its rise some sixty miles farther west than the north branch. Maryland's claim was reinforced by a survey commissioned by Frederick, Lord Baltimore, in 1770 and completed by Colonel Thomas Cresap, John Revely, and Dr. Charles Wheeler in 1772. But the region between the two forks of the Potomac remained in dispute between Maryland and Virginia until 1910 when it was decided by the United States Supreme Court against Maryland.[12] The Court based its decision on evidences of Maryland's frequent neglect to defend its western boundary claim and the resulting prescriptive rights of

Tidewater and Westward Expansion

the people living on the West Virginia side of the line arising out of long possession, custom, and traditional allegiance.

Until 1725 Maryland's western lands remained unsettled and even largely unexplored except for an occasional trapper or Indian trader. Tidewater Marylanders, looking to England for their economic and cultural contacts, were loath to venture into the heavily wooded regions beyond the fall line of the rivers. The area west of the headwaters of the Patapsco, Patuxent, and Gunpowder Rivers was described by the early map makers and explorers as consisting of the "barrens," or the Upper Piedmont Plateau, and successive formidable mountain ridges crossing the Province from northeast to southwest. The few trails that entered that area ran generally from northeast to southwest following the mountain valleys and provided no easy access from the tidewater region to Maryland's backlands.

In the western lands, Daniel Dulany first laid out in 1721 a tract named "Progress" extending some two miles along the east side of the Potomac below the mouth of the Monocacy River. And in 1725 Benjamin Tasker surveyed "Tasker's Chance" of 7,000 acres on the Monocacy. But not until 1729 was the first settlement made at Monocacy Village, situated near the later Creagerstown on the Monocacy trail. This trail ran from York in Pennsylvania through the Monocacy and Middletown valleys in Maryland to Williamsport on the Potomac and provided easy access into western Maryland for German immigrants from Philadelphia. As they found all the desirable tidewater lands already preempted, they moved out into the frontier areas beyond the fall line of the rivers, first settling in the mountain valleys west of the Susquehanna River along the Maryland-Pennsylvania border and then pushing southward to establish farm settlements in west central Maryland.

Western Maryland was therefore settled originally not by Marylanders but mainly by German immigrants who crossed the northern border of the Province and took up land in its intermontane valleys. In 1745 the town of Frederick was laid out on part of "Tasker's Chance," which had been patented by Benjamin Tasker in 1727 and sold to Daniel Dulany in 1744. To the new town Dulany gave land for churches and other public institutions. In the *Maryland Gazette* for September 1, 1747, he announced that he had "obtained a Patent for keeping a Fair at Frederick Town near Monocacy on the 21st day of October and the 10th day of May next, each Fair to continue three days, and for a Market to be held there every Saturday after the first of November next. All persons who will bring any Goods, Merchandize, Cattle or

Fort Frederick. View of south wall from outside, c 1920. Courtesy *Washington County Historical Society.*

Tidewater and Westward Expansion

anything else to the Said Fair or Market to sell shall be free and exempt from the payment of any toll, stallage, Piccage or any other charge for the term of Five years next ensueing this last day of August, 1747.—D. Dulany."

Dulany had the foresight to see the settlement possibilities as well as the speculative opportunities in western lands. At the time of his death in 1753 he owned more than 47,000 acres of land, of which 40,000 acres were situated in Frederick County. The importance of the new colonizing activity around Frederick was recognized by the legislature in 1748 when it created Frederick County, setting it off from Prince George's.

Already in the western part of the county a German immigrant, Jonathan Hagar, had been granted a tract of land which he named "Hagar's Delight." As other settlers arrived they laid out a town in 1762, named Elizabeth Town, in honor of Hagar's wife—a name which was changed to Hagerstown in 1814. The Germans who were attracted to the new county were offered liberal inducements to settle there, but they complained of the feudal exactions of the Proprietor, particularly his claims to quitrents. In the later political struggles between the popular and the proprietary parties, the settlers of the western counties usually espoused the cause of the people and resisted domination by the tidewater aristocracy, thus exhibiting the characteristics common to most of the frontiersmen in the American colonies.

The Germans became the dominant element in Maryland's frontier counties and retained their distinctive German culture well into the nineteenth century. Families cooperated in building primitive log cabins which served as the first homes of the German immigrants. They lived in close-knit families, each member necessarily helping the other to conquer the primitive forest and build a new way of life. Once established in village communities, they engaged in agricultural and handicraft pursuits, working as mechanics, harnessmakers and saddlers, weavers, tailors, tanners, shoemakers, papermakers, butchers, smiths, and iron workers. They were skillful and industrious agriculturists, noted for their large barns, their careful cultivation of the soil, and their use of animal fertilizer. Their principal farm crops were flax, corn, and wheat, much of which they sent overland by wagon to Philadelphia and Baltimore. In field labor the thrifty, industrious German women worked side by side with their husbands, raking hay, cultivating the tobacco plants, and harvesting the crops.

In their family life, the Germans retained their old-world fondness for sauerkraut and small beer. To this diet they added hominy, corn meal, cider, hog products, and many distinctive German recipes including *schnitzen* and *fastnachts*. When the settler's clothing wore out, he replaced it with handmade pantaloons, coat, leggings, and moccasins of deerskin. The women either wove or spun their dresses and petticoats of linsey-woolsey. The German women were noted for their scrupulously neat homes. The Reverend Andrew Burnaby, who traveled through the Maryland frontier communities in 1759 and 1760, reported that the people there "are subject to few diseases; are generally robust; and live in perfect liberty . . . and possess what many princes would give half their dominions for, health, content[ment] and tranquillity of mind."[13]

The settlers in western Maryland showed almost complete indifference to the politics of the colony. They were seldom bothered by the provincial government and for limited periods of time were not even subjected to the payment of quitrents. They remained a politically inert element in the life of the colony until the end of the colonial period. In the activities of the frontier churches—Lutheran, Reformed, and Moravian—they found virtually their only opportunity for political action.

The leading religious sect on the Maryland frontier was Lutheranism which, together with the Reformed and Moravian sects, the German immigrants brought from their homeland to Lord Baltimore's colony. Beginning in 1734, John Caspar Stoever, one of the two German Lutheran ministers in Pennsylvania, made annual visits to the Monocacy settlements in Maryland and in 1738 organized the first Lutheran congregation there.[14] A Lutheran congregation was formed in Frederick sometime between 1743 and 1746, possibly at the time when the town itself was laid out in 1745, making it the origin of the oldest Lutheran Synod in the nation. The first church building was constructed on a lot donated to the congregation by Daniel Dulany. As the importance of the Monocacy settlements waned, the center of Lutheranism in Maryland shifted from them to Frederick, from "the church in the hills" *(die Kirche am Geburge)* to "the church in the town" *(die Kirche an der stadt)*. The first Lutheran minister, a clergyman named Haushihl, arrived in Maryland and took up his pastoral duties in Frederick in 1752.

The Reformed denomination was first organized among German settlers in the upper Monocacy valley by a visiting clergyman, the Reverend Michael Schlatter, in 1747. Six years later, the Reformed churches in Frederick, Monocacy, and Conococheague received their first resident minister, the Reverend Theodore Frankenfeld. The Moravians, following the religious teachings of Count Nicholas Ludwig von

Zinzendorf who had founded a Moravian colony at Bethlehem, Pennsylvania, in 1741, engaged in zealous proselytizing in western Maryland, and there at Monocacy on land donated by Daniel Dulany they built their first church in 1749.

The long Sunday services, whether Lutheran, Reformed, or Moravian, in the German communities included music, both vocal and instrumental, and provided sometimes the only entertainment and opportunity for social intercourse available to the frontiersmen. For lack of resident pastors, the services were often conducted by the local schoolmaster or by itinerant clergymen, including some of the leading colonial preachers, for example, Henry M. Muhlenberg, who visited German Lutheran communities in Maryland in 1747, and Philip William Otterbein, who arrived in the Monocacy valley in 1760,[15] From Frederick the latter moved to Baltimore in 1774 to become pastor of the large Reformed Church where he took the lead in organizing a new sect called the United Brethren in Christ or, as it later became, the Evangelical United Brethren Church.

As population from tidewater Maryland advanced up the rivers into the frontier regions, the newcomers brought with them the Episcopalianism of the Established Church. An Episcopal chapel was built at Monocacy as early as 1737; ten years later the Maryland Assembly, in response to petitions from Anglicans in Frederick, appropriated funds for the construction of three Anglican churches in the area extending from Frederick to Conococheague creek. Because Episcopalianism was the established church, it flourished on public funds and seldom lacked church buildings and ministers, even in the remote frontier communities. Whenever the agencies of the secular government were established, the Anglican Church followed.

The tides of immigration flowing westward from the Chesapeake basin and southward from Pennsylvania thus gradually settled many of the unoccupied parts of Lord Baltimore's princely domain. They presaged future alterations of a fundamental character in the plantation economy and the social customs of the colony. Even the rising influence of Baltimore town, which was becoming a center of new industry, attested the changes which were subtly taking place in the economic and social life of tidewater Maryland. The tidewater gentry, however, still dominated the colony, and though many of them found both congenial public service and fortune in the proprietary party, others were growing increasingly restive under the exactions and restrictions imposed upon the colony by its foreign Proprietary.

Footnotes

[1] John Entick, *Present State of the British Empire*, London, 1774, IV, 438.

[2] Joseph Towne Wheeler, "Reading and other Recreations of Marylanders, 1700-1776," *Maryland Historical Magazine*, XXXVIII, Part 1, No. 1, March 1943, pp. 37-55, Part II, No. 2, June 1943, pp. 167-180. See also the same author's "Literary Culture in Eighteenth Century, Maryland, 1700-1776," *Maryland Historical Magazine*, vol. XXXVIII, No. 3, September 1943, pp. 273-276.

[3] Maryland, *Archives*, vol. IV, 189.

[4] *Ibid.*, vol. II, pp. 272-273.

[5] *Ibid.*, vol. II, 300.

[6] James Bisset, ed., *Abridgment and Collection of the Acts of Assembly of the Province of Maryland*, ... Philadelphia, 1759, pp. 130-131.

[7] *Pennsylvania Magazine of History*, XI, 63.

[8] Victor S. Clark, *History of Manufactures in the United States, 1607-1860*, Carnegie Institution of Washington, Washington, D.C., 1916, 173-174.

[9] Clarence P. Gould, *The Land System in Maryland, 1720-1765*, The Johns Hopkins University Press, Baltimore, 1913, 57.

[10] For details of this incident, see Kenneth P. Bailey, *Thomas Cresap: Maryland Frontiersman*, Boston, Massachusetts, 1944, 31-55.

[11] Thomas D. Cope, and H.W. Robinson, "When the Maryland-Pennsylvania Boundary Survey Changed from a Political and Legal Struggle into a Scientific and Technological Project," *Proceedings of the American Philosophical Society*, vol. 98, No. 6., December 1954, pp. 432-441.

[12] Maryland v. West Virginia, 217 U.S., 1-47, 1910.

[13] Andrew Burnaby, *Travels through the Middle Settlements in North America, 1759-1760*, T. Payne, London, 1765, 33.

[14] Abdel Ross Wentz, *The Lutheran Church of Frederick, Maryland, 1738-1938*, Evangelical Press, Harrisburg, 1938, 32.

[15] Carl D. Bell, *The Development of Western Maryland, 1715-1753*, M.A. thesis, University of Maryland, 1948.

Sources and Additional Reading

Bailey, Kenneth P., *Thomas Cresap: Maryland Frontiersman*, Christopher Publishing House, Boston, Massachusetts, 1944.

Bell, Carl D., *The Development of Western Maryland, 1715 to 1753*, M.A. thesis, University of Maryland, College Park, Maryland, 1948.

Bisset, James, ed., *Abridgment and Collection of the Acts of Assembly of the Province of Maryland, at Present in Force* ... William Bradford, Printer, Philadelphia, 1759.

Cope, Thomas D., and H.W. Robinson, "When the Maryland-Pennsylvania Boundary Survey Changed from a Political and Legal Struggle into a Scientific and Technological Project," *Proceedings of the American Philosophical Society,* vol. 98, No. 6, December 1954, pp. 432-441.

Culver, Francis Barnum, *Blooded Horses of Colonial Days: Classic Horse Matches in America before the Revolution,* Baltimore, 1922. Maryland, pp. [25]-[96].

Cunz, Dieter, *The Maryland Germans: A History,* Princeton University Press, Princeton, New Jersey, 1948.

Field, Thomas Meagher, ed., *Unpublished Letters of Charles Carroll of Carrollton, and of his Father, Charles Carroll of Doughoregan,* United States Catholic Historical Society. Monograph Series. Published by the United States Catholic Historical Society, New York, 1902.

Gould, C.P., *The Land System in Maryland, 1720-1765,* Johns Hopkins University Studies, Series 31, No. 1, Johns Hopkins Press, Baltimore, 1913.

Land, Aubrey C., "Economic Base and Social Structure: The Northern Chesapeake in the Eighteenth Century," *Journal of Economic History,* XXV, pp. 639-654 (December 1965).

Matthews, Edward B., "History of the Boundary Dispute between the Baltimores and Penns Resulting in the Original Mason and Dixon Line," *Maryland Geological Survey, Reports,* VII (1908), [105]-203.

Middleton, Arthur Pierce, *Tobacco Coast: A Maritime History of Chesapeake Bay in the Colonial Era,* Newport News, Virginia, 1953.

Mish, Mary Vernon, *Jonathan Hager, Founder,* rev. edn., Stouffer Printing Co., Hagerstown, 1962.

Nead, Daniel Wunderlich, *The Pennsylvania-German in the Settlement of Maryland,* New Era Printing Company, Lancaster, Pennsylvania, 1914.

Owens, Hamilton, *Baltimore on the Chesapeake,* Doubleday, Doran and Company, Inc., Garden City, New York, 1941.

Skaggs, David Curtis, *Roots of Maryland Democracy, 1753-1776,* Greenwood Press, Inc., Westport, Connecticut, 1973.

Wentz, Abdel Ross, *The Lutheran Church of Frederick, Maryland, 1738-1938,* Evangelical Press, Harrisburg, Pennsylvania, 1938.

CHAPTER XII

AN UNCOOPERATIVE COLONY

Soon after Frederick, the sixth Lord Baltimore, succeeded to the proprietary title in 1751, the venerable Samuel Ogle retired as governor of Maryland and his place was taken by Horatio Sharpe. Three months after Sharpe's arrival he received warning from London, addressed to all the colonial governors, to prepare for an attack upon the English frontier by the Indians and their French allies. The governors were instructed not to take the aggressive but to use force to protect English territory from invasion, and for this purpose they were advised to secure aid from their legislatures. Sharpe presented this letter to the Maryland Assembly and asked that it revive a law of 1704 which had levied a duty of threepence per hogshead on exported tobacco for the purchase of arms and ammunition; but his request was rejected. The Assembly deprecated the danger and informed the governor that "as there does not appear, at present, to be any pressing Occasion for imposing a Tax upon the People for these Purposes, we hope, that our Unwillingness to do it at this Time, will be rather ascribed to the real Motive of our Conduct, a Prudent Care of and Regard to, the Interest of our Constituents, than any Disinclination to the Service Recommended."

Contrary to the Assembly's opinion, the warning from London was justified and timely. War between the French and English empires was already preparing in the American wilderness. The French, expanding from their early settlements in the St. Lawrence valley, claimed all the territory drained by the Ohio River and its tributaries, considering that river system a vital link between their colonies in Canada and those on the Mississippi River. In 1749 France began to fence off this territory from the British; in that year the French governor of Canada sent Céléron de Bienville down the Ohio Valley to take official possession of it and to drive out British intruders. He took formal possession of the country but was unable to expel the British traders who crossed his path, and in 1752 the French, determined to protect their imperial claims, established a line of armed frontier posts at Presque Isle, Le Boeuf, and Venango reaching out from the Great Lakes southward toward the coveted valley.

But England also claimed this vast interior of the continent west of the Appalachian Mountains by the right of discovery and the sea-to-sea charters which she had granted to her seaboard colonies. In 1744, at a council held in Lancaster, Pennsylvania, the English were assigned control over the Ohio Valley by the Iroquois chiefs, who claimed suzerainty over it. English fur traders had already begun to build up a valuable trade in furs with the Indians in that valley, and in 1747 the English crown granted a half-million acres of land there to the newly formed Ohio Company for trade and colonization. In the following year, some 300 English traders were moving about through the forests of the Ohio country trafficking with the Indians and draining its rich fur and other resources eastward into the seaboard settlements. There the expanding empire of England was coming into conflict with the expanding empire of Louis XV.

In the American colonies the leadership in resistance to the French was taken by the Virginia government under pressure from land speculators and business interests who profited from the trade of the Ohio Valley. Governor Robert Dinwiddie of Virginia dispatched the young George Washington, a lieutenant in the Virginia militia, to the forts which the French had built in western Pennsylvania to warn them that they were encroaching upon lands claimed by England. When the French refused to heed this warning, Dinwiddie called upon the neighboring colonies in early 1754 for troops to aid in expelling the French. He suggested that the troops assemble at Wills Creek on the Maryland frontier and proceed westward under a Virginia commanding officer. At the same time, the Board of Trade directed the colonies to send commissioners to Albany to make plans for their common defense and to form alliances with friendly Indian tribes.

Governor Sharpe thereupon summoned the Maryland Assembly into session and laid before them both Dinwiddie's appeal for aid and the instructions from London. But the Assembly, after debating the matter for a week, reported that they failed to see that "any Invasion or hostile Attempt had been made against this or any other of his Majesty's Colonies." They considered it unnecessary, therefore, "to make any Provision for an armed Force which must inevitably load us with great Expence and which cannot, as we conceive, ... effectually cooperate, except in Case of an Invasion, with that of any other Colony." In response to the instructions from the Board of Trade, the Lower House voted £500 to be raised from the Proprietor's fees for licenses of hawkers, peddlers, and ordinaries (roadside inns) and to be spent in sending commissioners to the Albany Congress. But their proposal encountered resistance from both the Upper House and the Proprietor, who insisted that these fees, if they were to be collected again, must be restored to the Proprietor. The result was a deadlock between the two houses which blocked the legislation altogether. Since the Assembly thus refused both to furnish aid to Virginia and to authorize the governor to send commissioners to the Albany Congress, they were prorogued by the governor.

When the expedition under Captain Trent, which Dinwiddie had meanwhile sent out to the forks of the Ohio, was driven back by the French, Sharpe again convened the Maryland Assembly hoping that it would be impressed by the now more apparent danger and would vote money and men. This time the Assembly voted £3,000 but appropriated it again from money to be derived from licenses of hawkers and peddlers, thus insuring its defeat in the Upper House. Sharpe wrote to the Proprietor: "You will see that I am reduced to great Streights, by the People's determined Resolution to make Majesty's Service and his L'dp's Interest clash if by any means it can be so brought about." Sharp explained the Assembly's recalcitrance as due to the fact that (1) an election was approaching, and (2) "our people cd not as yet see things in their proper light & seemed to think the occassion of the present Dispute was who shd possess Lands the Lord knows where by the Determination of which they wd reap no benefit seeing the Lands were already granted by his Majesty to the Ohio Co." Maryland had a clearly defined western boundary and therefore could not expect to acquire from a war with the French any additional land. Nor could the colony expect to gain anything from supporting Virginia and the land operations of the Ohio Company. In these respects, her interests and policy coincided not with those of Virginia but with those of Pennsylvania, which adopted an attitude similar to that of Maryland's. The Maryland Assembly, however, did appropriate £150 to send two commissioners to Albany and made possible the selection of Benjamin Tasker, Jr., and Major Abraham Barnes for this mission. In general, its reluctance to join in collective effort against the French and their Indian allies gave early evidence of that individualism and spirit of local autonomy which stand out conspicuously in the later history of the colony and state.

When George Washington and his little band of embattled Virginians were obliged to surrender Fort Necessity in southwestern Pennsylvania to the French on July 4, 1754, thus exposing the American frontier to attack, Governor Sharpe again appealed to the Maryland Assembly. "The designs of the French must now be evident to everyone," he declared. "They have openly, in violation of all Treaties, invaded his Majesty's Territories, and committed most violent Acts of Hostility, by attacking and entirely defeating the Virginia troops under Col. Washington. In this Emergency, the Hopes and Expectations of our neighbors, whom in Duty, Honour, and Interest, we are engaged to support and defend, are fixed upon us for Assistance; and what must the World think of our Conduct or what Calamities may we not expect if, from an unreasonable Parsimony, we coldly look on, while they are cut to Pieces. The boundless ambition of the Common Enemy, and the cruel Rage of their savage Allies, now upon our Borders, flushed with Victory, indispensably require a vigorous and immediate Exertion of all our Powers, to check their Progress." Under this urging the Lower House voted £6,000 for defense but once more appropriated it from the licenses on hawkers, peddlers, and ordinaries. But this time so great was the emergency that the bill was approved by the Upper House and the Governor, though in doing so they violated explicit instructions from the Proprietor.

Sharpe now threw himself energetically into the preparation of colonial defense in cooperation with other like-minded colonial governors. He made plans to open a road all the way from Rock Creek to Wills Creek, he sent supplies of ammunition to Frederick, he began to recruit troops, and he instructed Colonel Thomas Cresap, who had established an Indian trading post on the north bank of the Potomac River at Oldtown five miles above the junction of its north and south branches, to purchase enough meat and flour to supply a force of one hundred men for a year. Cresap had already extended his trading operations west of Oldtown by constructing a storehouse at the junction of Wills Creek and the Potomac at the later site of Cumberland, and he had opened a narrow trail from that storehouse to a point called Turkey Foot. In 1752 he and Christopher Gist, with the help of a Delaware Indian named Nemacolin, extended this trail westward over difficult mountain country to the Monongahela.[1]

As hostilities with the French became more imminent, trails and wagon roads from tidewater Maryland to the west assumed new importance. Among these the two principal ones were the road from Georgetown to Frederick (the modern Route 240) and the other from Baltimore to Frederick (the modern Route 40). The increasing use made of these access routes to the west for the defense of the frontier stimulated the construction of roads and wagon travel and knit together more closely than ever before tidewater Maryland and its frontier settlements.

Meanwhile Sharpe's name was being pressed upon the crown in London by his two influential brothers, John and William, and by Lord Baltimore and Secretary Calvert for appointment as commander-in-chief of all the British forces in America, and he was commissioned to this position in July 1754. He received his commission in Williamsburg, where he conferred with Governor Dinwiddie of Virginia and Governor Arthur Dobbs of North Carolina. There they received word of a grant of £10,000 from the king, and they decided to use it to raise a force of 700 men and attack the strategically located Fort Duquesne which the French had built at the forks of the Ohio. When Sharpe returned to Annapolis, he began preparations for the attack and appealed to Governor Robert Hunter Morris of Pennsylvania, Governor William Shirley of Massachusetts, Governor Jonathan Belcher of New Jersey, and Governor James DeLancy of New York for assistance. He then proceeded to Wills Creek where the Marylanders had built a small fort poorly situated for defense purposes under a hill. This fort, originally named Fort Mount Pleasant, was soon renamed Fort Cumberland by its commander Colonel James Innes, in honor of the third son of George I, the Duke of Cumberland. The troops there numbered 300 and included a full Maryland company, 50 men from Virginia, and smaller contingents from New York and South Carolina. Virginia was guarding its own frontier with 100 men and voted £20,000 for colonial defense. New Jersey contributed £6,000 and New York £5,000. In this crisis the legislature of Pennsylvania, the only colony in which thus far any fighting had occurred, took no action because it was dominated by pacifist Quakers and was engaged in a bitter dispute with the Proprietor over paper money. Massachusetts and other New England colonies chose to utilize their military forces in the protection of their own frontiers

The English colonists were ill prepared to wage a war against even the weak and dispersed French forces in America. Few of them had any immediate experience of French enmity or were conscious of any resistance by the French to their own interests in the west. No roads ran through the dense forests and high mountain ranges that separated their seaboard capitals from the remote French garrisons in the St. Lawrence and Ohio valleys. They saw little need to put their settlements in a posture of defense, to organize a militia, to maintain frontier garrisons, and to provide munitions of war and a transport service. As each colony was loath to take measures for its own self defense, it was inhibited by rivalries with its neighbors from cooperating with them in a common defense. Militia officers were jealous of each other and resentful of the well disciplined British redcoats who now began to arrive and assume command positions over colonial troops. As Governor Sharpe reported, "The officers who bore His Majesty's commission would not deign to rank with those who served under his Governor's Commissions."

An Uncooperative Colony

Sharpe busied himself in overcoming these obstacles to united action. He ordered a new and better situated fort to be built at Wills Creek, and finding only one day's provisions there, he instructed Cresap to turn over his supplies to the fort. He then organized a commissary department, headed by Charles Dick, and set about procuring foodstuffs, arms, ammunition, and other supplies needed by the frontier forces. Realizing that "such Jealousies and Enmities subsisted between the officers of the Carolina Independants and the Virginia Regiment that their Meeting wouldshave been attended with innumerable Mischiefs and Confusion," he allowed these two forces to operate independently of each other. He also sought to eliminate extravagance and graft in the expenditure of colonial funds; one of Virginia's agents, Christopher Gist, was already using that colony's money to purchase goods for his own private trade with the Indians.

Despite these energetic preparations, Sharpe found the newly elected Maryland Assembly as uncooperative and unconcerned as its predecessors. The Assembly took under consideration the results of the Albany Congress, and after deliberating upon the Plan of Union which that Congress recommended to the colonies, unanimously rejected it "as manifestly tending to the Destruction of the Rights and Liberties of his Majesty's Subjects within this Province." In response to Governor Sharpe's urgent plea for appropriations to finance the defense of the colony, the house voted £7,000, of which £4,000 would be obtained from licenses issued to hawkers, peddlers, and keepers of ordinaries. When the Upper House and the Governor rejected this measure asserting the Proprietor's prior claim to these fees, the Assembly defiantly declared that these fees "are, and always have been, the undoubted right of the Country" and that "the Lord Proprietary of this Province, by his prerogative, can have no Right to impose himself any such Fine, Tax, or Duty, imposed by any Law of the Province, which now is or hereafter may expire, without the Consent of the Representatives in General Assembly." As a result of the deadlock on this question, the Assembly asked to be prorogued. Learning that royal troops were on their way to the American colonies, they abandoned all concern to protect the Province and decided to "let King George do it." Besides, they were influenced by the complacent attitude of the Pennsylvania legislature toward the war crisis and possibly also by the legislative opposition in that colony to the Proprietor over the currency issue. Sharpe was convinced that the conduct of Pennsylvania "influenced but too much I doubt their minds & Behavior & made them Averse ... to granting any further Supplies, unless by an Addition to the paper Cash already circulating in the Gov't to wh. scheme as it evidently appeared pregnant with many Evils & much Detriment to the province in general the Upper House & Assembly refused their concurrence."

Sharpe complied with the Assembly's request and prorogued it. He then regretfully abandoned his campaign preparations, largely because his own colony refused to support him. But the preparations which he had made helped his successor, General Edward Braddock, who was appointed in January 1755 by the crown to command the British forces in America and to protect the frontier against the French and their Indian allies. With him came two British regiments of Royal Americans who landed at Alexandria. Braddock immediately summoned the colonial governors to a conference at Alexandria and outlined his plan of operations against Fort Duquesne, Fort Niagara, and Crown Point. When he learned that no colony had contributed to the common fund, he was vexed and insisted that the governors once more solicit their assemblies. He wrote to Lord Halifax: "I cannot sufficiently express my indignation against the provinces of Pennsylvania and Maryland, whose interests being alike concerned in this Expedition, and much more so than any others on this continent, refuse to contribute anything toward the project."

The governors of several of the colonies had already decided to augment the British regiments with colonial recruits. But in the three colonies of Maryland, Pennsylvania, and Virginia, efforts to this end completely failed of results. Braddock therefore gave orders to enlist servants and secured many willing volunteers, though in doing so he encountered strong opposition from the planters and the government of Maryland. Sharpe tried in vain to persuade Braddock to revoke these orders because, as he wrote to Secretary Calvert, they imposed a hardship upon the planters, "as the Planters' Fortunes here consist in the number of their Servants who are purchased at high rates much as the Estates of an English Farmer do in the Multitude of Cattle."

Braddock's forces proceeded from Alexandria by way of Frederick to Fort Cumberland at the mouth of Wills Creek where they arrived in May with Fort Duquesne as their objective. But their conduct was so offensive as to arouse bitter resentment from the residents of the colony. Daniel Dulany wrote of Braddock's march through Maryland: "Many irregularities were committed by the troops in this Province, which nothing can excuse—our people were treated as slaves, and as arrogance unchecked knows no bounds, the military soon silenced the civil power, property became dependent on the moderation of a licentious soldiery triumphing over the sanction of laws, and the authority of magistracy."

After Braddock departed from Fort Cumberland on his westward march, Governor Sharpe again strongly urged the Maryland Assembly to grant more supplies to the expedition. In response to this appeal, the Lower House voted to raise £5,000 from the fees of licenses for ordinaries and by issuing bills of credit, but this measure was turned down again by the Upper House. Once more an appropriation for the defense of the Province was blocked by the perennial dispute between the Lower House and the proprietary party over the authority to collect these fees. Sharpe was anxiously concerned over the defense of the Province, and after failing to secure the support which he desired from the legislature, he tried to collect private contributions for the support of a military force of one or two hundred men, but his action was violently criticized by the Assembly. If the governor could thus raise money for a public purpose bypassing the legislature, they charged, he would destroy representative government in the Province and would deprive them of the power of the purse. This Assembly also quarreled with the governor on the Catholic question because of the appointment of the Catholic Attorney General of the Province, Henry Darnall, to the naval office at Patuxent, though Darnall qualified for the office by taking the required oaths. Once more the Province was thrown into a panic by the charge that the Catholics were plotting with the French for the destruction of the Province. The Catholics were even alleged to be organizing a slave insurrection. When the Assembly was finally prorogued, it was resentful and bitter toward the governor.

Braddock's disastrous defeat and death in battle with the French and Indians on the Monongahela River near Fort Duquesne in July 1755 left the English frontier undefended. Annapolis had been preparing to celebrate his victory and was thrown "into the greatest consternation" by the news of the rout of the British regulars. James Innes, who commanded the garrison at Fort Cumberland, sent a fragmentary report of it to Governor Dinwiddie on July 13, and five days later Captain Robert Orme reported it to Governor Sharpe from his bed at Fort Cumberland, in which he was recuperating from a wound in his thigh. Sharpe immediately summoned the Council in session, issued warnings to the Marylanders against a slave or convict uprising, and set out for Fort Cumberland. He learned that Colonel Dunbar, who had succeeded Braddock as commander of the British regiments, had decided to abandon the fort, and he met terrified frontiersmen who were retreating before the French and Indian menace. Dunbar's withdrawal to Philadelphia with the British troops and the independent companies from New York and South Carolina left Fort Cumberland in the hands of only a dwindling handful of troops from Virginia, North Carolina, and Maryland and created a great deal of bitterness in those colonies and in Pennsylvania because it exposed their frontiers to attack.

Sharpe now used the subscription money which he had collected to build a small fort on Tonoloway Creek and three small forts under North Mountain in the western part of Frederick County. Volunteer militia garrisoned them and patrolled the territory between them. But within a month after Dunbar's departure, the country for thirty miles below Fort Cumberland was deserted; by mid-October nearly one hundred Marylanders had been murdered or carried away as prisoners. The *Maryland Gazette,* published by Jonas Green at Annapolis, reported "Our Accounts from the Westward, are truly alarming: All the Slaughters, Scalpings, Burnings, and every other Barbarity and Mischief, that the mongrel *French,* Indians, or their Chieftain the Devil, can invent, are often perpetrated there, and approach us nigher and nigher." Dinwiddie proposed that Pennsylvania, Maryland, and Virginia cooperate in building a fort beyond the mountains, but the deadlock in Pennsylvania between Governor William Denny and the Assembly on the question of paper money prevented that Province from taking any action; and Governor Sharpe declined to convene the Maryland Assembly because, as he said, Pennsylvania's example "is too grateful to our Folks for me to give them an Opportunity of pursuing a similar scheme."

Only the crisis caused by Braddock's defeat and the resultant harassment of the Maryland frontier and decline in the sale of the Proprietor's western lands finally induced Lord Baltimore to waive his claim to the licenses on ordinaries, and his decision on this point did not reach Sharpe until the close of the year. Sharpe was thoroughly discouraged and wrote that "this Year's Experience I flatter myself has demonstrated that the Colonies are not to be depended upon for Assistance & unless the People are obliged by an Act of Parliament to furnish Horses, Waggons, & etc. to the utmost of their Power to forward any future Expedition it will be in vain to concert Plans for Conquest or undertake any Enterprise on the Continent of America."

Braddock's successor as commander-in-chief of the American forces was Governor Shirley of Massachusetts. He asked the colonies to send commissioners to New York to make plans for a spring campaign against the French and Indians. At that conference meeting in December, the colonies decided to make Crown Point their main objective and to launch attacks upon Quebec, Fort Duquesne, and the French posts on Lake Ontario. When Sharpe presented these plans to the Maryland Assembly, the Lower House voted £40,000 for military purposes and ordered that this sum be raised by taxing imported convicts and wine and spirits in the Province, but this proposal was vetoed by the Upper House. A compromise measure was then drafted levying upon every landowner—including the Proprietor, who was the largest landowner in the Province—a tax of one shilling upon every one hundred acres and double that amount from Catholics. Sharpe finally allowed himself to be persuaded that this supply bill was necessary to the preservation of the Province and gave it his reluctant approval. In justifying his action to the Proprietor, he explained that already the Proprietor had lost £1,600 in rent because his frontier lands had been abandoned by the settlers and he hinted at the possibility of tax evasion by pointing out that the law did not provide for assessors, as did a similar law passed in Pennsylvania.

Out of the £40,000 provided in this bill, the Maryland legislature set aside £11,000 to build a fort on North Mountain sixty miles east of Fort Cumberland, £25,000 for an expedition against Fort Duquesne, £3,000 to be used in negotiations with the southern Indians, and £1,000 as scalping money. Meanwhile, the English frontier of settlement from New England to the Carolinas was being pushed farther and farther eastward by the Indians. In Virginia, settlers were even deserting the area around Winchester in Frederick County. Colonel George Washington reported to Governor Dinwiddie in the spring of 1756, "You may expect by the time this comes to hand that without a considerable reinforcement, Frederick County will not be mistress of fifteen families. They are now retiring to the securest parts in droves of fifties." At the same time, the settlers around Carlisle, Pennsylvania, began to retreat eastward leaving the northwestern frontier of Maryland exposed to Indian attacks and making Conococheague the westernmost settlement in Maryland. In the following June, Governor Sharpe started to construct Fort Frederick located fourteen miles west of Conococheague on North Mountain near the Potomac River.

Meanwhile, England had formally declared war on France and appointed John Campbell, fourth Earl of Loudoun, as commander-in-chief in America. After the new commander arrived in New York with two skeleton infantry regiments, he and his agents proceeded to recruit troops, but when they enlisted servants of the Maryland planters, they encountered violent opposition and had many of their recruits forcibly wrested from them. As they lost Oswego to the French in August 1756, they were obliged to surrender to the French and Indians complete control over the region of the Great Lakes and Pennsylvania. The Maryland frontier was again harried and hundreds of settlers were driven as far east as South Mountain. Nevertheless, the Marylanders were slow to enlist in Loudoun's regiments, and the Maryland Assembly declined to comply with the governor's recommendations for the defense of the Province. The governor in disgust then prorogued the Assembly and wrote to Calvert: "The oftener they are convened the less tractable they grow & become more extravagant in their Demands on the Gov." [2]

French successes in America, the Mediterranean, and India resulted in the overthrow of the Newcastle ministry in England in November 1756 and the accession of William Pitt to power. The English government immediately began to make vigorous preparations for winning the war in America. Loudoun called a meeting of southern governors to convene at Philadelphia in March 1757 and there laid plans for an American campaign. He projected an attack upon Louisbourg, offered to send five companies of his Royal Americans to protect South Carolina, and entrusted the defense of the western frontier to Pennsylvania, Maryland, and Virginia, expecting Maryland to help open the line of communication between Fort Frederick and Fort Cumberland. But the Maryland Assembly still demurred and refused to garrison a fort so far west of the settled region as Fort Cumberland. Loudoun immediately protested to Governor Sharpe against "this unprecedented Step of the Assembly of your Province." Nevertheless, the following Assembly likewise refused to support a garrison at Fort Cumberland, and in November 1756 the Lower House, though it authorized an appropriation to maintain three hundred men, confined their service to Fort Frederick and Conocoheague and directed them not to obey any orders from Loudoun.

In the Maryland Assembly of thirty-eight voting members, Frederick County, which comprised the entire western section of the Province, with an estimated population of 25,000, had only three representatives. The legislature was dominated by its tidewater members and continued to be indifferent to the interests of western Maryland. Its recalcitrance was attributed by Sharpe to the influence of Pennsylvania's example. Writing to a correspondent in England, he explained that "To the Proceedings of the Assembly of that Province, & a few evil disposed Persons among ourselves I am endebted for all the Trouble that I have at times met with. It is not enough for them to be a Democracy themselves, but they would willingly have their neighbors in the same situation; however I congratulate myself on being vested with a Power which Mr. Denny wants, & I flatter myself that by my Steadiness & Integrity I shall convince every Man of common Understanding among us that the

Peoples Liberty & Proprieties would become very precarious if the Lower House of Assembly was alone to possess all the Power that is now distributed among the several Branches of our Legislature." The Assembly finally appropriated a meager £200 to be used in provisioning and quartering five companies of the Royal Americans in Annapolis, but when the governor ordered some of them to the frontier, members of the Assembly tried to prevent them from marching. At the time when the legislature adjourned, soldiers at Forts Cumberland and Frederick had gone without pay for eight months. General Loudoun, realizing that if the Maryland men were to remain on duty they would have to be paid by the British treasury, offered to guarantee their pay but stipulated his offer as a loan payable when the Assembly should come to their senses.

Under the inspired leadership of Pitt, England began to turn the war to her advantage. As British forces occupied French Acadia, Maryland received several hundred of the French deportees from that colony, who settled on the southern outskirts of Baltimore at a place long known as French Town. In 1758, English armies captured Louisbourg, Duquesne, and finally Fort Frontenac, and compelled the surrender of the entire chain of French forts in the Ohio Valley, breaking France's power in the west. In the following year, General Wolfe captured Quebec and in 1760 the English took Montreal. With its capture, England brought the Seven Years' War in America to a close.

The Peace of Paris of 1763 marked a turning point in the relations of Great Britain to her colonies. The mother country was confronted with the task of recasting her imperial policy, of providing efficient administrative machinery for her newly acquired world empire, and of readjusting the acts of trade to meet the new situation. Maryland's indifference to the French and Indian War and its use of the war to extort concessions from the governor had been matched by the actions of other colonies, which ignored royal requisitions for troops and money, evaded the commercial restrictions imposed by the British authorities, and continued to trade with the enemy throughout the war. The particularistic course of the colonial legislatures in America during the recent war had shown that the requisition system could not be depended upon to furnish a permanent revenue for a colonial military establishment, and the lawlessness of the colonial merchants had proved the need for reforming the administration of the trade laws. Parliament, therefore, under the leadership of George Grenville, proceeded to adopt an imperial policy which responded to the needs of British mercantile interests and the views of the Board of Trade. Moreover, the British government undertook to deal with the pressing Indian problem in America which was brought to an issue by the conspiracy of Pontiac.

As the French lost their empire in North America, their Indian allies west of the Appalachian Mountains intensified their hatred of the victorious British, their new masters. They now felt the loss of the generous gifts which they had customarily received from the French, they resented the abuses that they had long suffered at the hands of English traders, and their antagonism to the British was stimulated by French propaganda. In Pontiac, an influential Ottawa Chief, the Indians found an able champion, and under his leadership they rose against the English in May 1763.

After the British forces captured Fort Duquesne, changing its name to Fort Pitt, settlers immediately began to flock back into western Maryland. By 1759, they had settled the westernmost part of the colony as densely as before the war with the French, and they enjoyed there a quiet, peaceful life. But with the outbreak of Pontiac's rebellion, the Maryland frontiersmen were forced to take refuge in the nearest forts. A news item from Frederick in *The Maryland Gazette* for July 28, 1763, reported: "Every Day, for some Time past has offered the melancholy Scene of poor distressed families driving downwards through this Town, with their Effects, who have deserted their Plantations, for Fear of falling into the Cruel Hands of our Savage Enemies, now daily seen in the Woods. And never was Panic more general or forcible than that of the Back Inhabitants, whose Terrors, at this Time exceed what followed on the Defeat of General Braddock, when the frontiers lay open to the Incursions of both French and Indians." Sharpe at once dispatched several parties of militia to the frontier to subjugate the Indians. When Pontiac's conspiracy was soon afterward crushed, the western settlements quickly became peaceful again, but the frontiersmen now found their further westward advance and their lucrative trading activities blocked by the policy of the British government reserving the land west of the Alleghenies as an Indian hunting ground and prohibiting all white settlement in that region. The British thus replaced the French as barriers to the westward expansion of the seaboard colonies.

The French and Indian War and Pontiac's conspiracy emphasized to British policy makers that the American colonies could not be trusted to provide for their own defense. A strong force of British regulars would have to be maintained there to protect them from their enemies. Since the financial resources of the home government were already

An Uncooperative Colony

strained, these forces would have to be financed by the colonies. In the colonies the method of requisition which England had used had completely broken down during the war and must obviously be replaced by parliamentary taxation—a method which had been recommended by Governors Shirley, Sharpe, and Dinwiddie and by Generals Braddock and Loudoun. The British government therefore decided in 1763 to keep a standing army of 10,000 men in America and to tax the colonies for their support.

England's government, accustomed to legislating for a small and reasonably well united kingdom, now essayed therefore for the first time to legislate for an overseas empire with interests diverse from those of the mother country and offering few precedents for legislative wisdom in such matters. In the year after the Peace of Paris, Parliament passed the Sugar Act for the express purpose of raising revenue to defend and protect the American colonies. This act revised the old Molasses Act of 1733. Though it lowered the molasses duty from six to threepence per gallon, it provided for strict enforcement of the duty requirements. In addition, it levied duties upon sugar, coffee, wines, and other foreign commodities imported into the colonies. But the Sugar Act did not affect Maryland, whose chief industry was the raising of tobacco, not the distilling of rum, nor did the Currency Act, which was passed by the Grenville ministry and which forbade the colonies to issue paper money as legal tender, injure Maryland for Maryland's paper money was already backed by stock in the Bank of England. And the Quartering Act, which required the colonies to provide His Majesty's troops with quarters and certain supplies, did not involve Maryland since Britain chose not to station any troops there.

Since the revenue derived from the Sugar Act would furnish only about one-seventh of the cost of maintaining the army in America, the British government looked about for other sources of revenue. Finally in 1765 the insensitive and pettifogging Grenville introduced a Stamp Act which was enacted into law by Parliament almost without opposition.

Even before the enactment of the Stamp Act, the commercial colonies north of Maryland had organized an opposition to the new British measures of taxation and sought to enlist the support of the plantation provinces in their campaign. They expected to secure ready assistance from the tobacco growers of Virginia and Maryland, who were restive under their chronic indebtedness to British merchants. The planter Thomas Jefferson declared that in Virginia "these debts had become hereditary from father to son, for many generations, so that the planters were a species of property annexed to certain mercantile houses in London." The tobacco provinces responded the more readily to the appeals of the commercial provinces because of the unsatisfactory condition of crop prices and the scarcity of money. George Washington explained to a creditor that he had fallen "so much in arrears" because he had not "even tolerable crops" for three straight years, and when he had one it did not sell well. But these conditions were not directly attributable to the Sugar Act of 1764, and the southerly provinces did not render material support to the commercial provinces until after the passage of the Stamp Act.

The Stamp Act was more purely a fiscal measure than was the Sugar Act, and it fell on people in all the American provinces. This Act imposed duties on commercial papers of various kinds, on deeds, bonds, leases, and other legal documents, on pamphlets, newspapers and advertisements, and on articles of apprenticeship, liquor licenses, and other similar papers. The Act provided a common ground on which the planting provinces could join with the commercial provinces and furnished a basis for complaints against "taxation without representation" and "trial without jury." Moreover, by taxing pamphlets, newspapers, and other instrumentalities of public information and communication, it stirred up articulate organs of protest in the colonies.

On April 18, 1765, when news of the Stamp Act reached the colonies, *The Maryland Gazette* published the following ominous announcement: "This Gazette, No.1041, Begins the Twenty-first Year of Its Publication: But alas! must soon Droop and Expire, at least for some time, if the melancholy and alarming Accounts, we have just heard from the Northward, prove True, That an Act of Parliament is shortly to take Place laying a heavy and insupportable *STAMP DUTY* on all American Gazettes." The *Gazette* later reported that the people of Maryland were "much disgusted" because a "Notion had been entertained by many that Maryland was by its Charter particularly exempted from all Impositions except what should be laid by the Assembly." Lawyers in particular violently denounced the act, but Governor Sharpe felt that "their Warmth" would soon cool.

In August, Marylanders learned that Zachariah Hood, an Annapolis merchant, had been named stamp distributor for the colony. When he returned from England to Maryland, the people assembled in all parts of the Province to express their indignation. Charles Carroll of Carrollton wrote "Our stamp-master, Zachariah Hood, is hated and despised by everyone; he has been whipped, pilloried and hanged in effigy, in this place, Baltimore town, at the landing; the people seem determined not to buy his goods." In Annapolis the people made an effigy of Hood, placed it in a horse cart, and, to the tones of a solemn knell, paraded it through the streets, then hanged and burned it. Later a mob wrecked Hood's store at Annapolis and forced him to flee from the colony. Governor Sharpe believed that if Hood had been "a Person of any Note in the Province or connected with people of any Consequence," he would not have been treated so roughly. He wrote to Lord Baltimore: "I assure your Ldp. that when the People are so unanimous in opposing the execution of a Law as they are on this Occasion nothing but a Military Force can produce obedience to it."

Hood's friends in Maryland were quick to disclaim any intention of assisting him. Alexander Laing printed a notice in *The Maryland Gazette:* "Whoever says that I am appointed Deputy Stamp Master for Dorchester Somerset and Worcester Counties, is a Lyar; and I declare that I will not accept an Office so Detestable and Injurious to the Country." In New York, whence Hood had fled, the Sons of Liberty threatened him with violence unless he resigned his position and so forced him to do so. Hood did not return to Maryland until the storm had blown over.

Maryland meanwhile had received from Massachusetts a Circular Letter against the Stamp Act, and on the petition of many Maryland citizens, Sharpe summoned the Assembly into session. When it convened, it immediately appointed three members, Edward Tilghman, William Murdock, and Thomas Ringgold, to represent the colony in the Stamp Act Congress at New York and empowered them to join with the other colonies in a "General, and United, Dutiful, Loyal, and Humble Representation" to the King and Parliament against the Act and to "take Care that such Representation shall, humbly and decently, but expressly contain, an Assertion of the Rights of the Colonists, to be exempt from all and every Taxation and Impositions upon their Persons and Properties, to which they do not Consent in a Legislative Way, either by themselves, or their Representatives, by them freely chosen and appointed." They also adopted resolutions which, among other things, stressed the rights that Marylanders enjoyed under Magna Carta, the Petition of Right, and the Bill of Rights, as well as the Charter of Maryland granted to Cecil Lord Baltimore in 1632 exempting Marylanders from "any impositions, customs, or other taxations." "It is the Unanimous Opinion of this House," they declared, "that it cannot, with any Truth, or Propriety, be said, That the Freemen of this Province of Maryland are Represented in the British Parliament." Furthermore, they asserted that "the Representatives of the Freemen of this

Province, in their Legislative Capacity, together with the other Part of the Legislature, have the sole Right to lay Taxes and Impositions on the Inhabitants of this Province, or their Property and Effects; and that the Laying, Imposing, Levying, or Collecting, any Tax on, or from the Inhabitants of Maryland under Colour of any other Authority, is Unconstitutional, and a direct Violation of the Rights of the Freemen of this Province."

The temper of the people was shown by an incident that occurred when a tender belonging to His Majesty's sloop *Hornet* arrived in Annapolis. The officer of the tender, Mewbray, was taunted by John Hammond, one of the leading critics of England's policy in the Maryland Assembly, and became involved in a fight with him in an Annapolis tavern. He was then set upon by a mob and was wounded in the affray.

At this time Daniel Dulany the Younger published anonymously his pamphlet, "Considerations On The Propriety Of Imposing Taxes in the British Colonies." Dulany was one of the leading lawyers of Maryland, and his pamphlet was later glowingly eulogized by Pitt, the champion of the American cause, in a speech in the House of Commons. Dulany cogently presented the arguments of the colonists against the Stamp Act on both constitutional and economic grounds. Though he admitted the right of Parliament to impose external taxes upon the colonists under its power to regulate the trade of the empire, he denied its right to impose internal taxes upon them without their consent. Since the colonies enjoyed only "virtual representation" in Parliament—a representation which was no representation at all—they could not be taxed by Parliament. "It is an essential principle of the English Constitution," he declared, "that the subject shall not be taxed without his consent," and he pointed out that Parliament had not in any previous enactment made revenue its sole object.

This particular revenue measure, in addition, Dulany said, was inequitable, for it fell upon a Province "not in proportion to its wealth, but to the multiplicity of juridical forms, the quantity of vacant land, the frequency of transferring landed property, the extent of paper negotiations, the scarcity of money, and the number of debtors," and he argued that "the principal part of the revenue will be drawn from the poorest individuals in the poorest colonies, from mortgagers, obligors, and defendants." He strongly stressed the economic grievances of the colonists against the mother country, now aggravated by the Stamp Act, and cited the experience of the tobacco planter, who, he said, "pays a tax upon that produce of his land and labour consumed in Great Britain, more than six times the clear sum received by him for it, besides the expences of freight, commission, and other charges, and double freight, commission and charges upon the tobacco re-exported, by which the British merchants, mariners, and other British subjects are supported." Indeed, the balance of the colonial trade with the mother country was against the colonies and it could only be corrected if England encouraged, instead of discouraging, the trading activities of the colonies.

Dulany's pamphlet, showing literary skill, legal learning, and cogent logic, became at once one of the best defenses of colonial rights and exerted considerable effect both in the colonies and in England. Dulany, it should be noted, admitted the authority of Parliament over the colonies, but he recommended the development of colonial industry as a means of compelling England to abrogate this offensive tax measure. Already people in all the provinces, including Maryland, had begun to develop home manufacturing and they now determined to boycott English goods. It became the fashion for men and women to appear in homespun clothes.

As the day approached for the Stamp Act to take effect, it was anticipated that all business would stop. *The Maryland Gazette* appeared with the large headline "**EXPIRING** ' and ceased publication on October 10. On November 1 the public offices, customs houses, and nearly all the courts closed their doors because of lack of stamps, but the court in Frederick County continued defiantly to transact business without stamps. The Sons of Liberty in Frederick assembled to celebrate the court's independence. They carried through the streets a coffin bearing the inscription "The Stamp Act, Expired of A Mortal Stab Received from the Genius of Liberty In Frederick County Court, 23d November 1765 Aged 22 days," which they buried with great ceremony. By February 1766 an association of Sons of Liberty was formed in Baltimore, and soon afterward a similar association was organized in Annapolis under the leadership of Samuel Chase and William Paca. In response to their demands, many of the courts reopened and proceeded to conduct business without the stamps. For this action Samuel Chase was denounced by the more conservative elements as "a busy body, a restless incendiary, a ringleader of mobs, a foul mouthed and inflaming son of discord and faction, a promoter of the lawless excesses of the multitude." To these charges he defiantly replied: "I admit that I was one of those who committed to the flames in effigy the stamp distributor of this province, and who openly disputed the parliamentary right to tax the colonies, while you skulked in your houses, some of you asserting the parliamentary right and esteeming the Stamp Act as a beneficial law. Others of you meanly grumbled in your corners, not daring to speak of your sentiments."

Pressure both from the colonies and from the merchants in England whose economic interests were adversely affected by the colonial boycott impelled Parliament to repeal the Stamp Act. News of its repeal was received with rejoicing in Maryland. In Annapolis the day was spent in "mirth" and in drinking patriotic toasts. Chestertown started to collect a subscription to erect a monument at Annapolis in honor of Pitt, who had opposed the Act from the beginning. The Maryland Assembly adjourned after drinking "patriotic" toasts while the guns at the dock boomed a salute. Even Hood ventured back to Annapolis and reopened his business. And Sharpe wrote to the Proprietor, "I must also in Justice to the Inhabitants of this Province in general assure your Ldp that since the Repeal of the Stamp Act was notified to them they have not shown the least Signs of Discontent nor have Murmurings been heard among them, but as far as I can judge their Behavior has manifested the Highest Satisfaction at the late Measures of the British Legislature & while their Declarations have been expressive of unfeigned Loyalty & Gratitude to our most Gracious Sovereign & of the greatest Attachment to the Mother Country."

The Lower House of the Assembly voted to purchase a marble statue of Pitt to be set up in Annapolis, and both Houses sent separate messages to the King thanking him for consenting to the repeal of the Stamp Act. Its repeal seemed to restore harmonious relations between England and her American colonies, but it failed to settle any of the issues that it raised. And its repeal was accompanied by an ominous Declaratory Act in which Parliament claimed the right to make laws to bind the colonies in all cases whatsoever, thus seeking to dispose of the colonial arguments against "taxation without representation" and "external versus internal taxation." This foreshadowed future disagreements between England and the colonies over taxation.

In these disagreements Dulany took no part. He opposed no subsequent tax of the British government and eventually abandoned the American cause to give loyal support to the crown. Governor Sharpe also would not play a direct role in later relations between the colonies and the mother country, for in July 1768 he was obliged to resign from the office of chief executive of Maryland. It is difficult to determine the reasons for his dismissal, for he had always been on cordial relations with Lord Baltimore, Secretary Calvert, and the latter's successor, Hugh Hamersley. Secretary Hamersley explained to him on behalf of the Proprietor that "the workings of Nature, the Merit of his Brother in

Law, to himself particularly, and the Sollicitations of Relations have at length prevailed, and forced him to take the Painful Resolution of Delegating the Successor to Mr. Eden, for I am thoroughly satisfied, and he has Authorized me to say no other Successor would have been sent you by him, unless you had first desired it." Sharpe suspected that certain persons had been working against him in England; probably also the death of his influential brothers, John and William Sharpe, facilitated the Proprietor's action. Sharpe received the news of his dismissal graciously. He replied that he was prepared to remove to his "farm at a moment's warning" and pronounced the Proprietor's reasons for preferring Eden "very sufficient and satisfactory."

Sharpe had never been entirely happy as Maryland's governor. In 1760 he had written to his brother William: "I must confess I have often repented that I quitted the 20th Reg't to come to America but as I cannot it seems now hope to get into the Army again on a good Footing I shall endeavour to make the best of my Condition." The duties of his office required him to spend a considerable part of his salary, but he certainly lived very comfortably. He complained of his expenses in a letter written in 1757: "I am obliged to pay so much to Mr. Calvert out of my Sallary which no Governor before 1751 ever did, but really what with the Burden of these Expences & other incidental Charges which the late Ld Baltimore used to make an Allowance for out of the Fines & Forfeitures but which I defray out of my own purse, I really believe I am as ill off as any Governor on the Continent except those that are elective in some of the New England Republican Governments." His troubles were aggravated by the Maryland demonstrations against the Stamp Act and later against the Townshend Acts, as he complained to his brother, "Should not an End be speedily put to the Disputes and Jealousies now subsisting between Great Britain & her colonies lucky indeed will that Gov be that can act in such a manner as not to incur Censure either in America or at home, for my own part I think a private station with a moderate fortune is at such a time preferable to a Govern't especially to one where the Governor is responsible to so many."

In general, as the experience of Sharpe's predecessors had shown, the lot of a governor in colonial Maryland was not a happy one, for he often had to serve as mediator between a Proprietor who exercised the paternalism vested in him as lord of the manor and an irate "country" or popular party represented in the Assembly. Sharpe, as he complained, had found it a difficult task to please an absentee Proprietor, to carry out policies of the crown which brought the Marylanders to the verge of rebellion, and at the same time to remain on good terms with all factions in the Province. Besides, he was subjected to almost insatiable demands from the rapacious Proprietor for increased income from the Province and for special favors for the Proprietor's friends in England. He was loaded with such "saddles" or, in modern parlance, "kickbacks," being obliged to give £50 and £100 from time to time to several of Lord Baltimore's favorites.

Sharpe's position in Maryland during those turbulent times had been especially taxing. No Maryland governor had more staunchly supported the prerogatives of the Proprietor and the King; and even while doing so, he had retained the loyalty of the people. He had made a highly creditable record as governor, improving the standards of the clergy, promoting public education, improving the efficiency of the land office, encouraging military service during the French and Indian War, and developing a liberal attitude toward Roman Catholics.

At Sharpe's departure from the governorship, he was showered with messages of appreciation for his services. Judges, lawyers, clergymen, grand juries, public officials, and private citizens vied with each other in extending thanks to him. He wrote to his brother, "Had I obtained the good Opinion of the people here at the Expence of any Right of His Ldps or by not discharging my Duty to the Crown and punctually obeying the Orders communicated to me from time to time by His Majesty's Ministers I should consider the Compliments now paid me as a Reflection on my Conduct." The Assembly made the following comment on Sharpe's governorship: "Though a retrospection upon the Proceedings of this House will not permit us to say that Mr. Sharpe always paid a due regard to the interest of the Province, yet we must acknowledge it in our opinion, that his own inclination led him very much toward that desirable object." William Eddis, who came to the colony in 1769, wrote that Sharpe "by the invariable rectitude of his conduct, the affability of his manners, and his unremitting attention to the happiness and prosperity of Maryland, had established a well merited popularity, which, during an administration of sixteen years, continued in full force, and has secured to him the unabated love, and attachment of a grateful people."

Despite the harassments that he had endured and the complaints that he had voiced, Sharpe liked Maryland, and he determined to remain in the colony. He had built a beautiful country residence, Whitehall, on Chesapeake Bay eight miles from Annapolis, and to it he retired after leaving the governorship, spending his time in the management of his estate and the entertainment of his friends. But in 1773 he was called to England by family affairs. When the Maryland Assembly ordered the confiscation of the property of British subjects in 1780 at the height of the bitterness against loyalists, it exempted from seizure the property still belonging to Sharpe in the express hope that the popular ex-governor would return to Maryland as a citizen under the new government. But he never returned. He died at Hampstead in England in 1790, at the age of 72.

The international complications in which the mother country had become involved and its resulting assumption of new imperial responsibilities with its acquisition of the French empire in America brought into the open serious disagreements between Marylanders and their English suzerains and aggravated frictions between the two, which would lead to open ruptures and finally war in the 1770's. The high ingenuity and tact with which many of the proprietary agents, notably Governor Horatio Sharpe, sought to avert this eventuality proved ineffective in bringing about a durable reconciliation of the diverging interests of the two. The conception of mother country and colony as partners in empire was gradually dissolving.

Footnotes

[1] Bailey, *Thomas Cresap*, 94.

[2] James High, "The Earl of Loudoun and Horatio Sharpe, 1757 and 1758," *Maryland Historical Magazine*, vol. XLV, No. 1, March, 1950, pp. 14-32.

[3] Quoted by Lady Edgar, *A Colonial Governor in Maryland: Horatio Sharpe and His Times; 1753-1773*, Longmans, Green & Co. Ltd., London, New York, 1912, p. 249.

Sources and Additional Reading

Barker, Charles Albro, *The Background of the Revolution in Maryland*, New Haven, Yale University Press, 1940.

Browne, William Hand, ed., *The Archives of Maryland*, vols. I, II, III, Correspondence of Governor Sharpe, 1753-1771, Baltimore, 1888.

Edgar, Lady, *A Colonial Governor in Maryland: Horatio Sharpe and his Times, 1753-1773*, Longmans, Green & Co. Ltd., 1912.

Gurn, Joseph, *Charles Carroll of Carrollton, 1737-1832*, P.J. Kenedy & Sons, New York, [1932].

Land, Aubrey C., *The Dulanys of Maryland; a Biographical Study of Daniel Dulany, the Elder (1685-1753) and Daniel Dulany the Younger (1722-1797)*, Maryland Historical Society, Baltimore, 1955.

Rowland, Kate Mason, *The Life of Charles Carroll of Carrollton, 1737-1832, with his correspondence and public papers*, 2 vols., G.P. Putnam's Sons, New York, 1898.

Schultz, Edward T., *History of Freemasonry in Maryland, of All the Rites introduced into Maryland, from the Earliest Time to the Present . . .* , 4 vols., J.H. Medairy & Co., Baltimore, 1884-1887. A comprehensive, documentary work.

Silver, John Archer, *The Provisional Government of Maryland (1774-1777)*, Johns Hopkins University Studies, Series 13, No. 10, Johns Hopkins Press, Baltimore, 1895.

Smith, Ellen Hart, *Charles Carroll of Carrollton*, Harvard University Press, 1942.

Steiner, Bernard Christian, *Life and Administration of Sir Robert Eden*, Johns Hopkins University Studies, Series 16, Nos. 7-9, Johns Hopkins Press, Baltimore, 1898.

Wainwright, Nicholas B., *George Croghan, Wilderness Diplomat*, University of North Carolina Press, Chapel Hill, 1959.

CHAPTER XIII
WAR FOR INDEPENDENCE

Sharpe's successor as governor of Maryland, Robert Eden, took the prescribed oaths before the privy council in London in December 1768. He had served as a lieutenant and captain in the Cold Stream Guards fighting in Germany during the Seven Years' War. After the war he had married Caroline Calvert, daughter of the fifth Lord Baltimore and sister of Frederick, sixth Lord Baltimore. On June 5, 1769, Eden and his family arrived in Annapolis on the merchant ship *Lord Baltimore* and were ceremoniously received with a salute of seven guns. On the following morning, he exhibited his commission to the council, took the oath as governor, received the great seal of the Province from the retiring governor, and issued a proclamation in which he announced his arrival and continued in office all officials of the Province until further notice.[1]

Eden immediately made it his principal objective to win the allegiance and affection of the Marylanders. In this he was assisted by a naturally friendly and hospitable disposition which soon captivated the people of his colony. The new governor was elected, together with ex-Governor Sharpe, as one of the stewards of the Annapolis Jockey Club, and he entered heartily into the life of the provincial society. The society of Annapolis at this time was probably more polished and brilliant than that of any other capital of its size in the American colonies. According to William Eddis, who came to Maryland to take public office under Governor Eden at this time, it was especially noted for its great "number of fashionable and handsome women" and for its cultured social life. It was characterized by Jonathan Boucher, Anglican clergyman in Annapolis, as "the genteelist town in North America." There, between 1772 and 1774, the brilliant English-born architect, William Buckland, was constructing some of the finest specimens of domestic architecture to be found in colonial America, notably the Hammond House (now the Hammond-Harwood House), which has been described as "the most beautiful Georgian building in America."

Eden's commission from the Proprietor designated him, with the consent of George III, Lieutenant Governor and Chief Governor of the provinces of Maryland and Avalon and also commander-in-chief, both by sea and by land, of all the armed forces within their limits. He was authorized to appoint and remove officers, to summon, prorogue, and dissolve the Assembly, and with the Assembly make laws, provided they were not repugnant to the laws of England nor prejudicial to the Proprietor's interests. As the Proprietor's chief agent in the Province, he was entrusted there with the exercise of all the powers of the Proprietor.

Eden brought with him also instructions from the crown. These dealt entirely with the acts of trade. He was instructed to obey those acts and to make sure that officers in the Province gave bond to obey them. He was required to examine ship certificates and bills of lading, to transmit quarterly to England a list of vessels trading in the colony, to send to England and to the destination port of each vessel copies of her invoices, to seize vessels violating the navigation laws, to prevent the use of fraudulent and forged papers, to supply information desired by the Lords of Trade, and to see that no foreign-built ship traded with Maryland unless it operated under British registry. He was especially charged with preventing illicit trade with the East Indies and any other violation of the monopoly assigned to the East India Company. In trials involving breach of the revenue laws, he must make sure that all the jurymen were born in British dominions, and he must see to it that all the offices of the law courts and the treasury were filled only by native-born subjects of the king. If anyone owning property in Maryland attempted to dispose of it to a person not a native-born subject of the king, the governor must inform the crown of the transaction. He must comply with the requirements controlling the export of the so-called enumerated commodities and in particular must see that no wool was exported from the Province. He was warned that his failure to comply with these instructions would subject him to forfeiture of his bond, the payment of heavy fines, and the possible reversion of Lord Baltimore's charter to the crown.

These instructions to Eden from the crown dealing with revenue matters were supplemented by more general instructions from the Proprietor. In these instructions, Lord Baltimore, who was squandering his Maryland revenues in travel and debauchery, showed particular concern over the composition of the council, whose loyalty to the proprietary interests, as the experience of preceding proprietors had demonstrated, must be completely assured. In case vacancies in the council occurred, Eden must present names of nominees for the vacancies to Lord Baltimore, but he himself was not authorized to fill vacancies unless the membership of the council fell below six. Any appointments he might thus make either to the council or to other official positions in the Province would be provisional until they received Lord Baltimore's approval. Those nominated and appointed to offices in Maryland, the Proprietor stipulated, must be men "of good life, and well affected to our Church and State as by law established, and of good estates and abilities, and not necessitous persons or much in debt." The governor must also see that "God Almighty be devoutly and duly served throughout your government, the Book of Common Prayer, as by law established, read each Sunday and holiday, and the blessed sacrament be duly administered according to the rites of the Church of England."

Lord Baltimore also gave Eden specific advice as to which acts of the legislature would be adverse to the Proprietor's interest and must be resisted. These included acts disestablishing the church, acts which did not include clauses saving the rights of the Proprietor and suspending their operation until Baltimore could give his approval or disapproval, and acts concerning paper currency unless they were consistent with acts of Parliament on the subject. The governor was ordered to send copies of the proceedings of the council and assembly in Maryland to England. In case of his absence from the colony or death, his place would be taken temporarily by the eldest member of the council.

Before Eden arrived in Annapolis, the Parliament in London, under the misguided leadership of Charles Townshend, Chancellor of the Exchequer, had voted to impose upon the colonies a new tax—this time, an external tax in deference to the expressed predilections of the colonists. Duties were to be collected upon red and white lead, certain varieties of glass and paper, and tea imported into the colonies, and from the revenues thus collected Townshend proposed to pay the salaries of the royal officers in the colonies, thereby freeing them from dependence upon the colonial legislatures. The Townshend Act also provided for the efficient enforcement of the old Navigation Acts, which from 1660 onward had been tolerated by the colonies only because they had not been enforced. The revenues which the colonists would be required to pay under these reinvigorated acts would go to swell the British treasury.

Eden arrived in Maryland at an inauspicious time when the colonists were organizing their protest against the Townshend duties. The adjustment of the grievances of the colonists against the Stamp Act, which had occurred before Eden's arrival, had been followed by an interval of relaxed tensions between the colonies and the mother country, but the causes for conflict in principle and of struggle for power between the Lord Proprietor and his colonists in Maryland persisted. Soon afterward, John Dickinson of Pennsylvania wrote his "Letters from a Farmer" complaining that Parliament's new taxes which were imposed upon the colonies not merely for the regulation of trade but for raising money for imperial purposes constituted a dangerous innovation not warranted by the English constitution and threatening the growth of manufactures in

America. Under the leadership of the merchants of New England, the colonists, including those of Maryland, pledged themselves to non-importation and non-exportation agreements in an attempt to apply economic pressure upon Parliament. On the eve of Eden's arrival, the Virginia House of Burgesses passed resolutions claiming for the colonial legislatures the sole power of taxation. In order to prevent the Maryland legislature from subscribing to these resolutions, Eden did not summon it into session until the following November.

Eden acted wisely, for soon afterward he received intimations from Lord Hillsborough, who was handling colonial affairs in the cabinet in London, that the British government was planning to remove the duties on paints, glass, and paper. But until the colonists received definite word that Parliament had withdrawn the obnoxious duties, Maryland merchants continued to adhere to the non-importation and non-exportation agreements. When the British brig *Good Intent* arrived in Annapolis in January 1770, the Maryland merchants to whom the cargo was consigned refused to accept it. Eden endeavored, as he subsequently wrote, "as my duty to my sovereign and the colony demanded, to persuade them to reconsider the matter . . . but could not convince them of the impropriety of their conduct." The vessel accordingly was unable to discharge its cargo and returned to England.

When news reached Maryland in May 1770 that Parliament had actually voted to repeal the Townshend duties, the *Maryland Gazette,* which had been published since 1767 by Jonas Green's widow, Anna Catharine Green, hailed it as "proof of His Majesty's most gracious attention to the united petitions of his subjects, which cannot too much endear him to us." But Eden was not convinced that Parliament's action would satisfy the colonies, for George III had insisted upon retaining the tax on tea on the legalistic ground that "there must always be one tax to keep up the right." "From what I can observe," Eden reported, "I do not imagine that the taking off the duties on glass, paper and colors will put an end to the association while the duty on tea continues." Eden was right, for when the merchants of New York abandoned their non-importation agreement, a convention of Marylanders meeting in Talbot County condemned them for doing so, and a later convention at Annapolis decided to keep the Maryland association in force. When the Maryland Assembly finally convened, they resolved unanimously, in the spirit of the Virginia resolutions, "that the representatives of the freemen of Maryland, in their legislative capacity, with the assent of the other parts of the Legislature, have alone the right to lay taxes in Maryland."

War for Independence

In the mounting resistance of the American colonies to England's control over them, Marylanders generally did not assume a position of leadership but, instead, followed the lead of the more radical colonies, Massachusetts, Pennsylvania, and Virginia. But they developed grievances of their own against the mother country. Their mood of rebelliousness was now aggravated by the renewal of the controversy over the officers' fees. This disclosed once again an underlying antagonism between the popular party in Maryland and the proprietary party which was identified with England and with Lord Baltimore's friends in the colony, some of whom made plain that they regarded the Marylanders as uneducated and ill-bred provincials. In the privileges and virtual monopoly of fees which members of the proprietary party enjoyed, the colonists saw the ugly pretensions of a feudal landowning oligarchy battening on the labor of the colonists and exploiting them for its own ends. Through their monopoly of public offices, Carroll charged, the proprietary party was seeking "to establish a tyranny in a land of freedom." Colonial resentment against the fees system was compounded of class antagonism, jealousy, and frontier equalitarianism, and to its emotional content were added economic grievances caused by the worsening depression in the tobacco trade which occurred in the early 1770's. This local controversy over fees was a "curtain-raiser" for the approaching struggle of continental proportions against what was coming to be regarded as foreign overlordship.

The elective representatives of the people, representing the gentry or landholding class and serving without compensation, accordingly prepared to assert their independence of the executive authority. They resented and were ready to resist further exercise of this arbitrary authority, whether by the crown, by the Proprietor, or by their agents in the colony. In fact they were already beginning to think of themselves as no longer colonists of any foreign authority. Many of the leaders of this resistance against proprietary and other control from abroad found congenial companionship in the Masonic movement which was introduced into Maryland with the founding of the first lodge at Annapolis in 1749.

In all this, Marylanders, some motivated by the hope of financial gain, others by deeply felt philosophical reasons, were seeking to draw a proper line between their natural rights as freemen and Englishmen, on the one hand, and the prerogatives of proprietary monopoly and royal authority on the other. They hoped to draw this line by self-assertiveness and also by imposing such restraints as they possessed upon those who sought to curb their claimed rights as freemen and

Englishmen. Behind the justifications and rationalizations offered by the Baltimore family and by the crown, and despite their attempts to represent their policies as beneficial to the colonists, Marylanders were always conscious of the underlying fact of family and crown monopoly exercising final sovereign control over them. When that control became intolerable, they could no longer be satisfied with mere redress of specific grievances but would demand independence.

When Eden's first Assembly met, it took an intransigent position not only on the right of the colonists to be exempt from taxation from abroad but also on the matter of the officers' fees. The control of Maryland by the proprietary party, seated in office in pursuance of an ancient charter, was vigorously challenged by a new, aggressive group representing the popular party. Under the leadership of Samuel Chase and Thomas Johnson, about one-third of the members of the Assembly refused to extend the tobacco inspection and fees act of 1747, which after having been extended once in 1763 was now expiring. As before, the main target of their attack was the table of fees in the act which fixed the income of officials, and they complained with considerable reason that members of the council, which was dominated by the proprietary party, were monopolizing the principal offices. The Upper House, they declared, was showing too much "attachment . . . to the profits of office." Only one of the principal offices of the Province, that of Attorney General, was held by a person who was not a member of the council. Of the others, Daniel Dulany was Secretary of the Province, Walter Dulany was Commissary General, Daniel of St. Thomas Jenifer was Agent and Receiver General, John Beale Bordley was Judge of the Admiralty Court, William Fitzhugh was Treasurer of the Western Shore, William Hayward was Rent Roll Keeper of the Western Shore, and Benedict Calvert and George Stewart were Judges of the Land Office. These officers of the Province, then, besides being members of the governor's council, were also members of the bureaucracy of the Province. The fees which they derived from their offices were very large for those times, ranging from $4,000 a year for Judges of the Land Office to nearly $7,000 a year for the Commissary General. They quite naturally wanted the fees continued at the same lucrative rates fixed by law. At the same time, the Anglican clergy, who under the acts of 1747 and 1763 were supported by the "thirty-per-poll tax," renewed their demand for an increase in the tax support of the church. With the expiration of the act of 1763 they contended that the earlier law of 1702 fixing a forty-per-poll rate had entered again into force and that they should now be paid at this higher rate.

The old controversy of the 1730's and 1740's over the interlocking problem of tobacco inspection, officers' fees, and the support of the church, was therefore reopened. In a mood of compromise, the Assembly agreed to extend the expiring law for another year, until October 1, 1770, but at the next session the debate on the bill ended in a deadlock between the two houses. Governor Eden then prorogued the Assembly and, following the precedent which the fifth Lord Baltimore had set in 1733, while visiting the Province, undertook to settle the fees problem by proclamation. In this skillfully worded proclamation he forbade officers to take greater fees than they were entitled to take under the act of 1763 and so impliedly permitted them to take fees at least equal to those allowed by that act.

By this proclamation of November 26, 1770, the lines between the popular party and the proprietary party were again clearly drawn. It was immediately attacked by the leaders of the Assembly which met in 1771, including Edward Tilghman, Samuel Chase, William Paca, and Thomas Johnson. They contended that it was not justified by the charter and was contrary to earlier colonial statutes which provided that no money could be raised in the Province without the consent of the Assembly. The Assembly even declared that the Land Office performed public functions and could not be considered exempt from the fee-fixing powers of the Assembly. For its defiant action, the Assembly was then prorogued by the governor. For nearly two years it did not meet again and fees were paid in accordance with the governor's proclamation.[2]

Implicit in this controversy was strong antagonism to the church establishment in Maryland which, to the growing patriot group, symbolized taxation without representation. This phase of the opposition to the governor's proclamation was stressed at that time by Chase and Paca, who insisted that parish affairs and church taxes should be decided not by the Anglican hierarchy and the Proprietor but by the vestrymen of each parish. In 1773 the controversy was continued in the public press by Daniel Dulany the Younger, writing under the name of Antilon, and Charles Carroll of Carrollton, who called himself "First Citizen." Dulany had ably supported the popular cause in the dispute over the Stamp Act, but he now took the governor's side in the fees controversy, arguing in favor of it in the first of his Antilon articles published in the *Maryland Gazette* on January 7, 1773. He was answered by Carroll, representing the popular side of the issue, in the *Gazette* on February 4.

Carroll, a wealthy but disfranchised Catholic, saw in the dispute an opportunity to thrust at the Anglican Church and at the proprietary party which supported it and which had denied the franchise to Catholics, then numbering some 16,000 or only about one-fifteenth of the total white population of Maryland. The newspaper debate between Carroll and Dulany continued through the following June. Meanwhile the popular party was gaining ground, partly as a result of the vexation of the western Germans with the governor's proclamation favoring the Anglican Church. The cause of these German Lutherans and Pietists was represented in the General Assembly by Jonathan Hagar of Frederick County, whose election in 1771 marked the entrance of Maryland's German population into politics.

When the Assembly convened in November 1773, they passed a tobacco-inspection bill which was accepted by the Upper House though with an amendment limiting it to three instead of fourteen years. Both houses also agreed upon a bill requiring every taxable person in the Province to pay thirty pounds of tobacco or four shillings in currency annually to support the state church for the next twelve years. Both of these bills were signed by the governor and became law. They represented a victory for the popular party. But the two houses could not agree on a fees bill because it involved the fundamental question of the division of power between proprietary prerogative and popular rights. In October 1771 the Assembly, considering the governor's proclamation as a flagrant abuse of prerogative and a usurpation of the right of taxation which belonged to the Assembly, resolved unanimously that "the Representatives of the Freemen of this Province have the sole Right, with the Assent of the other Part of the Legislature, to impose and establish Taxes or Fees; and that the imposing, establishing or collecting any Taxes or Fees, on or from the Inhabitants of this Province under Colour or Pretence of any Proclamation issued by or in the Name of the Lord Proprietary or other Authority is arbitrary, unconstitutional and oppressive." They further specifically denounced the governor's proclamation as "illegal, arbitrary, unconstitutional and oppressive."[3] Fees nevertheless continued to be paid in accordance with the governor's proclamation until this controversy was merged in the larger question of independence.

From 1770 to 1773, the fees question generally monopolized the interest of the public and the attention of the legislature. The controversy over the salaries of the clergy was settled in 1773 when the legislature fixed the rate at thirty pounds of tobacco, but the dispute over the officers' fees remained unresolved. Eden had proposed that the Assembly improve the public roads of the Province but had not been able to get favorable action from the legislature. Nor did his repeated recommendations that the Assembly consider "the extensive utility which cannot fail to flow from an establishment in this province of a regular seminary for our youth, liberally instituted and supported" appeal to the legislature, which felt that "matters of an important nature more immediately affecting the welfare of the province demand attention more pressingly."

In 1771 the Proprietor, Frederick, the sixth Lord Baltimore, died in Naples, and with him the Baltimore title lapsed, for he left no legitimate heir. His career had been futile and unsavory. He has been described as "one of those worn-out beings, a hipped Englishman, who had lost all moral and physical taste. With an income of £30,000 he knew not how to enjoy it." Even his dissipations were petty and his literary efforts dull and foppish. His will revealed the existence of three illegitimate families. In his will he made his illegitimate son, Henry Harford, Proprietor of Maryland, and he transferred his personal estate to his sister Caroline, the wife of Governor Eden. The Maryland Assembly now established two new counties—Harford, named for the new Proprietor, and Caroline, named for Eden's wife. The county seat of the latter county, Denton, originally Edenton, perpetuates the name of Maryland's last proprietary governor.

After the disagreements over the Townshend duties, the relationship between the American colonies and England settled down into relative quiescence, but they were agitated again by the Tea Act. This act, inspired by the shortsighted Lord North, was devised to save the fortunes of the East India Company by giving it a monopoly of the business of selling tea in the colonies. After the Boston Tea Party and the Boston Port Bill, with which the British government sought to punish Massachusetts for the destruction of the East India Company's tea, the people of Annapolis sent resolutions of sympathy to those of Boston. They also chose a committee of correspondence to join with similar colonial committees elsewhere in seeking a redress of grievances from the home government. They demanded the repeal of the Boston Port Bill, called for the continuance of the non-importation agreements, and urged members of the legal profession to refuse to bring suit against any Marylander for debts owed to an Englishman. Meetings of citizens in Kent, Talbot, Baltimore, Frederick, and Charles Counties adopted similar resolutions. But, as Eddis reported, "The majority by which they were carried did not consist of the most respectable inhabitants." [4]

From delegates elected at such meetings throughout the colony was formed the first popular convention of the Province of Maryland, which met at Annapolis on June 22, 1774. Such a body seemed to be required in order to exercise surveillance over the actions and policies of England, for, as Charles Carroll of Carrollton had written a year before, "Our constitution is founded on jealousy and suspicion; its true spirit and full vigour cannot be preserved without the most watchful care and strictest vigilance of the representatives over the conduct of administration." [5]

This first convention grew out of the association which had been formed to resist the economic measures of the British government, and in its origin it was simply an association of the freemen of Maryland formed for the purpose of opposing those measures. It was attended by ninety-two members representing the people of the Province and elected by the freemen of the counties. When it met it became the only representative assembly in the Province, for the assembly of the proprietary government had been prorogued by the governor in the previous April and would not meet again under the proprietary regime. It functioned therefore as a provisional government, revolutionary in character and constituted extralegally, and until Eden's departure from the Province it existed side by side with the proprietary government.

This convention passed resolutions opposing the Boston Port Bill, endorsed the non-importation and non-exportation agreement, agreed to break off all trade with those who refused to join it, and urged merchants not to take advantage of it to raise their prices. They opened a subscription for the relief of the residents of Boston, who were now sealed off from the colonies by British troops, and appointed delegates "to attend a general congress of deputies from the colonies, at such time and place as may be agreed on, to effect one general plan of conduct, operating on the commercial connexion of the colonies with the mother country, for the relief of Boston and preservation of American liberty." Maryland thus early arranged to participate in the first Continental Congress whenever it might meet. But at this early stage the objective of the leaders of the resistance movement in Maryland, like that of Governor Eden, was simply to effect a peaceful accommodation with England.

Maryland's Tea Party was even more spectacular than that of Boston, though it came later. When the first tea vessel, the brigantine *Mary and Jane,* arrived in the Province, entering St. Mary's River with a cargo of East India Company tea consigned to merchants in Bladensburg and Georgetown, the vessel was turned back and compelled to return to England. A second tea vessel, the brig *Peggy Stewart,* sailed into the harbor of Annapolis with 2,320 pounds of tea on board in October 1774. Anthony Stewart, the owner of the vessel, paid the duty on it but was censured for doing so by a general meeting of the citizens of the town. Sensing the direction of public sentiment, he published an apology and offered to burn the tea publicly. But noting that public opinion was highly incensed against him, as shown in a later and larger meeting of citizens, Stewart, "from an anxious desire to preserve the public tranquility, as well as to ensure his own personal safety," went on board his vessel, ran it aground, and in view of all the people set fire to it with his own hands and let it burn to the water's edge. A second "tea party" was celebrated in Frederick County a few weeks later, and the tea was burned. And in July 1775, the ship *Totness,* with tea on board, ran aground near Annapolis and was burned For these acts Maryland was not penalized as Boston had been penalized for its Tea Party.

Almost in the light of the flaming *Peggy Stewart* Marylanders could read the defiant resolutions of the First Continental Congress which were adopted by the representatives of twelve colonies, Maryland included, meeting at Philadelphia just five days before. In these the colonists reaffirmed their claim to all the rights, liberties, and immunities of freeborn English subjects, demanded the repeal of certain specified acts of Parliament which they considered to be violative of their rights, and declared their intention of entering into a non-importation, non-consumption, and non-exportation agreement or association. In the Association which they subsequently formed, they pledged the colonies not to import any commodities from Great Britain and Ireland after December 1, 1774, nor to export any commodities to Great Britain and Ireland after September 10 of the following year, nor to have any dealings with any colony which refused to join or violated the Association.

These actions of the First Continental Congress were unanimously approved by a new Maryland Convention which met in November and which consisted of fifty-seven delegates chosen by the freemen of the Province. The members of this second convention of the provisional government resolved to carry out scrupulously the terms of the Association and to encourage the manufacture of woolens, linens, and cottons. To facilitate the enforcement of the Association, they organized committees of correspondence and observation and called upon the people to forget "all former differences about religion or politics, and all private animosities and quarrels of every kind" in order to unite in defense of their common rights and liberties. They agreed to support to the utmost any colony in which "the assumed power of parliament to tax the colonies shall be attempted to be carried into execution by force." They also organized a provincial militia explaining disarmingly that their purpose was to relieve the mother country of any expense in protecting the colony. This explanation seemed to be belied when they urged all the inhabitants of the colony, between the ages of sixteen and fifty, to form themselves into companies, choose officers, provide themselves with arms and ammunition, "and be in readiness to act in any emergency." Finally, they appointed delegates to the next Continental Congress and authorized them "to consent and agree to all measures which such Congress shall deem necessary and effectual to obtain a redress of American grievances."

These resolutions were generally endorsed and complied with by the people of Maryland. The freemen in the counties purchased arms and ammunition and formed militia companies. Committees of correspondence and observation were set up to enforce the provisions of the Association, and they did so by giving unfavorable publicity to violators, selling at auction goods imported from Great Britain in contravention of the Association, and censuring merchants who took advantage of the necessitous condition of their customers to raise their prices.

Governor Eden, reporting the sentiment of the Marylanders to London, wrote in December 1774: "I firmly believe that they will undergo any hardship sooner than acknowledge a right in the British Parliament [to impose internal taxation], and will persevere in their non-importation and non-exportation experiments, in spite of every inconvenience that they must consequently be exposed to, and the total loss of their trade." His estimate of their spirit was confirmed by the sharp decline in the value of imports from England into Maryland and Virginia from £528,738 in 1774 to only £1,921 in 1775.[6]

As by their own action Marylanders were deprived of English goods, they proceeded to open up a trade hitherto closed to them with Cuba and with the Dutch and French islands in the Caribbean where in exchange for tobacco and flour they could obtain muskets, gunpowder, coarse clothing, sugar, medicines, and canteens, twine, knives, and other military camp equipment.

A third provincial convention, chosen like its predecessors by the freemen of Maryland to carry forward the work of the provisional government while the proprietary government was faltering to its end, assembled in April 1775. The first act of the members was to proclaim their allegiance to the king "as the sovereign, constitutional guardian, and protector of the rights and liberties of all his subjects." They obviously did not look forward yet to withdrawal from the empire, though they were becoming increasingly suspicious of the crown's intentions toward them. Their general attitude was one of moderation, and they instructed the delegates who would represent the colony at the Second Continental Congress "not to proceed to the last extremity, unless in their judgments they shall be convinced that such measure is indispensably necessary for the safety and preservation of our lives and privileges," for, said they, they had "nothing so much at heart as a happy reconciliation of the differences between the mother country and the British Colonies in North America, upon a firm basis of constitutional freedom." At the same time, they urged Marylanders to continue to organize militia companies and collect arms and ammunition, and they asked Governor Eden to deliver the arms and ammunition of the Province into their hands, because, as they disingenuously said, they feared that they might be threatened by an uprising of slaves or "that some ship of war may arrive in the harbor of Annapolis, whose commander might probably have instructions to seize them." To this request the governor agreed to part and transferred a small quantity of arms to the militia officers of four counties.

Marylanders, like other colonists, were shocked into action by the news of bloodshed at Lexington and Concord and of the pitched battle between the king's redcoated regulars and colonial troops at Bunker Hill. To the newly formed continental army which assembled near Boston and was placed under the command of Washington, Maryland contributed two companies of riflemen. When the next or fourth Maryland convention met at Annapolis in July 1775, it met under war conditions. Although the proprietary government was still functioning, the new convention of Maryland, which was more representative than any of its predecessors, began to assume some of the civil and judicial authority of the governor. It acted as a high court in certain cases that were appealed to it from committees of correspondence, thus bypassing or superseding the proprietary courts. It recognized the authority of the Continental Congress, ordered the mobilization of forty companies of minutemen, and required that all ablebodied freemen, except clergymen, physicians, members of the governor's household, and conscientious objectors to war, should present themselves for service in the militia. It also issued an Association of the Freemen of Maryland calling upon all the residents of the Province to unite in repelling force and in preserving order. Following the example already set by Congress, the Convention authorized the issuance of bills of credit in the amount of $266,666 2/3 which were to be issued on the credit of the Province and would be redeemed on January 1, 1786. In order to secure an executive body that could function during the recess of the convention, they appointed a Council of Safety consisting of eight members from the

Eastern Shore and eight from the Western Shore. In its hands was placed control of the military forces of the Province and authority to do whatever it deemed best for the defense and security of the Province, and it was made a court of appeal.

It was this body which formed the first State Navy of Maryland in 1775, by pressing small sailing vessels from the merchant marine into state service. The vessels of this navy, never large in number or size of vessels, convoyed merchant ships, transported troops and supplies, served as patrol and observation vessels, and sought to prevent enemy marauders. The first vessel in Maryland's new navy was the *Defence,* armed with 22 six-pounder cannons. To it were added, by the spring of 1777, the row-galleys *Baltimore, Conqueror, Independence,* and *Chester,* the armed boat *Plater,* the tender *Amelia,* and the schooner *Dolphin.*

The powers which this convention assumed were of a sovereign nature. Although it still nominally respected the governor's authority and even advised the people of the Province to obey him, this convention was actually exercising executive, legislative, and judicial functions. The Council of Safety which it set up was an executive body which must either perform the same functions as the governor or replace him. But though the action of the convention was revolutionary, that body still professed loyalty to the Crown and Proprietor and was ostensibly only seeking redress of grievances within the imperial framework. In fact, however, it was supplanting the governor. As Eden saw power slipping from his hands, he needed all his natural inclination to moderation and tact to satisfy the demands of the popular party and yet keep Maryland under the Crown.

The next or fifth convention meeting at Annapolis in December 1775 declared that in their judgment the English constitution was the best known system "calculated to secure the liberty of the subject, to guard against despotism on the one hand and licentiousness on the other." They advised Maryland's delegates to the Continental Congress to "keep constantly in view the avowed end and purpose for which these colonies originally associated,—the redress of American grievances, and securing the rights of the colonists." They directed their delegates that in case any proposition should be made by the Crown or Parliament leading to a happy reconciliation on the grounds of constitutional freedom, they should do all in their power to further it and should not assent to any proposition of independence or foreign alliance or colonial federation leading to a separation from the mother country unless they should deem it absolutely necessary for the preservation of colonial liberties. Expressing strong attachment to the English Constitution and the House of Hanover, the convention disclaimed any desire for independence and insisted that their only purpose was to defend their lives and liberties.

At the same time, this convention took measures to put the colony in a stronger posture of defense. They prescribed a more efficient organization of the militia forces and provided for a battalion of regulars, seven independent companies, and two artillery companies at public expense. They authorized the establishment of a gun factory at Frederick and a saltpeter factory in each county, encouraged home manufacture of linen, lead, and other products, and authorized a new issue of bills of credit to replace the old in the amount of $535,111 1/9. The Association was made a test of loyalty to the colonial cause. If a freeman refused to sign it, he would be deprived of his arms or would be permitted to leave the country, taking his property with him. Thus Maryland prepared to join with the other colonies in a defensive war.

The actions of the Maryland convention were rendering Governor Eden's office superfluous. Meanwhile, the proprietary courts were conducting their business as usual, and the governor remained in Annapolis generally enjoying the respect of the colonists and using his influence in favor of conciliation and peace. But in March 1776, a circular letter and a private letter addressed to Governor Eden from Lord George Germain, Secretary of State for the Colonies, were intercepted commending Eden's attachment to the king and thanking him for one of his recent letters which contained "a great deal of very useful information" and a "confidential communication of the character of Individuals." In the letter from the blundering marplot, Germain, Eden was directed to give assistance to the British troops which were operating in the southern colonies.[7]

When the Maryland Council of Safety received these intercepted letters they showed them to the governor and requested to see the letters that he had been sending to the ministry in London. They also asked him to give a pledge that he would not slip out of the Province. He refused to show them the reports which he had been sending to the ministry but asserted "upon his honour that he had not endeavoured to inflame the ministry by traducing the characters of individuals." He also refused to promise that he would not leave Maryland because such a promise, he said, would be inconsistent with his duties as governor. But he said he had no intention of leaving as long as he could serve the cause of peace. This statement was accepted as satisfactory.

Maryland's leniency toward Eden was deplored by her neighbors. The Continental Congress ordered the Maryland Council of Safety to seize the governor, but the Council replied that they were opposed to interference in their internal affairs and had taken all the action that they deemed necessary. General Charles Lee of Virginia wrote to Benjamin Rush in Philadelphia, "What poor mortals are these Maryland

Council men! I hope the Congress will write a letter to the People of that Province at large, advising 'em to get rid of their damn'd Government. Their aim is to continue feudal Lords to a Tyrant." The Virginia legislature passed resolutions imputing Maryland's action "to some undue influence of Governor Eden under the mask of friendship to America and of the Proprietary interest in Maryland."

Maryland persisted in her conciliatory attitude toward England and seemed to lack enthusiasm for severing her last remaining tie with the mother country. Loyalty to England continued strong, particularly among the Anglican clergy. When the Reverend Jonathan Boucher outspokenly supported the royal government from his pulpit in Prince George's County, he was denounced by the popular leaders, Samuel Chase and William Paca, and his parish was closed. But he continued to preach for six months with his pistols on the pulpit cushion. He and his wife finally departed from Maryland in September 1775. They were only two of many Marylanders who were subjected to harassment, whose mail was tampered with, and to whom freedom of speech was denied by those whom they considered to be "violent fanatical spirits" who were bent upon running "things to the utmost extremity." [8] These latter included Maryland's two patriot newspapers, the older *Maryland Gazette* and the Maryland *Journal and Baltimore Advertiser,* which was established in Baltimore by William Goddard in 1773.

In response to a resolution of Congress recommending that they form a permanent government, the Maryland convention resolved "that the people of this province have the sole and exclusive right of regulating the internal government and policy of this province." They expressed a willingness, however, "to enter into further compact with the other colonies for the preservation of the constitutional rights of America," but as late as May 21, 1776, they felt that "a re-union with Great Britain on constitutional principles would most effectually secure the rights and liberties, and increase the strength and promote the happiness of the whole province." [9] The aversion to independence was especially strong among the Eastern Shoremen and the aristocratic planters of southern Maryland.

But partly by reason of the physical distance which separated Marylanders from London and partly by reason of the perversions of royal authority perpetrated by George III and condoned by Parliament, they were swinging by slow stages reluctantly into the current leading to independence. The sixth convention approved the dealings of the Council of Safety with Eden and reported that they found no evidence that the governor had been engaged in unfriendly correspondence with the ministry. But they suggested to him "that the Publick quiet and safety" required his departure and that they would allow him "to depart peaceably with all his effects." They also presented him with a complimentary address in which they expressed the hope that he would fairly represent the temper of the colonists when he arrived in England and that he would return to the government of the Province when relations between the colonies and the mother country were again peaceful. The governor, in reply, assured them that he would "still continue most sincerely to wish for the welfare and prosperity of Maryland, and, consequently, for a reconciliation with and constitutional dependency on Great Britain."

As arrangements were made for Eden's departure, the governor's Council held its last meeting on June 12, 1776, and adjourned forever. Thus the Upper House of Maryland's colonial legislature passed out of existence. Eleven days later, Eden, then only thirty-five years of age, embarked on his majesty's ship *Fowey* at Annapolis. He was escorted on board by the Council of Safety and was given an affectionate farewell. But the leave-taking of Maryland's last royal governor was marred by an unfortunate incident. During the preceding night, seven white servants and a deserter from one of Maryland's militia companies escaped and were taken on board the *Fowey*. When their escape was discovered the captain refused to surrender them, saying that his orders were "peremptory to receive all persons well affected and give them every protection." The Council of Safety then asked Eden to intervene, but he explained that "every exertion of my interest or interposition on this subject must prove ineffectual against the King's orders." The Council in reprisal therefore refused to put the governor's baggage on board and forced him to sail away without it.[10]

Marylanders were resolved to elect their own governing officials. After Eden's departure, the only vestiges of the Proprietor's authority that remained in Maryland were two officials of the Paper Currency Office, or Loan Office, as it was popularly called, William Eddis and John Clapham, and the officials in the Land Office headed by the judges Benedict Calvert and George Stewart. These two offices were regarded as quasi-private or proprietary agencies. The Land Office continued to be administered by proprietary officials for almost another year and to issue warrants and patents for land in the name of Henry Harford as Lord Proprietor of the Province. Eden returned to Maryland after the war ended and American independence was established, died there in 1784 at the age of forty-three, and was buried in Annapolis. Convivial, flirtatious, buoyant in disposition, he had faithfully fulfilled as governor the often ungrateful task of representing the interests of both England and the house of Baltimore in the twilight of their domination over the Maryland colony.

Maryland now had no physical obstacles to joining with the other colonies in declaring independence from Great Britain. Under the weak Henry Harford, lacking the name, the prestige, and the ability of his Baltimore predecessors, the proprietary government in Maryland had languished and finally disappeared. Maryland's colonial era thus ended. The Proprietor's prerogative was not destroyed by revolutionary action in Maryland; it had already lapsed into desuetude long before independence was declared. The substance was gone, and only the shadow of political control from abroad remained. Through the ineptitude of proprietary officials and the feeling of separateness from the mother country which had slowly developed, the colony of Maryland was irretrievably lost both to the Proprietor and to the crown of England. The long continued struggle against the proprietary government had readied the colonists for the eventual severance of all political ties and had slowly brought them to an acceptance of the need for revolutionary action to defend their interests. On the frontier of English settlement in America, they had acquired viewpoints and ways of living which were no longer compatible with an unsympathetic British rule. Sentiments of separatism had been a slow growth, but with the departure of Governor Eden, they were ready to flower into independence.

Maryland now assumed the status of a free state. Freed from political connection with the mother country, Marylanders assumed the right to mould their lives as they pleased without onerous limitations imposed from abroad. Henceforth, Maryland's commitment to independence of action and the free spirit would be one of its distinguishing characteristics.

In the case of Maryland, perhaps more than that of any other American colony of Great Britain, it can be said that the violence of rebellion was resorted to only after all the methods of reason had failed. Force was in truth the *ultima ratio*. The issue in the contest that had now opened up between mother country and colony was the entire imperial position of Britain in America, which was challenged by the Americans from Massachusetts to Georgia. The outcome would decide whether the colonies could successfully free themselves from the control of London.

Maryland's break with England came as a culmination of almost a century and a half of developing dissimilarities, evidenced by the struggles between the colonists and the Proprietor, by the economic grievances of the tobacco-planting class, and by the pervasive liberal ideas of the eighteenth-century Enlightenment. Under the influence of these ideas the colonists were inspired with a fervent antagonism to monarchism and imperialism. In the new cult of popular rights the planter class made common cause with the people of the Province. The emphasis upon election pledges, responsible legislative action, mass meetings, and popular associations produced a feeling of common cause between the gentry and the people, which was big with democratic implications. Almost all classes expected to benefit from the economic advantages which would accrue from independence. The tobacco economy of Maryland would be redeemed and her foreign trade would be freed from the shackles imposed by a jealous mother country which was obsessed with mercantilist ideas.

Popular dissatisfactions with an unresponsive British crown and popular aspirations for secession from it were effectively encouraged by a group of Maryland leaders, including notably Charles Carroll of Carrollton and Samuel Chase, who were convinced of the inevitableness of independence. In other colonies the movement for independence was also gathering strength. By the middle of May 1776, Massachusetts, Rhode Island, North Carolina, and Virginia had instructed their delegates in Congress to vote for independence, and on June 10 the delegates from Virginia introduced into Congress a resolution "to declare the colonies independent." As this momentous subject was thus introduced, the Maryland delegates—Thomas Stone, Matthew Tilghman, and John Rogers—asked the Maryland Council of Safety to call the Maryland convention into session in order to reach a decision as to Maryland's position. The delegates themselves enthusiastically favored independence, and Tilghman came from Philadelphia to stir up the people for it. As a result, on June 28 the Maryland convention unanimously voted to instruct their delegates in Philadelphia to join with the delegates from the other colonies in declaring "the United Colonies free and independent States; in forming such further compact and confederation between them; in making foreign alliances; and in adopting such other measures as shall be adjudged necessary for securing the liberties of America." But so jealous were Marylanders of independent statehood that the convention stipulated that in any new confederation that might be formed "the sole and exclusive right of regulating the internal government and police of this colony be reserved to the people thereof."

These new instructions were rushed to Philadelphia and were read to the Congress on July 1. On the same day that Congress, meeting as a Committee of the Whole, agreed to the Virginia resolution for indepen-

Charles Carroll of Carrollton

Samuel Chase

William Paca

Thomas Stone

The four Maryland signers of the Declaration of Independence. Photos by M.E. Warren from paintings by Thomas Sully. Courtesy *Maryland State House*

dence, the three delegates from Maryland who were then in attendance at the session—Paca, Stone, and Rogers—cast their votes for it. When another favorable vote on the same proposition was taken on the next day, Maryland's same three delegates again voted for the resolution reading as follows: "that these United Colonies are, and, of right, ought to be, Free and Independent States; that they are absolved from all allegiance to the British crown; and that all political connection between them and the state of Great Britain, is, and ought to be, totally dissolved." When the Declaration of Independence, drafted by Thomas Jefferson, was submitted to a vote on July 4, it was approved by the same three Maryland delegates. It was then engrossed and opened for signature on August 2, but by that time Maryland's delegation had changed. Paca and Stone were now joined by Samuel Chase and Charles Carroll of Carrollton, and these four signed the Declaration of Independence on behalf of Maryland.[11]

In the issue of independence, Paca and Stone had previously taken a cautious stance; Chase and Charles Carroll of Carrollton, however, had been outspoken advocates of independence. The impetuous Chase had represented the popular or "Country Party" against the Proprietary or "Court Party" ever since the Stamp Act. Carroll, one of the wealthiest men in the colonies, suffered from the political disabilities imposed upon Catholics under existing laws. The celebration of the mass was forbidden by law, Roman Catholic schools were prohibited, and Catholics were denied the right to bear arms. So unhappy was the lot of Catholics that their leaders, Charles Carroll and his cousin John Carroll, who had been educated in the Jesuit order in France, Belgium, and England, and who had just returned to Maryland in 1774, had applied to the king of France for a grant of land beyond the Mississippi River in the territory of Louisiana where they hoped to establish a new Catholic colony as Cecil Calvert had originally done in Maryland. But they found in the American resistance to England, waged for liberty of conscience and freedom of thought, a better solution and actively supported the cause of independence.

Maryland had slowly come to a decision to range herself with the other American colonies as an independent state. To this decision she had been impelled not only by the force of events which disclosed the widening breach between her own interests and those of the Proprietor but also by the liberal philosophy of the age which called in question the mother country—colony relationship. Marylanders were influenced by the natural-rights philosophy as well as by the deism and secularism of the era of the Enlightenment and had become restive under the restraints imposed by foreign authority and critical of established ways of doing things. As a result of these influences, they had acquired a new self-consciousness and aspirations for enlarged opportunities in self-government. Against both the proprietary and the royal prerogative, the Maryland House of Delegates had been long protesting and asserting at the same time the conviction that it, as the local representative of the people of the colony, should possess the keys of power. In this they were claiming their traditional rights of Englishmen and protesting against the perversion of these rights by a distant king and Parliament.[1][2]

To the theoretical arguments for revolutionary action against the mother country were added practical grievances arising from the dependence of the tobacco-planting class upon English middlemen who monopolized their major moneymaking crop and who kept them in a kind of debt bondage. But to this condition, it must be admitted, the planters themselves contributed by their own habits of luxurious and convivial living. Their resentment against their condition was associated also with a protest against the hereditary principle which made it possible not only for a hereditary monarch to deal with them in an irresponsible way but for a hereditary Proprietor to exploit the colony for his own dissolute purposes. The amount of income which the Proprietor drew from Maryland for his own use, it has been estimated, amounted to an 18 percent tax on Maryland's annual purchasing power in Great Britain.

One of the casualties of the struggle in which Marylanders now found themselves engaged would be the proprietary prerogative with all its financial perquisites which had been inherited from the conditions of the first founding of the colony and had become increasingly vexatious to the colonists. Their antagonism, latent and deep-seated, could not be conciliated by niggardly concessions from the king's ministers. Their protest was in part a revolution of taxpayers. In 1780 the Maryland legislature abolished quitrents forever.

The Maryland convention issued its own formal declaration of independence on July 3, 1776. In it that body set forth the violations of the rights of the colonists and proclaimed the withdrawal of their allegiance from the king of Great Britain. They also announced their intention of entering into closer union with other independent colonies, of forming alliances with foreign states, and of setting up a government for their new state. To accomplish this last object the convention ordered elections to be held to choose deputies to a constitutional convention. Though they recognized the authority of the people as the basis for their power, they excluded those in the military service from voting and retained the old system of property qualifications for the suffrage. They provided that "all freemen, above twenty-one years of age, being freeholders of not less than fifty acres of land, or having visible property in this colony to the value of £40 sterling, at the least," might vote for deputies in these elections. They assigned four delegates to each county except Frederick, which had the largest area and which was accordingly allowed to send four delegates from each of the two districts into which it was divided. For the first time they made separate provision for the towns of Baltimore and Annapolis by authorizing them to send two delegates each. Baltimore's importance had been considerably enhanced by the leading role which her ambitious merchants had taken in pressing for independence from Great Britain.

In a mood of exhilaration, not unmixed with a sober sense of responsibility, Marylanders now stood poised to assume the obligations of independent statehood. Maryland's first constitutional convention met at Annapolis on August 14, 1776. One of its first acts was to divide Frederick County into three counties—Frederick, Montgomery, and Washington—thus recognizing the growing population of the west. It then added its approval to the Declaration of Independence prepared by Congress and proceeded to appoint a committee "to prepare a declaration and charter of rights, and a plan of government agreeable to such rights as will best maintain peace and good order, and most effectually secure happiness and liberty to the people of this State." The committee included Matthew Tilghman, Charles Carroll, Barrister, Charles Carroll of Carrollton, William Paca, George Plater, Samuel Chase, and Robert Goldsborough. After preparing the documents they submitted them to the convention, which then adjourned to allow the people of the state to consider them.

The Declaration proclaimed that government comes from the people and exists solely for their good. It claimed for the people of Maryland the exclusive right to regulate their internal government and police and declared that they were entitled to the benefits of the common law of England and certain provisions of Magna Carta. It approved in general terms a framework of government for the state which would consist of legislative, judicial, and executive branches, asserted the rights of freedom of worship and freedom of the press, and condemned monopolies, hereditary honors, and titles of nobility.

The general principles set forth in this Declaration were carried out in the first constitution of the independent state of Maryland. The Constitution of 1776 reflected the jealousy of the executive power which was common among the former colonists of George III. The governor of

Maryland was to be elected by joint ballot of the two houses of the legislature, and he was not given any veto power over legislation. He would be elected for only a one-year term but could be reelected to serve three consecutive terms. He was required to own property worth at least £5,000 sterling, and he would be assisted by an executive council of four members chosen by both houses of the legislature. Each member of the council must possess property worth at least £1,500 sterling.

The constitution required property qualifications also for voting and for other offices than those of governor. To be able to vote a citizen must own 50 acres of land worth £30 in current money, and members of the General Assembly must be worth £500 sterling. The Lower House, or House of Delegates, was simply the continuation of the Lower House of the colonial assembly representing the counties as before and elected by voters who possessed the necessary age, residence, and property qualifications. It would consist of four members from each of the 19 counties of the state and two each from Annapolis and Baltimore.

The constitution gratified the patriot party by disestablishing the Anglican Church, by permitting the church tax to be assigned to a church of the taxpayer's choice, and by removing all civil disabilities against Catholics. It eliminated all tests for public office except an oath of fidelity to the state and a declaration of belief in the Christian religion. The provisions on religion contained in the Constitution of 1776 restored to Maryland the enviable distinction for tolerance on religious matters which it had enjoyed prior to the establishment of the Anglican Church in 1692. Among the other American states, six—New Hampshire, Connecticut, New Jersey, Georgia, North Carolina, and South Carolina—still maintained an established church; Massachusetts limited suffrage to Protestants, Delaware required an oath of belief in the Trinity, and Virginia did not adopt Jefferson's bill Establishing Religious Freedom until 1786. Maryland's example of religious toleration was surpassed only by New York, Pennsylvania, and Rhode Island, which had never discriminated against any religion since their founding.

In the new constitution, the Upper House, or Senate, replaced the council of the colonial governor, but senators were chosen not by the people, as in several other states, but by a college of electors who were chosen by the qualified voters. This method of indirect selection of senators by an electoral college was a unique feature of the Maryland constitution and provided the model for the method of choosing a president and a vice-president which was later incorporated in the Constitution of the United States. It was referred to approvingly in one of the

Federalist Papers, written either by Hamilton or Madison, as a successful example of the method of indirect election. The Maryland constitution required that electors possess property worth £50 sterling and senators property worth £1,000 sterling. It prescribed geographical representation for senators; nine must come from the Western Shore and six from the Eastern Shore. This provision, combined with the increase in the representation of Frederick County from four to twelve delegates, brought about a significant shift in the political power structure of the state from the Eastern Shore to the Western Shore.

The new constitution was approved by the constitutional convention in November 1776. It did not require ratification by the people but would go into effect as soon as a Senate and a House of Delegates could be elected. Meanwhile, the constitutional convention performed certain legislative acts. They instructed Maryland's delegates in Congress "to concur with the other United States, or a majority of them, in forming a confederation, and in making foreign alliances," provided, however, that such a confederation would not go into force without the assent of the Maryland Assembly and provided also that it did not deprive the state of the sole and exclusive right of regulating its own internal police. They were willing also that their delegates should "concur with the Congress, or a majority of them, in accommodating our unhappy differences with Great Britain," thus envisaging an ultimate reconciliation with her. Until peace could be achieved, on terms acceptable to the United States, however, the war must continue, and the convention agreed, in response to the solicitation of Congress, to augment the 4,000 troops which Maryland had already supplied to the American armies by contributing eight additional battalions to serve for the duration of the war.

Elections of delegates and senators under the new constitution were arranged by the Council of Safety, which exercised the interim executive authority of the state, but they did not proceed smoothly. They were held under war conditions when feeling between the supporters of the American cause and their Tory opponents was intense. As a result, disorders and intimidation of voters occurred in some places, notably in Baltimore where the Whig Club assumed the authority of government and drove the Tories out of town. But finally the newly elected delegates and senators assembled at Annapolis and organized the first General Assembly of the State of Maryland on February 5, 1777. The new constitution of the state then went into effect. Eight days later, the Assembly chose as governor Thomas Johnson, an iron manufacturer of Frederick, who was one of Maryland's delegates to Congress. With his inauguration on March 21,

Maryland's new independent state government began to function in all its branches and the revolutionary Council of Safety disbanded.

Maryland's future would depend upon the outcome of the clash of arms on the battlefields of the war, and her political course would be determined by her success in conducting the affairs of independent statehood. But in both respects she was engaged with twelve other Atlantic seaboard states, former colonies of England, in a joint effort of resistance to foreign control and experimentation with popular government. Her relations with those states would assume critical importance in the years ahead.

Footnotes

[1] Rosamond Randall Beirne, "Portrait of a Colonial Governor: Robert Eden, I–His Entrance," *Maryland Historical Magazine*, vol. XLV, No. 3, September 1950, pp. 153-175.

[2] James Haw, "Maryland Politics on the Eve of Revolution; The Provincial Controversy, 1770-1773," *Maryland Historical Magazine*, vol. 65, No. 2, Summer 1970, pp. 103-129.

[3] *Archives of Maryland*, vol. 63, 114.

[4] *Letters from America, 1769-1777.*

[5] Charles Carroll of Carrollton. "First Citizen," in *Maryland Gazette*, May 6, 1773.

[6] Arthur Meier Schlesinger, *The Colonial Merchants and the American Revolution, 1763-1776*, Columbia University Press, New York, 1918, p. 535.

[7] *Archives of Maryland*, vol. II, p. 344.

[8] James Christie, Jr., to Lieutenant Colonel Gabriel Christie, February 22, 1775, Robert Purviance, *A Narrative of Events Which Occurred in Baltimore Town during the Revolutionary War . . .*, Jos. Robinson, Baltimore, 1949, p. 37. See also Philip Evanson, "Jonathan Boucher: The Mind of an American Loyalist," *Maryland Historical Magazine*, vol. 58, No. 2, June 1963, pp. 123-136.

[9] *Proceedings of the Conventions of the Province of Maryland . . . in 1774, 1775, & 1776*, pp. 141-142.

[10] Rosamond Randall Beirne, "Portrait of a Colonial Governor: II–His Exit," *Maryland Historical Magazine*, vol. XLV, No. 4, December 1950, pp. 294-311.

[11] Albert Silverman, "William Paca, Signer, Governor, Jurist," *Maryland Historical Magazine*, vol. XXXVII, No. 1, March 1942, pp. 1-25.

[12] Charles A. Barker, "The Revolutionary Impulse in Maryland," *Maryland Historical Magazine*, vol. XXXVI, No. 2, June 1941, pp. 125-138.

Sources and Additional Reading

Beirne, Rosamond Randall, and John Henry Scarff, *William Buckland, 1734-1774, Architect of Virginia and Maryland*, Maryland Historical Society, Baltimore, 1958.

Boucher, Jonathan, *Reminiscences of an American Loyalist, 1738-1798,* Houghton, Mifflin, Boston, 1925.

Delaplaine, Edward S., *The Life of Thomas Johnson* ..., New York, Frederick H. Hitchcock, The Grafton Press, 1927.

Dole, Esther Mohr, *Maryland During the American Revolution,* Baltimore, privately printed, [Waverly Press], 1941.

Eddis, William, *Letters from America,* edited by Aubrey C. Land, Belknap Press of Harvard University, 1969.

Fisher, Richard D., "The Burning of the *Peggy Stewart,*" *Maryland Historical Magazine,* vol. V, No. 3, September 1910, pp. 235-245.

Hoffman, Ronald, *A Spirit of Dissension: Economics, Politics, and the Revolution in Maryland,* (Maryland Bicentennial Studies), Johns Hopkins University Press, 1973.

Leonard, Lewis A., *Life of Charles Carroll of Carrollton,* Moffat, Yard and Company, New York, 1918.

Onuf, Peter S., ed., *Maryland and the Empire, 1773: The Antilon—First Citizen Letters,* (Maryland Bicentennial Studies), Johns Hopkins University Press, Baltimore and London, 1974.

Province of Maryland, *Proceedings of the Conventions of the Province of Maryland Held at the City of Annapolis in 1774, 1775, and 1776,* James Lucas and E.K. Deaver, Baltimore, and Jonas Green, Annapolis, 1836.

Purviance, Robert, *A Narrative of Events Which Occurred in Baltimore Town during the Revolutionary War,* ... Jos. Robinson, Baltimore, 1949.

Riley, Elihu S., *Correspondence of "First Citizen"—Charles Carroll of Carrollton—and "Antilon"—Daniel Dulany, Jr., 1773, With a History of Governor Eden's Administration in Maryland, 1769-1776,* Baltimore, 1902.

Schlesinger, Arthur Meier, *The Colonial Merchants and the American Revolution, 1763-1776,* Columbia University Press, New York, 1918.

Sullivan, Kathryn, *Maryland and France, 1774-1789,* University of Pennsylvania Press, Philadelphia, 1936.

CHAPTER XIV

MARYLAND UNDER THE ARTICLES OF CONFEDERATION

Among all the former American colonies of Great Britain that were involved in the War for Independence, Maryland figured least prominently in the British plans of invasion. As a result, little actual fighting occurred on Maryland soil and the greater part of the fighting engaged in by Maryland troops was done beyond the borders of the state. Especially noteworthy was the support which Maryland privateers gave to the cause of independence. Baltimore, which possessed an abundance of both timber and iron, the two essentials for shipbuilding, built, equipped, and manned the first ships for the continental navy, and Maryland provided a state navy of twenty-five armed vessels for its own protection. When Congress authorized the use of privateers, Baltimore fitted out approximately 250 of these armed vessels to operate against England's navy and to seize guns, ammunition, and other supplies. These vessels were supplied with letters of marque and reprisal authorizing them to prey upon enemy commerce for their own personal enrichment. Of all the privateers that operated on behalf of the American states during the Revolution, Maryland furnished fifteen percent, thus ranking second after Massachusetts in privateering operations.[1]

Although popular opinion in Maryland was bitterly divided over the issue of independence, the new official government of the state cooperated wholeheartedly with neighboring states in the war against Great Britain. The commission which Congress appointed in February 1776 to visit Canada and win the support of that British colony in the struggle for independence included three Marylanders, Samuel Chase, Charles Carroll of Carrollton, and John Carroll, as well as Benjamin Franklin, but their efforts thus to make the war a truly continental cause proved unavailing, as also did the efforts of the continental armies sent to conquer the British armies in Canada.

Many of Maryland's militiamen, who were organized in forty companies in 1775, participated in the early military engagements under Washington around Boston. But it was during the New York campaign in the summer and fall of 1776 that the Maryland Line first distinguished itself. By launching a seemingly desperate assault upon the British at the battle of Long Island, they enabled the American troops under Washington to escape through the enshrouding fog. In this delaying action Colonel William Richardson, with his volunteers of the Maryland Line, was the last American officer to leave the field of action, and for this defense they received Washington's commendation. In the ensuing battles between the American and British forces at White Plains, Brandywine, Germantown, and Monmouth, Maryland troops under Colonel William Smallwood, Brigadier General Mordecai Gist, Colonel Otho Holland Williams, Lieutenant-Colonel Samuel Smith, Colonel William Richardson, Major John Eager Howard, and Major John Stewart distinguished themselves in military action.

In August 1777, when the great British fleet of more than 260 vessels under Admiral Sir William Howe appeared in Chesapeake Bay en route to Philadelphia, Maryland was thrown into a panic. But the fleet had no Maryland objective. It anchored for a short time off the mouth of the Patapsco and then proceeded to the Head of Elk where the British forces disembarked, marched overland, and established themselves in Philadelphia. As the British approached Philadelphia, the American Congress, which was sitting there, adjourned to Baltimore, taking the Continental Treasury with them. But the British occupation of Philadelphia soon ended. After the French entered the war against them as allies of the Americans, as they did following Burgoyne's surrender at Saratoga in October 1777, the British had to evacuate Philadelphia and transfer their military operations southward.

As the principal theater of conflict was transferred to the Carolinas in 1779, Maryland troops played an even more important role in the military engagements in the southern states than they had played in the fighting in the northern and middle states. Under their own commanders Gist, Smallwood, Williams, and Howard they participated in the battles at Camden, Cowpens, Guilford Court House, Hobkirk's Hill, Ninety-six, Eutaw Springs, and several minor encounters. The Chesapeake states became a theater of military operations in 1781 when Benedict Arnold, who had betrayed the American cause, made predatory raids into Virginia and then moved up Chesapeake Bay against Maryland. On both shores of the Bay the British fleet raided Maryland settlements, carrying off Negroes, pillaging houses, and burning property.

So effective were the Tory activities on the Eastern Shore that in 1777 much of the effort of the "Fifth Regiment of the Maryland Line" under the Quaker Colonel William Richardson was spent in attempts to control them. Nevertheless, during 1780 and 1781 the Eastern Shore and Chesapeake Bay were almost completely controlled by the friends of England. On the Eastern Shore the Established Church was very strong, and its preachers taught obedience to England and her laws. Chesapeake Bay with its scores of rivers, creeks, and islands afforded the Tories many havens of refuge and protection. In an attempt to suppress their destructive operations, Governor William Paca sent a naval expedition against the headquarters of the raiding parties at Devil's Island, and in the ensuing "Battle of the Barges" near the Tangier Islands on November 30, 1782, the Maryland forces suffered heavy losses.

The Tory raids drew the Marquis of Lafayette and his forces to Maryland to repel the British. To assist him, Maryland impressed some one-hundred transports and three small armed vessels, which, under the command of Captain James Nicholson of the Maryland navy, carried a large part of Lafayette's troops and equipment from the Head of Elk to Annapolis. As Lafayette prepared for a decisive thrust against the redcoats in Maryland, he secured much-needed food and other supplies for his men, and at Baltimore he pledged a part of his own private fortune in the amount of $10,000 for the purchase of supplies for his troops. He crossed the Patapsco at Elkridge, where he hanged a deserter as an example to discipline his troops, and proceeded to Richmond where he was joined by Generals Wayne and Washington. To promote the planned action against the British, Maryland collected another large fleet of transports which conveyed Washington's forces from the Head of Elk southward.

From Richmond the combined forces of Lafayette, Washington, and Wayne moved jointly to begin the siege of the British troops who had bottled up themselves under Cornwallis at Yorktown expecting that they would be rescued and transported away from their precarious position by British ships. But their hope was vain, for the British fleet had lost control of the Chesapeake to the French under Admiral de Grasse. The joint blockade of Cornwallis from the land by Washington and from the sea by de Grasse compelled him to surrender on October 17, 1781, bringing the war virtually to a close. The news of Cornwallis' surrender was immediately carried by a Marylander, Lieutenant Colonel Tench Tilghman, traveling by horse and by boat, to the Congress at Philadelphia where he arrived near midnight on October 24.[2]

A few mopping-up operations farther south were required to make the victory of the Americans complete. In January 1782, they forced the British to evacuate Wilmington; in July to abandon Savannah; and in December, Charleston. Meanwhile, after Yorktown, Lord North's cabinet had been replaced by one headed by the venerable Marquis of Rockingham and peace negotiations between British and American emissaries were initiated in Paris. These resulted in the conclusion of a provisional treaty of peace there in November 1782.

Like other states, Maryland permitted enlistment of Negro troops, and by 1778, Maryland's 2nd Brigade included 60 Negroes. Two years later, Maryland by law made free Negroes liable to draft and allowed slaves to serve in the army with the consent of their masters. Many black slaves were sent to serve in their masters' places, gaining freedom as a reward. Finally in 1781, the year of Yorktown, Maryland resolved to raise 750 Negro troops to be incorporated with the other troops and constituting 3.6 percent of Maryland's fighting forces under General Washington. Blacks sometimes served in regiments mainly white but also in all-black regiments, and some blacks served on the naval vessels of the states in their historic sea battles against the British.[3]

The measures necessitated by the war and the destruction that accompanied it had reduced Maryland's finances to a deplorable condition. In this crisis the state forbade the payment of all drafts upon the treasury, thus admitting that it was bankrupt and unable to pay its debts. As noted in the foregoing, in July 1777 the Maryland Convention issued currency in the amount of $266,666.66 2/3 to promote the manufacture of saltpeter and the construction of a powder mill, and in the following December they provided for a new currency issue in the amount of $535,111 1/9 to take up the first issue and to carry on war operations. Since none of this paper currency was supported by funds, it soon became practically worthless. At the same time, the paper money issued by the Continental Congress declined to less than one seventy-fifth of its face value and was, in the disparaging words of the day, "not worth a continental." Although the whole amount of coin in Maryland at that time probably did not exceed $100,000, the state promised to redeem its outstanding paper currency by January 1, 1786 with funds collected by taxation and other means.

The various methods of taxation to which the state resorted proved inadequate to supply the necessary funds. As a result, the general assembly of 1780 authorized the payment of taxes in commodities allowing them to be paid in pork, beef, wheat, flour, and tobacco. In 1782 the officers of the state were given the option of receiving their salaries in bills of credit or in wheat, and the legislature fixed the salary of the governor at 500 bushels of wheat each year. Another method which the state used in an attempt to redeem its finances was the confiscation of the property of the Tories who were still in Maryland or who had fled from the state.

As soon as Maryland fully committed itself to independence from Great Britain, it imposed restrictions upon persons who persisted in supporting the British cause. A law of July 4, 1776 prescribed death and forfeiture of property for all who gave aid and comfort to the enemy or engaged in war against the state, and this law was sometimes brutally enforced. Early in the following year the legislature suspended the writ of *habeas corpus.* In October 1777 an oath of allegiance was required of all free males in Maryland above the age of eighteen years, and those who refused to take the oath were required to pay a treble tax on their property for the rest of their lives and to suffer other disabilities. In early 1782 the legislature suspended the treble tax penalty and some of the disabilities, but not until 1789 did it repeal the requirement of the oath of allegiance of senators, attorneys, and other civil officers.

Beginning in November 1779 the House of Delegates made determined efforts to confiscate the property of the Tories and to use the proceeds from it for the conduct of the war and the business of the state. In these efforts some of the leaders were undoubtedly actuated by unworthy personal and emotional motives, and they were opposed by leaders of the Senate including Mathew Tilghman, Daniel of St. Thomas Jenifer, and Charles Carroll of Carrollton. But as the war spirit mounted, as popular resentment toward the Tories increased, and as the financial plight of the state became desperate, the act of confiscation was finally approved by the Senate in October 1780 in avowed retaliation for the plundering of the property of Marylanders and the refusal of the London merchants to honor bills of exchange drawn on them from the bank stock belonging to the state and invested in England. Maryland was the last of all the thirteen states to adopt such an act challenging the principle of the sanctity of private property.[4]

Bitterness toward the Tories sometimes took the form of personal persecution. William Goddard, editor of the *Maryland Journal and Baltimore Advertiser,* was assaulted for publishing a contributed letter sympathetic to the king and Parliament. Because the Anglican Church symbolized the British crown and many of its clergymen in Maryland defended the crown, the General Assembly in early 1779 transferred from the church to the local vestries control over all church properties; at the same time the legislature omitted to make any provision for the support of Anglican clergymen, thus ending the forty-per-poll tax of tobacco for their support.

To dispose of the confiscated loyalist property the state set up a board of commissioners of confiscated estates, and under their direction a great amount of the property was sold, most of it at public auction, between 1781 and 1783, and the proceeds were turned into the state treasury. After the war the Maryland Assembly was besieged with applications for indemnity for the seized property, one of the principal claimants being Henry Harford, who visited Maryland for this purpose and memorialized the legislature in December 1785 for compensation or restoration of his confiscated property. But the legislature decided "that the claims of the former proprietary ceased upon the Declaration of Independence." When the British government subsequently passed an act indemnifying American loyalists, it awarded Harford the sum of £90,000 for his lost Maryland properties.

Maryland's confiscation of loyalist property and its resort to other revenue devices did not prevent the credit of the state from steadily deteriorating. Citizens could not find satisfaction in improving their farms or carrying on routine trading operations when they could make as much as 36 percent in speculation. As a result, agriculture was neglected, commerce languished, and industry stagnated. Daniel of St. Thomas Jenifer was appointed Intendant of the Revenue, or treasurer of the state, in late 1781 and remained in this office until 1785, charged with the almost insuperable task of enforcing revenue measures which were intended to restore the solvency of the state. He was required to keep account of all income and expenditures of the state. In 1783, with the return of peace, the Maryland legislature abolished the payment of taxes in kind.

Under the treaty of peace with Great Britain, Maryland and the other states which had confiscated property from the royalists were expected to restore it, but they did not see fit to do so. Maryland, on the other hand, tried to collect funds in the amount of £29,478 which it had invested in the Bank of England before the war as a sinking fund for several issues of paper money—those of 1766, 1769, and 1773. Control over the stock was vested in three English merchants: Osgood Hanbury, Sylvanus Grove, and James Russell, who, after the termination of hostilities, refused to surrender the stock to the new government of Maryland, allegedly "on the advice of the officers of the crown of Great Britain."

The governor of Maryland therefore sent Samuel Chase abroad to demand payment. But neither Chase nor William Pinkney, who succeeded him in this mission, was able to persuade the trustees of Maryland's stock in the Bank of England to allow the Bank to reimburse the state unless Maryland would first compensate them for the confiscation of their property by Maryland during the war. The continuing pendency of this claim explains the leniency of Maryland, in contrast to the attitude of Virginia and other states, toward British creditors intent on the collection of their prewar debts. Maryland's conciliatory action in removing legal barriers to the recovery of these obligations was motivated by the hope that it would result in the recovery of her bank stock. But in the final settlement, which was made much later, the Lord Chancellor vested title to the stock in the crown as the lawful successor to the provincial government of Maryland. Thereupon the crown, as a gesture of good will in 1803, transferred to Maryland the ownership of the stock then valued at $648,484.34.[5]

Maryland's first governor, Thomas Johnson, served three one-year terms. He and three of his brothers had built the famous Catoctin iron furnace in 1774, which forged great quantities of cannon and shot for the American army during the war, to the great profit of the owners. While governor, he was also financially interested in the Illinois and Wabash land companies situated north of the Ohio River in territory claimed by Virginia. Upon the expiration of his third term as governor, when under the constitution he became ineligible for another term, he returned to the manufacture of iron and the practice of law at his home town, Frederick. As his successor, the second governor of Maryland, the legislature chose Thomas Sim Lee. When his three terms expired in 1782, the legislature elected William Paca as governor over Daniel of St. Thomas Jenifer. Soon after he took office, news of the provisional peace treaty reached Philadelphia and was officially communicated to the states by Robert R. Livingston, president of Congress. Governor Paca, in turn, issued a proclamation announcing the end of hostilities and appointing April 24 as a day of celebration. In the following month, the Maryland legislature authorized the sale of Maryland's small navy consisting of "the galley and the barges."

Almost immediately the House of Delegates and an influential group of citizens of Annapolis invited Congress to make that city the seat of government for the independent United States. There, in 1772, Governor Eden had laid the cornerstone of Maryland's new state house for which funds had been appropriated by the legislature of 1769. This "Stadt House," as it was called, was the third built on that site. The exact date when the building was completed is not known, but it was certainly finished by September 1775. When at the close of the war Maryland offered to present "the Stadt House and Public Circle in the City of Annapolis to the honorable Congress for their use," they also offered to donate the governor's mansion as a residence for the president of Congress, and to build "thirteen dwelling houses and other buildings for the residence of the delegates of each of the thirteen Confederate states" at an expense "not exceeding thirty thousand pounds specie." This offer was presented to Congress by two of Maryland's delegates, Daniel Carroll and James McHenry, and it was temporarily accepted. When Congress accordingly adjourned at Princeton, where it was then sitting, it agreed to meet at Annapolis in November 1783. Here Congress received the definitive treaty of peace between Great Britain and the United States, which had been signed at Paris on September 3.

Already General Washington had accepted the surrender of New York from Sir Guy Carleton. He then took leave of his troops and set out for Annapolis to resign the command of the army which had been entrusted to him more than eight years before. In traveling through New Jersey, Pennsylvania, and Maryland, he was received everywhere with acclamation as a victorious hero. As he approached Annapolis, the Maryland Assembly appointed a committee "to provide a proper house for the reception of His Excellency General Washington." They drew up and unanimously adopted an address to be presented to him. Upon his arrival they gave him a public dinner at the expense of the state and held a ball in his honor.

Congress had already arranged for the formal reception of Washington. In the state house at Annapolis on December 23, 1783, they received from him his resignation as commander-in-chief of the American army. While the president of Congress and the members remained "seated and covered" during the ceremony, Washington delivered a farewell speech and became a private citizen again.

One of Maryland's delegates, Major James McHenry, who had been surgeon general of the Continental army, described this dramatic event in a letter written immediately afterward, as follows:

... It was a solemn and affecting spectacle. ... The spectators all wept, and there was hardly a member of the Congress who did not drop tears. The General's hand which held the address shook as he read it. When he spoke of the officers who had composed his family, and recommended those who had continued in it ... to the favorable notice of Congress, he was obliged to support the paper with both hands. But when he commended the interests of his dearest country to Almighty God, and those who had the superintendence of them to his holy keeping, his voice faultered [sic] and sunk, and the whole house felt his agitations. After the pause which was necessary for him to recover himself, he proceeded to say in the most penetrating manner, "Having now finished the work assigned me I retire from the great theater of action, and bidding an affectionate farewell to this august body under whose orders I have so long acted, I here offer my commission and take leave of all the employments of public life." So saying he drew out from his bosom his commission and delivered it up to the President of the Congress.

Washington departed for his beloved Mount Vernon on the following day as Maryland, along with her sister states, prepared to face the tasks of peace. They would confront the future as united states because they had finally unanimously agreed in 1781 to be governed under Articles

George Washington resigning his commission as Commander-in-Chief of the Continental Army, December 23, 1783. Photo by M.E. Warren from a painting by Edwin White in 1859. Courtesy *Maryland State House*

of Confederation. In the consideration and final ratification of those Articles, extending over a period of three years, Maryland played an important part—a part which seemed obstructive at the time but which redounded to the national interest. It centered around the question of the ownership and disposition of the western or trans-Appalachian lands.

These lands were claimed by several of the seaboard states. Virginia's claims were based on her colonial charters of 1609 and 1624, on land grants west of the mountains made by Governors Dinwiddie and Dunmore, and on the conquest of the Illinois country by George Rogers Clark during the War for American Independence. The Carolinas and Georgia, under their original sea-to-sea charters, claimed western lands extending, after the Anglo-American treaty of peace, to the Mississippi River which was fixed by that treaty as the western boundary of the new nation. North of Virginia the states of Massachusetts and Connecticut insisted that by virtue of their colonial charters they were entitled to a Mississippi River boundary on the west, and New York advanced some tenuous claims. In some cases these claims overlapped and all of them became fertile sources of controversy.

The remaining six states, including Maryland, could not advance or support any claims to western lands, for their western boundaries were definitively marked. Early in the war, Congress had offered as an inducement to every noncommissioned officer and soldier who would enlist a bounty of twenty dollars and one hundred acres of land. Maryland refused to accept the proposition to give them one hundred acres of land because Maryland, unlike several other states, had no western lands that it could use for this purpose. If it accepted the proposal of Congress, it would be obliged to purchase lands from other states for its soldiers, probably at exorbitant prices. It offered therefore to substitute for the land bounty the sum of ten dollars, which was more than the price of the land. To this proposal Congress demurred pointing out that, if they accepted it, they would have to pay this more generous money equivalent to all the officers and soldiers. But they finally agreed to a compromise offering soldiers who enlisted for a three-year period of service a bounty of twenty dollars and those who enlisted for the duration of the war an additional bounty of one hundred acres of land. This proposal was acceptable to the Maryland Council of Safety, which accordingly proceeded to authorize the enlistment of Maryland troops for a three-year term.

But though this controversy over the use of lands as bounties for soldiers enlisting in the war was thus settled, Maryland went on to insist that the land question be dealt with as a national problem. The need of central control over the western lands of the various states was stressed in the debates in the Continental Congress as early as July 1, 1776, a few days before the adoption of the Declaration of Independence, by John Dickinson whose state, Pennsylvania, like Maryland, had a defined western limit.[6] Land speculators from Pennsylvania, Maryland, and New Jersey were interested in the Indiana Company and the Illinois-Wabash Company, which had staked out extensive areas within Virginia's charter limits and whose claims were denied by Virginia. The interests of these speculators coincided with the plans of those who desired to establish a strongly centralized Confederation. Maryland's case in particular was pressed by Thomas Johnson, Samuel Chase, Charles Carroll of Carrollton, and William Paca, all of whom were members of the companies that were developing and speculating in western lands.

In October 1777, one month before Congress referred the Articles of Confederation to the states for ratification, Maryland proposed that Congress should take over the western country. She supported a resolution in Congress declaring that the United States "shall have the sole and exclusive right and power to ascertain and fix the western boundary of such states as claim to the Mississippi or South Sea, and lay out the land beyond the boundary, so ascertained, into separate and independent states, from time to time, as the numbers and circumstances of the people thereof may require." [7] Maryland thus took the first step toward the assertion of national sovereignty over the western country, but she was the only state that supported it. On the other hand, the states that possessed western land claims succeeded in adding a clause to the Articles of Confederation assuring "that no State shall be deprived of territory for the benefit of the United States."

It seemed that Maryland was able to take a broad perspective on national problems which was impossible to states not similarly situated. From this time on, the states that possessed no western land claims, led by Maryland, carried on a persistent campaign to nationalize the western lands. They wished to deprive their rivals of the incalculable source of wealth and power which they possessed in the west. "Suppose, for instance, Virginia indisputably possessed of the extensive and fertile country to which she has set up a claim, what would be the probable consequences to Maryland?" asked the Maryland legislature in its instructions to its delegates in Congress in early 1779. It answered its own question: "Virginia, by selling on the most moderate terms, a small proportion of the lands in question, would draw into her treasury vast sums of money and ... would be enabled to lessen her taxes; lands comparatively cheap and taxes comparatively low [in comparison] with the lands and taxes of an adjacent State, would quickly drain the State, thus disadvantageously circumstanced, of its most useful inhabitants, its wealth; and its consequence, in the scale of the confederated States, would sink of course." Making a classic statement of the main issue, the Maryland legislature was convinced that this western country, "wrested from the common enemy by the blood and treasure of the thirteen States, should be considered as common property, subject to be parcelled out by Congress into free, convenient and independent governments, in such manner and at such times as the wisdom of that assembly shall hereafter direct." But Maryland qualified her demand for the surrender of the western lands with a condition that all grants and surveys made before the beginning of the war in these territories should be validated, thus preserving the interest of her own leaders who were members of the Illinois-Wabash and other western land companies.

Meanwhile Virginia was proceeding to make grants of land in her trans-Appalachian territories which Maryland and other states were insisting should be converted into a national domain. Two of Maryland's delegates in Congress, William Paca and George Plater, introduced a resolution in Congress in October 1779 calling upon Virginia "and all other states similarly circumstanced to forbear settling or issuing warrants for unappropriated lands." This resolution was adopted over the opposition of only Virginia and North Carolina, but it was so strongly resented by Virginia that she addressed a Remonstrance to Congress protesting against the claim of Congress to exercise jurisdiction over the lands which she claimed in the Ohio and Illinois country. In the same Remonstrance, however, she intimated that she would be willing to negotiate a settlement if she could thus remove "the ostensible causes of delay and the complete ratification of the Confederation," for until this question was settled, Maryland would not accept the Articles of Confederation, thus blocking the unanimous approval which would make it possible for them to go into effect.

Maryland's insistence upon making the cession of the western lands to the United States a condition to her ratification of the Articles of Confederation also had an effect upon New York, which in February 1780, in order to "facilitate the completion of the articles of confederation and perpetual union among the United States of America," instructed her delegates in Congress to make either a complete or a partial cession of her western lands as their own judgment dictated. Congress called upon other states to follow New York's example and at the same time entreated the legislature of Maryland to authorize their delegates to give their assent to the Articles. Upon the initiative of Maryland, Congress soon afterward declared that lands which should be ceded by the states to the United States should eventually be divided into states and admitted to membership in the federal union with the same rights as the older states, thus establishing the principle that federal territories would not be kept in a permanently colonial or subordinate status and foreshadowing the later Northwest Ordinance. As a further inducement, Congress offered to reimburse any state for the expenses which it had incurred in subduing or defending any part of its western territory during the war, making it easy in this way for Virginia to claim the expenses of the Clark expedition which had wrested the old northwest from the British without any aid from Congress or the Continental army.

Connecticut now offered to cede her western lands if she might retain jurisdiction over them, and Virginia came forward with an offer to cede all her lands northwest of the Ohio River on condition that they should be formed into republican states and that her continued possession of lands south of the Ohio River should be guaranteed to her. These land cessions of New York, Connecticut, and Virginia, though they were conditional, were sufficient to induce Maryland, the only state which had not yet ratified the Articles of Confederation, to do so. They were reinforced by the encouragement given by the French envoy, the Chevalier Anne C. de la Luzerne, who desired in the interests of France to bring about a union of the colonies. On the very day when New York made a formal offer of her lands to Congress (March 1, 1781), Maryland ratified the Articles and thus made the union of states complete. Appropriately, Congress, meeting in that same month at Philadelphia, elected a Marylander, John Hanson, the first president of the United States in Congress assembled under the Articles of Confederation. When Congress later formally accepted the land cession of Virginia, it did so on condition that Virginia would waive her demand for a guaranty of her claims south of the Ohio River. This condition was accepted by Virginia, and her delegates made an unconditional cession of all her western lands to Congress in March 1784.

To Maryland goes the principal credit for the formation of the national domain, which resulted from the land cessions by the states. In 1785, Massachusetts ceded both sovereignty and jurisdiction over her western lands to Congress, and Connecticut made a limited cession in the following year, reserving to herself the "Connecticut Reserve" or the "Western Reserve of Connecticut" in Ohio until 1800, when she finally ceded jurisdiction over it to Congress. South Carolina transferred her western lands to the United States in 1787 and North Carolina hers in 1790. Thanks to Maryland's efforts, during the period of the War for American Independence and the Confederation, all the thirteen states developed a common interest in the western country and a bond there which later united them after the unifying pressure of the war effort had ended. Out of these national lands Congress could now reward the soldiers of the continental army and thus encourage the process of settlement and occupation there.

Americans now turned their faces toward the west. In September 1776, Maryland's constitutional convention had officially erected the Upper and Lower Districts of Frederick County into two new counties, which they named Washington and Montgomery after the two American generals. When the Maryland Assembly wished to compensate the state's officers and soldiers who had fought in the war, they took over all the unassigned lands west of Fort Cumberland for this purpose in November 1781. They authorized the governor to appoint a surveyor to lay out these lands in lots of fifty acres each in 1787, and, as the surveyor, Francis Deakins, completed his work, the Assembly assigned four lots of fifty acres each to the officers and one to each private.

As the western lands were being settled, the older seaboard communities realized the importance of maintaining close ties with them and of becoming outlets for their products. The tidewater sections must open up new means of communication with the west. As they set up new governments, the former colonists of England emulated the pre-imperial pattern of English government harking back to precedents of localism, limited government, and decentralized authority which Englishmen had established long before the planting of colonies in America. But Marylanders, having established an independent state and being ambitious to promote its development in agriculture, manufacturing, and commerce, now partially abandoned their former commitment to principles of free individual action in favor of state aid. In Maryland's Declaration of Rights of 1776, they had declared that monopolies were "odious, contrary to the spirit of a free government and to the principles of commerce, and ought not to be suffered." But now, freed from the imperial regulations of trade and commerce which had been imposed upon them by London before the War for Independence, they looked to the state government for support for their enterprises.

Encouragement from the government in Annapolis took three forms: the granting of patent rights to inventors and of monopoly franchise privileges to certain transportation companies, direct loans of state funds to certain businesses, and the incorporation of private business companies. This last method, which had never been tried during the colonial period, was now used to encourage private businessmen who were promoting transportation facilities or were operating banks, insurance companies, and local public utility enterprises.

As early as 1762, George Washington had become interested in improving the navigation of the Potomac River between the Great Falls and Fort Cumberland as a part of his plans for the Ohio Company. But he and his associates were able to accomplish little at that time. In the year that finally brought the War for Independence to an end, the Maryland legislature appointed two surveyors, Charles Beatty and Normand Bruce, to estimate the expense of making the Potomac River "navigable through the several falls, and the time that the work might be performed in." When these two agents reported, in November 1783, that the river could be made navigable from the Great Falls to Fort Cumberland in two years at a cost of not more than $92,000, they stirred up a new interest in it.

Washington now recommended that the states of Virginia and Maryland appoint deputies to confer and agree upon a bill that would be acceptable to both states. As members of this commission, Virginia appointed Washington, General Gates, and Colonel Blakiston, and Maryland appointed Thomas Stone, Samuel Hughes, Charles Carroll of Carrollton, John Cadwalader, Samuel Chase, John De Butts, George Digges, Philip Key, Gustavus Scott, and Joseph Dashiel. They met at Annapolis in December 1784, with Washington as president and all the commissioners present except one. In the report which they prepared and submitted to the legislatures of Virginia and Maryland, they recommended that the two states join in forming a company to open the river and that each subscribe to the stock of the company in the amount of fifty shares. They also recommended that Pennsylvania be asked to lay out and improve a road from Fort Cumberland to the navigable part of the Youghiogheny River. Both states accepted these recommendations, passed the legislation suggested by the commission, and authorized the organization of a Potomac Company. The charter of this company provided that the capital stock should consist of 500 shares of £100 sterling each, commissioned the company to improve the navigation of the Potomac from tidewater to the highest practicable point on the North Branch or to Fort Cumberland, authorized it "to construct canals and erect such locks and perform such other works as they may judge necessary," and required that the work should be commenced within one year and completed within three years.

The company was organized and went into operation in May 1785, with Washington as its first president. He continued as president of the company until he was elected president of the United States. When the three years expired, the work had not progressed very far, and both Virginia and Maryland extended the terms of the charter for another three years. Again in 1790 they extended it for three years and continued to do so until 1820, when the company concluded that the undertaking was too gigantic for its resources and merged into the Chesapeake and Ohio Company.

Partly as a result of the activities of the Potomac Company, a native of Cecil County, Maryland, James Rumsey, carried on some interesting experiments in navigation on the Potomac River from 1784 to 1787. While working as an innkeeper at Bath in western Virginia, he met General George Washington who stopped at his hostel in September 1784 while riding through the village on a business trip. Rumsey showed him his working model of a pole-boat which he had designed to walk upstream against a current. It consisted of two small model boats with a paddle wheel between them which moved through water flowing rapidly through a flat-bottomed trough. The wheel was turned by the force of the current, and in turn it operated poles reaching from the outside gunwales of the connected boats to the bottom of the channel. The stronger the current, the faster the boat moved through the water. Rumsey's invention attracted Washington's interest and received his written endorsement, as follows:

I have seen the model of Mr. Rumsey's boat constructed to work against the stream; have examined the powers upon which it acts; have been an eye-witness to an actual experiment in running water of some rapidity, and give it as my opinion (although I had little faith before) that he has discovered the art of propelling boats by mechanism and small manual assistance against rapid currents; that the discovery is of vast importance, may be of the greatest usefulness in our inland navigation, and if it succeeds, of which I have no doubt, that the value of it is greatly enhanced by the simplicity of the works which, when seen and explained to, may be executed by the most common mechanic.

Acting presumably upon Washington's advice, Rumsey applied to Virginia for exclusive rights to use on its waters boats constructed in accordance with his model, and he received from that state in January 1785 a ten-year monopoly on the use of his invention. Soon afterward he similarly was granted by the Maryland Assembly the exclusive privilege of making and selling his craft "for navigating boats against the current of rapid rivers at a very small expense."

Rumsey was appointed by Washington as chief engineer of the Potomac Canal Company, and in early 1786 he and his brother-in-law, Joseph Barnes, allegedly made two unsuccessful attempts to operate a steam-propelled boat against the current of the Potomac. Later in that year, his pole-boat—apparently without any steam engine or boiler aboard—was given a public trial in which it moved about 200 yards upstream against the current. His main objective, it appears, was to move vessels through the water not by steam but by a process of jet propulsion, which had already been suggested by Benjamin Franklin in a paper on steamboats. Franklin had speculated that if a stream of water was driven out of the underwater hull of a boat at the stern, its reaction on the water in which the boat floated would drive the vessel forward or in the opposite direction to the flow of the water expelled from the boat. Rumsey tried out his jet propulsion steamboat in September 1787 with only equivocal results, for although the boat moved up the river at the rate of two miles per hour, the boat filled with steam and the test had to be abandoned.

Thereafter Rumsey carried on a bitter controversy with his principal rival, John Fitch, for the credit of operating the first steamboat and even made a trip to England in an unsuccessful effort to patent his invention. He did, however, design and patent a water-tube boiler in which the water was carried in narrow tubes bent in a spiral or zigzag form and was heated by fire or flame applied to the outside of it. This type of boiler later proved to have great value as steam pressures were increased to over 200 pounds to the square inch. Both Rumsey and Fitch unwittingly prepared the way for Robert Fulton's venture seventeen years later in developing the first commercially and financially successful steamboat on the Hudson River. Their ideas were freely pirated by Fulton.[8]

Maryland also became interested in constructing a canal that would connect the Chesapeake and Delaware Bays. Such a canal had been suggested by Dankers and Sluyter in their journal as early as 1679-1680, and after 1768 several routes were surveyed along the Chester, Bohemia, and Elk Rivers. When the route was surveyed in 1806 by Banjamin H. Latrobe, he declared that thirty-two surveys had already been made. Fifteen more were made before the canal was completed. The first legislative step was taken by the Maryland legislature in December 1789, when it passed a law to incorporate a company by the name of the Chesapeake and Delaware Canal Company and authorized certain individuals to cooperate with the states of Pennsylvania and Delaware in cutting a canal between Chesapeake Bay and the Delaware River and to open books for subscriptions to the amount of $500,000 in shares of $200 each. Not until May 1803 were a sufficient number of shares subscribed to complete the organization of the company. Maryland, through its sponsorship of the Potomac Canal and the Chesapeake and Delaware Canal, helped to pioneer the era of canal construction in the United States, which would reach its peak later in the 1830's.

The breakdown of the efforts of Maryland and Virginia to work out solutions to their common problems of navigation and trade helped to set in motion a chain of events that led to the adoption of the Constitution of the United States in 1787. As early as 1777, committees from the two states met in conference to consider jurisdiction over Chesapeake Bay and the navigation of the Potomac and Pocomoke Rivers, but they were unable to resolve their differences at this conference. Maryland soon afterward began to gain much of Virginia's foreign trade by the device of imposing lower tariff duties than her neighbor to the south. The ensuing tariff war between them began even while the War for Independence was being waged, and it was not terminated by the Articles of Confederation, for under the Articles Congress had no power to impose duties on imports without the assent of all the states. After the Articles of Confederation went into effect the Maryland Assembly, against the opposition of the Senate, voted to authorize Congress "to impose a duty of five *per centum ad valorem* on all imported goods . . . for the payment of the debt contracted by Congress during the war." But this proposal was not approved by all the states and so was not put in operation.

Each state was therefore left free either not to levy duties on imports or to levy such duties as it saw fit. As the tariff rivalries between the states became acute and the financial needs of the government mounted, Congress asked the states to authorize it to levy certain specified duties on spirits, wines, teas, pepper, sugar, molasses, cocoa, and coffee, and a duty of five *per cent ad valorem* on all other imported goods for a period of twenty-five years. To this request Maryland assented, and by 1786 was joined by eleven other states, but the consent of New York could not be obtained. Congress therefore remained impotent to curb interstate tariff rivalries, among them those that now developed between Maryland and Virginia and that complicated their already bitter rivalry over navigation on their common waters.

To solve this latter problem, Virginia appointed commissioners in 1784 to meet with commissioners from Maryland for the purpose of framing "such liberal and equitable regulations touching the jurisdiction and navigation of the waters of Chesapeake Bay, and the rivers Potomac and Pocomoke, as may be mutually advantageous to the two States." This action met with a favorable response in Annapolis where the Maryland Assembly named Thomas Johnson, Thomas Stone, Samuel Chase, and Daniel of St. Thomas Jenifer as commissioners to meet with Virginia's representatives, George Mason and Alexander Henderson, at Alexandria in March 1785. But at Washington's invitation the two state delegations met at Mount Vernon. There they agreed upon a compact which (1) declared the Chesapeake and Pocomoke common highways for the vessels of both states and (2) made the Potomac "a common highway to citizens of the United States and those in amity with the same States, trading to or from Virginia to Maryland." [9]

In this earliest—or, at least, one of the earliest—of interstate compacts, Maryland obtained a guaranty of free passage through the Virginia-controlled Capes of the Chesapeake. In return, Maryland gave Virginia a half-share in the management and use of the tidewater portions of the Potomac, including particularly its seafood resources. The compact, though disadvantageous to Maryland, was accepted by the Maryland Assembly. But the Assembly suggested that its terms be broadened to provide that the value of coin should be fixed at the same level in both states, that "duties on imports or exports, if laid, should be the same in both States," that representatives of the two states be appointed to confer on these subjects, and that the legislatures of Delaware and Pennsylvania likewise be invited to nominate commissioners for this same purpose. As these last two states promptly accepted the invitation, the Maryland legislature appointed commissioners in February 1786 "to meet commissioners from the States of Pennsylvania and Delaware, for the purpose of considering and digesting the most proper measures for improving the inland navigation of the Susquehannah [sic] River, and the waters communicating with it, and for effecting a navigable communication between the Bays of Chesapeake and Delaware, and also to confer on any other subject which may tend to promote the commerce and mutual convenience of the said States."

Already the propertied interests in many states were clamoring for a new constitutional convention and a strengthened central government. As early as 1782, the New York legislature passed resolutions, written by Alexander Hamilton, calling for a new convention. Washington repeatedly voiced a demand for stronger government. In 1785, the Massachusetts legislature instructed its delegates to persuade Congress to summon a convention. But the leadership in the movement for such a convention was taken by Virginia. When the legislature of that state took under consideration the compact with Maryland over the navigation of their common waterways, it appointed deputies to meet with representatives of "the other States in the Union, at a time and place to be agreed on, to take into consideration the trade of the United States, to examine the relative situation of trade of the said States, to consider how far a uniform system in their commercial regulations may be necessary to their common interest and their permanent harmony, and to report to the several States such an Act relative to this great object, as when unanimously ratified by them, will enable the United States in congress assembled effectually to provide for the same." Virginia was thus proposing that all the thirteen states that composed the Union should participate in the convention and suggested that the commissioners meet at Annapolis in September 1786.

This audacious proposal aroused considerable suspicion, particularly among northern merchants, who, though they wished to give Congress the power to regulate trade, questioned the motives and sincerity of Virginia. It evoked a mixed reaction in Maryland. The House of Delegates meeting in Annapolis immediately gave its approval, but the Senate refused to concur, explaining in a long message to the House that the proposed meeting "may be misunderstood or misrepresented in Europe, give umbrage to Congress, and disquiet the citizens of the United States, who may be thereby led erroneously to suspect that the great council of this country wants either the will or the wisdom to digest a proper uniform plan for the regulation of their commerce." The Senate feared that this meeting might be the forerunner of other meetings "which may have consequences which cannot be foreseen. Innovations in government, when not absolutely necessary, are dangerous, particularly to republics, generally too fond of novelties, and subject to change." But the Senate expressed a willingness to continue conferences and negotiations with Virginia, Pennsylvania, and Delaware "on the several subjects mentioned in the report of the commissioners of Virginia and Maryland."

Accordingly, when the convention met in Annapolis in September 1786, Maryland was unrepresented. Only five states sent delegates— New York, New Jersey, Delaware, Pennsylvania, and Virginia— though four others—New Hampshire, Massachusetts, Rhode Island, and North Carolina—had in fact appointed commissioners. John Dickinson, former president of Pennsylvania now residing in Delaware, was chosen president of the convention. With such a limited number of states in attendance, the convention declined to consider the general situation of the confederation and instead unanimously adopted a report of Alexander Hamilton which pointed out that important defects existed in the system of the federal government. It also recommended that the states there represented "themselves concur, and use their endeavors to procure the concurrence of the other States, in the appointment of commissioners, to meet at Philadelphia, on the second Monday in May next, to take into consideration the situation of the United States, to devise such further provisions as shall appear to them necessary to render the Constitution of the Federal Government adequate to the exigencies of the Union, and to report such an act for that purpose to the United States in Congress assembled."

Virginia promptly appointed George Washington, Patrick Henry, Edmund Randolph, John Blair, James Madison, George Mason, and George Wythe as commissioners to join with the deputies of the other states "in devising and discussing all such alterations and further provisions as may be necessary to render the Federal Constitution adequate to the exigencies of the Union." In Maryland both the House and the Senate approved the recommendation and agreed that it was "of the utmost importance, and most likely, with the least delay, to vest in the Federal Government those powers which are so necessary to give strength and stability to the union." But they adjourned without appointing deputies, and not until the governor convened them again in April 1787 did they resume consideration of this matter. They then chose Robert Hanson Harrison, Charles Carroll of Carrollton, Thomas Stone, James McHenry, and Thomas Sim Lee as "deputies to represent this State, for the purpose of revising the Federal Constitution."

Meanwhile the economic condition of the country was growing steadily worse. Because of the economic depression resulting from the war, the states were unable to contribute adequately to the support of the national government and to pay their share of the public debt. Some taxed imports from neighboring states; some treated the citizens of other states as aliens; some violated the treaties with England, France, and Holland; and some raised and equipped troops without the consent of Congress. The country was being rapidly drained of its specie, and insolvencies and bankruptcies became alarmingly numerous. The central government owed a debt of 42 million dollars, the annual interest on which was $2,415,956; the states had incurred large financial obligations, and many of the towns had contracted debts in furnishing men and supplies to the army. There was considerable agitation for the establishment of monarchy or for the partition of the Union into several confederacies. In Maryland the House of Delegates proposed to issue bills of credit in the amount of £350,000 redeemable in ten years; but the Senate rejected the suggestion and the controversy became so bitter that the House adjourned for two months so that the subject could be referred to the people. After a violent newspaper controversy, the people voted the proposal down. At this time news of the outbreak of Shays' Rebellion in Massachusetts arrived. It impelled many who had not been concerned hitherto to press for a stronger central government and gave the political leaders who had long been working for such a government a new leverage to use in consummating their program. In the midst of the ensuing turmoil, approaching anarchy, the convention assembled at Philadelphia in May 1787.

One of Maryland's delegates to the constitutional convention, Luther Martin, who served as a member of the special committee on representation, worked successfully for a compromise of the problem which nearly wrecked the convention involving the representation of the states in the national legislature. Upon the suggestion of Samuel Chase, Martin had been appointed Attorney General of Maryland in 1778, and in that office, in which he would serve for twenty-eight years, he had vigorously persecuted the Tories, had identified himself with the interests of the debtor class, and, along with Chase, had demanded new issues of paper money. In the constitutional convention at Philadelphia he championed the cause of the federalists or advocates of states' rights against the nationalists. He was particularly concerned to preserve the state of Maryland as a political entity and to prevent its absorption into an overpowering national union. The central government, he insisted, had been formed to preserve the state governments, not to govern individuals. As a result of his efforts, the convention provided for equal representation of the states in the Senate and representation according to population in the House of Representatives. To his efforts were largely due the guaranties of states' rights which survived in the constitution.

Maryland delegates also showed much interest in the proposal that Negroes should be counted in apportioning representation, which favored the slaveholding states. As Luther Martin, himself a slaveholder, explained, in objecting to this compromise, it increased the power of those states in proportion as they themselves violated the rights of freedom. At the time of the Declaration of Independence, slavery had existed in all the states. Vermont was the first state to abolish it, as she did in her state constitution in 1777. Massachusetts did the same in her constitution of 1780, declaring that "All men are born free and equal, and have certain natural, essential and inalienable rights, among which are the right of enjoying and defending their lives and liberties, and that of acquiring, possessing and protecting property." New Hampshire was later held to have abolished slavery by her constitution of 1783. Pennsylvania passed a gradual emancipation act in 1783, freeing all persons born in that state at the age of twenty-eight. Rhode Island, Connecticut, New York, and New Jersey also enacted legislation of this type at about the same time.

Meanwhile, the Quaker leader, John Woolman, was stressing the iniquity of slaveholding in his writings, particularly his *Considerations on the Keeping of Negroes,* published in 1754 and again in 1762, and in his "walking journey" through Delaware and the Eastern Shore of Maryland in 1766, he appealed to his coreligionists there to emancipate their slaves. In their opposition to slavery, the Quakers were soon reinforced by the work of Methodist leaders in Maryland, notably Bishop Asbury. For this and other reasons, many Maryland slaveholders manumitted their slaves, sometimes during their lifetime and sometimes in their wills.

Meanwhile, Maryland tried to prevent the further importation of Negro slaves into the state. From time to time it levied a poll tax on Negroes, and in 1780, when the state desperately needed additional revenue for war purposes, it levied a duty of 15 pounds of tobacco on every slave who had lived in the state for three years and 500 pounds of tobacco on every other. This tax measure thus discriminated against newly imported slaves. As the state's financial condition improved, the Maryland legislature adopted other methods of controlling the importation of Negroes. In 1783 it explicitly forbade any person "to import or bring into this State by land or water, a negro, mulatto, or other slave for sale, or to reside within this State; and any person brought into this State as a slave contrary to this Act, if a slave before, shall thereupon immediately cease to be a slave, and shall be free"; but it allowed citizens of other states to bring slaves into the state if they had a *bona fide* intention of settling in Maryland and it allowed slaveowners crossing Maryland to take their slaves with them. This Maryland act of 1783 was patterned after a Virginia act of 1778 which had forbidden all slave trade into Virginia from outside the state. But its explicit prohibitions against the foreign trade in slaves were not strictly enforced.

In the Philadelphia convention which drew up the new constitution for the United States in 1787, the subject of the slave trade was considered. Luther Martin proposed that the national government be authorized either to prohibit altogether or to impose a tax on the importation of slaves. In defending this proposition he said, according to Madison's notes: "As five slaves are to be counted as 3 free men in the apportionment of Representatives; such a clause wd leave an encouragement to this traffic. 2 slaves weakened one part of the Union which the other parts were bound to protect; the privilege of importing them was therefore unreasonable—3 was inconsistent with the principles of the revolution and dishonorable to the American character to have such a feature in the Constitution." But his proposal was opposed by Oliver Ellsworth and Roger Sherman of Connecticut, James Wilson of Pennsylvania, Rufus King and Elbridge Gerry of Massachusetts. It was therefore referred to a committee consisting of one member from each state; and, as a result, a compromise was adopted which prohibited limitation of the slave trade until 1808 but authorized the imposition of a tax upon it and, as a concession to the commercial states, eliminated the clause requiring a two-thirds vote of each House for the passage of a navigation act.

Only three of Maryland's five delegates signed the Constitution—James McHenry, Daniel of St. Thomas Jenifer, and Daniel Carroll, cousin of Charles Carroll of Carrollton. In November they submitted it to the Maryland legislature, which had been summoned by Governor William Smallwood for the purpose of receiving their report. Already opposition to it had appeared in Maryland, for two of Maryland's delegates, Luther Martin and John Francis Mercer, had left the convention before it was over and had returned to their state to explain their reasons for opposing it. They now headed a group in the legislature which opposed the constitution on the following grounds: that it gave the larger and wealthier states, such as Virginia, Pennsylvania, and Massachusetts, disproportionate power and that it entrusted the central government with too much power, particularly the power to lay duties upon imports into the states and to suspend the writ of *habeas corpus* in cases of rebellion. Besides Martin and Mercer, this group included Samuel Chase and William Pinkney.

But the state legislatures were not made the final ratifying authority by the Philadelphia convention. This power was lodged in state conventions to be specifically chosen for that purpose. Accordingly the Maryland legislature, despite strong opposition, ordered the election of delegates to a state convention to assemble in Annapolis in April 1788 for the purpose of approving or rejecting the document. A large majority of the delegates chosen to this convention were nationalists, favoring the Constitution. They elected George Plater of St. Mary's County as president and after only five days of debate ratified the constitution by a vote of 63 to 11, the eleven negative votes being cast by Jeremiah Chase, Samuel Chase, John F. Mercer, Benjamin Harrison, Charles Ridgely, Charles Ridgely of William, Edward Cockey, Nathan Cromwell, John Love, William Pinkney, and Luther Martin.

But one of the delegates who voted for the constitution, William Paca, a delegate from Harford County, had insisted upon adding amendments, and, after the ratification of the document, he was made chairman of a committee of thirteen to consider his amendments. The committee approved of twelve of them but did not report them to the Convention because they feared that, among other things "it might produce bad consequences in Virginia and the other States who had not ratified, where the opponents of the government might be equal or nearly equal in number to its friends." Maryland therefore circumspectly refrained from taking an open or leading part in the movement for a bill of rights, which was finally added to the constitution. In fact, in the crucial states of Massachusetts, Virginia, and New York, the majorities in the ratifying conventions opposed the constitution and were won over to its support only by the promise that, once the new government was established, amendments would be submitted to the states for ratification

Maryland was the seventh state to ratify the constitution. Because of her still pending claim against the Bank of England for recovery of her prewar stock in the Bank and her consequent compliance with the provisions of the treaty of peace regarding British debts, Maryland, unlike some of the other states, had no reason to fear possible action against her by the new federal courts provided for in the constitution. By the following September a sufficient number of states had ratified the constitution to enable Congress to select a time for the appointment of electors and the commencement of proceedings under the new frame of government. In preparation for this event, the General Assembly of Maryland divided the state into six districts: (1) St. Mary's, Charles, and Calvert Counties, (2) Kent, Talbot, Cecil, and Queen Anne's Counties, (3) Anne Arundel and Prince George's, (4) Baltimore and Harford Counties, (5) Somerset, Dorchester, Worcester, and Caroline Counties, and (6) Frederick, Washington, and Montgomery Counties. They provided for the selection of electors and of six representatives to Congress from these districts. "Every person coming to vote" for a representative, they declared, "shall have a right to vote for six persons," thus voting for the general ticket. Elections were not secret but were *viva voce*. The legislature provided further that Maryland's two senators "should be elected by a joint ballot of both Houses; and that no person should be elected a senator from this State, unless by a majority of the attending members of both Houses." They decided "that one senator should be a resident of the Western and the other of the Eastern Shore." In the resulting joint ballots, John Henry was chosen senator from the Eastern Shore, and Charles Carroll of Carrollton from the Western Shore. In drawing for the short and long terms, Carroll drew the two-year term and Henry the six-year term.

In the first elections for president and vice-president under the new constitution, Maryland cast her six electoral votes for George Washington for president and for Robert Hanson Harrison of Maryland for vice-president. When Congress finally organized itself in early April 1789, the Senate counted the electoral votes and declared that Washington was unanimously chosen president of the United States and John Adams vice-president. The president of the Senate then officially notified Washington of his election. As Washington set out from Mount Vernon for New

York (the seat of government) to assume his new duties, he received enthusiastic ovations along the way. On April 30, 1789, he took the oath of office in the Senate Chamber overlooking Wall Street in New York, where Congress was then sitting. Soon afterward, he appointed several Marylanders to important public offices, including Robert Hanson Harrison as associate justice of the Supreme Court and William Paca as judge of the United States District Court for Maryland.

Maryland thus took her place as one of the thirteen original members of the new federal union. Though, for reasons already noticed, the state had been responsible for delaying for four years the ratification of America's first constitution, the Articles of Confederation, she had fared well under the Articles. The state had developed satisfactory and effective techniques of self-government, its agencies of government had functioned smoothly under Governors Johnson, Lee, Paca, and Smallwood, and though it labored under the incubus of a large war debt, its economic condition was no more critical than that of other states. Nevertheless, majority sentiment in the state obviously favored a stronger central government, and Maryland did not play the same obstructive role in the events leading up to the ratification of the constitution of 1787 as she had played in delaying action on the Articles of Confederation. She had exerted her maximum leverage at that time as a small state by insisting upon the establishment of a national domain in the trans-Appalachian west, but she lacked both the means and the inclination to interpose similar objections to the ratification of the Philadelphia constitution. Indeed, Maryland, with the help of Virginia, had acted as a catalyst in precipitating the new constitution. In the struggle over its ratification, Maryland occupied an intermediate position between the large and the small states, going along with the majority in almost every case.[10]

Footnotes

[1] Fletcher Pratt, *The Navy: A History*, Doubleday, Doran & Company, Inc., Garden City, New York, 1938, p. 36.

[2] Homer Bast, "Tench Tilghman—Maryland Patriot," *Maryland Historical Magazine*, vol. XLII, No. 2, June 1947, pp. 71-94.

[3] Peter M. Bergman, *The Chronological History of the Negro in America*, The New American Library, New York and Toronto, 1969, pp. 55, 58; Phillip T. Drotning, *Black Heroes in Our Nation's History*, Cowles Book Company, Inc., New York, pp. 29-30; and W.B. Hartgrove, "The Negro Soldier in the American Revolution," *Journal of Negro History*, vol. I, No. 2, April 1916, p. 127.

[4] Rolfe Lyman Allen, *The Confiscation of British Property by the State of Maryland during the Revolution*, M.A. thesis, University of Maryland, 1935.

[5] Primary material on Maryland's attempt to recover her stock in the Bank of England will be found in Morris L. Radoff, *Calendar of Maryland State Papers: No. 2*,

The Bank Stock Papers, Publications of the Hall of Records Commission No. 5, Annapolis, 1947.

[6] John Dickinson, "Arguments ag^t. the Independence of these Colonies in Congress," cited in Merrill Jensen, *The Articles of Confederation: An Interpretation of the Social-Constitutional History of the American Revolution, 1774-1781,* The University of Wisconsin Press, Madison, 1940, p. 115.

[7] *Journals of Congress,* IX (1777), p. 807.

[8] James A. Padgett, ed., "Letters of James Rumsey," *Maryland Historical Magazine,* vol. XXXII, No. 1, March 1937, pp. 10-28; No. 2, June 1937, pp. 136-155; No. 3, September 1937, pp. 271-285.

[9] Printed in Scharf, *History of Maryland,* II, 531.

[10] Primary sources for the history of Maryland during the War for Independence include the following: William Hand Browne, ed., *Journal and Correspondence of the Maryland Council of Safety, Archives of Maryland,* vols. XIV, XVI, and XXI, Maryland Historical Society, Baltimore, 1893, 1897, 1901; Robert Purviance, *A Narrative of Events Which Occurred in Baltimore Town During the Revolutionary War,* Joseph Robinson, Baltimore, 1849; Bernard Christian Steiner, ed., *Journal and Correspondence of the State Council of Maryland, 1779-1781, Archives of Maryland,* vols. XLIII and XLV, Maryland Historical Society, Baltimore, 1924 and 1927.

Sources and Additional Reading

Adams, Herbert Baxter, *Maryland's Influence upon Land Cessions to the United States,* Johns Hopkins University Studies, Series 3, No. 1, J. Murphy, Baltimore, 1877; reprint 1973.

Black, J.W., *Maryland's Attitude in the Struggle for Canada,* Johns Hopkins University Studies, vol. 10, Johns Hopkins Press, Baltimore, 1892.

Bond, Beverley Waugh, *State Government in Maryland, 1777-1781,* Johns Hopkins University Studies, Series 23, Nos. 3, 4, Johns Hopkins Press, Baltimore, 1905.

Buchholz, Heinrich Ewald, *Governors of Maryland from the Revolution to the Year 1908.* With portrait supplement. Second edition. Williams and Wilkins Company, Baltimore, 1908.

Clarkson, Paul S., and R. Samuel Jett, *Luther Martin of Maryland,* Johns Hopkins University Press, Baltimore, 1970.

Crowl, Philip A., *Maryland During and After the Revolution: A Political and Economic Study,* The Johns Hopkins University Studies in Historical and Political Science, Series LXI, No. 1, Johns Hopkins Press, Baltimore, 1943.

Essary, J. Frederick, *Maryland in National Politics: From Charles Carroll to Albert C. Ritchie,* second edition, Baltimore, 1932.

Jensen, Merrill, *The Articles of Confederation: An Interpretation of the Social-Constitutional History of the American Revolution, 1774-1781,* University of Wisconsin Press, Madison, 1940.

———, "Cession of the Old Northwest," *Mississippi Valley Historical Review,* vol. XXIII, pp. 27-48 (June 1936).

Kremer, J. Bruce, *John Hanson of Mulberry Grove,* Albert & Charles Boni, Inc., New York, 1938.

Mayer, Brantz, ed., *Journal of Charles Carroll of Carrollton, during his Visit to Canada in 1776, as One of the Commissioners from Congress; with a Memoir and Notes.* Printed by John Murphy, for the Maryland Historical Society, Baltimore, 1876.

Nelson, Jacob A., *John Hanson and the Inseparable Union, . . .* Meador Publishing Company, Boston, 1939.

Padgett, James A., ed., "Letters of James Rumsey," *Maryland Historical Magazine,* vol., XXXII No. 1, March 1937, pp. 10-28; No. 2, June 1937, pp. 136-155; No. 3, September 1937, pp. 271-285, Baltimore.

Smith, Seymour Wemyss, *John Hanson, Our First President,* Brewer, Warren & Putnam, New York, 1932.

Steiner, Bernard Christian, *The Life and Correspondence of James McHenry, Secretary of War under Washington and Adams,* Cleveland, The Burrows Brothers Company, 1907.

———, "Maryland's Adoption of the Federal Constitution," *American Historical Review,* V, pp. 22-44 (October 1899), and pp. 207-224 (January 1900).

———, *Western Maryland in the Revolution,* Johns Hopkins University Studies, Series 20, No. 1, Johns Hopkins Press, Baltimore, 1902.

Steuart, Rieman, *A History of the Maryland Line in the Revolutionary War, 1775-1783,* Society of the Cincinnati of Maryland, 1969.

Treat, Payson Jackson, *The National Land System, 1785-1820,* E.B. Treat & Co., New York, 1910.

Turner, Ella May, *James Rumsey, Pioneer in Steam Navigation,* Mennonite Publishing House, Scottsdale, Pennsylvania, 1930.

Ward, George Washington, *The Early Development of the Chesapeake and Ohio Canal Project,* Johns Hopkins University Studies, Series 17, Nos. 9-11, Johns Hopkins Press, 1899.

Wheeler, Joseph Towne, *The Maryland Press, 1777-1790,* Baltimore, 1938.

CHAPTER XV

A STATE IN THE NEW UNION

When the new federal union of thirteen states was established under the constitution, Maryland, with a population of 319,728, according to the first national census in 1790, ranked sixth among them, being outnumbered by Virginia, Massachusette, Pennsylvania, North Carolina, and New York, in that order. Its population consisted of 208,649 whites, nearly half as many slaves numbering 103,036, and 8,043 free blacks. Though Maryland held only a little more than one percent of the total land area of the United States, it included more than eight percent of the people. In density of population it ranked third among the states, being exceeded only by Rhode Island and Connecticut.

But Maryland's population, calculated at 32.3 to the square mile, was still concentrated in the seaboard area and had only slightly penetrated into the western counties. In tidewater Maryland were situated all the largest population centers of the state including Elk Ridge Landing and Bladensburg, both of which were then accessible to seagoing vessels, Baltimore Town, Annapolis, Port Tobacco, Chestertown, Easton, and Oxford. Elk Ridge Landing, according to a British traveler, included "only about 15 houses, 2 stores, and a few shops for mechanics," but it was the seat of an iron industry which had been established in 1759 using local ore. In addition, this town, located seven miles from Baltimore on the south side of the Patapsco River, was a port of "deposit of all the tobacco raised for a considerable distance, where it was inspected and sent to Europe." In this business it was rivaled by Port Tobacco in Charles County, which was one of the chief seaports of the English colonies, with a busy, noisy, crowded waterfront at which ships from all over the world docked. On the Eastern Shore, Easton boasted a court house which was the most imposing building in the state, with the exception of the state house in Annapolis, and it was the center of an active social life.

The destinies of the state were regulated in pleasant and leisurely fashion by a few men of wealth and influence who set the tone of both society and politics. They gave Maryland its deserved reputation for gracious living and generous hospitality toward visitors. John Beale Bordley, a distinguished lawyer of Annapolis, farmed his 1,600 acres on Wye Island on a large scale, rotating tobacco with crops of wheat, hemp, flax, and cotton. At Wye House on the Eastern Shore, Edward Lloyd was reputed to own thirteen plantations of about 1,000 acres each. He even maintained a deer park in the English style. Near Baltimore Town, Colonel John Eager Howard, whose wealth was derived in part from Baltimore shipping, maintained an estate, Belvidere, whose palatial grounds extended from the present Franklin Street in Baltimore to North Avenue and included most of modern Baltimore's downtown business and residential section. Colonel John O'Donnell's estate east of Baltimore covered some 2,500 acres and was named Canton in deference to his interest in Far Eastern trade. In Howard County west of Baltimore was situated the principal estate of the Catholic Charles Carroll of Carrollton, who owned 300 slaves and was considered to be the wealthiest man in the nation. His estate, Doughoregan Manor, cultivated by slave labor, was and continues to be a show place for visitors. Of life at another of Carroll's estates, Brooklandwood, a visitor wrote, "We have four waiters at dinner which is always sumptuous; Terrapin, soup, fish, turkey, Galena fowls, omelette, ducks, corned beef, oysters stewed, carrots, turnips, potatoes, cabbage, parsnips, & c. . . . puddings, whips, sweetmeats, and thick cream. After dinner, American apples & c." Marylanders, it has been said, "would rather eat than fight but have a genius for both."

Maryland was an active competitor for the national capital under the new constitution. For this honor the state possessed certain strong claims. She occupied an intermediate position between the northern and the southern states, and the center of population of the United States was located in the vicinity of Baltimore. The state had helped to initiate the movement for a new constitution and had supported the results of that movement. The constitution itself had not located a national capital but had provided that "the seat of government of the United States" should be established in "such district (not exceeding ten miles square)" as should be ceded by particular states and accepted by Congress. Over this district Congress was given the power "to exercise exclusive legislation in all cases whatsoever."

Under the Articles of Confederation, Congress had met at Philadelphia, Baltimore, Lancaster, York, Princeton, Annapolis, Trenton, and New York. In 1783 Congressman Elbridge Gerry of Massachusetts proposed that the capital be located on or near the banks of the Delaware or Potomac Rivers, provided that a suitable place could be found for such a federal district and that the United States could secure exclusive jurisdiction over it. Congress subsequently took under consideration other proposals to locate the federal district either on the Delaware or the Potomac, but they reached no final decision. The new constitution, as already noted, refrained from suggesting a site for the seat of government. As early as December 23, 1788, soon after Congress organized itself under the constitution, the General Assembly of Maryland voted "to cede to congress a district of ten miles square, in this State, for the seat of the government of the United States." Virginia whose claims to the national capital were almost as strong as Maryland's, passed a similar resolution. But these offers did not arouse enthusiasm in Congress, where, instead, the House of Representatives declared "that the permanent seat of the government of the United States ought to be at some convenient place on the bank of the Susquehannah, in the State of Pennsylvania." Before the Senate could act upon this resolution, however, Congress adjourned.

Virginia and Maryland now resolved to offer money for the capital and to pool their efforts in order to obtain it. The Virginia legislature proposed in December 1789 to advance the sum of $120,000 "to the use of the general government and to be applied in such manner as Congress shall direct, towards erecting public buildings" on condition that the Maryland Assembly would advance not less than three-fifths of this sum. To this proposal the Maryland Assembly responded favorably, offering to advance the suggested sum of $72,000 for this purpose. In order to procure it, they instructed the treasurer of the Western Shore to sell "the reserved lands to the westward of Fort Cumberland" and also "the lands lying in Dorchester County, and now in the possession of the tribe of Choptank Indians."

Meanwhile, competition for the capital was mounting steadily, and the question of its location became entangled with other problems of national policy, specifically the problem of the state debts, which Hamilton and other northern leaders were insisting should be assumed by the national government. New York, Philadelphia, Trenton, and other places offered inducements to Congress for the capital, and Baltimore, going beyond the offer of the Maryland Assembly, offered an additional £20,000 to have the capital located within its limits. Finally, however, after a compromise arrangement between Hamilton and Jefferson, Congress decided on July 16, 1790 by a close vote of 32 to 29 that the capital should be located "on the river Potomac, at some place between the mouths of the Eastern Branch and the Conecocheague." This victory for the south was won at the sacrifice of the assumption bill, so distasteful to states such as Maryland and Virginia which had already paid off their war debts.

The actual selection of the site was left to President Washington. Later in the same year he visited Williamsport, Maryland, but did not like it. He finally chose the present site for the national capital. But since Congress had provided that the district must be located above the mouth of the Eastern Branch, he procured an amendment which authorized him to make "any part of the territory below the said limit, and above the mouth of Hunting Creek, a part of said district, so as to include a convenient part of the Eastern Branch and of the lands lying on the lower side thereof, and also the town of Alexandria, provided that no public buildings be erected otherwise than on the Maryland side of the Potomac." Washington then proceeded to appoint Thomas Johnson and Daniel Carroll of Maryland and Dr. David Stewart of Alexandria as commissioners to lay off "the Territory of Columbia." He entered into agreements with the owners of the land—most of which belonged to four planters, Daniel Carroll, David Burns, Samuel Davidson, and Notley Young—by which the owners retained every other lot and should receive £25 for every acre taken for public use with no allowance for land set aside for streets and alleys. Jenkins Hill on the east side of Goose Creek, the property of Daniel Carroll, was fixed as the site of the Capitol and "that part of the district called Hamburgh, near Burn's gate" was chosen for the president's house. The first commissioners called the new district "the Territory of Columbia" and the federal city "the City of Washington." The General Assembly of Maryland ceded to the national government in December 1791 that portion of the District of Columbia which lies on the north side of the Potomac, though it did not and could not vest in the United States any right of property in the soil except as the owners transferred it to the national government.

The principal rival to the new federal city was Georgetown, which the Maryland legislature had incorporated on December 25, 1789. The new capital therefore had difficulty in getting established. The sums of $120,000 and $72,000, which Virginia and Maryland respectively advanced to the government for the construction of public buildings there, were soon exhausted. The sale of lots in the District of Columbia did not proceed rapidly, and on December 23, 1793, the government made a contract with Robert Morris of Philadelphia and James Greenleaf of New York for the sale of 6,000 lots southwest and northwest of Massachusetts Avenue at £80 for each lot. The new city was in large part surveyed and laid out by a Marylander, Major Andrew Ellicott, assisted by a talented free Negro, Benjamin Banneker, and the new capitol building was originally designed successively by two other Marylanders, William Thornton and Benjamin H. Latrobe. The southeast cornerstone of the north wing of the capitol was laid on September 18,

1793 with Masonic honors. Washington presided over these ceremonies as Worshipful Master of Lodge No. 22, Virginia. At the conclusion of the exercises, "the whole company retired to an extensive booth, where an ox of 500 lbs. weight was barbecued, of which the company generally partook, with every abundance of other recreation."

But Morris and Greenleaf, who had purchased large tracts of land in the District, failed to make the first payment on their lands. At Washington's suggestion, Congress authorized a loan of $300,000 for the continuance and completion of the work on the public buildings, but the government's credit was so low that it could not secure the money. Washington thereupon wrote a letter to Governor John H. Stone of Maryland in 1796, asking the State of Maryland to lend $150,000. Maryland complied with this request, in part, offering to lend $100,000 for the erection of the capitol buildings if the three commissioners of the District would secure it with their bond. Maryland later lent additional sums of $100,000 and $50,000. By 1800, the public buildings were declared ready for occupancy and the government offices were moved from Philadelphia to the City of Washington. It was at that time, as has been aptly said, only an "ill-built little village in a vast swamp."

The population of Baltimore Town was reported to be 13,503 in the first national census. This town, situated on the north bank of the Patapsco River, fourteen miles from Chesapeake Bay, had not been founded until almost a century after the beginning of colonization in Maryland. A quarter century after its founding in 1729, the town was still surrounded by a board fence and included not more than 200 people. Established as a market place and an *entrepôt* for incoming and outgoing commodities, it grew up around the customs house. Its manufacturing and commercial activities were greatly stimulated by the War for Independence, as its furnaces, foundries, and forges supplied the weapons of war for the continental army. Its rise was also aided by the basic shift in the staples of Maryland's economy from tobacco to grain. This shift, together with Baltimore's continued role in the trade with the West Indies, saved it from the acute effects of the depression of 1785 from which the rest of the country suffered severely. A sugar refinery was built in Baltimore in 1784 to process the large quantities of raw sugar that were brought there as a consequence of the West Indian trade, and as commerce was resumed with Europe, refined sugar supplemented the exports of Maryland's tobacco, grain, and flour. By the close of the war, the population of Baltimore Town had grown to some 8,000, and it was beginning to rival Annapolis as the dominant population center in the state.

Two architects of Baltimore, Benjamin Henry Latrobe and Maximilian Godefroy, a temperamental French immigrant, assumed the mission of introducing modern architectural design into this country during the first two decades of the nineteenth century. Their efforts took form in such buildings in Baltimore as the Catholic Cathedral of the Assumption of the Blessed Virgin Mary by Latrobe, and the Baltimore Exchange and the Battle Monument by Godefroy, the latter commemorating the citizens who perished in the defense of the city in 1813. By developing and upholding high professional standards, they elevated architecture from its previous amateurishness to the profession which it became in the Jacksonian era, signalized by the Organization of the American Institute of Architects in 1835-1836. Latrobe, in particular, inspired a new appreciation of the dignity of classic simplicity, best exemplified perhaps in the capitol building in Washington, and he laid the basis for the architectural profession in America.

Baltimore owed its rising prosperity to its favorable geographical situation and its access to producing areas. It grew and prospered on the growing trade of the interior uplands. It served as the eastern terminus of the only practical road running west to the Ohio Valley. Over the Cumberland Road to Baltimore lumbered wagons from the Shenandoah Valley of Virginia and the valleys of western Maryland carrying grain and skins. Situated also on the only good road running north and south through the seaboard colonies, Baltimore became the commercial outlet for settlers in the back country of Pennsylvania and Virginia as well as Maryland. Over that road in 1783 a stagecoach provided passenger service from Baltimore to Philadelphia every day in the week except Saturday and Sunday, leaving at five o'clock and making the trip in 48 hours. The stage from Baltimore to Alexandria made only three round-trips a week, leaving Baltimore on Mondays, Wednesdays, and Fridays and returning on Tuesdays, Thursdays, and Saturdays.

Drawing raw materials from its rich hinterlands, the port on the Patapsco became a center of flour milling and shipping. To Baltimore came the grain from the farmers in southern Pennsylvania who found it more convenient to send their product on barges down the Susquehanna River than to haul it overland to Philadelphia. In 1771, a self-styled "Friend to Trade" complained in "An Address to the Merchants and Inhabitants of Pennsylvania" that "Baltimore town in Maryland has within a few years past carried off from this city [Philadelphia] almost the whole trade of Frederick, York, Bedford, and Cumberland Counties."[1] Using the products of the fertile wheat fields of the hinterlands of Pennsylvania, the Hagerstown and Middletown valleys of Maryland,

and the Shenandoah Valley of Virginia, Baltimore developed flour milling as its most important industry, utilizing the waterpower nearby. As early as 1795 it established the first American flour mill operated by steam, and by 1825, within a radius of twenty miles of the city, six flour mills could be found. One of these, situated at the fall line on the Patapsco River and owned by two industrious Quaker brothers named Ellicott, was described as follows by a French visitor in 1791:

> The wheat is hoisted to the upper floor by means of a machine whose mechanism is concealed; there it is spread out and descends to the mill stones. The flour falls into a room below and is carried by a mechanical contrivance to a place where it is put into barrels. The barrels are lifted away and loaded on wagons by the same machine which hoists the sacks of wheat to the upper floor.[2]

After the war, Baltimore Town developed an extensive commerce with Europe and the French West Indies. Its principal exports included flour, corn, salted meats, timber, and tobacco, and from the West Indies it imported quantities of sugar and molasses. In 1785 it opened up trade with the Far East when a Baltimore vessel, the *Pallas,* owned by Colonel John O'Donnell, arrived there from Canton with a cargo of silks, teas, and spices. At about that time, Baltimore achieved a rank of fifth among the ports of the United States, and in the single year 1795, a total of 6,085 vessels entered its harbor. Between 1790 and 1800, Baltimore's exports, chiefly wheat and tobacco, increased over sevenfold. In 1796 when Baltimore contained an approximate population of 15,000, it was erected into a city by the Maryland legislature. The opening up of these new lines of communication and trade tended to dilute the traditional plantation economy of Maryland and to counteract its traditional affinity with tidewater Virginia.

As Baltimore moved into new prominence in the state after the War for American Independence, it developed a distinguished social and cultural life of its own, displacing Annapolis. An English visitor to the city in 1796 remarked on its "spirit of improvement so congenial to a free and flourishing people" and noted that the streets resounded "with the busy hum of men."[3] President Washington described it as "the risingest town in America, except the Federal city." Early in the nineteenth century Baltimore had a Newtonian Society, formed to encourage the study of the natural sciences, an Economic Society to promote manufactures, and a music school and a dancing school established by French refugees. The Holliday Street Theater provided traveling theatrical troupes with the means to present such plays as "She Stoops to Conquer" and the "Comedy of Errors." A few years later, in 1814, Rembrandt Peale came from Philadelphia and founded the "Baltimore

Museum and Gallery of the Fine Arts," which still functions as the oldest museum building in the nation. There he displayed not only works of art but also the skeleton of a mastodon and other specimens in the natural sciences and even live animals in the garden. Here two years later he demonstrated the use of gas for illumination and made his museum the first building in Baltimore which was lighted with gas. He became one of the incorporators of the Gas Light Company of Baltimore, which was the first such company in the United States.[4]

Features of Baltimore which particularly impressed foreign visitors were its "neat houses of well made and well painted brick, delicately white doors with their shining knockers and handles" and "steps of clean white marble" and "the extreme beauty and stylish dress of its women." The houses in Baltimore were, in the main, built of red brick and were not pretentious. So glamorous and fashionable were the women that the English novelist, Mrs. Frances Trollope, who attended mass at the Roman Catholic Cathedral one morning in 1830, wrote that "excepting on a very brilliant Sunday morning at the Tuileries in Paris" she had never before seen "so many beautiful women at one glance." But it could hardly be said that Maryland possessed an aristocracy of flamboyant wealth, for its society was convivial and less stratified, for example, than that of Virginia. In 1824 not more than a dozen families possessed private carriages.

For protection from fires Baltimore depended upon volunteer fire companies in which membership was elective and which included some of Baltimore's most prominent citizens, who, at the sound of the fire alarm, turned out to pull the fire engine to the scene of the fire where they formed fire-fighting crews, passing water in leather buckets in relay lines to extinguish the fire. After the passing of Annapolis as the horse-racing center of Maryland around 1820, Baltimore took its place, and in 1830 a group of racing enthusiasts formed the Baltimore Jockey Club, which continued Maryland's preeminence in this sport.

Above the fall line of the rivers the towns of Maryland were few, small, and isolated. In Frederick, then called Fredericktown, nearly all the houses were built of brick, and the streets were laid out to run north and south, east and west intersecting each other at right angles. Near the Monocacy River some nine miles from Fredericktown, an immigrant from Germany, Johann Friedrich Amelung, arrived in Baltimore in 1784. Before the end of that year he acquired almost 1,900 acres of land comprising sections of old grants called Part of Gantt's Garden, Adam's Bones, Tobacco Hook, and I Don't Care What, and there built his new Bremen Glass works. With some one hundred fellow-German glassmakers employed in his factory, he began to produce glass of outstanding craftsmanship, consisting, according to his advertisement in the *Baltimore Advertiser,* of "all kinds of Glass-Wares, viz. Window-Glass, from the lowest to the finest sorts, white and green Bottles, Wine, and other Drinking Glasses, as also Optical Glasses, and Looking Glasses finished compleat." Near the foot of Sugar Loaf Mountain, Amelung built for himself a baronial castle of neo-Dutch colonial style and provided himself with his own blacksmith, baker, shoemaker, and even his own orchestra. On his New Bremen tract of some 2,100 acres he created a complete village for his workmen, who eventually numbered almost 400. So promising did this manufacturing enterprise seem that George Washington cited it in a letter to Jefferson in 1789 as a reason to proceed with opening up the navigation of the Potomac.[5]

Outside the towns, conditions of travel and living were primitive. The roads were full of sharp stones, mudholes, and ruts, often filled with tree trunks laid horizontally, and were sometimes virtually impassable by carriages. Drivers who conveyed passengers over these roads in their carriages for hire had to stop every three or four miles to give their horses water and a breathing spell. They crossed the streams on ferryboats which were large enough to hold both the carriage and its team of horses. The ferryman who propelled his boat across the stream did so by means of two ropes attached to fixed pulleys which ran alongside the boat on a cable stretched above the river to a tree on each bank. In sparsely settled western Maryland, few roads were suitable for wagons and only narrow paths led from one settlement to another.

In 1791, near Fredericktown, a traveler observed "the simplicity of the early days of colonial life." Here the typical farm home was "a narrow cabin, built of logs hardly rough-hewn, the chinks filled with clay and the only openings a door and a square hole covered by a sheet of oil-soaked paper." [6]

A few years later, as the Maryland hunter Meshach Browning recalled, he moved his young wife and daughter to Bear Creek Glades in Allegany County to a cabin which "had neither floor, chimney, nor door—a hole cut through the wall being the only way of getting in and out. After we arrived at our house," he recorded, "the first thing which greeted us was a very large rattlesnake which lay coiled up in the house, but which we soon despatched." The furniture in the cabin included a "primitive table made of a large sheet of maple-bark, tied down on two laths, to keep it from curling up at the sides; this was laid on a scaffold made by driving four small forks into our clay floor, on which little cross-poles were placed, to hold up the bark." In making preparations for supper, his wife followed the path to the spring, "situated on the edge of a large swamp, matted with high weeds, twisted with wild hops in all directions." Out rushed five wolves, but they were soon put to flight. At twilight the deer and bears came out into "the open glades, feeding leisurely in the cool evening air."

Meshach Browning's straightforward and often dramatic account of his life in Allegany County from the mid-1790's to the late 1830's is a near-classic in local history. First published in 1859, his *Forty-four Years of the Life of a Hunter* gives the authentic flavor of the Maryland frontier and entitles its author to rank as one of Maryland's literary figures. This autobiography is a tale of pioneer hardships, woodsman's lore, and the search for meat, skins, and furs in a country teeming with wildlife. Browning was a combination of Davy Crockett and an honest Baron Munchausen. Though he had only the barest rudiments of a formal education, he developed the frontiersman's qualities of physical courage and resourcefulness, and to them he added a genuine love for the natural beauty of western Maryland's mountains and glades.

The advantages of this happy hunting ground for settlers in western Maryland were soon interrupted by herds of cattle sent in by herders from Virginia and Pennsylvania to feed on the tall lush grass of the intervale meadows. The settlers waged a campaign of harassment against these intruders. The economy of this section of the state was primitive. Trade was carried on largely by barter in linsey, pork, beef, honey, corn, or skins. The settlers here took their politics seriously, carrying their hunting knives with them to elections. But they found in elections opportunities to meet with neighbors if only for quarrels. On this Maryland frontier, a man—or at least, a family—isolated from neighbors had to do all that was required for living. "One must be able to do a little of everything," one of these frontiersmen told a visitor. "In the course of time, one learns to handle fairly well the ax and the plane. With a few books on medicine, one can, if absolutely necessary, do without doctors, and the reading of the Bible can serve as a substitute for worship. As for society, it is less necessary than you think. When one has everything to do oneself, there remains little time for others and for pleasures." [7]

One of their principal pleasures was the revival service. At a Methodist evangelistic service in Middletown in 1791, as reported by the same visitor, an itinerant Methodist minister harangued his congregation "with a terrible vehemence." Speaking of the vengeance of God, he declared, "He will seize you by the throat in spite of your belated repentance and will hurl you headlong into the depths of hell." To this threat his congregation responded with "a frightful chorus of wailing.... Sometimes the women sprawl on the floor and strike their heads. Others become sick, and the whole congregation sees with holy rapture this conflict between the soul and the devil." [8]

This religious exhibitionism represented a frontier reaction to the religious and cultural ferment which agitated both the older and the newer settlements in America during the early years of independent statehood. As Maryland assumed its place among the states in the new nation, its social and economic conditions reflected both its colonial heritage and the changes engendered by the industrial revolution which was now beginning to affect American life. These conditions would largely determine the political stresses and strains within the state and the character of its participation in the political life of the nation.

Footnotes

[1] Paul H. Giddens, "Trade and Industry in Colonial Maryland, 1753-1769," *Maryland Historical Magazine*, vol. 4, 512-538; and Jane N. Garrett, "Philadelphia and Baltimore, 1790-1840: A Study of Intra-Regional Unity," *Maryland Historical Magazine*, vol. 55, No. 1, pp. 1-13, March 1960.

[2] Ferdinand-M. Bayard, *Travels of a Frenchman in Maryland and Virginia with a description of Philadelphia and Baltimore in 1791....* Translated and edited by Ben C. McCary, Williamsburg, Virginia [1950], 4.

[3] Francis Baily, quoted in Raphael Semmes, *Baltimore As Seen by Visitors, 1783-1860*, (Baltimore, 1953), 13.

[4] Latrobe Weston, "Art and Artists in Baltimore," *Maryland Historical Magazine*, vol. XXXIII, No. 3, September 1938, pp. 213-227.

[5] Dorothy Mackay Quynn, "Johann Friedrich Amelung at New Bremen," *Maryland Historical Magazine*, vol. XLIII, No. 3, September 1948, pp. 155-179.

[6] Ferdinand-M. Bayard, *Travels of a Frenchman in Maryland and Virginia...*, 16.

[7] *Ibid.*, 24.

[8] *Ibid.*, 28-29.

Sources and Additional Reading

Bayard, Ferdinand-M., *Travels of a Frenchman in Maryland and Virginia with a description of Philadelphia and Baltimore in 1791....* Translated and edited by Ben C. McCary, Williamsburg, Virginia [1950].

Bedini, Silvio A., *Life of Benjamin Banneker,* Scribner's, New York, 1972.

Bishop, J. Leander, *History of Manufactures in America,* vol. I, Edward Young and Company, Philadelphia, 1864.

Browning, Meshach, *Forty-four Years of the Life of a Hunter, Being Reminiscences of Meshach Browning, A Maryland Hunter Roughly Written Down by Himself: Revised and Illustrated by E. Stabler,* Philadelphia, 1928.

Clark, Victor S., *History of Manufactures in the United States,* 3 vols., New York, 1929.

Hamlin, Talbot, *Benjamin Henry Latrobe,* Oxford University Press, New York, 1955.

Hanna, Hugh Visson, *A Financial History of Maryland, 1789-1848,* Johns Hopkins University Studies in Historical and Political Science, Series XXV, nos. 8, 9, 10, The Johns Hopkins Press, Baltimore, 1907.

Livingood, James Weston, *The Philadelphia-Baltimore Trade Rivalry, 1780-1860,* Pennsylvania Historical and Museum Commission, Harrisburg, Pennsylvania, 1947; reprint 1970 (Arno).

Mathews, Catherine Van Cortlandt, *Andrew Ellicott: His Life and Letters,* Grafton Press, New York, 1908.

McKearin, George S. and Helen, *American Glass,* Crown Publishers, New York, 1941.

Renzulli, L. Marx, Jr., *Maryland, the Federalist Years,* Fairleigh Dickinson University Press, Rutherford, Madison, Teaneck, New Jersey, 1972.

Semmes, Raphael, *Baltimore as Seen by Visitors, 1783-1860,* Maryland Historical Society, Baltimore, 1953.

CHAPTER XVI

RELIGIOUS AND CULTURAL HAPPENINGS

When Maryland became an independent state in 1776, twelve of its seventeen counties were maintaining schools or academies which though poorly supported were offering secondary education to a limited number of pupils. In Maryland as in other states the wealthy people were accustomed to send their children to private schools or provide them with private tutors. Starting in 1807 the General Assembly incorporated societies dedicated to the education of orphans and poor children. The first fund to establish free schools was started in 1812 as part of an act to "incorporate a company to make a turnpike road leading to Cumberland and for extension of charters of the several Banks in this State and for other purposes." [1] Under this law the banks were required to subscribe money not only to build the road but also to pay a sum of $20,000 annually to be used for the support of the schools in each county.

Four years later provision was made for commissioners of schools in each county, and in 1820 another law required that poor children over eight years of age should be provided with three years of education at public expense.[2] But Baltimore did not establish a school system until 1829 when it rented two houses for this purpose. In these various educational arrangements, Maryland recognized the need of providing elementary education for children of both sexes, though keeping them separate in the schools.

Americans, newly freed from the incubus of foreign control, showed a new interest in education and turned to the founding of colleges. Before 1776 only nine colleges had been established in all the seaboard colonies of Great Britain, but four more were founded during the War for Independence and many others sprang into existence with the coming of peace.

Not until 1782 was the first college established in Maryland when the free school of Kent County was elevated into a college and was named Washington College "in honourable and perpetual memory of his excellency, General Washington, the illustrious and virtuous Commander-in-Chief of the Armies of the United States." The founding of this college was due to the efforts of Dr. William Smith, who after serving as provost of the University of Pennsylvania, became principal of the Kent

County School, which he thus raised to collegiate rank. By a law of 1784 Washington College was made the beneficiary of fines which the state collected from persons convicted of selling liquor without a license.[3]

In the following year, 1785, St. Johns College was founded at Annapolis as Maryland's second college, and to the new college were assigned the funds of King William's School, which had been established in 1694 as one of the earliest educational foundations in the American colonies. Maryland's latitudinarianism in religion was shown in the act incorporating the new college. In it the legislature stipulated that the college should be maintained, "upon a most liberal plan, for the benefit of youth of every religious denomination, who shall be freely admitted to equal privileges and advantages of education and to all the literary honors of the college, according to their merit, without requiring or enforcing any religious or civil test or urging their attendance upon any particular religious worship or service ... nor shall any preference be given in the choice of a principal, vice-principal, or other professor, master, or tutor, in the said college on account of his particular religious profession, having regard solely to his moral character and literary abilities and other necessary qualifications to fill the place for which he shall be chosen."

To launch the college and to solicit funds for it, a commission of outstanding religious leaders was appointed, including the Reverend Dr. William Smith, who was a noted Episcopal clergyman and an active Mason, the Reverend Patrick Allison, a Presbyterian clergyman, and the Reverend John Carroll, who would become, in 1788, the first Catholic bishop of the United States.[4] By act of the legislature in 1784, Washington College and St. Johns College were united under the name of the University of Maryland, and the state pledged a sum of £3,000 to be given annually and forever for their support. The funds for their support were to be collected from fees on marriage licenses, hawkers' licenses, licenses on ordinaries, and certain fines and forfeitures. By an act of 1798, the state appropriated a few hundred dollars of state funds each to several of the county schools and thus began to give public support to schools for secondary education. These included eight educational establishments, distributed as follows: Washington Academy, Eastern Academy, and Washington College on the Eastern Shore, Charlotte Hall, St. Johns College, and a projected Baltimore academy on the Western Shore, and the Frederick County School and Allegany County School for western Maryland. In 1811 the state assigned public funds also to the Hillsborough School in Caroline County; West Nottingham

Academy in Cecil County; a school then being built in Cambridge in Dorchester County; Hagerstown Academy, which had been incorporated in the preceding year; Centreville Academy in Queen Anne's County, and Rockville Academy in Montgomery County. On the Eastern Shore every county was supplied with a school, and all except Worcester received state aid. On the Western Shore, Charlotte Hall served the four counties of southern Maryland. All the other counties, except Baltimore, were provided with schools and all of them, except Harford, received state aid. Since Washington College was the only school in Kent County and St. Johns the only one in Anne Arundel County, these two institutions sank to the level of secondary schools and as the latter lost its state aid, the first University of Maryland ceased to exist.

But in 1812 the legislature established a second University of Maryland, based upon a previously existing "College of Medicine of Maryland" in Baltimore. This College of Medicine had been incorporated in 1807 and had been authorized at that time to maintain itself by a lottery of not over $40,000. Thus established, it became the fifth medical college in the country, being preceded by medical schools at the University of Pennsylvania, Harvard University, Dartmouth College, and the College of Physicians and Surgeons of New York.

This Maryland institution graduated its first class in 1810, and two years later it became the nucleus of the new University of Maryland. By the act of 1812, this College of Medicine of Maryland was given the power "to constitute, appoint, and annex to itself the other three colleges or faculties, viz., the faculty of divinity, the faculty of law, and the faculty of arts and sciences" and thus to become "the University of Maryland." The regents of the new university met and selected former Secretary of State Robert Smith as provost. They were authorized by the legislature to conduct lotteries of respectively $30,000 to finance their building and to purchase "a botanical garden, library, and apparatus" and $100,000 for the purchase of chemical and other equipment. They had already purchased a site for their college from Colonel John Eager Howard. The building which they constructed there at the corner of Lombard and Greene Streets in Baltimore in 1814-1815 was modeled after the Pantheon in Rome and continues in daily use as the oldest structure in the United States used for medical teaching.

The university never established a faculty of divinity, though it offered some lectures in this subject by a professor of theology from 1819 to 1823, and then discontinued them. It added a law department in 1822, but allowed it to lapse in 1843 and did not reopen it until

1869. Meanwhile, in 1826, the legislature had abolished the board of regents and substituted for them a board of trustees of twenty-one members who chose Chief Justice Roger Brooke Taney as provost of the university. But this action was resisted by the old board of regents who chose another provost and on the advice of their counsel, which included William Wirt and Daniel Webster, carried their case to the supreme court of the state. There, in 1839, the regents won their case in a decision reminiscent of the famous Dartmouth College case, which held that the legislature had violated the rights which it had conferred upon the university by its acts of 1807 and 1812 and had infringed the national constitution by impairing the obligation of contracts. The regents accordingly resumed the directive authority of the university, which now included a faculty of arts and sciences, formerly Baltimore College. But this faculty dwindled to one professor during the Civil War and soon afterward ceased to exist.

In 1840, a Maryland College of Pharmacy was established and was incorporated by the legislature in the following year. In 1844 it entered into a reciprocal arrangement for an exchange of lectures and courses with the faculty of physic of the University of Maryland and established its quarters in the building of this faculty. It later merged with the University of Maryland.

Much earlier, in 1819, the first dental lectures in America were delivered by a scholarly Baltimore dentist, Dr. Horace H. Hayden, before the medical class in the University of Maryland. Through his continuing efforts and those of a colleague, Dr. Chapin A. Harris, the Baltimore College of Dental Surgery was incorporated by the Maryland legislature in 1840 as the first institution in the world to give college instruction in this subject.[5] It became the prototype for a similar dental college founded five years later in Cincinnati and for five others founded before the Civil War. Not until 1882 did the University of Maryland establish a dental department.

Maryland was the third state to establish an agricultural college. The need for such an institution was emphasized by the State Agricultural Society in the early 1850's, and the project was strongly endorsed by Governor Lomas W. Ligon in his address to the General Assembly in 1856. In response, the legislature passed "An Act to establish and endow an Agricultural College in the State of Maryland" on March 6, 1856. It was established in College Park as a private institution, but the state agreed to contribute $6,000 annually to its support. After the enactment of the Morrill Act by Congress in 1862, the Maryland legislature designated the Maryland Agricultural College as a land-grant college to receive funds from the national government. Under a subsequent act in 1887 there was established, in connection with it, the first agricultural experiment station in the United States.

Between 1830 and 1842 at least eight seminaries or academies for girls were incorporated in Maryland. Among these one of the most important was the Patapsco Institute at Ellicott's Mills which was headed by Mrs. Almira Lincoln Phelps, sister of Emma Willard. As she herself explained, her Institute aimed "to enlighten, refine, and elevate the female mind and character." It sought to train the girls "to become useful rather than brilliant, patient rather than presuming." [6] A public high school for boys was not established in Baltimore until 1838 and two high schools for girls were opened there five years later.

In Baltimore the American Methodist Episcopal Church was born in 1784. The first convert to John Wesley's new religious sect who came to Maryland was Robert Strawbridge, who settled in Frederick County sometime before 1764. There on Sam's Creek, near the present New Windsor, in that part of Frederick County that was later erected into Carroll County, he set up his "Log Chapel," preached Methodism, and baptized converts. Soon afterward another preaching-place for Methodism was established at the home of Daniel Evans in Baltimore County near Baltimore Town. Other centers of Methodism were formed in Baltimore County including the Patapsco Neck Chapel in 1772, the Back River Meeting House in 1773, and the Middle River Chapel in the following year.

From these original meeting houses itinerant preachers of the new religion zealously carried their message throughout the Maryland countryside. In 1772 the first society was formed on the Eastern Shore at Solomon Hersey's house in Kent County, and two years later another at the house of John Fogwell near Sudlersville in Queen Anne's County. By that time ten Methodist chapels had been built—all under the leadership of Strawbridge. Methodism in Maryland was thus prepared for organization into larger units when Francis Asbury arrived in 1771. When the first annual conference was held in 1773, Maryland had more members of the new sect than any other colony. The figures of this conference showed 500 members in Maryland, 200 in New Jersey, 180 each in New York and Pennsylvania, and 100 in Virginia.

After he was designated as Wesley's "Assistant" in America, Asbury set out on horseback to tour Pennsylvania, New York, Delaware, and Maryland. Entering Baltimore in 1773, he preached in several private houses and began to raise funds to build a Methodist church in Baltimore. This building, completed in 1775, was the Lovely Lane Meeting

House, which served as the headquarters of the Fourth Methodist Conference in America in 1776.[7] By that time Baltimore reported 900 Methodists. The town had become the center of American Methodism. But in Annapolis, the so-called "Paris of America," Methodism could make little headway. Even Asbury hesitated to preach in that town where, as he wrote, "many people openly deny the Holy Scriptures, as well as the power of inward religion."

Methodism was not yet an independent, organized denomination. It was merely a revivalistic movement within the Church of England. But the American Methodists were propelled toward an independent organization by John Wesley's continued loyalty to the British cause in the American War for Independence. Accordingly, soon after the American colonies gained their independence from England, the Methodists gathered in their Lovely Lane Chapel in Baltimore on Christmas Eve in 1784, at the call of Asbury, to transform their scattered churches into "an independent Episcopal Church." For this purpose Dr. Thomas Coke had been ordained as a bishop and sent to America by Wesley. Sixty of the eighty-one Methodist ministers in the states attended this organizing conference. There the first Methodist Episcopal Church in America was organized; Asbury and Coke were elected the first American superintendents, later bishops; and a prayer book, known as the "Sunday Service," which had been sent over by Wesley, was adopted. "We are raised up to reform the continent and to spread scriptural holiness over these lands," the Methodist clergymen declared in the rules of Discipline which they there approved.

Even before the Christmas Conference, Asbury and Coke had laid plans to found a Methodist institution of higher learning. By the time of the Christmas Conference they had already received pledges of £5,000. The Conference named this forerunner of all Methodist educational institutions in America, Cokesbury College, in honor of the first two general superintendents and provided that it be established at Abingdon on Chesapeake Bay in Harford County. There the college was built. According to the bishops' circular of 1785 advertising the college, "We prohibit play in the strongest terms, and in this we have the two greatest writers on the subject that, perhaps, any age has produced (Mr. Locke and Mr. Rousseau) of our sentiments; for, though the latter was essentially mistaken in his religious system, yet his wisdom in other respects and extensive genius are indisputably acknowledged. The employments, therefore, which we have chosen for the recreation of the students are such as are of greatest public utility—agriculture and architecture." It may be added that "bathing" in Chesapeake Bay within the college enclosure was permitted, but only when a master or someone appointed by him was present. Only one boy was permitted to bathe at a time, nor was anyone allowed to remain in the water above a minute.

On this strict regimen was established the first Methodist institution of higher education in the United States. At the inauguration of the new college, lasting three days, Bishop Asbury preached three sermons, taking as his first text, "Trust in the Lord, and do good" (Psalms 37:3), as his second, "O thou man of God, there is death in the pot" (II Kings 4:40), and as his third, "They shall not labour in vain" (Isaiah 65:23). The beginnings of the college were carefully supervised by John Wesley in England and by Bishops Coke and Asbury in the United States. It was given a charter by the legislature in 1794 but lacked the financial resources and the enlightened leadership to sustain it. In Baltimore, Bishop Asbury himself, it is reported, "went from house to house, through the snow and cold, begging money" for the college. But the college was destroyed by fire in December 1795 and was then removed to Baltimore where one year later it was again leveled by fire. So ended this early Methodist venture in higher education.

But Methodism continued to pioneer in the establishment of institutions of higher learning in Maryland. When Cokesbury College was destroyed in 1796, Methodists waited twenty years before launching a second college. In Baltimore in 1816, the year of Bishop Asbury's death, they founded a college and named it for him. But it lacked financial resources and failed sometime before 1832. The Methodist Church also established the first college for women in Maryland, the Baltimore Female College in Baltimore, in 1849, for the purpose of educating young women in the arts and sciences and fitting them to become teachers. In 1860 this college was designated by the legislature as the first educational institution to be given aid by the state for the purpose of training teachers. Eight years later it lost its Methodist affiliation and became undenominational.

Like Methodism, Episcopalianism in Maryland severed its connections with England during the war. Though many of the leaders of the revolutionary movement in Maryland were members of the Anglican Communion, the majority of the clergy remained loyal to the British crown. In 1783 the church, hitherto known in Maryland as the Church of England, was organized officially as the Protestant Episcopal Church "agreeably to the principles of the American Revolution." Nine years later, meeting in convention at Annapolis, the leaders of the church, both lay and clerical, unanimously elected the Reverend Thomas John

Clagett as the first Episcopal bishop of Maryland. With his consecration in New York in September 1792, he became the first Episcopal bishop to be consecrated on American soil.

Contemporary with Bishop Clagett was the Protestant Episcopal clergyman, Mason Locke ("Parson") Weems, who won notoriety—if not fame—as the inventor of the cherry-tree anecdote of George Washington. He was born in Anne Arundel County in Maryland in 1759, served Episcopal parishes there from 1784 until 1792, and then, as an itinerant salesman, peddled his own and other books throughout Maryland and other eastern states until his death in 1825. As a book salesman he gained popularity, and sales, by comic patter, by playing the violin, and by exhorting his audiences with sermons by turn. His *Life of Washington*, which went through 70 editions in the nineteenth century, fixed the traditional pattern of the idealized Washington as a paragon of virtue and wisdom.

At Fountain Rock, the magnificent mansion of General Samuel Ringgold situated six miles south of Hagerstown, the Protestant Episcopal Church established the College of St. James in 1842, with the Reverend John Barrett Kerfoot as rector. This combined preparatory school and college, offering a curriculum strong in both secular and religious subjects, flourished until its students left to join the southern cause in 1861 and the institution itself was caught in the crossfire of Union and Confederate armies. The arrest of Rector Kerfoot and one of his staff members as Union sympathizers by General Jubal Early in 1864 ended the career of the institution, but its facilities were reopened in 1869 by Henry Onderdonk as a secondary school for boys under the name St. James School.

Maryland in its colonial past had responded only slightly to the proselytizing activities of Baptists. By 1772 there were only two churches of the Baptist denomination in Maryland. The first, situated at Chestnut Ridge about nine miles northwest of Baltimore, was organized in 1742 by the Reverend Henry Loveall who came from New Jersey to Maryland, but it disappeared during the War for American Independence. The census of 1790 showed the Baptists to be the weakest of the religious sects in Maryland with only 776 members in the entire state, the majority of whom were found on the Eastern Shore and in other rural areas.

The sect was badly torn between those who favored and those who opposed an educated ministry and missionary activity. The sector which favored these principles, largely confined to the Baltimore Association, established the Columbian College in the District of Columbia in 1821, starting with a theological school and adding a college department in the following year, but the college languished for lack of denominational support until the 1840's.

Maryland became the seat of several Catholic colleges and seminaries, perhaps because of its Catholic traditions going back to its early colonial beginnings. When Bishop John Carroll, heading the bishopric of Baltimore, which included jurisdiction over Catholic affairs in the entire nation, founded Georgetown College in 1789, it was situated in Maryland but was later incorporated in the District of Columbia when the District was separated from Maryland.

The first Catholic educational institution of collegiate rank established in what is now Maryland was St. Mary's College in Baltimore, which was founded in 1799 by the Reverend W.L. DuBourg, S.S., as a lay college, originally for students from the West Indies. It was closed in 1852 by the Superior General of the Sulpicians. The second Catholic college in the state and the third in the United States, Mount Saint Mary's College, was founded by a French priest, John Dubois, S.S., who came to the United States in 1791 as a refugee from the excesses of the French Revolution. In 1807 he purchased land near Emmitsburg at the foot of the Catoctin Mountain and there started a seminary and a school. The latter was at first limited to boys under fourteen years of age, but when Mount Saint Mary's was chartered by the General Assembly of Maryland in 1830, it was authorized to confer "any degree or degrees, in any of the faculties, arts, sciences and liberal professions except medicine, to which persons are usually admitted in other Colleges or Universities in America." Other Catholic colleges included St. Charles College near Ellicott City, begun in 1830 by the venerable Charles Carroll of Carrollton "for the education of young men of the Roman Catholic religion, for the ministry of the gospel," Loyola College in Baltimore, founded in 1852 as a Jesuit college for young men, and Woodstock College at Woodstock, a seminary for priests of the Society of Jesus, founded in 1869.[8]

Among Maryland's outstanding Catholic leaders Mother Elizabeth Ann Bayley Seton was canonized as the first Roman Catholic native-born saint in the United States in September 1975. She was born into an Episcopal family in New York, married in 1794 at the age of twenty, and bore five children before her husband died. She was then converted to Catholicism in Italy and after moving to Baltimore, established a school for girls there in 1808. But she is principally remembered as the foundress of the Sisters of Charity whose mother house is situated at Emmitsburg, some fifty miles west of Baltimore, and of St. Joseph's Academy situated at the same place.

Baltimore assumed a prominent place in the new Unitarian movement with the construction of the Unitarian Church at the corner of Charles and Franklin Streets, designed and built by the French architect, Maximilian Godefroy. From that pulpit in May 1819, the brilliant William Ellery Channing, minister of the Federal Street Church in Boston, speaking on the occasion of the ordination of Jared Sparks, a future president of Harvard University, preached a famous sermon on "Unitarian Christianity" in which he cast off many of the restraints of the old theology and vitalized the Unitarian movement in America.

As another type of educational institution, Annapolis was chosen by Secretary of the Navy, George Bancroft, in 1845 as the site of the national government's second defense service institution, the United States Naval Academy. The training of officers for the United States navy had been previously quite haphazard. It had been done almost entirely on board ship by so-called "schoolmasters" who accompanied the midshipmen on cruises but had no official status and no authority over them. To correct this situation and to professionalize the naval service, Bancroft obtained the transfer from the Army to his Department of a small fort at the mouth of the Severn River which had been built in 1808. The fort was situated in an area of some ten acres of land at Windmill Point, which was enclosed on all land sides by an eleven-foot wall, and its parapet was mounted with eight ancient guns. Bancroft refitted the ten or twelve buildings in the enclosure for educational purposes and selected a teaching staff headed by Commander Franklin Buchanan as Superintendent. Thus Annapolis became "The Cradle of the Navy."

Many of the churches and educational institutions in Maryland, during its history as a colony as well as its early history as a state, employed the lottery as a means of raising money for new buildings, purchasing burial lots, and financing other church activities. But the lottery system was susceptible of much abuse, as unscrupulous promoters used it for their own purposes and then absconded with the receipts before the drawing of the successful tickets. In addition, the system fell into disfavor with merchants who found themselves unable to compete with the attractions of the lottery. Maryland was slow to follow the lead of other states in intervening to control abuses of this system, but finally in 1792 the General Assembly assumed the authority to authorize lotteries and to outlaw all others. This law only introduced a measure of state regulation but did not prevent lotteries from flourishing. Under the sponsorship of Bishop John Carroll, the Catholic Cathedral in Baltimore was built with the proceeds of a lottery, which was advertised between 1801 and 1803.

Many Protestant organizations were also granted licenses to conduct lotteries. Similarly, the University of Maryland and Washington College benefited from lotteries, and the Washington Monument in Lafayette Square in Baltimore was built with proceeds from a gigantic lottery offering prizes ranging from $50,000 down to $5,000. Not until later did this practice come to be censured as immoral.[9]

In the field of journalism Maryland had distinguished itself while still a British colony, and it continued to be a leader among the states in the publication of newspapers. In 1773 a printer from Philadelphia, William Goddard, moved to Maryland and gave Baltimore its first newspaper, called the *Maryland Journal and Baltimore Advertiser* and later renamed the *Baltimore American and Daily Advertiser.* From 1775 to 1784 it was edited by his sister, Mary Katherine Goddard, with vigor and distinction. The immigration of Germans into Baltimore was sufficient to warrant the publication of one or possibly as many as three German-language newspapers there by the 1790's.[10] By 1810 when the first tabulation of the American newspaper press was prepared, Maryland had twenty-one newspapers. The oldest of these was the *Maryland Gazette,* which had been established in Annapolis in the year 1727 and had been published continuously since 1745, except for a brief interruption during the Stamp Act controversy. Of the twenty-one newspapers published in the state in 1810, all were weekly, except five dailies published in Baltimore, as follows: *Federal Gazette and Baltimore Advertiser, Whig, Federal Republican and Commercial Gazette, Evening Post,* and *American and Commercial Advertiser.* In number of newspapers published in that year, Maryland was surpassed only by four states: Pennsylvania with 73; New York with 67; Massachusetts with 32; and Virginia with 23. In the publication of daily newspapers, Baltimore ranked third among American cities, coming after Philadelphia with nine dailies and New York with seven. Rising to prominence somewhat later, *Niles Register,* owned and published by Hezekiah Niles in Baltimore from 1811 to 1837 and again from 1839 to 1848, gained a deserved national reputation as a weekly newspaper for its news and editorial opinion.

Among Baltimore's daily newspapers founded before the Civil War, the *Sun,* which was established by Arunah Shepherdson Abell in 1837, deserves special mention both because it set and maintained from the beginning a high standard of journalism and because it later came to wield great political influence. To the dismay of the editors of Baltimore's six other daily newspapers, Abell charged only a penny instead of sixpence for each copy of his newspaper, following the trend toward a penny press already established by the *New York Sun* and the *Philadelphia Public Ledger*. Within three years its circulation equalled that of all the other daily morning newspapers of Baltimore combined, and "Sunpaper" became synonymous with newspaper. In order to get the news speedily, Abell employed every means from carrier pigeons to chartered railroad cars, and he took advantage of the telegraph as soon as it became available. Out of these efforts eventually emerged the news-gathering network of the Associated Press.

Agriculture continued to be the leading activity of the state, but it became more diversified with the founding of the Maryland Agriculture Society in 1786. In 1819 Baltimore became the publishing headquarters of *The American Farmer,* a popular weekly magazine, which was the first journal devoted to agriculture published in the United States. Its founder and editor was John Stuart Skinner, who had accompanied Francis Scott Key on his mission to the British fleet at the bombardment of Fort McHenry in September 1814.

These achievements in journalism were notable, but Maryland remained backward in the field of literary journals, only two such journals, the short-lived *Portico* (1815-1819) and the *Red Book* (1819-1820) being published there before 1860. The latter was launched by John Pendleton Kennedy, then only twenty-three years of age, in collaboration with his friend, Peter Hoffman Cruse. It marked the beginning of Kennedy's literary career, which later gained him fame. With the demise of *The Red Book* in 1820, Kennedy was elected a representative from Baltimore to the Maryland House of Delegates, from which position he went on to serve for three terms as congressman. As Secretary of the Navy during the last months of President Millard Fillmore's administration, he despatched Commodore Matthew C. Perry on his historic mission to open up Japan to western commerce.

Kennedy's career as a successful Whig politican and public servant all but eclipsed his reputation as a writer. But while carrying on his multifarious public duties this versatile Baltimorean found time to publish his novel, *Swallow Barn,* in 1832, which revealed for the first time the romantic literary possibilities of Virginia's plantation life. His *Horseshoe Robinson*, published three years later and the most successful of his writings, dwelt on the historical experience of the South in the War for American Independence. For *Rob of the Bowl,* which he wrote as a labor of love and published in 1838, he turned to Maryland depicting events at Saint Mary's at the time of the feud between Catholics and Protestants under the third Lord Baltimore. He later produced

Quodlibet (1840), a satire on Jacksonian democracy, and a two-volume *Life of William Wirt* (1849).

The somber genius, Edgar Allen Poe, though born in Boston, had a Maryland parentage. His father, a traveling actor, had been cast off by his eminently respectable family in Baltimore when he went on the stage. His son, orphaned at an early age, was much associated with Baltimore during the brief twenty years of his active life. There he wrote his prize story, "The MS Found in a Bottle," which first brought him fame, and he contributed to the *Baltimore Saturday Visitor* before he moved to Richmond to assume the editorship of the *Southern Literary Messenger*. His dissipated career ended in the Baltimore City Hospital in October 1849, and he was buried in Baltimore in the churchyard of the Westminster Presbyterian Church.[11]

The distinction of being the first historian of Maryland is credited to John Leeds Bozman, whose *Sketch of the History of Maryland* was published in Baltimore in 1811.[12] Regarding it as unfortunate that "while almost every other state in the Union has had its historian, Maryland, though one of the earliest British colonies, has never yet had even its first provincial transactions developed to the inquiring reader," this Eastern Shore lawyer undertook the task of filling the gap.

While serving from 1789 to 1807 as deputy attorney general for Talbot and Caroline Counties under the Federalist leader of the Maryland Bar, Luther Martin, Bozman delved into the early history of the colony. He was an active member of the Masonic Lodge at Easton in Talbot County, and his history reveals both an anti-Puritan and an anti-Catholic bias. His history is indeed only a *Sketch,* for though conceived on a grand scale, it loses itself in the English background and devotes fewer than one hundred pages to the history of Maryland itself, tracing out only the first thirty years of the colony. His ambitious project remained uncompleted at his death in 1823, but in 1837 it was republished by the government of Maryland in two volumes, the latter containing his previously unpublished text which brought his history of Maryland to the date 1660.

Another essay at the history of Maryland was made by John Van Lear McMahon, whose *An Historical View of the Government of Maryland from its Colonization to the Present Day* was published in Baltimore in 1831. McMahon was born in Cumberland, educated as an attorney, and became an active political leader in the Jackson movement in Maryland in the 1820's. But he later broke with Jackson to support the Whig party and, after William Henry Harrison's death in 1841, was offered (but declined) the cabinet position of Attorney-General in

President John Tyler's cabinet. Of the projected two volumes of his *Historical View* only the first was ever published, and it covered the period from the founding of the colony only to 1776. As one of the leaders of the Maryland bar, McMahon gave a decidedly institutional and legalistic interpretation to Maryland's history.[13]

McMahon's *Historical View* was followed eighteen years later by James McSherry's *History of Maryland from 1634 to 1848*, published in Baltimore in 1849.

This trilogy of state histories by Bozman, McMahon, and McSherry, appearing between 1811 and 1849, denoted an awakened consciousness of the historical factors in the development of Maryland and a new interest in the background of current problems. This emerging attitude took form also in the founding of the Maryland Historical Society in 1844, with Brantz Mayer as president. The Maryland Historical Society was twelfth in order of founding among state historical societies, following in order those of Massachusetts (1791), New York (1804), Rhode Island and Maine (1822), New Hampshire (1823), Pennsylvania (1824), Connecticut (1825), Virginia (1831), Kentucky (1838), Georgia (1839), and Vermont (1840). At its formation it acquired the library of the Library Company of Baltimore, which had been organized in 1795 and which had flourished during the heyday of the private subscription library, that is, until the mid-1820's. It had been organized and operated almost exclusively for its members, but it finally yielded place to a new Mercantile Library Association, whose purpose was to provide opportunities for reading and study to young clerks and apprentices. It had already built up and maintained a collection of several thousand books for its members which it turned over to the Mercantile Library Association. The Association transferred them to the Maryland Historical Society when the latter was founded.[14]

Marylanders, as they developed increasing historical awareness, focused their attention mainly upon the history of the colony and the War for Independence. In the process, they enlarged their feelings of state pride and strengthened their conviction of the constitutional rights of the states and of Maryland's freedom to operate with maximum independence as a state within the federal structure, which was the essence of the states-rights doctrine. The opportunity which this doctrine afforded for diversity among the states was well illustrated in the case of Maryland. There the theological innovations introduced by Methodism and Unitarianism challenged the complacency of the older established religions. Churches took the lead in expanding Maryland's inadequate educational system and encouraged state action toward the same ends.

Footnotes

[1] *Laws of Maryland,* 1812, chap. 79.

[2] *Ibid.,* 1820, chap. 86.

[3] William Kilty, *The Laws of Maryland* ... Frederick Green, Annapolis, 1799, Chapter 37, Section 21.

[4] Bernard C. Steiner, *History of Education in Maryland,* Government Printing Office, Washington, D.C., 1894, pp. 95-99; and Tench Francis Tilghman, "The Founding of St. John's College, 1784-1789," *Maryland Historical Magazine,* vol. XLIV, No. 2, June 1949, pp. 75-92.

[5] Carl P. Lewis, Jr., "The Baltimore College of Dental Surgery and the Birth of Professional Dentistry, 1840," *Maryland Historical Magazine,* vol. 59, No. 3, September 1964, pp. 268-285.

[6] Mrs. Lincoln Phelps, *Hours with my Pupils,* Charles Scribner, New York, 1859, p. 31.

[7] N.C. Hughes, Jr., "The Methodist Christmas Conference: Baltimore, Dec. 24, 1784–Jan. 2, 1785," *Maryland Historical Magazine,* vol. 54, No. 3, September 1959, pp. 272-292.

A brief history of the beginnings of Methodism on the Eastern Shore is given in E.C. Hallman, *The Garden of Methodism,* Peninsula Annual Conference of the Methodist Church, no place [1948?], Chapter I.

[8] Thomas F. O'Connor, "The Founding of Mount Saint Mary's College, 1808-1835," *Maryland Historical Magazine,* vol. XLIII, No. 3, September 1948, pp. 197-209; and John J. Tierney, S.S., "St. Charles College: Foundation and Early Years," *ibid.,* vol. XLIII, No. 4, December 1948, pp. 294-311.

[9] John S. Ezell, "The Church Took a Chance," *ibid.,* December 1948, pp. 266-279.

[10] George C. Keidel, *Earliest German Newspapers of Baltimore* [J.H. Furst Company], Washington, D.C., 1927.

[11] John C. French, "Poe's Literary Baltimore," *Maryland Historical Magazine,* vol. XXXII, No. 2, June 1937, pp. 101-112.

[12] An earlier brief historical account of Maryland had been included in George Chalmers, *Political Annals of the Present United Colonies,* which was published in London in 1780. W.T. Brantly in Justin Winsor, *Narrative and Critical History of America,* vol. III, p. 559.

[13] John Thomson Mason, *Life of John Van Lear McMahon,* Eugene L. Didier, Baltimore, 1879.

[14] Jerry E. Patterson, "Brantz Mayer, Man of Letters," *Maryland Historical Magazine,* vol. 52, No. 4, December 1957, pp. 275-289; and Stuart C. Sherman, "The Library Company of Baltimore, 1795-1854," *ibid.,* vol. XXXIX, No. 1, March 1944, pp. 6-24.

Sources and Additional Reading

Armstrong, James Edward, *History of the Old Baltimore Conference from the Planting of Methodism in 1773 to the Division of the Conference in 1857,* King Brothers, Baltimore, 1907.

Bangs, Nathan, *A History of the Methodist Episcopal Church,* Lane and Sandford, New York, 1841.

Benjamin, Park, *The United States Naval Academy . . .* G.P. Putnam's Sons, New York and London, 1900.

Bibbins, Ruthella Mary, *How Methodism Came: The Beginnings of Methodism in England and America.* The American Methodist Historical Society of the Baltimore Annual Conference, Baltimore, 1945.

Bohnor, Charles H., *John Pendleton Kennedy, Gentleman from Baltimore,* Johns Hopkins Press, Baltimore, 1961.

Bozman, John Leeds, *The History of Maryland from its First Settlement, in 1633, to the Restoration in 1660, with a Copious Introduction and Notes and Illustrations,* 2 v., James Lucas & E.K. Deaver, Baltimore, 1837.

Brent, John Carroll, ed., *Biographical Sketch of the Most Reverend John Carroll, First Archbishop of Baltimore,* John Murphy, Baltimore, 1843.

Daniels, W.H., *History of Methodism in Great Britain and America,* Phillips and Hunt, New York, 1879.

De Barberey, Helène Baillys, *Elizabeth Seton,* translated by the Rev. Joseph B. Code, Macmillan Company, 1927, and Mother Seton Guild Press, Emmitsburg, Maryland, 1957.

Guilday, Peter, *The Life and Times of John Carroll, Archbishop of Baltimore (1735-1815),* The Encyclopedia Press, New York, 1922.

Hallman, E.C., *The Garden of Methodism,* Peninsula Annual Conference of the Methodist Church, no place [1948?].

Harrison, Samuel Alexander, *A Memoir of John Leeds Bozman,* Maryland Historical Society, Baltimore, 1888.

Hartman, Alfred Z., *History of Methodism in Maryland, 1770-1912,* Methodist Historical Society, Baltimore [1912?].

Herbermann, Charles G., *The Sulpicians in the United States,* The Encyclopedia Press, New York, 1916.

Keidel, George C., *Earliest German Newspapers of Baltimore,* J.H. Furst Co., Washington, D.C., 1927.

Luxon, Norval Neil, *Niles Weekly Register, News Magazine of the Nineteenth Century,* Baton Rouge, Louisiana State University Press, 1947.

Mason, John Thomson, *Life of John Van Lear McMahon,* John B. Remington Co., Baltimore, 1914.

McMahon, John Van Lear, *An Historical View of the Government of Maryland,* J. Lucas and E.K. Deaver, Baltimore, 1831.

McSherry, James, *History of Maryland from 1634 to 1848,* J. Murphy, Baltimore, 1849.

Melville, Annabelle M., *John Carroll of Baltimore: Founder of the American Catholic Hierarchy,* Charles Scribner's Sons, New York, 1955.

Phelps, Mrs. Lincoln, *Hours with My Pupils,* Charles Scribner, New York, 1959.

Soley, James Russell, *Historical Sketch of the United States Naval Academy...* Government Printing Office, Washington, 1876.

Steiner, Bernard Christian, *History of Education in Maryland,* Washington, Government Printing Office, 1894.

Wroth, Lawrence C., *Parson Weems; A Biographical and Critical Study,* Eichelberger Book Company, Baltimore, 1911.

CHAPTER XVII
A STAR-SPANGLED WAR

In the election of the first Congress Maryland supported the Federalists, favoring a strong central government. The congressional delegation which the state sent to Philadelphia consisted of six Federalist members of the House and two Federalist senators—John Henry from the Eastern Shore and Charles Carroll of Carrollton from the Western. When Alexander Hamilton proposed his centralizing fiscal measures to the new Congress Maryland endorsed the funding bill, which called for the consolidation of the various debts owed by the national government. On Hamilton's proposal that the central government assume the Revolutionary War debts of the states, Maryland was divided. This state, unlike certain others, had already made provision for discharging her war debt and showed reluctance now to help discharge the debts of less provident states. Members of Maryland's congressional delegation helped to defeat this measure in Congress. On Hamilton's proposal to establish a national bank Maryland opinion was also divided, half of Maryland's voting members in congress approving it and half opposing it.

The inauguration of the new national government coincided with the outbreak of a European cataclysm, the French Revolution, which would have serious and long-continued effects in America. Not only did it divide public opinion into pro-French and anti-French factions, but after the beginning of the Anglo-French war in 1793 it compelled the nation to put itself in a posture of defence. Washington, upon receiving news of the war, hastened from Mount Vernon to Philadelphia and summoned his cabinet together. Already the representative of the French Republic, Citizen Edmond Genêt, had arrived in the United States with instructions to fit out and commission privateers in American ports to prey upon British commerce. The Washington administration was confronted with the urgent necessity of adopting a policy toward the European war, now rapidly becoming worldwide.

Washington set forth the policy of the United States in his proclamation of neutrality, issued on April 22, 1793. But Genêt, despite the proclamation, continued defiantly to issue commissions to American vessels until Washington asked for his recall in the following year. Baltimore alone sent out between forty and fifty privateers under the

French flag to prey upon British ships. The French Revolution and its sequel, the Anglo-French war, besides dividing Maryland opinion into Anglophiles and Francophiles, as it also divided American opinion outside Maryland, led to two interesting developments. At the time when the involvement of the United States in the European War seemed imminent the Maryland legislature ceded to the national government a point of land called Whetstone Point in Baltimore on which the government proceeded to erect fortifications and a star-shaped fort of brick. Soon afterward this fort was named Fort McHenry in honor of Dr. James McHenry of Maryland, Washington's Secretary of War.

The French Revolution had another direct effect upon Maryland. In the French colony of Saint Domingue in the Caribbean the French Declaration of the Rights of Man and other decrees and orders of the French Assembly in favor of liberty and equality inspired the blacks to rise against their white masters, and in the course of the bloody civil war which broke out there and continued until 1795 several hundred white and mulatto refugees sought asylum in Baltimore. At first they were supported by private charity, but many of them later settled down in Baltimore and other Maryland towns and became citizens of the state strengthening both the Catholic complexion of the state and its pro-slavery elements. Many of them brought with them the habits and gentility of the French elite which they infused into Baltimore society.[1]

Maryland was drawn into the activity that accompanied the so-called Whisky Rebellion in 1794 when the national government was faced with a rebellion of the frontiersmen and whiskey-distillers in western Pennsylvania. These residents of the Pennsylvania counties of Alleghany, Fayette, Washington, and Westmoreland refused to comply with the excise laws passed by Congress and defied the revenue officers sent to enforce them. When the efforts of Pennsylvania to suppress the insurrection proved ineffective the Secretary of War instructed Maryland to equip and hold in readiness a militia force of about 5,500 men, and Washington threatened to employ the militia of Maryland, Virginia, Pennsylvania, and New Jersey to suppress the uprising. In the western counties of Maryland the frontiersmen were also rebellious. They were led by a Marylander named Bradford who put himself at the head of the insurgents for the purpose of resisting both the national and state governments.

To suppress this uprising in the west the government ordered the troops of Maryland and Virginia to assemble at Cumberland under the command of Governor Richard Henry Lee of Virginia. Washington issued a proclamation against the insurgents in September 1794, and in the following month he himself set out for Fort Cumberland to lead the army in person. But he concluded that his presence there was unnecessary because the insurrection was collapsing, and he soon returned to Philadelphia leaving Governor Lee of Virginia in command. Under Lee the troops then crossed the Allegheny Mountains and united with militia of Pennsylvania and New Jersey at Uniontown. As they advanced toward the west they saw the insurrection evaporate before them and end without the shedding of a drop of blood. In this case Maryland fully cooperated with her neighbor states to assert the power and authority of the national government. The Maryland legislature unanimously approved the action of the governor in responding to Washington's call for aid in suppressing these "violent and alarming proceedings."

Maryland seemed to be predominantly identifying itself with the Federalist policies of the Washington administration. A coalition of the landed slave-holding gentry, mainly Catholic in religion, with the urban commercial interests, representing the shipowners, merchants, lawyers, and bankers, constituted the source of Federalist power in the state. They largely dominated politics in the rural Eastern Shore, in southern Maryland, and in the town of Baltimore, soon to be incorporated as a city. Baltimore as the commercial and banking center of Maryland remained a stronghold of Federalism throughout the 1790's. But Federalist control was challenged by the new-rising class of small farmers, which were most numerous in the tidewater counties of the Western Shore including the counties of Baltimore, Anne Arundel, and Prince George's, and among the small merchants, artisans, and common laborers in Baltimore and other tidewater towns. This growing segment of public opinion in the state supported the Francophile and republican views of Jefferson and his followers and showed an almost frenzied interest in politics.

In the election of 1796 which highlighted the sharp cleavage between Federalists and Republicans the Federalists carried six of the ten districts in the state—one by a majority of only four votes. In the presidential poll the Maryland electors accordingly cast seven votes for John Adams of Massachusetts, who had been Washington's vice-president, four votes for Thomas Pinckney of South Carolina, four for Thomas Jefferson of Virginia, three for Aaron Burr of New York, and two for a favorite son of Maryland, Senator John Henry. Maryland's plurality vote for Adams was confirmed as reflecting the national preference when all the electoral votes were counted by the Senate in February

U.S. Practice Ship Constellation, c 1889. Courtesy Maryland Hall of Records Commission

1797 and it was discovered that Adams had received 71 votes thus gaining the presidency. The Federalists carried all the states north of Pennsylvania and in addition Delaware, the Republicans all the states from Virginia southward. The second highest number of electoral votes, 68, went to Jefferson, who thus was elected vice-president.

The Adams administration soon became involved in difficulties with France brought about by the capture of merchant vessels of the United States by French privateers during the European conflicts that followed in the wake of the French Revolution. In the resulting Franco-American naval war of 1798-1801 Adams summoned Washington from retirement and appointed him "lieutenant-general and commander-in-chief of all the armies raised and to be raised in the United States." In preparation for possible war the citizens of Annapolis collected subscriptions for the purpose of erecting a battery and a number of cannons, and they built and equipped two sloops of war, named the *Maryland* and the *Chesapeake*, for the government of the United States; Congress created a separate Department of the Navy in April 1798, and Adams selected a Marylander, Benjamin Stoddart, as the first Secretary of the new Department. Already Congress had authorized the construction of a navy to consist originally of three frigates. Of these the *Constellation* was built at Baltimore and was launched in September 1797. When Adams finally determined to send a second peace commission to France he included in it a Marylander, William Vans Murray, Minister Resident in the Netherlands. With him Adams sent Olliver Ellsworth, Chief Justice of the United States, and William R. Davie. Secretaries McHenry and Pickering quarreled with the President over these nominations, which were made without consultation with them, and other matters, and as a result they were practically forced out of the cabinet.

As during the European wars of the Federalist period the United States, taking commercial advantage of Europe's necessitous plight, became the world's principal neutral ocean carrier, Maryland's properity increased phenomenally. The export trade of the state in grain and tobacco centered in Baltimore, which had outdistanced other towns in the state in population reaching 26,114 in 1800. As Maryland's shippers got possession of their share of the lucrative foreign trade which was opened up to America by the European war the value of Maryland's exports rose to $5,686,191 in 1794, being exceeded among all the states only by those of Pennsylvania. Within the next five years Maryland's exports almost tripled in value reaching $16,299,609 in 1799. By this latter year Maryland's population totalled 349,692 and Baltimore ranked as the third commercial city in the United States.

In the hotly disputed presidential election of 1800 the Alien and Sedition Acts were a principal issue. In these acts the Adams administration resorted to drastic measures to curb the political opposition. The Alien act, giving the President power to deport all foreigners whom he considered dangerous to the country, was criticized by one of Maryland's representatives in the House, Samuel Smith, a wealthy merchant of Baltimore, as infringing upon the reserved right of the states themselves to regulate immigration. In Maryland, as also in Pennsylvania, it alienated the German voters who had been hitherto staunchly Federalist. But this act as well as the Sedition Act, which penalized persons who published malicious statements against Congress or the President, were generally approved by the Federalists in Maryland. Maryland took a definite Federalist position by refusing to endorse the Kentucky and Virginia resolutions, which asserted the right of a state to judge of the constitutionality of acts of the national government and to nullify those it considered to be unconstitutional.

Maryland was one of only four states—the others being Rhode Island, Virginia, and North Carolina—in which electors for president and vice-president were chosen by popular vote. In the election of 1800 the electoral vote of Maryland was equally divided between the Federalist Adams and the Republican Jefferson. Maryland's electors accordingly cast five votes for Adams, five for his Federalist running mate Charles C. Pinckney, five for Jefferson, and five for his party colleague Aaron Burr. When all the votes of the electoral college were counted Jefferson and Burr received an equal number—73 votes—and the Federalist candidates Adams 65 and Pinckney 64. Because of the tie between Jefferson and Burr and Burr's refusal to renounce the presidency and accept the office of vice-president for which his party had obviously intended him, the election was thrown into the House of Representatives where in such cases of a contested election each state was entitled to one vote, nine states being necessary for election. For the first thirty-five ballots continuing through five days and nights only eight states, not including Maryland, voted for Jefferson, but on the thirty-sixth ballot both Maryland and Vermont were persuaded to cast blank ballots thus making Jefferson president.[2]

Marylanders had clung to the Federalist party as long as it remained a dominant party, but soon after Jefferson's inauguration they began to espouse the cause of Republicanism which he led. Jefferson's political views appealed especially to Maryland's rural voters who favored state's rights, reduced taxation, governmental economy, and freedom of speech and press. After his inauguration Maryland Republicans succeeded in gaining control of the House of Delegates and in electing John F. Mercer as governor. The Jeffersonian party also elected five of Maryland's eight representatives in Congress. Under the leadership of this party Maryland now abolished the property qualification for voting which was required in the Constitution of 1776. The second article of that document provided that the members of the House of Delegates should be chosen by "all freemen, above twenty-one years of age, having a freehold of fifty acres of land in the county in which they offer to vote and residing therein, and all freemen having property in this State above the value of thirty pounds current money, and having resided in the county in which they offer to vote one whole year next preceding the election." In the convention of 1776 several attempts had been made to reduce this property qualification to five pounds or to abolish it altogether, but they failed, and this provision went almost unchallenged for twenty years.

But in 1797 Michael Taney, a Federalist from Calvert County, moved in the House of Delegates "to abolish all that part of the form of government which requires property as a qualification for voters or for office." This motion was approved by the House of Delegates but was rejected by the Senate. It was reintroduced in 1798 and 1799 and again encountered opposition in the Senate. But in 1801 after the Republicans had triumphantly secured a majority in both Houses they passed an amendment to the Constitution which partially modified the property qualifications. It provided "That every free white male citizen of this State, and no other, above twenty-one years of age, having resided twelve months in the county next preceding the election at which he offers to vote, and every free white male citizen of this State, above twenty-one years of age, and having obtained a residence of twelve months next preceding the election, in the city of Baltimore, or the city of Annapolis, and at which he offers to vote, shall have a right of suffrage, and shall vote by ballot, in the election of such county or city, or either of them, for Delegates to the General Assembly, Electors of the Senate and Sheriffs." But even the Republican legislature made no change in the property qualifications required for "persons to be appointed, or holding offices of profit or trust." Not until 1810 were these clauses in the constitution repealed.

The engulfing tide of Republicanism and the policies of its leader in the presidency, Jefferson, were bitterly distasteful to the distinguished Marylander, Samuel Chase, who had been appointed by President Washington as an associate justice of the Supreme Court in 1796. After going on the Court Chase abandoned his former ardent anti-Federalist views and consequently became a chief target of the Jeffersonians. A jurist of outstanding legal ability and absolute integrity and fearlessness he indulged in severe criticism of the Jefferson administration while charging a grand jury in Baltimore and for this action was brought before the Senate in Washington for impeachment in 1804. In this dramatic case he numbered among his defence counsel three leaders of the Maryland bar, Luther Martin, Robert Goodloe Harper, and Philip Barton Key. In the outcome the impeachment effort failed and Chase resumed his seat on the Court, serving there until his death six years later. He was one of the last to wear the costume of the Revolutionary era including knee breaches, a scarlet cloak, and a three-cornered hat, representing the survivals of a vanished day.

Maryland strongly supported the Republican party during the administrations of Jefferson and Madison. In the election of 1804 the Maryland electors cast their ballots as follows: Nine for the Republican candidates, Jefferson and George Clinton, and two for the Federalist candidates, Charles C. Pinckney and Rufus King. Maryland's vote presaged, though not quite adequately, Jefferson's overwhelming electoral victory, for Jefferson and Clinton received the electoral votes of all the states except Connecticut and Delaware and the two from Maryland.

Marylanders had been vitally concerned, as had Americans generally, with Jefferson's efforts to prevent the United States from becoming entangled in the European war which had reopened in 1803. As the British Orders in Council pinched American maritime commerce and as the British navy, which controlled the seas, violated America's neutral rights by seizing American vessels and impressing American seamen into British service, Jefferson dispatched a Marylander, William Pinkney, to London to reinforce his minister there, James Monroe, in securing redress of grievances. But he was not satisfied with the treaty which Pinkney and Monroe concluded with the British and refrained from submitting it to the Senate. Pinkney, one of Maryland's most brilliant lawyers, remained in London for five more years in largely fruitless efforts to reconcile Britain's war methods with America's neutral rights and was finally recalled in 1811 at his own request.

Meanwhile, in 1807, a Baltimore-built vessel, the *Chesapeake,* had become the innocent cause of an international incident which seriously worsened America's relations with England. This frigate had been recently constructed to serve as a unit in the American squadron to be used against the Barbary states. As it sailed out past the Virginia capes under command of Commodore Barron it was overhauled by a British frigate, the *Leopard,* Captain Humphreys, and was boarded by a British searching party, who removed four crew members from the *Chesapeake*. Of the four seamen who were thus impressed by the British as alleged deserters from the British vessels *Melampus* and *Halifax*, two were Maryland Negroes. This violation of an American vessel of war produced a violent anti-British reaction throughout the United States. Citizens of Annapolis and Baltimore adopted resolutions condemning it and offering to support "such measures as may be adopted by the government for avenging the present sanguinary insult, or for meeting the further hostilities which it gives room to expect."

The method which Jefferson now adopted to make the British respect America's rights as a neutral was the economic boycott, which had been used effectively against the British by the American colonists on several occasions in the decade preceding the War for Independence. When in pursuance of the President's recommendation Congress adopted an embargo act in December 1807, prohibiting all American vessels from sailing for foreign ports, Maryland generally obeyed it without protest and supported the Administration. But the embargo act worked special hardships upon New England where it virtually annihilated commerce and produced a strong sentiment for secession. Maryland's foreign commerce had been not much less than that of the northeastern states, but it was reduced from $14,298,984 in 1807 to only $2,721,106 by 1809. Nevertheless Maryland's representatives in Congress sustained the Administration and resisted the agitation of New England representatives for the repeal of the embargo. In January 1808 a town meeting in Baltimore adopted resolutions declaring "That the embargo was the wisest measure, which, under existing circumstances, could be opposed to those edicts [British Orders in Council], that its consequences have been important and beneficial, and that its complete success has been prevented by evasions which brand their perpetrators with indelible disgrace." The citizens of Baltimore announced further in these resolutions that they would "view with horror and resist to extremity any attempt to dissolve the union of these States, the basis of our unrivalled prosperity." The outcry against the embargo from New England, however, was so great that in February 1809 the act was repealed and for it was substituted a non-intercourse act which interdicted American trade only with Great Britain and France.[3]

Jefferson's embargo act stimulated the development of manufacturing in Maryland as in other states. In Baltimore it prompted the organization of the Union Manufacturing Company, the first successful textile mill in the state, with William Patterson, president of the Bank of Maryland, as its head. The census of 1810 reported a total of eleven cotton and woolen mills in the state. The outbreak of the second war against Great Britain two years later gave further impetus to the textile industry, particularly in the vicinity of Jones' Falls in Baltimore with its abundant water power. At that site in 1814 R. and A. McKim built the first steam-powered textile mill in the city. After the war these and other textile manufacturing plants in the state were sustained by a protective tariff.

Meanwhile the Maryland legislature, controlled by the Republicans, importuned Jefferson to accept a third term as president, but he declined. The majority of the members of the Republican party in Congress thereupon accepted Madison as Jefferson's successor and despite strong opposition succeeded in nominating him. In the election of 1808 the Maryland electors cast nine votes for Madison and George Clinton, and only two for the Federalist candidates, C.C. Pinckney and Rufus King. Maryland once again supported the winning candidate. It had the satisfaction of seeing Madison triumph over Pinckney by an electoral vote of 122 to 47. Maryland was rewarded with two positions in Madison's cabinet. Robert Smith of Baltimore, who had made a distinguished record as Secretary of the Navy throughout Jefferson's two administrations, became Secretary of State in the new administration, and William Pinkney became attorney general.

As the diplomatic ineptitude of Madison, particularly after his dismissal of Smith as Secretary of State in March 1811, swung the United States gradually into Napoleon's orbit and as Britain continued her impressments of American seamen and her depredations upon American commerce, public demand for war against Britain mounted. In Maryland, as elsewhere throughout the nation, opinion on this question was sharply divided. Both the necessity and the advantages of war were set forth in a declaration which a group of citizens of Baltimore drew up in a meeting at the Fountain Inn in May 1812. In these resolutions they declared that since Britain's conduct toward the United States showed "a determined hostility to our national rights" the United States had no alternative "but to choose between war and degradation." In the prosecution of such a war they pledged themselves "to support our government at every hazard." They felt an almost equal hostility toward France, whose conduct, they said, "has been scarcely less atrocious than that of England." If the negotiations with France should not terminate satisfactorily they hoped that "our government will direct the most active hostilities to be commenced against her for a redress of our grievances and the maintenance of our rights." As an exculpatory afterthought, they announced cryptically that "in our well-founded complaints against foreign nations, Russia and Sweden are not to be included!" [4]

Madison admitted the failure of his diplomatic efforts when he sent a message to Congress on June 1, 1812 calling for a declaration of war against Great Britain. But the president was leading a badly divided nation. His war resolution passed by a majority of only thirty in the House and six in the Senate. In this vote the Maryland delegation in the House was divided six to three in favor of war. Of Maryland's two senators Samuel Smith, brother of Robert Smith, voted for it and Philip Reed against it. This same division was reflected in the Maryland legislature. The Maryland Senate, which consisted of fifteen members who had been elected in 1811 and were all Republicans, resolved "That the war waged by the United States against Great Britain is just, necessary and politic, and ought to be supported by the united strength and resources of the nation, until the grand object is obtained for which it was declared." But the House of Delegates, which was also overwhelmingly Republican, adopted resolutions opposing the war. And in the presidential election later in that year Maryland cast only six of its eleven electoral votes for Madison, giving the remaining five to the Federalist candidate DeWitt Clinton.

Opponents of the administration had viewed with apprehension the drift of the unprepared nation toward a war in which it would be fighting against Britain in virtual alliance with Napoleon Bonaparte, emperor of the French. They deplored the militancy of the representatives of the west and south in Congress who were eager to use the war as a pretext for overrunning Canada and Florida and adding them to the Union. Virulent criticism of "Mr. Madison's War" was expressed by the *Federal Republican,* a newspaper published in Baltimore by Jacob Wagner and Alexander Contee Hanson. Soon after war was declared they printed a sharp editorial, running in part as follows: "Without funds, without taxes, without a navy, or adequate fortifications—with one hundred and fifty millions of our property in the hands of the declared enemy, without any of his in our power, and with a vast commerce afloat, our rulers have promulgated a war against the clear and decided sentiments of a vast majority of the nation. . . . We mean to represent in as strong colors as we are capable, that it is unnecessary, inexpedient and entered into from partial, personal, and as we believe motives bearing upon their front marks of undisguised foreign influence, which cannot be mistaken. We mean to use every constitutional argument and every legal means to render as odious and suspicious to the American people, as they deserve to be, the patrons and contrivers of this highly impolitic and destructive war, in the fullest persuasion that we shall be supported and ultimately applauded by nine-tenths of our countrymen, and that our silence would be treason to them. We detest and abhor the endeavors of faction to create civil contest through the pretext of a foreign war it has rashly and premeditately commenced, and we shall be ready cheerfully to hazard everything most dear, to frustrate anything leading to the prostration of civil rights, and the establishment of a system of terror and proscription announced in the government paper at Washington as the inevitable consequence of the measure now proclaimed. . . . We shall hereafter, as heretofore, unravel every intrigue and imposture which has beguiled or may be put forth to circumvent our fellow-citizens into the toils of the great earthly enemy of the human race. We are avowedly hostile to the presidency of James Madison, and we never will breathe under the dominion, direct or derivative, of Bonaparte. . . ."

Two days after the publication of this editorial on June 21, a well organized mob wrecked the printing office of the *Federal Republican* at the corner of Gay and Second Streets in Baltimore, destroyed the types and presses, and razed the building. According to a rival newspaper, "The Mayor of the City, the Judge of the Court of Oyer and Terminer and several magistrates and military officers, were present and witnessed this dreadful outrage which their *peaceful efforts* were insufficient to prevent, although it was generally known during the preceding day that the attack was meditated." As a result of this mob action Hanson and Wagner decided to print their newspaper in Georgetown and to issue it from Wagner's house on Charles Street in Baltimore. They provisioned the house with supplies of arms to withstand a siege and were joined by some 28 or 30 volunteers who undertook to maintain "the rights of person and property and defend the liberty of the press." But after the papers were distributed a mob gathered on July 27, stoned the house, and prepared to blow the building to pieces with cannon when the Mayor, Edward Johnson, and the Commander of the Militia, Brigadier General John Stricker appeared, arranged a truce, and secured the surrender of the beleaguered company. Twenty-three of them, including Hanson and General Henry Lee, father of Robert E. Lee, were lodged in the city jail. During the night the jail was stormed by a mob. Nine of the prisoners were beaten into insensibility. General James M. Lingan was killed, and General Lee was made a cripple for life. One of the prisoners was tarred and feathered. The mob then proceeded to the postoffice for the purpose of seizing copies of the current issue of the *Federal Republican* from the mails, but they were finally dispersed by a troop of horse.

This violent outbreak of the mob spirit to suppress newspaper criticism of the Madison administration's war policy caused citizens of St. Mary's, Charles, Prince George's, and Montgomery Counties to protest to Governor Robert Bowie against the "perfidy" and "cowardice" of Mayor Johnson and General Stricker, but they were assured by the Governor in reply that "those gentlemen not only fulfilled every legal duty incumbent upon them, but made every effort, even at the hazard of their lives, to prevent violence from being offered to the persons composing the armed association in Charles Street." The mob action was investigated by a joint committee of the two branches of the City Council and later by the Committee of Grievances and Courts of Justice in the General Assembly. As a result many presentments were made against individuals on both sides, but all were eventually acquitted.

This mob action was widely denounced as an attack upon the freedom of the press. Baltimore was nicknamed Mobtown, and the blame was laid on the city administration. The immediate effect of these mob excesses in Baltimore and of the growing resentment against the war was to give the Federalists the election in October 1812. They carried thirteen counties in the state—namely, St. Mary's, Charles, Prince George's, Calvert, Montgomery, Frederick, Allegany, Talbot, Caroline, Cecil, Dorchester, Somerset, and Worcester—and therefore elected a majority of the General Assembly. This Federalist majority was able on joint ballot to elect General Levin Winder as governor over Robert Bowie and to elect a Federalist as United States Senator. Hanson himself was elected to Congress and was later reimbursed for the losses which he had suffered at the hands of the mob.

Marylanders took a prominent part in many of the important military engagements of the second war against Great Britain, but they played an even more spectacular role in the war on the sea. Since Maryland had a long coastline which the national government was not prepared to defend, the state was obliged to equip a small navy on its own initiative and with its own resources. Within four months after the declaration of war Baltimore sent to sea forty-two armed vessels carrying about 330 guns and from 2,800 to 3,000 men. Baltimore clippers gained especial distinction in the naval operations of the war. The product of the skill of Baltimore shipbuilders, these streamlined vessels were described as "very low in the water, and broad in the beam; the masts are sloped very much backwards, and they sail exceedingly close to the wind." During the war Baltimore fitted out and dispatched more privateers to prey on enemy shipping than any other American port, and only a few of Baltimore's ships were ever taken.

So effective were these privateers that in December 1812 the British government issued an order in council declaring the Chesapeake and Delaware Bays blockaded, and in the following February Rear Admiral George Cockburn carried the war into those waters by bringing his fleet through the Virginia capes. In the next month the British government declared the whole coast of the United States, except Rhode Island, Massachusetts, and New Hampshire, to be blockaded. Throughout the rest of the year Admiral Cockburn harried the coasts of Maryland making shore incursions at Frenchtown near Elkton, at Havre-de-Grace in Harford County, on the Sassafras River, in St. Mary's County, on the Patuxent, at Kent Island, and at other places. In June he received reinforcements which brought his force in the Chesapeake up to eight ships of the line, twelve frigates, and many smaller vessels.

This concentration of British power in the Chesapeake boded no good for Maryland. In this crisis the Maryland governor begged the Secretary of War in the Madison administration, John Armstrong, to protect the state against certain attack. But Maryland was told that she must rely upon her own militia. In order to muster and pay the militia the legislature appropriated the sum of $100,000 "or so much thereof as may be necessary," and in anticipation of an attack ordered the records of the state to be moved from Annapolis to Upper Marlborough. The Mayor and City Council of Baltimore borrowed $500,000 with which to prepare for the defense of the city.

The anticipated attack on Baltimore did not occur until 1814, when the release of British troops on the continent of Europe after their victory over Napoleon enabled Britain to send reinforcements to the Chesapeake Bay. There they were assimilated to the military force under Major General Sir Robert Ross. Heartened by the arrival of these new forces the British naval squadron in the Chesapeake pursued the American gunboat flotilla under the renowned Captain Joshua Barney, a hero of the War for American Independence and one of Maryland's most distinguished naval officers. As the British naval vessels pursued the flotilla up the Patuxent toward Washington, the British land forces, numbering some 8,000, accompanied it on shore, marching parallel to the river. At Nottingham they forced Barney to blow up his gunboats and continue his retreat by land toward Washington. Ross and his army proceeded to Bladensburg where they found the American forces drawn up under General William Henry Winder in two or three futile lines on an open hillside. They easily routed them. Their objective was the national capital which they were determined to destroy in reprisal for the destruction of public buildings at York (Toronto) by an American raiding party in the previous year.

The British discovered that they were moving against an undefended city. The Americans had made no preparations for the defense of Washington conceiving that it had no importance from a military point of view. The British, accordingly, encountering only feeble resistance, entered Washington on August 24, 1814, and set fire to the Capitol and to the President's house. But they respected private property and committed no outrages. On the following day their work of destruction was checked by a sudden and terrific tempest which put out their fires. On August 26 they left the capital and regained their fleet without having a shot fired at them in their retreat. They had scored a signal triumph, not in terms of strategy but in terms of prestige.

The British operations in Maryland and the District of Columbia, whatever other advantages they might show, were proving useful as diversions in favor of Sir George Prevost's operations around Lake Champlain. The British forces therefore moved next against Baltimore for the purpose of securing booty, destroying its shipping, and seizing provisions. But they committed the tactical error of not moving directly from Washington to Baltimore on the heels of the retreating Maryland militia. Instead they chose to make a joint military and naval assault upon the city from the Patapsco estuary. On the eve of the anticipated British attack the Baltimore authorities entrusted the defense of the city to Senator Samuel Smith, a veteran of the Continental Army and a major general. Under his command slaves, free Negroes, and thousands of white citizens hastily threw up defensive fortifications; in and around the city were stationed some 7,000 militia, 1,200 marines and sailors, and 700 regular troops of the United States army—almost 9,000 armed men awaiting the enemy's attack. As they waited they received news that 56 British ships of the line, including such formidable battleships as the *Tonnant,* the *Dragon,* and the *Royal Oak,* each carrying 74 guns or more, had been sighted and that they were landing troops on the northern bank of the Patapsco to march against the city.

The Maryland militia, advancing to meet the British as they approached along the North Point Road killed many of them, including the British commander, General Ross. The forts guarding the harbor offered similarly effective resistance to the British men-of-war as they tried to reduce the forts below the town and open navigation for smaller ships of war. Against their assault Fort McHenry, commanded by Major George Armi-

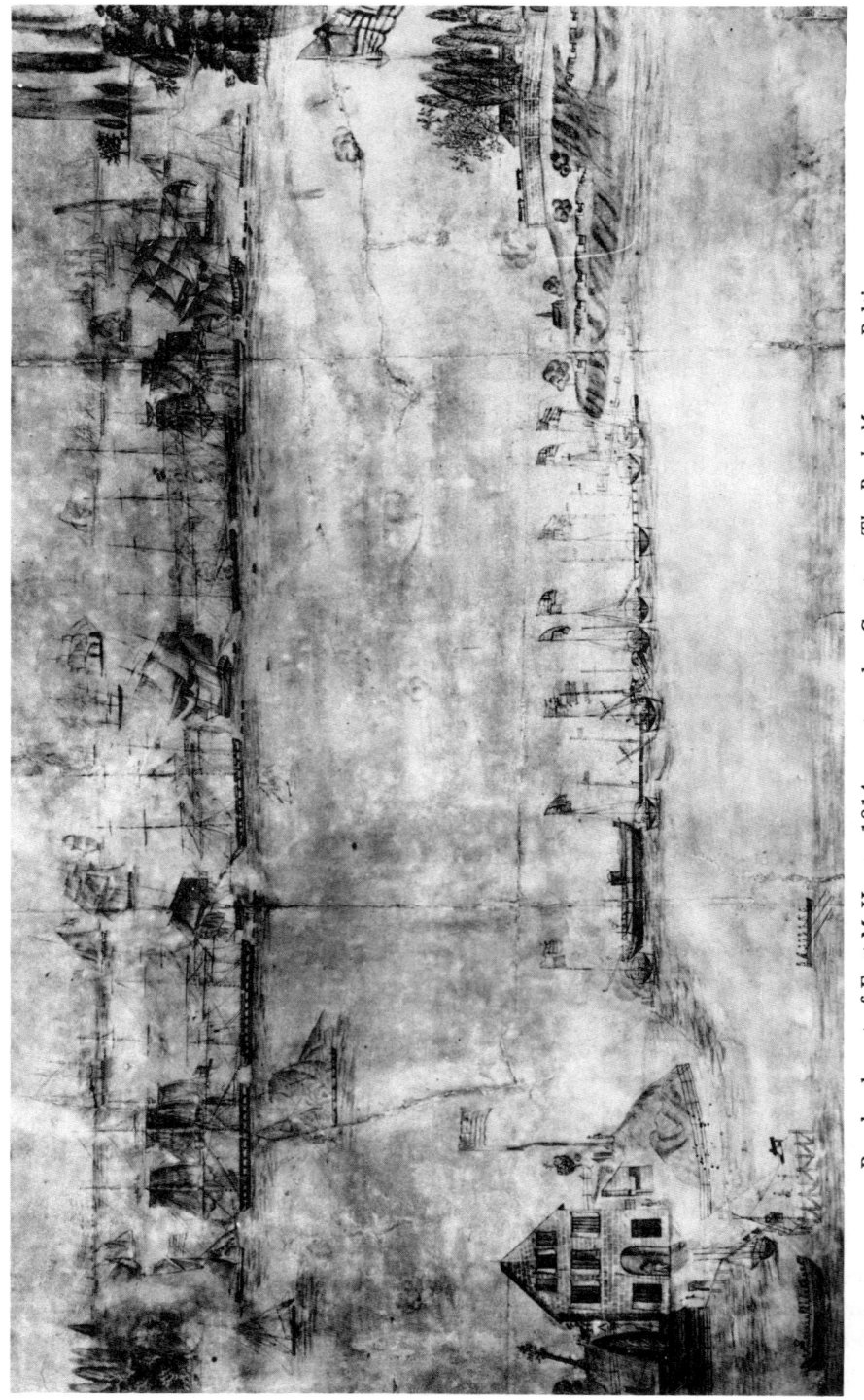

Bombardment of Fort McHenry, 1814; a watercolor. Courtesy *The Peale Museum*, Baltimore

A Star-Spangled War

stead, stood as an impregnable redoubt. As a result the effort of the British failed, and they abandoned both their land and naval operations against Baltimore. Embarking the remnant of their land forces the British vessels one by one spread their sails and moved down the Bay. Admiral Cockburn's squadron remained at anchor in the Bay until October when it sailed for Jamaica and New Orleans, arriving at the latter place in time to participate in the final disastrous defeat of British arms at the hands of General Andrew Jackson.

During the bombardment of Fort McHenry, Francis Scott Key composed the words of "The Star-Spangled Banner." Key was a native of Frederick County, was educated at St. John's College, and studied law in the office of his uncle, Philip Barton Key, in Annapolis. He began the practice of law at Frederick in 1800 but soon removed to Georgetown, a flourishing community of some 4,000 residents adjoining the new Federal City. The poet-lawyer composed "The Star-Spangled Banner" while on board a cartel vessel with the British fleet where he had gone on authorization of President Madison to secure the release of Dr. William Beanes. Beanes was a highly respected physician of Upper Marlborough, who on the withdrawal of the British from Washington was carried a prisoner on board their fleet.

Key promptly undertook to secure the release of Dr. Beanes. After obtaining the President's permission to visit the fleet he embarked at Baltimore, accompanied only by Colonel John S. Skinner, the government's agent for the exchange of prisoners in Baltimore. He succeeded in persuading both General Ross and Admiral Cockburn to release Dr. Beanes only after he showed them letters which he carried from the wounded British officers at Bladensburg testifying to the humanity and kindness with which they had been treated by Dr. Beanes. But Key and Skinner were told that they could not return to the American side until after the attack on Baltimore which was about to be made. During the bombardment they were advised by their British guards to "look well at the flag" because they would not see it waving over the fort in the morning.

Key and Skinner remained on deck of this cartel ship throughout the night of September 13-14 watching the British shells burst over the fort. When morning came and they saw that "our flag was still there," they were told that the attack on Baltimore had failed and that they could take Dr. Beanes and go whenever they pleased.

Though Key did not endorse the policies of the Madison administration and though he considered the war to be unnecessary he had been carried away by the excitement of the battle and had composed the words of the song which was finally made the official national anthem of the United States in 1931. As reported by his brother-in-law, Roger B. Taney, "he said he commenced it on the deck of their vessel, in the fervor of the moment, when he saw the enemy hastily retreating to their ships, and looked at the flag he had watched for so anxiously as the morning opened; that he had written some lines of brief notes, that would aid him in calling them to mind, upon the back of a letter which he happened to have in his pocket; and for some of the lines, as he proceeded, he was obliged to rely altogether on his memory; and that he finished it in the boat on his way to the shore, and wrote it out, as it now stands, at the hotel on the night he reached Baltimore and immediately after he arrived. He said that on the next morning, he took it to Captain Joshua N. [Joseph Hopper] Nicholson, commander of the Baltimore Fencibles and Chief Justice of the Baltimore Court, and one of the Judges of the Court of Appeals of Maryland, to ask him what he thought of it; that he was so much pleased with it that he immediately sent it to a printer, and directed copies to be struck off in handbill form." [5] Set to a British tune, "To Anacreon in Heaven," it was first sung in a Baltimore restaurant by Ferdinand Durang and thereafter regularly in the theater. In 1887 its composer was honored as far west as San Francisco where a memorial statue was erected to him in Golden Gate Park.

The flag which inspired Key to write "The Star-Spangled Banner" had been especially made by a Baltimore seamstress, the widow Mary Young Pickersgill, at the request of a committee composed of Commodore Barney, who was her brother-in-law, Brigadier General John Stricker, and Colonel Will McDonald. It was made large—twenty-nine by thirty-six feet—in order to be conspicuous and to be visible not only to the soldiers in Fort McHenry, where it was flown, but also to the land-based army under Major General Samuel Smith defending Baltimore at Hampstead Hill.

On the night of the British retreat Baltimore was a jubilant town. Her citizens might well feel proud of their successful defence of their city. And for the most part they had won the victory by themselves, without help from the national government. They had suffered only slight losses—20 killed, 90 wounded, and 40 or 50 prisoners—but they had inflicted much heavier losses on the enemy. Their successful resistance to the British helped to wipe out the disgrace of the disaster at Washington and probably hastened the end of the war.

The news of the peace treaty which the American commissioners concluded with the British agents at Ghent on December 24, 1814, was brought to Annapolis on February 13 by Christopher Hughes, who was a native of Baltimore and secretary to the commissioners. Immediately after he arrived in Annapolis with the news he set out for Washington. The coming of peace was wildly celebrated in Maryland. Cannons were discharged, the State House and other public buildings in Annapolis were "illuminated," and Baltimore arranged a general display of fireworks on the evening of February 15. The Maryland Senate adopted resolutions commending the President and justifying the war, and a mass meeting of citizens in Baltimore appointed a committee to carry to President Madison a congratulatory address upon the successful end of the war and upon his "enlightened wisdom and patriotic firmness." [6]

Maryland's contributions to the American effort in the War of 1812 had been notable. Out of a total of 250 vessels that sailed out of ports of the United States with privateering commissions between 1812 and 1814 to prey upon British commerce Baltimore contributed fifty-eight. The first seven privately owned armed privateers that sailed down the Chesapeake were:

Name of Schooner	Tonnage	Total Number of Prizes
Nonsuch	154	9
Rossie	206	20
Wasp	55	4
Highflyer	138	13
Comet	187	35
Globe	180	14
Dolphin	161	12

Others included the *Croghan* (132 tons), *Leonidas* (135 tons), *Amelia* (143 tons), *Java* (153 tons), *Saturn* (170 tons), *Vidette* (261 tons), *Charles* (283 tons), *Swift* (315 tons), *Eutaw* (330 tons), *Mammoth* (376 tons), *Harpy* (347 tons), *Maria* (346 tons), and *Chasseur* (356 tons).[7]

Many of Maryland's naval heroes of the War of 1812, including Stephen Decatur, John Rodgers, and Joshua Barney served on privateers before entering regular naval service. On one short voyage of privateering Commodore Barney on the schooner *Rossie,* 206 tons, captured 3,698 tons of shipping valued at $1,500,000, and took 217 prisoners. Another privateer, the *Chasseur,* popularly known as "the *Pride of Baltimore*," Captain Thomas Boyle, captured eighty vessels, thirty-two of which were equal in strength to his vessel and eighteen superior. Some of his prizes were of great value, three of them alone being valued at $400,000. Small wonder that the British regarded Baltimore as a "nest of pirates"! "The truculent savages of Baltimore must be tamed," demanded the London press.

After the war the *Chasseur,* rigged as a brig, sailed in the China trade and covered a run from Canton to the Virginia Capes in the astonishing time of 94 days with a record run of 84 days from Java Head. But after the Treaty of Ghent many of Maryland's famous privateers continued their depredations as outright pirates.

In proportion to population Maryland furnished a larger contingent of militia than any other state. For the support of the militia and for other war expenses between 1812 and 1814 the state expended almost $600,000. As a result both the state government and the city of Baltimore plunged into debt. "The claims of Maryland for her expenditures during the war," declared President Madison at the close of the war, "stood upon higher ground than those of any other State in the Union." In partial compensation for these claims Maryland was subsequently reimbursed by the national government in the amount of $307,122.

The War of 1812, fought ostensibly to vindicate the rights of American citizens and American commerce at sea, paradoxically resulted in an expansion of American interest in the West. Although Maryland possessed no territorial claims in the Ohio Valley it had made the interests of the trans-Appalachian region its own in the almost four-year-long controversy over the ratification of the Articles of Confederation. Its weight in the political balance of power might be expected to decline as new states were carved out of the national domain in the west and admitted to the Union, but Maryland did not react, as did New England, with jealousy and hatred against these states. By 1812 the thirteen states which had formed the Union had been joined by five new states, namely, Vermont, Kentucky, Tennessee, Ohio, and Louisiana, and other territories in the West were poised for admission as states. The future would tell how Maryland would adapt herself to new conditions of sectional rivalry in which the West would assume a crucial balance-of-power status.

Footnotes

[1] Walter Charlton Hartridge, "The Refugees from the Island of St. Domingo in Maryland," *Maryland Historical Magazine,* vol. XXXVIII, No. 2, June 1943, pp. 103-122.

[2] Edward G. Roddy, "Maryland and the Presidential Election of 1800," *ibid.,* vol. 56, No. 3, pp. 244-268.

[3] Dorothy M. Brown, "Embargo Politics in Maryland," *ibid.,* vol. 58, No. 3, September 1963, pp. 193-210.

[4] J. Thomas Scharf, *History of Maryland,* vol. II, pp. 633-634.

[5] A somewhat different version of the circumstances surrounding the composition of "The Star Spangled Banner" was written by J.S. Skinner who, as agent for prisoners, accompanied Key on board the British fleet. It was published in the *Maryland Historical Magazine,* vol. XXXII, No. 4, December 1937, pp. 340-347.

[6] For a modern account of the British capture of Washington and their subsequent repulse at Baltimore, see Charles G. Muller, *The Darkest Day: 1814,* J.B. Lippincott Company, Philadelphia, 1963.

[7] William Armstrong Fairburn, *Merchant Sail,* Fairburn Marine Educational Foundation, Inc., Center Lovell, Maine, 6 vols., 1945-1955, vol. II, pp. 831-832; and John Philips Cranwell and William Bowers Crane, *Men of Marque: A History of Private Armed Vessels Out of Baltimore During the War of 1812,* W.W. Norton & Company, Inc., New York, 1940.

Sources and Additional Reading

Cassell, Frank A., *Merchant Congressman in the Young Republic: Samuel Smith of Maryland, 1752-1839,* University of Wisconsin Press, Madison, 1971.

Chapelle, Howard Irving, *The Baltimore Clipper,* The Marine Research Society, Salem, Massachusetts, 1930.

Cranwell, John Philips, and William Bowers Crane, *Men of Marque: A History of Private Armed Vessels Out of Baltimore During the War of 1812,* W.W. Norton & Company Inc., New York, 1940.

Craven, Avery O., *Soil Exhaustion as a Factor in the Agricultural Histories of Virginia and Maryland,* University of Illinois Press, Urbana, 1926.

Cutler, Carl C., *Greyhounds of the Sea: The Story of the American Clipper Ship,* United States Naval Institute, Annapolis, 1961.

Delaplaine, Edward Schley, *Francis Scott Key, Life and Times,* Bibliography Press, Brooklyn, New York, 1937.

Fairburn, William Armstrong, *Merchant Sail,* Fairburn Marine Educational Foundation, Inc., Center Lovell, Maine, 6 vols., 1945-1955.

Footner, Hulbert, *Sailor of Fortune, the Life and Adventures of Commodore Barney, U.S.N.,* Harper's, New York, 1940.

Griffin, Charles C., "Privateering from Baltimore during the Spanish-American Wars of Independence," *Maryland Historical Magazine,* XXXV (March 1940), 1-25.

Kenly, John R., *Memoirs of a Maryland Volunteer in the War with Mexico, in the Years 1846-7-8,* J.B. Lippincott & Co., Philadelphia, 1873. The only published account of Marylanders in the Mexican War.

Marine, William M., *The British Invasion of Maryland, 1812-1815,* Society of the War of 1812 in Maryland, Baltimore, 1913; reprint 1965, Francis F. Bierne.

Muller, Charles G., *The Darkest Day, 1814: The Washington-Baltimore Campaign,* J.B., Lippincott Company, Philadelphia and New York, 1963.

Paine, Ralph D., *Joshua Barney, A Forgotten Hero of Blue Water,* Century Company, New York, 1924.

Pancake, John S., *Samuel Smith and the Politics of Business, 1752-1839,* University of Alabama Press, University, Alabama, 1972.

Paullin, Charles O., *Commodore John Rodgers . . .* The Arthur H. Clark Co., Cleveland, 1910.

Weller, N.I., *Commodore Joshua Barney: The Hero of the Battle of Bladensburg. Incidents of his Life Gleaned from Contemporaneous Sources.* Reprinted from the Records of the Columbia Historical Society. Read before the Society, May 10, 1910.

Weybright, Victor, *Spangled Banner: The Story of Francis Scott Key,* Farrar & Rinehart, Inc., New York, 1935.

CHAPTER XVIII
JACKSONIAN DEMOCRACY IN MARYLAND

Maryland was a weathervane of national political sentiment. As the state went in national elections, so went the nation. From the first election in 1788, Maryland was one of the few states that provided for the popular selection of presidential electors. In the equally balanced national contest of 1800, Maryland divided its votes equally between the two leading candidates. In other elections, from the first election of Washington in 1789 through the election of John Quincy Adams in 1824, the state cast the majority of its votes for the successful candidates for president and vice-president. If Maryland did not lead national opinion, it at least faithfully followed in its wake.

Much of the stress and strain in the politics of Maryland resulted from the growth of Baltimore in population and in economic strength. As the nineteenth century advanced, it became increasingly clear that Baltimore was not permitted by the state constitution to exercise as much influence as her population and economic position warranted. The constitution of 1776 made the state a confederation of counties and gave all of them an equal voice in the legislature without regard to population or wealth. Under that constitution each county in Maryland, whether large or small, sent four delegates to the House of Delegates, and the city of Annapolis and the town of Baltimore were each represented in the House by two delegates. Though Baltimore City and County were eventually contributing about one-third of the total tax income of the state and contained nearly one-fourth of the free population of the state, they were entitled to only six of the eighty members in the House of Delegates.

Under the constitution, representation in the Upper House of the state legislature, the Senate, also was based exclusively on geographical considerations. The method by which the members of the Senate were chosen was so indirect as to remove them from control by the people, for they were chosen by an electoral college. Every five years the qualified voters in each county selected *viva voce* two persons and the voters in Annapolis and Baltimore selected one person each to serve as members of an electoral college to choose the members of the State Senate. Each member of this electoral group must have resided for one year in his county, must own property in the state worth at least £50 in currency, and must be of the "most wise, sensible, and discreet of the people." This electoral college was "thus a half-size replica of the house of delegates." The electors chosen in this way were authorized by the constitution to select "by ballot, either out of their own body or the people at large, fifteen senators," who must have attained 25 years of age, "have resided in the State above three whole years," and have acquired real and personal property in Maryland above the value of £1,000 current money.

The members of the electoral college were required by the constitution to select nine senators from the Western Shore and six from the Eastern Shore. Since the constitution did not stipulate that the senators thus chosen should represent the counties, it was theoretically quite possible for all the senators representing either Shore to be chosen from only one county. Senators thus elected held office for five years, and the Senate as a whole was authorized to fill vacancies created during that period by the death or resignation of its members.

Under this arrangement the political party which won a majority of the senatorial electors could designate the entire fifteen members of the Senate. Since a joint ballot of the two Houses named the State Governor and the members of his Advisory Council, the political party that controlled the Senate possessed a fifteen-vote advantage toward control of the executive branch of the state government. As a result, the Maryland government was dominated by a narrow coterie of propertied lawyers, merchants, and landholders. The constitution enabled the smaller and less populous counties of the state to exercise considerably more power in the legislature than the larger counties could exercise. Kent and Calvert Counties, for example, with populations of around 10,000 each, were entitled to twice as much representation in the legislature as the City of Baltimore which had a population of around 65,000. A further inequity existed in the fact that when the constitution was adopted, Annapolis and Baltimore were made equal in the selection of electors, though Annapolis at that time had only between 230 and 260 votes while Baltimore had between 5,000 and 6,000. In the early decades of the nineteenth century, the disparity in population between the capital of the state and the state's principal port still further increased, particularly under the impetus given to the commercial activities of Baltimore by the War of 1812.

During the quarter century after the War of 1812, Marylanders were markedly affected by the new democratic spirit which was suffusing itself throughout the nation. As they accommodated themselves to it, they were constrained to make many changes in their constitutional system and in their accustomed economic and social ways of living.

These changes affected suffrage, finances, land tenure, schools, courts, internal improvements, and the aristocratic constitutional systems of the electoral college and the Senate.

In 1806, Maryland changed the method of voting for electors from *viva voce* to ballot, and four years later it abandoned the property qualifications of both electors and senators. But these changes failed to satisfy the growing demands of the popular party for a government that represented their interests. From the standpoint of that party, the inequity in the electoral college system became increasingly apparent. It enabled a minority of the people to control the government through their power to choose the fifteen senators for their five-year terms.

This system had not operated unfairly in the first quarter century of Maryland's history under the federal government. The Senates of 1791 and 1796 were Federalist and so reflected the popular will as expressed in the presidential elections. When Maryland voters swung over to the support of the Jeffersonian party, the senate also swung over. It became Republican in 1801 and remained Republican in 1806 and in 1811. In the wartime presidential election of 1812, the Maryland electors supported the reelection of Madison by the narrow majority of six to five. Though Maryland thus officially endorsed "Mr. Madison's War," a strong minority sympathized with the commercial states—New Hampshire, Massachusetts, Rhode Island, Connecticut, New York, New Jersey, and Delaware—which wished to repudiate the administration. Meanwhile, the Federalist opponents of Madison in Maryland had taken over the state government. They further strengthened their control over it in the elections of 1814 when the Federalists gained fifty-nine seats to only twenty-one for the Republicans in the Maryland House of Delegates and reelected Governor Winder over Robert Bowie.[1]

The Federalist party, thus rejuvenated by the local opposition to the war policies and conduct of the national administration, enjoyed a controlling position in the politics of Maryland longer than in almost any other state, though it did not throw the state into the opposition in national elections. The Federalists maintained their control over the House of Delegates in the elections of 1815, though by a smaller margin than before, and elected their candidate for governor, Charles Ridgely, though by a majority of only one vote on joint ballot of the two Houses in the legislature. Governor Ridgely had inherited from his uncle the imposing and beautiful ancestral estate, Hampton House, situated in the Dulaney Valley Road north of Baltimore, and he and his family of eleven children made it a center of a lively social life. A devotee of horse racing, he also owned a racetrack of his own at

Timonium on the York Road near Hampton. At his death, Governor Ridgely, like many of his slave-holding contemporaries, manumitted his slaves excepting only those who were either too young or too old to care for themselves.

In 1816 Maryland elected a Federalist Senate of fifteen members to hold office for the next five years. But the Federalist party in Maryland was badly divided between the "Coodies," led by Roger Brooke Taney who had supported Madison during the War of 1812, and the "Big Bugs" who had in varying degrees opposed the war. The latter group, which was led by Robert Goodloe Harper and Alexander Hanson, became the dominant group in 1816 and chose the governor. Partly because of the schism in the party, the Maryland electors cast all eight of their votes for James Monroe for president, the hand-picked choice of the Madison administration, who was duly elected. Although the Federalist party, after the defeat of their presidential candidate, Rufus King, in that election, never again nominated a candidate for the presidency, the Federalist party in Maryland continued strong. In the state elections of 1818 they again gained a majority of the seats in the House of Delegates.

But their triumph was short-lived. As the country entered upon the "era of Good Feelings" under the cautious Monroe, traditional party organizations weakened and eventually disappeared. It was a period when changing conditions and the emergence of new issues introduced new fluidities into the political situation and caused a decline of old party loyalties and the loosening of party discipline. In the Maryland elections of 1819 the Monroe Republicans or Democrats, as they were beginning to call themselves, triumphed, gaining a majority of four seats in the House of Delegates. Though they were unable to affect the Senate, which continued Federalist, they elected a Republican governor, Samuel Sprigg of Prince George's County, and chose Edward Lloyd and William Pinkney as United States Senators. In the election of 1820, the Republicans retained their legislative majority and reelected Governor Sprigg, and in the following year they gained a Republican landslide which gave them a majority of fifty-seven in the legislature and enabled them to reelect Sprigg for a third term as governor. In 1822 they further increased their majority to sixty-nine and chose Samuel Stevens of Talbot County as governor. They were able to keep him in office until 1825. In politics Maryland had become virtually a one-party state.

The Jacksonian party in Maryland owed its organization and its electoral triumph to the leadership of certain skillful organizers, including Roger Brooke Taney, a former Federalist. A son of the above-mentioned Michael Taney of conservative Calvert County, he was brought up in the tenets of Federalism. After serving for a short time in the Maryland House of Delegates, he moved to Frederick to practice law and was elected from that district to the State Senate where he served from 1816 to 1823. In the latter year he moved to Baltimore where pro-Jackson sentiment was developing and where he soon began to work in the Jackson organization.

The Republicans, whose star was in the ascendent, sought to make political capital out of the rising importance of Baltimore. As they gained influence in this growing metropolis, they attempted to raise Baltimore's representation in the House of Delegates from two to four. They also agitated for a constitutional amendment which would provide for direct election of the governor, thus allowing Baltimore, because of its large population, to exercise greater political influence in the state. They also attempted to delete from the constitution the oath required of officeholders affirming their belief in Christian doctrine and by this means to allow Jews to hold office. Members of the Jewish faith, numbering approximately 150 in the entire state, were acquiring power in banking and trading circles in Baltimore.

These proposals were bitterly opposed by the Federalists on the ground that they would diminish the power of the agricultural sector of the population, which was dominant in the Eastern Shore and southern Maryland, and transfer it to the mercantile, banking, and industrial interests, centered in Baltimore. The political schism reflected therefore a deep-lying geographical and economic division within the state. In it the sections of the State whose wealth depended upon an economy of large tobacco and wheat-growing plantations cultivated by slave labor were pitted against Baltimore, Annapolis, and the western counties whose residents were engaged in wheat farming on a small scale or in small industrial operations. The plantation counties persevered in their adherence to Federalism, but they could not effectively resist the power of numbers and the superior organizing skill of the leaders of the Democratic party, and they rapidly lost ground. After 1821, the Federalists abandoned organized opposition in most of the counties.

Under the influence of the new democracy, Maryland finally removed the limitations upon political activities of Jews. The initiative in this effort was taken by a Scottish immigrant, Thomas Kennedy, who was elected to the legislature in 1817 from Hagerstown. In the following year, his bill admitting Jews to the privilege of officeholding and removing other political disabilities from them was defeated by a vote of fifty to twenty-four, but subsequent legislatures revived the measure and debated it. The legislature of 1822 passed such a bill but could not make it final because of the constitutional requirement that an enactment of this sort must be confirmed by the next legislature. So strong was the opposition to this measure that out of the forty members of the legislature who voted for it, only sixteen were reelected. The movement to enfranchise the Jews gathered strength, however, Baltimore in particular strongly favoring it. Finally in 1824 the House, under prodding of Kennedy and a young Irish-Presbyterian member from Cumberland, John Van Lear McMahon, passed by a close vote of twenty-six to twenty-five the so-called "Jew Bill" which amended the constitution to relieve persons from political disqualifications because of religion. The next assembly ratified this amendment in 1825, thus making it possible for the first time for Jews in Maryland to vote and hold public office. Two Jews were immediately elected members of the Baltimore City Council.[2]

In national politics Maryland continued to move with the prevailing current of opinion. In the presidential election of 1820, the state's electors cast their eleven votes for Monroe, who received the unanimous votes of all the states except New Hampshire, which gave one vote to John Quincy Adams. Parties had ceased to exist. But though national politics seemed to be characterized by bipartisan harmony in Monroe's second administration, undersurface tensions were growing and an intense personal scramble for the presidency developed among several leading members of the Democratic party. In the presidential campaign of 1824, Maryland responded in large extent to the personality factors in the leading candidates, William H. Crawford, John Quincy Adams, Andrew Jackson, Harry Clay, and John C. Calhoun. The election results showed Adams strongest in southern Maryland and the Eastern Shore and Jackson the choice of Baltimore and the northern and western counties. Maryland gave a bare popular plurality to Adams over Jackson, but a majority—seven—of the Maryland electors nevertheless cast their votes for Jackson, three for Adams, and one for Crawford. Since the electoral votes of all the states when counted by the president of the Senate gave no presidential candidate a majority, this election of 1824, like the election of 1800, was thrown into the House of Representatives. There Maryland was one of thirteen states that voted for Adams and thus made him president. The electoral college had already chosen John C. Calhoun as vice-president by a more than two-thirds majority to which Maryland contributed ten votes.

As President Adams' popularity steadily diminished during his administration, new parties which were aligned behind either Adams or Jackson assumed clear shape in Maryland. They formed not primarily on economic or social issues but rather around the personalities of these two political leaders and the accompanying competition for political offices. The organization of the nascent parties was accomplished in 1827 at the first state conventions ever held in Maryland.

At the Jackson convention, which was held first, Taney was chosen as president of the Jackson Central Committee for Maryland and hence head of the Maryland Jackson party. He and his associates, all ambitious politicians riding the crest of the anti-Adams revolt, generally favored a low tariff, states rights, and an extension of the franchise. The Adams party, on the other hand, was drawn largely from the Republican officials of the state and from voters in southern Maryland and the Eastern Shore. They generally favored tariff protection for American industry and the use of public monies for roads, canals, and other public improvements.

This latter party prevailed in Maryland in the election of 1828. In the presidential poll of that year, Maryland was one of only three states outside Adams' own New England that favored his reelection—the other two being New Jersey and Delaware. And yet the popular majority for the Adams electors in Maryland over the Jackson electors was less than one thousand in a total vote of over 50,000. Maryland's electoral vote was therefore divided, six going to Adams and five to Jackson. In the national electoral vote Adams, receiving a total electoral vote of only 83, was overwhelmed by Jackson whose electoral vote was 178. For the first time in the history of Maryland as a state in the Union, it had backed a losing candidate for president, though, it should be noted, it had backed Adams by only a bare majority.

Following the presidential election of 1828, the contest between the Jackson and the anti-Jackson forces—soon to take the name of Whigs—continued to be close in Maryland for several years. In the state election of 1829, the Maryland voters gave the Jackson or Democratic party control of the state and elected as governor Thomas King Carroll, a cousin of Charles Carroll of Carrollton. In that election the Jackson forces placed eleven Jackson men in the state senate to only four anti-Jackson men.

But the leaders of the Jackson party in Maryland soon became disillusioned with the new president. Jackson's vetoes of the Maysville Road bill for the construction of a road in Ohio with federal funds and of a bill appropriating money for a road from Washington to Frederick showed him hostile to national government financing and internal improvements. His vetoes alienated many of his prominent Maryland supporters who were soliciting federal aid for canal construction and were pushing the Baltimore and Ohio Railroad to the west. As a result, the anti-Jackson party gained control of the Assembly in the next election and placed an anti-Jackson man, Daniel Martin of Talbot County, in the governor's chair. When Governor Martin died in the following year, he was succeeded by George Howard, a son of one of Maryland's early governors, John Eager Howard, and in the election of 1831, the voters increased the anti-Jackson majority in the state government and reelected Howard as governor. Out of this situation emerged the Whig party of Maryland.

The delay of the Democrats in capturing the state government is partly explained by the fact that Baltimore, which was a center of pro-Jackson sentiment, was denied political representation commensurate with its size and importance. The state senate elected in 1831 would be the last senate elected peaceably in accordance with the constitution. As the democratic movement headed by Jackson swept over the country, the electoral college system prescribed in the Maryland constitution of 1776 appeared to be inadequate to meet the needs of Maryland voters. The movement to abolish it centered largely in Baltimore and in the northern and western counties of the state.

As the plans were made for the presidential campaign of 1832, Maryland assumed pivotal importance. In fact, in that campaign—the first presidential campaign in which nominating conventions were held—all three of the important national political parties held their conventions in Baltimore. The first presidential nominating convention in the history of the United States was called by the anti-Masonic party. This party had originated in western New York state in 1826 as a result of the abduction of William Morgan, who was believed to have revealed the secrets of Freemasonry. The movement spread through the north and held a convention at Philadelphia in 1830 at which members made plans to hold a national convention in Baltimore in the following year to nominate candidates for the presidency and vice-presidency of the United States. This convention, when it assembled in the Athenaeum in Baltimore in September 1831, was largely motivated by anti-Jacksonism. It included representatives from Maine, New Hampshire, Vermont, Massachusetts, Rhode Island, Connecticut, New York, New Jersey, Pennsylvania, Ohio, Indiana, Delaware, and Maryland—thirteen states in all. They adopted no platform but nominated William Wirt of Maryland, former Attorney General of the United States—and a Mason—for the presidency.

In the following December, the National Republican party convened in Baltimore and nominated for the presidency Henry Clay, who was a Past Grand Master of the Masonic Lodge of Kentucky. In their resolutions they denounced the Jackson administration for its corruption and abuse of power, for its hostility to internal improvements, for its equivocation on the tariff question, and for its war on the Second Bank of the United States. The Democratic convention assembled at Baltimore in May 1832, confirmed the nomination of Jackson, who was a Past Grand Master of the Masonic Lodge of Tennessee, and named Van Buren as its candidate for the vice-presidency. This convention adopted no platform, for Jackson was their platform.

In the ensuing vote for presidential electors, the popular vote in Maryland was almost evenly divided between Clay and Jackson, the former receiving a majority of four votes out of a total of 38,316. Maryland's electoral vote was therefore divided, five going to Clay and three to Jackson. Maryland's native son, William Wirt, the candidate of the anti-Masonic Party, received only the seven electoral votes of Vermont. The Maryland state government remained in the hands of the National Republicans, and when the Whig party was formed, Maryland continued under its control.

Meanwhile Roger Brooke Taney, a son of Maryland and brother-in-law of Francis Scott Key, had played a large role in the Jackson administration. After serving as Attorney-General of Maryland, he had been appointed in 1831 as Attorney-General of the United States and in that position loyally supported the president in his campaign against the Second Bank of the United States, which Jackson denounced as an "octopus of finance" controlled by "foreign stockholders." After Jackson's reelection in 1832, Taney was transferred to the cabinet post of Secretary of the Treasury on an interim appointment and in that position carried out Jackson's order for the removal of government funds from the Bank. But when he was denied confirmation in that position by the Senate, he was forced out of office and returned to Baltimore to receive a tumultuous ovation. He was soon afterward nominated by Jackson as associate justice of the Supreme Court in place of another Marylander, Gabriel Duvall, who had just retired after twenty-four years of service on the court. But Taney's confirmation was blocked by Senators Henry Clay and Daniel Webster. In 1835, however, when the position of Chief Justice became vacant through the death of John Marshall, Taney was appointed and confirmed as Chief Justice, a position which he held for the next 28 years, until 1864.

In Maryland the Whig government failed to satisfy those groups who had found in Jackson a champion of the common people. Baltimore and the western counties had grown rapidly since the War of 1812, and they now pressed urgently for increased influence in the government of the state. As early as 1818, the legislature had taken under consideration a bill to amend the constitution so as to give Baltimore two additional members in the House of Delegates, but the bill had been defeated by the thinly populated counties. These counties refused to give the Democratic counties their proportionate share in the government of the state. They declined to surrender the power that they possessed. Though this subject was debated over and over again in the Assembly, it was not until 1835 that the legislature gave Baltimore two additional delegates.

But this concession was not enough. In the following year a Reform Convention, composed of delegates from Cecil, Harford, Baltimore, Frederick, Montgomery, and Washington Counties and Baltimore City, met and resolved to recommend to the people of Maryland (1) that they elect delegates pledged to reforming the constitution of the state, (2) that these delegates should provide for the summoning of a constitutional convention at Annapolis composed of members distributed equally among the several congressional districts of the state, and (3) that if the legislature did not arrange to call such a convention within forty days after the commencement of its session, they would again convene "for the adoption of such ulterior measures as may then be deemed expedient, just and proper, and may be best calculated, without the aid of the Legislature, to ensure the accomplishment of the desired results." This virtual ultimatum to the legislature precipitated a crisis in the state which was aggravated by the national political situation.[3]

As President Jackson's second term neared its end, the power of the administration was thrown behind the vice-president, Martin Van Buren, as his successor. Van Buren was nominated by the Democratic party as their presidential candidate at a convention held in Baltimore in May 1835. Against his candidacy the political opposition, consisting of former National Republicans and upholders of states rights, calling themselves Whigs, promptly rallied. The Whigs, though they were unable to agree upon a single candidate as their presidential standard-bearer, hoped to throw the election into the House of Representatives and there to defeat Van Buren. In Maryland this presidential campaign coincided with the election of electors to choose a new state senate. In all, forty electors were to be chosen—two from each of the nineteen counties of the state and one from each of the cities of Baltimore and Annapolis.

The election in Maryland resulted in victory for twenty-one Whig and nineteen Democratic or Van Buren electors. But these numbers did not accurately reflect popular sentiment. Chosen in accordance with the constitutional system of geographical apportionment, the twenty-one Whig electors represented ten counties having a total population of only 85,179 or, in federal numbers including three-fifths of the slaves, 138,020 while the nineteen Van Buren electors represented eight counties and the two cities which had a total population of 205,922, or in federal numbers, 267,669. A minority of the people of the state, in contravention of the will of the majority, had it in their power, therefore, through their Whig representatives in the electoral college to fix the political complexion of the state senate for the next five years and possibly even to put Maryland in the anti-Van Buren column in the presidential election.

But in opposition to this scheme the nineteen Van Buren electors determined to take advantage of the constitutional requirement that twenty-four electors were necessary to constitute a quorum. Several Democratic districts, therefore, including Frederick and Cecil Counties and Baltimore City instructed their electors not to proceed to the election of senators unless the Whig electors would agree to "such a thorough and radical reform of the Constitution of the State as will ensure to all citizens living under it equal political rights and privileges." Only in this way, they explained, could they "avoid the fate of being again compelled to submit for five years at least to the tyranny of a government wielded and controlled by a small and aristocratic minority of the people of the State." The nineteen Van Buren electors accordingly resolved that in accordance with their instructions and since they represented a majority of the voters of the state they would not participate in the election unless they received the privilege of naming eight members or a majority of the Senate. They pointed out that they represented "nearly three-fourths of the free white population, and two-thirds of the federal numbers of the State, and very much the largest portion of its territorial extent and wealth." They announced that they would not allow the election of a solid Whig senate. They realized that their refusal might "give some alarm to the timorous," but they felt that it would "produce less serious consequences than the perpetuation of existing evils for another five years." They demanded therefore that a convention be called "to reform our constitution."

The Van Buren electors, receiving no reply to these propositions from the Whig electors, left Annapolis and went home. They then issued an address to the people of the state alleging "that the government is based and administered on unjust and anti-republican principles; that the governor and senate are not elected directly by the people as they should be; that many of the officers have life tenures, contrary to sound political principle; and that in the formation of both branches of the legislature political power is apportioned arbitrarily without regard to any principle of moral or political justice. . . . A minority of one-fourth of the people having the right to elect a majority of the members of the legislature controls all the departments of government.... Can a government thus organized be termed republican?" they asked. For these reasons, they explained, they had declined to participate in the election of a senate and now returned their power to the people of the state recommending that the authority of all the civil and military officers of the state should be extended "until a convention, hereafter to be chosen, can be convened to amend the old or form an entire new government for the people of Maryland." They looked forward to "the great and inestimable advantage to be derived from a reorganization of our system and the substitution of wholesome democratic features for its present odious artistocratic ones."

Here was a revelation for Maryland of the explosive and disruptive character of Jacksonian democracy, of the new force of the people in public affairs.

To the defiant address of the Van Buren electors the Whig majority in the electoral college replied that the electors were "mere agents of the people of Maryland, selected for a specific purpose," and that they could not traffic among themselves on the subject of constitutional reform. "The moment it is attempted to force upon the people a new constitution in any other mode than that provided by the existing instrument, Maryland ceases to exist," they ominously declared. They showed that inequality of representation was not confined to Maryland and admitted that if constitutional reform was desired, many of the Whig electors would favor it by peaceful means. But they announced that they would do all in their power to avoid revolution and anarchy.

This was the very prospect that seemed now to threaten Maryland. "The hand of the disorganizer is uplifted to strike down our State Government and all its institutions; to suspend all our works of public improvement; to break our government into fragments, and go back into a state of nature," exclaimed one newspaper, referring to the dissident Van Buren electors. The grand jury of Allegany County presented the nineteen electors as "unfaithful public agents and disturbers of the public peace," and Governor Thomas W. Veazey denounced them as "recusant electors and their abettors." The propertied classes put themselves in a posture to resist revolution. A large public meeting in Cumberland resolved that "it would be wise in the people of the several districts of this county to meet and organize, so as to be ready at the first warning to carry into effect such measures as may be deemed most expedient to protect the rights of property and to preserve the liberties of the people." And the president of the meeting appointed a vigilance committee of nine "whose duty it shall be to communicate information of any revolutionary movements to the several committees appointed in other districts and to advise with them as to the best course to pursue." Two days later a large mass meeting was held in Monument Square in Baltimore at which "resolutions were adopted declaring that the Van Buren electors had "disregarded a high public trust, committed a high misdemeanor, and merit the severest reprobation." They had attempted "to introduce anarchy and revolution," had warred "against the peace, order, and happiness of society," had sacrificed "the best interest of the people of Maryland," had usurped the "sovereignty of the people," and had put in "jeopardy the vital principle of all republican institutions."

The Van Buren electors had raised the specter of a popular uprising against Maryland's constitutional system. They were supported by the urban and rural working class who formed the major element in the Jackson party. Their action was endorsed by a mass meeting of working men held in Monument Square in Baltimore in September 1836. The people, it was resolved at this meeting, have the power to change the constitution at will. The existing constitution, they declared, was "a blot upon the principles of republicanism and unworthy the respect of any American citizen." They urged that it be annulled or abolished and that a new one be provided "more consistent with the principles of republicanism and affording a better security of the rights and privileges of the whole people." They denounced those who opposed this change as a "power-loving aristocracy and grasping monopolists."

Such support, however, was not enough to vindicate the Van Buren electors. In the election of delegates to the new House, the Van Buren candidates were defeated, losing all the seats from Annapolis City, Anne Arundel and Queen Anne's Counties, and several from Washington, Harford, and Caroline Counties. In the new House they gained only nineteen seats to sixty for the Whigs. In the national election the Van Buren party in Maryland was also defeated. Between September 1836, when the Van Buren electors for the state senate had won a popular majority of over 3,000 in the state and had carried eight counties and Annapolis and Baltimore, and November 1836 when the presidential vote was taken, the Democratic party lost ground in Maryland. In the presidential election the Democrats carried only Baltimore and Cecil Counties and Baltimore City. The assault of the Van Burenites on Maryland's constitutional system had, at least temporarily, backfired against them.

Maryland's repudiation of Jackson in 1832 and of his candidate, Van Buren, in 1836 was undoubtedly due in part to the financial policy of his administration. In 1832 Jackson vetoed a bill rechartering the Bank

View of Annapolis from the State House in 1850, by Sachse.

Courtesy *Maryland Hall of Records Commission*

of the United States which had been chartered in 1816 to run for twenty years. He interpreted his subsequent reelection in that year as a mandate from the people to destroy the Bank and finding a compliant agent in Taney, he had removed the government deposits from the Bank. His war on the Bank, though it produced some national benefits, also encouraged speculation, disorganized the currency system of the country, and resulted in the transfer of national funds to the state banks. Though Jackson's action hastened the demise of an oppressive financial monopoly, at the same time it destroyed the only strong check upon further speculation. It brought disaster upon the banks of Baltimore, particularly upon the Bank of Maryland which was forced to suspend business in March 1835. This suspension so aroused Baltimore that a mob collected, attacked the homes of the president of the company, John Glenn, its counsel, Reverdy Johnson, and other officials of the company, caused damage of $102,552, and compelled the mayor to resign. Order was restored only when General Samuel Smith, then eighty-three years of age, placed himself at the head of the forces of law and order, issued orders to the firemen and to the citizens to preserve the peace, and secured the arrest of the leaders of the riots.

The Whigs hastened to take advantage of their electoral victory in 1836. Since a new senate had not been chosen, Governor Veazey issued a proclamation on the day after the election announcing "that the senate elected in September, 1831, continued to be the senate of Maryland, and will so continue until superseded by the election of successors, as constitutionally and lawfully provided for." He denounced the action of the Van Buren electors as preparing the way for "unspeakable calamities of anarchy, intestine commotion, and civil war" and announced that in order "to curb the spirit of anarchy, disorder, and revolution," he would "exert to the utmost all the powers" vested in him. To defend the governor in the exercise of these powers a volunteer military company, called the Planters' Guard, was organized at Upper Marlboro. The constitutional party thus set itself adamantly in opposition to constitutional change. In the national election Maryland cast all ten of her electoral votes for the Whig candidate, William Henry Harrison, for president. Maryland's candidate, however, came in only second best and had to allow the presidency to go to Van Buren.

The courageous Van Buren electors were now obliged to surrender. Several of them returned to Annapolis, took the required oaths, and enabled the electoral college to muster a quorum. The electors, whose complement was thus swelled to twenty-five members, proceeded to elect fifteen Whig senators, the Van Buren electors casting blank ballots. But the cause of constitutional reform was not defeated. A so-called Reform Convention assembled in Baltimore on November 16, 1836, including representatives from all the political divisions of the state except Allegany, Queen Anne's, and Somerset Counties. They first repelled the accusations of Governor Veazey that in agitating for constitutional reform they had done "anything inconsistent with their duties as peaceable citizens or in violation of the laws of the State." They then called for the following constitutional changes: (1) the governor should be elected directly by the people and his council should be abolished; (2) one senator from each county and one from the City of Baltimore should be elected directly by the people, (3) the House of Delegates should be reapportioned in order to give greater representation to the more populous districts, (4) all offices for life should be abolished, and (5) several minor state officials including clerks and registers should be elected directly by the people. The convention then adjourned, planning to meet again at Annapolis.

But this convention never found it necessary to meet again, for the assembly immediately entered upon the work of constitutional reform. They confirmed a law increasing Baltimore's delegation from two to four members and passed a law in March 1837 providing for many of the other demanded reforms. They gave the people the power of electing the governor, increased his term from one to three years, abolished the governor's council, and provided a Secretary of State to take the place of the clerk of the council. They abolished the electoral college and provided that one member of the senate should be chosen from each county and one from the City of Baltimore. Senators thereafter would be elected by the people. Their term was fixed at six years, one-third of them retiring from office at intervals of two years. Representation in the House of Delegates was reapportioned, five members being assigned to Baltimore City, Frederick, and Baltimore Counties; four to Anne Arundel, Dorchester, Somerset, Worcester, Prince George's, Harford, Montgomery, Carroll, and Washington; three to each of the remaining counties; and one to Annapolis. At every second census after the census of 1840 the delegates would be reapportioned in accordance with population. Baltimore would be entitled to as many delegates as the most populous county, and after 1840 the City of Annapolis would no longer have a separate representation in the House but would be considered a part of Anne Arundel County.

So it happened that most of the constitutional changes demanded by the intransigent Van Buren electors in 1836 were adopted in the following year. They and their friends claimed the credit for these changes, and their dramatic refusal to participate in the election of senators in 1836 undoubtedly highlighted the constitutional issue. It may well be, however, that their action rather hindered than helped the cause of constitutional reform, for it was of such a highhanded character as to repel many conservatives who otherwise would have supported the reform movement. Their action furthermore made the cause of constitutional reform in Maryland a part of Van Buren's campaign for the presidency, which not all advocates of constitutional change in Maryland could accept. By coupling it with national Democratic party politics, they forfeited all support of the Whigs, many of whom in the more populous counties appreciated the need of change, and they probably even alienated some Democrats who objected to Jackson's handpicked candidate for the presidency.

Maryland thus tardily swung into the democratic current of the times. The first state election held after the democratic constitutional innovations resulted in the election of William Grason, "the Queen Anne Farmer" and a Democrat, but the Democrats failed to gain a majority in the senate, the House of Delegates, or Maryland's delegation in Congress. In the elections in 1839, however, they captured the House. In the presidential campaign of 1840, Maryland's political importance was recognized by the Democrats who again held their nominating convention in Baltimore and there renominated Van Buren for the presidency. But in this "log cabin and hard cider" campaign, Maryland failed to give a majority of either its popular or its electoral votes to the Democratic candidate. Baltimore gave him a majority of thirty-one votes, but the state as a whole gave Harrison and Tyler a popular majority of almost 5,000. Maryland's electors therefore cast all ten of the state's electoral votes for the Whig candidates.

Despite the preference of Maryland voters for the Whig ticket in the national election of 1840, they turned the state government over to the Democrats in 1841 and kept them in control until 1843. In the state election in that year, the Democrats were obliged to yield to the Whigs, and in the election of the following year, the Whigs made a clean sweep of the state offices, carrying all the counties and towns of the Eastern Shore. Maryland's defection from the Democratic party was probably due in part to Tyler's independent course and the aggressive Whig leadership that was offered by Clay.

Maryland seemed to manifest a curious political irresolution in national and state elections as between the two major parties, but in this respect it reflected the indecisiveness which characterized the national political scene. From the viewpoint of partisan politics during the years from 1836 to 1840, the Whigs sought to defend the *status quo* which favored the privileged classes, but though they won the initial battles both in Maryland and in other states, they found it politically expedient to acknowledge the upthrust of the new forces in political life, to accept the inevitability of reform, and to identify themselves with it. Both major parties switched sides on a number of important issues.

Maryland's political importance was again recognized by the national parties in the campaign of 1844, for all three of them held their nominating conventions that year in Baltimore. The Whigs met there in early May and nominated Clay unanimously by resolution. The Democrats met there toward the end of the same month and amidst a great deal of excitement finally on the ninth ballot nominated James K. Polk of Tennessee, who was a neighbor and protegé of Jackson and who had served as speaker of the House of Representatives and governor of Tennessee. The news of his nomination was sent to Washington over the first telegraph line, a line which had recently been opened between Baltimore and Washington, and a congratulatory reply was received from Democratic members of Congress over the same wire. The Tyler faction, consisting mainly of officeholders of the Tyler administration, also held a convention in Baltimore, concurrently with the Democratic convention, and nominated Tyler for reelection, but Tyler soon withdrew from the campaign. In the campaign of 1844, Maryland again voted Whig, giving Clay a popular majority of over 3,000 and all the state's eight electoral votes. They also chose a Whig governor, Thomas G. Pratt.

In the national elections from 1828 through 1844, Maryland uniformly supported the anti-Jackson candidates, but in the election of state officers it had vacillated uncertainly between the Jackson and anti-Jackson parties. This deviation in state offices, though usually a very narrow one, continued after Polk's election in 1844. In 1845 Maryland's congressional delegation consisted of four Democrats and only two Whigs, but the state government was retained by the Whigs. The Whigs strengthened their position in 1846, but in 1847 had to surrender the governorship to a Democrat, Philip F. Thomas, who won by a small majority of 638 votes. In the presidential campaign of the following year, the Democrats held their national nominating convention again in Baltimore and nominated Lewis Cass of Michigan for the presidency, President Polk having declined to be considered for reelection. Maryland Whigs had already expressed a preference for General Zachary Taylor, a military hero of the Mexican War, and had put his name in nomination at a "Taylor State Convention" held in Baltimore. Taylor, whose wife, Margaret Smith Taylor, was a Marylander, was formally nominated by the Whig national convention at

Philadelphia in June. In the November election Maryland gave Taylor a popular majority of over 3,000 and all the state's eight electoral votes.

In every presidential election from Washington to Jackson, therefore, Maryland supported the winning candidate, but in the elections of 1828 through 1848 Maryland preferred the anti-Jackson or Whig presidential candidates. Only in the elections of 1840 and 1848 in this latter period, therefore, when Harrison and Taylor respectively were elected, did Maryland support the winning candidates. Maryland's favored candidates in the national elections from 1796 through 1848 are shown in the following table:

Maryland's Vote in Presidential Elections

Popular Vote	Electoral Vote	Elected
1796 ——	John Adams, Federalist	Adams
1800 ——	By abstaining in Congressional vote Maryland helped to elect Jefferson, Republican	Jefferson
1804 ——	Jefferson, Democrat–Republican	Jefferson
1808 ——	Madison, Democrat–Republican	Madison
1812 ——	Madison, " "	Madison
1816 ——	Monroe, " "	Monroe
1820 ——	Monroe, " "	Monroe
1824 ——	John Quincy Adams, " "	Adams
1828 Adams	John Quincy Adams, " "	Jackson
1832 Clay	Clay, Whig	Jackson
1836 Harrison	Harrison, Whig	Van Buren
1840 Harrison	Harrison, Whig	Harrison
1844 Clay	Clay, Whig	Polk
1848 Taylor	Taylor, Whig	Taylor

But in the state elections after 1832 Maryland was not consistently or overwhelmingly Whig. The Whig victories in state politics were often narrow, and frequently the Whigs had to surrender control of the state to the Democrats.

In national elections, therefore, Maryland generally assumed a conservative posture, in local politics a somewhat more liberal or at least flexible stand. This ambivalence in political action as between national levels and local levels again demonstrated the middle-of-the-road attitude of Marylanders whose border position between east and west, north and south, gave the state something of the character of all sections of the nation. It reflected not only her intermediate geographical location but also her radiating commercial ties with the states to the north, the south, and the west, and her expanding alliances with eastern financial interests, for politics, though it may be nothing more than an end in itself to the participants, must, in order to be effective, satisfy the majority of the underlying social and economic forces in a society.

Footnotes

[1] Victor Sapio, "Maryland's Federalist Revival, 1808-1812," *Maryland Historical Magazine*, vol. 64, No. 1, Spring 1969, p. 1-17.

[2] Emanuel Milton Altfeld, *The Jew's Struggle for Religious and Civil Liberty in Maryland*, M. Curlander, Baltimore, 1924.

[3] A. Clark Hagensick, "Revolution or Reform in 1836: Maryland's Preface to the Dorr Rebellion," *Maryland Historical Magazine*, vol. 57, No. 4, December 1962, pp. 346-366.

Sources and Additional Reading

Altfeld, Emanuel Milton, *The Jew's Struggle for Religious and Civil Liberty in Maryland*, M. Curlander, Baltimore, 1924.

Fein, Isaac M., *The Making of an American Jewish Community: The History of Baltimore Jewry from 1773 to 1920*, Jewish Publication Society of America, Philadelphia, 1971.

Kennedy, John P., *Memoirs of the Life of William Wirt* . . . 2 vols., Lea, Philadelphia, 1850.

Lewis, Walker, *Without Fear or Favor: A Biography of Chief Justice Roger Brooke Taney*, Houghton Mifflin Company, Boston, 1965.

McCarthy, Charles, *The Antimasonic Party: A Study of Political Antimasonry in the United States, 1827-1840*, Annual Report of the American Historical Association for the Year 1902, vol. 1, Washington, Government Printing Office, 1903, pp. 365-574.

Smith, Charles W., *Roger B. Taney: Jacksonian Jurist*, University of North Carolina Press, Chapel Hill, 1936.

Steiner, Bernard Christian, *The Electoral College for the Senate of Maryland and the Nineteen Van Buren Electors*, Annual Report for the Year 1895, American Historical Association, Washington, 1896, pp. 127-167.

——, *Life of Roger Brooke Taney, Chief Justice of the United States Supreme Court*, Williams & Wilkins Company, 1922.

Swisher, Carl Brent, *Roger B. Taney*, Macmillan Company, 1935.

Tuska, Gerald, "Know-Nothingism in Baltimore, 1854-1860," *Catholic Historical Review*, V, July 1925, pp. 217-241.

Tyler, Samuel, *Memoir of Roger Brooke Taney*, 2d revised and enlarged edition, John Murphy & Co., Baltimore, 1874.

CHAPTER XIX

NEW VENTURES IN TRANSPORTATION

The Potomac River as a route to the west had attracted the attention of enterprising colonists frequently during the colonial period. Its development as a channel of trade to the Ohio country seemed to become urgent as the Piedmont area of Maryland and Virginia attracted increasing numbers of settlers and as the tide of western migration, after the middle of the eighteenth century, moved into the valleys of the upper tributaries of the Potomac and Ohio Rivers. To open up means of transportation and communication with these new western settlements, after 1749 the Ohio Company blazed trails over the mountains to the headwaters of the Youghiogheny and the Monongahela Rivers. The Potomac River itself seemed to offer a natural means of ingress into the back country. But it was a narrow and winding stream obstructed by rapids and subject to wide fluctuations of water volume. Some means would have to be found to move river traffic around the rapids, and at certain places the riverbed itself would have to be deepened in order to make it commercially useful.

After America's victory in the War for Independence, the authority in the West which had been exercised by the English government devolved upon the state legislatures. Under George Washington's guidance, Maryland and Virginia appointed a joint committee to consider plans for improving the navigation of the Potomac. As noted earlier, Virginia chartered the Potomac Company for this purpose in October 1784 to run for five years, and months later a committee met, with Washington as its presiding officer, and organized the company. Early in the following year, the Maryland legislature confirmed the charter of the company and subscribed £5,000 to the venture. The company was made responsible for opening up the Potomac River to the highest point of navigation so as to make it navigable for boats carrying a load equivalent to fifty barrels of flour. Its minimum goal was Fort Cumberland, where river traffic could meet the improved Braddock Road leading into the Ohio River Valley.

The Potomac Company made a good beginning toward opening up the Potomac River to navigation. It built a canal fifty yards in length at House's Falls, five miles above Harpers Ferry, and a canal one mile long around Shenandoah Falls immediately above Harpers Ferry. But it encountered serious obstacles at the Great Falls, for the river at that point descends over 79 feet in only 1,200 yards and the shores are so steep as to make canal construction difficult. And yet the company succeeded in constructing a canal three-quarters of a mile long around the Great Falls on the Virginia side with locks at both ends. It built its last canal around the Little Falls on the Maryland shore, which ran more than two miles in length and was equipped with four locks. The company also deepened the river channel in several places, but soon after Washington's death, it fell into financial difficulties and became virtually bankrupt in 1802. Its activities had been hindered in Virginia by the proponents of the James River and Kanawha Canal and in Maryland by Baltimore's jealousy of a project which would benefit its rival ports of Georgetown and Alexandria. The company had also been plagued by a chronic shortage of laborers. But at this critical stage in the affairs of the Potomac Company, the state of Maryland subscribed to an additional one hundred shares of capital stock at £130 a share. With this sum the company was able to complete the work on the locks at the Great Falls, thus making the Potomac route navigable by small craft for approximately two hundred and twenty miles, from tidewater to the mouth of the Savage River.

The Potomac Company had planned to improve navigation on the tributaries of the Potomac, and it now constructed canals and locks around the five falls in the Shenandoah River near its junction with the Potomac, thus making the Shenandoah navigable for a distance of some two hundred miles southward from the Potomac. The company devoted some of its attention to dredging the Monocacy, the Conococheague, and the Antietam tributaries of the Potomac in Maryland. To increase its financial resources, the company was granted a loan by the state of Maryland in 1814 and was authorized to conduct a lottery, which, however, proved a dismal failure, netting the company a profit of only $486.03, instead of the anticipated $300,000. By this time the company's profits from the operation were inadequate even to discharge the interest payments. Its charter was extended from time to time by the General Assemblies of Virginia and Maryland, and in 1819, after an existence of thirty-five years, it applied to the Board of Public Works of Virginia for relief. It had not yet fully complied with the conditions of its charter. Between 1800 and 1822 traffic on the Potomac Canal averaged 633 boats a year, carrying 7,400 tons of produce and merchandise.[1] Nevertheless, the company had expended over $729,000 by 1822 and had paid only one small dividend of $3,890 in 1811. At all other times its profits had either been turned back into company operations or been applied to payment of interest on the loans contracted.

Because the development of the Potomac River and other works of internal improvement could not be adequately financed by private capital and state resources, and because they were deemed to have important military uses, the promoters of these works repeatedly turned to the national government for support. In 1805 the directors of the bankrupt Chesapeake and Delaware Canal Company, which had been organized to dig a canal connecting Chesapeake Bay with the Delaware River and Bay at the narrowest point of the Eastern Shore (Delmarva), appealed to Congress for assistance but received none. Plans of this sort were usually blocked by the constitutional scruples of the Republican administration. And yet in 1806 a bill for the construction of the National Road passed Congress and became law with the approval of President Jefferson. Two years later, Albert Gallatin, Secretary of the Treasury, upon instructions from Congress, presented a "Report on Roads and Canals," in which he recommended that the national government carry out a complete system of internal improvements over a period of ten years and expend twenty million dollars for that purpose. He proposed that the government launch these works and expend this money by purchasing stock in private companies on the assumption that private companies could do the work more efficiently than government engineers, and he suggested specifically that the government immediately purchase stock in the Chesapeake and Delaware Canal, the Dismal Swamp Canal, the Ohio Canal, and the Pittsburgh Road. The only immediate result of Gallatin's fervent and ambitious recommendations was the initiation of improvements by the government in the National Road west of Cumberland which began in 1811. Within the next six years this nationally sponsored road was completed to the Ohio River at Wheeling. But Congress, after launching this project, was distracted by the War of 1812 and took no action upon Gallatin's other recommendations.

With the return of peace, internal improvements once more became a major issue in politics. President Madison repeatedly emphasized it in his annual messages to Congress, though he deemed a constitutional amendment necessary to permit action by the national government. In 1817 both houses of Congress finally agreed upon a measure providing for a system of internal improvements by the national government without a constitutional amendment. From the bonus paid for the charter of the second Bank of the United States they created a permanent fund for the construction of roads and canals. But President Madison vetoed it on the last day of his presidency on the ground that the national government had no power under the constitution to undertake such works.

The states therefore took up this work themselves. Immediately New York began the Erie Canal, which when completed would make New York City the metropolis of the American seaboard. In this route to the west New York enjoyed several advantages over Maryland and Virginia. The route of the Erie Canal was more level than the Potomac River route, having only a 500-foot rise as compared with a 1,900-foot elevation on the Potomac route. Moreover, it led through a terrain in central New York State which was already well settled. At the same time (1816) the State of Virginia created a Board of Public Works which became interested in developing its own route to the west by means of river improvements in the James River and the construction of a canal to connect the James River with the Kanawha River. Maryland now turned to a Chesapeake and Ohio Canal, which would substitute a permanent artificial canal for the system of river improvements constructed by the Potomac Company.

The work of internal improvements by the national government, however, was not to be checked by Madison's pen, for it was urgently represented as an essential part of the "American System" which was gaining in public favor and was strongly favored by President Monroe. At the direction of Congress his Secretary of War, John C. Calhoun, who at this time held large national views, submitted a report, "Relative to Roads and Canals," in 1819 which went even further than Gallatin's earlier report in recommending an energetic federal program of internal improvements. He believed that the government possessed ample powers under the Constitution, and he suggested that it engage directly in the work of construction using the engineer corps to make the necessary surveys and plans and soldiers to do the actual work at a compensation a little below the average wages paid for such work in addition to their regular pay. But in spite of this report, the national government continued apathetic toward such projects.

Soon afterward Virginia took the first step toward the construction of a Chesapeake and Ohio Canal. The governor of Virginia recommended to his legislature the desirability of uniting the waters of the Potomac with those of the Ohio by a canal system. In response, the General Assembly of that state on January 8, 1820 requested the Board of Public Works to examine and report upon the most efficient means of improving the navigation of the Potomac River and establishing a communication by canals "between the Potomac and the Ohio on one side and the Potomac and the Rappahannock on the other." Accordingly Thomas Moore, chief engineer of the Board, surveyed the route and concluded that a canal from Georgetown to Cumberland was entirely practicable and would cost about $1,114,300. His report was transmitted to the General Assembly of Virginia which authorized the governor to appoint a committee to cooperate with a similar committee from Maryland. The legislature of Maryland immediately adopted a similar resolution.

A joint committee of the two states was then appointed and authorized "to examine the affairs of the Potomac Company, the state of the navigation of the Potomac River, and its susceptibility of improvement." The Committee was composed of Athanasius Fenwick, William Naylor, and Moses T. Hunter for Maryland, and William T.T. Mason and Eli Williams for Virginia. Holding their first meeting at Georgetown on July 2, 1821, they examined the books of the Potomac Company and concluded that it had failed to carry out its charter, that it had incurred a heavy debt, that it was hopelessly bankrupt, and that it should be given no further aid. They therefore recommended that its charter be annulled, that other means should be devised for improving the navigation of the river, and that the river channel be abandoned in favor of a continuous canal from tidewater to Cumberland. Proceeding then to western Maryland they began a survey of the route and concluded that a canal, thirty feet wide at the surface, twenty feet wide at the bottom, and holding three feet of water, could be constructed from Georgetown to Cumberland for $1,574,954.

This report was enthusiastically received by Maryland and Virginia, for the canal was expected to pay large dividends and to reduce the cost of transportation into the back country to approximately one-tenth its former cost. The General Assembly of Virginia passed a bill incorporating the "Potomac Canal Company" on February 22, 1823, and stipulated that it could not go into effect until confirmed by Maryland. Soon afterward the Maryland legislature took under consideration a bill to incorporate a new joint stock association called "The Potomac Canal Company" stipulating that Maryland, Virginia, and the District of Columbia should each subscribe one-third of the stock and that the canal should originate at Georgetown. But this measure was strenuously opposed by powerful Baltimore interests which feared that their trade would be injured by the canal. The city of Baltimore at that time was paying one-third of the taxes of the state, though it had only one-fourth of the delegates in the House of Delegates. Probably because of Baltimore's opposition, the Maryland legislature failed to pass the bill. The

Virginia Act therefore lapsed. This attempt by certain groups in Virginia and Maryland to construct a Potomac Canal had ended in failure.

As the Erie Canal advanced westward from Albany and public interest in all works of internal improvement increased, friends of the Potomac Canal project launched a series of popular meetings to stimulate interest in the enterprise and arranged a general meeting to be held in Washington in November 1823. This convention, which met in the Capitol, included thirty-eight representatives from Virginia, thirty-one from Maryland, twenty-four from the District of Columbia, one from Pennsylvania, and two or three honorary members from Ohio. Though one-third of the delegates who attended the convention came from Maryland, none of them represented the city of Baltimore. Dr. Joseph Kent, a highly respected member of Congress from Prince George's County, was chosen president of the convention.

This convention took action which prepared the way for the construction of the Chesapeake and Ohio Canal. It adopted resolutions endorsing the project of a canal to connect the Potomac with the West and petitioning Congress and the interested states to aid the project. It called specifically for a canal running from tidewater on the Potomac by way of Cumberland to the mouth of Savage River, thence to the Monongahela River, and eventually to Lake Erie and recommended that the states through which the canal would be constructed be permitted to connect their own canal systems with it by lateral canals. The convention estimated the total cost of the canal and its extension above Cumberland at $2,750,000, basing this estimate upon previous calculations and the cost of constructing the existing ninety-six miles of the Erie Canal ($1,792 a mile). The estimate for the 212 miles to the coal banks above Cumberland was about $13,000 per mile. The convention recommended that the entire cost of the canal project should be furnished as follows: 4/11 or $1,000,000 by the United States, 3/11 or $750,000 by Virginia, 2/11 or $500,000 by the District of Columbia, and 2/11 or $500,000 by Maryland. The members thus sought to enlist the efforts of the national government and to commit it to the enterprise. The convention then hopefully changed the name of the project to the Chesapeake and Ohio Canal and adopted a form for a charter which was to be submitted to the legislatures of Maryland, Virginia, Pennsylvania, and Ohio and to Congress. It also stressed the importance of hastening actual surveys of the canal route and prepared to open the books for subscriptions of stock.

To this convention of 1823 belongs the credit for finally launching the project which Washington had envisioned a half century before and of finally overcoming the scruples of the Monroe administration on the subject of internal improvements. When the draft charter of the new Chesapeake and Ohio Company was presented to the states, Virginia promptly approved it on January 27, 1824, but Maryland delayed because of the opposition of Baltimore, the indifference of some of the northern counties, and the strong resistance of the Eastern Shore counties. Baltimore, as noted above, feared that the canal would divert some of its western trade to Georgetown, designated as the eastern starting point of the canal. As the principal wheat-exporting port of the nation, Baltimore was engaged in competition with both Philadelphia and New York for the trade of the trans-Allegheny West. It was being thrust on the defensive by New York's construction of the Erie Canal, begun in 1817, which connected Albany with Buffalo, and by Pennsylvania's growing network of canals and inclined planes reaching out toward Pittsburgh. Under these circumstances Baltimore was in danger of losing western trade to its rival ports. On the other hand, it seemed clear that a canal extending inland from tidewater would provide the farmers of western Maryland with a cheaper means of transportation and would expedite the development of the coal-mining industry there. Lacking a canal, the coal miners of Allegany County had to transport their coal by wagon to Cumberland and there load it on boats to be floated down the Potomac River after the spring thaws.

At the suggestion of General Robert Goodloe Harper, the mayor of Baltimore, a meeting of citizens of Baltimore was held to consider the project, but Baltimore opposed it, preferring a canal which would connect her with the Susquehanna River and give her the trade of interior Pennsylvania. The Maryland legislature, however, appointed commissioners "to ascertain whether a water communication could be opened between the City of Baltimore and the projected Potomac Canal." When the commission determined that such a canal could be constructed connecting the canal at Georgetown with the Patapsco, Maryland made it a condition of her acceptance of the Chesapeake and Ohio Canal project that she should be given the privilege of constructing a branch canal to tap the main canal at some point in Maryland or the District of Columbia. After gaining this concession, Maryland confirmed the Virginia Act of incorporation on January 31, 1825.

President Monroe was impressed by the public support for a Potomac Canal which was manifested in the Chesapeake and Ohio Canal Convention. He pronounced in favor of national aid to internal improvement companies in his annual message to Congress on December 2, 1823 and recommended that Congress appropriate money to examine the unsurveyed route of the canal for the following three reasons, as expressed in his own words: (1) "A great portion of the produce of the very fertile country through which it would pass would find a market through that channel," (2) "Troops might be moved with great facility in war, with cannon and every kind of munition, and in either direction," and (3) "Connecting the Atlantic with the Western country in a line passing through the seat of the National Government, it would contribute essentially to strengthen the bond of union itself." Monroe apparently overcame his constitutional scruples by concluding that the works when completed could be turned over to the states or to private companies for operation.

Following Monroe's recommendation, Congress appropriated $30,000 for the necessary surveys of the Chesapeake and Ohio Canal route on April 3, 1824. In the following year, it also contributed to the stock of the Chesapeake and Delaware Canal Company judging it to be a work of national strategic and military utility.

The national government thus provisionally committed itself to the work of internal improvement. Monroe appointed a chief and two assistant engineers as a United States Board of Internal Improvement to make surveys and prepare estimates for the Chesapeake and Ohio Canal. The chief of this newly established United States Board was a Frenchman, General S. Bernard, head of the United States Corps of Engineers, and with him were associated Lieutenant Colonel Totten and John L. Sullivan, civil engineer. With the help of other army engineers and civil surveyors the Board undertook a meticulous survey of routes and costs of a canal between "the tide-waters of the Potomac and the head of navigation on the Ohio, and between the Ohio and Lake Erie." After both Virginia and Maryland endorsed the charter of the proposed company, Congress confirmed it, and Monroe signed the act on his last day in office as president. The remnant of the old Potomac Company gave its consent on March 16, 1825, and the Pennsylvania legislature sanctioned the canal project in the following February. The Potomac Company had already surrendered its charter to the Chesapeake and Ohio Canal Company. No legal obstacle to the organization of the new company remained.

The company was authorized to issue 60,000 shares of stock at $100 each totaling $6,000,000 and to construct a canal not less than forty feet wide at the surface, twenty-eight feet wide at the bottom, and four feet deep from tidewater on the Potomac to Cumberland or the mouth of Savage Creek and thence across the Allegheny Mountains to the Ohio River. The connection across the mountains could be made by canal, by inclined planes and railways, or by roads, and the company was authorized to connect the canal by a branch from Cumberland to the Savage River for the purpose of developing the newly discovered coal fields there. As a subsidiary operation, the Maryland legislature provided on March 6, 1825 for the organization of the "Maryland Canal Company" to construct a canal from the Potomac River to Baltimore and to receive $500,000 of state funds for this purpose. To satisfy all sections of the state, at least ostensibly, and thus to secure passage of this first general internal improvements act in Maryland's history, the state also subscribed $500,000 to the Chesapeake and Ohio Canal Company, promised a similar amount toward the construction of a canal from Baltimore to Yorkhaven, Pennsylvania, and pledged $200,000 for the improvement of the rivers of the Eastern Shore. Of these three items the state never appropriated money for any but the first.

Early in 1826 the Board of Internal Improvement, headed by General Bernard, presented a preliminary report in which they estimated that the eastern section of the canal alone extending from Georgetown to Cumberland would cost $6,085,000. This new estimate of the cost of the project considerably dampened the ardor of its proponents. They were dismayed when the Board, in its final report published in October 1826, estimated that a canal running on the north bank of the Potomac from Georgetown to Cumberland, then by way of Wills Creek across the highest ridge of the Alleghenies by a tunnel, and then through the valleys of the Casselman, the Youghiogheny, and the Monongahela Rivers to Pittsburgh would cost over $22,000,000.

The sponsors of the canal bestirred themselves to counteract the effects of this report. They called another meeting of the Chesapeake and Ohio Canal Convention in Washington in December 1826 and there proved to their own satisfaction that the section of the canal from Georgetown to Cumberland could be constructed for much less than the Board's estimate. At the request of about twenty members of Congress, President Adams appointed two topographical engineers to make another survey of the entire route from Georgetown to Cumberland. This new commission, after revising the estimates of the Board of Internal Improvement, calculated that the eastern section of the canal would cost only $4,479,346.93. Accordingly, the company opened its books for subscriptions on October 1, 1827 and in less than a month and a half received $1,500,000. In May 1828 Congress directed the Secretary of the Treasury to subscribe for 10,000 shares or one million dollars worth of the stock of the Chesapeake and Ohio Canal Company and to pay for it out of the dividends received from the stock of the United

States Bank. The District cities of Washington, Georgetown, and Alexandria had already subscribed respectively 10,000, 2,500, and 2,500 shares, totaling $1.5 million. The national government therefore really contributed two and one-half million dollars toward the enterprise. With this assured financial backing, the Chesapeake and Ohio Canal Company was formally organized in Washington in June 1828, with Charles F. Mercer of Virginia as president.

Elaborate preparations were made for the ceremony of breaking ground for the canal, and the site selected was the Little Falls, five miles west of Georgetown. On July 4, 1828, a procession of persons interested in the canal marched through Georgetown and then proceeded by Potomac River boats to the Little Falls where, before a distinguished company including the members of the Cabinet and all the diplomatic representatives of foreign powers in Washington, President Adams delivered an address and dug up the first spadeful of earth. Thus the canal was begun under the direct auspices of the national government. On the return trip down the Potomac, refreshments were served, and President Adams proposed the following toast: "To the Canal: Perseverance."

The sponsors of the canal would need perseverance, for they did not complete the canal to Cumberland until twenty-two years later. The Chesapeake and Ohio Canal never moved even one boat or cargo from the Chesapeake to the Ohio. On the same day the President of the United States was breaking ground at the Little Falls for the Chesapeake and Ohio Canal, Charles Carroll of Carrollton, the last surviving signer of the Declaration of Independence, was breaking ground at Baltimore for the new Baltimore and Ohio Railroad, which was to traverse a part of the route of the canal and to become its great rival.

The canal company immediately began to advertise for laborers in Great Britain, Germany, and the Netherlands, offering them "meat three times a day, a plenty of bread and vegetable, with a reasonable allowance of liquor and eight, ten or twelve dollars a month for wages." The president of the company, Charles F. Mercer, sent an agent abroad to recruit laborers, and they began to arrive in August 1829, coming over at the expense of the company under conditions of contract which bound them to a period of indentured service to the company. But these imported contract laborers were quarrelsome and proved very troublesome to the company. Many of them soon deserted the canal company to take work with the Baltimore and Ohio Railroad Company. Some of them also found the summer climate in Washington intolerable, fell sick, and became public charges. Their susceptibility to disease became especially disruptive of the company's operations in the summers of 1832 and 1833 when many of the laborers fled from the canal because of an outbreak of cholera. Besides, many of the imported Irish laborers brought with them their intercounty feuds from the homeland and engaged in actual pitched battles among themselves, which were settled only by the arrival of United States troops from Fort McHenry and the actual negotiation of treaties of peace between the opposing factions.

The company abandoned further importation of laborers toward the end of 1829 and thereafter suffered from acute labor shortages. In 1832 it decided not to use slave labor in constructing the canal. The company became involved in much litigation over canal rights, for it was unable to obtain some of the needed land at reasonable prices and some at any price at all. The company found Charles Carroll of Carrollton, for instance, who was interested in the Baltimore and Ohio Railroad, adamantly unwilling to part with any of his lands in the Potomac Valley.

The company, by concentrating on the lower section of the canal, was able to open a twenty-mile stretch between Georgetown and Seneca in the spring of 1831. By this time it had actually sold 36,094 shares valued at $3,609,400, and it awarded contracts for the construction of the first section of the canal. Its annual income consisted of about $52,000 from the operation of the completed parts of the canal and the tolls collected at the locks around the Great Falls and the Little Falls. By 1834 the company had expended $4,062,991, had been obliged to resort to the issue of promissory notes or scrip, and had completed only one hundred and six miles. It had done nothing with the section of seventy-eight miles between Williamsport and Cumberland.

Needing more money, some members of the company dispatched Richard Rush, former Secretary of the Treasury, to Europe to arrange a loan, which he eventually secured in the Netherlands. The canal company now encountered some unexpected obstacles. The most serious of these was the challenge presented by the Baltimore and Ohio Railroad Company, which had selected the Potomac River route for its roadbed to the west, and which, being an exclusively Maryland corporation, was considered to deserve the full backing of the state. The canal company consequently became an object of jealousy and hostility in the Maryland legislature. Moreover, being a federally chartered corporation, it began to lose its influence in Washington after the inauguration of Jackson, who opposed federally sponsored internal improvements.

The canal company now made urgent appeals to Congress and to the legislatures of Maryland, Virginia, and Pennsylvania for further aid.

Pennsylvania gave no support whatever to the project because of the opposition of influential persons in her eastern counties and particularly in Philadelphia. The interest and resources of Pennsylvania were already engrossed in her own system of public improvements which she was then completing. Virginia had not made any contributions to the Chesapeake and Ohio Canal project and was now constructing her own canal to connect the James River with the Kanawha. Maryland alone responded to the company's appeal for financial aid, and she did so only after the canal had won a legal battle with the railroad in the Court of Appeals recognizing the priority of the claim of the canal to the right-of-way from Point of Rocks to Harpers Ferry. Since this decision seriously jeopardized the future prospects of the railroad, the Maryland legislature stipulated that as a condition of further aid from the state, the canal must accept an accommodation with the railroad making the latter a stockholder in the amount of 2,500 shares in the canal company and providing for joint construction of the canal and the railroad to Harpers Ferry. As a result, the Maryland Assembly voted an additional subscription of $125,000 to the canal company in 1834, which was, however, insufficient to enable the company to discharge its accumulated debts.

With this now considerable support from Maryland, the canal, building jointly with the railroad west of Point of Rocks, reached Williamsport, a distance of eighty-six miles from Georgetown, in 1834. But new and complicated financial negotiations and several complete reorganizations of the company were required before work on the canal could be resumed and pushed westward. Maryland continued to be the principal supporter of the canal and agreed in March 1835 to lend an additional $2,000,000 to the canal company. But since this amount proved insufficient to complete the canal even to Cumberland, the company renewed its appeals to the legislature. Capitalizing upon the new general enthusiasm for internal improvements, the company secured in June 1836 from the Maryland legislature an additional subscription of $3,000,000 to its capital stock. This contribution formed a part of the appropriations authorized by the Maryland legislature in its internal improvements act of that year. In 1838 Maryland made a further subscription of $1,375,000 to the canal company. The canal project, which had begun as a nationally sponsored enterprise, had become Maryland's sole responsibility. The state now had control of the company and a mortgage on its property. Most of its financial contributions to the canal were made in the form of state bonds. At subsequent sessions the legislature gave it further aid.

After the canal reached Williamsport in 1834, five years elapsed before it reached Cacapon, the delay being due to the widespread labor unrest and the economic depression which appeared in 1837. By 1841 the canal was still fifty miles from Cumberland, and the company was begging a bankrupt state for further aid. In the following year the canal advanced a short distance beyond Hancock, having moved approximately 135 miles from Washington. By that time the construction work had cost over $10 million. Finally, in 1844, Maryland gave the company power to issue preferred bonds to the amount of $1,700,000, the purchasers of which received a mortgage on the canal, and with these funds the canal was extended to Cumberland in October 1850. As finally completed, the canal cost the state of Maryland alone over eleven million dollars, and, including the contributions of the federal government, the District of Columbia, and Virginia, its total cost amounted to almost $15 million.

The opening of the canal from Georgetown to Cumberland after twenty-two years of work was celebrated with appropriate ceremonies at Cumberland. "Five canal boats, laden with the rich products of the mines of Allegany, and *destined for Eastern markets*" passed "through the locks, amid the salvos of artillery . . . accompanied by the brilliant performances of the bands." This eastern section to Cumberland (the western section was never built) was approximately 184 miles in length, and it ran along the northern bank of the Potomac River from Rock Creek in the District of Columbia to Wills Creek at Cumberland. It included eleven stone aqueducts over the northern tributaries of the Potomac, seventy-five locks which had a maximum width of fifteen feet, and a quarter-mile-long tunnel. Along its course it gave at least temporary stimulus to the growth of such towns as Point of Rocks, Harpers Ferry, Williamsport, Hancock, and Cumberland. Over it moved all kinds of canal boats—scows, packets, barges, rafts, and other nondescript craft, carrying flour, wheat, corn, lumber, lime, stone, coal, and fertilizer.

At the time when the Chesapeake and Ohio Canal was completed, it was the largest canal in the United States. But it had long since been eclipsed by the Baltimore and Ohio Railroad, which had reached Cumberland eight years earlier. The railroad was Baltimore's answer to its urgent need for improved transportation facilities with the west.

Maryland's metropolis on the Patapsco, now rounding out the first century of its history, was one of the most flourishing commercial cities along the Atlantic seaboard. It owed its growth largely to its position as an entrepôt between the Susquehanna Valley and its own Maryland hinterland on the one hand and the world markets beckoning beyond the mouth of the Chesapeake on the other. In the days before efficient overland transportation, it served as the natural terminus of Susquehanna river trade from central Pennsylvania. But as the old northwest opened up, Baltimore was plunged into lively competition with New York and Philadelphia for the commerce of the back country. One of Baltimore's advantages in this competition was that she was situated some fifty or sixty miles nearer to the Ohio Valley than was Philadelphia and between 100 and 200 miles nearer than New York. Located on the Patapsco River 15.5 miles from Chesapeake Bay and 150 nautical miles from the Capes of the Bay, Baltimore, in comparison with her Atlantic coast rivals, is an inland port. Moreover, she had established good highway connections westward through Frederick with the National Road which was being pushed westward from Cumberland by the national government. But during the canal era Baltimore was not fortunately situated for establishing canal communications with the west. Hardly had the surveys for the Chesapeake and Ohio Canal been begun, when Baltimore's interest was attracted to the railroad as a substitute for the canal.

To two influential citizens of Baltimore, Philip Evan Thomas and George Brown, belongs the credit of introducing railroads for passenger and freight traffic into the United States. They began to study the new system of railroad transportation which was being built to connect Liverpool and Manchester in England and the two railroads which at this time were successfully operating in the United States—the one connecting the granite quarries at Quincy, Massachusetts, with the Neponset River, and the gravity railroad nine miles long extending from the coal mines at Mauch Chunk, Pennsylvania, to the Lehigh River. Thomas was a Quaker merchant of Baltimore and president of the Mechanics' Bank, and upon becoming interested in railroad transportation he resigned his position as one of Maryland's commissioners in the Chesapeake and Ohio Canal Company. Brown was a director in the Mechanics' Bank of Baltimore and worked with Thomas to promote railroad construction in Maryland.[2]

The Baltimore and Ohio Railroad owes its origin to a meeting of about twenty-five prominent Baltimoreans held on February 12, 1827, at Thomas's home to consider the advantages of the railroad over canals and turnpikes in stimulating Baltimore's commerce with the West. At this and subsequent meetings the members expressed concern over the efforts that New York and Philadelphia were making to divert the western trade from Baltimore and proposed that Baltimore counter these efforts by making use of the railroad. Its only competition for the western trade would then come from New Orleans. Moreover, they concluded that a railway system connecting Baltimore with the Ohio would provide a market for the products of the Chesapeake fisheries and oyster beds. They accordingly recommended "that measures be taken to construct a double railroad between the City of Baltimore and some suitable point on the Ohio River by the most eligible and direct route" and that a company should be incorporated for this purpose. They appointed a committee, headed by the aged Charles Carroll of Carrollton, to petition the legislature for a charter.

From their brothers, Evan Thomas and William Brown, who were in England, Thomas and Brown had been receiving information about the Liverpool and Manchester Railway. The Baltimoreans who were interested in the project now sent a deputation abroad to make a more thorough study of the railroads in England, and after receiving an encouraging report from them they resolved to apply to the Maryland legislature for an act of incorporation. This act was drafted by young John Van Lear McMahon, a representative from Allegany County, and passed the Maryland legislature on February 28, 1827. It provided that the company should be capitalized at $3 million and that it should reserve 10,000 shares in the company for the state of Maryland and 5,000 for the city of Baltimore. The remaining 15,000 shares were opened for subscription by individuals and corporations. Nine commissioners were appointed to receive subscriptions to the capital stock, and after the requisite amount had been sold, the stockholders were to elect twelve directors and they in turn a president. The directors and president were then given full authority over the company with power to appoint officers and all other agents, to increase the capital stock of the company, and to exercise the right of eminent domain in the construction of the railroad and the procurement of materials. But they must begin construction within two years and must complete the Maryland portion of the road within ten years. They were given the power to place on the railroad "all machines, wagons, vehicles or carriages of any description whatsoever which they may deem necessary or proper for the purposes of transportation," and to charge specified "tolls" for freight and passengers carried over the road. Another clause exempted the capital stock of the company from taxation by the state and provided for the payment of dividends to the stockholders "after deducting the necessary current and probable contingent expenses."

Subscriptions to the new company were received at the Mechanics' Bank in Baltimore and at banks in Frederick and Hagerstown between

March 20 and 31, 1827, and during that period 41,788 shares of stock were purchased by some 22,000 different individuals. The Baltimore and Ohio Railroad Company was then formally organized on April 24, 1827, with Philip E. Thomas as president, George Brown as treasurer, and Charles Carroll of Carrollton as a member of the board of directors. From the beginning, the company was subjected to a certain amount of direct control by both the state of Maryland and the city of Baltimore. As a stockholder in the company the state of Maryland, from this time onward until it sold its interest in the railroad in 1843, appointed a specified number of directors of the company to represent the public interest in this transportation project. Baltimore also was given two directors for its first subscription of 5,000 shares of stock; they were elected by joint ballot of both branches of the city council. Since the company proposed to operate not only in Maryland but also in Virginia and Pennsylvania, it applied to those states for a confirmation of its charter and received legislative endorsement from both.

After making preliminary surveys, the company decided to construct the railroad from Baltimore along the valley of the Patapsco to Point of Rocks on the Potomac, and on July 4, 1828, the "cornerstone" was laid by Charles Carroll of Carrollton, then ninety-one years of age. The ceremony was presided over by the Grand Masters of the Masonic Lodges of Maryland, Pennsylvania, and Virginia and was concluded "by pouring wine and oil, and scattering corn, upon the stone, with a correspondent invocation and response, followed by the Grand Masonic honors." With prophetic insight, one of the orators at the ceremony declaimed: "We are about opening the channel through which the commerce of the mighty country beyond the Allegheny must seek the ocean."

Immediately the company granted contracts for the grading and construction of the first twelve miles of the road. It received many free grants of land for the roadbed and of materials needed for constructing it. In 1828 the company received an additional subscription of $500,000 from the state of Maryland, but its appeals for aid from the national government were futile—partly because President Mercer of the Chesapeake and Ohio Canal Company was chairman of the Committee on Roads and Canals in the House of Representatives and partly because of President Jackson's declared opposition to national expenditures for works of internal improvement. The company opened the first division of the road on May 22, 1830, from Baltimore to Ellicott's Mills—a distance of 13¾ miles—and horses pulled over the tracks a dozen small carriages similar to stagecoaches.

The "Atlantic" locomotive was built by Phineas Davis at York, Pa., and went into operation on the Baltimore & Ohio Railroad in the summer of 1832. It is still in operating condition and is shown here pulling two double-decked Imlay coaches. This train was the first to enter the city of Washington and led the procession of trains on August 24, 1835. Courtesy *Association of American Railroads*, Washington, D.C.

With this first successful operation of vehicles on the railroad, the company was deluged with business and had almost ten times as much freight business as it was able to handle. On the rails which were laid, the company experimented with several different methods of moving its cars or rolling stock. One of the most picturesque "locomotives" used wind power. It was Evan Thomas' "Aeolus," which was propelled over the rails by a square sail. The first steam locomotive built in America made its trial run on this railroad in August 1830. Invented by Peter Cooper, who owned an iron works at Canton near Baltimore, it was called the "Tom Thumb" and consisted of an engine driven by steam from a boiler no larger than an ordinary kitchen hot-water tank and set vertically on the frame. This engine, having an overall weight of only a ton, pulled an open car, filled with the directors of the company and their friends, from Baltimore to Ellicott's Mills in one hour and twelve minutes and made the return trip, which was downhill, in fifty-seven minutes, attaining a maximum speed of fifteen miles an hour. With this run, Maryland inaugurated the first regular steam railroad service for passengers in the United States.

The railroad was opened to Frederick, a distance of sixty-one miles on December 1, 1831 and to Point of Rocks on April 1, 1832. There it began to tap Potomac River commerce and to come into direct competition with the Chesapeake and Ohio Canal. This stretch of the road from Baltimore to Point of Rocks—69 miles of track in all—was filled with steep grades and sharp curves; and the track was constructed of various materials and in various ways. Some of it consisted of iron rails on granite, some of iron rails on broken stone or on wooden sills, and some of log rails smoothed on one side and anchored with wooden sleepers. Within the next ten years almost all this portion of the road had to be reconstructed. Most of the rails used in this early construction were light iron straps which were spiked to a continuous curbing of cut stone or to wooden stringers laid on crossties, but the strap rails were abandoned after 1844 when the Mount Savage Iron Works in Maryland began to manufacture T rails which were demonstrably superior.

The rivalry of the Baltimore and Ohio Railroad with the Chesapeake and Ohio Canal Company for a right-of-way from Point of Rocks to Harpers Ferry was settled in favor of the canal company in 1832 when the Court of Appeals, by a vote of three to two, upheld the claim of the canal company to a prior right-of-way. The railroad, which was represented by some of Maryland's leading lawyers including Taney, McMahon, Reverdy Johnson, and John H.B. Latrobe, then made an effort to accommodate its differences with the canal by proposing an amalgamation of the two projects from Point of Rocks to Harpers Ferry, but its proposal was rejected by the canal company. The Maryland legislature then interceded to bring about a compromise. It embodied it in a law passed on March 22, 1833, which provided for the joint construction of the railroad and the canal between Point of Rocks and Harpers Ferry. The railroad company would subscribe for 2,500 shares of the stock of the canal company, and the canal company in turn would prepare the roadbed for the railroad. The canal would retain a right-of-way of fifty feet which, however, might be narrowed to forty feet where the passes would otherwise be too narrow for the railroad; and the railroad would have a strip not less than twenty feet in width. To supervise this arrangement and to harmonize the relations between the two companies under the compromise, the act created a board of commissioners composed of three engineers, one appointed by each company and the third by the president of the United States.

Under this arrangement, therefore, the railroad company paid $266,000 to the canal company for the cost of railroad construction and was able to reach a point on the Maryland shore opposite Harpers Ferry on December 1, 1834. At this point it connected with the Winchester and Potomac Railroad and tapped the agricultural resources of the Shenandoah Valley. But between Point of Rocks and Harpers Ferry, the railroad had to have its cars drawn by horses in order to protect the horses used on the canal from accidents with the locomotives. By the fall of 1834, the company added five more steam locomotives to the three already operating on the road and began to manufacture its own engines and to build its own repair shops.

In the compromise with the canal company, the railroad had agreed not to continue its road along the Potomac west of Harpers Ferry until the canal was finished to Cumberland. But in December 1835 it asked for aid from the state of Maryland and from the city of Baltimore to complete rail connections with Pittsburgh and Wheeling. Unless it could continue to build westward, it feared that Pittsburgh, Wheeling, and other growing western metropolises would begin to push rail construction eastward to meet the Baltimore and Ohio Railroad at Harpers Ferry. Indeed, Wheeling was prepared to expend $500,000 for this purpose. Baltimore, threatened with this competition, offered to supply the railroad with an additional $3 million whenever the railroad could reach an agreement with the canal company.

The railroad's appeal to the state of Maryland for aid was presented at a time when the general public enthusiasm for internal improvements was reaching its peak. This enthusiasm was shared by residents of the

Eastern Shore, who, however, were displeased by the lack of interest shown in internal improvements for their section of the state. All the major improvements that were being projected were Western Shore enterprises. The Eastern Shore counties, therefore, responded favorably to overtures from the state of Delaware for annexation to that state. When the Delaware legislature proposed that a commission be appointed, with the concurrence of the Maryland General Assembly, to discuss the advisability of such a merger, Eastern Shore delegates in the General Assembly supported the proposal and secured its passage through the House of Delegates by a majority of forty to twenty-four. In the Senate, a special committee composed of three Eastern Shoremen reported it favorably but saw it go down to defeat by one vote in the Senate as a whole.

Obviously, therefore, the state must include the Eastern Shore in its internal improvements program. When the Maryland legislature passed its general internal improvements act in June 1836, it included provision for an Eastern Shore railroad extending from Elkton to Crisfield. For Western Shore improvements it authorized the expenditure of eight million dollars, including additional subscriptions by the state of three million dollars each to the Baltimore and Ohio Railroad and to the Chesapeake and Ohio Canal Company. In this act, it released the railroad from the restriction which prevented it from building west of Harpers Ferry. This release was reluctantly accepted by the canal company.

When news of the enactment of this gigantic internal improvements program was announced, it was received with rejoicing in many parts of the state. Eastern Shore towns went wild with excitement at the prospect of a railroad, and Baltimore burst into an ecstasy of jubilation. It celebrated the event with a public dinner, fireworks, a salute of one hundred guns, a display of flags, and the ringing of church bells. Baltimore's enthusiasm was inspired principally by the prospects of the railroad, and the city immediately proceeded to borrow from the banks of Baltimore the money needed to pay the installments of its three-million-dollar subscription to the railroad's capital stock. Because of this subscription, the city's representation on the board of directors of the railroad company was increased to twelve. The state's contribution of three million dollars to the railroad under the internal improvements act was to be invested in preferred stock which would receive a perpetual annual dividend of six percent. Eventually about one million dollars worth of this stock came into the possession of Johns Hopkins University.

To procure the money needed for the additional capitalization of the railroad, the state issued $3,200,000 worth of bonds and undertook to sell them in Europe. For this purpose the president of the company, Louis McLane, went abroad and personally undertook to place the bonds with European banking houses. But he found investors wary because many of the American states, including Maryland, were suspending interest payments and some were even repudiating their debts under the stringent economic conditions of 1836. President McLane, who had served as Secretary of the Treasury and Secretary of State in Jackson's cabinet, had good banking connections abroad and finally arranged to deposit the state bonds with Baring Brothers and Company of London as security for a loan.

McLane had taken charge of the railroad at a difficult time in its history, for in 1836 it paid no dividends and in the following year the railroad, as well as many other works of internal improvement throughout the country, was almost thrown into bankruptcy by the financial panic. McLane had to levy money from the stockholders to keep the railroad in repair. The railroad also had to draw upon its credit with the city of Baltimore. The directors of the company offered its contractors and creditors certificates payable in city stock which had been deposited in certain banks of Baltimore by the city as security for the city's $3 million contribution to the railroad. These certificates were not paper money, but they circulated as such in denominations of from one dollar to one hundred dollars and were used quite generally for paying the workers engaged in construction of the railroad. They constituted virtual liens or shares in the city of Baltimore, and they depreciated in value, particularly after the Baltimore City Council refused to receive them in payment of taxes and other city charges. Ultimately the Maryland legislature forbade the railroad company to issue "anything in the nature of a bank note or other paper to be used for circulation as a currency." [3]

Meanwhile, as the railroad was threatened with legal challenges by the canal for the right-of-way west of Harpers Ferry, the company began to consider alternative routes. Virginia offered to pay $1,360,520 or two-fifths of the estimated costs if the company would carry the road into Virginia at Harpers Ferry and would continue it through that state to Cumberland and thence to Wheeling. This offer was so attractive that it was accepted by the stockholders and by the state of Maryland. With this aid the railroad began to build into Virginia and reached a point opposite Hancock in June 1842 and a point opposite Cumberland five months later.

The railroad was not extended west of Cumberland until the spring of 1849. It could not proceed farther westward because the company's legal right to construct the railroad in Maryland, Virginia, and Pennsylvania under its charters expired in 1843. Though the Maryland legislature promptly extended the time for the completion of the railroad within the state to 1863, the Virginia legislature failed to grant a satisfactory extension of time until 1837. Meanwhile the railroad continued to suffer financial difficulties. Some of the bonds of the state of Maryland which McLane had deposited with Baring Brothers in London were sold at a discount of fifteen percent in 1840 and netted the railroad company $21,583.68, all of which had to be used to pay accumulated interest charges. As the rest of the bonds proved unsalable in England, the company withheld its cash dividends after 1846 in order to finance the reconstruction of the existing road and its extension west of Cumberland.

The engineer of the company, Benjamin H. Latrobe, had already made surveys of the most practicable routes west of Cumberland, and after the resignation of President McLane in 1848, the new president, Thomas Swann, infused new enthusiasm into the company for the completion of the railroad to Wheeling. He finally induced Baring Brothers to purchase £200,000 of the Maryland State bonds which had been lying idle in their vaults, and in return the company issued £127,500 of six percent mortgage bonds to Baring Brothers for iron rails and an additional $1,128,731 to President Swann in six percent mortgage bonds made payable in July 1875. With these funds the railroad hired 3,500 laborers and 700 horses in 1850. By July of the following year, the tracks entered Piedmont, twenty-eight miles west of Cumberland; and on Christmas Eve, 1852, the road was completed into Wheeling. Baltimore was finally connected with the "western waters."

On this final section the railroad was carried through one of the steepest mountain regions in the eastern part of the United States. It crossed the Monongahela River on the largest iron bridge in America— 650 feet long—and between Cumberland and Wheeling it ran through eleven tunnels, one of which was more than half a mile in length, and over one hundred and thirteen bridges. Through service was formally opened on January 1, 1852, when the first train, loaded with 500 guests, made the complete trip from Baltimore to Wheeling. Thus completed, it was the longest railroad in America, extending 379 miles. It had cost a grand total of $15,628,963.24.

During the entire period of construction, the Baltimore and Ohio Railroad exerted an enormous effect upon the economic development of Maryland. When it reached Cumberland in 1842, it opened up the abundant iron and coal deposits of that region hitherto almost entirely unexploited. It contracted to deliver this coal and iron to ocean vessels in Baltimore and for that purpose constructed coal wharves at Locust

Point in Baltimore. By 1850 its shipments of coal eastward amounted to 132,534 tons. Soon afterward, mining companies began to open up coal beds in the region around Westernport, and in the following year the George's Creek Railway was begun, penetrating a rich coal basin and eventually connecting with the Baltimore and Ohio at Piedmont.

Iron also became an important commodity moving eastward over the railroad and by the middle of the century tens of thousands of tons of granite, lime, soapstone, and limestone were finding an eastern outlet over the railroad. Flour and tobacco, the principal agricultural products of the state, were carried over the road in constantly increasing quantities. In 1832, 12,610 tons of flour were transported by it from Ellicott's Mills and Frederick to Baltimore; ten years later this quantity had doubled, and by 1852 it reached the figure of 66,377 tons. During the same period shipments of tobacco increased from 174 tons in 1832 to 2,322 tons in 1848. Other bulk commodities handled by the railroad included livestock, lard, butter, whisky, leather, vegetables, and fruits.

The new transportation facilities offered by the railroad considerably stimulated the growth of the western towns. Both Frederick, which was located on a spur line, and Point of Rocks benefited from it, the latter becoming a point of transfer between river and railroad. Brunswick developed as a railroad town. Harpers Ferry became an important point of transshipment between Baltimore and the fertile Shenandoah Valley, which was serviced by the Potomac and Winchester Railroad. Frostburg grew from a village to a populous town, and Cumberland's population increased from 1,162 in 1830 to 6,105 in 1850. The railroad encouraged the construction of hotels and warehouses in Cumberland and increased travel over the National Road west of Cumberland. At Wheeling the railroad established connections with a daily line of boats which were operated by a company chartered by the Virginia legislature and which ran to Cincinnati and Louisville. But from Wheeling the railroad pushed farther to the westward, opening up new commercial possibilities all along its route. In 1857 it entered St. Louis.

The railroad exercised the greatest influence upon the growth of Baltimore, though in the early decades of the history of the railroad locomotives did not enter the central part of the city, probably because of the danger of fires from flying sparks. Instead, the locomotives were detached from the cars on the outskirts of the city and replaced by teams of horses or mules. Despite this handicap, between 1827 and 1853 the railroad carried to Baltimore from the west nearly two million tons of products which were either used by Baltimore manufacturers or distributed by Baltimore merchants. It either partly or wholly accounted for the growth of such manufacturing industries in Baltimore as iron and copper works, woolen, cotton, and flour mills, potteries and farm implements factories, distilleries and sugar refineries, and it carried thousands of tons of the finished products of these manufacturing establishments westward annually. By 1852 the westward traffic over the railroad included also large quantities of fish and oysters from Chesapeake Bay.

The railroad required the supporting services of rapid communication, and to meet this need a crew of men and mules and their equipment, employed by Samuel Finley Breese Morse and operated by Ezra Cornell, started in Baltimore in mid-October 1843 and began to dig a trench toward Washington following the route of the Baltimore and Washington Railroad, soon to be merged with the Baltimore and Ohio Railroad. In that trench they laid iron pipe enclosing insulated wires for the first experiment in telegraphic communication in America.

After more than five years of lobbying activity and demonstrations by the inventor, Morse had been able to obtain approval by Congress and a grant of $30,000 to finance the construction of this telegraph line. But underground lines soon proved impracticable, and Morse shifted to aerial lines supported by chestnut poles. At the official opening of his telegraph line, Morse, who had set up his receiving equipment in the Supreme Court chamber in the Capitol, received the message from Baltimore: "What hath God wrought?" Over this line a few days later Morse received the message that the Whig National Convention, then meeting in Baltimore, had nominated Henry Clay for President. He thus received the news an hour before the train from Baltimore arrived in Washington with it. When the Democratic National Convention met in Baltimore a week later, Morse posted news bulletins of the proceedings outside his room in the Capitol and was the first to report the nomination of James K. Polk as the choice of the convention.

The Baltimore headquarters of the telegraphic system was established in the Pratt Street station of the railroad, thus indicating its early usefulness to railroad service. In Baltimore the *Baltimore Patriot* was the first to publish daily telegraphic news reports from Washington. In the Mexican War this new system of instantaneous communication, first successfully demonstrated in Maryland, proved its utility and ultimately spread to almost every part of the nation.

Maryland, then, in the second quarter of the nineteenth century made a notable effort, by means of both water and rail transportation, to reach out and acquire the trade of the trans-Appalachian west. The state was slow to move into the era of internal improvements, partly because it had in its own Chesapeake Bay and its tributary streams an admirable system of natural waterways adequate for the needs of most of the populated parts of the state, and partly because the political question of the use of state funds for this purpose had first to be resolved. Public opinion long opposed the use of the power and credit of the state for the supposed general welfare, and when specific projects for internal improvements were proposed, they brought out all the sectional jealousies and resentments between the Eastern and Western Shores, between the southern and eastern counties and the northern and western counties, and between the agricultural and industrial sections of the state. The fear that Virginia and the District of Columbia would derive too many advantages from a Potomac canal impelled the Maryland legislature to disapprove of that project on two occasions. Baltimore was finally won over to it only by the promise of a lateral connection from the Potomac to the Patapsco, and having gained this concession, it soon turned to the preferred project of a railroad to the west.

In the very year, 1852, when the Baltimore and Ohio Railroad reached the Ohio River, another group of railroad enterprisers obtained from the Maryland General Assembly a charter for the construction of a railroad from Baltimore "to the town of Westminster, and thence westwardly to some point on the Monocacy River in the direction of Hagerstown." The organizers, calling themselves the Baltimore, Carroll, and Frederick Rail Road Company, soon changed the name to the Western Maryland Rail Road Company. Not until seven years later, however, was the first section of this railroad opened up, running a distance of only ten miles from Relay House to Owings Mills in Baltimore County. By 1873 it was completed to Williamsport, a distance of ninety miles, and there tapped the canal traffic of the Chesapeake and Ohio Canal. Under its new dynamic president, John Mifflin Hood, after 1874 the railroad was extended another 180 miles partly through construction of new roadbed and partly through absorption of other railroad lines to connect with the Philadelphia and Reading at Shippensburg and the Baltimore and Ohio at Cherry Run. Hood also developed Pen Mar as a summer resort in the Blue Ridge Mountains of Maryland and made it one of the most famous playgrounds in the East. The railroad had meanwhile required financing by Baltimore in the amount of nearly $9,000,000, and it later fell into the hands of George W. Gould who proposed to incorporate it in a transcontinental railroad system. Before Gould's scheme collapsed, he had acquired Port Covington on the Baltimore waterfront as a marine terminal for the railroad, had pushed the Western Maryland line on to Cumberland, and had taken over a railroad system which ran into the coal fields of West Virginia. From Cumberland the Western Maryland was constructed northwesterly as far as Connellsville on the outskirts of Pittsburgh. This Connellsville extension, which was completed in 1912, gave the Western Maryland the shortest railroad route between Baltimore and Pittsburgh and the lowest grade across the Alleghanies and made it the eastern tidewater outlet for the Pittsburgh and Lake Erie and the Pittsburgh and West Virginia Railroads.

After 1827, therefore, Maryland participated enthusiastically in the movement to open up new routes of transportation and communication to the west. In doing so, the state derived large benefits for its own economy. The canal and rail connections with the west broadened the state's outlook and contributed to the industrialization and urbanization of its life. Baltimore in particular, ceased to be just another tobacco port on tidewater and began to become integrated with the industrializing northern culture. This process was also furthered by the Chesapeake and Delaware Canal which moved Baltimore many miles closer to Philadelphia and New York.

A proposal for a canal connecting Chesapeake and Delaware Bays was one of the earliest canal projects that was urged upon the general government as a national effort. But it languished for twenty years while the principle of national aid to internal improvements was debated, and it was not completed until the height of the great burst of canal-building activity in 1829. The need for such a canal had been clearly demonstrated as a military defense requirement during the War of 1812, but it principally interested private citizens of Pennsylvania who conceived of it as a means of stimulating Philadelphia's commerce with the Susquehanna Valley and the Delmarva Peninsula, but it nevertheless received liberal aid from Congress between 1825 and 1829. Although only two miles of its 13.6-mile channel ran through Maryland, after its completion the canal became increasingly useful and attractive to Baltimore in its rivalry with Philadelphia for the trade of that area.

Baltimore also profited from the Susquehanna and Tidewater Canal which paralleled the Susquehanna River and gave Baltimore an advantage over Philadelphia in tapping the anthracite coal resources of eastern and central Pennsylvania. Maryland's principal port city was also connected with the anthracite region by the Northern Central Railroad which extended past York and Harrisburg to Sunbury. Baltimore's thrust westward and northward widened the breach which had long before opened up between this energetic industrializing metropolis and the planting interests of southern Maryland and the Eastern Shore and consequently strengthened its demand for representation in the General Assembly and a larger role in public affairs.

Though the Eastern Shore suffered a defeat of its hopes for a railroad in the financial depression of 1837, residents of the Eastern Shore obtained a charter in 1858 to build a connecting railroad running from the southern terminus of a Delaware railroad at Delmar through Salisbury to a fishing village on Tangier Sound called Somer's Cove, later to be named Crisfield for John W. Crisfield, president of the railroad. When completed after the Civil War, this railroad measurably expanded the trade and industry of the Eastern Shore.

Footnotes

[1] *American State Papers, Miscellaneous,* II, 988, cited in Victor S. Clark, *History of Manufactures in the United States, 1607-1860,* pp. 338-339.

[2] Alfred R. James, "Sidelights on the Founding of the Baltimore and Ohio Railroad," *Maryland Historical Magazine,* vol. XLVIII, No. 4, December 1953, pp. 267-309.

[3] For Louis McLane's accomplishments as president of the Baltimore and Ohio Railroad, see John A. Munroe, *Louis McLane, Federalist and Jacksonian,* Rutgers University Press, New Brunswick, New Jersey, 1973, chapters 15 and 17.

Sources and Additional Reading

Gray, Ralph D., *The National Waterway: A History of the Chesapeake and Delaware Canal, 1769-1965,* University of Illinois Press, Urbana, 1967.

Hungerford, Edward, *The Story of the Baltimore and Ohio Railroad, 1827-1927,* 2 vols., New York, G.P. Putnam's Sons, 1928.

Munroe, John A., *Louis McLane: Federalist and Jacksonian,* Rutgers University Press, New Brunswick, New Jersey, 1973.

Reizenstein, Milton, *The Economic History of the Baltimore and Ohio Railroad (1827-53),* Johns Hopkins University Studies, Series 15, Nos. 7, 8, Baltimore, 1897.

Sanderlin, Walter S., *The Great National Project: A History of the Chesapeake and Ohio Canal,* Johns Hopkins University Studies, Series LXIV, No. 1, Johns Hopkins Press, Baltimore, 1946.

Searight, Thomas B., *The Old Pike: A History of the National Road,* Uniontown, 1894.

Williams, Harold A., *The Western Maryland Railway Story: A Chronicle of the First Century—1852-1952,* Western Maryland Railway Company, Baltimore, 1952.

CHAPTER XX

FINANCIAL AND CONSTITUTIONAL CRISES

Maryland's internal improvements program, of which the Chesapeake and Ohio Canal and the Baltimore and Ohio Railroad were only two features, confronted the state with new and critical problems in public finance. Until the era of internal improvements, Maryland's financial needs had been moderate. In the Washington administration the state's debts, incurred in the War for Independence and the Confederation period and amounting to only a little more than $500,000, was assumed by the national government. The state had abandoned the general property tax in 1785, and as its tax needs continued small after 1790, it operated principally on the revenues derived from the proceeds of its stock in the national government, from the interest on its investments in the banks chartered by the legislature, and from the sale of licenses for marriages, hawkers and peddlers, keepers of ordinaries, retailers of spirituous liquors, and liquor sales at horse races. In 1813 the state, largely at the demand of the rural areas, first imposed a tax upon banks, the proceeds from which would be used to complete the National Road as far as Cumberland and to enable the counties of the state to establish free schools. But except for this tax, it imposed no new taxes during the war. To finance Maryland's expenditures in the War of 1812, the legislature chose to borrow $436,000 rather than tax the people of the state, and after the war the state was reimbursed in part by the national government for its war expenditures.

During the first third of a century of their experience as a state in the federal union, Marylanders enjoyed the unusual advantage of exemption from direct taxation. The state subsisted on its capital investment from which it derived enough income to meet the modest demands of state government. It made no attempt to use the taxing power to penalize the rich for the benefit of the poor, to redistribute wealth, or to finance welfare projects and public improvements except the law of 1813 taxing banks for road construction and for schools. Even under the strain of the business depression of 1819, it was loath to impose a direct tax. But finally in 1822 the legislature made a small direct levy upon the counties ranging from $19,468 for Baltimore County to only $320 for Caroline County and imposed upon the Levy Courts in each county the responsibility for collecting it from the owners of assessable property.

In lieu of other measures of direct taxation, in the search for additional sources of revenue, the legislature extended the license tax system to include additional sources, as, for example, auctioneers and business equipment, such as billiard tables. It also imposed a twenty-five percent tax on the fees in excess of $1,500 collected by officers such as clerks of courts and registers of wills, but since this law tended to perpetuate the inefficient and much-abused system of remunerating these officers with fees instead of salaries, the legislature soon abandoned it. Another law which Maryland adopted as a revenue measure imposed a license tax upon importers selling foreign goods in the original package, but this was struck down by Chief Justice John Marshall of the United States Supreme Court in *Brown versus Maryland* as violating the exclusive power of the national government to levy import duties. In a measure aimed particularly at the Baltimore branch of the Second Bank of the United States, the legislature also required a special tax from banks operating in Maryland without a charter from the state.

The only other new source of revenue which Maryland began to tap in this depression period was the state lotteries. Since 1792 the state had been licensing lotteries, but not until 1818 did it authorize lotteries to be conducted for the benefit of the public treasury. At the same time, the state bought out several large private lotteries, including one granted for the benefit of the Washington Monument in Baltimore and another for the University of Maryland. It sought at first to prohibit the sale in Maryland of lottery tickets issued by other states, but later, in 1832, abandoned this unenforceable prohibition in favor of a license system for sellers of lottery tickets. Three years later the state, by constitutional amendment, prohibited any further authorization of lotteries by the legislature and all dealings in lottery tickets.

Meanwhile, though state expenditures continued low, public opinion was gradually being converted to the proposition of state aid for internal improvements. Maryland's participation in such improvements had begun with the incorporation of the "Proprietors of the Susquehanna Canal" in 1784, when the state government first assumed the authority to charter corporations and thus put the advantage of its influence and its finances behind a favored company. This company was expected to render the Susquehanna River navigable to the Pennsylvania border, and to it Maryland made a loan of $30,000 in 1800, which was never repaid. But the state was much more interested in the prospects and work of the Potomac Company to which it originally subscribed £5,000. That company was indebted to Maryland for more than $150,000 in 1819 when it went out of existence. Soon afterward, in 1824, when work began on the Chesapeake and Delaware Canal, Maryland subscribed $50,000 to the stock of the company formed for that purpose. From this canal, which was finally opened for traffic in 1829, Maryland never received any financial return. The state also invested funds in two turnpike companies—the Baltimore and Frederick Turnpike Company and the Baltimore and York Turnpike Company. By 1825 Maryland had expended more than a quarter of a million dollars in various schemes of internal improvement. But it had financed them entirely from current revenues and had incurred no debt.

The lure of an ambitious program of internal development carried out under the auspices of the state inspired a large expansion of corporate enterprises, putting the state virtually in league with them for what was represented as the common good. As we have seen, all important internal improvements were carried on by companies incorporated by the state. In 1787 the Maryland legislature began to incorporate insurance companies, the first one being The Baltimore Insurance Fire-Company [sic], which was organized to "alleviate the distress of, and afford immediate relief to sufferers" from fire.[1] A volunteer fire company had been formed in Baltimore as early as 1763; for six years its entire apparatus consisted of leather buckets, but in 1769 it secured an engine which had been used on a Dutch vessel to throw water on the sails in order to increase the ship's speed. By 1828 this fire-fighting company, known as the Mechanical Company, had acquired enough apparatus to become incorporated. In order to reduce fire hazards, the Baltimore Insurance Fire-Company was given a monopoly of the storage of gunpowder and the authority to regulate chimney sweeps in Baltimore in 1791, and soon afterward it was given power to open subscriptions to the Baltimore Water Company to supply the town with water. By 1839 Maryland had incorporated twenty-three insurance companies with a total capitalization of $7,210,000.

Prior to 1852, Maryland incorporated 89 commercial banks and savings institutions, the first of which, the Bank of Maryland, was organized in 1790. Except for the two banks of the United States, which were chartered for twenty-year periods respectively in 1791 and 1816, all the banking in the country was carried on by institutions operating under state charters down to 1863. Before 1810, Maryland incorporated six banks of which four were located in Baltimore, one in Annapolis with branches in Easton and Frederick, and one in Hagerstown. In addition, Baltimore had a branch of the Bank of the United States. The presence and operations of this branch bank tended to stabilize financial conditions, but since it tended also to restrict the activities of the state banks, it became an object of strenuous protests. The closing of the first Bank of the United States in 1811 gave considerable satisfaction to the state banks and stimulated their expansion throughout the country. In Maryland this movement was further encouraged by the industrial growth of the state. In the single year 1810, the legislature granted five new charters for banks, of which four were located in Baltimore and the other in Elkton. By 1817 Maryland possessed twenty-two incorporated banks, having a nominal capital of $14,750,000 and headquarters in twelve of the counties.

But these state banks became the object of considerable popular resentment, and for almost exclusively political reasons the state began in 1813 to collect a revenue from its bank charters. As mentioned previously, it required certain banks to subscribe for stock in turnpike companies and asked all the banks of the state to pay a tax of 20 cents on each one hundred dollars of paid-in capital for the establishment of a general system of free schools for the state. Accordingly, the banks at Baltimore, Hagerstown, Conococheague, and Allegany formed the Cumberland Turnpike Road Company, and they later undertook the construction of the Boonsboro and Hagerstown turnpike. Other banks got an extension of their charters by agreeing to subscribe to the Frederick and Harpers Ferry road, the Williamsport and Hagerstown road, the Baltimore and Havre de Grace road, the Monocacy and Frederick road, the Rockville and Washington road, and others.

Debtor hostility to the banks as parasitical institutions was rampant. During the financial disorders of 1818, *Niles' Weekly Register,* published in Baltimore by Hezekiah Niles, complained that though many banks had become *"bankrupts,* yet their officers and stockholders roll in their coaches and impudently laugh at the miseries they have produced." In that year, the Maryland legislature passed the act, noted above, "to impose a tax on all banks or branches thereof in the State of Maryland not chartered by the Legislature." This act forbade banks which established an office or branch in the state without first obtaining the state's authority to issue notes except upon stamped paper procured from a state officer or to pay $15,000 annually in lieu of the tax. The direct object of the law was to tax the branch of the Second Bank of the United States which was located in Baltimore, and it was enacted as a result of the general hostility to the bank and the opposition to it of the state banks which were then passing through a difficult period and feared the competition and restraining influence of the Bank.

Other states had already enacted similar measures against the Bank of the United States and its branches for the same reasons. Indiana in its constitution of 1816 had prohibited the establishment of branches of any bank chartered outside the state; and the Illinois constitution of 1818 contained a similar clause. Tennessee imposed a tax of $50,000 on banks other than state banks doing business in the state in 1817; and in the same year Georgia laid a tax on every $100 of bank stock employed within the state and announced later that it was intended to apply only to branches of the Bank of the United States. In the following year North Carolina imposed an annual tax of $5,000 on the branches of the Bank. After the enactment of the Maryland law, Kentucky passed a law compelling each branch of the Bank in that state to pay $60,000 annually, and in 1819 Ohio imposed a tax of $50,000 on each branch.

Of all these acts the Maryland act was first held unconstitutional by the Supreme Court in the historic case of *McCulloch versus Maryland*. It was originally upheld by both the County Court of Baltimore County and the Maryland Court of Appeals, but an appeal was then taken on writ of error to the United States Supreme Court in September 1818. In the hearing before the Supreme Court the Maryland statute was challenged by the Bank's counsel which included two leaders of the Maryland bar, the arrogant William Pinkney and Attorney General William Wirt. The lawyers for Maryland upholding the state's authority against encroachments by an overriding central authority included Luther Martin, the leader of the Maryland bar. At that time the bar of Maryland was unsurpassed by that of any other state.

Pinkney's argument in defense of the Bank consumed three full days and represented the greatest legal achievement of his career. Justice Joseph Story wrote: "I never, in my whole life, heard a greater speech; it was worth a journey from Salem to hear it; his elocution was excessively vehement, but his eloquence was overwhelming. His language, his style, his figures, his arguments were most brilliant and sparkling. He spoke like a great statesman and patriot, and a sound constitutional lawyer. All the cobwebs of sophistry and metaphysics about State rights and State sovereignty he brushed away with a mighty besom."

Only three days after the close of Pinkney's argument Chief Justice Marshall rendered the unanimous judgment of the Court, in which he upheld the power of Congress to charter the Bank as an agency of the national government and held that since Congress had the exclusive right to control such an agency, the Maryland tax law was invalid. Though the Constitution did not specifically authorize the establishment of a bank, Marshall upheld the right of Congress to establish it under the implied powers clause, justifying it in the following potent language: "Let the end be legitimate, let it be within the scope of the Constitution, and all means which are appropriate, which are plainly adapted to that end, which are not prohibited, but consist with the letter and spirit of the Constitution, are constitutional." He denied the power of the state to tax such an agency of the national government because "the power to tax involves the power to destroy."

This decision, constituting a notable victory for the national government, was received with a storm of denunciation, *Niles Register* of Maryland declaring: "A deadly blow has been struck at the sovereignty of the States, and from a quarter so far removed from the people as to be hardly accessible to public opinion. . . . The principles established. . . are far more dangerous to the Union and happiness of the people of the United States than anything else that we ever had to fear from foreign invasion. A judicial decision which threatens to annihilate the sovereignties of the States: which will sanction any species of monopoly and make the productive many subservient to the unproductive few,—it creates a most disgusting monopoly."

The Bank of the United States, enormously strengthened by this decision, now began to exert a controlling influence over the state banks in Maryland and throughout the country. As early as 1830, however, its termination was anticipated, and as a result many applications for new banking charters were presented to the Maryland legislature. Between 1829 and 1836 Maryland chartered seventeen new banks and revived two others which had failed in 1821. Of these, nine were situated in Baltimore and the remaining ten were distributed through seven counties of the state. The oldest of all the state banks, the Bank of Maryland, which had been chartered in 1790, failed in 1834 because of excessive speculation and maladministration by its officers. During the panic of 1837 many other state banks failed or were forced to suspend operations. Those that continued in existence did not recover until the state itself again became solvent.

Maryland's subscriptions to the two major projects in which it became financially interested—the Chesapeake and Ohio Canal and the Baltimore and Ohio Railroad—did not prove seriously embarrassing to the state treasury, and in 1836, when the popular enthusiasm for internal improvements was mounting to its climax, the state, as noted in the previous chapter, provided for a broad program of such improvements costing $8 million to be raised by an issue of bonds redeemable in fifty years and to be sold abroad. In this act the state gave its support not only to the Baltimore and Ohio Railroad and the Chesapeake and Ohio Canal but also to the construction of a railroad from Baltimore to Yorkhaven, another from Baltimore to Washington, and another to run the entire length of the Eastern Shore. It made its contributions to the Chesapeake and Ohio Canal and the Baltimore and Ohio Railroad contingent upon the organization of a company sufficiently capitalized to complete the projected Baltimore-Washington Canal. When the financial depression of 1837 broke over the country, Maryland's total indebtedness amounted to the unprecedented figure of over $12 million, and by 1840 it exceeded $15 million, of which all but $240,000 had been incurred for internal improvements. These included the Chesapeake and Delaware Canal, the Tidewater Canal, the Chesapeake and Ohio Canal, the Baltimore and Washington Canal, the Baltimore and Susquehanna Railroad, the Annapolis and Elkridge Railroad, the Eastern Shore Railroad, and the Baltimore and Ohio Railroad. The state's bonds were unsalable abroad and were hawked about by the canal and railroad companies at such high discounts as to destroy the state's credit. From the sale of each $100 bond for the benefit of the Baltimore and Susquehanna Railroad Company, for example, the state received only $63.

This financial crisis was foreshadowed by the failure of the Bank of Maryland in 1834. By 1841 the credit of the state was completely gone, the treasury was empty, and Maryland could no longer borrow money even on a temporary loan. Two years later the legislature passed a bill to sell the state's public imprivements for $11.7 million, but received no offers. Maryland's financial situation became so bad that the legislature was obliged to resort to taxation just to pay the annual interest of over $600,000 on the state debt.

In its desperate search for new sources of revenue Maryland resorted to unusual expedients. In 1841 it imposed a tax of twenty cents for the first year and twenty-five cents for the next three years upon every $100 of real and personal property—the second attempt in the state's entire history to levy direct taxes upon the people; but this attempt was so novel, the sum needed so large, and the resistance of the large companies and of certain counties to the tax so strenuous that the state did not seriously attempt to enforce it. For three years Somerset, Worcester, and Calvert Counties submitted no tax returns.

The legislature also imposed an income tax for the first time since the War for Independence when a short-lived and unsuccessful tax of this sort had been levied. It now placed a low tax on all salaries and other incomes but allowed exemptions for the salaries of judges and clergymen and for all incomes of less than $500 annual value. For all public salaries and salaries paid by corporations, firms, and individuals, the legislature required the disbursing officers to withhold the tax and pay it over directly to the state treasurer. It allowed others to pay the tax on the basis of their sworn statements. For this purpose inheritances were treated as incomes and were taxed at the same rate as incomes. In 1845 the legislature enacted a Stamp Act which required stamps to be used on every business document above $100, but this measure was strenuously denounced as the "British Stamp Act" and encountered so much opposition, particularly from the Baltimore merchants, that it was soon repealed. The governor could not find persons to collect the taxes; in Carroll and Harford Counties anti-tax associations were formed, and considerable sentiment developed to repudiate the state's indebtedness.

Because of inefficient enforcement and popular resistance to these new tax measures they yielded only a disappointing $15,000 between 1841 and 1844, and in 1848 the income tax was abandoned. The state government was therefore driven into an austerity program. The separate fiscal system for the Eastern Shore, which was provided in the constitution of 1776, was abolished and the salaries of state officials were reduced, including that of the governor which was cut back from $4,200 to $2,000. In 1842 Maryland suspended payment of interest on its debt and for the next six years it failed to meet its interest payments. Under the new drastic tax measures the state gradually improved its financial condition and was able to resume payment of interest on the state debt on January 1, 1848. But though its credit had sunk low, Maryland, unlike some other states which had overcommitted themselves to internal improvements, did not repudiate its debt.

Maryland's trade and commerce had expanded notably between the end of the War for Independence and the War of 1812. Even during the second war against Britain, despite the British blockade and other interferences with American shipping, Maryland traders were able to carry on a profitable foreign trade. Maryland's principal center of foreign trade was Baltimore, which, because of its fine harbor and productive hinterland, established itself as the commercial metropolis of the state. In the boom year 1836 Maryland's total foreign commerce was valued at $10,807,312 and Maryland ranked among the top eight states in the nation in foreign trade. After the economic depression of the 1840's Maryland's foreign trade quickly recovered, reaching a value of $14,098,302 in 1853.

From the beginning of English settlement in the Chesapeake region the fisheries and local trading necessitated the construction of ships of all kinds, and Maryland became a center of an important shipbuilding industry, made possible by the abundance of cheap, good, and abundant timber. In the construction of vessels for the slave trade Chesapeake Bay shipyards early achieved considerable distinction. There the swiftest vessels, all brigs and schooners, built especially for this trade, were constructed. They had a between-deck space of from 5-2/3 to 6 feet, were divided by bulkheads into rooms for the male and female slaves, and provided space for as many as 600. Even before the War for American Independence, Chesapeake Bay shipyards acquired a worldwide fame for the construction of these fast vessels.

During the War of 1812 Baltimore shipbuilders developed the "Baltimore Clipper," a vessel ranging in size from 100 to 500 tons and rigged either as a schooner or as a brig. These vessels were designed primarily for speed, and many of them were pressed into service by attractive bounties as privateers during the war, giving Baltimore preeminence over other seaboard cities—Boston, New York, and Charleston—in this wartime activity. As the rivalry among them increased the vessels grew in size, were built with more and more sail spread, and were streamlined to beat everything that had gone before them in the merchant shipping field. Some of them attained a size of 2,400 tons, and they accomplished a revolution in the carrying trade of the world.

The most famous of the Baltimore clippers was the *Ann McKim*, constructed in 1833 at Fells Point in Baltimore for Isaac McKim. A vessel of 494 tons burthen, it has been acclaimed as the pioneer American clipper. In the California Gold Rush it sailed between Valparaíso in Chile and San Francisco and was one of the first gold-boom ships to sail through the Golden Gate. As the discovery of gold in California increased the need for these swift-moving cargo ships, American shipyards turned out clippers that exceeded both in size and sailing qualities everything that had gone before. Baltimore clippers "start from port," it was said, "before the wind had time to reach their sails and never allow it to come up with them." In the years between 1851 and 1856 Baltimore, Philadelphia, New York, and Boston sent out fleets of clippers which in sailing tonnage and beauty have never been surpassed. These "greyhounds of the sea" gave a great impetus to maritime commerce, boosted Baltimore into front rank as a commercial port, and provided an incentive for fixing it as the starting point of the Baltimore and Ohio Railroad, which could provide an outlet for the distribution of the commerce of Maryland's principal port. Many of them were built on order from foreign governments, and in their construction the large white oak trees growing on the Chesapeake peninsulas of Maryland proved particularly useful. The production of timber for the frames of vessels soon became a substantial industry in that region.

In the prosperous years after 1840 as many as fifteen shipyards kept busy turning out schooners, brigs, clippers, and steamboats on the shores of Baltimore harbor. Twenty to twenty-five vessels could be found on the stocks at a time. Some of the best vessels built in America were constructed in the Baltimore yards. In 1855 the Baltimore-built clipper *Mary*

Washington Monument, Baltimore, completed in 1829. Statues of John Eager Howard and General Lafayette are also on the site. Photo by M.E. Warren.

Whitridge, 978 tons, Captain Robert B. Cheesebrough, set a new record for a transatlantic crossing when it sailed from Baltimore to Liverpool in twelve days and ten hours. Though Chesapeake shipyards achieved wide reputation for building small, fast vessels, they never led in the production of sturdy merchant vessels of the type required in the transatlantic service. Only one line of sailing packets, inaugurated in 1843, operated between Baltimore and Liverpool, and it used packets built in northern shipyards. But though Baltimore shipbuilders could not compete successfully with northern shipbuilders in this type of vessel, they developed a large business in providing canalboats for use on the Chesapeake and Ohio Canal.[2]

Shipbuilding was only one of many industries which developed and expanded in Maryland during the three decades prior to the Civil War. One of the most profitable lines of foreign trade in which Baltimore pioneered was the trade with Latin America. By this trade the city introduced many exotic products into the United States and found an outlet for its manufactures. In its commerce with Latin America Baltimore possessed several advantages over other American ports. The city's staple export was flour, which was much desired in the countries to the south. Baltimore was more advantageously situated for the trade with that area than her east-coast rivals, New York and Philadelphia. As the most southern of the northern cities and the most western of the eastern cities it possessed both the products and the location to give it a large headstart in this trade. Finally, in the famed Baltimore clipper, trim-rigged and fleet, she developed a vessel admirably suited to this trade.

Baltimore opened up trade with the West Indies and the Guianas during the Napoleonic wars, and during the wars of independence in Latin America she secured trade with all the countries on the east coast of South America. In the War of 1812, when Chesapeake Bay was blockaded, her lines of trade with Latin America were temporarily closed, but in compensation she developed domestic manufactures as did other cities in America. Baltimore was one of the first American cities to establish cotton factories, and under the operation of the tariff of 1816, Baltimore's factories became prosperous and Baltimore's ships undertook to meet the demand for American cottons on the west coast of South America, particularly with Peru after that country gained its independence from Spain. An occasional Baltimore vessel made Lima a port of call on its route to China. By 1823 Baltimore was importing the largest part of the precious metals into the United States from the west coast of South America. In its trade with the east coast of South America Baltimore chiefly imported sugar, coffee, cacao, and indigo from Venezuela, the Guianas, and Brazil, and hides from Uruguay and Argentina.

Baltimore's principal export to the east coast of South America was flour, which formed sixty-eight percent of its total exports to that region in 1827 and fifty-nine percent in 1858. Until the Civil War Baltimore ranked second only to New York as a flour-exporting port, and it gained this position by reason of its Latin American trade. Between 1844 and 1847, for example, Baltimore exported more flour to Brazil than all other ports in this country combined, and it carried on most of this trade in Baltimore ships. In 1858 ninety-four percent of Baltimore's exports to Brazil was carried in her own vessels.

Baltimore's trade with Brazil became fairly stable because it was reciprocal, Brazil receiving Baltimore's flour and sending back full cargoes of coffee. So important was this trade to Baltimore that between 1841 and 1845 she imported eighty percent as much coffee as New York, and with the extension of the Baltimore and Ohio Railroad to Wheeling, her shipments of coffee into the west increased considerably. By 1850 Baltimore was receiving twenty percent of all the Brazilian coffee imported into the United States. Coffee was the most important element in Baltimore's import trade between 1825 and 1860, and by the latter year this trade was almost exclusively confined to Brazilian coffee. Only slightly less important was the sugar imported into Baltimore mainly from the islands in the West Indies.

During the Civil War the coffee trade of Baltimore suffered a serious loss, though its port was not blockaded. Baltimore's connection with the west was severed, for the Baltimore and Ohio Railroad was closed to traffic, and the depredations of Confederate privateers interfered with the direct trade between Baltimore and Brazil. During the Civil War Baltimore also lost its sugar trade with Latin America, which had centered chiefly in the Guianas, but it was able to reestablish this trade in 1871. Its trade in hides with the east coast of South America, which were imported principally from the Plata region, began to decline even before the Civil War and continued to decline after the war. By the outbreak of the Civil War, Baltimore's export trade with Venezuela had virtually ended.

By that date the six chief elements in Baltimore's foreign commerce were flour, grain, tobacco, guano, copper, and coffee. Of these, four figured prominently in the Latin American trade; and of these four, guano, or bird dung found on the islands off the west coast of South America, was by far the most important staple in the import trade of Baltimore with the west coast countries. Guano was the first commercial fertilizer used by agriculturists in the United States in any large amount, and the bulk of it came from Peru where it was subject to a government monopoly. The first regular importation of this commodity from Peru into the United States began in 1844 at Baltimore, which, because of its extensive trade with Latin America, was thus able to secure priority in this trade. The principal demand for this import in the United States came from the southern states, which needed it to restore fertility to their exhausted cotton and tobacco lands.

Baltimore became the headquarters for the importation and distribution of guano to the users of this fertilizer in the United States. An agent of the Peruvian government was stationed there to supervise its distribution. Through the port of Baltimore passed almost all the guano imported into this country. The farmers of Maryland, Virginia, and Delaware complained of the Peruvian monopoly which was so indispensable to their prosperity and urged the national government either to purchase the guano islands or to remove the restraints on the trade in some way. In 1854 the Maryland legislature passed a resolution petitioning the United States government to adopt measures "by which the present monopoly in the sale of guano in this State and other States of the Union may be removed and the agricultural interests of our country [be] thereby greatly promoted." This and other similar demands for the destruction of the Peruvian government monopoly and for the unrestricted importations of guano into this country impelled the national government in 1856 to authorize American citizens to take possession of hitherto undiscovered or unexploited guano islands, and it assimilated such islands to the coasting trade. As a result the United States acquired several such islands of its own and became increasingly independent of Peruvian sources.[3]

While Baltimore's guano trade was in its heyday, the Maryland legislature passed acts in 1846 and again in 1854 requiring the inspection of all foreign guano landed at Baltimore. But this inspection system alienated the Peruvian government, and the resulting coolness between them, together with the decline in Baltimore's export trade to Peru, caused the shifting of the guano agency from Baltimore to New York in 1856. Baltimore remained, however, the best guano market in the country until the outbreak of the Civil War, when her guano imports ceased through the loss of her markets in the Confederate states. In 1862 and 1863 she shipped her remaining supplies of guano to Great Britain and Spain. During the decade between 1852 and 1861 Baltimore's imports of Peruvian guano had been valued at over $14 million, and she probably imported and distributed more of it than any other American port. Her trade in guano was by far the most important branch of her import trade with the west coast of South America before the Civil War, but in addition she also imported from those countries considerable amounts of gold, copper, and silver.

In its overall commerce with foreign ports, Baltimore, as might have been expected, ranked especially high in the export of tobacco, shipping it mainly to the Netherlands, the ports of Germany, England, France, and Spain. Three-fifths of Baltimore's exports to the foreign world consisted of tobacco and flour, but aside from its large export trade in tobacco to European ports and in wheat and flour to Great Britain, the major part of Baltimore's foreign trading interest was directed toward Latin America, which was the one area in which Baltimore could successfully compete with New York. In summary, Baltimore's foreign trade was largely based upon the reciprocal exchange of tobacco and flour for the sugar and molasses of the West Indies, the coffee of Brazil, the copper ore of Cuba and Chile, the guano of Peru, and hides from Argentina. Maryland ships did not engage in the whaling industry in the South Pacific which was dominated by New Englanders.

The extensive foreign trade moving in and out of Baltimore rested upon a considerable industrial base. Baltimore's principal industry was the manufacture of men's clothing and its complementary processing operations including the cotton textile industry. Much of Baltimore's industrial energy on the eve of the Civil War also went into flour milling, sugar refining, iron manufacturing, and meat packing.

In 1858 Baltimore received over one million dollars worth of unwrought copper from South America for the use of her two smelting companies, the Baltimore and Cuba Smelting and Mining Company located at Locust Point and the Baltimore Copper Smelting Company at Canton. One of the incorporators of the latter company, founded in 1850, was a Maryland Quaker, Isaac Tyson, Jr., a pioneer engineer and metallurgist. These two companies, incorporated respectively in 1845 and 1850, were but two out of a grand total of 625 companies which were incorporated by the state of Maryland prior to 1852, indicating the scope of Maryland's financial and general business development during the first half of the century. Of this total of 625 companies, 137 were manufacturing companies, the first of which, the Union Manufacturing Company, was formed in 1808 to carry on and encourage the manufacture of necessary articles which had been hitherto imported from abroad. Of the total number of corporations created by the state, manufacturing companies comprised more than one-fifth. The first mining company was not organized in Maryland until 1829, when as a result of the opening up of the coal fields, the Baltimore and Pittston Coal Company was incorporated by the Maryland legislature. The first cargo of coal was shipped in 1843 by way of the canal and railroad to New York City where it undersold English coal and was adjudged the best quality of bituminous coal in the world.[4] Before 1852 fifty-one such mining companies had been incorporated.

Maryland, as noted previously, was able to resume interest payments on its debt in 1848, and by mid-century it was again adequately taking care of its financial problems. Thanks to the state's railroad system, Baltimore was prospering as a leading commercial center and shipping point for the coal, lumber, and agricultural products of a vast hinterland including the interior farm and mineral lands of Maryland, Pennsylvania, Virginia, and Ohio. Maryland was supplying the southern states with much of their breadstuffs and fertilizer, and Baltimore's trade with Latin America was approaching its zenith.

Prior to 1851, the Maryland legislature chartered a total of forty-seven commercial banks. Appreciating the need for new capital after the midpoint of the century, it authorized the incorporation of seventeen new banks between 1853 and 1858, having a combined capitalization of $3 million. In 1857 the banks of Baltimore, numbering thirty-one, formed a clearing house which began to operate in the following year.

In the great majority of the state bank charters issued before 1851, the legislature made the stockholders liable only to the extent of their paid-up capital investment. But when the state adopted a new constitution in 1851 it imposed double liability upon the members of banking corporations. In doing so it ran the risk that such a requirement might drive banking capital out of the state. In the convention that drew up the constitution of 1851 an attempt was made to subject the stockholders in trading, manufacturing, mining, and navigation corporations to the same double liability to which bank stockholders were being subjected, but this effort failed.

The state of Maryland exercised considerable control over the corporate business which it chartered. First, it usually chartered them for only short periods of time of from six to thirty years. In the constitutional convention of 1850-1851 an attempt was made to secure a constitutional provision that no charter of incorporation should last for more than twenty years, but it failed. Maryland's policy in this respect was much more conservative than that of New York, which chartered the Bank of Central New York at Utica for 4,050 years, the United States Bank at Buffalo for 200 years, the United States Bank of New York City for 62 years, two other banks for periods of 1,000 years, and several others for periods of 500 years. In its new constitution of 1851 Maryland made all laws and acts pertaining to corporations subject to alteration or repeal at any time.

The state also controlled certain corporations through its purchase of stock in them. This practice began in the early days of its history as a state when it derived from the investment of state funds a large part of the income required for the operation of the state government. From the first organization of the Baltimore and Ohio Railroad Company, for example, Maryland, as a stockholder in the company, appointed a certain number of the members of the board of directors. In 1847 it was entitled to select ten of the thirty directors of this company. The state attempted to regulate certain other public utility companies by reserving the right to require regular reports from them or to purchase the entire companies at the end of a certain period of time. In the charters of some companies it fixed the maximum toll which could be charged, and in numerous other ways it regulated their methods of doing business. It used them as a source of revenue. After 1814, for example, as already noted, it collected a tax upon paid-up bank capital stock, which it used to establish and support free schools in the counties of the state. This revenue became a very important item in the budget of the county schools and formed approximately one-third of the state's appropriation for this purpose.

Maryland conceived that its power to charter corporations should be used primarily for the development of the business and industry of the state. The charters which it issued were less liberal than those of many other states. Maryland made no effort to invite the incorporation of outside companies. The only such companies which it incorporated were three companies which were formed to carry on mining in Mexico, three to carry on mining near Lake Superior, and one or two others which received authority to operate outside the state. In general, Maryland intended the enterprises which it incorporated to operate within the state and for the benefit of citizens of the state. In this respect its motives in the use of the incorporating power were the same as those which impelled it to throw the credit of the state behind works of internal improvement starting with the Chesapeake and Delaware Canal and culminating in the "eight million dollar" internal improvements act of 1836.

The political and financial crises of the 1840's disclosed weaknesses in the constitution which Maryland had adopted in 1776 when it became a state. That constitution had provided in article 59 that it could be amended by the identical action of two successive legislatures, and in accordance with this procedure Maryland made many changes in its fundamental law at various times. By constitutional amendment it abolished the property qualification for voting and for officeholding. Partly as a result of the determined action of the Van Buren electors in 1836, the legislature soon afterward adopted an amendment reapportioning representation in the House of Delegates in favor of the more populous counties and the city of Baltimore, eliminating the electoral college for the selection of members of the state senate, and devolving upon the people the power to select the governor. But this far-reaching amendment of 1837 did not eliminate the demand for thoroughgoing constitutional revision. In fact, this and other amendments which had been added tended to destroy the unity of the constitution and to render it, as has been well said, a "shapeless mass of unintelligible and contradictory provisions."

Moreover, as the state forged ahead in commercial and industrial development, the constitution seemed to become an anachronism—poorly suited to the state's contemporary needs. During the first seventy-five years of Maryland's history as a state its social and economic life had been completely transformed. Since 1790 its population had almost doubled, reaching 583,034 in 1850, and it was differently distributed than it had been in 1790. Between 1820 and 1850 the number of Marylanders employed in manufacturing establishments almost doubled. By the latter year the annual production of these establishments was valued at nearly $32.5 million, making Maryland the sixth ranking industrial state in the nation. Baltimore had become the financial and commercial metropolis of the state and had increased its population from only 13,503 in 1790 to more than 100,000 in 1850. By that year the city possessed almost one-fourth of the total population of the state and more than one-third of its total wealth. During the three-quarters of a century since Maryland adopted its first constitution, the center of population and the center of economic activity in the state had shifted from the eastern and southern counties to the northern and western counties. But despite the constitutional changes of 1837, political power remained firmly rooted in the predominantly agricultural counties of the state.

But how could a new constitution be prepared? Could the legislature, which only possessed the power of amending the constitution, call a convention to frame a new one? Such a call would be an open act of revolution aimed at the overthrow of the very frame of government which limited their powers. Indeed, during the agitation for constitutional change in 1836, the legislature appointed a committee to inquire into the expediency of bringing charges of high treason against citizens who conspired against the constitution of the state. But, on the other hand, surely the people, acting through the legislature, possessed the right to change their constitution either in part or in whole at any time and in any way they wished.

Constitutional reform was in the air at mid-century. By 1850 eleven states—Massachusetts, New Hampshire, Connecticut, Rhode Island, New York, New Jersey, Pennsylvania, Virginia, South Carolina, Georgia, and Missouri—had held conventions for the purpose either of revising their constitutions or of preparing new ones, and in doing so they had acted without specific authorizations of their constitutions. In the year 1850 alone seven states—New Hampshire, Vermont, Michigan, Indiana, Ohio, Virginia, and Kentucky—held conventions to revise their constitutions or to frame new ones. In Maryland the controversy over constitutional reform became acute after the panic of 1837, for the panic and the ensuing bankruptcy of Maryland demonstrated that the legislature had played fast and loose with the finances and credit of the state. When the legislatures in the 1840's imposed new and unpopular tax measures they unwittingly gave further encouragement to the demand for constitutional change and furnished an issue to the anti-tax associations that were formed to resist the collection of the new taxes. Only a radical revision of the constitution, it seemed, would enable the people to impose checks upon the legislature in the future. In each election thereafter the issue of constitutional reform was bitterly fought over, and successive governors repeatedly urged the legislature to call a new constitutional convention.

Those who agitated for constitutional change demanded, first, an altered system of representation in the House of Delegates which would increase the representation of Baltimore and the more populous counties of the state, thus better reflecting their new economic importance. The amendment of 1837 had specified the number of seats for each county until the census of 1840 and had established a formula to be followed after that date, as follows: each county having less than 15,000 population would be entitled to three seats in the House of Delegates; each having a population from 15,000 to 25,000, four seats; 25,000 to 35,000, five seats; and 35,000 or over, six seats. By establishing a minimum delegation of three members, this formula gave more delegates in proportion to population to some smaller counties than to the larger. Caroline County, for example, which had the smallest population of Maryland's counties (only 7,806 in 1840), was entitled to one delegate for 2,602 inhabitants, whereas Frederick County, which had the largest population and so was entitled to six delegates, had only one delegate for 6,067 inhabitants. Representation therefore continued to be largely geographical. It was not based strictly upon equal representation by population.

As certain counties increased their population after 1840 they could not exceed the limit of six delegates allowed to each county and to the city of Baltimore. This limitation worked a special hardship on Baltimore which by 1850 had a population nearly four times as large as that of the most populous county. Baltimore included about one-fourth of the total population of the state, but its political position in the House of Delegates, where it had only one-sixteenth of the total representation, was not commensurate with either its population or its economic status.

Other demands of the advocates of constitutional change included limitation upon the power of the legislature to contract debts and pledge the public credit, reduction in governmental expenditures, popular election of all local officers, and reform and financial retrenchment in the judicial system of the state, which was considered too expensive. In 1844, for example, the cost of the Maryland judicial system amounted to $41,500, whereas that of Massachusetts serving a state population twice as large was only $25,750.

The opposition to these proposed constitutional changes and to the summoning of a new constitutional convention centered principally in the southern and eastern counties of the state, which were interested in the preservation of slavery and foresaw that a new constitution might alter the relationship between masters and slaves. These counties feared that a new constitution would base representation more strictly upon population and that Baltimore and the larger counties—which were leaders in the agitation for a new constitution—would deprive them of their privileged position in the government of the state. Whereas the northern and western counties, bordering upon the free state of Pennsylvania, had a slave population that was rapidly diminishing, the slave population of the southern counties was increasing, and the slaveholders there suspected that Baltimore and the northern counties were succumbing to the antislavery agitation. Their opposition to constitutional change was supported by the Whig party, which in general deplored any agitation of the slavery question and opposed any alteration in the existing system of representation.

To stimulate the movement for constitutional reform a state convention composed of delegates from several counties assembled in Baltimore in August 1845. They resolved to recommend that reform associations be organized in each election district in the state and that the people support no candidate "who will not pledge himself to vote for the call of a convention, the abolition of all useless offices, and the retrenchment of all unnecessary expenses." They rejected as "visionary" the suggestion that such a convention might agitate the slavery question "to the prejudice of the quiet and happiness of the public." Under considerable public pressure the legislature of 1845-1846 took under consideration a bill to refer to the people of the state the question of calling a constitutional convention, but this measure was strenuously opposed by the members from the smaller counties and was lost by a tie vote. The next legislature advised postponement of the question because of the state's financial embarrassment, but their failure to act did not silence the clamor of the reformers, who were most numerous in the Democratic party, for the summoning of a constitutional convention. In the gubernatorial election of 1847 they waged a vigorous campaign under the slogan "reform, retrenchment, and convention," with Philip F. Thomas of Talbot County as their candidate for governor, against the Whigs, who as a party generally opposed constitutional reform. They elected Thomas by a narrow margin of 709 votes, but lost both branches of the legislature to the Whigs, who declined to take any action on the subject.

Frustrated once more in their demand for a constitutional convention, the reform party began a still more violent agitation for "conventional reform." They held county conventions at Westminster, Snow Hill, and elsewhere. Delegates from conventions held in the counties of Washington, Frederick, Carroll, Baltimore, Harford, Caroline, Worcester, Somerset, Montgomery, Baltimore City, and Howard District met at Baltimore in July 1849 and resolved to support only those candidates for the state legislature who were "fully committed and pledged to vote for a bill providing for an immediate call of a convention to revise the present constitution." In general this action was endorsed by the northern and western counties and received almost unanimous support from the Democratic party. But it was strongly resisted by the counties of southern Maryland and the Eastern Shore, particularly by the Whigs in those counties.

But the Whig party in the state was beginning to show signs of weakening on this question. Though it gained majorities of twelve in the House and nine in the Senate in the election of 1849, it finally yielded to pressure from the governor and the reformers and voted to submit to the people of the state the question of calling a convention. The vote on this measure disclosed unanimous support for it by the representatives of Baltimore City and the counties of Baltimore, Harford, Cecil, Talbot, Frederick, Washington, Allegany, and Carroll; unanimous opposition to it by the representatives from St. Mary's, Calvert, Charles, Dorchester, Queen Anne's, Worcester, and Kent Counties; and division in the other county delegations. Before allowing the voters to decide the question whether a constitutional convention should or should not be called, the legislature stipulated that if ordered by the people, a convention should follow the same system of representation as was followed in the legislature, that it must not change the prevailing relationship between masters and slaves, and that if it drafted a new constitution, it must allow it to be submitted to the people for their approval. In the ensuing poll of the voters the call for a convention was approved by a popular majority of 18,833. Delegates were immediately chosen and the so-called "Reform Convention" assembled at Annapolis in November 1850.

The convention included a Whig majority of 55 to 48 Democrats, and it elected as chairman John G. Chapman of Charles County, a conservative Whig who had voted against the call for a convention. But members of the convention deferred to the popular will, and in the draft constitution which they framed they recognized the right of the people to resort to revolutionary procedures to alter their constitution. They agreed that the people "have at all times the inalienable right to alter, reform, or abolish their form of government in such manner as they may think expedient." In the matter of future changes the convention required that the legislature canvass the people of the state in regard to calling a convention every ten years.

The convention was dominated by the less populous counties of the Eastern Shore and southern Maryland—predominantly Whig—which were thoroughly committed to the institution of slavery and which largely controlled the public treasury through their disproportionately large representation. They were determined not to surrender control to the larger counties and the City of Baltimore. So great was the interest of southern Maryland in slavery that the question of secession was actually discussed there during the contest for seats in the convention. Thomas H. Hicks, a member from the Eastern Shore who later became the Civil War governor of Maryland, offered to the convention an amendment declaring "that any portion of the people of the State have the right to secede and unite themselves and the territory occupied by them to such adjoining State as they shall elect." This amendment received the support of 15 of the 27 votes cast by the Eastern Shore, but it was lost by a vote of 51 to 27.

The constitution as finally drafted recognized and protected slavery and forbade the legislature to pass "any law abolishing the relation of master or slave as it now exists in the state," thus allaying the apprehensions of the southern and eastern counties regarding the institution of slavery. After much debate the convention finally apportioned representation among the counties on the general basis of population but limited Baltimore City to four more delegates than the most populous county and stipulated that the whole number of delegates in the House of Delegates should never exceed eighty. This arrangement increased the representation of Baltimore City in the assembly from one-sixteenth to one-eighth of the total representation.

As to representation in the Senate, the convention continued in force the system embodied in the amendment of 1837 allowing each county and the city of Baltimore to choose one senator elected by the people. It also created a new county, Howard, out of the Howard District of Anne Arundel County.

The convention arranged to return to the system of annual sessions of the legislature, which had prevailed until 1846, but it provided that after three years the legislature should meet only biennially. It reaffirmed the prohibition, inherited from colonial days, forbidding any "minister or preacher of the Gospel of any denomination" from holding a seat in the General Assembly. It also prohibited the legislature from issuing any lottery grants and ordered the termination of all lottery schemes after April 1, 1859. This prohibition resulted in part from the increasing agitation against lotteries on moral grounds, which impelled Maryland now to align itself with other states that, starting with Pennsylvania in 1833, had abolished lotteries.

Profiting from the state's experience with its costly internal improvements program which had plunged the state temporarily into bankruptcy, the convention inserted in the new constitution an article prohibiting the legislature thereafter from contracting a debt unless at the same time it provided by law for a tax to pay the interest on the debt and to discharge it within fifteen years, and it limited the amount of any future such debt that might be contracted to $100,000. The constitution further forbade the legislature to involve the state in the construction of any future works of internal improvement or to give the credit of the state in aid of any individual, association, or corporation. To supervise all the public works in which the state was already interested either as a stockholder or as a creditor, the constitution provided for four Commissioners of Public Works to be elected by the voters.

In the clauses of the new constitution relating to the executive department, the convention provided for the election of a governor by popular vote and lengthened his term of office from three to four years.

But the new constitution added little to the powers of the governor and, like previous constitutions of the state, denied him the veto power. He was to be chosen in rotation from the three districts into which the state was divided, one on the Eastern Shore and two on the Western Shore. But the convention refused to continue the district system which had been followed for the election of the United States Senators and which had required that one senator should be chosen from the Eastern Shore and one from the Western Shore.

The new constitution effected several changes in the judicial system of the state. It provided for the election rather than the appointment of judges by joint ballot of the two Houses of the General Assembly, reduced the number of judicial districts in the state from six to four, and abolished imprisonment for debt. Until 1841 only the legislature of Maryland had the power to grant divorces, but in that year it gave the equity courts jurisdiction also over divorce cases, without, however, divesting itself of its jurisdiction in such cases. As late as 1849 the legislature granted twenty-one divorces. The constitutional convention now transferred this power exclusively to the equity courts.

The convention devoted some attention to the problem of public education in the state. At that time Maryland had no state system of public education but allowed each county and city to maintain its own schools. In 1798 the state had begun to contribute certain funds to their support, and in 1813, as noted heretofore, the Maryland legislature began to impose a tax upon banks as a school fund. When it consented to renew the charters of the banks operating within the state, it required them to pay annually $20,000 into a fund "for the purpose of supporting county schools." In the following year the legislature changed the tax to 20 cents on every $100 of paid-in capital stock of each bank and provided for the distribution of this so-called "Free School Fund" equally among the counties. Three years later the legislature appointed Commissioners of the School Fund for each county and thereafter disbursed the state school fund to them for the maintenance of the county schools. The state later set up a similar Commission for Baltimore City.

Under this arrangement Baltimore City rapidly forged ahead of the counties of the state in establishing and maintaining public schools. In 1826 it was authorized by the General Assembly to levy additional local taxes to maintain and expand its school system. The Baltimore City Council was empowered to elect six Commissioners of Public Schools, constituting a School Board, who were directed to divide the city into districts and to provide for the establishment and maintenance of schools in each district. Baltimore's schools were practically free to the children of residents of the city, the usual charge being only one dollar each quarter, and they were largely supported by city taxes.

The funds derived from the bank taxes proving wholly inadequate to provide a system of free primary education in the counties, the state proposed a comprehensive and fairly centralized system of public education in 1826, when the legislature authorized the establishment of a number of Lancastrian or monitorial schools at the primary level to take advantage of this cheap system of education. For the administration of this system the act provided for a state superintendent to be appointed by the governor and council, nine commissioners of primary schools for each county, and a corps of inspectors of primary schools. The commissioners were required to take steps to establish schools in the various school districts of their counties. But the acceptance of this system was made optional with the counties. It was approved by thirteen of them and rejected by six, Allegany, Caroline, Dorchester, Somerset, Washington, and Worcester.

This venture in public education soon collapsed as the Lancastrian system lost favor and financial support proved inadequate. The only funds which the state thereafter contributed to school purposes came from the "Free School Fund," but on two occasions this fund was supplemented by extraordinary increments of revenue. When Maryland was reimbursed by the national government for its expenditures during the War of 1812 it assigned the interest paid by the government to the financing of the public school system. Later in 1837 Maryland found another source of financial support for the local schools in the surplus revenue distributed to the states by the national government. Out of the amount which Maryland received, totaling $955,838.25, the state deposited $681,387.25 in certain banks and allocated the interest derived from it to the public school fund.

The public schools of the state, therefore, were largely financed by the local communities, and those in Baltimore City, which was the wealthiest school district in the state, were generally much superior to those in the counties. According to the census of 1850 the colleges, academies, and public schools of Maryland had a total enrollment of 45,025 and their total educational expenditures exceeded a half million dollars. Nevertheless, out of a total population of 208,043 over twenty years of age, the state reported 41,877 who could not read or write.

In considering the problem of public education the constitutional convention of 1850-1851 appointed a committee on education which in its report recommended the establishment of a permanent and adequate school fund and a uniform system of public schools throughout the state, including a state normal school, but this report was not acted upon by the convention. The opposition to it came from Baltimore City and the larger counties which considered that they had already made ample provision for schools under their local systems. It remained for Maryland's next constitutional convention meeting in 1864 to provide a state system of public education along the lines recommended by the committee in 1851.[5]

The constitutional convention of 1850-1851 concluded its work in mid-May 1851. Of the 103 members of the convention only 55 were believed to favor the adoption of the draft constitution. Even the president of the convention himself could not support it. Believing that no favorable vote on the constitution as a whole could be secured, the convention resorted to the expedient of endorsing each part separately and then submitted the whole document to the voters of the state for their action.

The constitution was remarkable for its democratic features. It required all state officers from governor to constable to be elected by popular vote. In general it was enthusiastically endorsed by the Democratic party newspapers of the state. The opposition to it centered largely in the counties of southern Maryland and the Eastern Shore. In the popular vote it was rejected by the counties of Anne Arundel, Charles, Calvert, Kent, Montgomery, Prince George's, Somerset, and St. Mary's. It was approved by the counties of the Eastern Shore by the narrow majority of 1,337 and throughout the state by a majority of 10,409 votes. It was in general a moderate document and benefited both in its formulation and in its passage through the voting process from the spirit of compromise which filled the air in 1850-1851. Harmony was the keynote of the time—on the slavery question, in politics, in intersectional competition. Agitation and violence were deplored.

Adopted under these circumstances the constitution could reasonably be expected to provide Maryland with a government well suited to the new requirements of the state, supporting its growing industrial economy, and responding to the desires of its increasing population. It signalized Maryland's final emergence from the financial trough of the 1840's and seemed to point the way toward a new and longed-for prosperity. The constitution provided for its own amendment by a convention chosen every ten years if the people so desired. It was never amended, however, and remained in force unchanged until superseded by the constitution of 1864.

In its consequences the constitution of 1851 strengthened the Democratic party organization in Maryland at the expense of the Whigs and hastened the demise of the Whig party. But at the same time it de-emphasized party politics by substantially reducing the number of appointive jobs, thus depriving a victorious party of political patronage. It tended to depoliticize politics by making politics less partisan. Moreover, by increasing the representation of Baltimore, which was more reform-minded than other parts of the state, it encouraged political and social innovations which had little to do with the traditional political parties and thus must be held partly accountable for the rise of the Know-Nothing movement.

Footnotes

[1] *Laws of Maryland, 1787,* April Session, ch. 20.

[2] Fairburn, *Merchant Sail,* vol. II, pp. 1183-1184, and 1288 ff.

[3] Vivian Wiser, "Improving Maryland's Agriculture, 1840-1860," *Maryland Historical Magazine,* vol. 64, No. 2, Summer 1969, pp. 105-132.

[4] *Niles Register,* LXV, 242.

[5] James Warner Harry, *The Maryland Constitution of 1851,* Johns Hopkins Studies in Historical and Political Science, vol. XX, Nos. 7, 8, Johns Hopkins Press, Baltimore, 1902.

Sources and Additional Reading

Blandi, Joseph G., *Maryland's Business Corporations; 1783-1852,* Johns Hopkins University Studies, Series 52, No. 3, Johns Hopkins Press, Baltimore, 1934.

Bryan, Alfred Cookman, *History of State Banking in Maryland,* Johns Hopkins University Studies, Series 17, Nos. 1-3, Johns Hopkins Press, Baltimore, 1899.

Debates and Proceedings of the Maryland Reform Convention to Revise the State Constitution, 2 vols., Annapolis, 1851.

Harry, James Warner, *The Maryland Constitution of 1851,* Johns Hopkins Studies in Historical and Political Science, vol. XX, Nos. 7, 8, Baltimore, 1902.

Rutter, F.R., *The South American Trade of Baltimore,* Johns Hopkins University Studies, Series 15, No. 9, Johns Hopkins Press, Baltimore, 1897.

CHAPTER XXI

PRELUDE TO CIVIL CONFLICT

Much of Maryland's political history has been determined by its geographical position as a border state. From the first establishment of the national union Maryland was cast in the role of mediator between the north, the south, and even the west, as sectional rivalries became intensified. Marylanders shared the viewpoints and interests of all those sections. The Maryland way was the way of compromise and accommodation. Like every borderland it has been an object of contention by rival factions.

At mid-century the mood of Maryland was conservative. This mood was reflected in the constitution which the state adopted in 1851. In national politics, as indicated above, the state's electors supported the Whig presidential candidates consistently through the election of 1848. Maryland was rapidly forging ahead as one of the leading industrial states, utilizing the raw materials of both west and south, and it supported the Whig party as a party bridging the interests of the sections. But despite its industrial growth Maryland in 1850 was still primarily an agricultural state, reporting 21,860 farms and an average acreage of 212, which was slightly above the national average. Its farms were valued at $87,178,545. In tobacco production Maryland was outdistanced among the states only by Virginia and Kentucky. It reported 1,726 tobacco plantations producing more than 3,000 pounds each. Its plantation economy rested upon the system of Negro slavery. Maryland therefore deplored any agitation of the slavery question and seemed disposed to accept the Compromise of 1850 as a final settlement of that question.

The Compromise of 1850, though it had seemed to augur a halcyon period of harmony between the rival sections of the Union, was soon followed by renewed political ferment. As plans were made for the presidential nominating conventions of 1852, Maryland again assumed importance as a pivotal state and was selected as the convention site by both political parties. Baltimore had been the choice of the Democratic party as its convention city in every campaign since 1832 when the party first began to hold nominating conventions. In 1852 the Democrats on their forty-ninth ballot nominated Franklin Pierce of New Hampshire as their presidential candidate. In their platform they prom-

Governor's House, United States Naval Academy, 1850. Courtesy *Maryland Hall of Records Commission*

ised "a faithful execution" of the Compromise measures of 1850, including the fugitive slave law, and they agreed to "resist all attempts at renewing, in Congress or out of it, the agitation of the slavery question." [1]

The Whig convention, which also met in Baltimore, selected John G. Chapman of Maryland as its permanent president and nominated General Winfield Scott for president on the fifty-third ballot. In their platform, which was the last to be adopted in the history of the party, they called for a return to the "great conservative principles" upon which the Union of states was based, including the limitation of federal authority, the reserved rights of the states, and freedom from all entangling alliances with foreign countries. On the Compromise of 1850 and the slavery question they expressed the same views as had the Democrats. But the Whig party had lost its appeal, and with the death of both Clay and Webster during the campaign, it lost its effective political leadership. In the election it suffered a considerable defeat in the popular vote and a still more decisive one in the electoral vote. For the first time in national elections even Maryland abandoned the Whig party and gave all eight of its electoral votes to Pierce, the candidate of compromise, a northerner with southern principles.

In this era of scarcely suppressed sectional antagonism Maryland, in casting about for new political affiliations, was swept into the current of the Native American movement. This was directed in part against the new European immigrants who flocked to America during the 1830's and 1840's, attracted by the opportunities for making a livelihood, particularly on the canals and railroads. Many of them fled from Ireland to escape starvation caused by the potato famine and benighted British rule. German immigrants were harried out of their home states by the reactionary rulers who regained control after the suppression of liberal movements in the revolutionary year of 1848. They settled in Baltimore and its environs, became largely merchants, artisans, and laborers, and retained their Germanism—their language and native customs—in cultural enclaves in their new urban environment. Some of them refused to be Americanized because they looked forward to returning to the Fatherland in a more liberal era.

By mid-century Maryland had a foreign-born population of 51,209, which was almost one-tenth of its total free population. Almost 25 percent of Baltimore's population were foreign-born—mostly Germans and Irish, the former outnumbering the latter about two to one. Of the 52,750 Germans in Baltimore in that year approximately 50 percent, or 26,936, were born in Germany.

Many of the new foreigners formed closely knit national organizations and began to play a role in local politics supporting the abolitionists. The intrusion of these new immigrant stocks into America, their persistence in their national customs, and, most important of all, their political activity, provoked strong resistance among already established Americans of older and different national stock. The antagonism to them was especially strong in the large cities where the least desirable newcomers remained stranded and where, with their lower European standards of living, they came into competition with American industrial workers. South of the Mason-Dixon line the opposition to them stemmed from the slavery system that prevailed there. They offered free labor which was incompatible with a slave-labor system.

The resistance to the new immigration soon became organized. During the 1840's Native Americans sent a few representatives to Congress from New York and Pennsylvania, and in September 1847 this party held a convention in Philadelphia, nominated a candidate for vice-president, and endorsed Zachary Taylor for president. In Maryland strong sentiments against the Catholics had been expressed from time to time, and in the constitutional convention of 1851 this hostility took the form of resentment against the influx of new immigrants. In the following year it was still further stimulated by the introduction into the legislature by a Catholic member, Martin J. Kerney, of a bill requiring school commissioners to make public school funds available to free religious schools.

The Order of United Americans was first organized in New York State in 1852 for the purpose of opposing the Catholic Church and of extending the term of residence required of immigrants before they could become naturalized American citizens. The order professed to oppose the Catholics not because of their religion but because of their political activity as members of a religious organization with headquarters abroad, and it declared that a Catholic for that reason could not be a good American citizen. It was founded as a secret organization, the calls for its meetings were never published, and it secured new members only by personal solicitation. A member who found a friend sympathetic with the purposes of the organization would take him into the august presence of "Sam"—the name by which the organization was known among its members. In this way members organized local councils in wards and counties, and these local councils were directed by state councils and by a National Council. The password was "Have you seen Sam?" and their motto was "Put none but Americans on guard tonight"—a saying attributed to Washington. Because the members refused to answer any questions about the organization, it was popularly called the Know Nothing party.

Baltimore, as a major port of entry for immigrants into the United States, as a traditional stronghold of anti-Catholicism, and as a professed neutral on the slavery controversy which was dividing the nation, was strongly attracted to the Know-Nothing movement, which supported Maryland's stance on these questions. The order first appeared in Baltimore in October 1852 with the formation of some local councils. It spread rapidly throughout the state, and within three months from the time the order started, it formed a grand council for the state.

Soon a new organization, called the United Sons of America, was launched at Baltimore. Composed of the same members to a large extent, it worked closely with the Know Nothing party. In 1852 and 1853 the members threw their weight against an attempt by the Catholics to pass through the legislature the Kerney bill to allot a certain portion of the school funds for the support of Catholic schools, and in 1854 they carried on propaganda against Carlo Bedini, the Papal legate, who was visiting Baltimore. In April they created a sensation by electing one of their friends as mayor of Hagerstown and choosing a Know Nothing Council there. Soon afterward they elected all their candidates to office in Cumberland. In October they campaigned against the Democratic candidates in Baltimore and triumphantly elected a mayor, Sam Hicks, and a majority in both branches of the City Council. In the state elections of that year they elected their candidate for governor by a majority of 33,000. At the same time they gained control of the state of Delaware, and in New York they polled over 122,000 votes in the state election. In all, the Know Nothings sent seventy-five of their members to Congress.

These victories were made possible largely by reason of the disappearance of the Whig party in 1852 and the factionalism within the Democratic party. Having revealed its strength, the order now gave up its secrecy and became an outright political party. As a political party it held primary elections and nominating conventions. After the party came out into the open, the Know Nothing Almanac of 1855 stated its objects to be "Anti-Romanism, Anti-Bedinism, Anti-Pope's Toeism, Anti-Nunneryism, Anti-Winking Virginism, Anti-Jesuitism, and Anti-the-Whole-Sacerdotal-Hierarchism with all its humbugging mummeries." [2] The National Council of the party held a convention at Philadelphia in June 1855 and there set forth a platform which was much more restrained and which was the first public statement of the principles of the party. This platform, besides calling for the maintenance of the Union and obedience to the constitution, demanded the restriction of immigration and more stringent naturalization laws. It expressed support of public schools and resistance to the "aggressive policy and the corrupting tendencies of the Roman Catholic Church." The slavery plank, though somewhat equivocal, actually favored the southern point of view, for it demanded that the existing laws on slavery should be maintained and that Congress should abstain from further legislation on the slavery question.

This platform was ratified by mass meetings of Know Nothings in Baltimore and elsewhere in Maryland. At this time, July 1855, the first state convention of the party in Maryland assembled in Baltimore and nominated candidates for state officers. In addition, party members in almost all the counties nominated Know Nothing candidates for local offices. They soon found their candidates strenuously opposed in some counties by fusion tickets backed by both Democrats and Whigs. In the ensuing campaign, which was marked by considerable rioting and the use of vicious campaign methods, Henry Winter Davis, who was the American party's candidate for Congress from the Fourth District, was made a special object of attack. He had been a prominent member of the Whig party in 1852 and had then eulogized the foreign-born citizen, but in 1853 he had become a member of the secret organization in Baltimore.

In the state election in 1855 the American party achieved almost complete success, sending the ebullient Davis to Congress and carrying Baltimore City and thirteen of the twenty-one counties of the state. But neither in this election nor in any subsequent election did they carry St. Mary's, Charles, and Prince George's Counties—which were probably predominantly Catholic. When the Maryland legislature assembled in January 1856, the Know Nothing party had a majority of fifty-four out of seventy-four members of the House of Delegates and eight out of the twelve newly elected members of the Senate. But the governorship remained in the hands of the Democratic party. As a result of the ensuing deadlock, no part of the Know Nothing program was carried out. No action was taken to break up the nunneries, for it was argued that the inmates were adequately protected by the writ of *habeas corpus;* similarly no action was taken upon proposals to revise the naturalization laws, for this was held to be solely within the jurisdiction of the national government.

The Know Nothing movement had shown its greatest strength in the east, but it soon spread to the south, even as far as Texas, where it became strong enough to carry one state election. In 1855 when the party gained its notable electoral victory in Maryland, it achieved conspicuous success in several other states. Know Nothings elected a governor in Massachusetts and gained important state offices in New Hampshire, Connecticut, Rhode Island, New York, and Kentucky. Encouraged by their success in the state elections of 1855, they held a convention at Philadelphia in February 1856 for the purpose of nominating presidential and vice-presidential candidates. They first adopted a platform which was considerably more moderate than their previous pronouncements. In it they asserted that "Americans must rule America; and to this end native-born citizens should be selected for all state, federal, and municipal offices of government employment, in preference to all others." Such persons, they insisted, should be free from any allegiance "to any foreign prince, potentate, or power." They called for a period of residence of twenty-one years as a prerequisite to naturalization, but they disclaimed any intention to interfere "with the vested rights of foreigners." They opposed "any union between Church and State," any "interference with religious faith or worship," and the requirement of test oaths for office. They straddled the slavery issue in favor of vague talk about the need for harmony and fraternal goodwill. After denouncing the Democratic administration then in power the convention, which included delegates from twenty-seven states (all but Maine, Vermont, South Carolina, and Georgia), nominated ex-President Millard Fillmore for president and Andrew J. Donelson of Tennessee as his running mate.

In 1856, for the first time since the Democratic party began to name its presidential and vice-presidential candidates in conventions, it failed to meet in Baltimore. This party, whose candidate Maryland had supported with its unanimous electoral vote in 1852, met at Cincinnati and after adopting a platform which contained, among other things, a strong repudiation of the principles of the American party, nominated James Buchanan for president. Soon afterward the Republican party held its first national convention at Pittsburgh and nominated as president John C. Fremont from the new state of California. Though it was predominantly a northern party, the convention included also delegates from Delaware, Maryland, Virginia, Kentucky, and the District of Columbia. The feeble remnant of the Whig party met in Baltimore—the only party in the campaign of 1856 which held its convention there—and accepted Fillmore and Donelson as its candidates.

Maryland was not to be won over to the Republican party. In the November election it gave Fremont only 281 votes. As in the south generally, the contest in Maryland was fought out between the Know

Nothing and the Democratic candidates. In Maryland it was a bitter campaign marked by considerably more rioting and bloodshed than the previous election; fourteen persons were killed and over 250 were wounded. Baltimore, where political tensions were especially bitter, continued to merit its nickname of "Mobtown." It often became the scene of actual pitched battles between rival volunteer fire companies which sometimes deliberately perpetrated arson in order to bring on fights. Baltimoreans could rightly be charged with having a low boiling point.

In the state elections the Know Nothings elected their candidate, Thomas Swann, former president of the Baltimore and Ohio railroad, as mayor of Baltimore and carried the city of Baltimore by over 7,000 majority and the state by 8,345. Maryland therefore cast its total electoral vote for Fillmore, but was the only state that gave him any electoral votes. The national election was won by Buchanan who carried all the slave states except Maryland and, in addition, the free states of Pennsylvania, New Jersey, Indiana, Illinois, and California.

The Know Nothing party found favor in Maryland largely because of the widespread resistance to the influx of foreign immigrants. Foreign immigration into the United States as a whole increased from 408,828 in 1851 to 460,474 in 1854, and it was directed to Baltimore and to other eastern seaports which were gateways to the West. The strength of the Know-Nothing movement in Maryland was accounted for in part by resistance to the seemingly overwhelming nature of the foreign invasion. The Know Nothing program also appealed to Marylanders because it straddled the slavery question. At a time when the old Whig party was disappearing and the Democratic party was rent by bitter sectional discord, this party offered a haven to those who had lost their political moorings. As a border state Maryland favored a policy of conciliation and appeasement on the slavery question and therefore approved of the Know Nothing presidential candidate, Fillmore, who had been a Whig and had favored the Compromise of 1850.

The Know Nothing party never carried another state election except in Maryland, and as a national party it waged its first and last campaign in 1856. It failed to realize its aspirations and served only as a temporary political phenomenon—a bridge, as it were, between the older parties and new parties then forming. With the defeat of the party in the national election, the National Council of the party met at Louisville and recommended "that the American party in each State and Territory and the District of Columbia be authorized to adopt such a plan of organization as respectively may be best suited to the views of the members of the party in their several localities." Accordingly in Maryland the party nominated candidates for state offices in 1857, selecting Thomas H. Hicks of the Eastern Shore as their candidate for governor. In the election the Know Nothings carried the state, electing Hicks, the other state officials, and four out of the six congressmen and retaining control of both houses of the legislature. But the new legislature contained many inexperienced men, and its principal achievement was to adopt a bill submitting to the people of the state the question of calling a new constitutional convention although there had been no agitation for such a convention and the legislature was not required to poll the citizens of the state on this question until 1861. Their purpose, it was alleged, was to concentrate more power in the hands of the Know Nothing governor and to base representation strictly upon population in order to give Baltimore a third of the representation in the legislature. But this proposal for a new constitutional convention was voted down by the people of the state.

In the election of 1858 the Know Nothings again succeeded in gaining control of Baltimore, reelecting Mayor Swann, and retaining a large majority in the City Council. Their only opponent, the Democratic party both in the city and in the state, was completely demoralized. But the Know Nothing party was likewise disintegrating in a scramble for office, and in the election of 1859 they retained control only of Baltimore, losing the remainder of the state. The Drmocrats now carried the counties outside Baltimore and gained control of the legislature. One of their first and most important acts was to pass a police bill which took the control of the Baltimore police out of the hands of the mayor and put it in the hands of a board of four commissioners appointed by the legislature. In setting up this board, they stipulated "that no Black Republican or endorser of the Helper Book [Hinton R. Helper's *The Impending Crisis*] should be appointed to any office under said Board." After the Democratic legislature thus took the Baltimore police force out of the hands of the city administration, the Know Nothings could make little headway in the election of 1860 and lost both the mayoralty and the City Council to so-called Reform candidates. The Know Nothing party had already disappeared elsewhere in the country. In the border states its members were absorbed into the Constitutional Union party whose program on the slavery question coincided with that of the Know Nothings. After the disappearance of that party following the election of 1860, many of the Know Nothings found their way into the Republican party.

The program of the Know Nothing party in Maryland was so provocative and the opposition to it so strong that all the elections in which it participated were marked by rioting, intimidation, violence, and fraud, for which the blame as between the opposing factions was probably equally divided. On balance, the Know Nothing regime in Baltimore produced some beneficial results for the city. Among other things it administered the finances well and carried out a good program of municipal improvements, including the purchase of Druid Hill Park, the construction of a new jail, the establishment of a paid fire department, and the founding of a "Floating School" to train sailors. In general, by emphasizing certain principles of American nationalism the American party also helped to prepare the way for the intensified national feeling which triumphed in the Civil War.

The Know Nothing movement was a transitory phenomenon in American politics, arising in a period when sectional tensions were mounting, and owed its popularity largely to the escapist nature of its program. It avoided taking a clear-cut position on the crucial questions of the day, namely Negro slavery and states' rights. If the sectional controversy on these questions reached a critical pass, Maryland as a border state would assuredly be deeply implicated.

Know-Nothingism was only one of many reform movements which agitated Maryland in the 1850's, a decade of social ferment and organized pressure for moral reform through legislative action. Several of the national temperance societies established branches in Maryland and crusaded against the evils of strong drink, generally with the support of the churches and the newspaper press. They campaigned for the strict enforcement of the laws (dating from 1835) against the sale of intoxicating liquor on Sundays and tried, unsuccessfully, to secure legislation enacting statewide prohibition of the sale of strong drink except in those election districts which voted to permit it. After Maine adopted statewide prohibition in 1846 and Ohio in 1850, Maryland temperance societies intensified their campaign, only to be countered by the business interests of Baltimore, including the liquor dealers, and by newspaper opposition to any such restriction of individual liberties. The Maryland legislature would go no further than enact a law in 1848 closing all saloons on Sunday, the opposition to the Prohibitory Liquor Bill prevailed, and Maryland did not join the lengthening roll of states committed to prohibition of the sale of intoxicating liquor.

This temperance movement was gradually eclipsed by the antislavery crusade. As the new constitution of the United States was going into effect in 1789, a group of Quakers in Baltimore organized the *Maryland Society for Promoting the Abolition of Slavery and the Relief of Poor*

Negroes and Others Unlawfully Held in Bondage on the principle that all men are created free and equal and that the Negro race is as capable of improvement as the white race. One of its petitions of that year was made the subject of a significant committee report in the Maryland House of Delegates. The committee held that every free community should try to bring about the abolition of slavery, but it opposed sudden and compulsory abolition and urged instead abolition "by silent and gradual steps, with the consent of the owner." But a proposal to this effect, when introduced into the House, encountered opposition from the delegates from the large slaveholding counties and was rejected by a vote of 39 to 15. When nothing resulted from this and other petitions of the Society, it resorted to other methods—methods which the House Committee on Grievances and Courts of Justics later pronounced indecent and unjustifiable. Consequently the Society had to be disbanded.[3]

As the time approached when under the national constitution it became possible for Congress to terminate the foreign slave trade, the Assembly of Maryland in 1805 instructed their senators and representatives to use their utmost exertion to put an end to all further importation of slaves into the United States. They sent the same recommendation to the governors of all the states, and in the following year they reaffirmed their opinion that the slave trade ought to be abolished. Finally in 1807, Congress passed an act prohibiting the further importation of slaves from abroad on the first day permitted by the constitution, namely January 1, 1808.

After the adoption of the constitution and while the slave trade into the United States was still flourishing, Maryland continued her efforts to regulate the interstate trade in slaves into her territory. In 1791 the legislature allowed citizens of Maryland who owned lands in Virginia, Delaware, or Pennsylvania, and who used slaves on those lands, to bring them into Maryland and to use them on their Maryland lands but not to sell them. They also authorized citizens of Maryland who acquired slaves by inheritance or marriage in other states to bring them into the state. As a special concession to its neighbor across the Potomac, Maryland permitted citizens of Virginia who owned lands in Maryland to bring in slaves to cultivate them. When the French residents of Haiti fled from the revolution there to Maryland in 1792, Maryland allowed them to retain their slaves but limited the number that they could keep after one year to five domestic servants for a family and three for a single person and stipulated that any slaves retained in excess of these limits would become free.

In 1796 the legislature embodied these and other provisions in a general act which served for many years thereafter as a kind of code on the subject of the interstate trade in slaves into Maryland. It again forbade the importation of slaves into the state for sale but allowed citizens of the United States who settled in Maryland to bring in the slaves which they owned at the time of their removal to the state if these slaves had previously resided in the United States for three full years. But it forbade the owner of such slaves to sell them until he had lived in Maryland for three years. The law also allowed residents of Maryland who inherited slaves in an adjoining state to bring them into Maryland for their own use but not for sale, and residents of an adjoining state who owned lands in Maryland to bring in their slaves to work on those lands only. All such importations of slaves must be properly reported to the county offices. In 1802 Maryland authorized citizens of the state to bring back into the state slaves whom they hired out for use in that portion of Maryland which had been ceded to the District of Columbia; but in the following year the legislature refused to extend this privilege to a citizen of Virginia.

Maryland thereafter frequently renewed its efforts to discourage the importation of slaves into the state. In 1831 the legislature once more forbade the importation into the state of any slave for sale or for residence there, making limited exception, however, for the temporary importation of those slaves from adjoining states who would be worked on farms not more than ten miles apart and were duly recorded by the county clerk. Any slaves imported contrary to the law would be given their freedom or would be sold to the Colonization Society for the sum of five dollars and prison fees and would be transported to Liberia. The legislature continued to allow the importation of slaves acquired in another state by marriage or bequest and in certain other cases, but it collected for the use of the Colonization Society a sum of $15.00 for each slave thus imported between the ages of 12 and 45 and $5.00 for each slave outside those limits. In 1835 it allowed citizens of either Maryland or Virginia who owned lands in both states to transfer their slaves at their pleasure, and three years later it authorized any citizen of Maryland and any person coming to Maryland to reside to bring in slaves for life from any part of the United States. In 1849 the legislature repealed all laws which prohibited or taxed the importation of slaves for life from any part of the United States. By 1850 Maryland contained over 90,000 slaves—some 10,000 fewer than it had contained fifty years before. By 1860 the number had still further declined to 87,000.

Meanwhile, some slaveowners were voluntarily emancipating their slaves, as they were permitted to do by an act of 1796. In 1797 Charles Carroll of Carrollton introduced into the Maryland Senate a bill which required the state to buy up all the female Negro children, educate them, and bind them out to service until they reached the age of twenty-eight. All males and all female slaves under forty-five years of age would become free at a designated date. But the bill did not pass. Two years later the manumission of slaves was stimulated by a decision of the General Court of Maryland allowing the children of slaves to present their claims to freedom and allowing the children of one free and one slave parent to follow the status of the mother, in accordance with the Roman law. From time to time thereafter the legislature considered gradual abolition, but in 1827 they reported that it was inexpedient. They believed, however, that Maryland would soon be relieved of "this grievous national calamity" through the plan of colonization; that is, the assisted deportation of the Negroes to Africa.

Still the movement for gradual emancipation continued. In 1832 the House received a memorial from citizens of Frederick County asking that all children born of slaves should be declared free after a certain time, but they took no final action on it. Finally in 1837 the legislature added an amendment to the state constitution declaring that the relation of master and slave should not be abolished except by a unanimous vote in each branch of two successive legislatures and that it should not be altered without full compensation to the slaveowners. By that year, therefore, it appears that sentiment in favor of the institution had crystallized. Maryland either did not care to do away with slavery, dreaded the problems created by a free black population, or expected too much of the plan of colonization.

The abolitionists made many attempts to prevent the exportation of slaves from Maryland. As a result of their petitions, a committee of the House, headed by William Pinkney, reported in 1798 that so long as the constitution recognized property in slaves the state could not prohibit their exportation, and the committee deplored such petitions as tending to undermine the docility of the slaves. Similarly in 1800 another committee of the House reported against interference with slave property though they favored the gradual removal of the black population from the state and the substitution of a system of white labor. They refused, therefore, to prohibit the sale and transportation of slaves to the south, but they favored legislation to prevent the separation of husband and wife and mother and child under a certain age. But this suggestion was rejected by the House.

Maryland was seriously concerned with the problems presented by the growing numbers of free Negroes in the state. In 1783 the legislature undertook to limit their civil rights by declaring that no freed slave and no descendants of a freed slave could vote at elections, could be elected or appointed to any office, could give evidence against any white person, or could "enjoy any other rights of a freeman, other than to hold property and to obtain redress in law or equity for any injury to his person or property." From time to time the legislature passed strict laws to prevent the fraudulent sale or transportation of free Negroes as slaves. In the general act of 1796 they imposed a penalty of $800 or work on the roads for not more than five years upon anyone who sold a free Negro into slavery. Later the legislature required that all purchasers of slaves for removal from the state must be given bills of sale fully identifying the slaves. In general, they refused to allow the removal from the state of Negro slaves entitled to their freedom within a definite term of years unless their owners would give good security to return them or free them at the expiration of their terms of service.

Free Negroes were denied the exercise of all political rights under a state law of 1802 which vested the political power of the state exclusively in free white male citizens. After the slave insurrection led by Nat Turner which occurred in Southampton County, Virginia, in the summer of 1831, and which resulted in the slaughter of several white persons, new limitations were imposed upon the activities of free Negroes in Maryland. Among these limitations were laws forbidding them to possess firearms or powder and to hold secret meetings. In 1841 slaveholders of Anne Arundel County held a large public meeting and resolved to summon a convention "of the persons favorable to the protection of the slaveholding interests in the State." When the Slave Holders Convention assembled in Annapolis early in the following year, it included representatives from every county in the state except Carroll, Allegany, Caroline, and Worcester. They adopted many recommendations favoring restrictions upon the free Negroes, most of which were subsequently enacted into law by the legislature.

By 1820 the free Negroes in Maryland formed one-fourth of the total number of Negroes in the state. Ten years later this fraction had increased to one-third, and Maryland had the largest number, 52,938 of free colored people of any state in the Union. By 1840 free Negroes constituted two-fifths of the total Negro population of Maryland, and by 1860 they numbered nearly 84,000 out of a total state population of 687,000.

Some of Maryland's free Negroes not only amassed considerable property, even property in Negro slaves, but gained some measure of intellectual distinction. One of Maryland's free Negroes who rose to prominence was Benjamin Banneker. Born of a free white mother and a slave father, he was enabled to attend a "pay" school near Ellicott's Mills and there attracted the attention of George Ellicott, who offered him the use of his personal library and tools. Banneker developed into an outstanding astronomer and mathematician. He published one of the first United States almanacs and assisted in surveying the District of Columbia.

Another Maryland Negro, Ira Frederick Aldridge, allegedly born in Bel Air in Harford County early in the nineteenth century, was apprenticed to a ship carpenter but, in some way not recorded came to the notice of the great English actor Edmund Kean on his visit to the United States in 1826 and returned to England with him. In England and on the continent of Europe Aldridge won great distinction as an actor in both tragic and comic roles, starring especially as Othello, Lear, and Macbeth, and for his acting talent he was awarded high honors by European governments and cultural organizations.

The free Negroes in Maryland had their own schools and religious organizations, but the census of 1860 revealed that only 1,355 free black children in Maryland were attending school. Negro education was neglected because of the general two-fold assumption by the dominant white slaveholding class that the Negro was uneducable and that if taught to read and write he would not be content to remain a docile member of the labor force. The education of Negro children was therefore left almost entirely to generous and dedicated Negro teachers, such as Daniel Coker who escaped from slavery to freedom and established a school for Negro children in Baltimore.

The segregation and subordination to which Maryland blacks were subjected led to the formation of black or "African" branches of the Methodist, Episcopal, Baptist, and Presbyterian churches early in the nineteenth century. In 1816 under the leadership of Daniel Coker, an African Methodist Episcopal Church was formed in Baltimore. The earliest Negro Episcopal congregation was the St. James First African Episcopal Church which was formed in 1824 by a black Episcopal clergyman, the Reverend William Levington, and incorporated under the laws of Maryland in 1828. Eight years later the First African Baptist Church was established at Old Town in Baltimore. During the 1840's an exclusively Negro Presbyterian Church was formed without any connections with the white Presbyterian church and one of its early ministers was the Reverend Hiram R. Revels, who five years after the end of the Civil War was elected by the state of Mississippi as the first Negro member of the Senate in Washington. By 1847 Baltimore had thirteen Negro congregations, some with as many as 1,000 members.[4]

Free Negroes, laboring under both racial and legal handicaps, ardently supported the cause of abolition, even assisting slaves to freedom by way of the Underground Railway at the risk of their own freedom. Over this Underground Railroad hundreds of fugitive slaves from Maryland and other states of the south found their way to freedom. Among the traffic managers on this transit route to freedom, one of the most active was Harriet Tubman, a Maryland slave born in Dorchester County on the Eastern Shore, who after escaping north in 1848 made nineteen perilous forays into the southern states on missions of liberation of her people and conducted more than 300 slaves to freedom north of the Mason-Dixon line. She never learned to read or write but established a notable record as a successful violator of the fugitive slave law.

Since the rapid increase in the number of free Negroes was very distasteful to the slaveholders and was deemed a threat to peace and order, the legislature began to give financial support to the American Colonization Society in 1827. This Society had been formed in Washington in 1816 for the purpose of transporting free Negroes from the United States and colonizing them in Africa. Its officers included several Marylanders—John Eager Howard, Samuel Smith, and Francis Scott Key. In 1831 a branch of this Society was organized in Baltimore under the auspices of a group of prominent Baltimore businessmen and was incorporated by the state. It immediately fitted out the *Orion* to make regular voyages to Liberia carrying Maryland Negroes. To these early Negro emigrants from Maryland the Society gave shoes, coffee, pots, hoes, flaxseeds, merchandise, hardwares, spades, and shovels and "$3.45 apiece to purchase an acre in the new world."[5] The Society opposed the emancipation of slaves unless arrangements were made for their deportation.

The Maryland legislature was encouraged by the Nat Turner insurrection to give financial assistance to this colonization project. Frightened by this uprising, the state decided to collaborate with the newly reorganized Maryland Colonization Society to facilitate the voluntary removal of Negroes already free and the forcible removal of those subsequently freed. Maryland continued to make annual appropriations to the Society up to the eve of the Civil War, but this project was an unqualified failure. The Society's threat of enforced deportation was never carried out, and the number of free Negroes who were willing to exchange America for Africa was very small. In this effort the Society acted independently of the national society.⁶ All adult emigrants to Liberia were required to sign a pledge to support the constitution of the colony in Liberia and to abstain from liquor. The Maryland Society retained the right to make the laws for the colony but gave the colonists a bill of rights which included freedom of religion, trial by jury, and the prohibition of slavery. It optimistically declared that its ultimate objective was the eradication of the institution of slavery, but its method proved extremely costly.

In 1834 the Maryland Colonization Society purchased territory in Liberia running 130 miles along the Atlantic Coast and indefinitely into the interior. Between 1831 and 1858 it colonized only 1,250 free Negroes in Liberia at a cost of $301,088 of which sum it received $255,703 from the state. The cost of removing each Negro therefore amounted to more than $2,400. But by this action Maryland assisted significantly in the founding of Liberia. It made larger contributions, financially and numerically, to the establishment of this first Negro republic in Africa than did several other states put together. "Maryland in Liberia," as Maryland's colony there was called, proclaimed its independence in 1854, but was annexed to the Republic of Liberia three years later and became Maryland County. In 1864 a Baltimore-born free Negro, Daniel Bashiel Warner, became the third president of Liberia and served a four-year term.

Slaves in Maryland were, in general, given better treatment than those required to labor in the more competitive economy of the states in the Deep South. In their free time the field hands could cultivate broomcorn in their little garden patches, make brooms, braid wheat straw into useful articles, trap rabbits, otters, foxes, and muskrats, and participate in the convivial "hoedowns." At Christmastime the old family servants would wait upon their master and mistress to wish them a Merry Christmas and to receive gifts of clothing or money as well as jugs of rum or gin for their own merrymakings in the slave quarters. There in the evenings they cleared the cabin floor and danced the jig or the juba, the latter a tribal import from Africa accompanied by vigorous shouts, cries, shuffling of feet, and hand clapping as the fiddler played and the slaves sang:

> Juba up and juba down,
> Juba all aroun' de town;
> Sift de meal, and gimme de husk;
> Bake de cake, and gimme de crus';
> Fry de pork, and gimme de skin;
> Ax me when I'm comin' ag'in;
>   Juba! hi, juba!

Juba in and juba out,
Juba, juba, all about;
Dinah, stir de possum fat;
Can't you hear de juba pot?
　　Juba![7]

The slave system created a sheltered social environment for the white women of Maryland. It largely exempted them from manual labor and encouraged them to indulge in a gay round of social activities. English visitors vying with each other to select the American city which displayed the most beautiful women agreed that "Baltimore held first place." [8]

Because of the chivalrous attitude which men were expected to show toward women in the plantation economy of the southern states, among which Maryland was numbered, women who were obliged to work engaged in such occupations as teaching, the preparation of food, the nursing and education of children, and the making of hats and dresses. Their status would be altered, however, by the Civil War, which brought out the initiative and independent spirit of Maryland women.

The controversy over slavery exerted a bitterly divisive effect upon some of the church organizations. The Catholic and Episcopal churches in Maryland were little disturbed by it and officially maintained a neutral position, but the Methodist church was badly shaken by it and when the national organization divided in northern and southern branches in 1845, the Maryland Methodists adhered to the northern branch, which opposed slavery. In the same year, Maryland Baptists sided with the Southern Baptist Convention. The Presbyterians succeeded in postponing a division until 1861, when some Maryland churches joined the newly formed Southern Presbyterian Church and others remained loyal to the northern organization.

In Maryland, as in the other border states, slavery as a labor system was gradually disappearing. These states were undergoing a process which had already worked itself out in the northern states, where a more temperate climate and the innovations of the factory system had rendered the slave labor system largely obsolete and where free labor was proving to be a superior method of production. Their experience was pointing toward a future which southern plantation interests, bound to their heavy investment in slaves and to their preoccupation with a single-crop economy, refused to accept. For the preservation of their system they relied upon constitutional safeguards which clearly recognized the pluralistic and diversified nature of American society but these were threatened by northern antislavery forces, which in 1860 gained control of the new Republican party.

Footnotes

[1] Douglas Bowers, "Ideology and Political Parties in Maryland, 1851-1856," *Maryland Historical Magazine*, vol. 64, No. 3, Fall 1969, pp. 197-217.

[2] Quoted in Laurence F. Schmeckebier, *History of the Know Nothing Party in Maryland*, Johns Hopkins Press, Baltimore, 1899; reprint 1973, p. 11.

[3] Kenneth L. Carroll, "Maryland Quakers and Slavery," *Maryland Historical Magazine*, vol. XLV, No. 3, September 1950, pp. 215-225.

[4] Carter Woodson, *History of the Negro Church*, Washington, 1921, p. 65; and Reverend George F. Bragg, *Men of Maryland*, Church Advocate Press, Baltimore, Maryland, 1925, pp. 21-26.

[5] W. McKenny, *Report to the Executive Committee of the Board, a List of Articles to be Distributed in Liberia*, Baltimore, 1832.

[6] Aaron Stopak, "The Maryland State Colonization Society: Independent State Action in the Colonization Movement," *Maryland Historical Society*, vol. 63, No. 3, September 1968, pp. 275-298.

[7] Beta Kaessmann, Harold Randall Manakee, and Joseph L. Wheeler, *My Maryland*, Maryland Historical Society, Baltimore, 1955, p. 117; Harold Courlander, *Negro Folk Music, U.S.A.*, Columbia University Press, New York and London, 1969, pp. 191-192; and Eileen Southern, *The Music of Black Americans: A History*, W.W. Norton & Company, Inc., New York, 1971, p. 121.

[8] M. Berger, *The British Traveler in America, 1836-60*, Columbia University Faculty of Political Science, Studies in History, Economics and Public Law, No. 502, Columbia University Press, New York, 1943, p. 77. See also Charles Dickens, *American Notes*, reprinted in *The Baltimore News*, May 7, 1922.

Sources and Additional Reading

Alexander, Archibald, *A History of Colonization on the Western Coast of Africa*, W.S. Martien, Philadelphia, 1849.

Bohner, Charles H., *John Pendleton Kennedy: Gentleman from Baltimore*, Johns Hopkins Press, Baltimore, 1961.

Bragg, Reverend George F., *Men of Maryland*, Church Advocate Press, Baltimore, Maryland, 1925.

Campbell, Penelope, *Maryland in Africa: The Maryland State Colonization Society, 1831-1857*, University of Illinois Press, Urbana, 1971.

Desmond, Humphrey J., *The Know-Nothing Party*, Washington, The New Century Press, 1903.

Douglass, Frederick, *My Bondage and My Freedom*, Miller, Orton and Mulligan, New York, 1855.

Eastman, Ernest, *A History of the State of Maryland in Liberia*, Monrovia, Liberia, 1946.

Forer, Philip S., *Frederick Douglass,* The Citadel Press, New York, 1969.

Jennings, Francis, *Early Activities of the Maryland Colonization Society,* Columbia University Press, New York, 1954.

Latrobe, John, *Maryland in Liberia,* Peabody Publication Fund, Baltimore, 1885.

Maryland, Board of World's Fair Managers, *Maryland, its Resources, Industries, and Institutions,* prepared for, by members of Johns Hopkins University and others, Sun Job Printing Office, Baltimore, 1893.

McConville, Mary St. Patrick, *Political Nativism in the State of Maryland, 1830-1860,* The Catholic University of America, Washington, 1928.

McKenny, W., *Report to the Executive Committee of the Board, A List of Articles to be Distributed in Liberia,* Baltimore, 1832.

Overdyke, W. Darrell, *The Know-Nothing Party in the South,* Louisiana State University Press, Baton Rouge, 1950.

Schmeckebier, Lawrence F., *History of the Know-Nothing Party in Maryland,* Johns Hopkins University Studies, Series 17, Nos. 4, 5, Johns Hopkins Press, Baltimore, 1899, reprint 1973.

Semmes, John Edward, *John H.B. Latrobe and His Times, 1803-1891,* Norman, Remington Co., Baltimore, 1917.

Tuckerman, Henry Theodore, *The Life of John Pendleton Kennedy,* G.P. Putnam & Sons, New York, 1871.

Woodson, Carter G., *History of the Negro Church,* Associated Publishers, Washington, 1921.

Wright, James Martin, *The Free Negro in Maryland, 1634-1860,* Columbia University Studies in History, Economics and Public Law, vol. XCVII, No. 3, Columbia University Press, New York, 1921.

CHAPTER XXII

THE BROTHERS' WAR

Maryland, by reason of its geographical situation and its economic interests, was cast in the role of a border state between North and South long before the shooting war between the sections began. It was a meeting ground where they came together, and it combined the qualities of both. Maryland was dependent upon foreign markets as were the commercial states to the north. But its staple export, tobacco, was the same as that of the southern states. Its intermediate position between the northern commercial states and the southern agricultural states would enable it to play a crucial role in the looming conflict. Baltimore, in particular, observed an astute English visitor in 1840, seemed to unite "the intelligence of the North with the frankness and generosity of the South," and to "avoid the mercenary spirit of the one and the reckless daring of the other."

In the early phases of the Civil War slavery was minimized as the central issue in the struggle. Emphasis was placed rather upon the preservation of the Union. But Maryland was a slave state. In this respect it had a closer kinship with the South than with the North. Its slave population dwindled after 1800, but by 1850 slaves still represented more than one-sixth of the population of the state. According to the national census for that year, they numbered 90,368 out of a total population of 583,034 and were concentrated in the tobacco-growing counties of Calvert, Charles, Prince George's, Anne Arundel, and St. Mary's. In these agricultural counties of southern Maryland were found 46.6 percent of the total slave population of the state. These counties and the counties of the Eastern Shore were bastions of Southern sympathy. They had escaped the rush of foreign immigrants. Their white populations had remained homogeneous and therefore largely unaffected by the ideas brought in by northern abolitionists and foreign groups who opposed slavery on ideological grounds. By 1860 Negro slaves constituted one-fifth of the population of the Eastern Shore.

But in northern and western Maryland slavery was on the way to extinction. In those sections it could not be adapted to the prevailing economy of small farming operations, manufacturing, and commerce.[1] In Baltimore, which itself occupied an intermediate position between the tidewater area and the western counties, public opinion on the

North-South question was almost equally divided. Strong opposition to the Southern position was expressed by the large German population, particularly in the daily German *Wecker,* the monthly *Die Fackel,* and *Turn Zeitung,* which were the only antislavery journals published in Maryland. As Baltimore preeminently the manufacturing center of the state, it ceased to need slave labor. Between 1830 and 1860 its slave population declined from approximately 6,000 to just over 2,000, and its free Negro population more than doubled in the same period, to over 25,000. Of the dwindling slave population of Baltimore some were employed as house servants, though their places were increasingly being taken by free Negroes, and many others, who possessed special skills or trades, were put out by their masters as contract laborers. Among this latter group was Frederick Douglass, born of a white father and a slave mother in Talbot County on the Eastern Shore of Maryland, who worked as a caulker in Baltimore shipyards until he escaped north. As a free man he joined William Lloyd Garrison in the abolitionist movement and used his extraordinary gifts in both publications and lecturing on behalf of the freedom of his race.[2] After the Civil War he would rise up to become one of the leaders of the freedmen and would serve as United States minister to Haiti by appointment of President Benjamin Harrison.

In western Maryland sentiment was predominantly opposed to slavery. The economy of that section had never depended upon tobacco culture or its concomitant slavery. When the German farmers there needed extra help on their farms they chose to call upon their neighbors rather than employ slave labor. Besides, some of the German religious sects, as for example, the Moravian, expressly forbade slaveholding. The few slaveholders in these mountainous counties were unable to prevent the escape of their slaves across the Mason-Dixon line into the free state of Pennsylvania, and they received little cooperation from officials of that state for the return of their runaways.

In general, slavery continued to flourish only in the tobacco counties, and it was becoming economically unprofitable in the manufacturing, commercial, and grain-growing areas of the state. Because Maryland (except in the tobacco counties) had less use for slave labor than states in the cotton south, it became a breeder of Negroes for the plantations in the deep south. Slave traders sought out runaway slaves and often kidnapped free Negroes for sale to the plantations of Alabama, Louisiana, and Mississippi. As late as 1857, fourteen slave traders were listed in the Baltimore City Directory.[3] But traders who engaged in this business were treated as social outcasts.

According to the census of 1860 the slaves in the state in that year numbered 87,189 out of a total population of 687,000. They were owned by some 16,000 slaveholders. Maryland's free Negro population meanwhile had risen from 74,723 in 1850 to 83,942. All told, nearly one-fourth of the total population of the state, or 171,131, were Negroes—87,000 slaves and 84,000 free. In almost every part of the state Negroes, whether slave or free, were segregated from the whites in public places, including churches. Free Negroes were required to carry their "free papers" with them at all times and to show them when travelling on ship lines or railroads.

During the 1850's the Fugitive Slave Law, *Uncle Tom's Cabin,* the Kansas-Nebraska bill, the struggle for Kansas between slaveholders and free-soilers, the Dred Scott decision—all these created serious divisions in public opinion in Maryland. Runaway slaves fleeing from Maryland could reach free soil very quickly, for Pennsylvania had abolished slavery during the Revolution. As early as 1798, Maryland legislators expressed concern over the escape of their slaves to Delaware, Pennsylvania, and New Jersey. In 1820 they passed a resolution calling attention of Congress to the aid which the Pennsylvanians were giving to runaway slaves, and they requested the members of Congress from Maryland to use their influence to secure legislation protecting the rights of slaveholders. In subsequent sessions the legislature entered into direct communication with the authorities of Pennsylvania, New Jersey, and Delaware to this end. In 1837 and again in 1843 the Assembly passed resolutions declaring that no state could abridge the rights guaranteed to all citizens by the United States Constitution and calling for a national law to make the rescue of a captured fugitive a criminal offense. Their demand for a national fugitive slave law was strengthened by the decision of the United States Supreme Court in the case of *Prigg versus Pennsylvania* in 1842, declaring a Pennsylvania statute of 1826 regulating the return of runaway bondsmen to be unconstitutional because only the Congress had the authority to legislate on this matter.

Such a law was enacted by Congress with the unanimous support of the Maryland delegation as a part of the Compromise of 1850. In the following year, Maryland was deeply agitated by the violation of this law by Pennsylvania in the so-called Christiana Riot. Edward Gorsuch, his son and a few friends, accompanied by United States Deputy Marshal Kline, traveled to Christiana in Lancaster County, Pennsylvania, to arrest and bring back to Baltimore County four fugitive slaves belonging to Gorsuch. Before they could serve warrants for the arrest of the slaves as they were legally entitled to do under the

Fugitive Slave Law, the Marylanders were set upon by a group of Negroes and abolitionists; Gorsuch was killed, his body mutilated, and his son was left for dead. For this violation of national law the perpetrators of the riot were brought to trial in Independence Hall in Philadelphia but were acquitted both by the federal court and later by the courts of Pennsylvania. Maryland slave interests were outraged at the mockery of these trials.

The decision of the Supreme Court in *Dred Scott versus Sandford* was handed down by Chief Justice Taney only a few days after Buchanan's inauguration. The case arose when Scott, a Missouri slave, sued for his freedom on the ground that he had been taken by his master, an army surgeon, into the free state of Illinois and later into the territory of Wisconsin. By his residence in those two places outside the area of slavery, his attorneys contended, he had been released from bondage. Dred Scott's leading counsel was Montgomery Blair of Maryland who was opposed by another Marylander, Reverdy Johnson. In the decision of the court Taney held that Scott was not a citizen of Missouri because he was a slave and he remained a slave despite his periods of residence in Wisconsin and Illinois. He then proceeded to invalidate the Missouri Compromise of 1820 on the ground that Congress had no constitutional authority to legislate on the question of slavery in the territories. Since the constitution recognized the right of property in slaves, Taney declared, the government was bound to protect the rights of the owner in his slaves.

Taney himself was not a slaveholder, for he had manumitted all his slaves except two some thirty years before the Dred Scott decision. As those two were too old to support themselves, he had provided for them as long as they lived. Quite apart from his personal views on the institution of slavery his decision in the Dred Scott case represented an impeccably literal and veracious construction of the constitution. But the decision, so hostile to the position taken by the Republican party, drove a wedge into the Democratic party and prepared the way for the split in the party between the northern and southern wings which appeared in 1860.

In Maryland the Dred Scott decision failed to create the elation that it evoked throughout the rest of the south. Maryland was inclined to take a middle-of-the-road attitude on all the issues that led up to the Civil War. It did not belong exclusively to any one section—south, north, or west. It was the mirror of a nation in quandary, deeply perplexed by the consequences of the failure of the authors of the national constitution to solve the problem of Negro slavery seventy years earlier and to make provision against a break-up of the federal union. Strong sentiment for states' rights and limited national government was found in Maryland. Maryland as the Free State was committed to the principle that the central government of the Union was the creature and not the master of the states which composed it. Conceiving the Union as essentially an alliance of free states united for certain specific purposes set forth in the constitution, Marylanders could scarcely deny the right of secession to any partner to the federal compact. At the same time Maryland was a slave state and lay south of the Mason-Dixon line. But Marylanders did not share the extreme viewpoints of the deep south on the slavery question, and they had built up and long maintained close connections—commercial as well as political —with the free states of the north and northwest.

Maryland's attitude toward the sectional controversy corresponded to its long tradition of moderation and compromise. From this attitude it was swayed in part by the influence of foreign immigrants and by other non-native Marylanders. Of Maryland's total free population of 515,918 in 1860, the foreign-born, coming mostly from Germany and Ireland, numbered 77,536, and they were favorably inclined toward the North. Of Maryland's population at that time, 24,386 were born in northern states, and of these all but 1,176 had migrated to Maryland from the free states of Pennsylvania, New York, New Jersey, and Massachusetts. Baltimore's textile mills used southern cotton, but her flour mills, thanks to the Baltimore and Ohio Railroad, milled the grain of the Old Northwest, where slavery had been abolished by the Ordinance of 1787. Baltimore merchants could see no profit for themselves in a division of the Union which might cause them to forfeit the trade of either the North or the South.

As the sectional tensions tightened into civil war, Maryland's role was rendered particularly difficult by her intermediate geographical situation. Besides, she surrounded the national capital on three sides. If Maryland cast her fortune with the South, Washington would be surrounded by enemy territory and cut off from communication with the North. Her attitudes and policies might have decisive importance on the outcome of the sectional struggle. In addition, the accession of Maryland to the southern cause would add some twenty percent to the South's total industrial output.

Just before the triumph of the anti-Know Nothing or Reform party, Maryland was the scene of one of the dramatic incidents leading to the Civil War. Early in July 1859, "Captain" John Brown, a fanatical abolitionist from Connecticut who had been engaging in guerrilla warfare against slaveholders in Kansas, appeared near Harpers Ferry with two of his sons and a son-in-law and under the assumed name of Isaac Smith rented a small farm on the Maryland side of the Potomac. There he ostensibly began farming operations. After receiving arms from his friends in the North, Brown and his party, now increased to eighteen in number, crossed the bridge connecting Harpers Ferry with the Maryland shore on Sunday night, October 16, 1859, and on reaching the other side, proceeded to take possession of the armory and arsenal of the United States. Their purpose was to use Harpers Ferry as a base for revolutionizing the entire slave population of the South. They would then lead the slaves to "freedom."

News of the attack was first brought to Baltimore by passengers on a Baltimore and Ohio train which passed through Harpers Ferry just after the raid. Immediately five companies of troops under command of Lieutenant-Colonel Egerton were dispatched to the scene of the disturbance, and at Sandy Hook, about one and one-half miles east of Harpers Ferry, they were joined by a detachment of marines commanded by Colonel Robert E. Lee, who ordered Egerton to remain on the Maryland side of the river while he proceeded with the marines to Harpers Ferry and occupied the armory grounds. Already several volunteer companies from Virginia and three from Frederick had arrived at Harpers Ferry and forced Brown's raiders to withdraw into the armory enclosure, taking with them eleven prisoners. After a short fight, Lee succeeded in breaking into the armory and capturing Brown and his associates. They escorted them to Charleston, Virginia, where soon afterward they were tried and indicted for conspiring with Negroes to cause an insurrection, for treason to the commonwealth of Virginia, and for murder. Brown and all his associates were found guilty and were hanged by the authorities of Virginia. It had been Brown's purpose to liberate the slaves, but he found no disposition among them to respond to his appeal.

Brown's suicidal assault on Harpers Ferry revived southern fears of a Negro insurrection and further intensified the already warlike bitterness between North and South. It evoked little sympathy in Maryland and prompted the Maryland legislature to appropriate $70,000 for the purchase of arms and other military equipment for distribution among the local military companies throughout the state to be used in suppressing Negro uprisings and resisting abolitionist propaganda. The platform of the "black" Republicans who agitated the slavery question and proposed to limit the further extension of slavery aroused almost no enthusiasm in Maryland. The legislature passed a resolution declaring that any combination of Maryland's representatives in Congress with the Republicans there would be contrary to the wishes of the people of the state.

When Congress was organized in December 1859, the Republicans supported John Sherman of Ohio as speaker, and after almost two months of voting, they came within four votes of electing him. They finally switched their support to another Republican, William Pennington of New Jersey, and succeeded in electing him speaker. Henry Winter Davis of Maryland cast his vote for Pennington, and for this action the Maryland legislature censured him in a resolution declaring that "Henry Winter Davis, acting in Congress as one of the representatives of this State by his vote for Pennington, the candidate of the Black Republican Party for the Speakership of the House of Representatives, has misrepresented the sentiments of all portions of this State, and thereby forfeited the confidence of her people." This resolution was adopted overwhelmingly by a vote of 62 to 1. In the next election held in the fall of 1860, Davis lost his seat in Congress.

In the presidential campaign of 1860, the Democratic party was hopelessly split. After several southern delegations withdrew from the Charleston convention, the party adjourned and reconvened in Baltimore in May to nominate Stephen A. Douglas of Illinois for president. The seceding Democrats nominated John C. Breckinridge of Kentucky. At Baltimore also the Constitutional Union party held its first and only national convention in the same month and after adopting a platform which vaguely called for support of "the Constitution of the country, the union of the States, and the enforcement of the laws," nominated John Bell of Tennessee for president. Maryland was represented by a delegation at the Republican convention in Chicago which nominated Abraham Lincoln of Illinois. For this nomination the leaders of the Maryland delegation, Francis P. Blair and his son, Montgomery Blair, were partly responsible.

In the election in the following November, Marylanders divided their vote almost equally between Breckinridge (42,482 votes), candidate of the Southern Democratic or secessionist party, and Bell (41,760 votes), representing the Constitutional Union party. Maryland therefore cast her eight electoral votes for Breckinridge. To the regular candidate of the Democratic party, Douglas, Maryland gave only 5,966 votes and to Lincoln only 2,294 votes. Two counties in the state gave Lincoln not a single vote. For Maryland, Lincoln was unacceptable as president.

In this crucial election, Maryland, like the nation as a whole, divided along sectional lines; the state was split between allegiance to the federal union under the constitution of 1787 and loyalty to the principle of state's rights which had now come to be identified with the institution of Negro slavery and which was therefore being pressed by the southern slaveholders at this particular juncture in the history of the nation. But Maryland had long been committed to the states' rights position, and the vote of the electorate in 1860 only confirmed the views often expressed by her leading public figures that Maryland recognized the right of secession against an overpowering central government. But the margin of secessionist strength was slight, for an almost equal number of voters favored the constitution and the preservation of the Union. In this latter direction Maryland was pulled by her industrial and financial ties with the north and west.

In that election Maryland's governor, Thomas H. Hicks, supported Bell. Hicks, a native of the Eastern Shore and a slaveholder, had been elected governor as a Know Nothing in 1857, and in his inaugural address, delivered in the Senate chamber in January 1858, he recommended Maryland's favorite project of transporting the Negroes beyond the national borders to the Caribbean Islands or to Africa. On the great question then agitating the country, he explained that "Maryland is devoted to the Union of all of the States" but had refused "to join with the misguided people of the northern states in their assaults on slavery."

Soon after Lincoln's election, all of the slaveholding states, including Maryland, were invited by South Carolina to send delegates to a convention to devise means of defending themselves against northern aggression and to take under consideration the question of seceding from the Union. The Maryland legislature in reply announced that Maryland declared its "fixed determination to cling to the Union so long as its principles can be preserved," but it assured "our brethren of South Carolina that should the hour ever arrive when the Union must be dissolved, Maryland will cast her lot with her sister states of the South and abide their fortune to the fullest extent." Before Lincoln could be inaugurated in March 1861, seven southern states—South Carolina, Mississippi, Florida, Alabama, Georgia, Louisiana, and Texas—had withdrawn from the Union. They expected Maryland soon to join them, and Jefferson Davis, president of the Confederacy, speaking at Richmond on February 22, 1861, predicted hopefully that "Maryland already united to us by hallowed ties and material interests will, when able to speak with an unstifled voice, unite her destiny with the South."

After Lincoln's election, Hicks was bombarded with petitions from people of the state urging him to summon the legislature into special session and to secure from the incoming Lincoln administration some guaranties of slavery. But Hicks rejected these suggestions. He and his party had lost control of the legislature to the Democrats in 1859, and he explained in a public statement on November 27, 1860, that, if called into session, the legislature would only increase excitement. Though he expressed sympathy with the South and indignation at the refusal of the North to enforce the Fugitive Slave laws, he counseled moderation. He distrusted the legislature. He knew that it had been elected eighteen months before the secession crisis became acute and that Speaker Kilbourn was openly advocating secession. Hicks' refusal to summon the legislature was approved by President Buchanan.

As the crisis of the civil war approached, the governor's actions and words were often inconsistent. He acted like a man trying to keep his footing on a log swirling in a midstream rapids. In a public proclamation early in January 1861, the temporizing Hicks condemned violations of the Fugitive Slave laws but at the same time condemned secession by the southern states as unjust and inexpedient. As a statement of the wisdom of a policy of inactivity, his proclamation received widespread approval in the North. But his only policy seemed to be one of opportunism. In this he undoubtedly reflected the indecision and perplexity of the people of his state. As for the Baltimore *Sun,* perhaps the most widely read newspaper in the state, its editor, Arunah S. Abell, sympathized with the South but opposed secession, but his partner was a Unionist in sympathies.

The vacillating Hicks meanwhile was holding long unofficial conferences with representatives from both northern and southern states. He carried on correspondence with the governors of Virginia, Tennessee, Kentucky, and Missouri. Though he admitted the abstract right of secession, he disapproved of immediate secession. And yet when the governor of Mississippi telegraphed Hicks that his state had withdrawn from the Union, Hicks wrote on the envelope, "Mississippi has seceded and gone to the devil." During those months he was a deeply troubled man. He deplored bloodshed and hasty action, and he became increasingly convinced that the national government would use force to bring the seceded states back into the Union. In that eventuality, Maryland would become a theater of war and would suffer bloodshed and destruction.

Hicks, together with officials of other border states, favored and worked for compromise between North and South. He sent a strong delegation of seven members to the peace conference that was held on the initiative of Virginia in Washington in February 1861. There twenty-one states, including all the southern states which had not seceded and most of the free states, were represented. Maryland was represented on the important Committee on Resolutions by Reverdy Johnson. The Maryland delegation deprecated secession, but they also opposed coercion of the seceded states. The report of the conference proposed an amendment to the Constitution containing seven sections as follows: (1) The Missouri Compromise line would be restored and would thus be embedded in the Constitution where it would be safe from adverse action by the Supreme Court. New states might come into the Union with or without slavery as they themselves might determine in their own constitutions; (2) no new territory would be acquired except by treaty, and such treaty would have to be ratified by four-fifths of all the members of the Senate; (3 and 4) the Supreme Court would be forbidden to interpret the Constitution in such a way as to give Congress power over slavery or to prevent the states from enforcing the Fugitive Slave Law; (5) Congress should provide compensation for escaped slaves; (6) the foreign slave trade should remain forever prohibited; and (7) no section of the Constitution, including these sections, should be amended or abolished without the consent of all the states.

But this compromise plan proposed by the peace conference was so similar to the plan which Senator John Crittenden of Kentucky had already presented and which had been vetoed by the president-elect that it passed almost unnoticed. This last attempt at compromise therefore ended in failure.

Meanwhile, rumors of a plot to seize the capital and prevent Lincoln's inauguration had been circulating. Anti-secessionists in the North looked to Maryland and particularly to its governor to resist this plot. Hicks himself believed the rumors and asked General Winfield Scott if he could secure two thousand arms from the national government to "meet an emergency if it shall arise." Scott himself took precautions to increase the number of troops in Washington. Hicks appeared before a committee of the House of Representatives set up in January 1861 to investigate whether "any secret organization hostile to the government of the United States existed." But his testimony was so vague that he appeared to have been unduly credulous. As Lincoln proceeded east from Springfield, he was warned in Philadelphia of plots against his life, and, against his better judgment, he permitted Allan Pinkerton, head of a detective agency, to convey him secretly through Baltimore to Washington where he was inaugurated president on March 4.

With Lincoln's inauguration the country entered upon a period of unprecedented turmoil and confusion. Hicks had two interviews with

Lincoln early in March and was probably consulted about cabinet appointments. Though he subsequently denied that he had recommended anyone to Lincoln, the pugnacious Marylander, Montgomery Blair, would hardly have been appointed postmaster-general in Lincoln's cabinet without Hicks' approval.

Thus far, Maryland's policy in the crisis had been one of conciliation and appeasement dictated by her geographical position as a border state and by her economic ties with both North and South. Two nations were facing each other—the United States, which had been established as independent since 1783; the other, the Confederate States which was newly claiming its independence. The apparent indecision of the Lincoln administration toward the upstart Confederacy to the south ended early in April when Lincoln, against the advice of all but one member of his cabinet, Blair, decided to send reinforcements to Fort Sumter in Charleston harbor and thus provoked the shooting war. What would have happened if South Carolina had quietly accepted Lincoln's decision, had withheld its gunfire, but had continued to maintain its legal position and its rights as a state in a new nation, is an interesting subject for speculation. Up to that time the legal position of the seceded states was unassailable, but in the matter of the reinforcement of Sumter they were maneuvered into firing the first shot.

Lincoln's call for 75,000 troops on April 15 imperiled the national capital. In order to protect it, a company of Baltimore Turners, members of the German *Turnverein,* secretly went to Washington, joined other companies of German volunteers from Washington and Georgetown, and held the city until the arrival of northern troops. Lincoln's call for troops dashed the hopes of the compromisers and drove four more slave states—Virginia, Arkansas, North Carolina, and Tennessee—out of the Union. Maryland was now more than ever isolated as one of only four slave states (the others were Delaware, Kentucky, and Missouri) that still remained in the Union. Would Maryland secede? Its defection to the Confederacy would isolate the nation's capital from the north. Hicks hurried to Washington and reported to Lincoln, General Scott, and Secretary of War Simon Cameron that the people of Maryland were intensely opposed to coercion of the southern states. From these officials he received assurances that Maryland troops would be used not for coercion but only for the defense of the "public property of the United States within the limits of the State of Maryland" and "for the protection of the Federal Capital."

When the governor returned to Baltimore, he found the city in a fever of excitement. Accordingly, both he and Mayor George William

Brown issued proclamations appealing to the people to maintain order and assuring them that no troops would pass through Baltimore except those intended for the defense of Washington. But so high were pro-southern feelings running that when the Massachusetts Sixth Regiment arrived in Baltimore on April 19, they were attacked by mobs. In the ensuing melee eight civilians and four soldiers were killed. The mayor made an ineffectual effort to curb this violence by marching at the head of the troops. Feeling against the Lincoln government was further stimulated at a mass meeting held that afternoon in Monument Square where Severn Teackle Wallis and other speakers, including Governor Hicks, opposed the coercion of the southern states. Hicks defiantly declared: "I am a Marylander, I love my State, and I love the Union, but I will suffer my right arm to be torn from my body before I will raise it to strike a sister state."

On that evening members of the militia left Baltimore and destroyed the bridges on the Philadelphia, Wilmington, and Baltimore and the Northern Central railroads, thus blocking the further entrance of troops into Baltimore from the north. They evidently received some kind of authorization from Hicks to commit these acts, though Hicks later denied that they had acted under his authority. Baltimore's Mayor Brown went to Washington to confer with Lincoln and received from him assurances that, if possible, the government would thereafter march its troops around and not through Baltimore. So intense was the popular reaction against the Lincoln government that when the news leaked out that members of the German *Turnverein* in Baltimore had volunteered to protect the government in Washington, a mob attacked the *Turnverein* hall, destroyed its equipment, and wrecked the presses of the two pro-Lincoln German newspapers, the *Turnzeitung* and *Wecker*.

Meanwhile, the City Council of Baltimore appropriated $500,000 for the defense of the city and made elaborate preparations to protect it against northern troops. Military companies were organized and drilled and quantities of arms were brought in from Virginia. When the Lincoln administration subsequently brought troops from the north through Maryland, it directed them from the mouth of the Susquehanna River to Annapolis by water and from there to Washington by the Baltimore and Ohio Railroad. The administration refused the demand of Governor Hicks that it forbid all government troops to pass through Maryland, for Maryland was the only means of ingress to the capital for northern troops. When General Benjamin Butler approached Annapolis with some Massachusetts volunteers, Hicks protested vigorously against this use of Maryland soil but was obliged to yield.

The Brothers' War

"The excitement here is terrible," reported the Maryland *Gazette* of Annapolis. "No man seems to know what should be done to avert the evil that has come upon us; and all admit that we are utterly powerless to offer any resistance." One by one, the southern cadets at the Naval Academy, on orders from their states, resigned and, confident of a glorious career in the new nation, left to fight with the Confederacy. Sometimes they were escorted to the Gate by their northern classmates who bade them a friendly goodbye. As Annapolis thus became involved in the war, the government loaded the remaining cadets and their gear on board the U.S.S. *Baltic* and transferred the entire Naval Academy to Newport, Rhode Island, for the duration of the war. It also took over the grounds and buildings of both the Academy and St. Johns College in Annapolis for the treatment of the wounded and for the housing of prisoners.

Maryland, proud of her title, "The Free State," was as strongly committed as were Virginia and her sister states in the new Confederacy to the principles of states' rights and the contract theory of the national constitution. Marylanders favored the preservation of the Union and opposed secession, but at the same time they desired the maintenance of southern rights and opposed coercion of the South. They shared the desire of citizens of the other border states—Delaware, Kentucky, and Missouri—to maintain a policy of armed neutrality and thus to serve as a buffer zone between the North and the South until a compromise settlement of the problems causing the war could be concluded.

The news of the resistance in Baltimore to the troops marching through the city soon spread through the south. It reached a young Baltimorean, the twenty-two-year-old James Ryder Randall, who was then teaching English at Poydras College in Louisiana. He was so emotionally stirred by the news that in an excited mood, which he later described as "a conflagration of the senses," he dashed off the nine stanzas of "Maryland, My Maryland!" It was a fiery castigation of the Lincoln government and an ode to the Confederacy. Set to different tunes it became an immediate hit, but when a Baltimore newspaper, *The South,* dared to publish it on May 31, 1861, the editor, Thomas Hall, was arrested for spreading seditious ideas. Its popularity in the Confederate camps was attested by an English combatant who wrote that in walking through the Confederate camps "we hear all kinds of drumming; and as for rival fifers! they . . . knew no tune except 'Dixie,' or the doleful and eternal 'My Maryland.' "[4] Both in Maryland and behind the Confederate lines it stimulated the secessionist cause and lived on long after the war to be selected by the General Assembly as the state song of Maryland finally in 1939.[5]

The demand for a special session of the legislature had now become so strong that Hicks could not ignore it. But when he issued his proclamation summoning it into session, he changed the place of meeting from Annapolis to Frederick where Union sentiment was stronger than in Annapolis. There the legislature met in the Court House on April 26. The governor's message to the legislature was noncommittal. Though he envisaged the possibility that Maryland might take "sides against the Federal Government" he disapproved of such action "at that time." He appeared to believe that a state could remain in the Union and yet refuse to take any part in the war. He favored neutrality for Maryland within the Union. His views were shared by the legislature, which was predominantly Democratic in both branches. They passed a resolution pleading that they were constitutionally unable to pass an act of secession and thus declined on their own authority to break away from the Union. But they spent much time in discussing preparations for the defense of the state, and they refused to take steps to repair the railroad bridges and thus to reopen communications with the North, since, as they asserted, to do so would offer "facilities for invasion . . . to the fanatical and excited multitudes of the northern cities . . . whose animosity to Baltimore and Maryland is measured by no standard known to Christian civilization, and who publicly threaten our destruction, without subordination even to the Federal authority." They also appointed a commission to confer with Lincoln and to protest against the treatment of Maryland as a "conquered province."

As time went on, this legislature became openly defiant of the Lincoln government. But meanwhile Governor Hicks drifted into a position of unconditional adherence to the Union. Whatever his previous hesitation, he now unmistakably showed his intention of supporting it, though he still advised against the passing of troops through Maryland as unwise and prejudicial to the growth of Union sentiment in the state. Lincoln now went much further, and gave General Winfield Scott, Commanding General of the Army, authority to suspend the writ of *habeas corpus* in order to protect the military line from Philadelphia to Washington. From May 13, 1861 to the end of the war in April 1865, Maryland was an occupied province. "Maryland's heart was with the Confederacy," concluded General Bradley Johnson, a Marylander who joined the southern cause, "but her body was bound and manacled to the Union." [6]

With both Annapolis and Baltimore in the hands of United States troops, the legislature virtually acknowledged its inability to change Lincoln's policy and adjourned to June 4. Hicks, who was now definitely cooperating with the administration, issued a call for four regiments to supply Maryland's quota under Lincoln's proclamation of April 15. Abandoning all hesitation, which had previously perhaps been more apparent than real, he began to collect all the "arms and accoutrements belonging to the State of Maryland." When the legislature reconvened, it condemned the governor's action and castigated him as a "military despot." Chief Justice Taney issued a writ in the case of John Merryman denying Lincoln's authority to suspend the writ of *habeas corpus,* "the most sacred writ known to the law," but Hicks, as well as Lincoln, refused to comply with it. Lincoln soon afterward requested Scott to occupy Frederick with troops, in order, as he later explained, to guard the town from an attack by "rebels at Harpers Ferry" and to prevent the sending of provisions from Frederick to the South.

The legislature had appointed a committee to see both Lincoln and Davis and to secure a cessation of hostilities until Congress could reassemble in Washington. The committee reported that the invasion of Virginia by government troops had rendered a visit to Lincoln futile, but the committee interviewed Davis and brought back from him expressions of good will and a statement that the Confederacy simply desired to be left alone. The legislature also passed resolutions protesting against Lincoln's suspension of the writ of *habeas corpus,* against the military occupation of Maryland, and against the war. Baltimore was now completely managed by the Lincoln authorities. Mayor Brown, the police commissioner, and the police marshal had been arrested. Under these circumstances, when Governor Hicks ordered a special election on June 13 for the purpose of selecting representatives to Congress, Maryland under duress chose an almost completely Unionist ticket.

The legislature was no longer on even formal terms of friendship with the governor, and after the defeat of the Union forces at Bull Run, all the members of the legislature (or a sufficient number to prevent the enactment of an order of secession) were ordered arrested by Secretary of War Cameron. Those who were regarded as dangerous to the war effort of the Lincoln administration were sent to northern prisons and those who were regarded as less hostile were required to take an oath of allegiance and were soon released. At the same time, Maryland's only States' Rights congressman, Henry May, was arrested by order of the Secretary of War. All these arrests received the unqualified endorsement of Governor Hicks. Not until November 1862, after the moderate Union victory at Antietam, were the members of the Maryland legislature who were still confined at Fort Warren in Boston Harbor set free.

At the same time, the police commissioners and the police marshal were released but without having had a trial or even a formal presentment of an indictment against them. The Baltimore *Sun,* dreading suppression by the authorities, lapsed into innocuousness. "Shut up" was the advice which its editor, Arunah S. Abell, gave to his staff, as a federal marshal closely scrutinized every edition, looking for an excuse to close it down.

Maryland, therefore, was kept in the Union largely through the efforts of Governor Hicks and the use of force by the Lincoln government. By reason of her geographical position as a border state and her economic ties with both North and South, she had originally worked for conciliation and appeasement of the sectional quarrel. After Lincoln's call to arms, Maryland wavered between a policy of secession and a policy of neutralism in the war. A decision in favor of the Union was finally forced upon her by Governor Hicks and national troops. But many Maryland families were distraught and divided by this decision, and their menfolk who were Confederate sympathizers quietly crossed the Potomac to enlist in the southern armies.

Among these latter was Colonel Harry Gilmor, who went on to win distinction as a partisan fighter in the Confederacy by his destructive raids into Maryland, even to the outskirts of Baltimore, and who later published an exciting record of his exploits.[7] Other supporters of the Confederacy were J.T. Scharf, who devoted his postwar career to indefatigable researches into the history of Maryland, and Severn Teackle Wallis, whose legal mentor had been William Wirt and who after the war became the outstanding leader of the Maryland bar. But John Pendleton Kennedy, who had been designated provost of the University of Maryland in 1850, staunchly supported the Lincoln administration and published a volume entitled *Mr. Ambrose's Letters on the Rebellion* in which he sought, not altogether successfully, to lay all the blame for the war upon the South, to disprove the claims of the southern states to the rights of secession, and to prepare the way for ultimate reconciliation of North and South after the abolition of Negro slavery. In attempting to refute the states' rights doctrine, Kennedy advanced the interesting argument that only the original thirteen states could be considered to have possessed sovereignty before the adoption of the Constitution and that all the remaining states in the Union, except Texas, were created by the original thirteen and could not therefore "resume" sovereignty, as they claimed to do in their acts of secession, because they had never possessed it, having been only territories of the nation at the time of the adoption of the Constitution.

Maryland now passed completely under the direct control of the national authorities, and Governor Hicks energetically cooperated with them, especially in stamping out disloyalty on the Eastern Shore. Maryland's capital, Annapolis, became the most important depot of the Lincoln government in the East for the exchange of prisoners; captive troops often arrived there in groups as large as six thousand at a time and were quartered either in the expropriated buildings of St. Johns College or at Camp Parole. Of the other border states Delaware likewise remained loyal to the Lincoln government, though not under coercion of government troops. Kentucky issued a declaration of neutrality in May 1861 and suffered no punitive action for it, but when its neutrality was violated by Confederate troops in September 1861, Kentucky declared for the Union. Missouri fought her own civil war, which resulted in the forcible overthrow of the pro-southern governor and the establishment of a Union government in July 1861.

In Maryland, political party organizations virtually disappeared. The Constitutional Union party ended its short existence perforce at the time of Lincoln's appeal to arms. The new Republican party attracted few followers and remained for some time an unimportant political force in the state. The Democratic party ceased to operate openly under the threat of bayonets, but a faction sympathetic to the Confederacy carried on its efforts quietly as a States' Rights party. The principal, indeed the only political, issue that divided citizens was loyalty or disloyalty to the Lincoln government. Those who were loyal to it formed the Union party early in 1861, directed by a State Central Committee of which Brantz Mayer was chairman. They denied the right of secession, justified the use of force to preserve the Union, and endorsed Lincoln's policies. Clearly representing only a minority of the population of the state, they defended Lincoln's virtual disfranchisement of the pro-Confederate majority and the resort to arbitrary arrest, to deportations beyond the lines, and to the presence of the military at the polls on the ground of the overriding supremacy of the Union. But even the Unionists held that the preservation of the Union must not be linked with the abolition of slavery.

A Union State Convention, which met in Baltimore in August, nominated Augustus W. Bradford for governor. He was known to be a staunch Union supporter but had been inactive in politics for the past fifteen years, a fact which perhaps assisted his nomination, for he had not been involved in the bitter political strife of the 1850's. A slaveholder, he carefully avoided the subject of emancipation during the campaign, though he admitted that a Lincoln victory in the war would end the slavery system.

The Maryland state elections held in November 1861 were supervised by agents of the Lincoln government, and General John A. Dix instructed the judges of election "to put to those who offer to poll such searching questions in regard to residence and citizenship as to detect traitors and without any violation of the constitution or laws of Maryland to prevent the pollution of the ballot-boxes by their votes." To circumvent "the constitution or laws of Maryland," which required the state to conduct its own elections, General Dix resorted to the policy of arresting Confederate sympathizers for rebellion and treason and holding them in jail until the election was over, thus effectually disfranchising them. As a result of the election thus conducted, the state government continued in the hands of officials who, like Governor Hicks, were friendly to the Lincoln administration. Bradford was chosen governor by a majority of over 31,000 votes. The new legislature was also loyal to the Union. By this election Maryland was definitely lost to the secessionists and henceforth was divided only between those who favored greater and those who favored less support to the Lincoln government in the prosecution of the war.[8]

The new legislature when called into special session by Governor Hicks in December 1861 accepted his recommendation and reversed practically all the actions taken by its predecessor, the so-called "rebel legislature." It appropriated money to indemnify the families of the members of the Sixth Massachusetts who had been killed or disabled in Baltimore; it passed resolutions expressing devotion to the Union and confidence in Lincoln; and it repudiated the claim made by Jefferson Davis in the previous February that Maryland, "will, when able to speak with an unstifled voice, unite her destiny with the South." When Hicks surrendered the governorship to Bradford in January 1862, the legislature passed a resolution thanking him for the "way he had met this solemn crisis in our national affairs" and for his loyalty to the Union. In the following December, Hicks was appointed to the United States Senate by Governor Bradford, and he represented Maryland there until his death in February 1865. As a senator he consistently supported the Lincoln administration. In a speech in the Senate in February 1863, he avowed that if the safety of the Union demanded it, "every rebel, North or South," should be put to death.

The war was playing havoc with the institution of slavery in Maryland by destroying the ties which bound the slaves to their masters. As a result Maryland was becoming neither a slave nor a free state. The slaveowners in Maryland naturally desired to receive some compensation for their property. Lincoln recommended compensated emancipation upon Congress in March 1862, and Congress approved the proposal, but Maryland and other border states declined it. In the following month (April 1862) Congress abolished slavery in the District of Columbia, an act which created a great furor in Maryland, particularly in the counties adjacent to the federal District. Maryland was now surrounded by free areas north and south, and slaveowners were severely limited in apprehending runaway slaves and in otherwise exercising coercive authority over their slaves.

Every politician who would succeed must follow more or less faithfully the doctrine that the end justifies the means, whether that end be the gaining and retaining of public office, the elimination of slavery, or the restoration of a rent union. Lincoln's commitment to these ends was deemed to justify any means, even to the use of military force. After his election to the presidency in November 1860, the Confederacy might have weakened his case for the use of force if it had abolished slavery and thus clearly exposed his policy simply as a war of conquest. His treatment of Maryland showed this to be the end toward which his policy was directed, and his long-sustained reluctance to make the elimination of slavery the explicit object of his administration and his consequent emphasis upon the restoration of the Union offered him a more plausible excuse for the use of military force.

The new abolitionist objective of the Lincoln administration placed the members of the Union party of Maryland in an embarrassing situation. Their loyalty to the Lincoln administration had been largely inspired by the aim of preserving the Union. How could they now logically support a war against slavery while maintaining Maryland as a slave state? Nevertheless, the militant or radical members of the Union party, which controlled the state, began to urge both emancipation and the summoning of a new convention to draw up a constitution that would replace the constitution of 1851 and would enable the Unionists to entrench themselves in power. Without such a convention slavery could not be banned in the state, for under the constitution of 1851 the legislature was forbidden to "pass any law abolishing the relation of master or slave, as it now exists in this state." The Union party therefore combined their demand for emancipation with their demand for a constitutional convention.

Meanwhile, one of the crucial battles of the war had been fought at Antietam, or Sharpsburg, in Maryland in September 1862. Since it resulted in a Union victory, though a very modest one, Lincoln took advantage of it to issue an emancipation proclamation freeing the slaves within the Confederate lines on January 1, 1863. This, of course, did

Antietam, September 1862, by Alexander Gardner. Courtesy *Library of Congress*

not affect the status of slaves in any area under the jurisdiction of the national authorities, including Maryland. But it made plain that the war was to be fought for more than the mere preservation of the Union.

Already, after the Confederate victory at the second battle of Bull Run in September 1862, Maryland had been invaded by Lee's army, which bivouacked at Frederick on its way to the north. In this center of Union sympathizers Lee and his men were most unwelcome, and as they marched out of town to the Hagerstown road, it is alleged, Mrs. Barbara Fritchie, then ninety-five years old, issued her defiant challenge to General "Stonewall" Jackson in sentiments which were soon afterward patriotically immortalized by the Quaker poet, John Greenleaf Whittier:

"Shoot, if you must, this old gray head,
But spare your country's flag," she said.[9]

On two later occasions Maryland became a battlefield of the war and temporarily found herself behind the Confederate lines. The state was invaded by General Lee as he dashed northward to meet the Lincoln forces under General Meade at Gettysburg in early July 1863, and it was crossed again by the Confederate forces as they retreated from Gettysburg southward across the Potomac. In the following year, when Grant and Lee were fighting in Virginia and Sherman and Johnston in Georgia, Maryland was again invaded—this time by General Jubal A. Early, who swept north from the valley of Virginia. His objective was to make a demonstration against Washington and thus relieve the pressure on Lee's armies around Richmond. He crossed the Potomac near Shepherdstown, occupied Hagerstown, and skirmished with Union troops near Frederick. There he defeated General Lew Wallace at Monocacy Junction on July 9, 1864, forcing Wallace to retreat in great disorder to Ellicott's Mills. The main Confederate force occupied Rockville and skirmished within sight of Washington. A small cavalry force under Colonel Gilmor burned Governor Bradford's country home five miles north of Baltimore and even raided Baltimore itself. Finally the main force recrossed the Potomac at Seneca and Poolesville carrying large amounts of booty with them.

On this as well as on earlier Confederate raids into Maryland, both the Chesapeake and Ohio Canal and the Baltimore and Ohio Railroad suffered considerable damage. Running through border territory they were exposed to assaults from both sides. The canal was repeatedly put out of operation by Confederate attacks, many of its boats were confiscated by the Lincoln government, and the wartime president of the Canal Company, Alfred Spates, was arrested three times for his sympathies and actions in support of the Confederacy.

During the first year of the war the Baltimore and Ohio Railroad was forced virtually to suspend traffic on its main line to the west and to forfeit much of its business to its rival, the Pennsylvania Railroad. Since the Baltimore and Ohio was the only railroad connecting Washington with the north and west its support was essential to the preservation of the Union government. Lincoln himself threatened it with competition by supporting a plan for government construction under his "war powers" of new railroad lines running north and west and paralleling the Baltimore and Ohio, but this plan was rendered unnecessary by the efficient support given to his government by officials of the railroad, particularly its energetic president, John W. Garrett.

Throughout the war the operations on the western line of the Baltimore and Ohio were seriously hampered by Confederate raids. The railroad lost much of its vital equipment, particularly engines, to General "Stonewall" Jackson at Harpers Ferry and Martinsburg, West Virginia. When Jackson abandoned Martinsburg, he transported overland with him in a prodigious land operation twelve Baltimore and Ohio camelback engines on drays drawn by forty horses and delivered them to Confederate railroads. Officials of the railroad were obliged to rebuild the Harpers Ferry bridge six times when it was destroyed either by military operations or by floods. Following General Rosecrans' disastrous defeat at Chickamauga, Secretary of War Stanton and Garrett collaborated in transferring almost fifteen thousand men by rail from tidewater Virginia to Tennessee where they turned the fortunes of war in the west. After the war the Baltimore and Ohio was reimbursed $3 million by Congress for its Civil War losses and it recovered the engines which had been taken south by Jackson.

The port of Baltimore, though it suffered little actual war devastation, was obliged to make difficult adjustments in its economic life. Early in the war its commerce was interdicted by the Lincoln government, and under the handicaps of government intervention, loss of southern trade, and depredations by Confederate privateers, the volume of business in the port seriously declined. But the city's shipbuilding industry enjoyed a real boom, and some other sectors of the economy of both Baltimore and the state as a whole profited from the war. Agriculture found ready markets for its output as thousands of farm workers were drawn to the fighting fronts and food demands increased. Many of the smaller service industries, such as tailoring and blacksmithing, which were useful to the army experienced unparalleled prosperity. Enoch Pratt's horseshoe and mule-shoe factory greatly expanded, and the basis for many other Maryland fortunes, including those of Johns Hopkins, George Peabody, and W.T. Walters, was laid during the war. After the war, Baltimore quickly recovered from its wartime dislocations and entered upon a new era of prosperity.

As opposition to the policies of the Lincoln government continued strong, Baltimore and the entire Western Shore of Maryland were placed under martial law in June 1863 and even social clubs were closed by the military authorities. During the war nine Baltimore newspapers were suppressed, either temporarily or permanently, and two of them were forced to stop publication because of the arrest of their editors. Only the *American,* the *Clipper,* and the *Sun* were published uninterruptedly throughout the war.

The election held in the fall of 1863 resulted in an overwhelming victory for the Union ticket and strengthened the forces in the state that were demanding emancipation of the slaves and the summoning of a new constitutional convention. Before the election Major-General Robert C. Schenck, who had been placed in command of the Middle Department, Eighth Army Corps, with headquarters in Baltimore, issued his General Order No. 53 in which he required all voters to take an oath to support the constitution and government of the United States and ordered the arrest of any southern sympathizers who attempted to vote in the election. The latter part of this order was immediately revoked by Lincoln, not, as he explained to Governor Bradford, because "it is wrong in principle, but because the military being, of necessity, exclusive judges as to who shall be arrested, the provision is liable to abuse." As a result of Schenck's order and of the consequent arrest of many leading citizens and even candidates for office, the vote was one-third smaller than in the election of 1861. Governor Bradford later complained bitterly to the legislature that "A part of the Army, which a generous people had supplied for a very different purpose, was on that day engaged in stifling the freedom of election in a faithful State, intimidating its sworn officers, violating the constitutional rights of its loyal citizens and obstructing the usual channels of communication between them and their Executive."

The legislature chosen in this election was overwhelmingly Unionist and contained a majority in favor of a constitutional convention and emancipation. It finally passed a bill providing for a special election to decide whether a constitutional convention should be called and to select the delegates to it. Since the outcome of the previous election had shown that the people of the state favored emancipation, the conservatives now in many places abandoned their opposition to it. Meanwhile, General Schenck, a Radical Republican, had resigned to take a seat in Congress and was succeeded by General Lew Wallace. Wallace issued no general military orders governing the election as Schenck had formerly done, but he publicly showed his sympathy for the Unconditional Union party, which was the name given to the group that advocated abolition of slavery. That party was successful in the election, the vote in favor of the convention being 31,593 and against it 19,524, giving a favorable majority of 12,069. But some two-thirds of the voters were disfranchised. Only 9,294 out of approximately 190,000 white voters in Baltimore voted in the election. The vote, limited as it was, showed that the Constitutional Union party had its strongest support in the northern and western counties and was weakest in the southern counties.

When the constitutional convention assembled at Annapolis in April 1864, it was dominated by the Unionists, who had a majority of 61 to only 35 Democrats, the latter coming exclusively from the southern counties and from the Eastern Shore. Nearly all of the Union Party members were pledged to unconditional emancipation. The members spent two months in debating at great length the questions of slavery and allegiance to the national government. Though they met in wartime their debates were remarkably free from personal recriminations; nevertheless, the delegates from the southern counties tenaciously clung to the doctrine of states' rights, a policy of conciliation toward the South, and a return to the political and economic conditions which existed before the war.

Early in June the convention recessed for a few days to allow members to attend the Union or Republican National Convention which met in Baltimore, endorsed the prosecution of the war, approved the measures and acts of the Lincoln administration, called for a constitutional amendment abolishing slavery, and nominated Lincoln for reelection with Andrew Johnson of Tennessee as his running mate. In July the convention's work was interrupted by Early's raid into Maryland. The raid caused great excitement throughout the state—especially after Wallace's defeat at Monocacy. Frederick, then called Fredericktown, saved itself by collecting from its five banks a sum of $200,000 on the promise that its residents would be taxed over the years to reimburse the banks and by delivering this amount to the Confederate general to prevent him from sacking the city. The citizens of Frederick did not finally discharge their debt to the banks until 1951.[10]

When the constitutional convention was able to reconvene after Early's raid, the Unionist majority showed a new spirit of vindictiveness. They passed a resolution requesting the president "to assess upon known sympathizers with the rebellion resident in this state the total amount of all losses and spoliations sustained by loyal citizens of the United States resident in this state, by reason of the recent rebel raid, to compensate loyal sufferers." Soon afterward they demanded that all who refused to take the oath of allegiance or who openly expressed sympathy with the invasion of the state should be either banished beyond the lines of the army or imprisoned for the duration of the war.

The convention had already abolished slavery in the state by incorporating in the new constitution the substance of what later became the thirteenth amendment to the national constitution. Hereafter in this state, they declared, "there shall be neither slavery nor involuntary servitude, except in punishment of crime, whereof the party shall have been duly convicted, and all persons held to service or labor as slaves are hereby declared free." They adopted this article by a party vote of 53 to 27 and over the protests of the minority who wished to compensate the slaveowners on the ground that slaves were private property and ought not to be taken for public use without compensation. To this proposition the Baltimore delegates especially objected, for Baltimore would have been obliged to pay a large share of the resulting increased taxation and would have received only a small part of the compensation. Upon the suggestion of the Democratic minority the convention turned to the solution of national compensation which Lincoln favored. They adopted a motion declaring that the "General Assembly shall have power to receive from the United States any grant or donation of land, money or securities for any purpose designated by the United States, and shall administer or distribute the same according to the conditions of the said grant." But Maryland slaveowners never received any compensation from the national government.

On the question of the relationship between Maryland and the national government, the convention after a long debate provided that "the Constitution of the United States and the laws made in pursuance thereof, being the supreme law of the land, every citizen of this state owes paramount allegiance to the Constitution and Government of the United States, and is not bound by any law or ordinance of this state in contravention or subversion thereof." Every voter was required to take an "ironclad oath," and such an oath was specifically required of "the president, directors, trustees, or agents of corporations created or authorized by the laws of this State, teachers or superintendents of the public schools, colleges, or other institutions of learning; attorneys-at-law, jurors, and such other persons as the General Assembly shall from time to time prescribe." The judges of election were given the sole power to determine who could vote.

The constitution allowed forfeiture of estate for treason which had not theretofore been allowed in Maryland. It denied the franchise and the privilege of holding office to all southern sympathizers and other disloyal persons by declaring that no person who had been in armed hostility to the United States or had enlisted in the service "of the so-called 'Confederate States or armies' " or had in any manner adhered to or befriended those engaged in armed hostility to the United States or had even expressed a desire for the triumph of the South "shall ever be entitled to vote at any election to be held in this State, or to hold any office of honor, profit or trust under the laws of this State." Test oaths of allegiance both to Maryland and to the United States were required for officeholding, and these must include a declaration of belief either in the Christian religion or in the existence of God and in a future state of rewards and punishments. Persons elected to office were required to take an oath stating that they had not aided those in rebellion against the United States and promising to oppose all political combinations having for their object the dissolution of the Union.

The constitution confined the suffrage to free white male citizens and required a uniform registration of the names of the voters of the state—a new thing in Maryland's politics. It did away with the old gubernatorial districts from each of which the governor was chosen in turn; it raised the governor's salary from $3,600 to $4,000, created the office of Lieutenant Governor, and gave him the tasks of presiding over the Senate and of succeeding the Governor in case of the latter's "death, resignation, removal from the state, or other disqualification." It also created the office of Attorney General, which had been abolished by the constitution of 1851. In the matter of representation the new constitution changed the system which was adopted in 1851 and which made the entire population—white and black, slave and free —the basis for representation. Under the direction of the Baltimore delegates the constitution now made the white population the exclusive basis for representation in the House of Delegates. Until the next census Baltimore City was to have 18 delegates and the counties a total of 62.

The constitution also continued the provisions of the constitution of 1851 which prohibited the state from giving its credit to aid works of internal improvement, and it authorized the state government to dispose of its interest in the Baltimore and Ohio Railroad, in other works of internal improvement, and in banking corporations. In the expectation that Maryland by reason of its loyalty to the Union would receive part of the new state of West Virginia or Loudoun County, Virginia, or a part of the eastern shore of Virginia, the constitution empowered the General

Assembly "to accept the cession of any territory contiguous to this state from the states of Virginia and West Virginia, or from the United States, with the consent of Congress and of the inhabitants of such ceded territory." But this provision never had any practical significance.

The educational provisions of the new constitution were especially noteworthy, for they established the foundations for Maryland's public educational system. The state had previously done little to provide public schools beyond recognizing its obligation to do so. Governor Ligon had declared in his message to the legislature in 1856: "The system of public instruction in Maryland (if we except the city of Baltimore, whose public schools are an honor to the State and reflect the highest credit upon all intrusted with their management) is in a state of the most utter and hopeless prostration. Our plan of public instruction must be constructed anew, made uniform in its operations throughout the State, supported more liberally by State and county resources, and, above all, it should be made subject to some controlling, supervisory power."

The basis for such a centralized system of education for the state was laid in the constitution of 1864. It provided for the first time for a state system of education authorizing the Governor to appoint a State Superintendent of Public Instruction for a term of four years at a salary of $2,500. It created a State Board of Education consisting of the Governor, the Lieutenant Governor, the Speaker of the House of Delegates, and the Superintendent of Public Instruction and empowered them to appoint school commissioners in each county. The General Assembly was authorized to provide a uniform system of schools by which a free school would be established in each school district for at least six months in each year. To finance the schools an annual tax of ten cents was to be levied on each $100 of real and personal property throughout the state and distributed among the counties in proportion to their population between the ages of five and twenty and a further tax of five cents on each $100 was to be levied and invested until a School Fund of $6,000,000 was formed. An attempt was made by the minority in the convention to prohibit the application of the School Fund to education of Negroes, but it was overwhelmingly defeated.

In preparation for submitting the new constitution to the voters of the state for their approval or disapproval, the convention required all voters in the election to take the test oaths prescribed in the constitution for all future elections and required the General Assembly to "provide by law for taking the votes of soldiers in the army of the United States serving in the field." After adopting the constitution by a vote of 53 to 26, the convention adjourned on September 6.

The campaign for the ratification of the constitution was stormy and fierce. The constitution was endorsed by President Lincoln, but many of the more conservative members of the Union party, who were critical of the Lincoln administration, opposed it, and the Democrats strenuously campaigned against it. Reverdy Johnson, a member of the Unconditional Union party, criticized the requirement of the test oath in the vote on the constitution. The thirty-five minority members of the convention published a unanimous protest "To the Voters of Maryland" condemning the failure of the constitution to compensate slaveowners and criticizing the provisions providing for paramount allegiance to the United States government, the test oaths, the increase in the legislative representation of Baltimore City, and the soldiers' vote. The Democrats, who had sufficiently reorganized their party to hold a state convention in Baltimore in September 1864 declared their unanimous opposition to it. In the elections which were held on October 12-13 the constitution was defeated by a majority of 1,995, but the soldiers were yet to be polled. When these were added, the constitution was declared ratified by the small majority of 375 in a total vote of 59,973. Governor Bradford declared the new constitution adopted on October 30, 1864.

At the beginning of the war Maryland had been disposed to favor secession. Maryland had found herself deeply implicated in questions serious enough to produce bloody internecine struggle—questions involving the relations between the white and the black races and the constitutional relationship between the national and the state governments. Viewing with approval the separatist actions of the slave states, Maryland had tried first to play a mediating role between North and South and then fell back into a position of neutrality. But when Marylanders veered too overtly toward support of the Confederate cause, they were constrained by the force of the government in Washington and by the strong-handed action of Governor Hicks to remain loyal to the Lincoln administration. The Republican party which had mustered less than three percent of the Maryland votes in 1860, had gathered strength as the pro-slavery voters were disfranchised and the Union armies won their military victories. By 1863 it had come under the firm control of the emancipationist wing headed by Henry Winter Davis and in the following year was strong enough to force through a new state constitution abolishing slavery without compensation to slaveowners. That constitution was a product of war passions, and its principal purpose was to perpetuate the ascendancy of the Union party in the state.

On the matter of the relation of the state to the central government, the constitution of 1864 established the novel principle that citizens of the state owed paramount allegiance to the government of the United States and were not bound by any law of the state which contravened the constitution and laws of that government. It thus accepted the philosophy of centralism and represented the logical culmination of the decision that Maryland's officials made in 1861 to back the cause of the Union. With the support of this new constitution, narrowly adopted, when Grant's army finally took Richmond the militantly anti-Confederate party was in control of Maryland, prepared to take political advantage of the opportunities which Reconstruction would bring.

Maryland's official commitment to the cause of the Union did not effectually silence the deep resentment of citizens of the Free State against the coercive policies of the Lincoln administration. That resentment was echoed long afterward by Maryland's gadfly journalist, Henry L. Mencken, who charged that Lincoln's claim in his Gettysburg address that the war was fought for the cause of self-determination was hypocrisy, for, said he, the war resulted in "the destruction of the old sovereignty of the States, i.e., of the people of the States. The Confederates went into battle an absolutely free people; they came out with their freedom subject to the supervision and vote of the rest of the country."[11] The imposition of military rule upon the South, though it may ultimately have promoted the spirit of nationalism, weakened the constitutional system of the conception of free states which Maryland had long cherished.

Footnotes

[1] Avery O. Craven, *Soil Exhaustion as a Factor in the Agricultural History of Virginia and Maryland,* University of Illinois Press, Urbana, 1926, p. 67.

[2] Frederick Douglass, *Life and Times of Frederick Douglass,* Hartford, 1884, p. 225.

[3] Frederic Bancroft, *Slave-Trading in the Old South,* J.H. Furst Company, Baltimore, 1931, p. 122.

[4] An English Combatant, *Battlefields of the South from Bull Run to Fredericksburgh* (New York, 1864), p. 308.

[5] All nine stanzas of "Maryland, My Maryland" are printed in Appendix IV. Upon its official adoption as the state song, the first five and the ninth verses were omitted as being too warlike. Other Civil War songs in or about Maryland are described in Raphael Semmes, "Civil War Song Sheets," *Maryland Historical Magazine,* vol. XXXVIII, No. 3, September 1943, pp. 205-228.

[6] Clement A. Evans, ed., *Confederate Military History: A Library of Confederate States History,* 12 vols., Confederate Publishing Company, Atlanta, 1899, II, *Maryland,* p. 17.

[7] Colonel Harry Gilmor, *Four Years in the Saddle* [New York, Harper and Brothers, 1866].

[8] Charles L. Wagandt, "Election by Sword and Ballot: The Emancipationist Victory of 1863," *Maryland Historical Magazine,* vol. 59, No. 2, June 1964, pp. 143-164.

[9] The pros and cons of this incident are reviewed with scholarly finality by Dorothy Mackay Quynn and William Rogers Quynn, "Barbara Frietschie," *ibid.,* vol. XXXVII, pp. 227-254 (September 1942), and 400-413 (December 1942).

[10] Richard R. Duncan, "Maryland's Reaction to Early's Raid in 1864: A Summer of Bitterness," *ibid.,* vol. 64, No. 3, Fall 1969, pp. 248-279.

[11] *Prejudices: Third Series,* New York, 1922, p. 175.

Sources and Additional Reading

Baker, Jean H., *The Politics of Continuity: Maryland Political Parties from 1858 to 1870,* Johns Hopkins University Press, Baltimore, 1973.

Bancroft, Frederic, *Slave Trading in the Old South,* J.H. Furst Company, Baltimore, 1931.

Brown, George William, *Baltimore and the 19th of April, 1861,* Johns Hopkins University Studies, Series III, extra volume, N. Murray, Baltimore, 1887.

Clark, Charles B., *Politics in Maryland during the Civil War,* Chestertown, Maryland, 1952.

Cuthbert, Norma B., ed., *Lincoln and the Baltimore Plot, 1861,* Huntington Library, San Marino, California, 1949.

Debates of the Constitutional Convention of the State of Maryland, 1864, 3 vols., Annapolis, 1864.

Douglass, Frederick, *Life and Times of Frederick Douglass,* Park Publishing Company, Hartford, Connecticut, 1882.

Evans, General Clement A., ed., *Confederate Military History,* 12 vols., vol. II, *Maryland,* Confederate Publishing Company, Atlanta, Georgia, 1899.

Gilmor, Colonel Harry, *Four Years in the Saddle,* Harper and Brothers, [New York], 1866.

Goldsborough, William W., *The Maryland Line in the Confederate States Army, 1861-1865,* Kelly, Piet and Company, Baltimore, 1869; reprint 1972.

Hanaford, Phebe A., *The Life of George Peabody,* B.B. Russell, Boston, 1870.

Hart, Richard H., *Enoch Pratt: The Story of a Plain Man,* Enoch Pratt Free Library, Baltimore, 1935.

Henig, Gerald S., *Henry Winter Davis: Antebellum and Civil War Congressman from Maryland,* Twayne Publishers, Inc., New York, 1973.

Hensel, W.N., *The Christiana Riot and the Treason Trials of 1851: An Historical Sketch: Prepared and Published for the Commemoration of These Events,* September 9, 1911; reprint 1969.

Manakee, Harold R., *Maryland in the Civil War,* Maryland Historical Society, Baltimore, 1961.

Murfin, James V., *The Gleam of Bayonets: The Battle of Antietam and the Maryland Campaign of 1862,* maps by James D. Bowlby, introduction by James I. Robertson, Jr., Thomas Yoseloff, New York, 1965.

Proceedings of the State Convention of Maryland to Frame a New Constitution, Annapolis, 1864.

Radcliffe, George L.P., *Governor Hicks of Maryland and the Civil War,* Johns Hopkins University Studies, Series 19, Nos. 11, 12, Baltimore, 1901. Especially valuable because most of the manuscript materials used by Senator Radcliffe in preparing this study were subsequently burned.

Seabrook, William L.W., *Maryland's Great Part in Saving the Union: The Loyalty of Her Governor, Thomas Holliday Hicks, and a Majority of Her People...,* American Sentinel Company, Westminster, Maryland, 1913.

Steiner, Bernard Christian, *Life of Henry Winter Davis,* John Murphy Company, Baltimore, 1916.

Summers, Festus P., *The Baltimore and Ohio in the Civil War,* Putnam's, New York, 1939.

Wagandt, Charles Lewis, *The Mighty Revolution: Negro Emancipation in Maryland, 1862-1864,* The Johns Hopkins Press, Baltimore, 1964.

Wallis, S. Teackle, *Correspondence between S. Teackle Wallis, esq., of Baltimore and the Hon. John Sherman, of the U.S. Senate, Concerning the Arrest of Members of the Maryland Legislature and the Mayor and Police Commissioners of Baltimore, in 1861.* Baltimore 1863.

CHAPTER XXIII
A PAINFUL RECONCILIATION

A brothers' war was bitterly fought in Maryland after 1861. It had a seriously disruptive effect upon every phase of the life of the state. The Maryland Diocese of the Protestant Episcopal Church, for example, which numbered approximately 11,000 parishioners, was rent over the question of supporting the Lincoln government, many refusing to follow the unyielding pro-Union leadership of Bishop William R. Whittingham. As mentioned previously, Annapolis, which was strongly pro-southern in its sentiments, lost the Naval Academy to Newport, Rhode Island, and only after considerable difficulty recovered it after the war. Some 20,000 sons of Maryland fought as volunteers in the Confederate armies during the war; approximately 50,000 either volunteered or were drafted to fight in Lincoln's army. The first election held after the adoption of the constitution of 1864 naturally resulted in a victory for the Union party, whose candidate for governor was Thomas Swann of Baltimore. He won the election by a majority of 8,511. In the presidential election of that year Maryland gave Lincoln a popular majority of 7,432 votes (after the soldiers' vote was counted) and all seven of its electoral votes. But Lincoln's victory in Maryland was made possible only by his overwhelming majority in Baltimore, for he received only a minority of the popular vote in the rest of the state. As a result of the election, Maryland's congressional delegation included three Union party representatives and two Democrats, the latter representing Cecil and St. Mary's Counties. Making allowance for the requirement of test oaths for voting and for the pressures exerted by the national government, it was clear that the Democratic party had made a good showing in the election.

The Union party, having secured a large majority in the House of Delegates and a majority in the Senate, proceeded to ratify the Thirteenth Amendment abolishing slavery and then to remove all the disabilities of the Negroes except the one disqualifying them from being witnesses in cases where white persons were concerned and the one authorizing Negroes to be sold for crime for the period that a white man might be confined in the penitentiary for the same offense. Early in 1865 they passed a registration bill, famous in the history of the state, which authorized the governor to appoint three citizens to register the voters in each ward or election district and in the camps of the soldiers and sailors of the state. The Union party consolidated its position just in time, for after Grant's capture of Richmond on April 3, 1865, the surviving Marylanders who had served in the Confederate armies began to return home in large numbers. The Union party became alarmed that these southern sympathizers might join the Democrats to drive them from power. The *Baltimore American* demanded that "the more conspicuous leaders of the Rebellion, civil and military, should be awarded the extreme penalty of the law. Nothing short of expiation on the gallows would satisfy the simplest demands of justice." The Baltimore City Council protested against allowing rebels to return to the city, and Cumberland organized a vigilance committee to keep them away. The Union party, fearing this increment of Democratic votes, deliberately kept alive the hatreds of the past in order to retain power.

Thus began the tragedies of the Reconstruction period. The magnanimity which Lincoln was prepared to show the conquered South ended with his assassination in mid-April 1865. John Wilkes Booth, who fired the fatal shot at the president in Ford's Theater in Washington, escaped through southern Maryland. He and his fellow conspirators planned to meet, after accomplishing their plan, at Surrattsville (Clinton), Maryland, and to proceed from thence to Port Tobacco and across the Potomac into the Southland. But Booth had broken his leg in his jump from Lincoln's box onto the stage and had to seek medical help from Dr. Samuel Mudd, who lived at Bryantown, in Charles County. On the night of April 22 Booth and a companion succeeded in eluding the river patrol at Nanjemoy Creek and crossed the Potomac, but they were overtaken by government forces at Port Royal, Virginia. There Booth took refuge in a barn and lost his life when it was set on fire. As a result of the subsequent trial before a military court of the persons accused by the government of complicity in the assassination of Lincoln, Dr. Mudd was imprisoned and Mrs. Mary E. Surratt was hanged. A brief was prepared in defense of Mrs. Surratt by Maryland's senator, Reverdy Johnson, who was attempting to curb the vindictiveness and prejudices of the Reconstruction period, but he was denied a hearing by the military court. Dr. Mudd was pardoned in 1869 by President Johnson and more than a century later, in 1973, the Maryland legislature declared him "innocent of any complicity in the assassination" of Lincoln.

In preparing for the Maryland state elections of November 1865, the officers of registration drafted a list of twenty-five questions "which formed such a strict catechism of political faith and activity that a

Democrat who was once tainted" with disloyalty would be unable to subscribe to it and would thus be debarred from voting. This list, as enacted into law by the legislature, included such questions as the following:

XIV. Have you ever contributed money, goods, provisions, labor or any such thing, to procure food, clothing, implements of war or any such thing for the enemies of the United States or the so-called 'Confederate States' or armies?

XIX. Have you ever declared your desire for the triumph of said enemies over the armies of the United States?

XXIII. During the rebellion, when the armies were engaged in battle, did you wish the success of the armies of the United States or those of the rebels?

XXIV. Have you voted at all the elections held since the year 1861, and if not, give your reasons?

XXV. Have you, in taking this oath or in answering any questions propounded to you, held any mental reservation or used any evasion whatever?

This test of political orthodoxy was designed to exclude all ex-Confederates and southern sympathizers from registering. The Democratic party protested against it to the State Court of Appeals but without success, and later the Democratic state central committee called upon the people of the state to oppose it, charging that it was "in marked contrast and hostility to the wise and just policy of conciliation which distinguishes the dealings of President Johnson with the Southern States." Nevertheless, the registry test was applied with the result that it disfranchised probably one-half of the voters of the state. Out of a total voting population of approximately 95,000 in Baltimore City, for example, only 10,842 registered and of these only about one-half, 5,504, voted. As a result of this farcical election the Unconditional Union party gained a large majority in the legislature of 1866 and further strengthened its power in the state.

Meanwhile, the Democrats and the Baltimore *Sun*, a recognized advocate of the Conservative Unionists, had launched a campaign against the registry law and the Union party. They objected to those provisions of the constitution of 1864 which made this law possible; they called it an *ex post facto* law which was for that reason contrary to the United States Constitution; and they denounced it as unjust because it disfranchised a majority of the voting population of the state and was based, as they alleged, upon political vindictiveness. In order to organize their protest against it, they held an anti-registry law convention in Baltimore in January 1866, presided over by Montgomery Blair, at which they denounced the law and appointed a committee, headed by Blair, to present their grievances to the legislature. The Democratic minority in the Senate also protested against the law, pointing out that "petitions are pouring in signed by men of all shades of political opinion, for some legislative action. Meetings are held in every county in the State." But this Democratic agitation was bitterly resisted by Unionists, who felt that, in the blunt words of the Frederick *Examiner,* "we can get along without the assistance of rebels or traitors. They deserted the State in the hour of trial, and we have no need of their service now that all danger is over." These sentiments were shared by the legislature, and as a result it took no action on the complaints of the Democrats.

But already a reaction against the Union party in Maryland was setting in, encouraged by the developing impasse between President Johnson and the Radical Republican Congress. The do-nothing policy of the Union legislature, combined with the conservative-radical division in national politics, created a schism in the Union party in Maryland which proved fatal to the party. Its continuance in power was further endangered when the Provost Marshal General's Office of the Middle Department, Union Army, in Baltimore, closed on January 12, 1866, thus terminating federal intervention in the state. But the Unionists refused to abandon their proscriptive policies, and they proceeded to organize for more effective action. After Johnson threw down the gauntlet to Congress by vetoing the Freedmen's Bureau bill in March 1866, the Unionists in Maryland organized themselves at a mass meeting held in the Front Street Theater in Baltimore. They endorsed the registry law and called for its rigid enforcement. For the first time since 1860 they formed a permanent state organization under the name Republican.

The Democrats and some of the conservative Unionists had already held a mass meeting in the Maryland Institute on February 26, 1866, and endorsed President Johnson's "restoration policy." Calling themselves the Democratic-Conservative party, they attracted to their membership many of the Conservative Unionists, including Senator Reverdy Johnson and even Governor Swann. Swann announced his decision in the Baltimore *American* on May 12, 1866, saying that he was "for keeping the control of this government in the hands of loyal men exclusively," that he supported President Johnson, and that he opposed "universal negro suffrage and the extreme radicalism of certain men in Congress and in our own State, who have been striving to shape the platform of the Union party in the interests of negro suffrage." The governor thus deserted the old Union party mainly because of the Negro question and possibly because he may have hoped to receive the senatorship from the Democratic-Conservative Alliance in return for the repeal of the registry law.

Though Governor Swann had supported the Registration Act at the time of its adoption, he now abandoned it. Having the authority under the constitution of 1864 to appoint the registering officials and thus to exercise final control over the voting lists, he proceeded to appoint new registers and judges of election in each district, and he instructed them to interpret the registry law liberally and to let the people register and vote. In the six-weeks' period of registration, Swann's officials nearly doubled the number of legal voters. This action, of course, threatened the Republican ascendancy in the state and, it was feared, might provoke riots in Baltimore, which was controlled by the Radicals. To forestall this danger, Major General Edward R. Canby, whose department included Maryland, kept his troops in readiness there and Governor Swann, after conferring with President Johnson, brought General Grant himself to Baltimore. The ensuing election passed off quietly, however, and resulted in an overwhelming defeat of the Radicals in both Baltimore City and throughout the state. They elected only one Congressman and surrendered to the Conservatives two-thirds majorities in both houses of the legislature. This "quiet revolution" was attributable more to Governor Swann than to any other person, and he was denounced by the Radicals after their defeat as a traitor to their cause who had "stopped short of no species of villainy which promised success to the unholy plot he conceived to wrest from loyal men the power placed into their hands." The proximity of the federal military forces prepared to act on behalf of the governor must also have contributed to this Conservative-Democrat victory. The precedent for such military interposition had been established by the Lincoln administration in 1861 and 1862.

The electoral defeat of the Radical Republicans led to enraged demands for Congressional intervention in Maryland to restore the supremacy of the Unionist forces. But such intervention could not be justified in a state which in fact had never seceded. Nevertheless, the triumph in Maryland, and concurrently in Kentucky, of the party which had supported the Confederates in the Civil War, stiffened the determination of the radicals in Congress, led by Thaddeus Stevens, to impose military reconstruction upon the seceded states and clinched the argument in favor of severity as against leniency toward the South.

To Governor Swann was largely due the comeback of the Democratic party in Maryland. The Democratic-Conservative party now came into power with a two-thirds majority in each house and a governor who shared their political views. When Swann opened the new General Assembly in January 1867, he defended the state against the charge that it was permitting mistreatment of the Negroes though he opposed Negro suffrage and the Fourteenth Amendment. He approved President Johnson's plan to leave Negro suffrage and other methods of reconstruction in the hands of the states, thus reaffirming Maryland's commitment to its traditional Free State position. The General Assembly immediately passed a resolution approving the reconstruction policy of President Johnson and the action of Governor Swann in supporting it. They also endorsed the governor's "just and liberal execution . . . of the existing Registry Law of this state [as] a concurrence with the sentiments of a great majority of the people of this State, and a proper recognition of their inalienable right to participate in its Government by the exercise of the elective franchise." The legislature accordingly restored to full citizenship and the right to vote and hold office all persons deprived of these rights by the constitution of 1864. The Democratic-Conservative majority even rejected a minority proposal barring from the franchise men who had fought in the Confederate army or navy. Thus the legislature impliedly approved Governor Swann's action in disregarding the registry law. Henceforth all that would be required of voters would be a simple oath of allegiance, and judges of election must register all persons qualified to vote and must receive all votes of persons so registered.

The legislature and the governor now connived in a political maneuver which was typical of the reprehensible practices of the Reconstruction period. In order to carry out the alleged preelection bargain between the Democratic-Conservative party and Governor Swann, the legislature chose Swann as senator. But in order to do so they had to repeal the law which required that one of the senators should be a resident of the Eastern Shore. They then reenacted this law immediately after choosing Swann. But this scheme was blocked by the Radical Republicans, who secretly plotted to have the Senate in Washington refuse to seat Swann on the ground that his election was a result of a bargain with the disloyal faction in Maryland and had violated the law requiring one senator to be elected from the Eastern Shore. Swann's successor in the governorship, Lieutenant Governor Dr. Christopher C. Cox, who had remained loyal to the Republican party, would then appoint John A.J. Creswell as senator in Swann's place and would use his influence against the enactment of a bill to hold a new constitutional convention to replace the Radical constitution of 1864. When news of this scheme leaked out, Swann formally declined the election to the Senate because, as he said, of the solicitation of friends and his conviction that his paramount duty was to the state. Accordingly the legislature chose Philip Francis Thomas as senator, but when he was not allowed to take his seat in the Senate on the ground that he had "voluntarily given aid, countenance, and encouragement to persons engaged in armed hostility to the United States," namely, had given his son $10 to go South during the war, the legislature replaced him with General George Vickers.

After Swann declined the senatorship, the legislature proceeded to carry out his recommendations that a new constitution be adopted. Both houses of the legislature passed by two-thirds majorities a bill to poll the people of the state upon the question of calling a convention to frame a new constitution. In their call for this election, to be held in April 1867, they provided that "every person entitled to vote for delegates to the General Assembly [should] vote on the question of a call for a convention, to frame a new constitution and form of government, with a clause therein prohibiting the legislature from making any law providing for payment by this State for persons heretofore held as slaves." The Republicans in Maryland strenuously objected to this call for an election to change the constitution and they insisted that no constitutional change should be made except by "impartial manhood suffrage without regard to color." Since this was not done, they appealed to Congress "to organize a loyal State government with impartial suffrage." But they received no satisfaction from Congress and were unable to prevent the election from being held, though they nominated no candidates for it. Of the 58,718 votes cast in the election, 34,534 favored a convention and 24,136 opposed it. As the election resulted in a victory for the Democratic-Conservative party, the Republicans abandoned their plan to hold a rival constitutional convention wisely deciding to await the new constitution and to defeat it at the polls if it did not contain a provision for universal manhood suffrage.

Preparations were immediately made for the summoning of a convention to propose a fourth constitution for Maryland. All of the previous constitutions of the state, adopted respectively in 1776, 1851, and 1864 with the exception of the first, had been made in an illegal manner; that is to say, they violated the revision clauses of the preceding constitution, and the constitution of 1867 was no exception. The convention which met to draft it included 118 delegates, all of whom belonged to the Democratic-Conservative party. It assembled at Annapolis on May 8, 1867, and chose judge Richard B. Carmichael of Queen Anne's County as its president. Both he and every other member of the convention then took an oath to support the constitution and laws of Maryland, to "bear true allegiance to the United States, and support, protect and defend the Constitution, Laws and Government thereof as the supreme law of the land, any law of ordinance of this or any State to the contrary notwithstanding," and "to protect and defend the Union of the United States" against all political combinations seeking to dissolve or destroy it. So the members of the convention repelled the Radical charge of disloyalty and guaranteed their allegiance to the Union. On June 29 the convention was honored with a visit from President Johnson whom they enthusiastically and fulsomely welcomed.

Though Maryland was now controlled by the Democratic party and officially supported the reconstruction policies of the Democratic executive rather than the Republican Congress in Washington, it had remained loyal to the Union and was therefore allowed by Congress to handle its own postwar problems of governmental reorganization. Since Maryland had never been out of the Union, it could not be forced by a Radical Congress to meet prescribed conditions for readmittance to the Union. While Congress was busily setting up military governments in the conquered states of the South, the constitutional convention at Annapolis proceeded to draw up a constitution which in general embodied the views of the Democratic party in the Reconstruction period. At the very outset it reaffirmed the Democratic view on the national-state relationship by incorporating verbatim in Article III the tenth amendment to the national constitution declaring that "powers not delegated to the United States by the Constitution thereof, nor prohibited by it to the States, are reserved to the States respectively or to the people thereof." In another article they impliedly condemned Lincoln's war policy of intervention in the state by declaring "That the provisions of the Constitution of the United States, and of this State, apply, as well at time of war, as in time of peace; and any departure therefrom, or violation thereof, under the plea of necessity, or any other plea, is subversive of good Government, and tends to anarchy and despotism."

The new constitution did away with the punitive provisions of the constitution of 1864 by abolishing the test oaths. It merely required officeholders to take an oath to support the Constitution of the United States and the constitution and laws of Maryland and to discharge faithfully their duties as officials. It prescribed a uniform registration of the voters of the state and made such registration conclusive evidence of the right to vote. But it reserved this right to white male citizens. Whereas the constitution of 1864 had made the white population the basis for representation in the General Assembly, the new constitution made the whole population the basis; that is, though not allowing the Negroes to vote, it allowed them to be counted for purposes of representation in the General Assembly and so in effect increased the power of the southern counties where Negroes were most numerous. It reaffirmed the Thirteenth Amendment by declaring that "slavery shall not be reestablished in this State, but having been abolished, under the policy and authority of the United States, compensation, in consideration thereof, is due from the United States." In these provisions also the constitution reflected the policies of the Democratic party and of President Johnson. But it removed the disqualification of Negroes to serve as witnesses in any cases on account of race or color and prohibited poll taxes.

The convention gave little time, in comparison with the time given by the constitutional convention of 1850-1851, to debating the matter of apportionment of representation in the House of Delegates. On this question it worked out a formula which operated to the disadvantage of Baltimore City and to the advantage of the less populous counties of the state, as follows: Each county having a population of 18,000 or less would have two delegates, those with a population of from 18,000 to 28,000 would have three, 28,000 to 40,000 would have four, 40,000 to 55,000 would have five, and over 55,000 would have six. But Baltimore City, which included one-third of the population of the state, was entitled to send to the House of Delegates only six delegates from each of its three legislative districts or a total of eighteen, which was only a little more than one-fifth of the total number of delegates. As a further condition upon representation in the legislature, the constitution revived a provision which had been omitted from the constitution of 1864 making any minister or preacher of the Gospel or of any religious creed or belief ineligible for membership in the General Assembly in order to keep church and state separate. The constitution also created a new county, the first since the creation of Howard County in 1850. The provision establishing Wicomico County, with Salisbury as its county seat, was inserted to gratify local pride in Salisbury and to increase the representation of the southern counties in the legislature.

In its judiciary provisions the constitution legislated all the judges out of office and did away with the Court of Appeals. It reduced the number of judicial circuits from thirteen to eight and constituted the eight chief justices of the circuits as the Court of Appeals. These judges were to be elected by the people of each circuit respectively. The convention also legislated all other state officials out of office and provided that a new state election should be held in 1867 and every fourth year thereafter for the election of a governor and other state officials. It gave the veto power to the governor and required a three-fifths vote in both houses of the legislature to override his veto. It raised his salary from $4,000 to $4,500 and abolished the office of lieutenant governor. It provided for an entirely new government for the city of Baltimore, which would be set up under new elections to be held in October 1867 and prohibited the city from creating any debt or lending its credit without specific authorization of the General Assembly and the approval of the people. In the matter of education, the constitution let stand the enlightened provisions of the previous constitution and simply required that the General Assembly should at its first session "by Law establish throughout the State a thorough and efficient system of Free Public Schools."

This constitution could be amended in two ways. First, the legislature might pass amendments by a three-fifths vote in each house and submit them to the people; and, second, in the year 1887 and every twentieth year thereafter the people should be given an opportunity to vote on the question of calling a new convention to alter the constitution. When the convention finished its labors, it adopted the constitution by a vote of 100 to 4 and then submitted it to the people of the state. In the election the constitution was adopted by an overwhelming majority. Out of a total vote of 70,215, the vote in favor was 47,152 and against, 23,086. Even the Republican opposition was almost negligible. When in pursuance of the constitution the Baltimore elections were held, the Democratic-Conservatives captured the city government, and at the state election on November 5 their candidate for governor, Oden Bowie, was elected over his Republican opponent by a majority of 22,050, the largest ever given to any candidate. Every member of the General Assembly chosen in that election was a Democrat.

As a young man Bowie had won distinction for gallantry in action in the war against Mexico. When he ran for election to the Maryland Senate in 1861 he had been deprived of victory by the military intervention of the Lincoln government at the polls. He had meanwhile been elected president of the Baltimore and Potomac Railroad in 1860 and through his business skill and energy he made it a successful line. He remained president of the railroad until his death. During the Civil War he had supported the Southern cause but disapproved of secession. His election completed the self-reconstruction of Maryland.

In this way Maryland adjusted its fundamental law to the requirements of the postwar political situation under the auspices of the

Democratic party and without interference by either Congress or the president. The success which the Republicans had enjoyed in Maryland under the constitution of 1864 had been short-lived. Their radicalism, particularly on the question of Negro suffrage, alienated the predominantly conservative opinion in the state and threw the government of the state into the hands of the Democratic party. But so strongly was this self-reconstruction of Maryland resented by the powerful Radical Republicans who now controlled Congress that that body gave serious consideration to moving "the United States Naval Academy from its present location in the state of Maryland to some point in a loyal state." But, fortunately for Maryland, this move failed. The Radical Republican Congress proceeded to initiate proceedings of impeachment against President Johnson, but in the ensuing trial before the Senate the president was successfully defended by, among other counsel, Maryland's Senator Reverdy Johnson. Soon afterward the president sent Johnson to England where as minister he negotiated a treaty for the adjustment of the *Alabama* claims, afterward rejected by the Senate.

Under the circumstances, in the election of 1868, Maryland supported Governor Horatio Seymour of New York, the Democratic candidate for the presidency, giving him a popular majority of more than two to one and all its electoral votes. Besides Maryland the only other former slave states that gave their electoral votes to Seymour over Grant were Delaware, Kentucky, and Louisiana, all the rest of them being under control of the military authorities and therefore perforce Republican. In 1868, for the first time since the beginning of national nominating conventions, no major party held its convention in Baltimore.

Meanwhile, Maryland under conservative Democratic control had to give consideration to the proposed Fourteenth Amendment to the constitution which had been approved by the Radical Republican Congress and referred to the states for their action in June 1866. It was opposed by the Maryland legislature on the grounds that, as stated in the majority report of the joint committee of the two houses, (1) the proposed amendment had not passed Congress by the required two-thirds majority because the Congress which had approved it was a Congress from which eleven southern states had been excluded, (2) section 3 punishing ex-Confederates was an *ex post facto* law and therefore unconstitutional, (3) the South had sincerely believed in state's rights and secession, and (4) section 4 prohibiting compensation for slaves was unacceptable to the state. Moreover Maryland did not want to abandon its hope of receiving compensation for its emancipated slaves nor to approve a Congressional plan that would force the southern states to give suffrage to the Negroes under penalty of losing a part of their representation in Congress. But a sufficient number of states in the North and in the militarily occupied South ratified the amendment to warrant Secretary of State Seward in proclaiming in July 1868 that it had received the approval of twenty-nine states and was therefore in effect. But Maryland continued to refuse to ratify the amendment and did not finally do so until 1959, leaving at that time only California and Kentucky as states which still withheld their approval.

Meanwhile, the movement among Radical Republicans for a constitutional amendment that would assure Negro suffrage in the South and continued Radical control of Congress was gathering momentum. When the Fifteenth Amendment forbidding the states to deny voting privileges to citizens of the United States "on account of race, color, or previous condition of servitude" was passed by Congress and referred to the states for their approval in February 1869, Maryland refused to ratify it. Governor Bowie in his annual message to the legislature objected to it on the ground that it deprived the states of their full control over the right of suffrage and that the states must retain this control in order to operate efficiently. Without control of the suffrage, he insisted, the states could not exercise the powers of local government which the constitution intended them to exercise. In accordance with the governor's recommendation, the Maryland legislature then rejected the amendment by a unanimous vote in both houses. Maryland's dominant party, the Democratic, was obviously hostile to any attempt to legislate civil and political equality for the Negroes. This Fifteenth Amendment was ratified only by those states which had negligible Negro populations or were dominated by "carpet-bag" governments, but it was rejected by the border states Maryland, Delaware, Kentucky, and Tennessee, as well as by the Pacific Coast states California and Oregon, who opposed the enfranchisement of the Chinese. Nevertheless, in March 1870 Secretary of State Seward proclaimed that this amendment had been ratified by the necessary number of states and had thus been made a part of the constitution. Of the states which he named as having ratified it, three—Virginia, Mississippi, and Texas—had been obliged to do so as a condition of their readmission to representation in Congress. Maryland waited more than one hundred years and finally ratified the Fifteenth Amendment in 1973.

The adoption of this Fifteenth Amendment purportedly enfranchising the Negroes did not overthrow the power of the Democratic party in Maryland, for ways of circumventing it were found. After the amendment was put into effect, some Negroes in Maryland were allowed to vote in local elections for the first time in the spring of 1870 and in the congressional elections held that fall. But still the Democrats carried the state by a majority of almost 20,000 votes and gained control of all but four counties. From 1870 to 1892 Maryland was subjected to the application of the Federal Enforcement Acts which were passed in 1870 and 1871 and which placed officials of the national government in positions of surveillance over registration and voting procedures in the former slave states in all elections for officials of the national government. Every two years during that period, Maryland elections were therefore supervised by marshals and other election officials from Washington who were charged with responsibility for ensuring that Negroes were allowed to vote.

But Negroes in Maryland continued to protest that they were not fairly treated even by the Republican party in the state nor given their rightful share of state and national patronage. They contrasted the discrimination to which they felt they were subjected with the equality of rights which the Democrats were eagerly conferring upon the German and Irish citizens of the state. But they professed continued loyalty to the Republican party and voted almost without exception for it. During the post-Civil War period they comprised more than fifty percent of the membership of that party. In Baltimore by 1890 they were sufficiently numerous to elect a Negro Republican, Harry S. Cummings, as a member of the Baltimore City Council, making him the first Negro to hold an elective office in Maryland.

In the years following the emancipation of the blacks, many of the freedmen moved from the plantation counties to Baltimore and the larger towns to enjoy the supposed advantages of urban living. As a result, the Negro population of Baltimore increased far out of proportion to the increase in the counties. In the decade 1860-1870, Baltimore's Negro population grew by 12,000, in the next decade by 14,000, and in the decade of the 1880's by 25,000. In Baltimore Negroes were allowed to ride only on the front platforms of the streetcars where they were unprotected from the weather and were not provided with seats. But a black man from New York challenged this system in 1870. When he was ejected from a seat on one of the cars, he brought suit against the street railway company and was awarded damages. As a result, the company put on several cars marked "colored persons admitted into this car," but it did not restrict their use to Negro passengers. When a second suit was brought in 1871 by a Negro who, after having offered to pay his fare was ejected from a car reserved for whites, he was awarded damages of $40 by a jury. Thereafter all the streetcars were thrown open to both Negroes and white persons.

Though the Maryland law against the intermarriage of whites and free Negroes was repealed with the general repeal of Maryland's "black" code by the legislature in 1867, the law was reenacted in 1884 prohibiting the marriage of whites and blacks to the third generation under penalty of imprisonment of from eighteen months to ten years. This law was upheld by the courts. Other legal discriminations either survived or were reenacted. A state law prohibited Negroes from practicing law in the state, but this was held in 1885 by the supreme court in Baltimore to violate recent rulings of the Supreme Court that black men must be admitted to practice law despite the word "white" in the Maryland code. When the state bar was opened to black lawyers in 1885 the Law School of the University of Maryland began to admit Negro applicants, graduating its first two Negroes in 1889. As another legal disability of the black race in Maryland, Negro women were not given the same privileges in court as white women to name the father in bastardy cases. But this also was changed in 1888 when a new code of general public law was quietly adopted omitting the word "white" in the jury law, the bastardy law, and the law relating to admission to the bar.

The events of the early Reconstruction period, especially those surrounding the adoption of the constitution of 1867, made it highly improbable that the Republicans would regain control of the state for many years. The acknowledged leader of the Republican party during more than two decades after the Civil War was John A.J. Creswell of Cecil County, who served as a representative in Congress from 1863 to 1865 and as senator in Washington from 1865 until he entered Grant's cabinet as postmaster general in 1869. After five years in that position, he retired to practice law in Elkton but occupied a dominant position in Maryland's Republican party until his death in 1891.[1]

After the Union government ended in 1866, Marylanders did not elect a Republican governor for thirty years. During that period they consistently chose not only Democrat governors but also Democratic legislatures. After the adoption of the constitution of 1867, the Republicans had either very small or no representation in Maryland's congressional delegation and did not gain equal representation with the Democrats in that delegation until 1895. And not until 1896 did they send a Republican senator to Washington. The Republican party continued as a distinct minority party in Maryland almost to the end of the century.

Because of the radical nature of the reconstruction measures, based upon bayonet rule over the conquered southern states, many of the "war Democrats" who had cooperated with the Republicans now returned to their old party allegiance. The conservative Unionists in Maryland, who after 1864 organized the Democratic-Conservative party, once more moved into the Democratic party. The Democratic party in Maryland in those years was a conservative party, emphasizing state's rights as against national authority, believing generally in a minimum of governmental interference in the life of citizens, staunchly upholding property rights, opposing radical action on the race question, and working in close alliance with the growing business and industrial interests of the state. In the Democratic party the sympathies and interests of both rural and urban Maryland merged. The eminently respectable and conservative nature of the Democratic party was embodied in its candidate for governor in the state elections held in the fall of 1871. William Pinkney Whyte, a grandson of William Pinkney, was elected governor by a majority of about 15,000 votes and was inaugurated in the following January. During the 1850's he had won notoriety by exposing election frauds perpetrated by the Know Nothings. During the Civil War he had supported the Confederacy. He was a "Democrat of the old school" and a personification of propriety and decorum.

Soon after Governor Whyte's inauguration, the revolt within the Republican party against the renomination of President Grant erupted in the Liberal Republican convention which met at Cincinnati and nominated Horace Greeley of New York for president. In July the Democratic party held its national convention in Baltimore and accepted Greeley as their candidate. In the ensuing popular election, the Maryland voters favored Greeley over Grant but by less than a thousand majority. As Greeley died a few days after the election, Maryland cast her eight electoral votes for another Democratic candidate, Thomas A. Hendricks of Indiana.

After Grant's inauguration for his second term, the Maryland legislature elected Governor Whyte to represent Maryland in the Senate. He therefore resigned from the governorship, and as senator took a leading part in party caucuses and legislative measures. During his service there, which continued until 1881, he opposed the greenback movement and favored resumption of specie payments in order to stabilize the credit of the government. As a member of the Senate committee on the District of Columbia he helped in setting up the commissioner system of government for Washington in 1874 which replaced the mayoral system. Upon Whyte's resignation as governor of Maryland, the legislature chose James Black Groome to complete his term ending in January

1876. After Groome finished the term, he was elected to the Senate for the six-year term beginning in March 1879.

None of the national nominating conventions met in Baltimore in 1876, and thereafter neither of the major political parties selected Baltimore as the site of its convention until the Democrats met there in 1912. In a political sense, Baltimore lost its attractiveness and prestige as a convention city after 1872. In the contest of 1876 between the Republican candidate for the presidency, Rutherford B. Hayes of Ohio, and the Democratic candidate, Samuel J. Tilden of New York, Maryland gave the Democratic candidate a majority of almost 20,000 votes. The Maryland returns were not called in question in the exciting count of the electoral votes by the Electoral Commission which agitated the country until March 2, 1877, when the president *pro tem* of the Senate declared that Hayes had been elected. All of Maryland's electoral votes had been cast for Tilden.

Meanwhile, Governor Groome had been succeeded in the State House in Annapolis by John Lee Carroll, who was a great-grandson of Charles Carroll of Carrollton and owner of Doughoregan, the ancestral home. In a campaign which was marked by fraud, bribery, intimidation, and some anti-Catholic agitation against Carroll, he was elected over his Republican rival by a majority of about 10,000 out of a total of 157,984 votes. He served the full four-year term from January 1876 to January 1880.

The uncertainty surrounding the presidential election, leading even to apprehension of civil war, did not end with the inauguration of President Hayes in March 1877, and was aggravated by agitation over the currency, business failures, labor-management conflicts, and unrest among the farmers. As the four-years' depression was bearing down with especial hardship upon the railroads, the Baltimore and Ohio Railroad Company notified its employes on July 11, 1877 that because of "the depression in the general business interests of the country" it was reducing "the present compensation of all officers and employees of every grade in the service of the company" by ten percent where the amount of their wages exceeded one dollar per day. They explained that they had delayed action until after their competitors, the Pennsylvania, the New York Central and Hudson River, and New York and Erie companies had made similar reductions in pay and that they hoped that every employee "will cheerfully recognize the necessity of the reduction and earnestly cooperate in every measure of judicious economy necessary to aid in maintaining effectively the usefulness and success of the company."

But the employees, who already nursed grievances against the personnel policies of the company and its lax safeguards of personal security, did not accept the wage reduction supinely, and on July 16, when it was to become effective, they refused to work along the entire line of the road. To counter their resistance the company hired strike-breakers and with the aid of the police, succeeded in running the trains in and out of Baltimore. But at Martinsburg, West Virginia, one of the principal junctions of the railroad, service was interrupted when the strikers dragged strike-breakers from the engines and completely tied up train service. The railroad then appealed to Governor Henry Matthews of West Virginia. When the militia of that state proved unable to restore order, the governor asked the aid of President Hayes, and at the same time John W. Garrett, who was president of the Baltimore and Ohio Railroad, likewise appealed to the president. In response to these appeals, Hayes issued a proclamation ordering all persons responsible for domestic violence and obstruction of the law "to disperse and retire peaceably to their respective abodes." His government also dispatched eight companies of infantry from Forts McHenry and Washington to Martinsburg, and under their protection two trains were started from there on July 19; one of them arrived safely at Baltimore, but the other was stopped by strikers at Keyser.

Meanwhile, the strike was spreading into the Ohio Valley affecting the Pittsburgh and Fort Wayne, the Lake Shore and Michigan Southern, the Ohio and Mississippi, and the Cincinnati, Hamilton and Dayton Railroads. To check the spreading strike, troops were called out in both Pennsylvania and New York. As the strike continued, no freight trains moved out of Baltimore, and perishable freight began to spoil. At Cumberland a mob stopped freight trains, broke open the cars and uncoupled the engines, and the rioters were joined by reinforcements from Martinsburg. When the news reached Baltimore that the strike at Cumberland was assuming dangerous proportions, Governor Carroll conferred with the officers of the Baltimore and Ohio Railroad and was finally persuaded reluctantly to send the state militia to Cumberland. He accordingly sent Brigadier General James Herbert, commanding the First Brigade, to Cumberland to suppress "riot and lawlessness on the line of the Baltimore and Ohio Railroad in this State." He also issued a proclamation ordering citizens "to abstain from acts of lawlessness and to aid the lawful authorities in the maintenance of peace and order."

But as the Maryland troops marched from the Baltimore armory to the Camden Street Station to entrain for Cumberland, hundreds of excited citizens blocked their progress and pelted them with stones and other missiles. They also tore up the tracks leading out of the station and destroyed the railroad switches. The enraged crowd, estimated at 2,000 persons, confined the sixth regiment in its armory at the corner of Fayette and Front Streets, but after they were fired upon, they were forced back. In this encounter ten civilians were killed and 25 wounded, and 12 members of the regiment were wounded. When the troops arrived at Camden Station, Governor Carroll, at the behest of Mayor Ferdinand C. Latrobe of Baltimore, revoked the orders dispatching them to Cumberland. A mob meanwhile gathered around the station calling out the names of the railroad officials with cries of "hang them," "shoot them," "burn them out." Probably numbering 15,000, they destroyed several locomotives, burned three passenger cars, and set fire to the passenger platform.

While this riot was in progress, Governor Carroll telegraphed to President Hayes stating that he could not disperse the rioters who had "taken possession of the Baltimore and Ohio Railroad depot." He called upon the president "to furnish the force necessary to protect the State against domestic violence," since the legislature of the state was not in session and could not "be convened in time to meet the emergency." Accordingly, the president dispatched troops from Fort McHenry, Fortress Monroe, Fort Columbus, and New York harbor and marines from the Washington navy yard and ordered them to report to Major General Winfield S. Hancock at Baltimore "to act under the orders of Governor Carroll in quelling the riot at that point." As a result, Governor Carroll was able to inform the Secretary of War on July 21 that order had been restored. Nevertheless, on the following day General Hancock, commander of the military division of the Atlantic, reached Baltimore, and stationed nearly 2,000 United States troops there together with about 600 marines. In addition, Maryland regiments were recruited to their maximum, and the police commissioners of Baltimore selected 500 special policemen. The saloons of the city were closed for several days, and business was suspended. The governor issued proclamations calling for the maintenance of public order and forbidding citizens to gather in crowds. At the same time, President Hayes issued a proclamation against the rioters.

By July 23 the strike had spread all over the eastern part of the country, becoming most serious at Pittsburgh. There rioters burned all the depots and shops of the Pennsylvania Railroad, destroyed 125 locomotives, and demolished hundreds of railroad cars. They drove a regiment of Pennsylvania militia, hurriedly dispatched from Philadelphia, into the engine house, and set the building on fire, causing losses to the Pennsylvania Railroad Company in Pittsburgh estimated at $3,000,000. In Maryland the expenses of suppressing the riots mounted to $85,000. By July 28 the strike was ended and regular train service was resumed under the protection of local posses and troops. The boatmen on the Chesapeake and Ohio Canal had also threatened to strike but were prevented from doing so by the president of the company, Arthur Pue Gorman, and the 7th regiment. As a sequel to the strike, a Workingmen's Party was formed in Baltimore, and in the elections of October 1877 the Workingmen's candidate for mayor polled 17,367 votes. But the election was safely carried by the Democratic candidate who received a vote of 51,091. Nevertheless, both the Republican and the Democratic parties thereafter tried to outbid each other for the support of labor.[2]

As a result of the growing strength of labor organizations, the Maryland legislature was obliged to modify its labor law in 1884. When Maryland became independent of Great Britain, it adopted the harsh English law which treated union activities as criminal conspiracy. In 1821 the Maryland Court of Appeals, interpreting this law in *State v. Buchanan,* held indictable "(1) a conspiracy (by two or more) to raise their wages, either of whom might legally have done so," and (2) "a malicious conspiracy to impoverish or ruin a third person in his trade or profession." Under this decision labor actions were not brought into the courts but were legally considered to come exclusively under police control. But this law did not seriously inhibit the growth of labor organizations and activities. Finally in 1884 the legislature, partly on Gorman's initiative, passed two laws legalizing them. The first declared that an act of a combination formed in "furtherance of a trade dispute between employers and workmen shall not be indictable as a conspiracy, if such act committed by one person would not be punishable as an offense (nothing in this section shall affect the law relating to riot, unlawful assembly, breach of peace, or any offense against any person or against property)." The second permitted the incorporation of trade unions "to promote the well-being of their every day life, and for mutual assistance in securing the most favorable conditions for the labor of their members." As a result of these laws, labor unions first became a legal factor in Maryland. In 1892 labor won another victory when it secured the enactment of a law legalizing and protecting union labels; but not until 1911 did the legislature pass an act requiring the "public printer" to affix the label of the International Typographical Union to all public printing.

In national politics the Hayes administration had meanwhile withdrawn the military forces of occupation from the last three southern

A Painful Reconciliation

states and allowed them to return to the fold of the Democratic party. The South now became "solid" for the Democrats and seemed likely to confront the Republicans with a strong challenge to their continued control as the presidential election of 1880 approached. In the election Maryland favored the candidate of the Democratic party, Winfield S. Hancock of Pennsylvania, over the Republican candidate, James A. Garfield of Ohio, and gave him a majority of over 15,000 popular votes and all its electoral votes.

The Democratic party of Maryland chose as their candidate for governor in 1880 a former United States senator from Maryland, William Thomas Hamilton of Hagerstown, and elected him by a majority of more than 22,000 votes. During the Civil War he had upheld the right of the South to secede, and as governor he threw his weight against the influence of the Chesapeake and Ohio Canal in state affairs.

At the expiration of Hamilton's four-year term, the Democrats turned for governor to one of Maryland's most distinguished political figures, Robert M. McLane, a son of Louis McLane who had been Jackson's Secretary of the Treasury. From 1853 to 1855 Robert McLane had served by appointment of President Pierce simultaneously as commissioner to China, Japan, Siam, Korea, and Cochin China. In 1859 he was appointed envoy extraordinary and minister plenipotentiary to Mexico with "discretionary authority to recognize the government of President Juárez, if, on his arrival in Mexico, he should find it entitled to such recognition." This he did, and he continued in Mexico until December 1860. He was elected to Congress in 1879 and served there until 1883, when he was nominated for governor by the Democratic party of Maryland and was elected. But in 1885, while he was serving as governor, he was offered the position of minister to France by President Cleveland and turned over the governorship to the president of the Senate, Henry Lloyd, a native of the Eastern Shore, who served out the remainder of McLane's term.

The Democratic party to which Maryland had steadfastly adhered since 1867 finally triumphed in national politics in 1884. In the campaign of that year which preceded this triumph, Maryland did not take an active or controversial role. It was not given a chance to serve as host to any of the national conventions, for these were now being held in the midwestern cities of Chicago, Cincinnati, Indianapolis, and other cities which were closer to the national center of population and national political power than was Baltimore. But for the first time Maryland showed an electoral interest in the National Prohibition party which had been holding national conventions since 1872. A Maryland branch of the Women's Christian Temperance Union had been started in Maryland as early as 1879 under the leadership of Mrs. J.C. Thomas.[3]

In the convention of the National Prohibition party which was held at Pittsburgh in 1884, a Marylander, William Daniel, was chosen as the vice-presidential nominee, and his party for the first time made a showing in the popular vote in Maryland, polling almost 3,000 votes. But in the major contest in that sordid election between the Democratic nominee, Grover Cleveland of New York, and the Republican nominee, James G. Blaine of Maine, Maryland once again supported the Democratic ticket, giving Cleveland a popular majority of more than 11,000 over Blaine and all eight of its electoral votes.

As a result of the Maryland state election in November 1887, Governor Lloyd turned the governor's chair over to another Democrat, Elihu Emory Jackson, a native of Salisbury. In that era when opposition to business monopolies was strong, Governor Jackson, who before becoming active in politics had built at Delmar one of the largest lumber businesses in the country, urged upon the legislature a policy opposing the consolidation of railroad companies. He believed that legislative barriers should be raised against the railroad mergers as stifling competition. He also tried to make the railroad companies and other large corporations assume a larger share of the tax burden of the state. State control of business monopolies which were "public in nature though privately owned and managed" had been approved by the Supreme Court in *Munn versus Illinois* and other so-called Granger cases in 1877, but as such business monopolies became increasingly interstate in character, national control over them seemed urgently needed. Maryland was a state in which business monopoly was becoming a serious problem, particularly among the railroads, and Governor Jackson in joining in the demand for governmental regulation was supporting the program of his party. This demand had already resulted in the enactment of the Interstate Commerce Act in 1887.

Again in the presidential election of 1888, Maryland gave a majority of its popular vote and all its eight electoral votes to the Democratic candidate, Cleveland, who was, however, defeated by the Republican candidate, Benjamin Harrison of Indiana. In that election Maryland gave almost 5,000 votes to the presidential candidate of the National Prohibition party, which polled votes in all but one of the states for a total of almost a quarter of a million. In the next presidential election when Cleveland and Harrison again opposed each other, Maryland further increased its popular vote for the Democratic candidate and gave him all eight of its electoral votes. As the returns of that election revealed, Marylanders showed little interest in the Populist party which had nominated a presidential candidate for the first time and which represented the frustrations and demands of the agricultural midwest and south. But Maryland increased its support of the National Prohibition party.

When Governor Jackson retired from the governorship in 1892, he was succeeded by another leader of the Democratic party of Maryland, Frank Brown, a native of Carroll County. He had been appointed postmaster of Baltimore by President Cleveland in 1886, and under his administration the postoffice substation system and mail collection by carts were introduced into Baltimore. He was nominated by the Democrats in the summer of 1891 and at the election held on November 3 was elected over the Republican candidate. In 1894 during his administration, a coal strike broke out at Frostburg. It was a part of the general ferment that affected the coal-mining sections of the country during that year of hard times. When it appeared that the local authorities would not be able to maintain order and protect property, Governor Brown sent the Fourth and Fifth regiments there by special trains on July 6 and had the town posted with proclamations against destructive strike action. The governor himself went to Frostburg and conferred with the strike leaders. As a result, Maryland suffered no violence or property destruction during these disturbances. Later in the same year he provided special trains to move the remnants of the famous Coxey's army rapidly through Maryland after they were expelled from Washington.

After Maryland adopted its constitution of 1867, the Democratic party enjoyed an uninterrupted lease of power in the state for almost thirty years. All nine of the governors from 1869 to 1896 were active in the Democratic party before they were nominated for governor and the legislatures during those years consistently included Democratic majorities in both houses. The congressional delegations that Maryland sent to Washington were overwhelmingly Democratic, including, in all that span of time, only seven different Republican congressmen and not one Republican senator. During this period Maryland experienced no political scandals and no widespread corruption.

Democratic domination of the state was made possible in large part by the working alliance that was formed sometime in 1870 by Arthur Pue Gorman of Laurel and Isaac Freeman Rasin of Baltimore. Gorman was born in Howard County of Irish ancestry and started his political career as a page boy in the House of Representatives. Through the influence of Stephen A. Douglas he became postmaster of the Senate but lost this position in 1866 because of his sympathies with President Johnson. He served six years in the Maryland House of Delegates, from 1869 to 1875, becoming speaker in 1871. Through the influence of Governor Whyte, he became president of the Chesapeake and Ohio Canal Company in 1872 and from that vantage point began to build up a Democratic rural machine in the counties.

Isaac Freeman Rasin, a native of Kent County, had identified himself with the Know Nothing party in Baltimore in the 1850's but later shifted to the Democratic party. After 1867 when he was elected clerk of the Court of Common Pleas in Baltimore and in his later appointive positions as naval officer of the Port of Baltimore (1886-1890) and as insurance commissioner of Maryland (1892-1895), he made himself the boss of the Democratic party in Baltimore and chief dispenser of patronage. From the time when this crafty political manipulator formed his alliance with Gorman, these two worked together to control the Democratic party in the state.

Under Gorman's presidency from 1872 to 1882 the Chesapeake and Ohio Canal Company achieved unprecedented prosperity and finally gave promise of fulfilling the hopes of its founders. In this position, Gorman, who continued to serve in the House of Delegates and after 1875 in the Maryland Senate, was able to exert considerable political pressure and to become one of the most influential men in the Democratic party in Maryland. Throughout his career he showed great hostility to the Baltimore and Ohio Railroad, thus reflecting not only the interests of the Canal Company which he headed but also the growing public resentment against monopolistic business practices. During his administration the canal company reached the peak of its prosperity and influence. It was able to discharge a considerable part of its bonded indebtedness and to make notable improvements in its facilities, including the installation of a telephone line along the entire length of the waterway. At the time when this line was constructed, 1879, it was the longest single circuit in existence.

In 1880, while Gorman was a member of the state senate, he maneuvered William Pinkney Whyte out of his seat in the United States Senate and won the seat for himself. After entering the Senate, he continued his antagonism to Whyte, who was now serving as mayor of Baltimore. In 1882 the Gorman forces defeated the ticket of judges who had been selected by Whyte from the judges already in office to run for election in Baltimore, proposed instead a slate of so-called reform judges who would presumably not be under Whyte's influence, and elected these new judges.

A Painful Reconciliation

In the critical presidential election of 1884, Gorman served as chairman of the Democratic National Executive Committee and so efficiently conducted Cleveland's successful campaign that he was given control over national patronage in Maryland and so strengthened his already powerful political organization. He was reelected to the Senate by the Maryland legislature in 1886, and in the Senate three years later he led the Democratic resistance to the Federal Elections bill—the so-called Force Bill—which would have authorized federal enforcement of the election requirements of the Fourteenth Amendment in the South. In the election of 1892 Gorman again managed Cleveland's campaign, which again turned out successfully. In the state election in that year, Gorman himself was reelected to the Senate, defeating Governor Jackson.

But both Gorman's party regularity and his skill in political maneuvering were put to the test in Cleveland's second administration when under his leadership the Senate so amended the Democratic tariff measure passed by the House as to evoke a public criticism from President Cleveland. The Senate amendments for which Gorman was responsible placed coal, sugar, and iron ore on the duty list, and for this action the Senate was denounced by Cleveland for abandoning "Democratic principle." Gorman must be credited with the high tariff features of this Wilson-Gorman tariff act of 1894. The imposition of a tariff on sugar, reversing the free-sugar provision of the McKinley tariff passed four years before, had much to do with sparking the rebellion that broke out in Cuba in 1895.

Maryland was a stronghold of Democratic party strength, having become such partly as a continuation of a Democratic allegiance which antedated the Civil War and partly as a reaction against the Republican extremism of the Civil War and immediate postwar periods. But its commitment to the Democratic party had certain disadvantages, for as it ceased to be a doubtful state in politics it also ceased to be a pivotal state—a state in which political factions had to be cultivated and appeased by the national political parties. Maryland could be taken for granted. For this reason Baltimore lost its appeal as a convention city for the political parties after 1872, and Maryland leaders received fewer appointments to presidential cabinets and the Supreme Court bench than before the Civil War. Whereas Maryland had been represented in the cabinets of ten presidents before the war—Washington, Adams, Jefferson, Madison, Monroe, Jackson, Tyler, Taylor, Fillmore, and Buchanan—from 1861 to 1897 it was represented in the cabinets of only two—Lincoln and Grant. Five Marylanders sat on the Supreme

Court prior to the Civil War, one of whom, Taney, served as chief justice, but after Taney's appointment in 1836, no Marylander sat on the Court until the appointment of a Maryland Negro, Thurgood Marshall, as associate justice of the Supreme Court by President Lyndon Johnson in 1967. After 1868 no Marylander was nominated for the presidency of the United States by either of the major parties until 1892, when Gorman's name was put in nomination without his consent. During the two Cleveland administrations Maryland achieved some national notoriety, if not prestige, because of Gorman's influence in the national councils of his party.

And yet, despite Maryland's overt record as a Democratic state, the margins of Democratic strength at the polls in presidential elections were sometimes not large, and in the Congress which opened in Washington in 1889, half of Maryland's delegation in the House was Republican. The long tenure of Democratic officeholding might be interrupted, particularly as the feuds of Civil War days were forgotten. To this eventuality the growing public dissatisfaction with the policies of the Democratic administration in Washington during the last two years of Cleveland's second term contributed. The financial depression of 1893, the labor unrest that accompanied it, the rumblings of revolt among the farmers, the tariff controversy between the parties—all these aroused strong feelings against the party in power and threatened the continuance of Democratic control in Maryland.

Footnotes

[1] Robert V. Friedenberg, "John A.J. Creswell of Maryland: Reformer in the Post Office," *Maryland Historical Magazine*, vol. 64, No. 2, Summer 1969, pp. 133-143.

[2] Clifton K. Yearley, Jr., "The Baltimore and Ohio Railroad Strike of 1877," *ibid.*, vol. 51, No. 3, September 1956, pp. 188-211.

[3] *Thoughts Memorial of Mary Whitall Thomas*, D.W. Glass and Company, Baltimore, 1888, p. 3.

Sources and Additional Reading

Brackett, Jeffrey C., *The Negro in Maryland,* Johns Hopkins University Studies, extra volume 6, Johns Hopkins University, Baltimore, 1889.

———, *Notes on the Progress of the Colored People of Maryland since the War. A Supplement to The Negro in Maryland: A Study of the Institution of Slavery.* Johns Hopkins University Studies, Series 8, Nos. 7-9, Johns Hopkins University, Baltimore, 1890; reprint 1973.

Kent, Frank Richardson, *The Story of Maryland Politics: An Outline History of the Big Political Battles of the State from 1864 to 1910, with Sketches and Incidents of the Men and Measures That Figured as Factors, and the Names of Most of Those Who Held Office in That Period,* Thomas and Evans Printing Co., Baltimore, 1911; reprint 1968.

Lambert, John R., Jr., "Reconstruction to World War I," *The Old Line State: A History of Maryland,* ed., Morris U.L. Radoff, vol. I of "Library of American Lives," Historical Record Association, Hopkinsville, Ky., 1956.

Myers, William Starr, *The Maryland Constitution of 1864,* Johns Hopkins University Studies in Historical and Political Science, Series XIX, Nos. 8, 9, The Johns Hopkins Press, Baltimore, 1901.

———, *The Self-Reconstruction of Maryland, 1864-1867,* Johns Hopkins University Studies, Series 27, Nos., 1, 2, Johns Hopkins University, Baltimore, 1909.

Perlman, Philip B., *Debates of the Maryland Constitutional Convention of 1867,* Hepbron and Haydon, Baltimore, 1923.

Proceedings of the State Convention of Maryland to Frame a New Constitution, Annapolis, 1867.

Quarles, Benjamin, *Narrative of the Life of Frederick Douglass, an American Slave,* The Belknap Press, Cambridge, Massachusetts, 1960.

Steiner, Bernard Christian, *Life of Reverdy Johnson,* Norman, Remington Co., Baltimore [1914].

View of Baltimore City from Federal Hill. The steamboat *Georgia*, one of the first four vessels of the Old Bay Line, is entering harbor at the right of the print. Lithograph by E. Sachse, Baltimore, 1859. Courtesy of Enoch Pratt Free Library, Baltimore

CHAPTER XXIV

ECONOMIC GROWTH

The importance of all the Atlantic seaboard states in the Union declined with the admission of new states in the west, as the New England Federalists had early foreseen. Maryland, as one of only thirteen states in 1789, played a larger role in national affairs than she played as one of thirty-seven states in 1870 or one of forty-five in 1900. Some time in the 1880's the state reached the 1,000,000 mark in population, and by 1900 it doubled its population of 1850 to reach 1,188,044. But because of the increase in population of the rest of the country, Maryland's rank among the states according to population declined from sixth place in 1790 to twentieth in 1870 and twenty-sixth in 1900. Meanwhile, the geographical center of population of the nation shifted from a point 23 miles east of Baltimore in 1790 to a point in central Indiana in 1900, leaving Maryland far behind and indicating the diminishing influence of the state in the life of the nation.

During the nineteenth century the balance between the rural and urban population of the state changed in favor of the latter. In the census of 1900 almost half the people of the state were classified as urban dwellers. Baltimore, which had a population of only 26,514 at the beginning of the century, numbered more than half a million inhabitants in 1900, having increased its population almost twenty-fold during the century. In 1870 it was the fifth city in population in the nation, but it dropped to sixth in 1880 and remained in that rank at the end of the century. In its role as the metropolis of Maryland it attracted large numbers of both whites and Negroes from the rural hinterland, the agricultural counties of the state. As a principal port city and industrial center it also offered inducements to immigrants from the Old World, 150,000 of whom settled in Baltimore between 1860 and 1920. By the latter date more than one-third of the entire population of Baltimore was either foreign-born or first-generation Americans.

Baltimore was by far the largest concentration of people in the state, for in 1900 Maryland had only three other population centers numbering more than 10,000. These were Cumberland, Hagerstown, and Annapolis. As the population of the state and its principal city had thus grown, the density of population in the state increased from only 32 to the square mile in 1790 to almost 120 to the square mile in 1900. As a result of both the growth of population and the increasing urbanization of the state, agriculture, which had been Maryland's principal economic activity well into the nineteenth century, yielded primacy to manufacturing, mining, trade, and transportation.

Agriculture in Maryland was adversely affected by the opening up of new farmlands in the Mississippi Valley. From twenty-third place among the states in the value of its agricultural production in 1870 Maryland slipped to twenty-sixth place in 1880, to twenty-seventh in 1890, and to twenty-ninth in 1900. Whereas in 1870 of the total number of people in the state engaged in gainful employment approximately one-third were employed in agriculture, by 1900 this fraction had declined to one-fifth. Maryland's tobacco production in 1900 was no greater than it had been in 1840, and it had suffered severe fluctuations during the intervening period. In 1900 Maryland ranked only eighth among the states in the production of this crop, being surpassed by Kentucky, North Carolina, Virginia, Ohio, Tennessee, Wisconsin, and Pennsylvania. By the close of the nineteenth century 44 percent of the land area of the state was still covered with timber, but much of it no longer had a market value. In this product Maryland had earlier succumbed to competition from the new West. Although Maryland's lumber industry had low rank in the nation as a whole, nevertheless the products of that industry in 1900 were valued at more than $2.5 million. Of Maryland's 46,012 farms, 3,041 were reported as dairy farms in 1900, but Maryland was not ranked among the first ten dairy states in the census of that year. At the close of the century, Maryland stood only twenty-first among the states in the production of wheat and twenty-fifth in the production of corn.

But farming, with its subsidiary occupations, continued to be a basic industry of the state. Of Maryland's total land area more than five million acres, or almost 82 percent, remained in farms in 1900. This acreage had continued fairly constant since 1850. The highest proportion of farmland was found in Kent, Queen Anne's, Talbot, and Caroline Counties on the Eastern Shore and Carroll and Howard Counties in the north central part of the state. The lowest proportion was found in the northwestern and southeastern counties. Allegany County had a smaller proportion of farmland than any other area of the state except Baltimore City.

But the size of Maryland's farms had diminished. No longer did Maryland farmers carry on a plantation economy. During the latter half of the nineteenth century the average size of the farms in the state was reduced by almost one-half, and by the end of the century Maryland had only 79 "farms" of more than 1,000 acres. As a result, during that period the number of farms more than doubled, increasing from only 21,860 in 1850 to 46,012 in 1900. In the average size of its farms Maryland in the latter year ranked twenty-eighth among the states. Despite more than two and a half centuries of intensive and almost continuous cultivation, the value of Maryland's farmland was calculated at more than the national average. In this respect Maryland ranked twenty-second among the states. Its livestock alone in 1900 were valued at almost $21 million, and Maryland's agricultural production as a whole in that year was valued at almost $44 million—a figure which was roughly equivalent to the value of the farm production each of Virginia, Massachusetts, and New Jersey.

As Marylanders saw their agricultural activities and output eclipsed by the new states of the west, they turned increasingly to manufacturing, trade, and transportation. Like many other states of the Union rimming the Atlantic, as Maryland yielded agricultural primacy to the Mississippi Valley it found its economic salvation in industrialization. The role of the state was consequently transformed from one of producing agricultural raw materials to one of transporting and processing them. This shift proceeded rapidly after the Civil War.

Maryland's intensified emphasis upon manufacturing was shown by its rise in manufacturing industry from fourteenth to thirteenth place in the nation between 1870 and 1880. By the latter year its manufactures were valued at almost $107 million, and the number of Marylanders engaged in manufacturing and mining was only slightly larger than the number who were employed in agriculture. By 1890 Maryland's manufactures were valued at almost $172 million and in value of manufactured product Maryland ranked first among the states classed in the southern group in the census reports of that year. Its leading manufactures were men's clothing, masonry, canned fruits and vegetables, flour and grist-mill products, fertilizers, malt and distilled liquors, and tin, copper, and sheet-iron manufactures. Baltimore as the industrial metropolis of the state was the leading industrial city in that part of the nation lying south of the Mason-Dixon line and the Ohio River. It ranked eighth among American cities in the value of its manufactures in both 1880 and 1890 and was responsible for 82.5 percent of the total manufactures of the state. The Baltimore of the 1880's and 1890's, with its odoriferous industry, its delicious seafood cuisine, its street life, and its railroading, was later vividly and affectionately described by Henry L. Mencken in his two volumes of reminiscences, *Happy Days*, published in 1940, and *Newspaper Days,* published in 1942.

During the two decades between 1880 and 1900, the amount of capital invested in manufacturing in Maryland almost tripled. Of the state's total number of gainfully employed persons in the latter year, 48.9 percent were engaged in manufacturing, trade, and transportation and Maryland's manufactures were valued at $242.5 million or more than five and a half times as much as its agricultural products. During that same period the number of manufacturing establishments in Baltimore increased by 75 percent and the value of capital investment in manufacturing in the city more than tripled. But Baltimore's contribution to Maryland's manufactured output declined from 82.5 percent in 1890 to 66.5 percent in 1900 as during that decade Maryland's industry dispersed itself somewhat more generally over the state. Though Maryland's growth in manufacturing during the latter four decades of the century seemed phenomenal, it merely kept pace with the rate of national industrialization in general. In the value of its manufactures Maryland ranked fourteenth among the states in both 1890 and 1900.

Maryland's industrial growth gave Baltimore, with its superb port and railroad facilities, a preeminent position as a center of commerce and transportation at the close of the nineteenth century. The value of its foreign trade quadrupled between 1870 and 1900. It became not only a principal outlet in foreign trade for the raw materials and manufactured goods of a vast hinterland area but also a leading distributor of these products in domestic markets, particularly in the southern states. Maryland's decision to turn its back on the plantation economy of the south and to throw in its lot with the industrial north had been made for it by the Lincoln government, and after the war it joined in the effort by northern industrial and investment interests to develop the newly opened resources of the south, as signalized particularly by Baltimore's leadership during the Reconstruction period in organizing both the Atlantic Coast Line and the Seaboard Air Line to provide her with railroad connections with the southern Atlantic states. Baltimore became the broker or middleman between north and south, continuing its traditional role as a border state and earning for itself the title "Gateway to the South." Its commercial interests in the south, which burgeoned after the Civil War, were reinforced by large investments of Baltimore capital in southern enterprises, including railroads, municipal streetcar systems, cotton mills, and mines.[1]

In terms of value of product Maryland's leading industry in the last decade of the century was the manufacture of men's clothing. This industry had received its impetus from Baltimore's early interest in cotton goods manufacture. In Baltimore and its vicinity several cotton mills had operated from the pioneer days of cotton spinning in America, and in the days of the Chesapeake clippers many of them turned to the manufacture of duck. About four-fifths of all this fabric made in the United States was produced in the mills in and around Baltimore. By 1890 Baltimore ranked sixth among the cities of the United States in the manufacture of men's clothing, much of which was manufactured in so-called "sweat shops" under the "putting-out" or contracting system, by which merchant employers distributed cloth to journeyman tailors who assumed the responsibility for making up the suits in their own shops with the aid of seamstresses. But this system was gradually replaced by the factory system which permitted the use of even more refined processes of division of labor. The census of 1900 reported 139 establishments in Maryland for the manufacture of men's clothing, employing 9 percent of the wage earners of the state. Their total output was valued at $17.3 million.[2]

The second ranking industry in the state in 1900 was the canning and preserving of fruits and vegetables, which reported 271 establishments and a total output valued at almost $12 million. During the decade 1890-1900 the value of the products of this industry increased by 66.7 percent. Maryland led all the states in 1900 in quantity of canned vegetables, producing 26.2 percent of the total national output.

The commercial canning of corn began in Baltimore in 1839. This and other canning operations in Maryland were stimulated by government orders during the Civil War. In 1861 experiments conducted in Baltimore proved that the canning of fruits and vegetables could be carried on at higher temperatures than formerly. This discovery made possible an increase in the range of products that could be packed and reduced the loss from spoilage. The canning industry in Maryland had two seasons—from June until September when it specialized in canning fruits and vegetables, and from September to June when it canned oysters and other seafood, destined for markets in China, Japan, and Europe. The industry required the establishment of several subsidiary industries. To meet the demands of this industry, Baltimore manufactured nearly 30 million cans annually in the late 1860's, some six printing establishments were kept in operation by printing labels, and kilns were built to convert the oystershells into lime. In the early 1890's a large tinplate mill was erected at Baltimore principally to serve the needs of the canning industry. The mechanization of the canning industry, as well as of other industries, was opposed by organized labor on the ground that machines would displace workingmen, but despite their resistance, new machines, as for example, a can-making machine, a capping machine, a pea-huller, and a labeling machine, were developed and introduced.[3]

Maryland canneries turned out the following canned vegetables, in order of value—tomatoes, corn, peas, beans, sweet potatoes, succotash, pumpkins, and okra. In the canning of tomatoes and beans Maryland outdistanced all the other states in 1900, and was outranked only by California in the canning of fruits. Maryland canneries specialized in the following canned fruits, again in order of value—peaches, pears, apples, strawberries, blackberries, raspberries, and cherries. After the discovery of the quick-freezing process for preserving fruits and vegetables in the late 1920's, the canneries yielded place to freezing plants.

The canning of oysters was started in Baltimore by Thomas Kensett in 1820. By 1850 oysters were being canned at one or two other Chesapeake fishing ports. The original "cove" oysters which were thus canned were found in coves on the west side of Chesapeake Bay above the Potomac. In 1858 Louis McMurray of Baltimore did away with the old hand-shucking process by first scalding the oysters. Soon afterward this scalding process was replaced by a steam process. In 1900 Maryland led all the other states in the canning of oysters. It doubled the number of its oyster canneries between 1890 and 1900 and in the latter year was turning out canned oyster products valued at almost $2.5 million. Some of Maryland's oyster canneries employed as many as 500 persons. Both in quantity and value Maryland's canned oyster product formed over 50 percent of the totals for the country.

Maryland's fishing industry centers in the Bay ports of Crisfield (which is sometimes called Maryland's "seafood capital"), Smith Island, Deal Island, Tilghman Island, Cambridge, Rock Hall, Baltimore, Annapolis, Solomons, and Rock Point. The oystermen detach the oysters from the bed of the Bay and its estuaries by means of either tongs or dredges. They then bring the oysters to the packing houses to be shucked, packed in tin containers of one, three or five gallons, and transported to markets throughout the United States. After the oyster season ends in March, the fishermen begin to catch hard and soft-shell crabs using either trotlines or traps for the hard crabs and scraping tools for the soft ones. Both professional watermen and amateur sportsmen find a great variety of other seafood in Maryland's waters—shad, striped bass, river herring, croakers, and Maryland's own distinctive diamond-back terrapin, a delicately fleshed water-turtle.

In value of product Maryland's third ranking industry in 1900 was the manufacture of tobacco. Baltimore ranked as the second most important center for the manufacture of smoking tobacco. A conspicuous characteristic of American industry during the era after 1870 was its tendency to fall into the hands of monopolies or near monopolies. At the turn of the century, for example, sixteen of the twenty breweries in Baltimore belonged to the Maryland Brewery Company. Similarly Maryland tobacco was taken over by large tobacco corporations, which offered the advantages of steady and, as it is so well called, a "suggestible" market, making possible a standard product, quantity production, and highly efficient methods of distribution. Until about 1890 tobacco manufacture was in the hands of small producers and a few larger firms, one of which was owned and operated by the father of Henry L. Mencken. But in that year the five principal cigarette factories in the country were merged in the American Tobacco Company. So began the great tobacco trust which eventually, by ruthless methods, acquired almost a complete monopoly of the manufacture of not only cigarettes but also plug and smoking tobacco, snuff, and cigars. Even the retailing of these tobacco products was taken over on a virtual monopoly basis by the United Cigar Stores, a chain of distributing agencies which sold directly to consumers. By 1907 the American Tobacco Company controlled about 75 percent of the entire American trade in cigarettes, plug, chewing and smoking tobacco, and snuff, and about 25 percent of the cigar industry. As a $450 million business organized as a "trust" of the vertical sort it carried on the complete circle of tobacco manufacture from ownership or control of tobacco lands to the marketing of the finished product. Maryland's Senator Gorman was a heavy investor in the American Tobacco Company and the Consolidated Tobacco Company. From them he and other stockholders reaped fabulous profits. By the end of 1905 his shares in the first of these companies, the American Tobacco Company, were worth $400 a share on a par value of $100 and were paying a twenty percent annual dividend.

Maryland's fourth ranking industry in 1900 was iron and steel with nine establishments and products valued at $8.7 million. The iron industry began in Maryland in 1649 when iron ore was smelted on the lower Patuxent. Iron smelting furnaces were built along a belt of ores running from Prince George's through Cecil County, and they produced charcoal pig iron of high quality. One of these smelters, the Principio Furnaces, situated in Cecil County, manufactured cannon and ordnance for the government during the War of 1812. Rolling mills were later built, and the mill at Mount Savage rolled the first heavy rails made in the United States. Abbott Brothers' rolling mill, located at Canton, manufactured armor plate for Union vessels after 1861 and made the armor for John Ericsson's *Monitor*. This mill made the same contribution to the military operations of the Lincoln government as the Tredegar Iron Works at Richmond made to those of the Confederacy. But the Canton mill could not roll armor more than 1.5 inches thick, as compared with twelve-inch plates which were being rolled at Sheffield at that time for the British navy. In 1864 it had to yield superiority to the New Soho Works at Pittsburgh which were equipped to furnish the government with armor plates from three to twelve inches in thickness and up to 20 feet in length.

During the 1870's the charcoal-iron industry in Maryland lost ground in relation to the industry as a whole though it maintained its output at former levels. Baltimore continued, as it had since colonial days, to be the state's leading furnace center. Of the 39,000 tons of iron made in Maryland in 1875, some 16,000 tons were smelted in Baltimore. By 1882 out of a total iron production of 54,524 tons for the state, Baltimore produced 24,462 tons. But Maryland's small-furnace industry could not compete with the new iron and steel industry which was growing up in western Pennsylvania, Ohio, and Indiana and which drew ore from the Mesabi range in the Lake Superior district. Finally in 1891 the old Principio Furnace, which had been built in 1723, was obliged to go out of business.

Between 1880 and 1890 Maryland made the transition from the small-furnace era, which had survived from the eighteenth century and which had produced charcoal iron, to the period of large-scale production using mostly foreign ores. As manufacturers of iron rails began to experiment with chrome ore and manganese in the puddling furnaces for developing especially hard steel for rails, Maryland began to open up some mines producing chromite of iron. Still another use for this metal was found when the government ordered an experimental lot of projectiles to be made of chrome iron in order to test their armor-penetrating qualities. In 1884 the Baltimore mills began to bring in ores from eastern Cuba. Three years later the Pennsylvania Steel Company, which had its headquarters near Harrisburg, purchased the tract of land at Sparrows Point on Chesapeake Bay, six miles from Baltimore, and proceeded to erect a large plant to smelt ores which it, along with the Bethlehem Iron Company, was acquiring in Cuba. In this operation the participating companies brought fuel and ore together at tidewater. Their principal foreign sources of supply for iron ore, aside from Cuba, were Spain and Algiers, and in 1890 the Baltimore mills alone imported 481,000 tons of ore. These ores were mined in countries where labor was cheap, and since they were carried across the Atlantic often as ballast or as a return cargo for outgoing grain ships, they were transported at less cost than the railroad freight on ore from interior mines in the United States.

During 1889 the first of the four giant furnaces of the Pennsylvania Steel Company at Sparrows Point went into operation and began to produce iron. In the following year Maryland made almost 100,000 tons of pig iron, representing an increase of 60 percent over the quantity produced ten years before. By 1892 the Sparrows Point furnaces made their first steel and soon were built up to a producing capacity of 400,000 tons of steel annually. To supplement these operations the company also built a shipyard at Sparrows Point. The Sparrows Point plant was nominally owned by the Maryland Steel Company, but was controlled by the Pennsylvania Steel Company. During the financial depression of 1893, both companies, finding themselves unable to meet the heavy expenses which they had incurred in building the plant at Sparrows Point, went into the hands of receivers but were soon reorganized into a condition of solvency. During the depression the iron industry throughout the United States, in company with most other business enterprises, experienced serious setbacks, and iron production sank to its lowest point since 1885. Maryland was one of only three states which maintained their pre-depression level of production.

When the Pennsylvania-Maryland Steel Company was reorganized in 1895 it was operating eight blast furnaces which had a total annual capacity of 558,000 tons of pig iron; it also owned a mill for manufacturing rails, a shipbuilding and bridge-building plant, and iron mines in Cuba. In 1898 during the war with Spain, the Sparrows Point plant was deprived of its Cuban source of iron ore and was able to work to only about half its capacity. But it rapidly expanded production after the war and by 1900 was sending bridges to Norway, Australia, India, Japan, and other foreign markets. Half of the rails which were made at Sparrows Point were bought by foreign customers.

Despite the depression of the 1890's and the dislocation of the industry caused by the war with Spain, the value of Maryland's output of iron and steel during the decade between 1890 and 1900 increased by 204.6 percent. According to the census of 1900 Maryland ranked eleventh among the states in the value of its iron and steel manufactures, reported at $8.7 million. This figure represented almost a threefold gain since 1890. The capital investment in this industry in 1900 amounted to almost $3.8 million. Maryland's largest single iron and steel product was rolled iron and steel in which the state ranked tenth, the value of its production amounting to $5.5 million.

Like the tobacco industry, the tidewater steel industry fell under the control of great corporations. By 1903 during the boom period of the Pennsylvania Steel Company, the company was capitalized at $50 million and it erected by-product coke ovens which made it independent of outside fuel supplies. Its only tidewater competition was the Bethlehem Steel Company. This latter company was organized in 1899, and two years later it was acquired by Charles M. Schwab. In 1905 the Bethlehem Steel Corporation was formed with a capital of $30 million, and it was authorized by its charter to build and repair ships and marine engines as well as to manufacture iron and steel. It was already a large producer of armor, ordnance, ammunition, and naval vessels, and soon afterward it began to produce open-hearth steel rails. Between 1913 and 1917 this corporation acquired the Fore River Ship Yards at Quincy, Massachusetts, iron mines in Chile, and finally the Pennsylvania Steel Company, which was itself an amalgamation of the Pennsylvania and the Maryland companies and was capitalized at over $56 million at the time of the transfer. As it acquired the Sparrows Point plants it owned five shipyards. This tidewater steel industry rivalled that of the midwest centering around Pittsburgh, Wheeling, and Cleveland.

Subsidiary to Maryland's iron and steel industry was the tinplate industry which was established at Baltimore largely to meet the needs of the local canning industry. By 1897 the leaders of the industry organized to regulate the distribution of their product, to reduce competition, and to defend the tariff on tin. In 1898 the American Tinplate Company was formed with a capital of $50 million, and it acquired 39 plants in different parts of the country representing 90 percent of the nation's productive capacity in tinplate. A competing company was formed in 1899, called the National Enameling and Stamping Company to combine the four principal enamel and tinplate factories, including one at Baltimore. These were merged into the United States Steel Corporation when it was formed in 1901 through the financial manipulations of J. Pierpont Morgan as America's first "billion-dollar" corporation.

A related industry was shipbuilding. The American shipbuilding industry in general had been almost ruined by the Civil War. At the end of the war its revival was prevented by the high labor costs in the shipbuilding seaports of the East Coast, including Baltimore. But in 1880 Baltimore reported seventeen shipyards, and at Cambridge, Pocomoke City, Solomons Island, and other Bay ports, shipyards were engaged either in repairing vessels or in building bay and river vessels of small size. Most of the building and repairing of the canalboats was done at Cumberland. In the single year 1873 ninety-one new boats were built in Cumberland for the freight traffic on the Chesapeake and Ohio Canal, and three years later six steam vessels began to operate on the canal. By 1880 Cumberland had six firms engaged year-round in the building and repairing of canalboats. But this industry declined as the coal fields of western Maryland became exhausted and the canal thus lost its principal freight. The canal went into bankruptcy in 1890, was taken over by the Baltimore and Ohio Railroad, and thereafter gradually fell into disuse. In 1938 it was put up as collateral by the railroad in its application for a Reconstruction Finance Corporation loan and was turned over to the national government for $2 million. In the following year it was dedicated as a national park.

Even before the Civil War Baltimore had ventured into the construction of iron ships, for which industry it seemed favorably situated. This work was interrupted by the war but was resumed in 1872 when two iron vessels were constructed. Four years later Baltimore established a yard for the construction of iron ships. In the 1890's shipbuilding, which had previously been a separate industry, became a branch of the steel industry. As a principal use of iron and steel it began to attract the interest of the large iron and steel manufacturers and was swept into the movement for vertical trusts which characterized American business activity during that period. The Sparrows Point Works were involved in this merger, as already described. In 1890 the Sparrows Point shipyard built the first oil tank steamer constructed in the United States. Two-thirds of the new vessels built during the 1890's in shipyards on the Atlantic Coast were built of steel. By 1900 Maryland had 47 shipbuilding establishments, of which four built only iron and steel vessels, as compared with only 34 in 1890, and was turning out ships valued at $4.1 million a year. In this industry Maryland ranked seventh among the states. In the building of iron and steel ships it ranked second.

Another leading industry of Maryland at the close of the century was the manufacture of foundry and machine tools, a product of the iron and steel industry. Copper smelting had declined to negligible importance. Before the Civil War most of the copper imported into the United States was brought in from Chile and Cuba and Baltimore took the lead among the eastern cities of the United States in the smelting, refining, and rolling of these ores and concentrates. After the war this industry shifted to the west, particularly Pittsburgh and Cleveland, and still later to New York, but Baltimore smelters continued to be involved in the reduction of some copper ores from Cuba and Chile.

Maryland showed considerable gains in flour milling during the 1890's. In 1890 it reported 335 flour and grist mills, but by 1900 it could boast

407 such establishments with an output valued at more than $8 million. Similarly, Maryland's animal-slaughtering industry increased from 17 establishments in 1890 to 82 in 1900. The capital investment in that industry during the decade increased by almost fifty percent, and the value of its product approximately doubled. By 1900 it had become the sixth largest industry in the state in terms of value of product.

Beginning several decades before the Civil War Maryland farmers had increasingly depended upon fertilizers to restore or maintain the productive capacity of their soils as they had to compete with the new lush soils of the Mississippi Valley. They experimented first with crushed bone, and then, as we have noted, turned to guano from South America. Before the Civil War Maryland lost its primacy in the use and distribution of Peruvian guano. As early as 1850 Baltimore pioneered in the manufacture of chemical fertilizers in the United States when P.S. Chappell and William Davison first began to carry on experiments with them. These fertilizers gained in importance as imports of Peruvian guano declined, and in the decade after 1869 this industry developed remarkably in Maryland. By the close of that decade, Maryland was the leading state in the Union in the manufacture of fertilizers, having 48 factories and turning out products valued at almost $5.8 million. Its principal rivals in the commercial fertilizer industry were Virginia, South Carolina, and Georgia. These states possessed large quantities of phosphate rock, ammonium sulphate, and cotton seed meal which formed the principal ingredients of commercial fertilizers and they were located close to the markets in the southern cotton fields which were the principal users of fertilizers. In 1895 the first great fertilizer corporation was organized—the Virginia-Carolina Chemical Company—and by the end of the century it owned thirty-one fertilizer factories scattered along the Atlantic Coast from Baltimore to Savannah. By 1905 it was powerful enough to challenge the fertilizer syndicate of Germany and to acquire large potash concessions in that country, thus becoming independent of the German trust. Maryland retained its leadership in this industry over all other states until 1904, when it fell into second place. Maryland was maintaining the fertility of its agricultural land only by the extensive use of fertilizers. According to the census of 1900 it was expending on fertilizers six percent of the total value of its agricultural products. This was a higher percentage than that of any other state except South Carolina.

At the end of the 1890's Maryland's malt liquor industry was capitalized at more than $13.8 million as compared with only $5.8 million at the beginning of the decade, and in the amount of its distilled liquor output Maryland ranked sixth among the states, specializing in rye whiskey. In 1819 Major John Adlum, of Wilton Farm near Georgetown, had found the first Catawba grapevine growing in the garden of an inn at Clarksburg, Maryland, and he had taken cuttings from it and developed them for wine-making in his vineyard on Rock Creek. Using these original vines, native to Maryland, the wine industry grew to large proportions in Ohio and New York, but it remained negligible in Maryland. In 1823 Adlum published the first book produced in the United States on the culture of grapes, entitled *A Memoir on the Cultivation of the Vine in America and the Best Mode of Making Wine.*

Maryland as one of the leading industrial states in the Union shared in the prosperity that accompanied industrialization. In 1870 the state was burdened with a total public debt of over $29 million and in respect of per capita public indebtedness had the unenviable rank of sixth among the states. But during the next decade it made a phenomenal reduction in its public debt of 62 percent, and as a result its per capita rank among the states in this respect declined from sixth to twenty-seventh. In per capita wealth Maryland ranked fifteenth among the states in 1880. Its total wealth increased from $1,085 million in 1890 to $3,391 million in 1922, or on a per capita basis, from $1,043 in 1890 to $2,728 in 1922. Since manufacturing had taken precedence over farming as the principal occupation of the state, Maryland did not experience the agrarian discontent and violence that appeared in the predominantly agricultural sections of the country during the 1890's nor did it subscribe to radical movements. In the election of 1892 Maryland gave only 796 votes to the Populist candidate for president, James B. Weaver, which was a smaller total popular vote than that of any other state except Delaware, New Hampshire, Rhode Island, and Vermont.

But many of the industries in Maryland were no longer exclusively Maryland industries, for they had become parts of larger business combinations. Maryland's Senator Gorman took a leading part in devising the Interstate Commerce legislation in 1887 which sought to curb railway monopoly, but Maryland was not as much affected by problems of railroad monopoly as were the larger states of the west and south. In 1880 Maryland ranked only twenty-seventh among the states in railroad mileage. The state was geographically small enough to benefit from competition among its three leading railways—the Baltimore and Ohio, the Pennsylvania, and the Western Maryland. In the regulation of other monopoly industries, which seemed to be increasingly called for by public opinion, Maryland was disposed to proceed slowly. Its mood was disciplined and conservative.

As Baltimore grew into one of the principal manufacturing and commercial metropolises of the nation after the Civil War, it experienced the same consequences of industrialization and urbanization as other comparable cities, New York, Boston, and Philadelphia. It found itself confronted with common problems of a social and political nature which accompanied its industrial transformation. Urbanization caused a loss, on the one hand, of individualism, which had characterized the antebellum era of the merchant-entrepreneurs, and a gain, on the other hand, of civic consciousness and of concern for people as groups. Baltimore's growing industries absorbed many of the new populations which were attracted from the Maryland countryside to its principal port and from European countries to the shores of Chesapeake Bay, but industrialization also created conditions of child labor, long working hours, unsanitary working conditions, and problems of urban congestion.

Grievances caused by these conditions inspired the organization of the Knights of Labor which made rapid progress in organizing workingmen in the decade 1877-1886. But in Maryland as elsewhere the labor organization of the Knights quickly crumbled away after 1886, to be succeeded by the American Federation of Labor. Maryland's industrial progress was seriously disrupted by strikes in 1877, 1883, 1886-1887, 1892, 1895-1896, and 1900, aimed in general at higher wages and shorter working hours and resulting in some cases in a reduction of the work day to nine hours. The unions affiliated with the American Federation of Labor took the lead in pressing for legislation favorable to manual workers and succeeded in obtaining a nine-hour day for municipal workers in 1892 and a further reduction to eight hours in 1898. In 1894 a law was passed prohibiting the employment of children under twelve years of age except in canneries.[4]

Attention was focused upon the living conditions in Baltimore's slum areas not only by the labor organizations but also by public-spirited citizens. Among the latter the Reverend Thomas M. Beadenkopf, a Congregational minister of German immigrant parentage, became concerned over the lack of bathing facilities for poor families and opened the first public bathhouse at Canton in 1893, patterned after those that had been built two years earlier in New York, which were the first in the United States.[5] Other bathhouses were built by the philanthropy of Henry Walters and were opened to public use after 1900. A further refinement of this system was the construction of tent bathhouses which were set up near fire hydrants in hot summer weather, thus taking the baths directly to the people in crowded districts.

The lines of Maryland's future economic development were clearly prefigured as the twentieth century opened. By 1910 the urban popula-

Economic Growth 507

tion of the state had passed the 50 percent mark in relation to rural population. The trend toward urban concentration continued, reaching 60 percent of the total population of the state in 1920. By the latter year Maryland's total population had almost reached 1.5 million, but its relative rank among the states in population had declined from twenty-sixth in 1900 to twenty-eighth in 1920. Meanwhile, however, the number of residents per square mile rose from 119.5 in 1900 to 145.8 in 1920. In the latter year Baltimore City alone contained 50.6 percent of the total population of the state.

But the growth of Baltimore had not kept pace with that of other large cities of the country. On a windy Sunday morning in February 1904 the city was swept by a fire which burned for more than thirty hours. Before it was finally brought under control, it destroyed over 1,500 buildings valued at nearly $150 million and covering almost 140 acres in the downtown district of the city. The Baltimore Fire Department summoned help from Washington, Baltimore and Anne Arundel Counties, Philadelphia, Wilmington, York, Harrisburg, Altoona, and even New York City. For the first time since the railroad riots of 1877, the Board of Police Commissioners were obliged to call out units of the Maryland National Guard to assist the police. Four of Baltimore's newspapers—the *Sun,* the *Evening News,* the *Herald,* and the *American*— were burned out and had to use publishing facilities of Washington newspapers for even weeks thereafter. As a result of the fire, five Baltimore stock insurance companies failed. This greatest disaster in Baltimore's history gave the city an opportunity to widen its streets in the burnt area, and to replace rotting wharves and antiquated business buildings with modern structures. The gigantic task of improving and rebuilding the burnt district extended over several years.[6]

The trends established during the latter half of the nineteenth century, militating against agricultural in relation to industrial activities, continued into the twentieth century. By 1920 the agricultural population comprised only 40 percent of the total population of the state as compared with a national percentage of 48.6. Of Maryland's gainfully employed workers the agricultural workers formed approximately one-fifth until 1920 when the number declined to only 15.9 percent or one-sixth, reflecting the severe depression that afflicted the nation's agricultural life in the years after World War I. By 1920 the average size of farms in Maryland sank below 100 acres for the first time, and between 1910 and 1920 the total farm acreage of the state decreased by almost 300,000 acres, or 5.9 percent. Agriculture as one sector of Maryland's economy was definitely losing ground in relation to other sectors.

However, one phase of agriculture, the dairy industry, was stimulated by the demands created by cities and industry. Its growth was further encouraged by the organization of the Maryland Milk Producers Association in 1908. With the expansion of highways and motor transportation facilities the dairy industry became a $20 million industry in the late 1920's and between 1929 and 1933 accounted for 29 percent of the total gross income of Maryland farms. By that time it was the leading agricultural enterprise in Maryland. The growth of this industry in turn stimulated the production of corn, hay, alfalfa, and other forage crops.

In the 1930's the old colonial controversy over "trash" in Maryland's tobacco was reopened. After being cured in the barn, the tobacco leaves were customarily stripped from the stalk and packed under pressure in large hogsheads, which were then either rolled or shipped to market and there sold from samples taken from the hogshead. As Baltimore became the commercial metropolis of the state it had emerged as the dominant tobacco market where growers could store their hogsheads of tobacco to await a favorable turn in the market.

The American Tobacco Company and the French government were the largest purchasers of Maryland tobacco, but in 1933 the former company dropped its purchases from 14,000 hogsheads to only 4,000 and the French government, which operated a tobacco monopoly, bought none. When local tobacco growers in Upper Marlboro instituted inquiries, they found that their purchasers objected to the method of buying tobacco only from hogshead samples. A French official in charge of a cigarette factory showed a Maryland visitor a yard littered with rocks, rusty plowshares, and other pieces of "trash" which he said had been found in Maryland tobacco.

Soon afterward, the tobacco-marketing system was revolutionized when Frank M. and R.L. Hall built an immense shed in Upper Marlboro and invited the tobacco growers to bring their tobacco to it and sell it loose. Thus originated the Marlboro Tobacco Market, bypassing both the need for pressing machines and the Baltimore market. There they could show buyers the exact quality of the tobacco to be sold, free of deception. The buyers themselves subsequently built packing plants near the market where, after purchasing the loose-leaf tobacco, they could pack the tobacco in hogsheads and send it to their own warehouses and factories. As a result Baltimore lost to Upper Marlboro its priority as the tobacco market of the state.

The latter half of the nineteenth century had been a period of unprecedented manufacturing and business activity in Maryland, and this activity greatly accelerated in the twentieth century. During the first decade of the new century, while the population of the state was increasing by 9 percent, its manufactures increased in value by 49.6 percent. But because of the extraordinary growth of manufacturing in other parts of the nation, Maryland's contribution to the national production in terms of value declined from 1.6 percent in 1904 to 1.5 percent in 1909. The value of Maryland's manufactured products, as disclosed in the census of 1910, exceeded $315 million. In this respect it ranked fifteenth among the states, having declined from fourteenth place in 1900. Maryland's manufacturing industry was still situated predominantly in Baltimore, but during the first decade of the twentieth century that city's contribution to the manufactures of the state still further declined from 66.5 in 1900 to 59.2 in 1910. During that period Baltimore as a manufacturing center slipped from eighth city in the nation to thirteenth.

The manufacture of clothing continued to be the most important industry in the state, employing 20.8 percent of the total number of employees engaged in manufacturing and turning out products which accounted for 13.1 percent in value of the total manufactures of the state. In this line of manufactures Maryland contributed 8.3 percent of the total national product and ranked fourth among the states. This entire industry was carried on in Baltimore.

By 1910 Maryland's second ranking industry was no longer canning and preserving but the manufacture of copper, tin, and sheet iron products, valued at almost $17 million. In this industry Maryland ranked fifth among the states. But these manufactures were only slightly more valuable than the products of Maryland's third industry—the canning of fruits, vegetables, and oysters, which comprised 468 establishments and turned out a product worth $13.7 million. In this industry Maryland was edged out of second place by New York between 1900 and 1910. In terms of value of product Maryland ranked third among the states, being surpassed only by California and New York. The output of this industry in Maryland comprised 14.4 percent of the total national product.

Slaughtering and meat packing came fourth among Maryland's industries in 1910 with an output valued at $13.6 million. Between 1904 and 1909 this industry showed an almost 100 percent gain, and Maryland took rank as seventeenth among the states. The lumber and timber industry in Maryland consisted largely of logging plants, mills turning out rough lumber, shingles, cooperage materials, and finished lumber products, including doors, sashes, blinds, and packing boxes. In this industry Maryland ranked thirty-first among the states, and its lumber and timber product had a value of more than $12 million.

Foundry and machine-shop products ranked sixth among Maryland's industries in 1910. They included a wide variety of manufactures, such as gas and water meters, hardware, plumbers' supplies, structural ironwork, and canning machinery. Next in importance were tobacco manufactures in which 263 establishments in Maryland specialized. Fertilizers were produced at 41 establishments in the state and were valued in 1910 at $9.6 million. In the fertilizer industry Maryland ranked second among the states, being outranked only by Georgia. In shipbuilding Maryland ranked ninth, in the manufacture of glass and musical instruments tenth, in chemicals eleventh, in pottery twelfth, in paper and wood pulp thirteenth, in leather products fifteenth, in both the paint and varnish and the printing and publishing industries sixteenth, in the manufacture of boots and shoes eighteenth, in flour milling twenty-first, in the production of soap twenty-third, and in the brick and tile industry twenty-seventh. Such was the diversity of Maryland's manufactures.

The most important mining operation in Maryland was the production of bituminous coal. Of the total value of Maryland's mines amounting to almost $5.8 million in 1910 almost 78 percent represented the value of the product of bituminous mines. It represented a capital investment of almost $22.9 million, and in the production of this fuel Maryland ranked sixteenth among the states.

Maryland's entire economy was greatly stimulated, as was the general economy of the nation, by World War I. It benefited from the war-born demand for foodstuffs and fighting materials and, at least in the short run, by the inflation in values that accompanied the war. Maryland's agricultural production in 1919 reached the fabulous value of $158 million, which was almost two and a half times its prewar value. Its vegetable production in 1920 was valued at the sixth highest among the states.

But even in those boom years, in terms of the total value of its farm crops Maryland ranked only thirty-second among the states. Its agricultural development was almost negligible in comparison with the growth of its industrial machine in the war years. During World War I the value of Maryland's canning and preserving industry increased by more than 58 percent, the value of the products of its cereal mills more than doubled, and the value of its output of cotton goods almost tripled. In 1919 Maryland still outranked all other states except Georgia in fertilizer production, and its product was valued at more than $37 million. During the war the value per ton had approximately doubled. Maryland's distilled liquor industry made phenomenal gains, increasing its production from only 2.6 million gallons in 1915 to 26.7 million gallons in 1918, or a gain of more than 1,000 percent. Between 1916 and 1919 Maryland shipyards increased the tonnage of their launched steel ships from 45,833 to 131,012, or 185.8 percent. In 1919 the Sparrows Point yards launched sixteen vessels and Baltimore yards ten—most of them intended for war operations. During the war Maryland developed a new aircraft industry. In the census reports of 1910 this industry was so new that the data on it was reported under "motorcycles, bicycles, and parts." In 1919 Maryland had only one aircraft establishment manufacturing monoplanes, byplanes, triplanes, and balloons.

Maryland's total industrial production more than doubled in value during the war years, rising from $315.6 million in 1914 to $873.9 million in 1919. The capital investment in Maryland industries also doubled, increasing from $293 million in 1914 to $619 million in 1919. Baltimore, and Maryland generally, profited considerably from the opening up of the Panama Canal in 1914, which offered new opportunities in trade between the east and west coasts of the United States and brought the west coast of South America thousands of miles nearer to the Chesapeake. Because of Baltimore's new potentialities as an industrial center, many local industries—notably the steel, tinplate, and petroleum companies—expanded their facilities. The largest industrial alcohol plant in the world was established there. Two of the three trunk-line railroads of Baltimore built their own docking facilities, and the other constructed an immense grain elevator. As new industries and new capital flowed into Baltimore, the city's industrial output tremendously increased, tripling in value between 1914 and 1939 and considerably outstripping that of the nation as a whole.

In the latter year Baltimore's commercial connections with northern seaboard cities were expanded when the Chesapeake and Delaware Canal was deepened to 27 feet and a second entrance to the canal was completed. By that year Baltimore had become the seventh industrial city in the nation and it ranked second to New York among east coast ports in total foreign-trade tonnage and second in the entire nation in the volume of imports. It was a port-of-call for approximately 65 steamship lines for an all-time record. During that year 3,288 vessels entered its harbor and 3,816 departed. By 1940 it was the third port in the country in total waterborne commerce, and though it lost this rank during World War II, it regained it by the end of 1946.

In the seventy years between 1870 and 1940 Marylanders had been drawn increasingly into the ambit of machine production. The economic, social, and even political life of the state was transformed by industrialization and urbanization. In the decade between 1910 and 1920 Maryland's cities of over 10,000 population increased to five as Frederick passed the 10,000 mark. Western Maryland also came to occupy a new place in the life of the state as a producer of fuel for industry. Of the 126 mining enterprises in the state in 1928, 58 were coal mines located in Allegany and Garrett Counties. They accounted for 84.5 percent of the total value of Maryland's mineral products. This section of the state also developed new industries of its own supplementary to railroad and canal operations. In addition, as early as 1911 the rayon industry, which is a kind of link between the chemical and the textile industries, began production. By 1929 it was concentrated in the hands of some eight or nine corporations. Among them was the Celanese Corporation which operated a large factory at Cumberland. Factory production was almost a monopoly of Maryland's cities. Its five cities having more than 10,000 inhabitants, though they included 56.2 percent of the total population of the state, accounted for 82.3 percent of its manufactures.

The fundamental shift in the economy of the state from agriculture to industry and from a predominantly farming population to an industrial population, coinciding as it did with similar shifts in Maryland's neighbors in the Middle Atlantic region, tended to detract to a degree from the proud uniqueness of the Maryland way of life and to open up necessary channels of change. These would lead into political action, which while responding to Maryland's middle-border states, would still further reduce her weight in national politics.

Footnotes

[1] Charles Hirschfeld, *Baltimore, 1870-1900*, pp. 32-34.

[2] *Ibid.*, pp. 41-42, 56-59. See also Eleanor S. Bruckey, "The Development of Baltimore Business, 1880-1914," *Maryland Historical Magazine*, vol. 64, No. 1, Spring 1969, pp. 18-42, and vol. 64, No. 2, Summer 1969, pp. 144-160.

[3] Hirschfeld, *cit. sup.*, pp. 48-50.

[4] *Laws of the State of Maryland, 1894*, Ch. 317.

[5] Anne Beadenkopf, "The Baltimore Public Baths and the Founder, the Rev. Thomas M. Beadenkopf," *Maryland Historical Magazine*, vol. XLV, No. 3, September 1950, pp. 201-214.

[6] James B. Crooks, "The Baltimore Fire and Baltimore Reform," *Ibid.*, vol. 65, No. 1, Spring 1970, pp. 1-17.

Sources and Additional Reading

French, H. Findlay, and Ralph J. Robinson, *Baltimore Industrial Development, 1919-1950,* privately printed, Baltimore, Schneidereith and Sons, 1964.

Gary, James A., and others, *A Sketch of the History of Manufactures in Maryland,* Merchants and Manufacturers Association, Baltimore, 1882.

Hirschfeld, Charles, *Baltimore, 1870-1900: Studies in Social History,* The Johns Hopkins University Studies in Historical and Political Science, Series LIX, No. 2, The Johns Hopkins Press, Baltimore, 1941.

Hollander, Jacob Harry, *The Financial History of Baltimore,* Johns Hopkins University Studies, Extra Volume 20, Johns Hopkins Press, Baltimore, 1899.

Rea, Leonard O., *The Financial History of Baltimore, 1900-1926,* Johns Hopkins University Studies, Series 47, No. 3, Johns Hopkins Press, Baltimore, 1929.

Williams, Harold A., *Baltimore Afire,* Schneidereith, Baltimore, 1954, Great Baltimore Fire of February 7 and 8, 1904. Illustrations.

CHAPTER XXV

THE SEESAW OF POLITICS

Under the constitution of 1867 the Democratic party had succeeded in gaining control of the political machinery of the state—control which it maintained for more than twenty-five years. From 1870 until the election of a Republican governor in 1895 Democrats occupied all major state offices and dominated both houses of the legislature. During that quarter century Maryland regularly supported the Democratic candidates in national presidential elections and was represented in Congress by sixty-seven Democrats out of a total of seventy-seven.

But Maryland's border character as an intermediate state between north and south, east and west continued to influence its political history.

During that period Maryland unlike the majority of the former slave states, developed and maintained a vigorous two-party system, for Maryland Republicans skillfully capitalized upon the Civil Rights amendments to utilize the voting power of Negroes to the advantage of their party. Republicans remained a minority party, however, until 1895 when their party won control of the state from the practically all-white Democratic party. Their growing strength throughout the period rendered Democratic control of the state more apparent than real and inhibited feelings of complacency on the part of the majority party. On a few occasions Republicans were prevented from gaining control only by the effectiveness and voting majority of the Democratic organization in the city of Baltimore.

The supremacy of the Democratic party in Maryland, controlled after 1880 by the Gorman-Rasin organization, came to an end in the mid-1890's. With its defeat Maryland returned to a two-party system for the first time in more than a quarter of a century. A restive younger generation in the Democratic party challenged the old leadership of the organization and in doing so created enough disaffection to defeat it. In part, the Democratic defeat in Maryland in 1895 reflected popular dissatisfaction with the leadership of the national Democratic party which had struggled for two years under the incubus of severe economic depression. Moreover, Senator Gorman's independent course in opposing both the gold and tariff policies of the Cleveland administration alienated both the president himself and an important sector of the

Democratic party in Maryland. These dissident elements included the Baltimore *Sun,* which was controlled by its politically powerful publisher, Edwin F. Abell, and which condemned Gorman's break with the Cleveland administration, and the Baltimore and Ohio Railroad, whose counsel John K. Cowen, later president of the company, opposed Gorman because of the latter's hostility to the railroad. The long span of Democratic control in the state made the party vulnerable in times of economic depression such as occurred after 1893. As the Democratic party went down to defeat in those years of hard times, the Republican party was the beneficiary of the demand of the voters for a change.

The nine Democratic governors that Maryland elected after adopting the constitution of 1867 represented all sections of the state except western Maryland. One had been elected from southern Maryland, three from the Eastern Shore, three from Baltimore, and two from north central Maryland. The Democratic organization concentrated its efforts on all these sections to the neglect of western Maryland. While the Democratic machine led by Gorman and Rasin dominated the state, as it did after 1880, Republican leaders such as Charles Joseph Bonaparte and Lloyd Lowndes sought to counter its influence by building up the Republican party organization. Cresswell's successor as leader of the party after the former's death in 1891 was James Albert Gary, a businessman engaged in cotton manufacturing, banking, and insurance, who would become postmaster general in McKinley's cabinet in 1897. Other able leaders of the party in the 1890's included George L. Wellington, Sidney E. Mudd in southern Maryland, and William T. Malster in Baltimore. In reorganizing their party they directed their efforts toward all sections of the state, including western Maryland, and showed more interest in the Negro vote in southern Maryland and Baltimore City than the Democrats had shown.

Republicans in Baltimore interested in reform campaigned vigorously against the Democratic ring which was allied with the vice ring and was riddled with graft. Among them, Bonaparte, a grandson of Napoleon Bonaparte's brother Jerome and the beauteous Baltimore belle Betsey Patterson, whose marriage had been terminated by order of the Emperor, had long been a leading member of the Baltimore Reform League and the Civil Service Reform Association of Maryland. He was associated in the civil service reform movement with such national figures as Carl Schurz, Dorman B. Eaton, and George William Curtis. For twenty years Bonaparte waged a persistent battle to reform and purify the Baltimore city government. His close associates in this campaign included Cowen and Severn Teackle Wallis, who, though Democrats, were distressed by the corruption of the city's political machine. Their efforts bore fruit in the election of 1895, which was acknowledged to be the first honest election in a quarter of a century or more. In that campaign both western Maryland and the Republican party won a notable victory when Marylanders elected Lloyd Lowndes as the first governor of the state from western Maryland and the state's first Republican chief executive.

Lowndes, though born in West Virginia, had long been identified with the mercantile and mining interests of Cumberland, from which he acquired considerable wealth. Public-spirited and warmhearted, he made friends easily and gained wide distinction in western Maryland. As a member of Congress in 1872 he broke with his party to become one of only six Republicans who voted against the Civil Rights bill. Though defeated in 1874, he had continued active in the organization and work of the Republican party throughout the state and was boosted as the candidate of the Republican party and of certain dissatisfied Democrats for the governorship in 1895. In the election in the fall he was supported not only by his own party followers but also by many independent Democrats and outdistanced his Democratic rival for the governorship by more than 18,000 votes. The Republicans also gained a majority of 70 to 21 in the House of Delegates and in Baltimore elected both the city council and the mayor.

This Republican victory foreshadowed Maryland's action in the presidential campaign in the next year. In the election Maryland rejected the free-silver Democratic candidate, William J. Bryan, and gave a comfortable popular majority and all eight of its electoral votes to the Republican candidate, William McKinley of Ohio, who in addition, carried three other border states—Delaware, West Virginia, and Kentucky. In that election Maryland gave pluralities to Republican candidates in all but five counties of the state and chose Republican congressmen in all six districts. For the first time in its history, Maryland sent a unanimously Republican delegation to the national House of Representatives. The Maryland legislature also replaced one of its Democratic senators in Washington with a Republican, George L. Wellington. Fortunately for Maryland's other Democratic senator, Gorman, he did not come up for election in that sad year for his party. In the election Maryland gave almost 6,000 popular votes to one of her own citizens, Joshua Levering, who had been nominated for the presidency by the Prohibition party.

Maryland's swing to the Republican party in 1895 and 1896 marked a revolution in the politics of the state and relegated the Gorman-Rasin organization to the background. In January 1898 the legislature voted Gorman out of his senate seat and replaced him with Louis E. McComas, who as a Republican congressman from Maryland in 1890 had worked for the Federal Elections bill that Gorman had helped to defeat. Within a little more than a quarter of a century the Republican party in Maryland had moved from abject defeat to complete control of the state. But the Republican victory represented rather the repudiation of a Democratic political organization, both state and national, that appeared to have outlived its usefulness than a basic reversal of Maryland's political orientation.

The Republican success was short-lived. Governor Lowndes himself gave an enlightened administration. Under his leadership the legislature first adopted the Australian or secret ballot in 1896. Another accomplishment of his administration was the enactment of a new Baltimore City Charter Law. This charter was drawn up by a non-partisan commission appointed by Mayor Malster to replace the old charter of 1796. In 1851 Baltimore had been detached from Baltimore County and given separate status, and it continued thereafter to operate under its old charter, simply maintaining the offices provided for under county government, with the exception of those in the executive branch who were called Mayor and Council rather than Board of County Commissioners, and performing in addition to its municipal services the services rendered by counties elsewhere in the state. The new charter of 1898 provided for a reorganization of the city government and consolidation of its agencies. It retained the traditional municipal framework of a mayor and a bicameral council and set up eight departments of the city government as follows: (1) Finance, (2) Law, (3) Public Safety, (4) Public Improvements, (5) Public Parks and Squares, (6) Education, (7) Charities and Corrections, and (8) Review and Assessments. Embodying most of the provisions of modern city charters, it was intended to make possible a more efficient administration of Maryland's principal city. It served the city until 1918, when, in pursuance of a constitutional amendment adopted by the voters of the state, Baltimore adopted its own charter.

The Republican administration soon became fouled up in scandals as it sought to build up a political machine and entrench itself in power through abuse of patronage and fraudulent census enumerations. At the same time it alienated traditionalist voters by repealing the so-called "Eastern Shore Law," which required that one of Maryland's two senators come from the Eastern Shore, and by the strenuous Republican efforts to increase and mobilize the Negro vote. The scandals opened up a schism in the Republican party and produced an open breach between Governor Lowndes and Mayor Malster on the one hand and Charles Bonaparte and Senator Wellington on the other. The political extremism of state officials also provoked a general public reaction in favor of the Democratic party.

The state Republican convention of 1899 nominated Lowndes for reelection, though no Maryland governor under the constitution of 1867 had ever been reelected. In the election in the fall of that year Lowndes was defeated by the Democratic candidate, John Walter Smith, of Worcester County, by a majority of 12,123 votes. Smith's victory brought success to the entire Democratic state ticket and put the state once more under the control of that party. In the House of Delegates the Democrats gained a majority of 65 to only 26 Republicans and regained control of the state senate. But Maryland's essential conservatism and opposition to the Democratic free-silver campaign kept it in the Republican column in the presidential election in the following year. The state gave McKinley and Theodore Roosevelt a popular majority of over 14,000 and all eight of its electoral votes.

Maryland's revived importance as a factor in national Republican circles was attested when President McKinley immediately appointed Gary to his cabinet as postmaster general. For the first time since 1874, a Marylander sat in the cabinet in Washington. Henceforth the Republican and Democratic parties in Maryland would compete for popular favor under conditions approaching equality. This was the long-run result of the brief Republican rule from 1896 to 1900. That the Republicans still constituted a formidable factor in Maryland politics was shown by the presidential election of 1904 in which the Republican candidate, Theodore Roosevelt, edged out a narrow victory of 51 votes in Maryland over his Democratic rival, Alton B. Parker.

Meanwhile, Gorman and Rasin had been carefully rebuilding Democratic party organization in the state. The new Democratic governor called a special session of the legislature to meet at Annapolis in March 1901 to provide for correcting the errors which had occurred in the enumeration of the United States census taken in the state in 1900, to enact legislation that would correct abuses in the state's election law, and to give greater authority to the mayor and council of Baltimore in dealing with sewerage and other sanitary matters. When the legislature convened in special session it complied with the governor's recommendations. It provided for taking a state census which proved that frauds had occurred, it passed a new election law, and it gave the executive authorities of Baltimore the added authority which they requested.

Governor Smith also secured the revision of the public school law to provide for bipartisan membership on all the county school boards in an attempt to lessen political influence on the schools. In 1902 Gorman, who had been out of political office since his defeat in 1899, was reelected to the Senate, and in the national Democratic convention of 1904 he received a scattering of votes for the presidential nomination.

The national census of 1900 reported 235,064 Negroes in Maryland out of a total population of 1,188,044. Negroes comprised approximately one-fifth of the population of the state. When the Negroes were permitted to vote they supported Republican candidates. Accordingly, when the Democrats returned to power they bestirred themselves actively to limit the participation of Negroes in politics as a means of weakening the opposition party. Their efforts were directed not only at the disfranchisement of Negroes but at the maintenance and even the extension of measures of racial segregation. This program soon proved to have considerable voter appeal, as the Democratic party unabashedly announced its intention of keeping the "ignorant and corrupt negro" from participating actively in politics. They pushed this issue strongly after President Roosevelt entertained the Negro educator Booker T. Washington at dinner at the White House in October 1901 and thus ostensibly committed the Republican party to social equality of the races. They were also encouraged by the action of the Virginia Constitutional Convention in 1901 in disfranchising Negroes.

Aside from the political advantages which the Democrats hoped to gain by limiting voting privileges of Negroes, they rationalized their effort as aimed at confining political power to the literate and propertied sector of the population as had been done in the early history of the Republic. In this movement Gorman took the lead, primarily at the outset for the purpose of diminishing Republican power and regaining his seat in the Senate. The latter object he obtained when he was elected by the Maryland legislature in November 1901 for a fourth term in the Senate. On his initiative, John Prentiss Poe, legal counsel of the State Democratic Central Committee and Dean of the Faculty of the Law School of the University of Maryland, drew up a proposed amendment to the constitution which required voters to be able to read or interpret the constitution and excluded from the franchise anyone whose ancestor had not voted in elections before January 1, 1869. Obviously the Democrats in sponsoring this measure, which was more extreme than any adopted by Maryland in the Reconstruction period, feared that a resurgence of Republican rule would produce serious racial dislocations in Maryland and threaten white supremacy.

Meanwhile, the Democrats had nominated, as Governor Smith's successor, Edwin Warfield of Howard County, who was owner of the *Ellicott City Times.* He conducted an anti-Negro campaign, characterizing the election as "a contest for the supremacy of the white race in Maryland" and was elected in November 1903 with a plurality of 12,625 over his Republican opponent. He opposed the Poe amendment —not on principle but because he felt it should include property qualifications as well as literacy tests for voting. The Baltimore *Sun,* which had now returned to the Democratic fold, editorially pronounced the Negro a "menace, not only politically but in other respects." Senator Gorman actively campaigned for the proposed amendment, and on this question parted company with his Democratic colleague in the Senate, the flamboyant Jew, Isidor Rayner. As the campaign progressed, the sectional implications of the amendment became clearer; it would favor the rural areas, where Gorman's political strength lay, at the expense of Baltimore, threatening the influence of the Baltimore political machine over Negro and foreign voters. It was opposed by most of the Baltimore newspapers and by the Republican party which held a firm line of opposition to it under the leadership of Bonaparte. When the amendment was submitted to the voters in the fall of 1905 it was defeated, receiving an especially heavy adverse vote in Baltimore.

Obviously the Democratic party machine in Maryland was badly deranged. Gorman had led the unsuccessful fight in the Senate against the ratification of the canal treaty with Panama, he had finally broken his alliance with Rasin going back to the 1870's, he had alienated his Democratic colleague in the Senate, and he had lost the backing of the people in the vote on the Poe amendment. His death at the early age of sixty-seven in June 1906 and Rasin's death in the following March highlighted the need for new leadership of Maryland's dominant party. Moreover, the temper of the times required more active leadership along so-called progressive lines than either Gorman or Rasin had been able to furnish. That a progressive program could be achieved within the existing constitutional system and without resort to illegal or violent action was demonstrated in 1907 when Marylanders voting in a statewide plebiscite decided that no new constitutional convention was needed.

The new reform leadership was provided by Austin Lane Crothers, a native of Cecil County, who was named by the Democratic state convention for governor in August 1907. In the ensuing poll he was elected by a majority of more than 9,000 votes over the Republican nominee, George R. Gaither. With the aid of overwhelmingly large majorities in both the Senate and the House of Delegates, his administration was able to enact a direct primary elections law, a corrupt-practices law, a highway-building law, and an act setting up a Public Utilities Commission.

Maryland thus kept step, at least legislatively, with the "progressive" movement of the period. But the Democratic party in the state remained largely a state machine. It was not able to throw Maryland into the Democratic column in national elections. One of the leaders of the Republican party in Maryland, Bonaparte, was appointed Secretary of the Navy in Roosevelt's cabinet in July 1905, and late in the following year was moved into the office of Attorney General. As Attorney General in Roosevelt's cabinet during the "trust-busting" campaign, he initiated and successfully carried through antitrust suits against many large corporations.

The Democrats, having reestablished themselves in the state government in 1900, controlled the state administration until 1912 but were unable to prevent the state from giving its popular vote to Republican presidential candidates. In 1908 Maryland gave a popular plurality to the Republican candidate, William H. Taft, though, because of the electoral district system prevailing in the state, it gave only two of its eight electoral votes to Taft and the remaining six to the Democratic candidate, William J. Bryan. As Governor Crothers' successor the Democrats in Maryland nominated in 1911 the son of the late Senator Gorman, but in the election held that fall their candidate lost the governorship to the Republican candidate, Phillips Lee Goldsborough, by a narrow margin of some 3,000 votes. Goldsborough, a native of Cambridge in Dorchester County, thus became Maryland's second Republican governor since the adoption of the constitution of 1867. But the legislature which was elected at the same time was overwhelmingly Democratic, and all six members of Maryland's congressional delegation were Democratic.

This Republican victory in the election of 1911 was therefore quite limited. In national politics the Republican party was wracked by the schism between the Taft and the Roosevelt factions. As between these two candidates, both of whom ran for the presidency in the election of 1912, Maryland favored Roosevelt over Taft and gave the two candidates a combined total of votes slightly exceeding its popular vote for the Democratic candidate, Woodrow Wilson. But Maryland's plurality and therefore eight or all its electoral votes went to Wilson, who became the Democratic party's second president since the Civil War. While Goldsborough was governor, Maryland became the first state to hold a popular vote for United States senator after the adoption of the Seventeenth Amendment to the constitution and elected a Democrat, Blair Lee, to that position in November 1913. In the same year, after the death of Senator Rayner, Maryland sent a Republican senator, William P. Jackson, to Washington.

The progressive impulse in both national and state politics culminated in Governor Goldsborough's administration in the adoption of a notable Workmen's Compensation Law in 1914. Since the economic crisis of the 1890's the demand for legislation especially designed to benefit labor had steadily grown and political pressure by labor organizations had mounted. In the early part of the century Maryland had experimented with laws providing for the voluntary arbitration of industrial disputes. In 1904 the legislature entrusted the Chief of the Bureau of Statistics and Information with power to mediate, arbitrate, or investigate such disputes. The legislature of 1916 amended this law to authorize the State Board of Labor and Statistics "to promote the voluntary arbitration, mediation and conciliation of controversies and disputes between employers and employees, and to avoid resort to lockouts, boycotts, black-lists, discriminations and legal proceedings in or arising out of such controversies and disputes and matters of employment." But already Maryland had adopted legislation of a different sort to satisfy laboring men and to avert labor troubles.

Under the common law the employer was required to perform certain duties toward his employees. If his negligence in any of these matters caused the injury of a workman he was liable to action at law by the worker, and he could advance three defenses to such a suit: (1) that the workman in entering his employ assumed the risks of the employment, (2) that the workman's safety was jeopardized by his fellow employees in their common employment—the fellow-servant rule of the common law, and (3) that the workman himself was guilty of contributory negligence. The first attempt made in the United States to mitigate this common-law system in favor of the workers by means of workmen's compensation legislation was made in Maryland, when the legislature passed the first workmen's compensation law in the United States in 1902. Introduced by Senator David J. Lewis, a former miner of Allegany County, it created a Cooperative Insurance Fund for the benefit of those employed in "coal or clay mining, quarrying, steam or street railroads ... and any incorporated town, city or county engaged in the work of constructing any sewer, excavation or other physical structure, or the contractors of any such town." Within these rather narrowly defined limits the act applied to about 10,000 workmen. It made employers liable for "death or injury caused by the negligence of the employer or by that of any servant or employee of such employer" unless they contributed to the insurance fund. It stipulated that half of the contributions should be deducted from the wages of the employees and provided a benefit of $1,000 for the death of an employee occurring "in the course of employment and by causes arising therein." It contained no provision for compensation for permanent or temporary injury. As a piece of social legislation it was, of course, rudimentary, but it was important as a precursor of future laws.

This law remained in force for nearly two years and was then held unconstitutional by Judge Henry Stockbridge of the Court of Common Pleas of Baltimore City because it denied to the employee a jury trial when he wished to recover for the negligence of the employer. As the law was thus killed, the Insurance Commissioner closed the accounts of the Insurance Fund and filed a final report with the governor in May 1904, showing that during the almost two years that the law had been in operation he had collected $5,313.90 from the nine companies which had joined and that he had paid out benefits of $5,000 for five deaths.

After this initial piece of social legislation was declared unconstitutional, several years elapsed before another attempt was made to set up a system of workmen's compensation. In 1910 the legislature passed a second act establishing a new cooperative relief fund but limited to clay and coal mining in Allegany and Garrett Counties. It established a compulsory, cooperative insurance scheme but obviated the constitutional difficulty by allowing the employee to sue in the courts if he renounced all benefits from the Relief Fund. This Maryland law was upheld in the Maryland courts and proved quite effective until superseded by subsequent acts.

Both the principle and the system of workmen's compensation had been steadily opposed by the Merchants and Manufacturers Association of Baltimore as impairing their ability to compete with businesses in states which lacked this system. But the advocates of workmen's compensation contended that industrial accidents could not be avoided and that they must therefore be reckoned as a part of the cost of production. Their cause was espoused by clergymen, publicists, and some businessmen and lawyers, who warned that if this solution was not accepted by the businessmen in a "humane, common sense and economic manner, it would be settled for them with a vengeance by the demagogue, agitator and socialist." In each of the presidential elections of 1904 and 1908 Maryland gave approximately 2,300 votes to the Socialist candidate for the presidency, Eugene V. Debs.

Governor Crothers set in motion in early 1911 a procedure for drafting a new and broader workmen's compensation law. He appointed a commission to study the question and draft a bill. The commission, after studying the compensation laws of several other states in the Union and of foreign countries, finally presented a bill which had been drafted by Senator Lewis. Lewis had earlier been a member of the Socialist party, and he still advocated government ownership of the telephone, telegraph, and railroad industries. In the following year the legislature enacted a new workmen's compensation law which was based on optional participation by employers. It made it possible "for any employer to make a contract in writing with any employee whereby the parties may agree that the employee shall become insured against accident occurring in the course of employment which results in personal injury or death." The act prescribed that the death benefit would amount to three times the annual wages but not less than $1,000 and that the benefit for total disability would amount to at least fifty percent of the wages during disability.

But this elective or optional compensation act and other partial measures of workmen's compensation were superseded by the new Workmen's Compensation Act of 1914, passed during Governor Goldsborough's administration. During the years between 1911 and 1914, the question of compensation for injuries suffered in industrial work was a leading issue in Maryland politics. During those years twenty-two states passed workmen's compensation laws. Since Maryland's law of 1912 was proving ineffective and the demand for broader legislation was increasing, both political parties pledged themselves to the enactment of new workmen's compensation legislation in 1914. In campaigning for it, Senator Lewis declared, "For fourteen years I have been working to bring about a workmen's compensation law. For ten years, perhaps I was considered 'a crank,' a dreamer. But the time has come when every thoughtful person is in favor of a compensation law. It has simply been a matter of educating the public."

Governor Goldsborough accordingly appointed a commission in May 1913 to study employers' liability and workmen's compensation legislation and to submit an administration bill to the legislature. The bill which the Commission submitted six months later was modeled upon an act prepared by the Conference of Commissioners on Uniform State Laws. But since it was opposed by organized labor it was withdrawn, and a compromise bill was substituted for it modeled upon the Workmen's Compensation Act of New York, which was supported by both employers and labor. This bill was enacted into law by the Maryland legislature and went into effect in November 1914.

The purpose of the Workmen's Compensation Act of 1914, as stated in the preamble, was "first, to relieve the taxpayers of the State of the burden of providing for the care of injured employees and their dependents; second, to dispense with the common-law system of recovery by employees for personal injuries, a system inconsistent with modern industrial conditions; and third, to make certain relief to workmen engaged in specified extra-hazardous work who were injured while in the course of and arising out of their employment, regardless of the question of fault." The act itself provided for a compulsory system of compensation insurance in extra-hazardous employments and an elective system for all other employments in the state.

But this Maryland law provided a low scale of benefits, which made it, in practice, less than satisfactory to labor. For example, it provided for only a fifty percent wage as a benefit during disability and continued this limited benefit for only eight years. It also discontinued all death benefits to a widow or widower at the end of eight years. It required employers either to insure their employees in the State Accident Fund, in an old-line insurance company, or in a mutual insurance association. The act set up the State Accident Fund which operated as a straight insurance system and was based upon the experience and organization of private insurance companies. For the first three years the full cost of its administration was borne by the state. The law as a whole was administered by the State Industrial Accident Commission, a bipartisan body of three commissioners who were appointed by the governor for terms of six years.

This law was a landmark in the history of Maryland labor legislation. In 1920 it was amended to increase the disability benefits of an employee to two-thirds of his average weekly wage. Its provisions were further liberalized in amendments in 1929 and 1931, but it remained the basic law of the state on workmen's compensation until superseded by legislation in the New Deal era.

The Democrats regained the governorship of Maryland in the elections in late 1915 when their candidate for governor, Emerson C. Harrington of Dorchester County, triumphed over the Republican candidate by a majority of some 3,000 votes. During his administration the United States went to war against Germany and her allies, and as Maryland's war governor he had the responsibility, which he discharged creditably, of preparing the state and mobilizing its resources for war. In the presidential election of 1916, in which the issue of war or peace seemed predominant, Maryland supported President Wilson for reelection with a popular majority of more than 21,000 votes.

One of Governor Harrington's administrative innovations was an executive budget, the first in the history of the state. Maryland became the first state in the Union to adopt the "executive" budget and to make it a component part of the constitution. In 1915, as the state was running further into debt and its system of finance was becoming more and more complicated, both parties endorsed a budget; but the Democratic convention went a step further and appointed a nonpartisan committee headed by Dr. Frank J. Goodnow, president of the Johns Hopkins University, to frame a budget bill. In January 1916 the committee presented a budget plan and recommended its passage as an amendment to the constitution. The plan was accordingly referred to the people and was ratified by a vote of 77,478 to 37,100. Under it the governor was required to submit to the legislature within twenty days after the opening of the session two budgets, one for each of the ensuing fiscal years. The control over the formulation of the budget which was thus entrusted to the governor enabled him to exercise a sometimes decisive influence in legislation.

Another innovation of Governor Harrington's administration was the establishmentt of two new state agencies, the Law Department and the Conservation Commission. His administration, however, was sharply challenged by the Republicans, who were able to increase their representation in the Maryland delegation in Congress to three and thus equal the Democratic representation. During the last two years of his governorship he was confronted by a Republican majority in the House of Delegates which was elected as an incident in the Republican reaction against the foreign policies of the Wilson administration in Washington.

As mentioned earlier, Maryland had joined in the agitation after the Civil War for national legislation prohibiting the sale of intoxicating liquor and had participated in the presidential campaigns of the Prohibition party from 1872 onward. It was not a leader in that movement and gave its maximum number of popular votes, 5,922, to the presidential candidate of that party in 1896. This election represented the highwater mark of the Prohibition party in Maryland. Thereafter the influence of the party declined. Under the barrage of propaganda spread by anti-saloon agitators and because of the wartime demands for grain, Maryland adopted local option in 1917 but did not adopt statewide prohibition until it was forced to do so by the Eighteenth Amendment to the national constitution in 1920. The attitude of Marylanders toward it was dictated by their tradition of toleration. They believed in the freedom of individual conscience and action. As citizens of a Free State, they did not want to be told what they should or should not drink.

The Seesaw of Politics

Prohibition and its enforcement legislation, the Volstead Act, immediately became a burning issue in Maryland politics. In the first statewide election held after the adoption of the Eighteenth Amendment, Harry W. Nice, the Republican candidate for governor, declared that he would oppose enforcement legislation by the state unless it was approved by a referendum of the people. The Democratic candidate for governor, Albert C. Ritchie, also took a strong states'-rights position. He opposed the Eighteenth Amendment because, as he said, it dealt "with a matter that ought to be left to the people of the states," but since it had been made a part of the constitution of the nation he pledged to enforce it if elected governor. He regarded the liquor question as a problem to be dealt with on a local basis rather than by national action and defeated the Republican candidate, Nice, by the narrow margin of 165 votes in the election of November 1919.

Marylanders had shown little interest in the spreading campaign to extend voting privileges to women. Beginning in 1871 the leaders of the national woman suffrage movement carried their campaign into Baltimore, where they won the support of the *Baltimore American and Commercial Advertiser* but evoked little response from Marylanders generally. Not until 1889 was Maryland represented at the National Suffrage Convention. Women were admitted, however, to some of Maryland's institutions of higher learning, specifically the Colleges of Law and Dentistry, the State Normal School, the Women's College of Baltimore, and the Medical School but to no other department of Johns Hopkins University. The women's rights movement was stimulated also by the increase in the number of women gainfully employed, for between 1870 and 1880 the number of women in gainful occupations in Maryland increased from only 11 percent to 16.5 percent. The greatest increase took place in the professions, including nursing, teaching, and medicine, but women were not admitted as lawyers to the Maryland bar until 1902. Many working women also found employment in Maryland's new factories, though at wages generally lower than those of men.

Though Maryland produced no outstanding national leaders of the women's rights movement during the nineteenth century, Maryland women slowly gained rights of legal equality with men. The laws of the state in this case, based as they were upon the common law of England, permitted the husband to possess his wife's personal property, rents, and real property. When a woman married she surrendered these property rights to her husband. But the legal status of women was gradually liberalized during the nineteenth century. By legislation in 1842 married women gained the right to make wills, provided they obtained the consent of their husbands, and the right to have property in real estate or slaves, though they were still required to allow their husbands to control and manage the slaves.[1] Not until the close of the century, however, were married women given the right to hold property for their separate use.[2]

The achievement of women's suffrage has been decidedly a twentieth-century victory. It began with action by the legislature in 1900 admitting women to vote on certain municipal questions in the Annapolis election. By that time women were voting in all state elections in four other states, Wyoming, Colorado, Idaho, and Utah. A bill to open up the franchise to Maryland women in state elections was defeated in the legislature in 1910 and again in 1912 but finally passed the Senate both in 1916 and in 1918 only to be defeated in the House of Delegates. Women's suffrage eventually came to Maryland only through the adoption of the Nineteenth Amendment to the national constitution in 1919, but even then the Maryland congressional delegation opposed it by a vote of four to two. The Democratic party in Maryland opposed the amendment in its platform in 1920 and the new governor, Albert C. Ritchie, a Democrat, refused to support it largely on the ground that the amendment represented an unwarranted and unconstitutional imposition of the authority of the national government upon the state. As a result Maryland failed to rank among the thirty-six states needed to bring the amendment into effect, but accepted women's suffrage only after it was proclaimed to be in effect for the nation as a whole.

Both the Senate and the House of Delegates chosen in the election of 1919 were safely Democratic. But Maryland's Congressional delegation continued to be equally divided—three Republicans and three Democrats—and in the presidential election of 1920 Maryland gave overwhelming endorsement to the Republican candidate, Warren G. Harding. In the next Congressional election, in 1921, Maryland sent to Congress a predominantly Republican delegation—four Republicans to two Democrats—for the first time in its history. In national politics Maryland remained safely Republican throughout the 1920's, giving its electoral vote to Calvin Coolidge in 1924 and to Herbert Hoover in 1928.

Ritchie exercised a decisive influence upon Maryland state politics until he was defeated in his bid for a fifth term as governor in 1934. He was a graduate of Johns Hopkins University, class of 1896, and took his law degree two years later from the University of Maryland Law

School. He then began the practice of law in Baltimore with the firm of Steele, Semmes, Corey, and Bond, and became a member of that firm in 1900. From 1903 to 1910 he served by appointment as Assistant City Solicitor of Baltimore. In 1903 he formed his own law firm and continued as a member of it until he was elected governor. From 1907 until he became governor, he served also as professor of law at the University of Maryland Law School. In 1910 he became Assistant General Counsel to the Public Service Commission and in this position represented the Baltimore consumers in their successful fight for cheaper gas and electricity. In 1915 he was nominated in the direct primary for Attorney General of Maryland and was elected to this office by a majority of 25,000. In this position, which he occupied from 1915 to 1919, he organized the first State Law Department of Maryland, which assumed responsibility for handling the legal work of all the state departments except that of the Public Service Commission. Early in 1918, while the United States was involved in World War II, Ritchie was appointed General Counsel to the United States War Industries Board, and soon after he left this position, he was nominated for governor of Maryland.

When Ritchie was inaugurated governor he became the beneficiary of a change in the office of governor which had been gradually occurring through the years since the Civil War. The office had experienced a considerable accretion of power. Under the constitution of 1776, adopted at a time when the reaction against Maryland's experience with the powerful colonial governor was strong, the state's governor was subordinated to the legislature. He was elected annually on joint ballot by the two houses of the legislature and was made ineligible to serve more than three successive terms and ineligible for reelection until four years after the expiration of his third term. In the constitutional amendments of 1837 the governor was made elective by popular vote for a term of three years and was made ineligible to succeed himself. His council was abolished, and he was vested with the whole executive power of the state. Thus he was relieved in part from his dependence upon the legislature. In the constitution of 1851 he remained nominally the head of the executive department, but he was deprived of much of both his administrative authority and his judicial power. By the terms of the constitution of 1864 the governor's authority and position remained virtually the same, but with the framing of the constitution of 1867, his powers received their greatest advance.

Under that constitution the governor was required to examine the Treasurer and Comptroller under oath "on all matters pertaining to their respective offices." He was given the general power of nominating and, by and with the advice and consent of the Senate, appointing "all civil and military officers ... whose appointment or election is not otherwise herein provided for." He was specifically empowered to appoint, by and with the advice and consent of the Senate, the State Librarian and the Commissioner of the Land Office, and he was given the authority to "remove for incompetency, or misconduct, all civil officers who received appointment from the Executive for a term of years," thus having his removal power broadened. In this constitution the governor for the first time was given the power of veto—a power which the chief executive in nineteen other states possessed at that time—and his veto could be overridden only by a three-fifths vote of each house. Maryland thus became one of the last of the original states to adopt the veto.

The constitution of 1867 gave an impetus to the growth of the governorship over that of the legislative branch of the government and started a tendency which eventually made the governor the leading figure in the state government. As the power of the governor increased, that of the legislature decreased. To the governor, therefore, gravitated the responsibility for the state government. If he misuses his power he is subject to impeachment by the legislature, and he is always quadrennially responsible to the people at the polls. Until the opening of the twentieth century, candidates for governor were nominated in party conventions, but as many states at that time introduced the direct primary system in order to combat the evils of the convention system and to secure a greater amount of popular control over the government, Maryland in 1908-1910 adopted it for all statewide elections except that of governor. In the gubernatorial nominations thereafter a kind of indirect primary system was used. The candidate for governor in each party was nominated by a party convention made up of delegates elected in primaries by the direct vote of the registered voters belonging to that party. After the passage of the Quadrennial or Fewer Elections Amendment in 1922, the governor, members of the Assembly, and other state officers were elected in the even years between presidential elections, and most state and county officers had their terms lengthened to four years. The person having a plurality of votes and meeting the constitutional qualifications is declared governor. In the event of a tie, the governor is chosen from the contestants by joint majority vote of the Senate and the House of Delegates. In case of the death, resignation, removal, or other disqualification of the governor, the vacancy may be filled for the remainder of the governor's term by the General Assembly if it is in session. But if the vacancy occurs during a recess of the legislature, the office is assumed by the President of the Senate and, after him, the Speaker of the House.

The governor, though he serves as the executive head of the state, does not exercise all executive power since there are several other officers in the administration, for example the Attorney General, Comptroller, and Treasurer, who are elected independently of him and over whom he exercises only incomplete control. He must take care that the laws are faithfully executed, and in doing so he may "call out the militia." In addition to the governor there are only three state executive officers who are popularly elected: the Attorney General, the Comptroller, and, since 1970, the Lieutenant Governor. (The Treasurer is elected by the legislature.) But the governor has been given the power of inspecting the books and papers of the Comptroller and of removing him for cause after a hearing during a recess of the Assembly. The Attorney General is the only elected executive officer who can be said to be at all independent of the governor. Of the other executive officers the governor selects his running mate, the Lieutenant Governor, for election by the voters, and he appoints his Secretary of State by and with the advice and consent of the Senate and may remove him.

Since the beginning of the twentieth century, the governor's power of appointment has been broadened with the establishment, in accordance with the general trend throughout the United States, of an increasingly large number of commissions and boards. In 1935 the governor had part in the appointment of about 66 offices, boards, and commissions with a total membership of over 300. The legislature has almost abdicated its powers of appointment, retaining sole power of appointing only the Treasurer. The governor is authorized to make many appointments alone and without confirmation by the Senate or any other body. This practice began with the creation of the State Roads Commission in 1908 and was continued when the act creating the commission was amended in 1918. In the act as amended, the State Roads Commission was reduced to three members who were appointed by the governor without confirmation by the Senate. The practice thus established was greatly extended by subsequent legislatures. The governor was given the sole power to appoint a long list of state officers, including the State Auditor, Bank Commissioner, Insurance Commissioner, Conservation Commissioner, Commissioner of State Employment and Registration, Commissioner of Mental Hygiene, Purchasing Agent, Commissioner of Labor and Statistics, State Industrial Accident Commission, State Tax Commission, Public Service Commission, State

Department of Education, State Roads Commission, Board of State Aid and Charities, and the Maryland Racing Commission. The offices which are filled by appointment by the governor without confirmation comprise from 40 to 50 percent of the total number of state administrative agencies. This practice has followed the modern trend, apparent in both state and national government, toward aggrandizement of executive agencies of government, and though it has had the perhaps wholesome effect of emphasizing executive and party responsibility, it has correspondingly derogated from the powers of the legislature, by whose authority, ironically, these changes have been made.

From time to time, the governor of Maryland has been given authority by the legislature to supervise or direct the work of various state agencies, and he can often determine their budget allotments or require reports from them at regular periods. In addition, his powers of removal and suspension of state officers have been gradually expanded since the constitution of 1776, and under the constitution of 1867, as noted heretofore, he was given broad powers to remove officers appointed by him. Under certain circumstances, for example, he may even remove the Comptroller and the Treasurer, two officers who are not appointed by him but are elected by the people and by the legislature respectively. Nevertheless, he may not remove the Attorney General who is elected by the people, nor County Boards of Education, nor Justices of the Peace, nor State's Attorneys, nor Sheriffs. His power to remove local officials is indeed quite limited.

By 1920 the number of administrative and executive agencies in the state government had multiplied so bewilderingly that a governmental reorganization became necessary. Governor Ritchie, on the basis of his experience as Attorney General and of the recommendations of competent authorities, became convinced that the administration should be simplified, and in 1921, during his first term, he appointed the Maryland State Reorganization Commission composed of 108 men and women from all parts of the state, headed by Judge Charles A. Burke, to make a survey of the administrative departments and to suggest changes in the interest of efficiency and economy. A small subcommittee of eight under the chairmanship of Judge Burke performed the actual work.

They ascertained that there were at that time 77 separate and independent state administrative agencies of which 60 were boards and commissions ranging in membership from two to thirty. The appointments to these boards were made in various ways; in length they ranged from two to nine years, and thirteen of them had an indefinite term.

Related agencies were not grouped together; for example, the Commissioners of Fisheries, Board of Shellfish Commissioners, and the Commander of the State Fishery Force were wholly separated. Some state agencies which had once been set up by the legislature had virtually ceased to exist, such as the Weigher of Tomatoes, the Inspector of Hay and Straw, and the State Agriculture Lime Board. Some of these agencies were not compelled to make any report or to maintain any records. In an attempt to simplify this maze of officers, boards, and commissions and to reduce the expense of government, the Reorganization Commission submitted recommendations which were endorsed by the Democratic Convention and became the leading plank in the party platform in September 1921. At the opening of the next session of the legislature, they were introduced in the form of a bill and enacted into law in February 1922.

Under this act the state executive and administrative agencies were reduced to nineteen. Some boards and commissions were replaced by single commissioners, and those performing similar services were consolidated. This plan reduced the expenses of government by more than $100,000 a year. The following nineteen administrative departments were established: (1) The Executive Department, (2) the Finance Department, (3) the Department of Law, (4) the Department of Education, headed by the State Board of Education, (5) the University of Maryland, (6) the Department of Militia, (7) the Department of Welfare, (8) the Department of Charities, which was subsequently abolished, (9) the Department of Health, headed by the State Board of Health, (10) the Department of Public Works, (11) the Commissioner of Motor Vehicles, (12) the Conservation Department, (13) the Department of Public Utilities, consisting of the Public Service Commission, (14) the State Industrial Accident Commission, (15) the Commissioner of Labor and Statistics, (16) the Department of State Employment and Registration, (17) the Inspector of Tobacco, (18) the Maryland State Board of Censors, and (19) the Maryland Racing Commission. An Advisory Council of thirteen officials was also established to meet with the governor for the consideration of general state policies and finances; it was composed of the following: the Comptroller, the Treasurer, the Attorney General, the Chairman of the State Board of Education, the President of the Board of Agriculture, the Director of Welfare, the Director of Charities, the Director of Health, the Director of Public Works, the Commissioner of Motor Vehicles, the Police Commissioner of Baltimore City, the Conservation Commissioner, and the Commissioner of State Employment and Registration.

Governor Ritchie took an outspokenly states'-rights position on the prohibition question. In 1920 he declared himself in favor of legislation that would permit the manufacture of beer and light wines, and for this he was attacked by the Superintendent of the Anti-Saloon League of Maryland, George W. Crabbe, as "a menace to the good morals of the State of Maryland." At governors' conferences with both President Harding and President Coolidge, he took the position that the Volstead law was "an unnecessary and drastic federal infringement" on Maryland and the personal rights of its citizens. He advocated turning "the whole question back to the states so that each may settle it in accordance with the will of its own people." Indeed, under his leadership, Maryland refused to adopt a state enforcement act of the Eighteenth Amendment on the ground that if the prohibition of intoxicating liquors was to be enforced in Maryland, the responsibility for enforcing it rested solely with the national government.

Ritchie stressed also his states'-rights convictions in the coal miners' strike of 1922 when he declined to respond favorably to President Harding's call upon the governors of all the coal-producing states to send troops to the mines. Instead, Governor Ritchie took the position that the strike should be settled by mutual agreement rather than by physical force, and he was able to effect a settlement by this means. In the election held in November 1923, Ritchie was reelected for a second term, the first Maryland governor to win this distinction since 1838, when Maryland first began to choose its governors by popular vote. During the entire period until 1923 no Democratic governor had been renominated and no governor of either party had been reelected. Ritchie's plurality in the election of 1923 was over 40,000. He was reelected in November 1926 by a majority of nearly 60,000, the largest ever received by a candidate for governor in Maryland's history.

The handsome and articulate governor of Maryland was becoming a national figure and a recognized spokesman for citizens throughout the country who opposed the further erosion of the authority of the states and the concomitant concentration of power in the central government in Washington. He was carrying on the states'-rights tradition that had been established by Maryland's Luther Martin in the Philadelphia convention of 1787 and that had impelled many Marylanders to support the Southern Confederacy in 1861. The states, Ritchie warned, in a speech at the Jefferson Day banquet of the National Democratic Club in New York in April 1924, "are fast losing rights ... without which our form of government cannot endure." For those rights was being substituted "an incompetent, extravagant, un-American control radiating from Washington."

He defended "the right of the people of each state, so long as they do not hurt their neighbors or injure society, to determine their own conduct and mode of living for themselves." In an address in the following year at the Annual Conference of Governors, meeting in Maine, he denounced "Federal aid" as a "misnomer" and as a costly pretext for centralized control over functions "reserved to the states under the Constitution." Such control, he asserted, impairs the initiative of the states and results "in standardization in affairs which ought to be settled by the home people of each State, in accordance with their home wants and needs."

These views reflected the states'-right philosophy which had characterized Maryland's conception of the federal-state relationship ever since the Articles of Confederation. And yet within this historical sequence Ritchie drew a distinction between that philosophy as represented by the pre-Civil War doctrines of nullification and secession and the contemporary need to resist the imposition by the national government of schemes "of social control, to regulate human conduct and relations, and to secure the moral well-being of the individual by forcing upon all the people the social precepts and ideas of groups or classes of the people." National legislation and bureaucratic intervention by agencies of the national government in the affairs of the states were, he protested, upsetting the constitutional equilibrium between the central government and the state governments and were threatening to destroy our "dual form of government" composed of "an indestructible Union" of "indestructible states." [3]

Even the banking history of Maryland reflects the persistence of the spirit of local initiative and control which has long been characteristic of the Free State. Membership of state banks in the Federal Reserve System was optional, but from the time of the inauguration of that system in 1913 to 1919, no Maryland banking institutions joined it. They preferred to remain under state regulation which stipulated lower capital requirements, imposed fewer restrictions, and involved less "red tape." Even as late as 1936, only ten Maryland banks belonged to the Federal Reserve System, representing the largest number up to that time. Even after the establishment of the Federal Deposit Insurance Corporation, many state banks in Maryland refused to join it and to take advantage of the deposits guaranty offered through it by the national government. Ultimately, however, the state's banking laws were amended to conform to the requirements of the national authority under pain of withdrawal of insurance privileges from the state banks. Although the legal control over state banks remained with the Maryland Bank Commissioner, actual control thus passed over to the FDIC, involving, among other things, regulation of advertising, the fixing of the rate of interest on deposits, and constraints upon banks to join the Federal Reserve System in a calculated effort to eliminate state banking systems.

Ritchie represented Maryland as a delegate-at-large at the Democratic nominating conventions of 1920 and 1924. In 1928 he was an active contender for the Democratic presidential nomination but was finally persuaded to support Alfred E. Smith of New York. But he was an acknowledged leader of the states'-rights forces in the Democratic party and the movement to repeal the Eighteenth Amendment. His availability as a candidate for either the presidential or the vice-presidential nomination grew as the Democratic convention of 1932 approached. When he was outmaneuvered for the presidency by the forces of Governor Franklin D. Roosevelt of New York, who was also a champion of states' rights and a reduction of governmental bureaucracy, he declined the vice-presidential nomination. He helped to elect Roosevelt but soon turned against the centralization, the paternalism, and the welfare philosophy of the New Deal.

And yet Ritchie's solution for the crisis of depression which swept over the country after 1929 was not much different from that of the New Deal. His answer to the problem of unemployment was to reduce the state budget but at the same time to apply the savings to financing a $12 million state bond issue for unemployment relief in Baltimore City. At the 1929 session of the legislature he carried through a reduction in the tax rate which completed a 30 percent reduction in the decade 1920-1930 and represented the lowest state tax rate since 1912. In his depression budget of 1933 he further reduced the tax rate, thus accomplishing a 36 percent reduction during his fourteen-year administration. But during his total tenure of Maryland's governorship, the state's funded debt increased by $24.5 million. Between 1922 and 1929 Maryland's debt increased by almost $4.4 million, or on a per capita basis, rose from $14.90 to 17.04. Under Ritchie's leadership, however, Maryland's debt record was not as wild as that of certain other states. In per capita share of the state's debt Maryland was outranked by thirteen other states in 1922 but by eighteen in 1929.

Although some individuals and some private enterprises in Maryland suffered severely from the economic deflation after 1929, the state as a whole withstood it remarkably well. Maryland's proportion of bank failures between 1928 and 1932 was consistently lower than the national total; in 1931, for example, when 11 percent of the banks in the United States failed, Maryland's percentage of bank failures was only 8 percent, or 18 banks out of a total of 226.[4] Later, however, as the number of bank failures throughout the nation mounted, Governor Ritchie, following examples set by the governors of Michigan and Indiana, proclaimed a bank holiday for February 25, 1933, and extended it up to the national bank holiday proclaimed by President Roosevelt on March 5. Despite this precautionary measure, fourteen banks in Maryland failed in 1933, involving nearly $100 million in liabilities and comprising largely banks in Baltimore and its suburbs.

Throughout Ritchie's four terms as governor, he had a state legislature which was consistently controlled by the Democratic party. Maryland's congressional delegation during his era was also predominantly Democratic. Ritchie gave Maryland a national reputation as a leading Democratic state, but in fact, though his personal victories were large, he considerably outran his party in state elections. From 1921 to 1923 Maryland was represented in the Senate in Washington by two Republican senators and from 1923 to 1927 and from 1929 to 1935 by one Republican senator.

In the election of November 1934, Ritchie was defeated in his campaign for a fifth term as Maryland's governor. The victor in that election was Harry W. Nice, a Republican attorney from Baltimore, who had held several public offices in Baltimore, including Secretary to the Mayor, member of the Baltimore City Council, Supervisor of Elections, Judge of the Appeal Tax Court, and State's Attorney for Baltimore City. He had been serving in this last position when he was nominated for governor by the Republicans in 1919 but, as noted previously, had been defeated then by Ritchie by only 165 votes. He was nominated again by his party to run against Ritchie in 1934 and this time triumphed over him by more than 6,000 votes. In his administration his campaign promises of tax reduction were not fulfilled. Instead, during his single term as governor, Maryland's net funded debt was increased by $21.6 million to reach a new high level of $46.1 million at the end of his administration.

In the election of November 1938, Nice was defeated for reelection by Herbert R. O'Conor. O'Conor had been elected State's Attorney for Baltimore City in 1923 and had been reelected to that position in 1926 and again in 1930 by a majority of 100,000 votes, the largest majority ever given to a candidate for public office in Baltimore City. In 1934 he was elected Attorney General and in 1938 was nominated as the Democratic candidate for governor. He was elected by a plurality of 66,277 votes, and in the same election the Maryland electorate reduced the Republican membership in the State Senate to only 6 and in the House of Delegates to only 16, its lowest point since 1900. As O'Conor's administration coincided with preparations for World War II, Maryland shared in the war-induced prosperity. At the close of O'Conor's first term, Maryland was reported to be the only state in the Union with a balanced budget, a large surplus, and falling taxes.[5] Governor O'Conor was reelected in 1942 after the United States went to war, and at the expiration of his second term in 1946 was elected to the United States Senate.

After the Gorman political machine had been checked by the voters of the state in 1895, Maryland had become again a two-party state. But in the Ritchie era the Democratic monopoly in state politics was again largely reestablished, and it continued, except in the governorship under Nice, until 1950, when the Republican mayor of Baltimore, Theodore R. McKeldin, ran for governor and defeated the incumbent Democrat, William Preston Lane, Jr., receiving 57.3 percent of the total vote. At that time the list of registered voters in Maryland showed 623,800 Democrats and only 243,400 Republicans. Since the Civil War Republicans had controlled the Maryland House of Delegates for only six years (1896-1900, 1918-1920) and the State Senate for only two years (1898-1900). The state had not elected a Republican governor since 1934 or a Republican senator since 1928. The election of 1950 brought about a new resurgence of Republicanism in Maryland. As Governor McKeldin once remarked, "Republicans only get into office in Maryland when the Democrats split."

The explanation of Maryland's political schizophrenia must be sought in its history as a border state, being neither overwhelmingly Southern Democratic nor overwhelmingly Northern Republican. It can be attributed in part to the sectional rivalry between the predominantly Democratic eastern counties and the city of Baltimore, on the one hand, and the western Republican counties, on the other. It is accounted for also by the changing programs and philosophies of the national political parties. As Marylanders saw the Democratic party under the New Deal administration in Washington abandon traditional liberalism or *laissez-faireism*, accept the concept of welfare statism, and renounce the states'-rights views which were championed by Governor Ritchie, they became confirmed in their own conservative, states'-rights views. They cherished Maryland's distinction as the Free State, that is, free from outside interference, and therefore supported the party in national politics which most clearly stood for individualism and states' rights.

A predominantly Democratic state committed to Jeffersonian principles, Maryland found itself caught in the crossfire during the Roosevelt presidency between too diametrically opposed philosophies of statecraft. The state's traditional political stance was challenged by President Franklin D. Roosevelt, while at the height of his national popularity. In the presidential election of 1936 Roosevelt carried Maryland against his Republican rival, Alfred M. Landon, by a better than three to two majority, but two years later, when he sought to use his presidential influence in the Democratic primary in Maryland, he foundered. Maryland, like many other states whose representatives in Congress were marked for purging by Roosevelt in the mid-term election of 1938, refused to become the victim of Roosevelt's resentment over the defeat of his attempt to "pack" the Supreme Court or the tool of his plan to remodel the Democratic party into what he called a "liberal, forward-looking, progressive" party.

Roosevelt's target in that election was Maryland's Senator Millard Tydings who was running for election to a third term. Many of his New Deal measures had been opposed by senators who, like Tydings, represented the states'-rights viewpoint and distrusted the central government. Against the Maryland senator Roosevelt pitted Congressman David J. Lewis, who had authored Maryland's Workmen's Compensation system and who had run for the Senate in 1916 but had been defeated by his Republican opponent, Joseph I. France. Tydings' victory was virtually assured when President Roosevelt and half his cabinet invaded the state to campaign against him in the primary, for the senator was able to appeal shrewdly to his constituents to keep the Free State free from outside intervention. He easily won both the primary nomination of his party and reelection to a third and ultimately a fourth term in the Senate, serving longer in that body than any other senator in Maryland's history.

In Maryland state politics the Democratic party adhered to a conservative line as befitted the party that had written the constitution of 1867. Representing the political elements that had emerged triumphant in the struggle over reconstruction after the Civil War, the party leadership, dominated by Gorman and Rasin, made it a primary objective to avoid innovation and disturbance. Theirs was a Bourbon party which opposed extensions of the franchise to Negroes and the propertyless and that jealously guarded the right of the state to manage its own affairs free from interference by the national government. This latter states'-right tenet was fundamental in the constitution of 1867 and was ably defended by Governor Ritchie into the 1930's.

The Republican party, on the other hand, while out of office championed limited reform measures and during its brief periods of officeholding provided the state with moderate, not radical, leadership. Maryland, whether under Democratic or Republican direction, was slow to respond to the pressure of the Populists, Muckrakers, and Progressives to intrude the government, whether state or national, into the traditional relationship between employers and employees and between producers and consumers, Maryland's philosophy of statecraft could generally be characterized as consistently *laissez-faire*.

Footnotes

[1] *Laws of Maryland, 1842*, chap. 293.

[2] *Ibid.*, chap. 457.

[3] Albert C. Ritchie, "John Marshall: Would he Save the States to-day as he did the Union in other Days?" Address at the Dinner of the Lawyers' Club of New York City on the 125th Anniversary of the appointment of John Marshall as Chief Justice of the Supreme Court of the United States, Wednesday, January 20, 1926. Other addresses of the same tenor by Ritchie were his address at the annual dinner of the New York Southern Society, December 10, 1924, entitled "The Two Political Parties, Their Past, Their Present, and What of Their Future," and his address at the Institute of Public Affairs, University of Virginia, August 14, 1929, "The Enforcement of the Eighteenth Amendment and the Volstead Act from the Point of View of the Individual States."

[4] Joseph T. Elvore, *State Bank Failures in Maryland*, M.A. thesis, University of Maryland, 1936. pp. 20-22.

[5] *New York Herald Tribune Magazine*, July 5, 1942, p. 7.

Sources and Additional Reading

Bishop, Joseph Bucklin, *Charles Joseph Bonaparte: His Life and Public Services*, New York, Charles Scribner's Sons, 1922.

Callcott, Margaret Law, *The Negro in Maryland Politics, 1870-1912*. The Johns Hopkins University Studies in Historical and Political Science, Eighty-Seventh Series, Johns Hopkins Press, Baltimore, 1969.

Goldman, Eric F., *Charles J. Bonaparte, Patrician Reformer, His Earlier Career*, Johns Hopkins Press, Baltimore, 1943.

Johnson, Gerald W., Frank R. Kent, H.L. Mencken, and Hamilton Owens, *The Sunpapers of Baltimore*, Alfred A. Knopf, New York, 1937.

Kent, Frank R., *The Story of Maryland Politics*, Thomas and Evans Printing Company, Baltimore, 1911.

Kirwin, Harry W., *The Inevitable Success: Herbert R. O'Conor*, The Newman Press, Westminster, Maryland, 1962.

Lambert, John R., *Arthur Pue Gorman,* Louisiana State University Press, Baton Rouge, 1953.

Lauchheimer, Malcolm H., *The Labor Law of Maryland,* Johns Hopkins University Studies, Series 37, No. 2, Johns Hopkins Press, Baltimore, 1919.

Rohr, Charles James, *The Governor of Maryland,* Johns Hopkins University Studies in Historical and Political Science, vol. 50, No. 3, Johns Hopkins Press, Baltimore, 1932.

Singleton, Evelyn Ellen, *Workmen's Compensation in Maryland,* Johns Hopkins University Studies, Series 53, No. 2, Johns Hopkins Press, Baltimore, 1935.

CHAPTER XXVI

EDUCATION AND RECREATION

In the census of 1860 Maryland ranked twenty-fourth among the thirty-three states of the Union in total expenditures for education and twenty-third in expenditures on public education. The wartime constitution of 1864 laid the basis for a thorough reorganization of Maryland's system of public education. Implementing the constitutional provisions on education, in 1865 Maryland enacted a law entitled "A Uniform System of Public Instruction for the State of Maryland," which was largely drafted by Dr. Libertus Van Bokkelen, who was to become Maryland's first superintendent of schools and who advocated an educational system wholly controlled by the state.

This act provided for a state board of education consisting of the governor, lieutenant governor, speaker of the House of Delegates, and state superintendent of education. To this board was given supervision over all colleges and schools which were receiving state aid. They could prescribe the textbooks to be used, could draw up a uniform code of bylaws for the guidance of county school boards, and could appoint the school commissioners in each county. Each county was required to maintain one high school, providing instruction for both "males and females in the higher branches of English and scientific education, and in the Latin and Greek languages and mathematics, sufficient to prepare youth to enter any one of the state colleges under the control of the council of the University of Maryland."

Under the act of 1865, the state undertook to collect an annual tax of fifteen cents on every one hundred dollars for school purposes and to distribute it among the counties and the city of Baltimore in proportion to their populations between five and twenty years of age. Accordingly, by 1870 Maryland rose to fifteenth place among the states in expenditures for public education.

The educational plan of Van Bokkelen envisaged the establishment of several teacher-training institutions, and under his plan the Maryland State Normal School was organized at Baltimore in 1865. Maryland thus became the first state south of the Mason-Dixon line to establish and maintain a normal school. This Maryland State Normal School was moved to a new building at Carrollton and Lafayette Avenues in 1876 and remained there until it was transferred to Towson in 1915. In 1924 the Baltimore City Training School, which had been formed in 1901 to train teachers for the Baltimore City schools, was consolidated with the normal school. A second teachers' college was authorized by the legislature in 1902 and was established at Frostburg. A third was founded at Salisbury on the Eastern Shore in 1925.

The "separate and equal" doctrine, which was approved by the Supreme Court in *Plessy versus Ferguson* in 1896 as defining official policy in the treatment of whites and Negroes, reflected the facts of life in racially segregated Maryland. Under this doctrine, provision for teacher-training schools for Negroes was deemed necessary. In 1908 the state took over the Baltimore Normal School, which had been a private normal school for Negroes since 1867, moved it to Bowie, and eventually recognized it as one of the state teachers' colleges. But the necessity for racial segregation was weakened when the Maryland Court of Appeals ordered the admission of Negroes to the law school of the University of Maryland in Baltimore in 1935 and to the university's nursing school, also in Baltimore, in 1950. Both of these cases were contested by the University of Maryland, which, under the presidency of H. Clifton ("Curley") Byrd, a native of Crisfield on the Eastern Shore, had made phenomenal growth and had achieved academic distinction among state universities. The university opposed admission of Negroes to the College Park campus until the Supreme Court ruled in 1954 that segregated public education was unconstitutional.

In 1870, when the census disclosed that more than one-seventh of the total population of the state over the age of ten were illiterate, the majority being Negroes, Governor Oden Bowie reminded the legislature that a portion of Maryland's population consisted of black freedmen, who might sometime gain the franchise and ought therefore to be given education that would prevent them from being "misled by the crafts and clamors of designing and unscrupulous politicians." He did not propose to increase taxes for the purpose of educating the black population but recommended instead that the taxes paid by Negroes be used for the establishment and maintenance of public schools for Negro children. As the conservative Baltimore *Sun* observed, "Without taking into account any higher considerations, it is evident we cannot afford to let the colored people among us go uneducated. There is a duty to them as well as ourselves in that matter." But when the state collected less than $5,000 under this law during the first year, this method of financing Negro schools had to be abandoned. In its place the legislature, controlled by the Democrats, required each county to establish a free public school for Negro children in each election district and appropriated $50,000 annually for their support. In 1878 this appropriation was doubled, the increase being deducted from the appropriation for the white schools. Many of the Negro schools in Baltimore were conducted in buildings erected by the Freedmen's Bureau. By 1873 Negro schools were available in all the counties of Maryland, but by 1892 eleven counties, all of which had large Negro populations, were contributing nothing to their Negro schools but were leaving them to operate entirely on state appropriations and private donations.

The state system of education established by the constitution of 1864 and the implementing legislation of 1865 were soon superseded by a new constitution and by a new basic educational law enacted in 1868. The constitution of 1867 simply required that the state establish "a thorough and efficient System of Free Public Schools." The act of 1868 provided for neither a state superintendent of schools nor a state board of education. Instead, it recognized the educational autonomy of the counties and allowed them to exercise almost complete control over the public schools within their jurisdiction. However, the act retained the requirement of county high schools. This requirement hastened the transformation of several of the county academies into county high schools, but by 1874 Governor Whyte was still calling for the establishment of high schools in all the counties. Laws of 1870 and 1872 reestablished the state board of education, but not until 1900 was the office of State Superintendent of Public Education revived.

In a few of the larger population centers of the state, foreign-language groups had established private schools for the education of their children in their native languages even before the War for American Independence. Lutheran, Reformed, and German-Catholic congregations maintained church schools in the German language in Baltimore. Among these one of the earliest was a Lutheran school which was started by the Zion Church in 1769. Revitalized in 1836 by the new pastor, Heinrich Scheib, it became one of the most influential and progressive schools in Baltimore and persistently adhered to its basic principle of instruction in both the German and English languages. Another important private German and English school was conducted in Baltimore by Friedrich Knapp who came to Baltimore in 1850 as a revolutionary refugee from Germany; one of his pupils was Henry L. Mencken.

These and several smaller German private schools in Baltimore flourished in the decade after the Civil War, but all of them disappeared soon after the mid-1880's because of competition from the Baltimore public schools. The German population in Baltimore was so large that in 1873 they persuaded the city authorities to establish a German-English school in the public school system. By 1897, 6,780 pupils, or over one-tenth of the total number of pupils enrolled in the public schools of the city, attended the German-English schools, which then numbered seven. But the interest in these schools and public support for them dwindled after 1900 and ceased altogether after the United States went to war against Germany in 1917. This branch of Baltimore's public school system then ended. Meanwhile, largely through the example and persistent pressure of the German *Turnverein* in Baltimore, the city school system adopted school gymnastics in 1895 as a complement to academic education.

In 1871 Baltimore's first kindergarten was established by Eli Lamb in his school on Lombard Street. It was designed for children too young to learn the three R's, and he secured Miss Elizabeth Peabody of Boston to administer it. Lamb later collaborated with officials of Johns Hopkins University in founding the Baltimore Training School for Kindergarten Teachers. In 1893 kindergartens were organized for summer recreation of the children of Baltimore, and at the turn of the century kindergartens were opened in both white and Negro schools. By 1920 the Baltimore school system added a full-time supervisor of kindergartens and made the education of five-year-old children an integral part of the school system. Kindergartens were not, however, incorporated into the state school system.

Only in Baltimore did the problem of assimilating and educating the foreign-born constitute a major problem. Elsewhere in the state the proportion of foreign-born to native-born was small. Whereas in 1900 the foreign-born formed 13.5 percent of the population of Baltimore, in the state as a whole they formed only 9.3 percent, and their numbers dwindled to only 8.1 percent in 1910. In the rural areas of the state in the latter year, the foreign-born formed only 3.7 percent of the population. In that year approximately 80 percent of the residents of the state had been born within its borders.

In 1890, 15.7 percent of Maryland's population ten years of age and over were still unable to read and write. In percentage of illiteracy Maryland showed a slightly worse record than the national average and ranked fifteenth among the states. In other words, its percentage of illiteracy was exceeded by that of only fourteen other states, all of which were situated either in the south or the far west. But among the white population over ten years of age in Maryland in 1890 illiteracy was reported at only seven percent whereas among the blacks it exceeded fifty percent. In respect of literacy, Maryland's Negroes were only slightly better off than the Negroes in twelve other southern states. By 1900, of Maryland's total population over ten years of age, 11.1 percent were illiterate. Its percentage of illiteracy was exceeded by that of seventeen other states, all of which were located either in the south or in the west and southwest. But the percentage of illiteracy among its Negro population remained high—35.2 percent. This percentage had been reduced, however, from 50.1 in 1890. In 1910 Maryland's rate of illiteracy for all persons, white and black over ten years of age, was 7.2 percent, which was slightly below the national average (7.7 percent). Its rate of illiteracy was exceeded by that of seventeen other states. But the rate of illiteracy among Maryland Negroes was 23.4 percent. By 1930 Maryland's proportion of illiteracy in its white population declined to only 1.3 percent but for the Negro population it stood at 11.4 percent.

The extension of the state's supervision over education, including the certification of teachers and the accreditation of all public schools, which has occurred largely in the twentieth century, was made possible by the public education act of 1916. This act resulted from a thorough survey of "Public Education in Maryland" which was authorized by the legislature and was directed by Dr. Abraham Flexner for the General Education Board of New York. It devastatingly reported that the state's system of public education, though "in the main soundly conceived, yields on the whole extremely unsatisfactory results. A few counties possess good and steadily improving schools; a good school may be found here and there in other counties. But the large majority of the schools are poor; teachers are, for the most part, poorly trained; instruction is ineffective and obsolete; children attend school with disastrous irregularity; school buildings are far too often in unsatisfactory condition, school grounds frequently neglected and untidy." The survey reported that the average annual salary of teachers, exclusive of those in Baltimore City, ranged from $271 in St. Mary's County to $662 in Baltimore County. In only two counties did this average salary exceed $450 a year.[1]

Among the many recommendations made by this survey was one calling for a strengthened State Department of Education. To carry out the recommendations, Dr. Albert S. Cook was appointed in 1920 by Governor Ritchie as State Superintendent of Education. Convinced that the county was the proper unit for educational administration and should be retained as such, he undertook to correct inequality in educational opportunity in the state through the equalization fund, which allocated state aid to those counties that showed the greatest needs. A teacher-retirement system was introduced in 1927 under which both teachers and the state contribute to a fund for old-age annuities, the so-called normal schools were converted into teachers' colleges, and the more prosperous counties were encouraged to develop their own supervisory personnel and corresponding independence from state supervision.

Through the Equalization Fund, which was first set up in 1922, the state undertook to enable each county to provide a minimum program of education. Under it the state supplemented the school funds of the more backward counties to enable them to meet a minimum prescribed program for schools. This system, which came to be known nationally as the "Maryland Plan," was intended to equalize educational opportunities and financial support of education throughout the state. Through this system, which was a part of Governor Ritchie's thoroughgoing educational reform, increased numbers of pupils were transported to school and the high school curricula were broadened to include such nonacademic subjects as agriculture and industrial arts. Additional funds were later received from the national government for support of schools in so-called "federally impacted areas," that is, areas in which employes of the national government are served by the Maryland schools, as, for example, United States army bases located in Maryland.

Under the new educational act of 1916 which resulted from the Flexner survey, the system of secondary education underwent an extraordinary expansion. It was encouraged by the enactment of child-labor laws, the extension of school-age requirements, the elimination of payment of public money to private academies, and increased state aid to the counties for public high schools. Between 1905 and 1953 the number of pupils enrolled in accredited high schools in the state increased from 2,049 to 138,728, or more than 67 times.

These high schools replaced the older academies, and though they at first took over the traditional classical curricula of the academies they soon broadened their course offerings. Baltimore had pioneered in opening the Baltimore Polytechnic Institute in 1883, which was the first manual training school in the United States wholly supported by public funds, and Baltimore County had introduced the teaching of agriculture and domestic sciences into its public school curriculum. After Maryland accepted the Smith-Hughes Act in 1918, it quite generally broadened its secondary schools program to include not only agriculture and home economics but also many other vocational courses, as, for example, courses in commercial subjects and industrial arts. A "1941 Survey of the Maryland Public Schools and Teachers Colleges," conducted by the Maryland State School Survey Commission, recommended for the Maryland schools an "enriched educational program which will help every pupil in Maryland to realize as fully as possible the blessings of American democracy and will prepare him in the best possible way to meet the immediate emergencies and those which may follow at the close of the present conflict." But Maryland carefully refrained from imposing a uniform statewide curriculum upon all the schools of the state. Its educational system remained predominantly a county system. Its conception of the role of the state in public education has been partly supervisory, partly guidance, and partly *laissez faire*.

Public funds have also gone into the establishment of a relatively new type of educational organization—the junior college. Maryland's first junior college, Mount St. Agnes, was founded early in the 1900's but remained a private institution. In the early 1940's the State Teachers Colleges began to treat the first two years of their program as junior college curricula, and several counties later began to operate junior colleges with public funds.

Maryland had survived the threat of having the United States Naval Academy wrested from her by Congress during the crucial Reconstruction period. The new superintendent, Admiral David Porter, secured additional funds from Congress to rehabilitate the buildings, to add new ones, and to expand the grounds at the expense of St. Johns College. But as the navy went into the doldrums in the 1870's and 1880's, the Academy suffered loss of public interest and reduction of appropriations. Not until the United States once more felt the imperative need for a new navy in the 1890's did the Academy come to be appreciated as an educational institution essential to the defense of the nation.

The Van Bokkelen law provided also for a University of Maryland which would consist of St. Johns College, Washington College, the Maryland Agricultural College, and other colleges that were to be established. Both St. Johns College at Annapolis and Washington College in Chestertown, though private colleges, were receiving some state support. The policy of granting state subsidies to private colleges was challenged in 1884 on principle by Governor William T. Hamilton who advocated instead an expanded system of public education. But the policy nevertheless continued to be followed.

After 1864 the Maryland Agricultural College at College Park was owned jointly by its private stockholders and by the state of Maryland. After the main building there was destroyed by fire in 1914, the state, on the recommendation of Governor Phillips Lee Goldsborough, contributed to the construction of a new building, then foreclosed the mortgage, and made the college a state institution in 1916, changing its name to Maryland State College.

The consolidation of this institution with the Colleges of Medicine and Dentistry in Baltimore into a state university was recommended by several of Maryland's governors during the first two decades of the twentieth century, but it was not achieved until 1920 during Governor Ritchie's administration. In that year a bill to merge the University of Maryland in Baltimore with the Maryland State Agricultural College in College Park was introduced by the Speaker of the House of Delegates, Millard E. Tydings. It passed the House unanimously, was approved by the Senate, and was reluctantly signed by an unsympathetic governor. Four years later Ritchie tried unsuccessfully to return the professional schools in Baltimore to private ownership and to limit the College Park branch strictly to agricultural education, in which he was deeply interested.

The census of 1870 showed that Methodism was the largest religious denomination in Maryland, followed in order by the Episcopal, Roman Catholic, Baptist, Lutheran, and Presbyterian. Several of these religious bodies moved vigorously into the field of higher education. Western Maryland College originated as the ambitious undertaking of Fayette R. Buell, a schoolteacher from New York, who was conducting a private academy in Westminster in the closing months of the Civil War. He obtained the patronage of the Methodist Protestant Church, selected as its first president the Reverend Dr. James Thomas Ward, a retired minister of that church, and had the cornerstone of the first building laid on September 6, 1866, by the master of the Door to Virtue Lodge of Freemasons. It was the first college south of the Mason-Dixon line to admit both young men and young women but kept them strictly separated in living quarters, dining hall, and classrooms. As the president of the college wrote in 1894, "the design of this arrangement was not to carry out strictly the coeducational idea. . . . The course of study is not the same for both [sexes], although the difference is mainly in the substitution of French for Greek for the ladies; the recitations are conducted separately and the gentlemen live in a building separate from the main building in which the ladies reside. In chapel, dining hall, and, once a month, in the reception parlor, they meet in the presence of teachers. The arrangement has worked admirably," concluded President Lewis. "The presence of both sexes is inspiring and restraining in its influence, while the limitations have served to relieve the natural embarrassment often found in working together." [2] Western Maryland College became one of the first collegiate institutions in the country to develop a coordinated program in physical education, and in the mid-1890's it constructed the first college gymnasium in the state.

At Westminister also the Methodists established the Westminster Theological Seminary in 1882 for the purpose of training ministers. This institution, as it grew and flourished, was transferred to the campus of the American University in Washington, D.C., in 1959.

The background of Goucher College was also Methodist. It began in 1888 as the Women's College of Baltimore City, which was founded to commemorate the centennial in 1884 of the Methodist Episcopal Church in Baltimore and was supported from the beginning by a wealthy Methodist clergyman of Baltimore, the Reverend John F. Goucher, who became its president in 1890 and for whom it was eventually named. Especially notable has been its pioneering work in physical education, political science, and vocational guidance for women. The college was originally located on St. Paul Street between 22nd and 24th Streets, but was later moved to Towson.

Morgan State College was chartered as the Edmonston and Centenary Biblical Institute in 1866 primarily to prepare Negroes for the ministry of the Methodist Episcopal Church. It was enabled to qualify for collegiate status in 1890 through a gift of money from Dr. Littleton F. Morgan, a Methodist clergyman of Baltimore, and thereafter took his name. It became a part of the educational system of the state by act of the legislature in 1939 when it sold its physical property to the state for $225,000 and was named Morgan State College. Another of its early sponsors was the same Methodist clergyman for whom Goucher College was named. Morgan State College was operated by the state as an institution of higher learning for Negroes, and at the time it was taken over by the state, it had an enrollment of almost 1,100 students. Its name was changed to Morgan State University in July 1975.

A branch of this Negro institution was established in 1887 at Princess Anne for the education of Negroes on the Eastern Shore and was named the Delaware Conference Academy. It was leased by the state as an agricultural college for Negroes in 1892, and it was taken over by the state in 1925 to serve as the Negro branch of the University of Maryland entitled to receive federal land grant aid under the Morrill Act. To it was given a new title, Maryland State College.

Johns Hopkins University, a pioneer institution in graduate instruction in the United States, was incorporated in Baltimore in 1867 by the philanthropy of Johns Hopkins, who, coming from Annapolis to Baltimore as a young man, laid the basis for a large fortune in the grocery business and later in railroad investments. At his death in the early 1870's, this wealthy Quaker bequeathed to the University some $3.5 million, including his Baltimore estate of 330 acres called Clifton and 15,000 shares of common stock of the Baltimore and Ohio Railroad. In the same will be bequeathed a similar amount to the establishment of a new hospital to be named for him.

Johns Hopkins University, under the leadership of its first president, Daniel Coit Gilman, who had been president of the University of California, attracted a galaxy of outstanding professors, including Ira Remsen in chemistry, G. Stanley Hall in psychology, Simon Newcomb in mathematics and astronomy, Herbert Baxter Adams in history, and Richard T. Ely in political economy. To the faculty of its medical school, which opened in the fall of 1893, came the distinguished William H. Welch, William Osler, William S. Halsted, and Howard A. Kelly, the so-called "big four." From the beginning Johns Hopkins was a university in the true meaning of the word, specializing in graduate instruction, research, and seminars and modeled on the German university system. Johns Hopkins University established the German scientific method in American education. Its first building, located at Howard and Little Ross Streets, opened its doors for students in the fall of 1876. Several additional buildings were subsequently constructed in the area of Howard and Monument Streets, but later the university was moved to spacious grounds on North Charles Street.

Johns Hopkins Hospital was not opened until 1889 but soon acquired an international reputation through the work of its distinguished staff. Four years after the founding of the hospital, the Johns Hopkins Medical School was opened, with Dr. Welch as dean and with women as well as men students. Among American institutions the Johns Hopkins Hospital and Johns Hopkins Medical School were unique in emphasizing the need for original research and in experimenting in methods of diagnosis and treatment of bodily malfunctions. Their example was subsequently followed by other medical schools and hospitals. The Hopkins Hospital and Medical staff each showed a proficiency with the pen as well as with the scalpel and authored books which bridged the gap between science and literature. Their devotion to medical science was matched by their interest in adventure and scholarship, and this interest continued to be expressed in the work of Dr. J. Hall Pleasants, Dr. Hulbert Footner, Dr. Hugh Young, and many others.

The Catholic University of America was established in Washington in 1885 by action of a committee of the American Catholic hierarchy of which Baltimore-born Archbishop James Gibbons of the Baltimore diocese was chairman. Although Gibbons himself preferred Philadelphia as a site of the new university, he officiated at the laying of the cornerstone in Washington in 1888 as a cardinal, having meanwhile been made a prince of the church by Pope Leo XIII as the second American cardinal. Gibbons later served for many years as chancellor of the university and took a deep interest in it. He was a consistently strong advocate of separation of church and state, attributing the strength and growth of the American Catholic Church to this constitutional requirement.

In the years following the Civil War Maryland, and especially Baltimore, moved into a new position of prominence in the art world under the encouragement of such patrons of the arts as William T. Walters, who founded the Walters Art Gallery, Charles James Madison Eaton, and J. Latimer Hoffman. The paintings of Alfred Jacob Miller, continuing until his death in 1874, depicted Indian life and turned the attention of his students toward historical themes. Among his disciples Frank B. Mayer won distinction with his "The Burning of the *Peggy Stewart*" and "The Founding of Maryland," which are displayed in the State House in Annapolis. Among Baltimore's portrait painters may be mentioned Louis Dieterich, John Dabour, Oscar and Paul Hallwig, and Harper Pennington. Baltimore's sculptors of distinction included William H. Rinehart and Ephraim Keyser.

Maryland continued its outstanding tradition in newspaper journalism after the Civil War. By 1880 Baltimore had eleven daily newspapers, of which two were published in the German language. Negro journalism was well represented by the *Afro-American,* which was started in 1892. An epochal advance in the mechanics of printing was made in 1886 when Ottmar Mergenthaler of Baltimore invented the linotype machine. The operator of this machine, by manipulating the keys, could produce a matrix for each line of type, which when pressed forward against a bar of molten metal cast a slug that could then be used for printing. By 1900 approximately 8,000 of these machines were being used in printing establishments in the United States, and about 1,000 new machines were being put into operation each year. This invention supplied an impetus to many other mechanical improvements in printing and gave Maryland distinction in this field. In 1919 Maryland reported 18 daily newspapers and 104 weekly newspapers and periodicals.

The incomparable Henry L. Mencken, writing prolifically as a member of the *Sunpapers* staff, brought notoriety to Maryland with his poniard pen. Belonging to the political school of Governor Ritchie, Mencken defended individualism and private morality as against statism and state-dictated morality. In 1908, while still in his twenties, he published his book on Nietsche, which was notable for its clarity of expression and foreshadowed the precision and literary charm of his later works. *The American Language: An Inquiry into the Development of English in the United States,* which he published in 1919, was a treatise of prodigious scholarship which he expanded in subsequent revisions until it reached almost 800 pages in the fourth. As he himself declared, he delighted to fling his ego into the face of the world. His pungent style in his columns, "The Free Lance" and "The Smart Set," and his editorial contributions to the old *American Mercury,* lit the torches of flaming youth in the 1920's, and his volumes of *Prejudices,* running through six series and marked by witty originality and devastating sarcasm, exploded the complacencies of the "boobocracy." Mencken "had a way," one of his associates observed, "of putting into print the things that most people confine to conversations among their intimates.... He seldom failed to shock the local public with his damning frankness." [3]

Mencken relinquished the editorship of the *American Mercury* in 1933. His monumental compilation, *A New Dictionary of Quotations on Historical Principles from Ancient and Modern Sources,* running to 1,347 pages, occupied in its preparation twenty-four years of his leisure time. Meanwhile, he published such lurid essays as "The Sahara of the Bozart" and "Theodore Roosevelt: An Autopsy." He established a wide reputation as a scourge of fraud, as an exposer of self-deception. But his caustic strictures upon the foibles of his contemporaries were supported with facts, and despite his acidulous barbed and brilliant writing, were tempered by the charitableness of a large-souled and convivial nature. In Mencken's autobiographical works, *Happy Days* and *Newspaper Days,* he created and relived an enchanted Baltimore thrilling with life in all its myriad forms. He loved its streets and people, and for him and his readers he personalized and humanized his native city. Despite his German lineage, he could reply to the most confirmed Maryland traditionalists, "I too belong."

But Mencken spoke to a much larger audience than his native Maryland. In the state's attitude of respect and veneration for him it exemplified its traditional tolerance of nonconformity and its commitment to individual rights and local responsibility. Mencken, as himself a member of the "Smart Set," could load witty castigation upon the "booboisie" and made them like it, but when the importance of the "booboisie" as voters was proven by Franklin D. Roosevelt after 1932, both Mencken and the tradition of Maryland gentility were forever defeated.

But to the day of his death in 1956 his fame as the sage of Baltimore remained secure.

Much earlier, in the post-Civil War era, Baltimore had become the home of the Georgia-born poet Sidney Lanier, who came there at the invitation of Asger Hamerik, director of the Peabody Orchestra, to become first flutist in the orchestra. In 1879 he was asked by President Gilman to join the faculty of Johns Hopkins University as lecturer in English literature. During his Baltimore period he wrote most of his best-known poems, including "Sunrise," "The Marshes of Glynn," "The Symphony," "Psalm of the West," "Ballad of Trees and the Master," and his "Ode to the Johns Hopkins University." With his death at the early age of 39 perished the authentic poet of the South and one of the nation's most sensitive spirits. He is honored by a bronze monument sculptured by Hans Schuler and situated on Charles Street between the Homewood House and University Parkway, which was dedicated in 1942.

A native Marylander, Severn Teackle Wallis, like his contemporary, John Pendleton Kennedy, not only played prominent roles in politics but established a considerable reputation in the field of prose literature. In the early 1870's Wallis became a leader in the reform movement within the Democratic party opposing the Rasin-Gorman leadership and their "ring," and he was nominated for attorney general by this independent group. His collected prose works, including sketches of his travels in Spain, fill four volumes.

An early Maryland novel was *Emily Chester*, written by Anne Moncure Crane of Baltimore and published anonymously in Boston in 1864. It went through ten editions and was translated into German. Another author who did most of his writing in Baltimore was Richard Malcolm Johnston (1822-1898), who wrote short stories and several novels idealizing antebellum life in the South. He also published a biography of his friend, Alexander H. Stephens, vice-president of the Confederacy.

A Delaware writer, George Alfred Townsend, used Maryland locales in his novels, *The Entailed Hat, Katy of Catoctin,* and *Tales of the Chesapeake,* but his reputation rests mainly upon his perceptive newspaper reporting during the Civil War in which he used the pseudonym "Gath." Local pride in the literary productions of other Eastern Shore writers has recently been gratified in the publication of a selective compilation of their prose and verse.[4]

Maryland, particularly Annapolis, provides the setting for a considerable part of a tender and dramatic tale of the Revolution, *Richard Carvel,* written in the Victorian manner by the St. Louis-born romancer

Winston Churchill and first published in 1899. Churchill's interest in Maryland stemmed from his years at the Naval Academy from which he graduated in 1894. The gay conviviality of the social life of Annapolis centering around Carvel Hall in the 1760's and 1770's is recounted with nostalgic charm against the background of the gathering Revolutionary storm.

In the twentieth century literary distinction in the field of *belles lettres* has come to Maryland through the work of several authors beside Mencken. Van Wyck Mason, though descended from a Massachusetts family, is associated with Maryland, for after a youth and young manhood spent in travel, he settled in Baltimore with his family in 1929. He has published many of his widely read short stories and historical novels, including *Three Harbors* (1937), *Stars on the Sea* (1940), and his *Major North* series, which he began to publish in 1931. Some of his other novels have appeared under the pseudonym "Ward Weaver" *(Hang My Wreath)* and "Geoffrey Coffin."

Hulbert Footner, though born in Canada and a longtime resident of New York City, found his literary milieu in the Maryland countryside where the Chesapeake laves the sandy beaches and the green fields yield their abundant harvests. He has added to Maryland's literary distinction with his delightful *Charles Gift,* a "biography" of the historic house situated in Calvert County near Solomons Island and the Patuxent River which he first saw in 1916 and purchased as a summer home for himself and his family. His biography of Commodore Joshua Barney of Maryland was written in 1940, and his *Maryland Main and the Eastern Shore,* published in 1942, is another portrait of a portion of his beloved Maryland. From his pen have also flowed several novels and detective stories.

Another Maryland author, James Mallahan Cain, has deep roots in the state. His early stories had a setting in California and other parts of the Far West, but in his *Past All Dishonor* (1946), his principal character is a young graduate of St. Johns College in Annapolis who as a Confederate spy becomes involved in the lusty life of Virginia City, Nevada. And the locale of his *Galatea* (1953) is southern Maryland. Some of his fast-moving tales, full of human insights and artistry, have achieved success both in Hollywood and on Broadway. These include especially *The Postman Always Rings Twice* and *Mildred Pierce.* Cain has been acclaimed by critics as the best literary examplar of the "hardboiled" school of detective-murder fiction, ranking in this respect above another Maryland author, Dashiel Hammett.

Another author, who, though born in Maryland won fame in California, is Upton Beall Sinclair. His novel *The Jungle,* published in 1906, has been credited with starting the militant consumers' movement of modern times leading to the creation of the Food and Drug Administration in Washington. His later novel, *Dragon's Teeth,* won him the Pulitzer Prize for literature in 1943, and he later ran for governor of California on the Socialist ticket. He died in 1968.

Baltimore's distinguished twentieth-century poetess, Lizette Woodworth Reese, a longtime teacher of English at Western High School in Baltimore, is best known for her slender volume of poems entitled *A Branch of May* published in 1887, and she added to her fame with her sonnet "Tears" published in *Scribner's* in 1899. She also published two prose works, *A Victorian Village* and *The York Road.* She died in 1935.

To make these and other books available to readers, Maryland pioneered in the traveling library or "bookmobile" as early as 1907. The first bookmobiles were horse-drawn wagons used on country trails in western Maryland. Three years later the Washington County free traveling library was established, and it distributed books from a truck fitted with shelves outside the body. Meanwhile, Baltimore had been supplied with a magnificent free public library through the philanthropy of Enoch Pratt (1808-1896), a New Englander by birth, who became a Baltimore iron and coal merchant, financier, and patron of the arts.

The habits of gregariousness and conviviality which were noted by visitors to Maryland before the War for American Independence remained a conspicuous trait of Marylanders. It was expressed in social balls and dances, in the sport of horse racing, and in the social and literary clubs. Of the latter the famous South River Club at Annapolis, which was organized in the eighteenth century, continued and still meets as reputedly the oldest social club still in existence in the United States. Among Baltimore's famous clubs the Wednesday Club was socially the most notable. It originated in a birthday party given by Otto Sutro on February 24, 1858, in his bachelor quarters on Charles Street. To its meetings, which combined serious musical and dramatic productions with boisterous tomfoolery, came the elite of Baltimore, including some of the foremost professional musicians and playwrights of the day. The meetings in Sutro's home were abandoned after his marriage, but the club continued to meet, its membership augmented by some of the most famous names in music, literature, and art. In 1879 the club built a combined clubhouse-theater where outstanding operettas, plays, and musical numbers were presented. After many years of distinguished contribution to Baltimore's social and cultural life, the club's headquarters was sold in 1886 as a result of dissension among the stockholders, and it subsequently was destroyed by fire.[5]

Education and Recreation

Marylanders have been sports enthusiasts since early colonial days. The Maryland Jockey Club, dating from the mid-eighteenth century, is America's oldest racing association. Preakness Day, which is celebrated in May each year by the Jockey Club at the Pimlico racetrack in Baltimore, has been a leading sports event since 1873. This historic race, named for the horse that won the first stakes race at Pimlico three years earlier, is preceded by the Powder Puff Preakness, a race limited to lady jockeys. The winner of the main event, the Preakness, is awarded the coveted Woodlawn Vase by the governor of Maryland, and the winning horse is draped with a blanket of Black-Eyed Susans, the state flower. Among all the horses that have run this historic course, the most famous was Man o' War, which in his race there in 1920 ran the fastest mile ever run at Pimlico. The Laurel Race Course, situated in Anne Arundel County near Laurel, was opened in 1911 and is the scene of annual international horse racing events. Maryland has become one of the nation's principal producers of thoroughbred horses. By 1960 horse-breeding and training farms occupied over 55,000 acres in Maryland.

Another popular sporting event is the Maryland Hunt Cup race, which evolved from a challenge issued by the Elkridge Foxhunting Club to the Green Spring Valley Hunt in 1894 to a cross-country steeplechase over a four-mile course. It continues as a strictly non-professional annual race over courses marked out in the Worthington Valley and attended by thousands of spectators.

The game of baseball, which was invented in Cooperstown, New York, reached Baltimore in 1859 when A. Henry Pohlemus organized a team called the Baltimore Excelsiors. Maryland teams have actively participated in baseball almost from the beginning of this game as an organized professional sport. In 1872, one year after the formation of the National Association of Professional Baseball Players, Baltimore placed a team called the Lord Baltimores on the diamond. But the Lord Baltimores were soon discredited by a scandal. Professional baseball was revived in Maryland in 1882 when Harry Vonderhorst, a Baltimore brewer, organized a team as a means of selling beer to patrons of the game, and in the following year his team took the name Orioles. Not until the team was taken over, however, by a new owner and manager, Edward ("Foxy Ned") Hanlon, did it begin to set baseball records. Under his leadership the Orioles developed the hit-and-run play, sacrifice hits, and base stealing—innovations which revolutionized the game. Hanlon later served from 1916 to his death in 1937 as a member of Baltimore's Park Board and was its president after 1931.[6]

His successor as manager of the Baltimore Orioles was the youthful John McGraw, then only 26 years old. He later qualified with four other baseball "greats" who got their start in Baltimore to be included in baseball's Hall of Fame at Cooperstown. Others were Willie Keeler, famous place-hitter around 1900, who originated the saying "Hit 'em where they ain't"; George Herman ("Babe") Ruth, idolized as the "King of Swat," who established the all-time home-run record with 714 runs over a 21-year span in the major leagues; and two from Maryland's Eastern Shore, Franklin ("Home Run") Baker and Jimmy Foxx. In the 1960's professional baseball became so popular that Baltimoreans fortunate enough to possess season tickets in the 60,000-seat stadium for Oriole games even bequeathed them to their heirs in their wills.

The game of lacrosse, which was a favorite sport of the North American aborigines, was first organized in Maryland at Baltimore in 1882. Lacrosse teams at Johns Hopkins University, the University of Maryland, and the Naval Academy consistently attract large crowds of spectators. The St. Johns College lacrosse team achieved world championship in 1931. In football the Baltimore Colts won national acclaim after 1957 with "Johnny" Unitas as their quarterback.

From colonial days both education and recreation have been important features of the life-style of Marylanders, and the opportunities and facilities for both have been greatly expanded in this twentieth century.

Footnotes

[1] Abraham Flexner and Frank P. Bachman, *Public Education in Maryland: A Report to the Maryland Educational Survey Commission*, General Education Board, New York, 2d edition, 1916, p. XVI. See also Raymond S. Sweeney, "Public Education in Maryland in the Progressive Era," *Maryland Historical Magazine*, vol. 62, No. 1, March 1967, pp. 28-46.

[2] B.C. Steiner, ed., "History of Education in Maryland," *Contributions to American Educational History*, No. 19 (Government Printing Office, Washington, 1894, pp. 191-193.)

[3] Francis F. Beirne, *The Amiable Baltimoreans*, p. 321.

[4] Harold D. Jopp and R.H. Ingersoll, eds., *Shoremen: An Anthology of Eastern Shore Prose and Verse*, Tidewater Publishers, Cambridge, Maryland, 1974.

[5] Ottilie Sutro, "The Wednesday Club: A Brief Sketch from Authentic Sources," *Maryland Historical Magazine*, vol. XXXVIII, No. 1, March 1943, pp. 60-68.

[6] John H. Lancaster, "Baltimore, a Pioneer in Organized Baseball," *ibid.*, vol. XXXV, No. 1, March 1940, pp. 32-55.

Sources and Additional Reading

American Council on Education, *Higher Education in Maryland*, Washington, D.C., 1947.

Beirne, Francis F., *The Amiable Baltimoreans*, E.P. Dutton & Co., New York, 1951.

Bready, James H., *The Home Team: 100 Years of Baseball in Baltimore*, Baltimore: the Author, 1958.

Callcott, George H., *A History of the University of Maryland*, Maryland Historical Society, Baltimore, 1966.

Creamer, Robert W., *Babe: the Legend Comes to Life*, Simon and Schuster, New York, 1974.

Cushing, Harvey, *The Life of Sir William Osler*, Clarendon Press, Oxford, 1925.

Fleming, Donald Harnish, *William H. Welch and the Rise of Modern Medicine*, Little, Brown and Company, Boston, 1954.

Flexner, Abraham, *Daniel Coit Gilman, Creator of the American Type of University*, Harcourt, Brace and Company, New York, 1946.

———, and Frank P. Bachman, *Public Education in Maryland: A Report to the Maryland Educational Survey Commission*, General Education Board, New York, 2d edition, 1916.

Forgue, Guy J., *Letters of H.L. Mencken*, Alfred Knopf, New York, 1961.

Franklin, Fabian, *The Life of Daniel Coit Gilman*, Dodd, Mead and Co., 1910.

French, John C., *A History of the University Founded by Johns Hopkins*, Johns Hopkins Press, Baltimore, 1946.

Gibbons, James Cardinal, *A Retrospect of Fifty Years*, John Murphy Co., Baltimore, 1916.

Gilman, Daniel Coit, *The Launching of a University and Other Papers: A Sheaf of Remembrances*, Dodd, Mead & Company, New York, 1906.

Greene, Lee, *The Johnny Unitas Story*, G.P. Putnam's Sons, New York, 1962.

Hawkins, Hugh, *Pioneer: A History of Johns Hopkins University, 1874-1889*, Cornell University Press, Ithaca, New York, 1960.

Jopp, Harold D., and R.H. Ingersoll, eds., *Shoremen: An Anthology of Eastern Shore Prose and Verse,* Tidewater Publishers, Cambridge, Maryland, 1974.

Knipp, Anna Henbeck, and Thaddeus P. Thomas, *The History of Goucher College,* Baltimore, 1938.

Leonhart, James Chancellor, *One Hundred Years of the Baltimore City College,* H.G. Roebuck & Son, Baltimore, 1939.

Lieb, Frederick G., *The Baltimore Orioles: The History of a Colorful Team in Baltimore and St. Louis,* G.P. Putnam's Sons, New York, 1955.

MacCallum, William G., *William Stewart Halsted, Surgeon,* Johns Hopkins Press, Baltimore, 1930.

Manchester, William, *Disturber of the Peace: The Life of H.L. Mencken,* Harper & Brothers, Publishers, New York, 1950.

Rose, Stuart, *The Maryland Hunt Cup,* Huntington Press, New York, 1931.

Rossell, Lieutenant Colonel John E., Jr., *History of the Maryland Hunt Cup, 1894-1954,* Sporting Press, Baltimore, Maryland, 1954.

Stedman, Edmund Clarence, and Stephen B. Weeks, *Literary Estimate and Bibliography of Richard Malcolm Johnston,* Harrisburg Publishing Co., Harrisburg, Pennsylvania, 1898.

Steiner, Bernard Christian, ed., "History of Education in Maryland," *Contributions to American Educational History,* No. 19, Government Printing Office, Washington, 1894.

Thayer, William Sydney, *Osler and Other Papers,* Johns Hopkins Press, Baltimore, 1931.

Wagenheim, Kal, *Babe Ruth: His Life and Legend,* Praeger Publishers, New York, Washington, 1974.

Wallis, Severn Teackle, *Writings,* 4 vols., John Murphy & Co., 1896.

Weyand, Alexander M., and Milton R. Roberts, *The Lacrosse Story,* M. and A. Herman, Baltimore, Maryland, 1965.

CHAPTER XXVII

MARYLAND IN WORLD WAR II

Maryland's geographical position, facing the Atlantic theater of military operations and adjoining the national capital, which might become an enemy air objective, gave it reason for close involvement in World War II. To lessen the damage of threatened enemy attack upon Washington, the Baltimore and Ohio Railroad assisted the national government in transferring valuable materials and several government offices out of Washington to new locations throughout the country immediately after the Japanese attack on Pearl Harbor on December 7, 1941. During the war the Baltimore and Ohio not only transported its normal bulk commodities, petroleum and coal, but over its 1,095 miles of track in Maryland hauled thousands of tons of miscellaneous equipment and materials for shipment overseas through its marine terminals at Curtis Bay and Locust Point. Similarly, the Western Maryland Railway, which provides a rail outlet for the bituminous coal and grain region of Maryland, Pennsylvania, and West Virginia, transported these commodities to its tidewater terminal at Port Covington, Baltimore, for shipment overseas.

Maryland was not only an essential link in the supply lines for men and equipment needed on the fighting fronts, but served as a constituent element in the Army's Third Service Command. That Command, which had been originally created in 1920 at the end of World War I, included virtually all army operations in Maryland, Pennsylvania, Virginia, and, until May 1942, the District of Columbia. To it were assigned large responsibilities for the security of both the state and the nation. With headquarters in Baltimore, it had the duty of coordinating and performing the housekeeping functions for most of the military operations in Maryland. It arranged for transportation inland of pro-Axis sympathizers away from the sensitive coastal area and gave security checks to workers employed in war industries in Maryland. The whining of air-raid sirens in daytime alarms drove citizens from their desks and workbenches into shelter areas and at nighttime cooped them up in their homes under blackout conditions.

Chesapeake Bay was closed twice by action of German submarines—for two days in June 1942 and for three days in September 1942. The authorities of the Third Service Command, working through state guard units, organizations of "Minute Men," and the military forces under their command, kept the state in a condition of combat readiness, but Marylanders fortunately experienced only vicariously the rigors of war. In the growing length of wartime casualties as well as in its civilian contribution to the winning of the war, however, Maryland exerted an influence reaching all over the world. Wherever United States troops were stationed, Marylanders were found manning base depots in Allied countries, occupying front-line positions in fighting territory, and conquering islands as the war progressed across the Pacific Ocean toward Japan.

Meanwhile, the economy of the state buzzed with wartime activity, as war plants maintained around-the-clock schedules of production and workers vied with one another in promoting the war effort not only through overtime work but also through purchases of war bonds. The prosperity and growth of Baltimore in particular were enormously stimulated by World War II as it became an important port of embarkation for the fighting fronts and a builder of Liberty and Victory ships for the war effort. In its shipyards, airplane factories and other war industries, even former "unemployables" found work at high wages. To the city the wartime expansion of industry attracted thousands of people from most of the other eastern states. Its steel mills glowed red throughout the nights, obsolete railroad rolling stock was pressed into service, and under war contracts Maryland's diversified industry turned out quantities of heavy-duty tires, x-ray machines, railroad brake shoes, cartridge cases, chemicals, communications equipment, food containers, and a myriad other necessities of war. The state's readiness and facilities for war production were attested by the amount of war contracts it received from the national government, totaling over $5.5 billion and placing it fourth among the states of the nation in value of contracts received in proportion to population. Of the total, over 75 percent went to industry in the Baltimore metropolitan district ranking Baltimore tenth among the cities of the nation in the value of its war contracts.

Long before World War II the national government, as it assumed new responsibilities, had expanded its personnel requirements and multiplied its bureaucracy, especially under the exigencies of the depression years after 1929. As a result, government agencies spilled over from Washington into neighboring states, including Maryland. In the early 1930's Maryland was selected by the Roosevelt administration as the site of an experiment in government housing. A supposedly model city was built by the Resettlement Administration with funds made available by the national government, at Greenbelt, located some fifteen miles from Washington in Prince George's County, for selected residents who met certain requirements of low income, religious preferences, and career interests. Built partly by relief workers it was conceived by its planner, Rexford G. Tugwell, a disciple of the collectivist Thorstein Veblen, as a method of stimulating a back-to-the-land movement by providing the advantages of urban living to a rural community. But to the extent that this objective was accomplished it was done only by continued heavy subsidies from the national government. In 1952 the government divested itself of this responsibility by disposing of Greenbelt at 53 percent of its estimated cost to a consortium of the residents.[1]

The Department of Agriculture's Bureau of Animal Industry established a small experiment station at Bethesda as early as 1897, and transferred its operations to the Beltsville area in Prince George's County in 1910. By 1928 other bureaus of the Department of Agriculture had transferred some of their offices and laboratories to Beltsville, and ultimately the Department of Agriculture moved virtually all its scientific work to this Agricultural Research Center.

Responding to the wartime emergency, Maryland farmers, though deprived of 30 percent of their labor force by migrations from the farms and by the needs of the government, nevertheless produced 40 percent more food than in the prewar period. The agricultural commodities which they produced in unprecedented quantities included milk, poultry and eggs, soybeans, sweet corn, tomatoes, and truck garden crops. To meet the labor shortages, women and children worked in the fields and performed other farm tasks, and in critical harvest periods German prisoners of war were released from prison camps in Maryland and sent into the field. Farmers suffered from the rationing and, ultimately, the actual lack of new essential farm machinery. These shortages became especially serious in the dairy industry in Harford County, the principal supplier of dairy products to Baltimore. To meet the shortage of machinery farmers kept obsolete farm equipment in repair and shared pieces of scarce machinery with their neighbors in cooperative arrangements.

Over Maryland's highways long truck convoys of young soldiers streamed to ports of embarkation. Maryland's principal overseas fighting force in World War II was the 29th Infantry Division which was, however, not limited to Maryland troops but included also national guard units from Virginia, Pennsylvania, and the District of Columbia. This force, through much of its history reaching back into the colonial past, had been linked with the Free State. One of its units, the

115th Infantry, traced its lineage to early militia units formed in western Maryland to defend its frontier. To it belonged two companies which marched to the defense of Boston in 1775 and which, as the Maryland Line, later protected General Washington's retreat from Long Island. Another component of the 29th Infantry Division, the 175th Infantry, had been originally organized by Mordecai Gist in Baltimore in 1774 and had fought in several battles of the War for American Independence. In the War of 1812 it had participated in the unsuccessful defense of Bladensburg and in the defense of Baltimore. Still other predecessor units of the 29th Division fought at Antietam, Cold Harbor, and Petersburg during the Civil War.

But the modern 29th Infantry Division was a product of World War I and came to be known as the Blue and Gray, symbolizing the melding of the Union and the Confederacy. Troops of this division fought in the Alsace sector with French troops in World War I and later participated in the Meuse-Argonne offensive. In February 1941, more than ten months before the Japanese air force attacked Pearl Harbor, the 29th Infantry Division was activated for service in the threatened World War II, under a Marylander, Major General Milton A. Reckord, and later under Major General Leonard T. Gerow it participated in the allied landing on the Normandy Coast of France on June 6, 1944 in the greatest amphibious assault in military history. The gallantry and sacrifice of the men of that division on that day "made of the sands and bluffs of Normandy a place forever Maryland." [2]

After that bloody but successful exploit, marking the beginning of the land assault on Adolf Hitler's *Festung Europa,* the 29th moved on to invest the heavily defended port city of Brest and then, after crossing France, participated in bitter fighting in the Netherlands and in northwestern Germany. In the latter area they were given temporary duties of military government and then joined in the victorious push to the Elbe River which marked the dividing line between the armies of the United States and those of the Soviet Union. At the end of the war the division was demobilized at Camp Kilmer, New Jersey, on January 16, 1946. It had suffered casualties of 19,814 men, or approximately 140 percent, and had captured 38,912 prisoners of war. But it had also won richly merited honors for bravery in action.

In compliance with the Army's policy in World War II of locating its hospital units as close to the scenes of combat as possible, the Johns Hopkins Hospital and the University of Maryland Medical School, which had operated base hospital groups in World War I, volunteered their services in the far-flung battle areas of World War II. They organized four General Hospital units, all of which contributed their medical, surgical, and psychiatric expertise to the rehabilitation of war victims in the Pacific Theater. The two General Hospital Units of the Johns Hopkins Hospital—the 18th and the 118th—operated there, the former in New Zealand, the Fiji Islands, and India, and the latter in Australia and the Philippines. The two units from the University of Maryland Medical School in Baltimore, the 42nd and the 142nd, were assigned successively, the former to Australia and Japan, and the latter to New Zealand, the Fiji Islands, and India. In addition, a volunteer General Hospital unit, the 56th, which was organized independently by Baltimore physicians, gave relief in England to the wounded veterans of the North African campaign and on the continent at Liege after D-day, often carrying on their dedicated mission of saving lives under U-1 and U-2 attacks. Many of the wounded veterans whose lives were thus saved in the theaters of military action were later provided with rehabilitation and reconditioning for civilian life at the Forest Glen Section of the Walter Reed General Hospital which occupied the site and used the facilities of the National Park College, a finishing school for young women near Silver Spring in Montgomery County, Maryland.

Not far from the Walter Reed Hospital in Montgomery County, the Navy constructed and dedicated its world-famous Naval Medical Center in 1942, for the purpose of providing medical and dental care to navy, marine corps, and coast-guard personnel. Especially notable was the research work in depth which the Center carried on during the war in the special diseases and injuries incident to the war.

Maryland supplied the locations, facilities, and much of the personnel for war activities that supported the fighting forces in World War II. At the Aberdeen Proving Ground, occupying most of Gunpowder Neck some thirty-five miles northeast of Baltimore, enormous quantities of war material, ranging from small ammunition to heavy tanks, were tested and many new types of military equipment were designed and manufactured before being shipped to the armed forces overseas. This base had been established at Aberdeen in late 1917 and, with additional increments of land, comprised by 1943 almost 71,000 acres, including some 34,600 acres of water. Though far removed from the fighting fronts, the Proving Ground heard the sound of almost continuous gunfire throughout the war as missile-testing operations were carried on. In this and other centers of war activity, the Federal Housing Administration and local construction agencies built hundreds of small frame houses for civilian employees, and near them colonies of trailer camps appeared for the accommodation of construction workers. The racing crowds which had brought a seasonal peacetime prosperity to placid Havre de Grace disappeared, but their places were taken by a heavy influx of year-round war workers. When the national government appropriated 50,000 acres of the best lands in Harford County, the authorities of the county refused school facilities for the children of government workers until the national government agreed to build several schools to accommodate the newcomers.

Maryland also provided at Camp Springs in Prince George's County a site for a new Army air base, later christened Andrews Air Force Base, which was intended for the air defense of Washington. A reservation of some 4,700 acres, it was located midway between the county seat of Prince George's County, Upper Marlboro, and Washington. By mid-1943 this base was serving as a training field for Air Force fighter squadrons and was equipped with a control tower capable of handling eighty to one hundred planes simultaneously either for taking off or for landing. After World War II it continued to be maintained as one of the most important army air stations in the nation.

Almost all the advances in chemical warfare which the United States made during World War II resulted from work done in Maryland at the Army Chemical Center situated at the Edgewood Arsenal on over 11,000 acres adjoining the Aberdeen Proving Ground on the peninsula of Gunpowder Neck. This government reservation was established in 1917 as a center for the development of poison gases after the introduction of gas warfare by the German Army. There specialists developed and manufactured enormous quantities of materiel needed in both the offensive and defensive aspects of toxic warfare, including flame throwers, incendiary bombs, and mechanical smoke generators. Supplementing their work was the highly secret experimentation in biological warfare, of both an offensive and a defensive nature, which was carried on by the Army's Chemical Warfare Service at Camp Detrick situated near Frederick.

An indispensable supporting service for the fighting forces was provided by the Army Map Service, which was located in Montgomery County near the District of Columbia line. During World War II this Army agency produced some 30,000 different maps and published approximately 500 million copies for use of land, air, and naval forces. The Navy's counterpart of this agency, the Hydrographic Office, faced with a similarly desperate need for map aids to navigation, was transferred to Maryland soon after the Japanese attack on Pearl Harbor and was located at Suitland in Prince George's County.

At Camp Albert C. Ritchie, near Cascade in Washington County, the Army operated a secret intelligence center for the training of interrogators, interpreters, translators, and counterintelligence teams. After the war the Army allowed it to revert to its prewar use as a training center for the Maryland National Guard. The supersecret Office of Strategic Services, headed by Colonel (later Major General) William J. Donovan, also maintained five espionage training centers in Maryland, specifically one near Thurmont in Frederick County, another at Lothian Farm near Clinton in Prince George's County, another at Smith Point on the Potomac River in Charles County, another at the Congressional Country Club near Bethesda in Montgomery County, and another at various estates near Glencoe in Baltimore County.

In number of Army personnel processed and trained and in variety of functions performed, the most important installation of the armed services in Maryland in World War II was Fort George G. Meade, which occupied an area of almost 14,000 acres situated in the Jessup-Odenton section of Anne Arundel County some seventeen miles southwest of Baltimore. It had originally been authorized and established in 1917 for training World War I draftees. In World War II its principal function was to train Army Ground Force troops, but it was also involved in many related activities. During the war Fort Meade handled in all over 3.5 million service men and women, inducting them into the service, providing them with basic training or dispatching them to other training centers, and finally discharging them from the service. In a special section Fort Meade also maintained an internment camp accommodating hundreds of nationals of the enemy nations, Japan, Germany, and Italy who had been judged by legal investigating bodies to be too dangerous to the nation's safety to be allowed to remain at large. There they were kept under strict surveillance.

Other permanent military installations in Maryland include the Holabird Signal Depot, or Camp Holabird, which had functioned in World War I as a principal depot for supplying motor equipment to the field forces. But in 1943 it was taken over by the Signal Corps and given the responsibility for training Signal Corps personnel and for providing and shipping communications equipment to the armed forces. It became the largest military installation in the world handling army signal equipment. It occupies 354 acres situated within the city limits of Baltimore.

The Curtis Bay Ordnance Depot, another military installation situated in Baltimore, was devoted to the preparation of ammunition for small arms during World War II. The Curtis Bay center, originally established in 1899, served exclusively as a Coast Guard Yard, the only one of its kind in the nation, until 1941 when it was transferred to the Navy to concentrate its efforts upon ship construction, repair of ships, and training programs for coast guardsmen. For powder, nitric and sulfuric acid, and other explosive chemicals, the Navy depended upon the Naval Powder Factory, a government reservation of some 3,100 acres which had been located at Indian Head in Charles County in 1890 and which had contributed substantial amounts of powder to World War I.

The shipping requirements of World War II made Baltimore one of the busiest ports in the nation. It was designated by the Army's Chief of Transportation in July 1942 as a Cargo Port of Embarkation for the handling of supplies to be shipped abroad to the fighting forces of the United States and its allies and to the civilian populations of friendly nations under Lend-Lease. Implementing this order the War Department acquired preferential rights to the harbor piers belonging to the Canton Railroad Company and use of the harbor lines of the Pennsylvania Railroad, the Baltimore and Ohio Railroad, and the Western Maryland Railway. Baltimore thus became the principal port for the entire Third Service Command. As the volume of shipping multiplied, the Baltimore Cargo Port was obliged to acquire additional berthing space for its vessels. During the war years it supervised the loading of 724 army and 201 commercial outbound vessels and unloaded 233 inbound vessels, handling in all about seven million tons of army cargo.

World War II caused a tremendous expansion of the activities of the Navy Department in Maryland. When President Roosevelt proclaimed a limited national emergency in 1939, the Navy Department was operating only five offices in the Baltimore area, but it rapidly both expanded the number and increased their facilities as the nation prepared for the oncoming war. The shipbuilding facilities in the Patapsco yards were made available to the government, and down their ways slid many of the most important cargo and transport vessels needed in the war effort against the Axis powers. As a result of the mounting production of ships, aircraft, and almost countless other supplies needed in the military preparedness campaign and later in the war itself, the Navy assumed large inspection responsibilities in the Baltimore and Hagerstown areas, as the industrial plants in these areas turned out an increasing volume of production for the Navy.

Even before the war, the Navy Department had arranged for the construction of a model testing basin for ships at Carderock in Montgomery County. When completed in July 1939, two months before the outbreak of the war in Europe, this David W. Taylor Model Basin was the largest and most completely equipped ship- and aircraft-testing facility in the world, for it included, beside ship-testing basins, a wind tunnel for testing aircraft. Naval aircraft were also rigorously tested under actual flying conditions at the Naval Air Station comprising about 8,000 acres of land lying between Harper Creek and the Patuxent River near Cedar Point. To service this greatest naval aircraft-testing range in the nation, the Navy rebuilt and extended the old Washington, Brandywine and Point Lookout Railroad some thirty miles from Mechanicsville to the Naval base, at a cost of $1,000,000. By the end of the war this base had a personnel complement of about 14,000, doubling the prewar population of St. Mary's County.

The Naval Air Station formed a vital link in a naval defense system extending from the mouth of the Potomac to the Severn. It included the naval-testing base near Chesapeake Beach, the torpedo-testing base at Point Lookout, the huge naval powder factory at Indian Head, the government radio station near Cheltenham, the Naval Academy and the naval engineering experiment station at Annapolis, the naval radio station at Greenbury Point, and the ordnance and Coast Guard depots at Curtis Bay. Maryland formed a part of the Fifth Naval District with headquarters at Norfolk, Virginia, and for administrative purposes was assigned by the Navy Department to two subordinate commands. Within the Potomac River Naval Command fell the entire Potomac River up to Great Falls, and the counties of Prince George's, Montgomery, St. Mary's, Calvert, and Charles. The Severn River Naval Command consisted of Anne Arundel County and was headed by the Superintendent of the Naval Academy.

Under the exigencies of the wartime demand for officers, the Naval Academy accelerated its schedules of graduation. The needs of the Navy for trained personnel were also met at the huge Naval Training Center which was established on the grounds of the Jacob Tome Institute near Port Deposit in Cecil County in 1942 and named for Commodore William Bainbridge, one of the commanding officers of the historic frigate *Constitution*. Near Solomons in Calvert County the Navy maintained a base for the training of fighters in amphibious warfare.

Especially vital to victory in the war was the contribution of the Bethlehem Steel Company. The Sparrows Point plant of this enormous industrial complex, with central offices in Bethlehem, Pennsylvania, was the second largest producer of steel in the nation and in its steel-processing operations it turned out a great variety of iron and steel products ranging from nails to Liberty ships. From the launching of the first Liberty ship in 1941 until the end of the war, the Bethlehem-Fairfield Shipyard built 384 Liberty ships, 30 Landing Ship Tanks, and 94 Victory ships. The elapsed time between keel-laying and launching was meanwhile reduced from 244 days to fewer than 30. By September 1943, this yard was launching a ship every 35 hours.

From some 300 factories throughout the nation materials ranging from delicate navigation instruments to porcelain dishes poured into Baltimore to be used in this gigantic ship-assembly operation at the Bethlehem-Fairfield plant. In that plant the rumbling cranes, the warning whistles, the hissing steam, and the clattering machines engaged in riveting and welding the plates onto the ships' hulls presented a deafening scene of wartime activity. Between 1942 and 1945 Baltimore shipbuilders launched an unprecedented total of 600 vessels.

The airplanes produced by the Glenn L. Martin Company at Middle River and other sites in the Baltimore area and by the Fairchild Aircraft Division in Hagerstown utilized the latest aeronautical techniques and made essential contributions to the needs of the fighting forces. Martin's *Marauders* and *Mariners* proved spectacularly successful on bombing missions in both the European and Pacific theaters, and the *Mars,* of which six only were built before the end of the war, was the largest cargo plane designed up to that time, having a payload capacity of almost 75 tons. Its hull was larger than the *Ark* which had brought Lord Baltimore's wayfarers to Maryland in 1634. The Fairchild plant at Hagerstown also built large cargo planes, particularly the *Flying Boxcar,* as well as bombers and fighting planes.

World War II brought serious dislocations into the life of southern Maryland. Farmers who were obliged by shortages of Negro labor to seek work in defense plants found their former Negro farmhands earning more than they themselves could earn under the pay scales of the national government. As the Navy took over thousands of acres of land in St. Mary's County, these lands had to be removed from the tax rolls, but the expenses of the county constantly mounted. The Naval Air Station at Cedar Point and other government installations at Indian Head in Charles County and at Camp Springs near Upper Marlboro drained the farms of their labor supply and brought acute food shortages. Although the price of many farm products was frozen, the wages of farm laborers had to be increased because of the competitive level of wages in war industries. As a result of these wartime changes, St. Mary's lost some of its old, unhurried ways, and the Maryland counties surrounding the national capital—namely Prince George's and Charles— began to be absorbed into the new regional Washington complex.

Among the geographical regions of Maryland the Eastern Shore was least affected by World War II. It responded to the war effort by establishing the Kent Defense Corporation at Chestertown financed by local investors to make munitions and employing some 1,800 people, mostly women. But although this was the only strictly defense industry on the Eastern Shore, other industries there, especially boatbuilding and the canning industry, were stimulated by the war into a new prosperity.

But Maryland made contributions to the national effort in the war in more than material ways. In an effort to cement the Anglo-American alliance against the Axis powers, Anthony Eden, the British Foreign Secretary and a direct descendent of Maryland's last royal governor, came to Annapolis in March 1943 and addressed the Maryland House of Delegates. The war was reflected also in literary productions of Marylanders. Among the twelve reporters assigned by the *Sunpapers* to cover the war fronts, Mark S. Watson received a Pulitzer Prize for his telegraphic reporting in 1944. In 1941 a Maryland native of Mt. Savage, Lawrence A. Finzel, while employed by the Associated Press, received a Pulitzer Prize for his report of his adventures with the British fleet in the Mediterranean. Sergeant Karl J. Shapiro, a Baltimorean who served in Australia in the Medical Corps during World War II, wrote two volumes of verse, *Person, Place and Thing* and *V-Letter and Other Poems,* which were published by Reynal and Hitchcock, Inc., and Commander Frederick J. Bell, a Baltimorean of the regular navy, wrote in *Condition Red* a description of destroyer action in the Pacific, which was published by Longmans, Green and Company.

World War II wrought many fundamental changes in the economy and ways of life in Maryland. Luxurious plantation houses of a former day, used as country homes by wealthy Baltimoreans, were either neglected or demolished and their spacious grounds filled with crowded new dwellings.

The influx of a transient trailer population into Baltimore for work in war industries prompted a feature writer for the Baltimore *Sun,* Lee McCardell, to predict sadly, in June 1942, that "many of the newcomers obviously don't and never will belong to the Baltimore that you have known for the last ten, twenty, thirty years. . . . Between them and the war you may not recognize Baltimore in 1962." Much of the western shore of the tidewater region was partially metropolitanized by urban sprawl as Washington and Baltimore experienced unprecedented population increases and transportation facilities from those metropolises north and south multiplied.

Footnotes

[1] George A. Warner, *Greenbelt: The Cooperative Community, An Experience in Democratic Living,* Exposition Press, New York, 1954; and Leslie Gene Hunter, "Greenbelt, Maryland: A City on a Hill," *Maryland Historical Magazine,* vol. 63, No. 2, June 1968, pp. 105-136.

[2] War Records Division, Maryland Historical Society, *Maryland in World War II,* vol. I, Military Participation, Baltimore, 1950, p. 6.

Sources and Additional Reading

Maryland Historical Society, War Records Division, *Maryland in World War II,* vol. I, *Military Participation,* Baltimore, 1950.

Warner, George A., *Greenbelt: The Cooperative Community, An Experience in Democratic Living,* Exposition Press, New York, 1954.

CHAPTER XXVIII

THE FREE STATE IN THE BICENTENNIAL YEAR

The bicentennial of the emergence of the United States as a separate nation marks also the bicentennial of the independence of Maryland as a Free State in that nation. Long before Marylanders gained their independence, they aspired to exercise the full responsibilities of self-government. They developed a yearning for independent statehood which, if less militant than that of their neighbors in the Old Dominion, nevertheless inspired their resistance to a parasitical proprietary rule and their final adherence to the cause of national independence in 1776. They acquired fame for their steadfastness in that course through the exploits of their Old Line troops during the War for Independence, and throughout their experience of statehood they have generally emphasized the importance of limiting central authority in the interest of the largest possible measure of individual decision and local autonomy. Marylanders have been unwilling to accept the doctrine that they must give up their freedoms in order to gain or to preserve their rights. They have not only upheld their rights against the claimed powers of the general government, yielding occasionally only under irresistible pressure, but they have also often insisted upon carrying over this principle into their attitude toward the administration of state affairs.

Maryland has made and cherished its record as a defender of the federal system of government, which limits the powers of the national administration to delegated powers and retains all residual powers in the states. The theory of federal government to which Maryland has been conspicuously committed ever since the War for American Independence emphasizes the wide options of experimentation and of policy that are and must remain open to the components of that system. Under that theory the states retain their full powers and range of action, except in those areas which they have voluntarily transferred to the central government.

This is not to suggest that Maryland has established a unique record of isolationism in relation to other states in the Union in either its economic, social, or political life. On the contrary, it has cooperated with adjoining states and with successive administrations in Washington in promoting policies of national benefit in all these areas of action. Maryland has wholeheartedly participated in the national experience throughout the last 200 years as a member of a national union in which it retains its innate prerogatives as a Free State. To that national experience Maryland and Marylanders have made many notable and, indeed, unique contributions.

With the increasing popularity and use in recent years of the interstate compact as a device for interstate cooperation, Maryland has found it expedient to join in such arrangements with neighboring states for joint handling of their common problems. One of the oldest of these is the Potomac River Fisheries Commission, which grew out of a joint plan concluded by Maryland and Virginia in the late eighteenth century and which was regularized as an interstate compact in 1958 to establish and maintain a program of conservation and improvement of the seafood resources of the Potomac River. Maryland also is a member of the Interstate Commission on the Potomac River Basin which was organized as an interstate compact under Act of Congress in 1940 to include Maryland, Virginia, Pennsylvania, West Virginia, the District of Columbia, and the national government. By a similar arrangement, Maryland in 1967 joined with Pennsylvania, New York, and the national government in the Susquehanna River Basin Commission. Maryland also cooperates with fourteen other Atlantic seaboard states in the Atlantic States Marine Fisheries Commission, which was organized in 1941 under an interstate compact to concern itself in an advisory way with the marine fisheries problems of the entire Atlantic coast. Two other such compacts of which Maryland is a member are the Interstate Oil Compact, which was concluded in 1935, and the Interstate Mining Commission, which Maryland joined in 1973.

But from Luther Martin and Samuel Chase to Albert Ritchie and Millard Tydings, Maryland has remained committed to the philosophy of a Free State in a federal union of states, to the principle of a conglomerate rather than a monolithic or consolidated nation. The state constitution, which was originally adopted in 1867, is called the Free State Constitution partly because it freed the slaves in Maryland but mainly because it reasserted in classic terminology the federal theory of the prerogatives of the state in relation to the general government.

Marylanders later, during the governorship of Ritchie, popularized the name "The Free State" to symbolize and justify their resistance to national prohibition of intoxicating liquor. Though Maryland had ratified the Eighteenth Amendment in 1918, the conviction of individual liberty and states' rights was so strong that it adopted no enforcement legislation and instead challenged the national authorities themselves to enforce the national law in the state. When given an opportunity in

1933, Maryland promptly ratified the Twenty-first Amendment repealing the Eighteenth Amendment. Nor has Maryland yet (1976) ratified either the Seventeenth Amendment, providing for direct popular election of senators, or the Nineteenth Amendment, providing suffrage for women, though it is, of course, bound to follow them since they were duly ratified by the necessary three-fourths of the states.

In the national presidential contests of this twentieth century Maryland has supported the national consensus in every election except those of 1904, 1908, and 1948, and has shown itself to be, with those few exceptions, an accurate gauge of American political thought. From 1912 to 1948 Maryland voters followed the national trend in every election by supporting the winning candidate, whether Democratic or Republican, but in 1948 they gave a majority to the loser, Thomas Dewey of New York, over President Harry Truman by a slight margin. They sustained their preference for the Republican party in the two ensuing presidential elections with General Dwight Eisenhower as the candidate, giving him 55.48 percent of the popular vote in 1952 and increasing this percentage to 60.0 to reelect him in 1956. But in the presidential campaigns from 1960 to 1972, Maryland gave its majority support to the Democratic candidates, John F. Kennedy in 1960, Lyndon Johnson in 1964, and Hubert Humphrey in 1968, as summarized in the following table.

Election	Maryland's Vote	
	Democrat	Republican
1940	F. Roosevelt 284,546	Wilkie 269,534
	electoral votes 8	none
1944	F. Roosevelt 315,490	Dewey 292,949
	electoral votes 8	none
1948	Truman 286,521	Dewey 294,814
		electoral votes 8
1952	Stevenson 395,337	Eisenhower 499,424
		electoral votes 9
1956	Stevenson 372,613	Eisenhower 559,738
		electoral votes 9
1960	Kennedy 565,808	Nixon 489,538
	electoral votes 9	
1964	Johnson 730,912	Goldwater 385,495
	electoral votes 10	
1968	Humphrey 538,310	Nixon 517,995
	electoral votes 10	
		American Independent
		178,734 (15%)
1972	McGovern 505,781	Nixon 839,305 (62%)
		electoral votes 10

The decisions of the United States Supreme Court, headed by Chief Justice Earl Warren, outlawing racial segregation in public schools and endorsing the principle of one-man one-vote have caused traumatic dislocations in the society and politics of Maryland. Racial polarization, both legal and social, has been a fact of life in Maryland since early colonial times and has been handled through processes of segregation, which were endorsed by the United States Supreme Court in the leading case of *Plessy versus Ferguson* in 1896. The effective reversal of that decision by the Warren court in *Brown versus Topeka Board of Education* in 1954 necessitated changes of a critical nature in patterns of life in Maryland. That decision, along with subsequent implementing national legislation in the areas of education, housing, and employment, required the elimination of ethnic racial pockets in the interest of a more homogeneous American population.

Throughout the history of Maryland, as indeed also of other societies, various ethnic, religious and racial groups have tended to form their own communities, partly because of their common economic levels, partly because of manifestations of discrimination directed against them by already established groups, partly because people choose to mingle with those who share common interests with them, and partly because of the clannish habits of the old families of these groups. In Baltimore these factors have produced a Chinatown, a Little Italy, a Polish sector, a little Bohemia, an Irish Belt, and the Jewish section. Baltimore, like other Atlantic Coast ports which were points of debarkation for millions of white immigrants of foreign nationality, occasionally had reacted emotionally and violently against the intrusion of foreign nationalities into the state, thus breaching Maryland's vaunted theory of toleration, but eventually Marylanders allowed these newcomers to commingle with them in the normal life of the state without molestation.

Much more serious has been the challenge of Negro-white integration involving not the acceptance of foreigners but of native-born Americans of the black race. Throughout most of the history of the state, white Marylanders have been free to form their own social institutions, to determine the structure of their government, and to fix the character of their business relationships with one another, but now they were being required, under pressures from the national government, to limit their freedom of action and to admit a large and hitherto virtually alien race into partnership in determining these matters of highest individual and state concern. The Maryland melting pot of nationalities must now become also a melting pot of races.

This ideal of racial integration, which was so casually imposed by the Warren Supreme Court, was resisted by traditionalists of both races, black and white, who were proud of their respective cultural heritages and who insisted upon maintaining the purity of the races and the uncorrupted integrity of their own culture patterns. The Negro leaders who resisted assimilation pointed out that the experience of other societies demonstrates that through mixture with a white civilization, the black element becomes diluted and may eventually disappear. To many of them integration means absorption into the white society and consequent loss of racial identity. When imposed upon society by superior authority, they regarded it as simply a form of institutionalized white racism, but their alternative, namely continued segregation, when previously tried by both the Maryland Colonization Society and by Lincoln, had foundered on the obstacle of finding a suitable homeland for black people.

In Maryland white critics of the Supreme Court's decision questioned not only the objective of racial homogeneity but also the application of the coercive power of the national government to achieve it. The volume of resistance by the whites was probably roughly indicated by the 43 percent of the popular vote that they gave to George Wallace of Alabama, segregationist candidate for president of the United States, in the statewide Democratic primary of 1964.[1] In the demonstrations against forced racial integration the revitalized Ku Klux Klan once again became active in Maryland.

The great nineteenth-century Maryland-born champion of Negro rights, Frederick Douglass, had criticized "the colored people of this country" for "saying so much of race and color as a basis of their claims to justice." Their emancipation, he insisted, had been won "not because the victim of slavery was a Negro, but because the Negro is, and of right ought to be, a man—a brother of all other men, a child of the common Father of mankind, and, therefore, ... entitled to justice, liberty and equality before the law, to education and to an equal chance with all other men in the race of life and in the pursuit of happiness."[2] This continued to be the objective of Negro civil-rights organizations. Among them the lead was taken by the Maryland branches of the National Association for the Advancement of Colored People (NAACP), which was headed for many years by a distinguished Negro civil-rights leader, Mrs. Lillie M. Jackson.

But in its modern phase this objective has become entangled with the drive also for the social and even the economic equality of all citizens, thus calling for correction of social injustices by vigorous government enforcement action and calling in question some hitherto accepted property rights. From the requirement of legal equality for Negroes in public education, as set forth in the Supreme Court's decision, black leaders could easily infer also the requirement of social and economic equality as their constitutional right.

Many of the black riots and other demonstrations which marred the racial picture in Maryland during the 1960's were motivated by local grievances, stemming from both social and, in some lingering cases, legal restrictions upon the actions of Negroes and from unfulfilled promises of remedial action by state and local officials. Racial conflict between Negroes and whites broke out in Cambridge and led to the occupation of the city by the National Guard in 1963 and again in 1964. Governor Spiro Agnew denounced H. Rap Brown, an advocate of segregation and leader of the Student Non-Violent Coordinating Committee, as their instigator for a recent speech which he had made in Cambridge, and he threatened to use police action thereafter to stop speakers who were using inflammatory language. In Baltimore the 1960's brought sit-ins and other demonstrations by Baltimore's black population, including the students of Morgan State and Coppin State Colleges, against white-only restaurants, department stores, and theaters. In Maryland's largest city where the census of 1960 showed a Negro population of 326,589, or 34.8 percent of the total population of 939,024, the racial problem was complicated by a high rate of unemployment among Negroes.

This situation was soon put on the way to legislative solution by the Warren Court's decision applying the principle of one-man one-vote to matters of political representation. A legislative apportionment carried through in Maryland in 1966 brought the Maryland General Assembly into line with the Supreme Court's principle. It increased the representation for Maryland's cities and the burgeoning suburbs adjoining Baltimore and Washington from 55 percent to 75 percent in the House of Delegates and from 34 percent to 75 percent in the Senate and thus proportionately reduced the representation of the rural areas of the state. In the following year, the reconstituted legislature repealed a 300-year-old statute barring interracial marriages and by enacting a fair-housing act made Maryland the first state south of the Mason-Dixon line to adopt legislation limiting racial discrimination in new housing.

The black population of the state, numbering approximately 700,000, amounts to almost one-fifth of its total population and constitutes three percent of the black population of the nation. In comparison with the experience of other states situated south of the Mason-Dixon line, Maryland, except for a few lurid incidents, made the transition from a segregated society into an avowedly racially integrated society with a minimum of social dislocation, revealing in the process the existence of an unexpectedly large reservoir of respect and goodwill between blacks and whites. To produce such a measure of racial desegregation as has been achieved since 1954 has required the application of legal pressure and moral prodding, but it has also revealed, at least in Baltimore, the existence of a widespread tolerance of racial diversity which seems natural to a society that has been faced throughout its history with the task of reconciling divergent religions and nationalist views and moulding large numbers of foreign immigrants to the Maryland way.

The process of desegregation in Maryland was facilitated by the guiding influence of the Maryland Commission on Interracial Problems and Relations, appointed by Governor Theodore R. McKeldin in 1952, and by the Baltimore Commission on Human Relations, appointed by Mayor Thomas J. D'Alesandro of Baltimore. Maryland leaders, while seeking to preserve quality performance and to reward competence, have striven toward the national goal of legal equality of blacks and whites. As they have qualified themselves for public recognition, individual Negroes have been recognized, facilities for Negro education have been improved, slum housing has been razed and replaced by acceptable government housing, and legal justice (except in certain perhaps exaggerated cases) has been meted out to minority persons.

In the controversy as between the "melting-pot" concept on the one hand or the preservation of cultural integrity on the other, the former seemingly has triumphed. This was a logical climax to a long-continued drive to eliminate second-class citizenship and represented the latest stage in a two-hundred-year evolution of the state and the nation toward the Jeffersonian concept of legal and civil equality of all citizens.

But legislation of a reformatory character can be expected to have only a slight influence in modifying public attitudes and may not become embodied in custom for many decades. Maryland's posture of desegregation obviously involves a measure of "tokenism," of compliance with the letter though not the spirit of racial partnership between whites and Negroes. In other words, "black and white speak but do not reach each other." [3] In view of Maryland's long experience of racial bipolarization, it would be premature to expect the opposite.

In the 1960's Maryland implemented the legal processes of racial integration in its public school system as required by policies of the national government, but several counties, particularly Somerset, Talbot,

Worcester, and Dorchester, all situated on the Eastern Shore, gave only token compliance. Following the trend in other states, Maryland converted its six state colleges—Bowie, Coppin, Frostburg, Morgan, Salisbury, and Towson—to liberal arts institutions and soon afterward, in 1963, committed them to racial integration, but, as it has turned out, the three previously white colleges—Frostburg, Salisbury, and Towson—have continued predominantly white, and the other three, which were previously black, have continued black. The degree of integration achieved in this state college system was estimated in 1971 at no more than 10.4 percent, in 1972 at less than 12 percent, and in 1974 at 12.5 percent.[4]

Despite the enforcement actions of both the state and the national administrations, racial segregation has persisted as a way of life in many of Maryland's cities, notably in Baltimore, whence the whites have fled to the outskirts and formed a white suburban ring around the old urban center. During the 20 years between 1952 and 1972 Baltimore City lost almost one quarter of its white population each decade, and the city was almost abandoned to those who were too poor to move. As a result of this white exodus to the suburbs, the central city, though it has retained its daytime character as a business metropolis, has lost a large majority of its white residents. As those that remain choose to send their children to private white schools, Negroes constitute 83 percent of the pupils enrolled in the public school system. In the 1955-1965 decade 65 manufacturing industries moved from Baltimore City to Baltimore County.[5] In the early 1970's when the Negro population of Baltimore reached 48 percent, the neighboring counties were still 93 percent white. The pattern of population distribution shows that the blacks and the whites were slightly more separated in 1970 than in 1960.[6] In residential living arrangements segregation still in fact prevails. In the port of Baltimore dock labor had long been racially integrated, but the white International Longshoremen's Union refused to accept black members until forced to do so by court action.

Baltimore City has accordingly been left with declining employment, a lowered tax base, and increased competition from an almost all-white suburban and affluent Baltimore County. If the population movement out of the central city continues, Baltimore County, it is predicted, will outstrip Baltimore City as the state's largest political subdivision by 1990. According to the 1970 census, 44 percent of the black families in Baltimore were receiving some sort of public assistance. As a result of the ensuing urban blight, many of Baltimore's famous restaurants closed their doors, and the city forfeited its reputation for fine foods. Central city shopping centers have steadily lost ground to suburban shopping centers. The change in the complexion of the inner city has even been accompanied by a decline of interest in the previously popular spectator sports and a significant reduction in attendance at the stadium games of the Orioles and the Colts. Coincident with this decline has been a large increase in the crime rate, particularly homicides.

The great majority of Maryland black people are striving earnestly to adjust themselves to ways of living of which their slave ancestors never had a foretaste and to which they themselves were unaccustomed before the modern civil rights movement. The newly established legal relationship between Negroes and whites has created a favorable climate for the encouragement of black capitalism, that is, Negro ownership and management of commercial enterprises. As a result, new oppostunities are opening up for black entrepreneurship in the food industry, medical services, and other businesses, as well as in law, journalism, medicine, and other professions. Negroes also occupy management-level positions in many Maryland branches of national business organizations.

Traditional Marylanders continue to cling to their habits of social exclusivism and conviviality with congenial associates, and they refuse to allow their conviction of quality to be diluted by the masses and pressures of the new democracy. Descendants of Maryland's colonial gentry or of her nineteenth-century millionaires still maintain the traditions of their genteel society in the rolling, verdant horse country of the Green Spring Valley and the Worthington Valley north of Baltimore. In 1936 a lower-echelon member of this society, the twice-wedded and divorced Wallis Warfield Simpson, made a romantic "pitch" for a king and shook the British empire with her attachment to King Edward VIII, leading to his abdication of the throne. "Fashionable" society in Maryland is still exclusively white, but a new middle-class black society is emerging, which is creating its own inner social strata.

Until the 1930's Maryland's black population, insofar as they had voted, had generally supported the Republican party of Lincoln and of emancipation, but under the impact of the Great Depression after 1930 and the New Deal measures of the Franklin Roosevelt administration, they generally swung over to the Democratic party. Their numbers in Maryland were tremendously increased during World War II as they were attracted from the southern states by the prospect of jobs in Maryland's war industries.

The continued overwhelming preponderance of Democrats over Republicans in the Baltimore voting lists, however, has weakened the political leverage of black politicians, for the white leaders of the Democratic party demonstrated that they could win elections without using Negro candidates to gain the Negro vote. Moreover, blacks were showing the same record of abstinence from voting as whites except when race was perceived as an issue in a campaign.

Shrewd black candidates for public office accordingly sometimes find it necessary to reach out for white votes by moderating their pro-black campaign promises. But the Congress of Racial Equality (CORE) has eliminated its white supporting members and converted itself into an all-black organization, even demanding an independent black school system and advocating the nationwide continuance of two societies, one white, the other black.

As early as 1890, a Negro, Harry S. Cummings, was elected to the Baltimore city council, but at the state level blacks gained election to the legislature only after the Supreme Court's decision in the *Brown* case in 1954. By 1973 a total of 18 blacks were serving in the Maryland state legislature, four in the Senate and 14 in the House of Delegates. In 1967 a Negro, Joseph C. Howard, was elected a judge on Baltimore's highest city court for a term of 15 years. Three years later, Parren Mitchell, who in 1950 as a Negro student from West Baltimore won his suit against the University of Maryland for admission to the graduate school of sociology at the College Park campus, was elected as Maryland's first black member of the United States House of Representatives. He expressed his philosophy of politics as follows: "In white areas I'm always asked if I'll represent all the people. The answer is yes. But I'll do more for blacks because blacks need more." [7]

For Maryland's transition from segregation to integration in racial matters the black community gives much credit to Republican Governor Theodore R. McKeldin. He was the tenth child of an Irish immigrant father who worked as a stonemason and later became a Baltimore policeman. After a defeat for mayor of Baltimore in 1939 and a defeat for governor in 1942, McKeldin gained the mayor's office in 1943, defeating the Democratic incumbent, Howard Jackson, in a city where the registration was 5 to 1 Democratic. In 1951 he defeated William Preston Lane's bid for reelection as governor by the largest majority in Maryland's history to become the state's third Republican governor. After serving the constitutional limit of two terms as governor, he returned to politics to serve again as mayor of Baltimore from 1963 to 1967. He possessed a talent for almost evangelical oratory but was flexible in his political views and did little to build up the Republican party in the state. Upon his retirement as governor in 1958, the Democrats regained the governorship with J. Millard Tawes of Crisfield as their candidate, and he was reelected in 1962.

To meet the increasing costs of state government in a period of inflation of prices and values, Governor Lane had recommended a two percent retail sales tax in his "Message on Additional Revenue Requirements" in February 1947. His recommendation was accepted and enacted into law by the legislature in an attempt to keep the state government solvent and operating on a pay-as-you-go basis. But the sales tax aroused strong public opposition. "Pennies for Lane" boxes were installed in stores, and the governor was derisively showered with pennies whenever he made a personal appearance. But by means of the sales tax he was able to show a balanced budget in 1948.

Although McKeldin in campaigning against Lane in 1951 promised to repeal the sales tax, he failed to do so after his election, explaining that he had "made a mistake" in promising it. With the additional revenues from this source he, like Governor Lane, carried out a program of vigorous state action. Lane, a lawyer and publisher from Hagerstown, brought to realization the Chesapeake Bay Bridge connecting Annapolis with Kent Island and the Eastern Shore, which had been under consideration for more than forty years. The opening of this seven-mile bridge, the William Preston Lane, Jr. Memorial Bridge, gave large commercial advantages to Baltimore in its traditional rivalry with Philadelphia for the products and trade of the Eastern Shore.

During McKeldin's governorship, the Friendship Airport, later renamed the Baltimore-Washington International Airport, was completed and the Harbor Tunnel under the Baltimore harbor was constructed. The opening of the airport at Friendship, located some eight miles south of the city and costing $15 million, increased the air freight and passenger traffic of Baltimore and supplemented the facilities of the municipal airport, which was located on the waterfront south of Canton and which accommodated both land and sea planes. The Harbor Tunnel enabled north-south highway traffic to move speedily through Baltimore. Costing $130 million, it was the largest single project that the state had ever undertaken, completely eclipsing in scope the earlier Chesapeake and Ohio Canal.

McKeldin put his prestige as governor behind the State of Israel and thus set a precedent for Maryland's concern with foreign affairs which was followed by the Maryland legislature in 1974 when it adopted a resolution opposing any relinquishment or dilution of United States sovereignty over the Panama Canal Zone in Central America, an interoceanic maritime facility which had been a tremendous boon to Baltimore's port industry ever since it was opened to world trade in 1914. Copies of the resolution were sent to all the other states of the Union.

As the national presidential campaign of 1952 approached, Maryland, a traditionally Democratic state with a Republican governor, became especially interesting to national Republican party managers, and Governor McKeldin was invited to make the nominating speech for Eisenhower at the Republican convention in Chicago. Although in both of McKeldin's terms the state legislature continued to be consistently Democratic, Maryland's congressional delegation was split between Republicans and Democrats, and the state was represented in the Senate by two Republicans, John Marshall Butler and J. Glenn Beall. Though a nominal Republican, McKeldin, after returning to the mayor's office in Baltimore, supported President Johnson for reelection in 1964 and in return collected nineteen million dollars from the administration in Washington for Baltimore's Inner Harbor Redevelopment Project, to which McKeldin had committed his administration in his inaugural speech.

The Maryland constitution of 1867 required that the General Assembly must, at twenty-year intervals, submit to the voters of the state the question as to whether or not a convention should be held for the purpose of revising the constitution. When the General Assembly polled the voters in 1887 and again in 1907, the majority opposed a new constitutional convention. In the reorganization of the state government which was made in 1922, a constitutional amendment was adopted providing that the next poll of the voters on the question of holding a constitutional convention should be postponed from 1927 to 1930 and should be held every twenty years thereafter. When the poll was taken in 1930, the majority of citizens who voted on the question voted in favor of a convention, but their wishes were ignored by the General Assembly on the ground that whereas a majority of those voting on the question of a convention had favored it, they did not constitute a majority of those voting at the same time in the election for governor. In 1950 the question of a convention was again submitted to the voters and again turned down. When the voters were confronted with a draft of a proposed new constitution in elections in 1968, they rejected it overwhelmingly, preferring to continue to operate their government in accordance with the venerable and respected document of 1867. They followed a similarly conservative course by voting down a proposed increase of the governor's salary from $25,000 to $45,000 in the election of 1974.

The standard-bearer and consistent loser of the Democratic party in eleven campaigns for state offices in Maryland during the 1950's and 1960's was George P. Mahoney, son of a Baltimore policeman, who had organized and made himself wealthy in a construction business. Mahoney made his third bid for governor in 1952 but went down to defeat in the Eisenhower landslide. He ran for the United States Senate in 1956 and again fell under the weight of another Eisenhower victory. In the election of 1966, Mahoney won the Democratic nomination for governor but his campaign proved so divisive that he was again defeated, this time by Republican Spiro T. Agnew.

Agnew had a phenomenally rapid rise in politics, going from a four-year term as elected county executive in Baltimore County from 1962 to 1966, to governor of Maryland in 1967. Son of a Greek immigrant who operated a restaurant in Baltimore, Agnew attended Johns Hopkins University and earned a law degree from the University of Baltimore after returning from army service in World War II. As governor, working with a Democratic majority in both houses of the legislature, he supported open-housing legislation which when enacted into law, as noted above, was the first such legislation passed by any state south of the Mason-Dixon line. For the first time in Maryland's history, he integrated the governor's staff with blacks and whites. But in the Baltimore race riots of April 1968, he took a stiff and popular stand in defense of law and order, which commended him to Republican party leaders. Dealing with the delicate race question, Agnew warned that "the goal of equal opportunity had been replaced by the goal of instantaneous economic equality." Partly for this reason and partly because of his symbolic middle-state base, Maryland being considered neither North nor South, he was chosen vice-president on the Republican ticket with presidential candidate, Richard M. Nixon, a ticket which proved victorious in the election in November 1968. When Agnew took the office of vice-president of the United States in the following January, he became the first Marylander to occupy that office.

Since Taney's death in 1864, no Marylander had been appointed to the Supreme Court in Washington until President Lyndon Johnson selected a Maryland Negro, Thurgood Marshall, as an associate justice in 1967. No Marylander served in a president's cabinet after Charles J. Bonaparte left the Roosevelt administration in 1908 until President Eisenhower appointed William P. Rogers as attorney general in 1957. But neither he nor two other cabinet officers subsequently appointed from Maryland—Clark Clifford as Secretary of Defense by President Johnson and Rogers C.B. Morton as Secretary of the Interior by President Nixon—were born in Maryland.

As vice-president, Agnew, in his often-expressed views on the problems of the period, spoke for the American people. But after he began to make speeches against the public news media, blaming them for biased and inaccurate reporting, he was charged with having followed throughout his public career a practice, not unknown among Maryland public officials, of augmenting his official income with outside earnings without due regard for conflict-of-interest implications. Angew chose not to defend himself and resigned from the vice-presidency in October 1973. It was rumored that the politicians who placed him on the Republican ticket with Nixon knew of his vulnerability in this respect and had seen in it, as they hoped, a means of keeping him in tow.

In the quarter-century before the bicentennial year, government at all levels in the United States—national, state, and local—grew at unprecedented rates in number of personnel employed, in budgetary requirements, and in dominant influence over the private sector of the nation. Between 1954 and 1974, the share of the Gross National Product appropriated by the public sector increased from 26.5 percent to 32.8 percent or almost one-third of the nation's total annual production. Most of this growth occurred in the state and local bureaucracies.[8]

This tremendous expansion of governmental power, which was responsible for spending vast sums of money, offered temptations to public officials who were charged with selecting sites for new government buildings, applying zoning regulations, determining the routes of new highways, and reaching official decisions on many other matters which would favor one or another special interest. To these temptations which presented themselves in a prevailing milieu of a general breakdown of ethics and morals, officials, in Maryland as elsewhere, sometimes succumbed, corrupted by the exorbitant power which was vested in the jobs in which they found themselves.

When Agnew resigned as governor of Maryland in January 1969 to become vice-president of the United States, a Democratic leader in the legislature, Marvin Mandel, was chosen by the legislature to replace him and was subsequently elected to a full four-year term in November 1970. From 1776 until the adoption of the Constitution of 1867, all of Maryland's governors had been Episcopalians, 27 in all, except for two Roman Catholics (Thomas Sim Lee, 1779-1782, and Enoch Lowe, 1851-1854), one Presbyterian (Levin Winder, 1812-1816), and two Methodists (Thomas H. Hicks, 1858-1862, and Augustus W. Bradford, 1862-1866). Thereafter, under the constitution of 1867, the list of governors included eleven Episcopalians, six Presbyterians, three Roman Catholics, and three Methodists. Marvin Mandel became Maryland's first Jewish governor. He took over the administration of a state bureaucracy which had enormously expanded since Governor Ritchie's reorganization in 1922. He was confronted with a vastly proliferated and cumbersome state organization including no fewer than 248 agencies and departments. He proceeded to consolidate them into eleven departments headed by cabinet-level secretaries. Maryland thus became one of the few states in the nation to adopt the cabinet system of state administration. These departments include (1) Natural Resources, (2) Planning, (3) Budget and Fiscal Planning, (4) Health and Mental Hygiene, (5) Employment and Social Services, (6) Public Safety and Correctional Services, (7) Personnel, (8) Licensing and Regulation, (9) Economic and Community Development, (10) General Services, and (11) Agriculture. His administration has also reorganized the Metropolitan Transit Authority to prepare for mass transit systems in the Washington-Baltimore complex, and has adopted comprehensive programs for environmental protection.[9]

In Maryland the township system of New England never appeared, and local government remains the responsibility of counties and incorporated municipalities. The county government, under existing constitutional and statutory provisions, serves as an administrative unit for statewide programs and handles the judicial and record-keeping functions for the geographical area of the county. The municipal government is responsible, under the law and municipal regulations, for public safety and public health, for the construction and maintenance of public thoroughfares and buildings, and for certain protective fire and police services. Of the general revenues raised by Maryland's local governments in the fiscal year 1970-1971, local property taxes supplied more than half. In addition, the counties and Baltimore City have been authorized by the state legislature to levy local income taxes, which are imposed at percentages ranging from 20 to 50 percent of the state income tax and which are levied and collected in conjunction with the state tax.

Under conditions of inflation and expanding budgetary requirements, the state saw fit to return to the lottery system of raising revenues in 1972. Two years later, the Maryland state government took over the full responsibility for property-tax assessments and for appeals from them. Since then, the state has followed the practice of increasing property-tax assessments and by this method has been able to make significant increases in its income without resort to increased levels of taxation. But the state government shares a substantial portion of its revenue receipts with the counties and with Baltimore City. Only five states pass on a greater percentage of general state revenues to local governments than does Maryland. The state has also assumed responsibility for all public-school construction, thereby relieving the counties and Baltimore City of a heavy financial burden.[10] In addition, the state has relieved the Baltimore City government of the responsibility for mass transit, the port, the Baltimore-Washington Airport, and the share of welfare costs which are not supplied by the national government. The Maryland tax law requirement that for every $100 of tax assessment 21 cents shall be collected and devoted to retirement of the public debt provides a guaranty of the credit standing of the state.

The Maryland style reflects three and a half centuries of traditional living and does not easily accommodate itself to innovations whether they are imposed from outside or introduced by newcomers into the state or even by "alien" sectors within the state. Marylanders prefer the old ways of doing things. Baltimore, for example, was the last major city in the nation to adopt parking meters, not accepting them until 1956. But Maryland's complacencies have been severely shaken by the imperatives of social and political change which have been impressed upon the state with increasingly compulsive force. Many of those required changes can be attributed to shifts in national policy, for, like other states in the federal complex, Maryland, laboring under its own domestic competitions and contradictions, finds that its actions are increasingly determined by the objectives of national interest that are defined by administrations and bureaucracies in Washington and that the range of choices remaining open to it for independent action as a free state are correspondingly restricted.

Footnotes

[1] Wallace was shot, but not fatally injured, in Laurel, Maryland, in May 1972.

[2] Quoted in George F. Bragg, *Men of Maryland*, pp. 60-61.

[3] Jane Matz, *Report on Baltimore Civil Disorders,* April 1968, Middle Atlantic Region, American Friends Service Committee, Baltimore, September 1968, p. 33.

[4] Report of Trustees of the State Colleges, Eighth through Eleventh Annual Reports, 1971-1974, Appendix VI.

[5] Daniel Conway and Natalie Lobe, Regional Planning Council, Baltimore, *Patterns of Change in Manufacturing Industry, Baltimore Region, 1955-1965.* October 1968, p. 18.

[6] Regional Planning Council, *General Development Plan for the Baltimore Region,* 1972, p. 87.

[7] *News-American,* Baltimore, June 13, 1973.

[8] Advisory Commission on Intergovernmental Relations, "Trends in Fiscal Federalism, 1954-1974," Washington, D.C. February 1975.

[9] Other legislative and administrative achievements of Governor Mandel are noted in the State of Maryland, *Manual, 1973-1974,* pp. 5-9.

[10] Will S. Myers, Senior Analyst, Advisory Commission on Intergovernmental Relations, Washington, D.C., letter to author, August 11, 1975.

Sources and Additional Reading

Bard, Harry, *Maryland State and Government: Its New Dynamics,* Tidewater Publishers, Cambridge, Maryland, 1974.

Hollander Foundation, Sidney, *Toward Equality: Baltimore's Progress Report,* Sidney Hollander Foundation, Inc., Baltimore, Maryland, 1960. A condensed record of the process of desegregation in Maryland, 1946-1958.

Maryland-National Capital Park and Planning Commission, *Looking Ahead, 1958-1980: A General Plan for the Maryland-Washington Regional District,* Riverdale and Silver Spring, Maryland, 1957.

Motz, Jane, *Report on Baltimore Civil Disorders, April 1968,* Middle Atlantic Region, American Friends Service Committee, Baltimore, September 1968.

U.S. Department of the Interior, *The Nation's River: A Report on the Potomac,* Washington, 1968.

———, Potomac Planning Task Force, *The Potomac: A Report on Its Imperiled Future and a Guide for Its Orderly Development,* Government Printing Office, Washington, 1967.

CHAPTER XXIX

TRENDS INTO THE FUTURE

Maryland is a virtually one-city state. The economy of that city, Baltimore, depends upon its port, which represents an investment of some $500 million in piers, warehouses, channels, shipbuilding and repair yards, as well as an elaborate complex of harborside industries. Here the American Sugar Company operates its main refinery, and other large companies carry on their industrial operations. Through the port the very life of the city pulsates. It is the city's biggest industry.

The port of Baltimore is also the greatest single physical asset of the state as a whole. According to studies made by the University of Maryland, the economic impact of the port upon the state increased from $1.6 billion in 1966 to $2.5 billion in 1973. In the latter year, the port was responsible for nearly 170,000 jobs, or one-tenth of the total number of jobs in the state, and also for almost one-tenth of the total Gross State Product (9.89 percent of $25.1 billion).[1]

As noted earlier, Baltimore enjoys a more advantageous situation than its rival ports on the Atlantic seacoast in relation to the producers and markets of the heartland of the continent. Its distance from Chicago, for example, is only 796 miles, as compared with 817 miles for Philadelphia and 899 miles for New York, with consequently lower freight charges on both foreign and domestic cargoes. But Baltimore lost this advantage when in 1963 the Supreme Court abolished its advantageous freight-rate differential after 86 years and granted parity to New York, Boston, and southern ports on freight-rate charges on railborne cargo moving to and from the midwest.

Nevertheless, in spite of this blow, by 1970 the port of Baltimore had increased its overseas traffic by 21.8 percent to surpass Philadelphia and become the third Atlantic coast port after New York and Norfolk. In the following year, it broke its own record of the previous year by handling in all nearly 43 million tons of cargo, the largest single commodity being iron ore. Baltimore's imports of iron ore, mainly for the Bethlehem Steel Company at Sparrows Point, are now being exceeded by petroleum imports as Baltimore's largest tonnage commodity, and the Bethlehem Steel shipyards are now building enormous oil tankers of as much as 265,000 deadweight tons. Grain exports, which once were the principal export commodity of the port, still retain their importance and in 1973 reached an all-time high of approximately 150 million bushels.

Among the ports of the nation Baltimore ranks third in total value of waterborne foreign trade and fourth in volume. Among all the Atlantic and Gulf ports it stands second in handling container cargoes, coming only after New York in this respect. It is also the leading world port of entry for the importation of foreign-made automobiles, having unloaded as many as 315,000 in one year. In both imports and exports the trade of the port is increasing, particularly in the handling of containerized cargoes in which Baltimore was a pioneer.

The port of Baltimore contains more than 100 covered and open piers and can handle approximately 200 vessels at one time. It possesses two routes of access from the Atlantic, one by way of Chesapeake Bay, a distance of 150 miles, and the other by way of Delaware Bay and the toll-free Chesapeake and Delaware Ship Canal, a distance of 125 miles. This latter canal was privately operated for ninety years after its opening in 1829 and was then purchased by the national government in 1919 and enlarged to accommodate increased traffic. Of the total number of vessels which call at Baltimore's wharves, some 40 percent use the Chesapeake and Delaware Canal.[2] It annually accommodates more traffic than the Panama Canal in both number of ships and tonnage of cargo carried.

Most of the marine terminals at the port in Baltimore are privately owned. The ore piers of the Baltimore and Ohio, the Pennsylvania, and the Western Maryland Railroads, and the independent facility operated by the Cottman Company can handle almost 10,000 tons per hour. The port's three grain elevators can store over 13 million bushels, and the grain piers can load some 450,000 bushels per hour. Shipbuilding and ship repair have long been an essential part of the port's operation. By 1963 more than 500 new vessels had gone down the ways of the Bethlehem Steel Company's shipbuilding plant at Sparrows Point, and the port possesses, in general, modern facilities for servicing all types of oceangoing vessels. The piers and drydocks of Bethlehem can accommodate 23 vessels at the same time. In 1950 Baltimore installed a harbor radar system on the Municipal Pier, thus becoming the first port on the East Coast and the third port in the world to provide this facility.

After World War II Baltimore profited from the expanded foreign commerce engendered by the national program of relief and rehabilitation of the war-devastated foreign countries and foreign aid to underdeveloped countries. But by the mid-1950's the port and the downtown business district of Baltimore showed critical signs of decay. Because the railroads, which had long dominated Baltimore's waterfront, had allowed the dock facilities to deteriorate, the Maryland General Assembly established the Maryland Port Authority in 1956 and charged it with the responsibility of coordinating the effort of city, state, and private groups on behalf of Maryland's ports. Its name was changed to the Maryland Port Administration in 1971, when it was put under the jurisdiction of the newly created cabinet-level State Department of Transportation.

The responsibility of this five-man authority, which is appointed by the governor, extends to building and operating pier facilities which may be required in the public interest, the carrying out of trade solicitation and promotional programs, and cooperation with the private operators of Baltimore's existing port and terminal facilities in modernizing the port, in meeting the competitive efforts of other ports on the Atlantic seaboard, and in preventing diversion of commerce from Maryland ports to Great Lakes ports which were opened up to oceanic commerce by the St. Lawrence Seaway. Since the Maryland Port Authority, now Administration, was formed, it has allocated more than $100 million into revitalizing Baltimore's port facilities besides encouraging private investment. It represents the interests of the state in Baltimore's 45-mile waterfront and also in other Maryland ocean ports. Among these latter the most important is the newly developed port for oceanborne ships on the Choptank River at Cambridge on the Eastern Shore which engages mainly in the preparation and shipping of frozen fish. Salisbury has also made overtures to the Maryland Port Administration for assistance in dredging the Wicomico River on the Eastern Shore in order to make it navigable again for oceangoing vessels.

The port of Baltimore and the various marine industries of the entire Chesapeake Bay area are faced with serious problems caused by water shortage, silting of river and bay estuaries, pollution, and other environmental changes. As the outlet of a network of river systems, the "drowned river basin" of the Chesapeake receives a large discharge of sediment from denuded upriver forest areas. After the War for American Independence the Ellicott brothers, John and Andrew, found it necessary to deepen the water surrounding their Baltimore wharf, and for this purpose they developed a so-called "Mud Machine." [3] Frequent dredging of the main channels of the harbor is increasingly required to keep them freely navigable by large vessels and to avoid the fate which long ago befell many of Maryland's best harbors of the colonial era as, for example, Elk Ridge Landing on the Patapsco, Piscataway on Piscataway Creek, Bladensburg on the Eastern Branch of the Anacostia River, and Port Tobacco on Port Tobacco River, all of which have been lost to commerce through silting. In the course of the last two centuries of the use of Baltimore's harbor, sedimentation has already moved the head of navigation some seven miles downstream, from Elk Ridge Landing to the Hanover Street Bridge in Baltimore.[4]

Modern dredging operations to maintain deep-water channels in the port of Baltimore and in Chesapeake Bay have been accompanied by vigilant efforts since 1950 to combat the release of oil wastes, the dumping of ballast and bilge water, the discharge of industrial wastes from shoreline factories, and other pollution abuses. Other effective measures of reducing water pollution, as recommended by the Baltimore Regional Planning Council, include "sedimentation control at construction sites, diversion of silt and fertilizer runoff to farm ponds, enforcement of laws restricting the dumping of untreated waste, and increasing public ownership of parkland along rivers and streams."[5] In their antipollution measures, however, the environmentalists sometimes come into conflict with the ambitions of the port authorities, both public and private, particularly in the plans for the dredging of the ship channels from 42 to 50 feet and for the disposal of the dredged matter.

Pollution of the Chesapeake waters, along with the increasing salinity of the Bay, commercial overharvesting, and multiplication of predators, has already taken a heavy toll of marine life, especially oysters. In the book on Maryland and its resources which Johns Hopkins University prepared for the World's Fair at Chicago in 1893, it boasted that from the time when "the business of packing oysters for shipment to the interior was established in 1834 nearly four hundred million bushels of oysters have been taken from our waters."[6]

The production of Chesapeake Bay's famous oysters reached its peak in the mid-1800's but has since steadily declined to less than one-fifth its former level because, in part, of oyster wars and indiscriminate harvesting, but mainly water pollution. To help prevent further depletion of the oyster beds, Maryland in 1890 set a minimum legal size of two and a half inches for market oysters and later raised it to three inches. The state has also instituted other conservation measures, but enforcement agencies find the independent-minded Chesapeake "watermen" unsympathetic to control measures and uncooperative in complying with them. The plight of the entire marine industry of the Bay was worsened by the devastation wrought by tropical storm *Agnes* in 1972. Oystering in particular still remains a depressed industry but can be restored through proper measures of conservation.

Like the marine occupations, agriculture no longer plays the same large role that it once played in the economy of the state. In the twenty years after 1951, the total number of Maryland farms declined by one-half and the total farm acreage dropped by almost one-fourth. Agricultural production in general by 1975 was accounting for only 14 percent of the gross economic product of the state and its future was clouded by the increasing diversion of the best farmlands to industry and to housing developments. Tobacco has long since lost its preeminence as Maryland's principal commercial cash agricultural crop and now ranks a poor fifth, being outclassed by poultry, dairy products, grains, and cattle.[7] By 1971 Maryland was supplying only 1.7 percent of the total national production of tobacco.[8]

The migration of people both into and within Maryland has caused radical shifts in types of agricultural production since World War II. As Anne Arundel and Prince George's Counties have acquired larger populations, they have lost their rank as eighth and ninth, respectively, among Maryland agricultural counties and have slipped to twentieth and nineteenth, respectively. By 1969, in terms of farm-product sales, the nine counties of the Eastern Shore accounted for more than half of the total production of the state because of their expanded production of corn, soybeans, vegetables, and chickens. The farm production of the five counties of southern Maryland declined from 16 to 8 percent of the state's total between 1939 and 1969 and that of the Piedmont region from 42 to 29 percent. Maryland continues to be a deficit food-producing state.[9] This condition can be expected to worsen as population increases and as the amount of land available and profitable for agricultural uses correspondingly diminishes.

In order to keep fertile agricultural land in production and out of the hands of real estate developers the state adopted in the early 1960's a reduced tax-assessment system for farmland, and by changes in the tax law in 1973, it gave such land further preferential treatment in tax assessment.[10] These concessions have encouraged environmentalists to advocate the "conservation easement," a private, voluntary device which enables landowners to restrict or prohibit future development rights and future changes in land use. Since this easement reduces the value of the land, the owners are compensated by tax advantages. The Baltimore Regional Council has made the interesting recommendation in its *General Development Plan for the Baltimore Region* that "conservation districts, either public or as a syndication of landholders, be created to acquire the interest, either in fee or less than fee, to land within the district and sell or lease back the land for agricultural purposes." (P. 35). Among the hereditary landowners in the Green Spring and Worthington Valleys it appears that some such "syndication" or compact has already been informally adopted because of their unanimous resistance to the blandishments of land speculators.

The growth rate of manufacturing has also declined from the high point that it reached during the 1950's. "It is the non-commodity producing sectors—public administration, trade, professional services—that presently account for a full 75 percent of Maryland employment and have boosted Maryland's nationwide ranking to seventeenth among the states in total employment," explains the Maryland Department of Economic and Community Development.[11] The economy of the state therefore is based no longer upon the processes of primary production but rather upon secondary services and is therefore critically dependent upon the policies of government—national, state, and local—in the areas of tax policy, health services, employment guaranties, and welfare responsibilities in general.

Government at all levels is the largest employer in Maryland, accounting for 26 percent of all employed persons as compared to only 14 percent for the nation as a whole. The majority of them, however, are employed either within or outside the state in agencies of the national government, for Maryland itself ranks only twentieth among the states for workers in state employment and thirteenth for workers in local government. Maryland ranks third among the states, however, coming after New York and California, in the number of state residents who are employed by the general government.[12]

In terms of per capita personal income Maryland ranked eleventh among the fifty states of the Union in 1971 and in family income fifth, being outdistanced only by Alaska, Connecticut, Hawaii, and New Jersey. Montgomery County showed at that time the highest family income rate in the nation, with a figure of $16,700 income per family as compared with the national average of $9,500. Government employment is a large contributing factor to this result. In the Maryland counties of Prince George's and Montgomery bordering on the District of Columbia, 32 percent of the residents are employed by government, including national, state, and local. But approximately 10 percent of the population of the state, or 75,000 families, live below the poverty level of $4,000, of whom two-fifths live in Baltimore City and one-third in the rural areas of the Eastern Shore, southern Maryland, and western Maryland.[13]

In the mid-1950's Baltimore was a complacent city largely unconcerned with racial pressures, deteriorating public services, and spreading slums. Its tradition of gentility, it was felt, would gloss over imperfections and derelictions. The initiative for change came from a group of central-city businessmen of large vision and business acumen, who, under the leadership of J. Jefferson Miller, constituted themselves a Committee for Downtown, Incorporated, to devise ways and means by which downtown Baltimore could once again compete with its own suburbs. They persuaded Mayor D'Alesandro to work cooperatively with them through the city Department of Planning in renovating and modernizing a limited area—33 acres—of the downtown business district, and, at their own expense and with a contribution from the Greater Baltimore Committee, they financed a plan for a unified complex of new office-building towers, two high-rise apartment towers, a theater, a hotel, plazas, and retail shops in the heart of Baltimore's business district with the hope that such a complex would encourage similar private action for renewal of neighboring areas.

Charles Center, as the new planned development was called, was originally planned as an exclusively private enterprise, requiring only a bond issue of $25 million to cover public costs, largely for purchase of land and for administrative expenses, but eventually and reluctantly the promoters changed this policy and received approximately $23 million from the national agency for urban renewal. Even when only partially completed in the early 1970's, this privately inspired and largely independent, self-help development block in Baltimore's central city soon began to contribute almost $3 million annually in city real estate taxes, which was approximately six times the amount paid by the same distressed area in 1958. This increased tax revenue, it was estimated, would enable the city to recoup its costs within nine years.

Charles Center has served as a catalyst for imitative programs of urban renewal in other run-down areas of the city. In particular, it has inspired the Inner Harbor project for the rebuilding of some 240 acres surrounding the harbor basin and involving funds from the city, state, and national governments. Five major new buildings were begun there in 1973 costing more than $80 million and including a Science Center, the Christ Church Harbor Apartments, the United States Fidelity and Guaranty Building, the International Business Machines (I.B.M.) building, and a 30-story, pentagon-shaped World Trade Center overlooking the harbor and the city. To these, other modern buildings, along with a new campus for the Community College of Baltimore, museums, libraries, harbor-tour facilities, and shopping centers with specialty shops, theaters, and restaurants, are being added in the Inner Harbor district in a program which, it is anticipated, will carry forward far beyond the bicentennial year, will cost an estimated $250 million when completed, and will enable the metropolitan area of Maryland to sustain a competitive position in national and world commerce.

Both in the Inner Harbor renewal area and elsewhere in the city, Baltimore's Department of Housing and Community Development initiated in 1973 a plan by which substantial brick row houses and other residential properties which had been acquired by the city through tax-delinquency sales could be placed in the hands of "homesteaders" at a price of one dollar each and a commitment to rehabilitate the property within a specified time limit. The same agency is also creating, in cooperation with private developers, a new residential community in the hitherto undeveloped Coldspring section of northwestern Baltimore and in other city sites. Of the total budget of this Baltimore municipal agency, the national government supplies almost 40 percent.[14]

Maryland's physical progress, especially in the area of residential construction, has been retarded by the ultraconservatism of Baltimore's banking institutions, whose failure to keep pace with Maryland's requirements for developmental funds has provided a pretext for intervention by national housing authorities and other administrators of national aid programs operating in the banking field. In the Inner Harbor development project, in the larger Metro-Center plan of the Baltimore Department of Planning for the rehabilitation of more than 1,000 acres of residential property in downtown Baltimore, and in other city programs of slum clearance, street improvements, and expanded recreational facilities, emphasis is being placed, as it was in the original Charles Center plan, upon neighborhood initiative, responsibility, and cooperation, thus preserving Maryland's long tradition of local enterprise.

These development plans have been guided by the City Planning Commission and include a master plan of transportation designed to move traffic rapidly into and out of the downtown area through use of radial and ring streets. The gains which Baltimore makes through the rehabilitation of its harbor-related economy redound to the advantage not only of Baltimore but of the entire state. Since 1960 the Gross State Product of Maryland has more than tripled, rising from an estimated 8.1 billion to $25.1 billion in 1974. Some two-thirds of the jobs in the Greater Baltimore complex are located in Baltimore City, which is both the commercial and financial hub of the entire region. Because downtown employment is largely commuter employment, much of the tangible advantage is drained out of Baltimore into the suburban counties, especially Baltimore County, which is a preferred residential area for city workers.

The Greater Baltimore area is expected to have a population of approximately 3.1 million by 1985. For Baltimore City the situation of declining population, deteriorating central city, diminishing tax base, and wealthy suburbs has encouraged proposals for a merger of the city with Baltimore County. To the city this seems to be both a logical solution to its problems and a fair proposition since the prosperity of the county flows largely from the port and industry of the city. But it has evoked little enthusiasm in Baltimore County which is reluctant to "bail out" the city. Because of the moves that have already been made to rehabilitate the inner city, it appears that the city-to-county migration may be diminishing, for although middle-class Negroes are joining the trek to suburbia, middle-class whites are beginning in slow numbers to return to the city.

Population forecasts indicate that if current birth rates and population movements continue, Maryland will show a population of 5.5 million by the year 2,000. Its population increase of 821,000 between 1960 and 1970 was accounted for by both natural increase—53 percent—and immigration into the state from other states and the District of Columbia—47 percent. In that decade the black population of Prince George's County alone almost doubled, representing an overflow from the Federal District, which in 1970 was three-fourths black, and Montgomery County made only slightly smaller population gains. The metropolitan complex of Washington and its surrounding area had an estimated population of more than three million in 1972 and is expected to reach at least five million by the year 2,000.[15]

The most highly urbanized counties of Maryland are Baltimore, Prince George's, and Montgomery. Their character is being radically altered by the processes of metropolitan elephantiasis or urban sprawl emanating from Baltimore and Washington which is gradually absorbing them into a developing economic and cultural Megalopolis to form a part of a continuity of settlement extending from Greater Washington northward to New York and even beyond into southern New England. Greater Baltimore and the Greater Washington complex form two links in a chain of metropolitan growth which constitutes the nation's single largest concentration of population, commerce, industry and cultural activities. Baltimore and Washington are reaching out for each other, declared the Baltimore *Sun* in 1959, "like octopuses, sending out tentacles of freeway, sewerage lines, and industrial zones" in a process which was already creating a maze of urban problems in the intervening area.[16] With the destiny of this so-called "big street," or Washington-Boston corridor of population, transportation, and industry, the destiny of both coastal and Piedmont Maryland is inextricably connected, linked as they are by busy railroad lines, superhighways, air-flight patterns, and common corporate interests. Accepting this situation, Maryland planners, both public and private, have sought to influence it through processes of planned growth. The goals of the public planners are stated to be as follows:

1. *In the Physical Sector*
   To counter growth with high quality developmental concepts that optimize human diversity and service and minimize land consumption.
2. *In the Economic Sector*
   To stimulate the local economy and broaden the region's economic base, to provide jobs for the area's labor force, to reduce reliance on a single dominant form of employment, and to provide an adequate tax base.
3. *In the Social Sector*
   To upgrade the region's human resources to enhance the opportunity of the individual and the family to participate in and contribute to the social structure of the region.
4. *In the Governmental Sector*
   To increase the management capacity and responsibilities of the region's public institutions. [17]

To achieve these goals the Maryland state government has provided official planning councils covering all the geographical regions of the state except Frederick County. Maryland has long served as a partner of the District of Columbia in the Maryland National Capital Park and Planning Commission, the planning jurisdiction of which was enlarged in 1957 to include not only the District of Columbia and a large portion of Prince George's County but also all of Montgomery County. The overall planning operations for the Washington metropolitan area are carried on by the Metropolitan Washington Council of Governments, a voluntary organization of 15 major local governments of the Washington area which are represented by governing officials, state legislators, and members of Congress from those local areas. It is essentially an agency of those local governments and possesses only advisory functions, but its recommendations are submitted to the regional planning agencies, which include the above-mentioned Maryland-National Capital Park and Planning Commission as well as the National Capital Planning Commission and the Northern Virginia Planning District Commission for application each to its own district. The Metropolitan Washington Council of Governments provided in 1974 a *Reexamination of the Year 2000 Policies Plan* which updated *A Policies Plan for The Year 2000*, issued by its predecessor organization, the National Capital Regional Planning Council in 1961.

Falling in with the general trend toward public planning at both national and local levels, the General Assembly of Maryland created in 1963 a Regional Planning Council to prepare a comprehensive plan for Baltimore City and the five adjoining counties, Anne Arundel, Baltimore, Carroll, Harford, and Howard. Their efforts have taken form in a variety of planning studies including a *General Development Plan for the Baltimore Region* in December 1972 and many other plans for counties and municipalities within the region. Their master plan includes recommendations for the physical development of their district as a whole, emphasizing requirements for open space, transportation facilities, elimination of substandard housing, control of flooding and silting, industrial parks, and adequate health, recreational, and educational facilities. They have also concerned themselves with zoning regulations and have made recommendations for land use by land developers. They generally lack enforcement authority, but some of their conclusions are embodied in zoning ordinances which have legal force.

The planners have designed a mosaic of urban and suburban communities rationally organized and rationally related to each other. As their plans are adopted only after public hearings, they presumably respond to the wishes of the residents both actual and potential as to the conditions indispensable to the good life in these communities. A continuous population corridor between Washington and Baltimore does not appear to be an imminent possibility, for Washington is expanding more along the Potomac watercourse rather than toward Baltimore and Baltimore's suburbs are extending outward on a north-south axis. Howard County, lying almost directly on the Washington-Baltimore axis, contains only two settled areas of more than 2,500 population, Ellicott City and Columbia, the latter of which is an artifically created developer's dream.

The new planned city of Columbia, situated in the open country of Howard some fifteen miles southwest of Baltimore, represents an attempt by a private developer, James W. Rouse, to direct the urban sprawl from the usual form of random suburbias into a planned community. This new city, which is expected to attract 110,000 residents when completed in 1981, includes residential, recreational, business and industrial areas, with many kinds of community services. It was conceived as Maryland's answer in part to the problems of the decaying inner city and to the inconveniences, trials, and even dangers of metropolitan living. It is organized as a cluster of villages to emphasize local responsibility and the easy availability of all the facilities that are fundamentally needed for satisfactory modern living. Since its location was not fixed by the imperatives of trade and commerce, the success of this still experimental planned community may depend upon the continuance of growth and expansion of the national government as the principal patron of Maryland's suburbias.

Maryland is also involved in the planning of the development of the Eastern Shore. In 1964 a Delmarva Advisory Council was formed by the governors of the three states of the Delmarva Peninsula—Delaware, Maryland, and Virginia—to serve as "a permanent organization for the future development of the Peninsula." It functions in this way for nine Maryland counties on the Eastern Shore, for the three counties of Delaware, and for the two counties of Eastern Shore Virginia. It makes recommendations for tri-state cooperation in the fields of education, water pollution, housing for low and moderate-income groups, conservation of natural resources, tourism, unemployment, health facilities, the fishing industry, and many others. Of especial concern to this Council has been the need to preserve the railroad system of the peninsula which has been operating under conditions of depression.[18]

The Tri-County Council for Southern Maryland was created in 1965 and was organized by act of the General Assembly in the following year. But its regional development plan for the three counties of southern Maryland—St. Mary's, Charles, and Calvert—was prepared for it by the Maryland Department of State Planning and dated July 1974. Except for the regional planning which has been done for it by the Maryland Department of Planning, this Council has mainly concerned itself with promoting tourism and advising prospective groups interested in the area, but it refrains from central planning because in the words of its executive director, it has confidence "in the ability of the people to decide what's best for them."

Western Maryland has seemed to call for especial attention from planning agencies as constituting a sector of the larger national problem of Appalachia. The *Appalachian Maryland Development Plan,* as drafted by the Tri-County Council for Western Maryland, Incorporated, therefore emphasizes the need for better housing and health facilities, more industrialization, and more effective exploitation and at the same time better conservation of the rich natural resources of the region, comprising Garrett, Allegany, and Washington Counties.[19] Many of these recommendations relate equally well to problems which also concern adjoining counties of West Virginia, Pennsylvania, and other parts of the Appalachian region generally. The population of Appalachian Maryland, reported at a little less than 210,000 in 1974, is expected to reach approximately 228,000 by 1980, for a gain of only 9 percent.[20]

Formerly a cultural and economic projection of Piedmont Maryland, this region has become increasingly oriented toward the Pittsburgh metropolis of southwestern Pennsylvania.

These public planning activities have been criticized as mere exercises in Utopianism and as leading toward ever-increasing and compulsory uniformity. When they fail to take account of guidelines laid down by the planning agencies of the national government, they can be expected to fail, for in these planning operations, as well as in many other state and local policies, Maryland is being drawn more and more into the engulfing vortex of central power.

Indicative of the relationship of the state to the national government are the figures which show the contribution of the residents of Maryland to the revenues of the national government as compared to the share which Maryland receives in the expenditures of the national government for production, services, and activities in the state or for payments to residents of the state. In the fiscal years 1965-1967 Maryland contributed roughly an annual average of $2.79 billion to the national government and received in return an average of $3.24 billion. Maryland ranked ninth among the states in the amount of per capita revenue which it allocated to the national government and eighth in amount of funds which it received in return from the national government.[21]

In 1970 Maryland received $4.5 billion from the national government and this allocation was increased to $5.5 billion two years later. At that time Maryland ranked fourteenth among the states in the amount of disbursements which it received from the administration in Washington. But it ranked only forty-first among the states in the amount of funds received from that source on a per capita basis. Of the $5.5 billion which Maryland received in 1972, $1.4 billion represented outlays by the national government in Baltimore City, more than $1.3 billion in Montgomery County, and more than $.8 billion in Prince George's County.[22]

In 1974 the outlays of the national government to all the states totaled $281.5 billion, and of this amount Maryland received $6.78 billion, or 2.4 percent, ranking eleventh among the states. Of Maryland's share in this exchange $1.56 billion went to Baltimore City and $1.05 to Prince George's County.[23] In that year the national government was supplying almost 49 percent of the total amount of over $232 million which Maryland expended in its programs of unemployment benefits and social services.[24]

These disbursements of the national government to the states almost always have strings attached to them in the form of guidelines or more mandatory restrictions. The conditions attached to most aid grants from the national government to the states have increased its leverage over state and local budgetary decisions with the result that by 1974 more than 85 percent of the matching funds supplied by the national government to local agencies had strings attached to them. By 1974 the national government was supplying more than one-quarter of the general budget requirements of state and local governments.[25]

Maryland's proximity to the national capital and the consequent high visibility of projects of the national government serve as a constant challenge to Maryland's claims as a Free State, and the long cycle of national crises through which the nation has passed since World War II, from the Cold War to the so-called energy crisis, has argued in favor of central power. The tremendous expansion of the implied powers of the national government as differentiated from its explicit powers has posed difficult problems for Maryland and has not only weakened the responsibility of state and local authorities for the conduct of state and local affairs but has provoked feelings of inadequacy, demoralization, and hopelessness, in some cases at these levels. A prime requirement of state and local agencies, it seems, is to fit their policies and programs into conformity with national standards.

The forebodings of Maryland's leaders from Luther Martin to Albert Ritchie and Millard Tydings as to Maryland's loss of identity and its absorption into a larger entity, first the Union of States and in modern times an amorphous, undifferentiated Atlantic regional Megalopolis and a national governmental leviathan, seem finally to be finding their justification, but no longer do they excite concern. Nevertheless, the quiet, somnolent little towns of Tidewater and Piedmont Maryland which lie outside the metropolitan areas of Baltimore and Washington and which have found it difficult to accept even supermarkets, will only with great reluctance and slowly adjust themselves to the requirements of life in Megalopolis. While they profess to be committed to progress, they take a dim view of too rapid progress and cannot reconcile themselves easily to an equation of progress with industry and public planning, both of which appear to be integral attributes of the new America.

The increasing mobility of the American population is meanwhile diluting the sense of being a Marylander. The restlessness of the people as they move from state to state is producing a rootlessness which tends to diminish pride in one's own region. The breakdown of the sense of one's identity with a local community and even with one's own native state is one of the phenomena of the post-World War II era. In 1970 the percentage of people who moved across state lines was the highest in twenty years. In the case of Maryland, this condition of transiency is intensified by the movement of incoming and outgoing civil servants who work in Baltimore and Washington. These people often feel unrelated to any single community, and though they may involve themselves temporarily in local school matters affecting their children, they develop little love for the state in which they live and no deeply rooted understanding of its history and traditions, for they have had no real contact with these things. They are, essentially, tourists shuttling about from job to job and even taking their vacations on the road. Americans no longer write paeans to "Home, Sweet Home" and the "Old Oaken Bucket." Their homes are on wheels, and the "Old Oaken Bucket" is filled with ice and bottles of beer and cola ready to travel.

Under the conditions produced by this mobile society, local points of interest and pride of excellence may become dimmed and their stabilizing social values lost. A people on the loose is thereby deprived of the balance and tolerance which are found in settled communities. Disorganized migrants who flood into such a community may change its character abruptly and irredeemably before moving on to another, where they repeat the process. This process is having a marked effect upon the social situation in Greater Washington and Greater Baltimore, much less so in the smaller communities of the state. As new populations are attracted to the cities and new megalopolises are thus formed, the problems of rootlessness become further aggravated. In the mishmash of the new urban conglomerates the uniquenesses of individuals often become submerged, and as this phenomenon multiplies, affecting all states, it may result in a congeries of states that can be differentiated from each other not by cultural nor even by economic distinctions but only by their differing histories. Local needs can still be met most effectively by local committees and local officials, for all the problems of life ultimately resolve themselves into individual and local problems. In this spirit Governor McKeldin used to enjoin Marylanders to "think and act like Marylanders and not as mere suburbanites of Washington." That is the Maryland spirit.

Footnotes

[1] Maryland Department of Transportation, *Port of Baltimore Bulletin,* "Special Report," May 1975, pp. 2-7.

[2] Ralph D. Gray, *The National Waterway: A History of the Chesapeake and Delaware Canal, 1769-1965,* University of Illinois Press, Urbana, 1967, p. 256.

[3] See series of articles by Ralph J. Robinson, "How Baltimore Became a Port," *Baltimore,* June-November 1955, Maryland Department, Enoch Pratt Free Library, Baltimore.

[4] L.C. Gottschalk, "Sedimentation in a Great Harbor," *Soil Conservation*, vol. X, No. 1, July 1944; reprinted by United States Department of Agriculture, Soil Conservation Service, Washington, D.C.

[5] *General Development Plan for the Baltimore Region*, Baltimore, 1972, p. 2.

[6] Maryland, Board of World's Fair Managers, *Maryland, Its Resources, Industries and Institutions*, Baltimore, 1893, p. [264].

[7] Department of Economic and Community Development, *An Economic and Social Atlas of Maryland*. Department of Geography, University of Maryland, 1974, p. 37.

[8] John W. Wysong, *Adjustments and Changes in the Geographical Location and Product-Mix of the Maryland Farm Industry, 1939-1969*, University of Maryland Agricultural Experiment Station, College Park, Maryland, Miscellaneous Publication 832, April 1974, p. IV.

[9] *Ibid.*, p. V-VI.

[10] Advisory Commission on Intergovernmental Relations, "The Property Tax in a Changing Environment: Selected State Studies, Maryland," Information Report, M-83, Washington, D.C., March 1974.

[11] *An Economic and Social Atlas of Maryland, Statistical Supplement*, University of Maryland, College Park, 1974, p. ii.

[12] Department of Economic and Community Development, *An Economic and Social Atlas of Maryland*, University of Maryland, p. 75.

[13] *Ibid.*, 1974, pp. 63-65.

[14] Department of Housing and Community Development, Annual Report 1973, p. [35].

[15] Metropolitan Washington Council of Governments, *Reexamination of the Year 2000 Policies Plan*, vol. 1, p. 15.

[16] Baltimore *Sun*, August 21, 1959.

[17] Tri-County Council for Southern Maryland. Preliminary Draft, Regional Plan, July 1974, p. 1. This plan was prepared by the Maryland State Department of Planning.

[18] Delmarva Advisory Council, *Overall Economic Development Program Update, 1974-1975*.

[19] Tri-County Council for Western Maryland, Incorporated, *Appalachian Maryland Development Plan, Fiscal Year, 1975*, updated from an earlier 1972-73 version.

[20] *Ibid.*, pp. V-16.

[21] Harriet J. Halper and I.M. Labovitz, *Federal Revenues and Expenditures in the Several States: Averages for the Fiscal Years 1965-1967*, Library of Congress, Legislative Service, Washington, D.C., 1968.

[22] Maryland, Department of Economic and Community Development, *Maryland Statistical Abstract, 1973*, Annapolis [1974], pp. 215-225.

[23] *Federal Outlays, Fiscal Year 1974, Maryland*, Office of Economic Opportunity.

[24] Department of Employment and Social Services, *Report to the Governor for the Year July 1, 1973—June 30, 1974*, Baltimore, p. 57.

[25] Advisory Commission on Intergovernmental Relations, *Trends in Fiscal Federalism, 1954-1974*, Commission Report M-86, Washington, D.C., 1975, p. 2.

Sources and Additional Reading

Maryland, Department of Economic and Community Development, *An Economic and Social Atlas of Maryland*, Department of Geography, University of Maryland, College Park, Maryland [1974].

———, *Maryland Statistical Abstract, 1973*, Annapolis [1974].

Maryland National Capital Park and Planning Commission, *Looking Ahead, 1958-1980: A General Plan for the Maryland Washington Regional District*, 1957.

Regional Planning Council, *General Development Plan for the Baltimore Region*, December 1972, Regional Planning Council, 701 St. Paul Street, Baltimore, Maryland, 21202.

APPENDICES

APPENDIX I

NAMES AND ORIGINS OF COUNTIES

County	Year	Derivation of Name	County Seat
Allegany	1789	Oolikhanna, beautiful stream.	Cumberland
Anne Arundel	1650	Wife of Cecil, Second Lord Baltimore.	Annapolis
Baltimore City	1850	(Was part of Baltimore County until 1850, when it became a separate political division of the state.)	
Baltimore County	1659	Proprietor's Irish barony.	Towson
Calvert, originally Patuxent	1654	Family name of the Proprietary.	Prince Frederick
Caroline	1773	Sister of the last Lord Baltimore, Lady Caroline Eden.	Denton
Carroll	1835	Charles Carroll of Carrollton.	Westminster
Cecil	1674	Second Lord Baltimore.	Elkton
Charles	1658	Charles Calvert, son of Cecil, Second Lord Baltimore.	La Plata
Dorchester	1668/9	Earl of Dorset, friend of the Calverts.	But Port Tobacco until 1895. Cambridge
Frederick	1748	The last Lord Baltimore.	Frederick
Garrett	1872	John W. Garrett.	Oakland
Harford	1773	Henry Harford, last Proprietary.	Bel Air
Howard	1851	Colonel John Eager Howard.	Ellicott City
Kent (probably)	1640	Kent County, England.	Chestertown
Montgomery	1776	General Richard Montgomery.	Rockville
Prince George's	1695	Prince George of Denmark, husband of Queen Anne of England.	Upper Marlboro
Queen Anne's	1706	Queen Anne of England.	Centreville
St. Mary's	1637	Mary, the mother of Jesus.	Leonardtown
Somerset	1666	Mary Somerset, sister of Cecil, Second Lord Baltimore.	Princess Anne
Talbot	1661	Grace Talbot, daughter of George, First Lord Baltimore.	Easton
Washington	1776	General George Washington.	Hagerstown
Wicomico	1867	Wicko-mekee, village on a stream.	Salisbury
Worcester	1742	Earl of Worcester.	Snow Hill

(*Maryland Manual*, Hall of Records Commission, Annapolis, and Edward B. Mathews, *The Counties of Maryland*, Maryland Geological Survey, Special Publication vol. III, Part 5, Baltimore, 1907.)

APPENDIX II

PROPRIETORS AND GOVERNORS OF MARYLAND

BARONS OF BALTIMORE AND LORDS PROPRIETARY

1580(?)-1632   George Calvert, created First Lord Baltimore in February 1625. Petitioned for grant of land north of the Potomac.[1]

1605-1675   Cecilius Calvert, Second Lord Baltimore. Succeeded to title on death of George, April 15, 1632. Granted Charter of Maryland on June 20, 1632.

1637-1715   Charles Calvert, Third Lord Baltimore. Succeeded to title on death of Cecilius, November 30, 1675.

1679-1715   Benedict Leonard Calvert, Fourth Lord Baltimore. Succeeded to title on death of Charles, February 21, 1715.

1699-1751   Charles Calvert, Fifth Lord Baltimore. Succeeded to title on death of Benedict Leonard, April 16, 1715.

1732-1771   Frederick Calvert, Sixth Lord Baltimore. Succeeded to title on death of Charles, April 24, 1751.

1760-1834   Henry Harford. Harford did not succeed to the title when Frederick died on September 4, 1771, because he was an illegitimate son. He was bequeathed the Province of Maryland in Frederick's will. After the Revolution, Harford relinquished his claim to Maryland in return for a monetary grant from the General Assembly.

COLONIAL GOVERNORS

Prior to the granting of the Charter to Cecilius Calvert, Captain William Claiborne, acting under a commission from the King, had established a trading post and plantation on Kent Island in 1631. He was driven from the Island by Leonard Calvert a few months after the colonists landed.

PROPRIETARY GOVERNMENT

1634-1644/5   Leonard Calvert
Calvert had occasion to leave the colony several times, usually for a month or two but once for over a year. During his absences the following men governed the Province: 1637/8 and 1638, John Lewger; 1638 and 1641, Captain Thomas Cornwaleys; 1643-1644, Giles Brent; 1644, William Brainthwait.

1644/5-1646   Captain Richard Ingle
Usurped the government and maintained control until about the middle of 1646.

1646   Captain Edward Hill
Elected Governor by the Council while Leonard Calvert was still in Virginia. He also claimed to have a commission from Calvert. His appointment was illegal, as he was not a member of the Council when elected, and Calvert was out of the Province when the commission was issued. He does seem to have held office, however, for he later attempted to collect certain fees and emoluments which were due him by virtue of his service.

1646-1647   Leonard Calvert

1647-1648/9   Thomas Greene

---

[1] James W. Foster, the most recent biographer of George Calvert, gives "about 1580" as the date of birth (*Maryland Historical Magazine*, Vol. 55, p. 264). Others have given dates ranging from 1578/9 to 1584.

1649-1651/2	Captain William Stone During absences from the Province he left the following men to act in his place: 1649, Thomas Greene; 1650, Thomas Hatton.
1652	Parliamentary Commissioners
1652-1654	Captain William Stone
1654-1657	Commissioners appointed by Parliamentary Commissioners
1657-1660	Josias Fendall Appointed Luke Barber to serve in his place while he was absent from the Province from June 1657 to February 1657/8.
1660-1661	Philip Calvert
1661-1676	Charles Calvert Left Philip Calvert, William Calvert, Jerome White and Baker Brooke as deputies governing the Colony from May 1669 to November 1670 while he was in England. On November 30, 1675, his father died, and be became Lord Proprietary.
1676	Jesse Wharton Cecilius Calvert, infant son of the Lord Proprietary, was the nominal Governor from June to October 1676, but, actually, the Province was governed by the Deputy Governors.
1676-1679	Thomas Notley Succeeded Wharton as Deputy Governor, and later, in October 1676, was commissioned as Governor by the Lord Proprietary.
1678/9-1684	Charles Calvert, Lord Proprietary Calvert was definitely back in the Province by January 1678/9, perhaps earlier, but he appears to have permitted Notley to retain the title of Governor until his death in April 1679.
1684-1688	Council of Deputy Governors Benedict Leonard Calvert, infant son of the Lord Proprietary, was commissioned Governor, but the duties were actually performed by the Deputies. The Deputies named in the commission were George Talbot, Thomas Tailler, Colonel Vincent Lowe, Colonel William Stevens, Colonel William Burgess, Major Nicholas Sewall, and John Darnall. Most of them served the entire period indicated, but there were a few changes.
1688-1689	William Joseph Named as President of the Council of Deputies in a commission from the Lord Proprietary.

ROYAL GOVERNMENT

1689-1690	John Coode Leader of the Protestant Associators who seized the government on August 1, 1689.
1690-1692	Nehemiah Blakiston Appointed President of the Committee for the Government of Maryland when Coode went to England.
1692-1693	Sir Lionel Copley
1693	Sir Thomas Lawrence Elected Governor after death of Copley, but had served only a week or two when Sir Edmund Andros arrived in Maryland to assume control.
1693	Sir Edmund Andros Remained in Maryland about ten days before returning to Virginia.

1693-1694	Colonel Nicholas Greenberry Appointed President of the Council by Andros.
1694-1698/9	Sir Francis Nicholson.
1698/9-1702	Colonel Nathaniel Blakiston
1702-1704	Thomas Tench Appointed President of the Council by Blakiston.
1704-1709	Colonel John Seymour
1709-1714	Major General Edward Lloyd Elected President of the Council when Colonel Francis Jenkins, who was senior member of the Council and thus entitled to succeed Seymour, failed to assert his right promptly.
1714-1715	John Hart

RESTORATION OF THE PROPRIETARY GOVERNMENT

1715-1720	John Hart
1720	Thomas Brooke Became President of the Council by virtue of his seniority when Hart returned to England.
1720-1727	Charles Calvert
1727-1731	Benedict Leonard Calvert
1731-1732	Samuel Ogle
1732-1733	Charles Calvert, Lord Proprietary
1733-1742	Samuel Ogle
1742-1746/7	Thomas Bladen
1746/7-1752	Samuel Ogle
1752-1753	Benjamin Tasker Became President of the Council upon the death of Governor Ogle.
1753-1769	Horatio Sharpe
1769-1776	Robert Eden Eden was in England from May to November 1774, during which time Richard Lee, President of the Council, governed the Province. Lee also governed the Province briefly in 1776 during the interval between the departure of Eden and the assumption of the government by the Convention.

GOVERNORS OF THE STATE OF MARYLAND

Elected Under the Constitution of 1776 by the Legislature for One Year[2]

Thomas Johnson, No Party, 1777-1779.
Thomas Sim Lee, No Party, 1779-1782. Federalist, 1792-1794.
William Paca, No Party, 1782-1785.
William Smallwood, No Party, 1785-1788.
John Eager Howard, Federalist, 1788-1791.
George Plater, Federalist, 1791-1792.
John H. Stone, Federalist, 1794-1797.
John Henry, Federalist, 1797-1798.
Benjamin Ogle, Federalist, 1798-1801.

---

[2] Under the Constitution of 1776, the Governor was elected annually on the second Monday in November. He could be re-elected for two additional terms. Thomas Johnson, the State's first governor, was elected on February 13, 1777, after the Constitution of 1776 became operative.

John Francis Mercer, Democrat, 1801-1803.
Robert Bowie, Democrat, 1803-1806, 1811-1812.
Robert Wright, Democrat, 1806-1809.
Edward Lloyd, Democrat, 1809-1811.
Levin Winder, Federalist, 1812-1816.
Charles Ridgely of Hampton, Federalist, 1816-1819.
Charles Goldsborough, Federalist, 1819.
Samuel Sprigg, Democrat, 1819-1822.
Samuel Stevens, Jr., Democrat, 1822-1826.
Joseph Kent, Democrat, 1826-1829.
Daniel Martin, Anti-Jackson, 1829-1830, 1831.
Thomas King Carroll, Jackson, Democrat, 1830-1831.
George Howard, Anti-Jackson, 1831-1833.
James Thomas, Anti-Jackson, 1833-1836.
Thomas W. Veazey, Whig, 1836-1839.

Elected by the People for Three Years Under the Constitution of 1776 as amended in 1838

William Grason, Democrat, 1839-1842.
Francis Thomas, Democrat, 1842-1845.
Thomas G. Pratt, Whig, 1845-1848.
Philip Francis Thomas, Democrat, 1848-1851.
Enoch Louis Lowe, Democrat, 1851-1854.

Elected Under the Constitution of 1851 by the People for Four Years

Thomas Watkins Ligon, Democrat, 1854-1858.
Thomas Holliday Hicks, Native American, 1858-1862.
Augustus W. Bradford, Unionist, 1862-1866.

Elected Under the Constitution of 1864 by the People for Four Years

Thomas Swann, Unionist-Democrat, 1866-1869.

Elected Under the Constitution of 1867 by the People for Four Years

Oden Bowie, Democrat, 1869-1872.
William Pinkney Whyte, Democrat, 1872-1874.
James Black Groome, Democrat, 1874-1876.
John Lee Carroll, Democrat, 1876-1880.
William T. Hamilton, Democrat, 1880-1884.
Robert M. McLane, Democrat, 1884-1885.
Henry Lloyd, Democrat, 1885-1888.
Elihu E. Jackson, Democrat, 1888-1892.
Frank Brown, Democrat, 1892-1896.
Lloyd Lowndes, Republican, 1896-1900.
John Walter Smith, Democrat, 1900-1904.
Edwin Warfield, Democrat, 1904-1908.
Austin L. Crothers, Democrat, 1908-1912.
Phillips Lee Goldsborough, Republican, 1912-1916.
Emerson C. Harrington, Democrat, 1916-1920.
Albert C. Ritchie, Democrat, 1920-1935.
Harry W. Nice, Republican, 1935-1939.
Herbert R. O'Conor, Democrat, 1939-1947.
William Preston Lane, Jr., Democrat, 1947-1951.
Theodore R. McKeldin, Republican, 1951-1959.
J. Millard Tawes, Democrat, 1959-1967.
Spiro T. Agnew, Republican, 1967-1969.
Marvin Mandel, Democrat, 1969-

APPENDIX III
SITES OF MAJOR PRESIDENTIAL NOMINATING CONVENTIONS
1832-1972

	Anti-Masonic	National Republican	Democratic
1832	Baltimore (1831)	Baltimore	Baltimore
1836			Baltimore
1840		(Whig) Harrisburg	Baltimore
1844		Baltimore	Baltimore
1848	(Know Nothing) Philadelphia (1847)	Philadelphia	Baltimore
1852		Baltimore	Baltimore
1856	(Know Nothing) Philadelphia	(Republican) Pittsburgh (Whig) Baltimore	Cincinnati
1860	(Constitutional Union) Baltimore	Chicago	Charleston and Baltimore
1864		Baltimore	Chicago
1868		Chicago	New York
1872	(Liberal Republican) Cincinnati	Philadelphia	Baltimore
1876		Cincinnati	St. Louis
1880		Chicago	Cincinnati
1884	(Greenback) Indianapolis	Chicago	Chicago
1888		Chicago	St. Louis
1892		Minneapolis	Chicago
1896		St. Louis	Chicago
1900		Philadelphia	Kansas City
1904		Chicago	St. Louis
1908		Chicago	Denver
1912	(Progressive) Chicago	Chicago	Baltimore
1916	Chicago	Chicago	St. Louis
1920		Chicago	San Francisco
1924	(Progressive) Cleveland	Cleveland	New York
1928	(Socialist) New York	Kansas City	Houston
1932		Chicago	Chicago
1936		Cleveland	Philadelphia
1940		Philadelphia	Chicago
1944		Chicago	Chicago
1948		Philadelphia	Philadelphia
1952		Chicago	Chicago
1956		San Francisco	Chicago
1960		Chicago	Los Angles
1964		San Francisco	Atlantic City
1968		Miami Beach	Chicago
1972		Miami Beach	Miami Beach

APPENDIX IV

MARYLAND, MY MARYLAND!

James Ryder Randall, 1861

The despot's heel is on thy shore,
    Maryland!
His torch is at thy temple door,
    Maryland!
Avenge the patriotic gore
That flecked the streets of Baltimore,
And be the battle queen of yore,
    Maryland! My Maryland!

Hark to an exiled son's appeal,
    Maryland!
My mother State! to thee I kneel,
    Maryland!
For life and death, for woe and weal,
Thy peerless chivalry reveal,
And gird thy beauteous limbs with steel,
    Maryland! My Maryland!

Thou wilt not cower in the dust,
    Maryland!
Thy beaming sword shall never rust,
    Maryland!
Remember Carroll's sacred trust,
Remember Howard's warlike thrust,—
And all thy slumberers with the just,
    Maryland! My Maryland!

Come! 'tis the red dawn of the day,
    Maryland!
Come with thy panoplied array,
    Maryland!
With Ringgold's spirit for the fray,
With Watson's blood at Monterey,
With fearless Loew and dashing May,
    Maryland! My Maryland!

Come! for thy shield is bright and strong,
    Maryland!
Come! for thy dalliance does thee wrong,
    Maryland!
Come to thy own heroic throng,
Stalking with Liberty along,
And chaunt thy deathless slogan song,
    Maryland! My Maryland!

Dear Mother! burst the tyrant's chain,
    Maryland!
Virginia should not call in vain,
    Maryland!
She meets her sisters on the plain—
"Sic semper!" 'tis the proud refrain
That baffles minions back again,
    Maryland! My Maryland!

I see the blush upon thy cheek,
    Maryland!
For thou wast ever bravely meek,
    Maryland!
But lo! there surges forth a shriek
From hill to hill, from creek to creek—
Potomac calls to Chesapeake,
    Maryland! My Maryland!

Thou wilt not yield the Vandal toll,
    Maryland!
Thou wilt not crook to his control,
    Maryland!
Better the fire upon thee roll,
Better the blade, the shot, the bowl,
Than crucifixion of the soul,
    Maryland! My Maryland!

I hear the distant thunder-hum,
    Maryland!
The Old Line Bugle, fife and drum,
    Maryland!
She is not dead, nor deaf, nor dumb—
Huzza! she spurns the Northern scum!
She breathes! she burns! she'll come! she'll come!
    Maryland! My Maryland!

APPENDIX V
CHECK LIST OF MARYLAND COUNTY HISTORIES

Allegany County

Thomas, James W., and Thomas John Chew Williams, *History of Allegany County, Maryland*, 2 vols., L.R. Titsworth and Company [Cumberland], 1923.

Anne Arundel County

Riley, Elihu Samuel, *A History of Anne Arundel County in Maryland*, Charles G. Feldmeyer, Publisher, Annapolis, 1905.

Baltimore City

Hall, Clayton Colman, ed., *Baltimore: Its History and Its People*, 3 vols., Lewis Historical Publishing Company, New York and Chicago, 1912, vol. I.

Scharf, John Thomas, *Chronicles of Baltimore: Being a Complete History of "Baltimore town" and Baltimore City from the Earliest Period to the Present Time*, Turnbull Brothers, Baltimore, 1874.

Baltimore City and County

Scharf, John Thomas, *History of Baltimore City and County . . . Including Biographical Sketches of Representative Men*, 2 vols., Louis H. Everts, Philadelphia, 1881; reprint 1971.

Baltimore County

Board of Education of Baltimore County, Alvin V. Burgess and Norris A. King, Cochairmen, *Baltimore County: Its People and Progress*, Towson, Maryland, 1953.

Huttenhauer, Helen G., and G. Alfred Helwig, *Baltimore County in the State and Nation*, Baltimore County, Board of Education, Towson, Maryland, 1962.

Calvert County

Stein, Charles Francis, *A History of Calvert County, Maryland*, Calvert County Historical Society, Baltimore, 1960.

Caroline County

Caroline County Schools, Laura C. Cochrane, et el., *History of Caroline County, Maryland from Its Beginning*, J.W. Stowell Printing Co., Federalsburg, Maryland [1920]; reprint, 1971.

Cecil County

Gifford, G.E., Jr., *Cecil County, Maryland, 1608-1850* . . . Rising Sun, Maryland, 1974.

Johnston, George, *History of Cecil County, Maryland*, Elkton, 1881; reprint 1967.

Miller, Alice Etta, *Cecil County, Maryland: A Study in Local History*, C. and L. Printing and Specialty Co., Elkton, Maryland, 1949.

Charles County

Klapthor, Margaret Brown, and Paul Dennis Brown, *History of Charles County, Maryland*, Charles County Tercentenary, Inc., La Plata, Maryland, 1958.

Dorchester County

Jones, Elias, *History of Dorchester County, Maryland*, Williams and Wilkins Company, Baltimore, 1902; revised edition, Read-Taylor, Baltimore, 1925; reprint, Tidewater Publishers, Cambridge, Maryland, 1966.

Frederick County

Williams, Thomas John Chew, *History of Frederick County, Maryland*, 2 vols., L. Titsworth, Frederick, 1910; reprint, 1967.

Harford County

Preston, Waller Wilkes, *History of Harford County, Maryland*, Press of Sun Book Office, Baltimore, 1901.

Howard County

Stein, Charles Francis, Jr., *Origin and History of Howard County, Maryland*, Howard County Historical Society, Baltimore, 1972.

Kent County

Hanson, George Adolphus, *Old Kent: the Eastern Shore of Maryland*, J.P. Des Forges, Baltimore, 1876; reprint, R.H. Collins, Chestertown, 1936, and Regional Publishing Company, 1967.

Usilton, Frederick G., *History of Kent County, Maryland, 1630-1916* [privately printed, 1916(?)].

Montgomery County

Boyd, Thomas Hulings Stockton, *The History of Montgomery County, Maryland, from Its Earliest Settlement in 1650 to 1879*, Baltimore, 1879; reprinted by Regional Publishing Company, Baltimore, 1968.

Prince George's County

Hienton, Louise Joyner, *Prince George's Heritage: Sidelights on the Early History of Prince George's County, Maryland, from 1696 to 1800*, Maryland Historical Society [1972].

Queen Anne's County

Emory, Frederic, *Queen Anne's County: Its Early History and Development*, published in the *Centreville Observer*, 1886, typescript copy in Maryland Department, Enoch Pratt Free Library, Baltimore, 1936.

St. Mary's County

No county history

Somerset County

Torrence, Clayton, *Old Somerset on the Eastern Shore of Maryland; A Study in Foundations and Founders*, Whittet and Shepperson, Richmond, Virginia, 1935; reprint 1966.

Talbot County

Tilghman, Oswald, *History of Talbot County, Maryland, 1661-1861*, 2 vols., Williams and Wilkins Company, Baltimore, 1915; reprint 1967.

Washington County

Williams, Thomas John Chew, *A History of Washington County, Maryland*, J.M. Runk and L.R. Titsworth, Hagerstown, 1906; reprint 1968.

Wicomico County

No county history

Worcester County

No county history

INDEX

INDEX

Local place names are situated in Maryland unless otherwise indicated.

Abell, Arunah Shepherdson, 312, 313, 443, 450
Abell, Edwin F., 515
Aberdeen, 565
Aberdeen Proving Ground, 565, 566
Abingdon, 307
Accident, 16
Accomac Indians, 20
"Act concerning Religion" ("Toleration Act"), 72, 87, 89, 90-2, 94, 101, 103, 104, 113, 114, 144
Adams, The Reverend Alexander, 145
Adams, Herbert Baxter, 551
Addison, Colonel Thomas, 176
Adlum, Major John, 505
Agnew, Spiro, Gov. of Md., 578, 585, 586
Albany Congress, 213, 214, 217
Aldridge, Ira Frederick, 429
Alexandria, Va., 218, 280, 293, 295, 363, 371
Allegany County, 11-4, 298, 299, 331, 352, 357, 368, 374, 376, 408, 412, 428, 494, 512, 522, 523, 601
Allegheny Plateau and Mountains, 12, 321, 369, 387
Allison, Reverend Patrick, 303
Alsop, George, 22, 178
Altamont, 13
Altham, John, S.J., 44, 45, 56, 66
Amadas, Philip, 26
Amelung, Johann Friedrich, 297
American Colonization Society, 430
American Farmer, 313
American Federation of Labor, 506
American Independence, War for, 143, 198, 200, 262, 263-68, 271, 275, 279, 294, 296, 302, 307, 309, 327, 332, 362, 389, 395-97, 437, 544, 556, 564, 570, 592
Anabaptists, 89
Anacostia River, 15, 593

Ancient and Honorable Tuesday Club, 195
Andrews Air Force Base, 566
Anglican Church, 51, 95, 114, 129, 142-44, 146, 149, 164, 168, 172-74, 176, 178, 182-86, 188, 189, 209, 237, 240-42, 250, 258, 263, 266, 307, 308
Ann McKim, clipper, 397
Annapolis, 5, 16, 146, 147, 149, 150, 169, 172-74, 181, 182, 185, 186, 193-95, 216, 219, 220, 223, 226-30, 232, 235, 237-39, 243-45, 247, 249, 251, 257-59, 264, 268, 269, 275, 276, 279, 281, 285, 290, 291, 294, 296, 297, 303, 307, 311, 312, 323, 325, 327, 332, 335-37, 341, 345, 350, 351, 353, 356, 357, 391, 395, 409, 446-48, 451, 458, 466, 472, 473, 481, 493, 498, 518, 527, 548, 550, 554-56, 569, 571, 582
Annapolis Jockey Club, 194, 235
Anne Arundel County, 6, 65, 97, 99, 102, 103, 105, 111, 195, 202, 286, 304, 309, 321, 353, 357, 410, 413, 428, 435, 507, 557, 567, 569, 594, 600
Anne Arundel, Lady, 75, 97
Anne Arundel Town. See Annapolis.
Annemessex Bay, 116
Annemessex River, 110, 116
Anne, Queen of England, 143, 147, 163, 164, 203
Antietam, 13, 363, 449, 453, 564
Anti-Masonic movement, 348, 349
Anti-Saloon League of Md., 534
Anti-slavery movement, 424-27
Archihau, 45
Ark and *Dove*, 37, 42, 44, 45, 47, 66, 89, 195, 570
Armistead, Major George, 333, 335
Articles of Confederation, 269, 271-74, 279, 287, 291, 338, 535
Asbury, Bishop Francis, 284, 306-08
Assawoman Bay, 2

619

Association, non-importation and non-exportation, 238, 244-47, 249
Atlantic States Marine Fisheries Commission, 574
Avalon, 36-38, 86, 235

Backbone Mountain, 2, 13
Bacon, Nathaniel, 133, 134
Bainbridge, Commodore William, 569
Baker, Franklin, 558
Baltimore American and Daily Advertiser. See *Maryland Journal and Baltimore Advertiser.*
Baltimore and Cuba Smelting and Mining Co., 402
Baltimore and Ohio Railroad, 8, 14, 347, 371-86, 389, 394, 395, 397, 400, 404, 422, 439, 440, 446, 455, 456, 460, 481, 482, 488, 503, 505, 515, 551, 561, 568, 591
Baltimore and Pittston Coal Co., 402
Baltimore City Training School, 542
Baltimore clipper, 331, 332, 397, 399, 497
Baltimore College of Dental Surgery, 305
Baltimore Colts, 558, 581
Baltimore Commission on Human Relations, 579
Baltimore Committee for Downtown, Inc., 596
Baltimore Copper Smelting Co., 402
Baltimore County, 9, 11, 17, 105, 111, 146, 193, 199, 243, 286, 304, 306, 321, 341, 350, 353, 357, 389, 393, 408, 437, 507, 517, 546, 547, 580, 585, 597, 598, 600
Baltimore Harbor Tunnel, 583
Baltimore Insurance Fire-Co., 391
Baltimore Orioles, 557, 558, 581
Baltimore Polytechnic Institute, 547
Baltimore Reform League, 515
Baltimore Regional Planning Council, 593, 594, 600
Baltimore Town and City, 4, 8, 9, 11, 14-6, 22, 193, 197, 207, 209, 215, 223, 226, 229, 257-59, 262-64, 290-92, 294-97, 302, 306-10, 312-15, 320, 321, 323-28, 330-33, 335-38, 341, 342, 345, 346, 348-51, 353, 356-59, 366-68, 370, 371, 374-77,

Baltimore Town and City *(cont.)*
380-87, 390-92, 394-97, 399-401, 403, 405-15, 417, 419-24, 429-32, 435, 436, 439-41, 444-52, 455-62, 466, 468-70, 474-76, 478-83, 485, 487-89, 493-98, 500, 502-09, 511, 514-18, 520, 527, 529, 536-38, 542-46, 549-58, 561, 564, 565, 567, 568, 570, 571, 576, 578-82, 585, 587, 588, 590-98, 600, 602-04
Baltimore-Washington International Airport (Friendship Airport), 583, 588
Baltimore Water Co., 39
Bancroft, George, 311
Bank of England, 187, 225, 267, 286
Bank of Maryland, 327, 356, 391, 394, 395
Banneker, Benjamin, 293, 429
Baptist Denomination, 309, 310, 429, 432, 549
Baring Brothers, 382, 383
Barlowe, Arthur, 26
Barnes, Major Abraham, 214
Barnes, Joseph, 277
Barney, Captain Joshua, 332, 336, 337, 555
Battle of the Severn, 100-02, 104
Beadenkopf, The Reverend Thomas M., 506
Beall, Brooks, 16
Beall, J. Glenn, 584
Beall, Ninian, 144
Beanes, Dr. William, 335
Beatty, Charles, 276
Beckler, Edward, 55
Bedini, Carlo, 419
Bel Air, 429
Belcher, Jonathan, Gov. of N.J., 216
Bell, Frederick J., 571
Beltsville, 563
Bennett, Richard, 65, 98-103
Berkeley, Lord John, 122
Berkeley, Sir William, Gov. of Va., 78, 83, 95, 116, 133
Bernard, General S., 369, 370
Bethesda, 16, 563, 567
Bethlehem Steel Co., 500, 502, 569, 590, 591
Bienville, Céléron de, 212
Big Savage Mountain, 12
Blackiston's Island (St. Clement's Island), 45, 46

Index

Bladen, Thomas, Gov. of Md., 151, 187, 201
Bladen, William, 151
Bladensburg, 145, 244, 290, 332, 335, 564, 593
Blair, Francis P., 441
Blair, John, 282
Blair, Montgomery, 438, 441, 445, 468
Blakiston, Nathaniel, Gov. of Md., 154, 155, 163
Blakiston, Nehemiah, 139, 142
Bloemmaert, Samuel, 120
Blount, William, 59
Blue Ridge, 12-4
Board of Trade, English, 213, 224, 236
Bohemia, 34
Bohemia River, 278
Bonaparte, Charles Joseph, 515, 518, 520, 521, 585
Boonsboro, 392
Booth, John Wilkes, 467
Bordley, John Beale, 240, 290
Bordley, Thomas, 181, 182
Boston Port Bill, 243, 244
Boston Tea Party, 243, 245
Boucher, Jonathan, 235, 250
Bowie, 9
Bowie, Oden, Gov. of Md., 475, 477, 543
Bowie, Robert, Gov. of Md., 331, 343
Bowie State College, 543, 580
Bownas, Samuel, 119
Boyle, Captain Thomas, 337
Bozman, John Leeds, 314
Braddock, General Edward, 218-20, 224, 225
Bradford, Andrew, 151, 152
Bradford, Augustus W., Gov. of Md., 451, 452, 455, 457, 462, 586
Bradford, William, 152
Brainthwait, William, 63
Bray, The Reverend Thomas, 143, 173
Brent, Giles, 59, 63, 64, 75-81, 84
Brent, Mistress Margaret, 82-4
Britton, William, 59
Brooke, Baker, 106, 108, 132
Brooke, Robert, 95, 99, 110
Brooke, Thomas, 15
Brown, Frank, Gov. of Md., 487
Brown, George, 375-77
Brown, George William, 445, 446, 449
Brown, Dr. Gustavus, 7
Brown, H. Rap, 578
Brown, "Captain" John, 439, 440
Brown vs Maryland, 390
Brown vs Topeka Board of Education, 576, 682
Browning, Meshach, 298, 299
Bruce, Normand, 276
Brunswick, 199, 384
Bryantown, 467
Buchan, The Reverend James, 145
Buchanan, Commander Franklin, 311
Buckland, William, 235
Buell, Fayette R., 549
Burke, Judge Charles A., 532
Burnaby, The Reverend Andrew, 208
Butler, John, 54, 55
Butler, John Marshall, 584
Byllinge, Edward, 122
Byrd, Harry Clifton, 543

Cabot, John, 24, 26
Cacapon, 374
Cadwalader, John, 276
Cain, James Mallahan, 555
Calhoun, John C., 346, 365
Calvert, Benedict, 240, 251
Calvert, Benedict Leonard, 4th Lord Baltimore, 125, 137, 164, 165, 184
Calvert, Caroline, wife of Robert Eden, 235, 243
Calvert, Cecil (Cecilius), 2nd Baron of Baltimore, 6, 15, 22, 23, 33, 37, 38, 40-3, 47, 48, 50, 52-7, 62, 65, 66, 68-72, 74-84, 86-92, 94-9, 101-08, 110, 111, 113, 114, 118, 120, 126, 129-35, 175, 177, 227, 255
Calvert, Cecil, uncle of the 6th Lord Baltimore, 201
Calvert, Charles, 3rd Lord Baltimore, 108, 110, 112, 114, 115, 121-126, 129-32, 134-40, 149, 156, 161, 164, 177, 198, 199, 203, 313
Calvert, Charles, 5th Lord Baltimore, 165, 168, 170-73, 175-77, 180, 181, 183-88, 198-201, 203, 204, 235, 241
Calvert, Charles, Gov. of Md., 176, 178, 182-84
Calvert, Frederick, 6th Lord Baltimore, 198, 199, 201, 203, 204, 212-14, 217, 220, 221, 227, 230-32, 235-37, 239, 243, 251, 252, 256

Calvert, George, 1st Baron of Baltimore, 33-9, 44, 147
Calvert, George, son of George Calvert, 1st Baron of Baltimore, 42, 52
Calvert, Leonard, Gov. of Md., 42, 45-7, 50-60, 62-5, 67, 69-71, 75, 77-83, 89, 107, 108, 195
Calvert, Philip, 103-08, 110, 116
Calvert, William, 108, 132
Calvert County, 6, 99, 102, 105, 111, 132, 134, 139, 286, 325, 331, 342, 344, 395, 409, 413, 435, 555, 569, 601
Cambridge, 4, 15, 498, 502, 521, 578, 592
Cameron, Simon, Secretary of War, 445, 449
Camp Albert C. Ritchie, 566
Campbell, John, Earl of Loudoun, 221-23, 225
Camp Springs, 566, 570
Canby, Major General Edward R., 470
Canton, 291, 379, 402, 499, 500, 505, 583
Canton Railroad Co., 568
Carderock, 568
Carmichael, Richard B., 472
Caroline County, 243, 286, 303, 314, 331, 353, 389, 406, 408, 412, 428, 494
Carre, Sir Robert, 122
Carroll, Charles, 139, 162, 169-72, 175, 177, 193
Carroll, Charles, Barrister, 257
Carroll, Charles, of Carrollton, 225, 239, 241, 242, 244, 253, 255, 257, 266, 272, 276, 282, 285, 286, 291, 310, 319, 347, 371, 372, 376, 377, 427, 481
Carroll, Daniel, 269, 285, 293
Carroll, The Reverend John, 255, 262, 303, 310, 311
Carroll, John Lee, Gov. of Md., 481-83
Carroll, Thomas King, Gov. of Md., 347
Carroll County, 9, 193, 306, 357, 396, 408, 428, 487, 494, 600
Carteret, Sir George, 122
Cartwright, Colonel George, 122
Cascade, 566
Casselman River, 13, 370
Catholicism, 24, 42, 43, 66, 69-72, 133, 134, 137-39, 142, 143, 146, 147, 149, 168-72, 174-76, 219, 221, 232,

Catholicism *(cont.)*
242, 255, 258, 310, 313, 320, 418-20, 432, 481, 544, 549, 551, 552, 586
Catholic University of America, 551
Catoctin Creek, 13, 15
Catoctin Mountain, 9, 11, 12, 310
Cauther, James, 64
Cecil County, 9, 11, 111, 118, 146, 147, 169, 277, 286, 304, 331, 350, 351, 353, 408, 466, 479, 499, 520, 569
Cecil, Sir Robert, 29, 33
Cedar Point, 569, 570
Channing, William Ellery, 311
Chapman, John G., 409, 417
Charles, Cape, 8, 124, 375
Charles Center, Baltimore, 596, 597
Charles County, 6, 7, 15, 65, 85, 95, 99, 105, 110, 111, 135, 144, 145, 202, 243, 286, 290, 331, 409, 413, 420, 435, 467, 567-70, 601
Charles I, King of England, 34, 36-8, 40, 41, 74, 78, 94, 113, 120
Charles II, King of England, 96, 107, 122, 123, 152
Chase, Jeremiah, 285
Chase, Samuel, 229, 240, 241, 250, 253, 255, 257, 262, 267, 272, 276, 279, 283, 285, 325, 326, 574
Cheltenham, 569
Chesapeake, 323, 326, 327
Chesapeake and Delaware Canal, 278, 279, 354, 369, 387, 390, 391, 395, 404, 511, 591
Chesapeake and Ohio Canal, 14, 277, 365-75, 377, 379-81, 386, 387, 389, 394, 395, 399, 455, 484, 485, 488, 503, 583
Chesapeake Bay, 1-5, 8, 9, 13, 15, 21, 23, 24, 27, 28, 31, 36, 38, 40, 41, 44, 45, 52, 111, 112, 116, 117, 124, 126, 161, 162, 193, 194, 197, 209, 232, 263, 264, 278-80, 294, 307, 332, 335, 364, 371, 375, 376, 385, 386, 396, 397, 399, 498, 500, 506, 511, 555, 561, 591-93
Chesapeake Bay Bridge, 5, 582
Chesapeake Bay Bridge-Tunnel, 5
Chesapeake Beach, 569
Cheseldyne, Kenelm, 139, 142
Chester River, 14, 278
Chestertown, 4, 194, 230, 290, 548, 571

Index 623

Chincoteague Bay, 1-3
Choptank Island, 111
Choptank River, 15, 48, 111, 197, 592
Chowan River, 38
Christiana, Fort, 120
Christiana Riot, 437, 438
Christison, Wenlocke, 115, 116
Church of England. See Anglican Church.
Churchill, Winston, 55
Clagett, The Reverend Thomas John, 308, 309
Claiborne, William, 40, 41, 44, 45, 51-5, 65, 78, 79, 87, 98-101
Clapham, John, 251
Clark, George Rogers, 271, 274
Clarke, (Clerk), Robert, Surveyor General, 47, 59
Clarksburg, 505
Clifford, Clark, 585
Clinton. See Surrattsville
Cloberry, William, and Co., 40, 51-3, 55, 81
Cockatrice, vessel, 53
Cockburn, Rear Admiral George, 332, 335
Cockey, Edward, 285
Coke, The Reverend Thomas, 307, 308
Coker, Daniel, 429
Cokesbury College, 307, 308
College of Medicine of Md., 304, 549
College of St. James, 309
College Park, 305, 543, 548, 549, 582
Collier Mountain, 12
Columbia, 600
Compton, Henry, Bishop of London, 143
Congress of Racial Equality, 582
Connecticut, 16, 153, 258, 271, 274, 283, 284, 290, 326, 343, 348, 406, 421, 595
Connecticut River, 31
Conococheague River, 15, 208, 209, 221, 222, 292, 363, 392
Conservative Unionist Party, 468, 469
Constellation, ship, 322, 323
Continental Congress, 245-50, 253, 259
Conventions, sites of nominating, 613
Coode, John, 135, 138, 139, 142, 153, 163
Cook, Dr. Albert S., 546
Cook, Ebenezer, 185
Cooper, Peter, 379
Copley, Sir Lionel, Gov. of Md., 140, 142, 146, 154

Copley, Thomas, S.J. (alias Philip Fisher, S.J.), 56, 66-8, 70, 78, 80, 84, 85
Coppin State College, 578, 580
Cornell, Ezra, 385
Cornwaleys, Thomas, 42, 56, 57, 59, 63, 64, 76, 77, 79, 80, 81, 89, 104
Cottman Co., 591
Council for New England, 31, 36
Counties, names and origins of Maryland, 608
County histories, Maryland, 615, 616
Coursey, Henry, 108, 132
Covington, Port, 386
Cowen, John K., 515
Cox, Christopher C., 471
Crabbe, George W., 534
Crane, Anne Moncure, 554
Creagerstown, 205
Cresap, Daniel, 12
Cresap, Colonel Thomas, 12, 203, 204, 215, 217
Creswell, John A.J., 471, 479, 515
Crisfield, 381, 388, 498, 543, 582
Crisfield, John W., 388
Cromwell, Nathan, 285
Cromwell, Oliver, 81, 86, 98-100, 102, 103
Crosland (Crossland), Alice, wife of George Calvert, 86
Crothers, Austin Lane, Gov. of Md., 520, 521, 523, 524
Cruse, Peter Hoffman, 313
Cuba, 246, 500, 501, 503
Cumberland, 13-5, 215, 216, 218-20, 222, 223, 275, 276, 292, 302, 314, 320, 321, 346, 352, 362, 364, 366-75, 380, 382-84, 387, 389, 419, 467, 482, 483, 493, 502, 503, 512, 516
Cumberland Turnpike Road Co., 392
Cumberland Valley, Pa., 12
Cummings, Harry S., 478, 582
Cummins, Edward, 84
Curtis Bay Ordnance Depot, 567, 569

Dabour, John, 552
D'Alesandro, Thomas J., 579, 596
Dale, Sir Thomas, 31
Danckaerts (Dankers), Jasper, 117, 278
Daniel, William, 486
Dans Mountain, 12
Darnall, Henry, 132, 139, 164, 175, 219

Dashiel, Joseph, 276
Davenant, Sir William, 96
David W. Taylor Model Basin, 568
Davis, Henry Winter, 420, 441, 462
Davis, Jefferson, Pres. of the Confederate States, 442, 449, 452
Davis, John, 27
Davyes (Davis), William, 134, 135
Dawson, Will, 15
Deakins, Francis, 275
Deakins, William, 16
DeButts, John, 276
Decatur, Stephen, 337
Declaration of Independence, 255, 257, 283, 371
Deer Park, 13
DeLancy, James, Gov. of N.Y., 216
Delaware Bay, 2, 31, 38, 116, 120-22, 124, 126, 278, 280, 332, 364, 591
Delaware, Colony and State, 1, 126, 146, 203, 204, 258, 280, 281, 284, 306, 323, 326, 343, 347, 348, 381, 388, 401, 419, 421, 425, 437, 445, 447, 451, 477, 505, 516, 601
Delaware River, 31, 64, 121-24, 126, 203, 291, 364
Delmar, 486
Delmarva Advisory Council, 601
Delmarva Peninsula, 4, 5, 387, 601
Democratic Party, 345-51, 353, 358-60, 385, 409, 413, 415, 417, 419-23, 438, 441, 443, 448, 451, 459, 462, 466-76, 478-80, 484-90, 514-21, 525, 526, 528, 533, 534, 536-40, 554, 575, 581, 582, 584-86
Dennis, Robert, 98
Denny, William, Gov. of Pa., 220, 222
Denton, 243
Dick, Charles, 217
Dickinson, John, 237, 272, 281
Dieterich, Louis, 552
Digges, George, 276
Dinwiddie, Robert, Gov. of Va., 213, 214, 216, 219-21, 225, 271
District of Columbia. See Washington.
Dix, General John A., 452
Dixon, Jeremiah, 204
Dobbs, Arthur, Gov. of N.C., 216
Donovan, Major General William J., 567
Dorchester County, 4, 15, 202, 227, 286, 292, 304, 331, 357, 409, 412, 430, 521, 525, 580

Doughty, The Reverend Francis, 144
Douglass, Frederick, 436, 577
Dove. See *Ark* and *Dove*.
Drake, Sir Francis, 25, 26
Dred Scott vs Sanford, 437, 438
Dubois, The Reverend John, 310
DuBourg, The Reverend W.L., 310
Dulany, Daniel, the Elder, 175, 176, 181-83, 187, 188, 195, 199, 203, 205, 207-09
Dulany, Daniel, the Younger, 198, 218, 228-30, 240, 242
Dulany, Walter, 240
Dunbar, Colonel Thomas, 219, 220
Dundalk, 16
Duquesne, Fort, 216, 218-20, 223, 224
Durang, Ferdinand, 336
Durham, Bishop of, 108
Dutch West India Co., 31, 118, 120, 121
Duvall, Gabriel, 349

Eagle Rock, 13
Early, General Jubal A., 309, 455, 458
East India Co., 27, 36, 236, 243, 244
Easton, 290, 314, 391
Eaton, Charles James Madison, 552
Eddis, William, 232, 235, 243, 251
Eden, Anthony, 571
Eden, Robert, Gov. of Md., 172, 187, 231, 235-38, 240-44, 246-52, 268
Edgemont, 14
Edgewood Arsenal, 566
Edict of Nantes, Revocation of, 137
Eisenhower, Dwight D., Pres. of the U.S., 575, 584, 585
Elizabeth I, Queen of England, 25-7, 33
Elk Ridge, 194, 264, 395, 592
Elk River, 118, 278
Elkin, John, 63
Elkton, 9, 332, 381, 392, 479
Ellicott, Andrew, 293, 592
Ellicott City, 11, 310, 600
Ellicott City Times, 520
Ellicott, George, 429
Ellicott, John, 592
Ellicott's Mills, 377, 379, 384, 429, 455
Ellsworth, Oliver, 284
Eltonhead, William, 101, 107
Ely, Richard T., 551
Emmitsburg, 146, 310
English Consul, 15

Index

Entick, The Reverend John, 194
Episcopalianism, 308, 309, 429, 432, 466, 549, 586
Evangelical United Brethren Church, 209
Evans, Daniel, 306
Evans, William, 108
Evelin, Captain George, 53-5, 57
Evelin, Captain Robert, 59

Fairchild Aircraft Division, 570
Fear River, Cape, 29
Federal Deposit Insurance Corp., 535
Federalist Party, 319, 321, 323-26, 329, 331, 343-45, 360, 493
Federal Republican, Baltimore, 329-31
Federal Reserve System, 535, 536
Fell, William, 197
Fells Point, 197, 397
Fendall, Josias, 103-08, 121, 129, 133-35, 139
Fenwick, Athanasius, 366
Fenwick, Cuthbert, 59, 94
Fenwick, John, 122
Fiddlesburg, 16
Finzel, Lawrence A., 571
Fisher, Father S.J., 85 See Copley, Thomas, S.J.
Fitch, John, 278
Fitzhugh, William, 240
Fleet, Captain Henry, 23, 45, 46, 53
Flexner, Dr. Abraham, 546, 547
Florida, 5, 27, 28, 42
Footner, Dr. Hulbert, 551, 555
Ford, Mary, 80
Fowey, ship, 251
Fowler, Henry, 7
Fox, George, 116
Foxx, Jimmy, 558
France, 24, 25, 33, 34, 37, 138-40, 149, 152-54, 156-58, 161, 162, 175, 188, 212-16, 218, 219, 221-24, 255, 263, 264, 274, 282, 319, 320, 323, 327-29, 402
France, Joseph I., 539
Frankenfeld, The Reverend Theodore, 208
Franklin, Benjamin, 184, 262, 278
Frederick, 205, 207-09, 215, 218, 249, 259, 268, 297, 298, 335, 345, 347, 375, 376, 379, 384, 391, 392, 440, 448, 449, 455, 458, 512, 566

Frederick County, 9, 11, 112, 194, 202, 207, 220, 222, 229, 242, 243, 245, 257, 259, 275, 286, 306, 331, 335, 350, 351, 357, 406, 408, 427, 567, 599
Frederick *Examiner*, 69
Frederick, Fort, 221-23
Frederick, Lord North, 243
French and Indian War, 12, 198, 212-24, 232
Frenchtown, 332
Fritchie, Barbara, 455
Frobisher, Martin, 27
Frostburg, 384, 487, 543
Frostburg State College, 580
Fugitive Slave Law, 437, 438, 443, 444
Fuller, William, 100, 101, 104, 107

Gaither, George R., 520
Garrett County, 11-4, 512, 523, 601
Garrett, John W., 456, 482
Garrison, William Lloyd, 436
Gary, James Albert; 515, 518
Geddes, Andrew, 150
Genêt, Citizen Edward, 319
George I, King of England, 164, 165, 169, 170
George G. Meade, Fort, 567
George, Joshua, 181
George III, King of England, 230, 235, 236, 238, 246, 250, 256, 257
George's Creek, 13, 14
George's Creek Railway, 384
Georgetown College (University), 310
Georgetown, D.C., 15, 215, 244, 293, 330, 335, 363, 366, 368, 370-74
Gerard, Thomas, 59, 81, 84, 89, 105-07, 139
Gerow, Major General Leonard T., 564
Gerry, Elbridge, 284, 291
Ghent, Treaty of, 336, 338
Gibbons, James Cardinal, 551, 552
Gilbert, Sir Humphrey, 26
Gilman, Daniel Coit, 551, 554
Gilmor, Harry, 450, 455
Gist, Christopher, 215, 217
Gist, General Mordecai, 263, 564
Glencoe, 567
Glenn, John, 356
Glenn L. Martin Co., 569
Goddard, Mary Katherine, 312

Goddard, William, 250, 266, 312
Godefroy, Maximilian, 295, 311
Godfrey, George, 135
Godyn, Samuel, 120
Goldsborough, Phillips Lee, Gov. of Md., 521, 522, 524, 548
Goldsborough, Robert, 257
Gondomar, Count (Diego Sarmiento de Acuña), 30, 34
Goodnow, Dr. Frank J., 526
Gorman, Arthur Pue, 484, 487, 489, 490, 499, 505, 514-21, 538, 539, 554
Gorsuch, Edward, 437, 438
Goucher, The Reverend John F., 550
Goucher College, 550
Gould, George W., 386
Governors, Maryland, 611, 612
Grason, William, Gov. of Md., 358
Great Backbone Mountain, 12
Great Britain, Imperial policy, 15, 224, 228, 230, 236, 237, 327
Great Falls, Potomac River, 276, 363, 372, 569
Green, Anna Catharine, 238
Green, Jonas, 220
Greene, Thomas, Proprietary Governor, 81-6, 96
Greenleaf, James, 293, 294
Greenbelt, 563
Greenbury Point, 569
Green Mountain, 12
Green Spring Valley, 581, 595
Grenville, George, 223
Groome, James Black, Gov. of Md., 480, 481
Guano, 400, 401, 504
Guilford, Francis, Lord, 165, 169, 172, 176
Gunpowder Neck, 565, 566
Gunpowder River, 9, 205

Hagar, Jonathan, 207, 242
Hagerstown, 12, 14, 207, 295, 309, 345, 376, 386, 391, 392, 419, 455, 485, 493, 568, 570, 583
Hall, Frank M. and R.L., 508
Hall, G. Stanley, 551
Hall, The Reverend Henry, 174
Hall, Thomas, 447
Hallwig, Oscar and Paul, 552
Halsted, William S., 551

Hamersley, Hugh, 230
Hamilton, Dr. Alexander, 195
Hamilton, Alexander, 259, 280, 281, 292, 319
Hamilton, Andrew, 168
Hamilton, William Thomas, Gov. of Md., 485, 548
Hammett, Dashiel, 555
Hammond, John, 103
Hancock, 14, 374
Hancock, Major General Winfield S., 483, 485
Hanlon, Edward, 557
Hanson, Alexander Contee, 329-31, 344
Hanson, John, 7, 274
Hardwicke, Lord Chancellor, 203, 204
Harford County, 9, 15, 243, 285, 286, 304, 307, 332, 350, 353, 357, 396, 408, 429, 563, 566, 600
Harford, Henry, Proprietor, 243, 251, 252, 267
Harper, Robert Goodloe, 326, 344, 368
Harpers Ferry, 13, 362, 373, 374, 379-82, 384, 392, 440, 449, 456
Harrington, Emerson C., Gov. of Md., 525, 526
Harris, Dr. Chapin A., 305
Harrison, Benjamin, 285
Harrison, Benjamin, Pres. of the U.S., 436
Harrison, Robert Hanson, 282, 286, 287
Harrison, William Henry, 314
Hart, Captain John, Gov. of Md., 159, 164, 165, 169-78, 180, 200
Harvey, Sir John, Gov. of Va., 44, 45, 51, 53
Hatch, John, 107
Hatteras, Cape, 20
Hatton, Thomas, 87, 99, 101
Havre-de-Grace, 332, 392, 566
Hawkins, Captain John, 26
Hawley, Jerome, 42, 54
Hayden, Dr. Horace H., 305
Hayes, Rutherford B., Pres. of the U.S., 481-85
Hayward, William, 240
Heamans, Captain Roger, 103
Helper, Hinton R., 423
Henderson, Alexander, 280
Henderson, The Reverend Jacob, 174, 183
Henlopen, Cape, 120, 124, 203

Index 627

Henrietta Maria, Queen of England, 35, 38
Henry, Cape, 3, 8, 124, 375
Henry, John, 286, 319, 321
Henry, Patrick, 282
Herbert, Brigadier General James, 482
Herrman, Augustine, 117, 121, 124, 147
Herrman, Casper August, 147
Herrman, Ephraim, 117
Hicks, Thomas Holliday, Gov. of Md., 409, 423, 442-46, 448-52, 462, 586
Hill, Captain Edward, Proprietary Governor, 81-3
Hill, The Reverend Matthew, 144
Hoffman, J. Latimer, 552
Holabird, Signal Depot (Camp Holabird), 567
Hood, John Mifflin, 386
Hood, Zachariah, 226, 227, 230
Hopkins, Johns, 457, 550
Horse racing, 194, 195, 297, 557
Howard County, 9, 11, 193, 290, 408, 410, 474, 487, 494, 520, 600
Howard, George, Gov. of Md., 348
Howard, John Eager, 263, 290, 304, 348, 430
Howard, Joseph C., 582
Howard, Lord, of Effingham, Gov. of Va., 126
Howard, Michael, 181
Howe, Admiral Sir William, 263
Hudson, Henry, 120
Hudson River, 31, 38, 118, 120, 122
Hughes, Christopher, 336
Hughes, Samuel, 276
Hunter, Moses T., 366
Hunting Creek, 3, 293

Indian Head, 15, 558-70
Ingle, Richard, 70, 76-80, 83, 86
Inner Harbor Redevelopment Project, Baltimore, 584, 596, 597
Innes, Colonel James, 216, 219
Interstate Commission on the Potomac River Basin, 574
Invincible Armada, 28
Ireland, Irish, 33, 35, 58, 137, 139, 142, 145, 160, 169, 173, 182, 417, 439, 478, 487, 576, 582
Isle of Wight, 44
Issue, 15

Jackson, Andrew, 314, 335, 344, 346-50, 353, 358-60, 372, 377, 485, 489
Jackson, Elihu Emory, Gov. of Md., 486, 487, 489
Jackson, Lillie M., 577
Jackson, William P., 522
James I, King of England, 27, 28, 30, 31, 33-6, 74
James II, Duke of York and King of England, 122-24, 126, 127, 137, 138, 140, 142, 202
James, The Reverend Richard, 51
James River, Va., 29, 30, 38, 46
James River and Kanawha Canal Company, Va., 363, 365, 373
Jamestown, Va., 29-31, 37, 44, 78
Jefferson, Thomas, 225, 258, 292, 298, 321, 323-28, 343, 360, 364, 489, 538, 579
Jenifer, Daniel, of St. Thomas, 7, 240, 266-68, 280, 285
Jennings, Edmund, 203
Jessup, 567
Jews, 345, 346, 576, 586
Johns Hopkins Hospital, 551, 564, 565
Johns Hopkins Medical School, 551
Johns Hopkins University, 381, 526-28, 545, 550, 551, 554, 558, 585, 593
Johnson, Andrew, Pres. of the U.S., 467-74, 476, 488
Johnson, General Bradley, 448
Johnson, Edward, 330, 331
Johnson, Lyndon B., Pres. of the U.S., 490, 575, 584, 585
Johnson, Reverdy, 356, 379, 438, 444, 462, 467, 469, 476
Johnson, Thomas, Gov. of Md., 240, 241, 259, 268, 272, 279, 286, 293
Johnston, Richard Malcolm, 554
Jones, Evan, 151
Joppa, 194
Joseph, William, 125, 137
Jousting Tournaments, 7
Jowles, Henry, 139

Keeler, Willie, 558
Kelly, Howard A., 551
Kennedy, John Pendleton, 313, 314, 450, 554
Kennedy, Thomas, 345

Kensett, Thomas, 498
Kent County, 15, 59, 60, 97, 105, 111, 168, 243, 286, 302, 304, 306, 342, 409, 413, 488, 494
Kent County, Del., 203
Kent Defense Corp., 571
Kent Island (Winston's Island), 5, 24, 41, 44, 51-7, 62, 63, 65, 66, 79, 82, 84, 110, 332, 582
Kent, Dr. Joseph, 367
Kerfoot, The Reverend John Barrett, 309
Kerney, Martin J., 418, 419
Key, Francis Scott, 313, 335, 336, 349, 430
Key, Philip Barton, 276, 326, 335
Keyser, Ephraim, 552
Kieft, Wilhelm, Gov. of New Amsterdam, 120
King, Rufus, 284
King William's School, Annapolis, 150, 159, 172, 303
Knapp, Friedrich, 544
Knights of Labor, 506
Know-Nothing Movement, 414, 417-24, 442, 480, 488

Labadie, Jean de, 117
Labadists, 117-20
Lafayette, Marquis de, 264
Laing, Alexander, 227
Lamb, Eli, 545
Lancaster, Pa., 213, 291
Lane, Ralph, 26, 28
Lane, William Preston, Jr., Gov. of Md., 538, 582, 583
Langford, John, 59, 103
Lanier, Sidney, 554
La Plata, 7
Latrobe, Benjamin H., 278, 293, 295, 383
Latrobe, Ferdinand C., 483
Latrobe, John H.B., 379
Laud, William, Archbishop of Canterbury, 31, 74
Laurel, 9, 195, 487, 557
Laurel Hill, 12
Lawson, William, 65
Le Boeuf, Fort, 212
Lee, Blair, 521
Lee, General Charles, 249
Lee, Henry, 330

Lee, Richard Henry, Gov. of Va., 320, 321
Lee, Robert E., Colonel and General, 330, 440, 455
Lee, Thomas Sim, Gov. of Md., 268, 282, 286, 586
Leonardtown, 6
Leopard, 326
Levering, Joshua, 516
Levington, The Reverend William, 429
Lewger, John, 54, 56, 58, 80, 81, 83, 89
Lewis, David J., 522, 524, 539
Lewis, William, 89, 101
Library Company of Baltimore, 315
Ligon, Lomas W., Gov. of Md., 305, 461
Linchester, 3
Lincoln, Abraham, Pres. of the U.S., 441-47, 449-53, 455-59, 462, 463, 466, 467, 470, 473, 475, 489, 496, 500, 577, 581
Lingan, General James M., 330
Liverpool, England, 8, 375, 376, 399
Lloyd, Edward, 97, 164, 198, 291, 344
Lloyd, Henry, Gov. of Md., 485
London, 26, 29, 30, 33, 38, 144, 155, 156, 158, 159, 162, 163, 176, 181, 184, 186, 187, 226, 235, 237, 249, 250, 252, 266, 326, 337, 382
London Company, 29, 31
Long Parliament, England, 74
Long Tayle, pinnace, 53
Lords Commissioners for Foreign Plantations, 41, 55, 79, 103, 112, 114, 126, 152
Lotteries, 304, 311, 312, 363, 390, 410, 587
Loudoun, Earl of. See Campbell, John
Louis XIV, King of France, 137, 154
Love, John, 285
Loveall, The Reverend Henry, 309
Lovely Lane Meeting House, 306, 307
Lowe, Enoch, Gov. of Md., 586
Lowndes, Lloyd, Gov. of Md., 515-18
Loyola College, Baltimore, 310
Lutheranism, 146, 182, 208, 209, 544, 549

MacNamara, Thomas, 169, 170, 175
Madison, James, 258, 282, 284, 328-32, 335, 337, 338, 343, 344, 360, 364, 365, 489

Index

Magothy River, 15
Mahoney, George P., 584
Makemie, The Reverend Francis, 144, 145
Malster, William T., 515, 517, 518
Manchester, 9
Mandel, Marvin, Gov. of Md., 586
Manokin River, 110, 116, 145
Markham, William, 124
Marlboro, 15, 194
Marlboro Tobacco Market, 508
Marshall, Thurgood, 490, 585
Martin, Daniel, Gov. of Md., 348
Martin, Luther, 283-85, 314, 326, 393, 534, 574, 603
Martin Mountain, 12
Martinsburg, W. Va., 482
Mary, daughter of the Tayac, 84
Maryland Agricultural College, 305, 548
Maryland Agriculture, 494, 495, 507, 508, 510, 594
Maryland, America in Miniature, 1, 17
Maryland, Assembly, 47, 55-63, 68, 69, 72, 81, 82, 84, 87, 88, 90-2, 96-100, 102, 104-08, 111, 113, 125, 129-39, 142, 146, 147, 150-56, 159, 161, 168-78, 180-83, 185-87, 195, 196, 199-201, 209, 212-15, 217-20, 222, 223, 226, 227, 230-33, 236-38, 240-42, 347, 350, 357, 373, 380, 410, 425, 437
Maryland Association, 132, 138, 139, 142, 150, 163
Maryland, Banks, 302, 356, 389-92, 394, 403, 411, 412, 460
Maryland Bicentennial Commission, ix, xiii
Maryland, boundaries, 1, 38, 65, 123-26
Maryland Brewery Company, 499
Maryland Canal Company, 370
Maryland, Charter of, 38-41, 51, 126, 129, 140, 164, 175, 177, 181, 187, 204, 226, 227
Maryland, climate, 2
Maryland, Coastal Plain—Southern Maryland, 2, 3, 6-9
Maryland Colonization Society, 426, 430, 431, 577
Maryland Commission on Interracial Problems, 579
Maryland, Conditions of Plantation, 66, 69, 71, 86, 95

Maryland, Constitution of 1776, 257-59, 325, 341, 342, 345, 346, 348, 350-53, 404-06, 472, 529, 532
Maryland, Constitution of 1851, 405-13, 460, 472, 529
Maryland, Constitution of 1864, 413, 457-62, 466, 470-72, 474, 476, 529, 542, 544
Maryland, Constitution of 1867, 472-75, 479, 487, 514, 520, 521, 529, 530, 532, 539, 544, 574, 584, 586
Maryland, Conventions, 244-50, 253, 256
Maryland Council, 156, 164, 169, 172, 174-77, 179-82, 185, 188
Maryland, Council of Safety, 247-51, 253, 259, 260, 271
Maryland Counties, names and origins of, 608
Maryland County Histories, check list of, 615, 616
Maryland, crime and punishment, 61, 62
Maryland, Declaration of Rights, 72
Maryland, Eastern Shore, 2-6, 8, 20, 55, 62, 65, 144-46, 160, 162, 174, 198, 200, 201, 248, 250, 258, 263, 284, 286, 290, 291, 303, 304, 306, 309, 314, 319, 321, 342, 345-47, 370, 381, 386, 388, 394-96, 408, 409, 411, 413, 423, 430, 435, 436, 442, 451, 458, 471, 485, 494, 515, 517, 543, 550, 554, 558, 570, 571, 580, 582, 592, 594, 595, 601
Maryland, education in, 133, 147, 149, 150, 159, 172, 243, 302-12, 389, 392, 411-13, 429, 461, 475, 519, 542-51
Maryland, effect of laws of England in, 39, 57, 58, 61, 64, 81, 130, 178, 182, 190, 484
Maryland, "Free State," 43, 92, 252, 439, 447, 463, 471, 526, 535, 538, 539, 563, 573, 574, 603
Maryland Gazette, The, 152, 184, 188, 205, 220, 224, 226, 227, 229, 238, 241, 312, 447
Maryland, General Assembly, 292, 293, 302, 305, 310, 311, 331, 380-83, 386, 388, 410, 411, 428, 447, 460, 461, 470-75, 478, 484, 514, 530, 531, 578, 582-84, 586, 592, 600, 601
Maryland Geological Survey, 13

Maryland, Germans in, 146, 182, 194, 198, 202, 205, 207-09, 242, 312, 324, 417, 436, 439, 445, 446, 506, 545, 552
Maryland, Governors, 396, 410, 411, 611, 612
Maryland, Great Seal of, 80, 86, 88, 104, 108, 235
Maryland Historical Society, 315
Maryland, House of Delegates, 258, 259, 264, 268, 279-82, 313, 325, 329, 341, 343-45, 350, 353, 357, 358, 366, 381, 405-07, 410, 420, 425, 427, 460, 466, 474, 488, 516, 518, 520, 526, 528, 530, 537, 538, 542, 549, 571, 578, 582
Maryland Hunt Cup Race, 557
Maryland, Indians in, 20, 21, 23, 24, 45-8, 52-6, 62-71, 84, 88, 89, 115, 116, 132-35, 138, 139, 169, 212
Maryland, Jesuits in, 22, 44, 47, 52, 56, 66-72, 85, 87, 102, 103, 114, 174
Maryland Jockey Club, 557
Maryland *Journal and Baltimore Advertiser*, 250, 266, 298, 312, 467, 527
Maryland, land policy, 42, 47, 50, 55, 66, 68, 69, 72, 78, 102, 104, 198, 199, 221, 251
Maryland, laws of, 39, 56-8, 77, 136, 168, 169, 176, 181
Maryland local government, 57, 97, 111, 112, 477, 587
Maryland, location and geography, 1, 2, 415, 439, 445, 450, 561
Maryland, manorial system, 16, 50, 66, 68, 202
Maryland, manufacturing, 159, 160, 185, 196, 197, 327, 328, 399, 436, 439, 495-505, 508-11
Maryland Milk Producers Association, 508
Maryland, My Maryland, 614
Maryland-National Capital Park and Planning Commission, 599
Maryland, Navy, 248, 262, 331
Maryland Nominating Conventions sites of, 613
Maryland, oaths of office, 85, 460
Maryland, officers' fees, 58, 129, 177-81, 185, 187, 188, 199, 202, 239, 240-42
Maryland, organized labor in, 484, 497, 506, 522

Maryland, paper currency in, 184-87, 189, 247, 249, 265, 267
Maryland, Piedmont Plateau, 2, 9, 11, 20, 177, 193, 205, 362, 594, 599, 602, 603
Maryland, "plundering time," 76, 79, 81, 82, 87, 94, 104
Maryland, population, 16, 17, 142, 196, 290, 341, 405, 407, 410, 417, 426, 428, 435-37, 439, 474, 478, 493, 506, 507, 512, 519, 543, 545, 578, 598, 601
Maryland Port Authority (Maryland Port Administration), 592
Maryland, privateering, 319, 331, 332, 337, 338
Maryland Proprietors, 609-11
Maryland, Puritans in, 65, 94-7, 100-04, 106, 107, 129
Maryland, Senate, 258, 259, 266, 281, 282, 325, 329, 337, 341-45, 347, 348, 351-53, 356-58, 381, 410, 420, 466, 475, 488, 518, 520, 528, 530, 531, 538, 549, 578, 582
Maryland State College, 549
Maryland State Normal School, 542
Maryland Steel Company, 501
Maryland, Western Maryland (Appalachian Region), 2, 11-5, 205, 208, 209, 298, 299, 435, 436, 512, 515, 516, 538, 556, 563, 595, 601
Maryland, wildlife, 21-3, 50, 298, 299
Mary Whitridge, clipper, 397, 398
Mason, Charles, 204
Mason-Dixon line, 1, 12, 204, 418, 430, 436, 439, 495, 542, 549, 578, 585
Mason, George, 280, 282
Masonic Order, 239, 294, 303, 314, 348, 349, 377, 549
Mason, Van Wyck, 555
Mason, William T.T., 366
Massachusetts, colony and state, 6, 16, 43, 51, 60, 94, 112, 115, 116, 144, 153, 158, 216, 220, 227, 239, 243, 253, 258, 271, 274, 280, 281, 283-86, 290, 291, 312, 332, 343, 348, 406, 407, 421, 439, 555
Mattapanient, 57, 60
Mattawoman Creek, 110
Matthews, Samuel, 103, 104
May, Cape, 122
May, Henry, 449

Mayer, Brantz, 315, 451
Mayer, Frank B., 552
McCardell, Lee, 571
McComas, Louis E., 517
McCulloch vs Maryland, 393
McGraw, John, 557
McHenry, Fort, 313, 320, 333, 335, 336, 372, 482, 483
McHenry, James, 269, 282, 285, 320, 323
McKeesport, Pa., 13
McKeldin, Theodore R., 538, 579, 582-84, 604
McKim, Isaac, 397
McKinley, William, Pres. of the U.S., 515, 516, 518
McLane, Louis, 382, 383, 485
McLane, Robert M., Gov. of Md., 485
McMahon, John Van Lear, 89, 168, 314, 315, 346, 376, 379
McMurray, Louis, 498
McSherry, James, 315
Meadow Mountain, 12, 13
Mechanics' Bank, Baltimore, 375, 376
Mechanicsville, 569
Mencken, Henry L., 463, 495, 499, 544, 552, 553, 555
Mercantile Library Association, 315
Mercer, Charles F., 371, 377
Mercer, John Francis, 285, 325
Merchants and Manufacturers Association of Baltimore, 523
Mergenthaler, Ottmar, 552
Merryman, in re John, 449
Methodism, 284, 299, 306-08, 315, 429, 432, 549, 550, 586
Meverick, Samuel, 122
Middletown, 12, 205, 295
Miller, Alfred Jacob, 552
Miller, J. Jefferson, 596
Mississippi River, 13, 20, 175, 212, 271, 272
Mitchell, Parren, 582
Monocacy River, 9, 15, 146, 205, 208, 209, 297, 363, 386, 392
Monongahela River, 13, 215, 219, 362, 367, 370, 383
Montgomery County, 9, 11, 17, 193, 257, 275, 286, 304, 331, 350, 357, 408, 413, 565-69, 595, 598, 599, 602
Moore, Thomas, 366
Moravianism, 146, 208, 209, 436

More, Henry, Provincial of Society of Jesus in England, 70, 71
Morecroft, John, 131
Morgan, Dr. Littleton F., 550
Morgan State College (University), 550, 578, 580
Morris, Robert, 293, 294
Morris, Robert Hunter, Gov. of Pa., 216
Morse, Samuel Finley Breese, 385
Morton, Rogers C.B., 585
Mount Airy, 9
Mount Saint Mary's College, 310
Mount Savage, 499, 571
Mudd, Dr. Samuel, 467
Mudd, Sidney E., 515
Muhlenberg, The Reverend Henry M., 209
Murdock, William, 227
Murray, William Vans, 323
Mynne, Anne, 33

Nanjemoy Creek, 15, 144, 467
Nanticoke Indians, 20, 48, 63, 65
Nanticoke River, 15, 111, 197
"Narrows," 13
National Association for the Advancement of Colored People, 577
National Park College, 565
Naval Academy, 11, 311, 447, 466, 476, 548, 555, 558, 569
Naval Air Station, 569, 570
Naval Powder Factory, 568
Naval Training Center, 569
Navigation Acts, 80, 88, 156, 161, 163, 196, 237
Naylor, William, 366
Neale, Captain James, 76, 77, 122
Necessity, Fort, 214
Negroes, 31, 132, 143, 160, 161, 163, 169, 173, 185, 193, 195, 196, 265, 283, 284, 290, 291, 327, 333, 344, 407-10, 415, 417-20, 422-32, 435-40, 442, 450, 452, 453, 455, 457, 459, 461, 462, 466, 471, 473-75, 477-80, 490, 493, 514, 515, 517, 519, 520, 539, 543-46, 550, 552, 570, 574, 576-82, 598
Negro Mountain, 12
Nemacolin, 215
New Amsterdam (N.Y.), 118, 120-22, 144
New Bremen, 298

New Castle (New Amstel), Del., 118, 121-26, 150, 203
Newcomb, Simon, 551
Newfoundland, 26, 36-8, 163
New Jersey, 16, 123, 216, 258, 269, 272, 281, 283, 306, 320, 321, 343, 347, 348, 406, 422, 437, 439, 440, 495, 564, 595
New Sweden Company, 120, 121
New Windsor, 306
New York, 5, 16, 20, 122, 123, 153, 158, 161, 162, 185, 216, 219-21, 227, 258, 262, 269, 271, 273, 274, 279, 280, 283, 286, 287, 290-92, 306, 309, 312, 343, 348, 365, 368, 375, 397, 399-402, 406, 418, 419, 421, 439, 482, 503, 505, 506, 509, 524, 536, 549, 557, 574, 590, 591, 595, 598
Nice, Harry W., Gov. of Md., 527, 537, 538
Nicholett, Charles, 130
Nicholson, Francis, Gov. of Md., 146, 147, 149, 150, 154, 163, 172
Nicholson, Captain James, 264
Nicholson, Joseph Hopper, 336
Nicolls, Colonel Richard, 122
Niles, Hezekiah, 312, 392
Niles Register, 312, 392, 394
Nixon, Richard M., Pres. of the U.S., 575, 585, 586
North Carolina, 26, 38, 60, 220, 253, 258, 271, 273, 275, 281, 290, 324, 494
North Mountain, 12, 220, 221
Notley, Thomas, 131, 135
Nuthead, Dinah, 150
Nuthead, William, 139, 150

O'Conor, Herbert R., Gov. of Md., 537, 538
Odenton, 567
O'Donnell, Colonel John, 291, 296
Ogle, Samuel, Gov. of Md., 187, 194, 203, 212
Ohio Company, 213, 214, 362
Ohio River, 13, 212-14, 216, 295, 338, 362, 364, 365, 369, 371, 375, 376, 386, 495
Oldtown, 215
Onderdonk, Henry, 309

Orange, Fort (Albany, N.Y.), 120
Orme, Captain Robert, 219
Osler, William, 551
Otterbein, The Reverend Philip William, 209
Owings Mills, 386
Oxford, 194, 290

Paca, William, Gov. of Md., 229, 241, 250, 255, 257, 264, 268, 272, 273, 285, 287
Palatinate, 36, 39
Pallas, vessel, 296
Palmer, Edward, 147
Palmer's Island, 55, 64, 65, 147
Panama Canal, 511, 520, 583, 591
Parker, Edward, 76, 77
Parks, William, 152, 184
Parr's Ridge, 9
Patapsco River, 8, 9, 15, 22, 68, 111, 138, 193, 197, 205, 263, 264, 290, 294-96, 333, 368, 374, 375, 377, 386, 568, 592
Patterson, Betsey, 515
Patterson, William, 327
Patuxent County, 102, 110, 111
Patuxent Indians, 67
Patuxent River, 9, 15, 21, 52, 53, 65, 95, 101, 104, 110, 145, 162, 193, 205, 332, 499, 555
Peabody, Elizabeth, 545
Peabody, George, 457
Peace of Paris, 1763, 223-25
Peale, Rembrandt, 296
Peggy Stewart, vessel, 244, 245
Pen Mar, 12, 14, 386
Penn, William, 122-26, 137
Pennington, Harper, 552
Pennsylvania, colony and state, 1, 6, 9, 11-3, 146, 161, 169, 170, 184, 185, 193, 198, 202-04, 208, 209, 214, 216-18, 220-22, 237, 238, 258, 269, 272, 276, 278, 280, 281, 283-85, 290, 292, 295, 299, 306, 312, 320-24, 348, 367-70, 372, 373, 375, 377, 382, 387, 390, 403, 406, 407, 410, 418, 422, 425, 436-39, 482, 494, 500, 561, 563, 569, 574, 601, 602
Pennsylvania Railroad, 8, 456, 481, 483, 484, 505, 568, 591

Index 633

Pennsylvania Steel Company, 501, 502
Peter, Jafer, 65
Phelps, Almira Lincoln, 306
Philadelphia, 150, 164, 168, 184, 203, 205, 207, 219, 222, 245, 253, 263, 264, 268, 274, 282-85, 287, 291, 292, 294, 296, 312, 319, 321, 348, 360, 368, 373, 374, 387, 397, 399, 418, 419, 421, 438, 444, 448, 483, 506, 507, 534, 552, 582, 590
Pickersgill, Mary Young, 336
Piedmont, 383, 384
Pile, John, 86
Pinkney, William, 267, 285, 326, 328, 344, 393, 427, 480
Piscataway Indians, 20, 46, 48, 67, 71, 132
Piscataway River, 15, 68, 592
Pitt, William, 222, 223, 228, 230
Pittsburgh, 13, 368, 370, 380, 387, 421, 483, 484, 486, 500, 502, 503, 602
Plater, George, 257, 273, 285
Pleasants, Dr. J. Hall, 551
Plessy vs Ferguson, 543, 576
Plymouth Company, 29, 31, 43
Pocahontas, 84
Pocomoke Bay, 117
Pocomoke Indians, 65
Pocomoke River, 1-3, 15, 53, 117, 279, 280
Poe, Edgar Allen, 314
Poe, John Prentiss, 519, 520
Pohlemus, A. Henry, 557
Point Comfort, 30, 45
Point of Rocks, 373, 374, 377, 379, 380, 384
Point Lookout, 9, 569
Pontiac's Conspiracy, 224
Popham, Sir John, 29
Port Deposit, 11, 569
Port Tobacco, 6, 7, 68, 144, 290, 467, 593
Porter, Admiral David, 548
Potomac and Winchester Railroad, 384
Potomac Company, 276, 277, 362, 363, 365, 366, 369, 390
Potomac River, 1-3, 6, 9, 13-5, 21-3, 29, 38, 44-6, 54, 65, 68, 110, 132, 162, 193, 198, 204, 215, 221, 275-77, 279, 280, 291-93, 298, 362, 364-72, 374, 377, 379, 380, 386, 425, 440,

Potomac River *(cont.)* 450, 455, 467, 498, 567, 569, 574, 600
Potomac River Fisheries Commission, 574
Potomac River Naval Command, 569
Pott, John, Gov. of Va., 40
Powhatan, 21, 29
Pratt, Enoch, 456, 556
Pratt, Thomas G., Gov. of Md., 359
Preakness Day, 557
Presbyterianism, 129, 144-46, 429, 432, 549, 586
Presque Isle, 212
Preston, 3
Preston, Richard, 100, 101, 104
Price, John, 106
Prince Frederick, 15
Prince George's County, 6, 9, 15, 17, 110, 145, 193, 194, 202, 207, 250, 286, 321, 331, 344, 357, 367, 413, 420, 435, 499, 563, 566, 567, 569, 594, 595, 598, 599, 602
Princess Anne, 15, 550
Princeton, N.J., 291
Principio Company, 197, 499, 500
Prohibition Party, 485-87, 516, 526, 527
Proprietors, Maryland, 609-11
Providence, Puritan settlement, 95-7, 99, 103

Quakers, 114-16, 118, 129, 142, 143, 194, 216, 284, 551
Queen Anne's County, 15, 286, 304, 306, 353, 357, 409, 472, 494

Raleigh, Sir Walter, 26, 27
Randall, James Ryder, 447
Randolph, Edmund, 282
Randolph, Edward, 163
Rappahannock River, Va., 126, 366
Rasin, Isaac Freeman, 487, 514-16, 518, 520, 539, 554
Rayner, Isidor, 520, 522
Reading, Thomas, 151
Reckord, Major General Milton A., 564
Red Book, 313
Reed, Philip, 329

Reese, Lizette Woodworth, 556
Reformation, ship, 76, 79
Reformed Church, 208, 209
Rehoboth, Del., 145
Remsen, Ira, 551
Republican Party, 421, 423, 432, 438, 440, 441, 458, 462, 469-73, 475-81, 484-86, 490, 514-21, 525-27, 538-40, 575, 581, 582, 584, 585
Revels, The Reverend Hiram R., 429
Revely, John, 204
Rhode Island, 16, 43, 89, 116, 253, 281, 283, 290, 324, 332, 343, 348, 406, 421, 447, 466, 505
Richardson, Colonel William, 263
Richmond, Va., 30, 455, 461, 467, 500
Ridgely, Charles, 285, 343
Ridgely, Charles, of William, 285
Rinehart, William H., 552
Ringgold, General Samuel, 309
Ringgold, Thomas, 227
Rising Sun, 15
Ritchie, Albert C., Gov. of Md., 527, 528, 532, 534, 536-39, 546, 547, 549, 552, 574, 586, 603
Roanoke Island, N.C., 26, 27
Rock Creek, 215, 505
Rock Hall, 498
Rockville, 11, 392, 455
Rodgers, John, 337
Rogers, John, 253, 255
Rogers, William P., 585
Rolfe, John, 30, 84
Roosevelt, Franklin D., Pres. of the U.S., 536-39, 553, 562, 568, 575, 581
Roosevelt, Theodore, Pres. of the U.S., 518, 519, 521, 585
Ross, Major General Sir Robert, 332, 333, 335
Rousby, Christopher, 125, 126
Rouse, James W., 600
Rumsey, James, 277, 278
Rupert, Prince, 75, 76
Rush, Benjamin, 249
Rush, Richard, 372
Ruth, George Herman ("Babe"), 558

St. Clement's Hundred, 60, 97
St. George's Hundred, 60
St. George's River. See St. Mary's River.
St. Helen, vessel, 53
St. Inigoes, 85, 97
St. John's College, 303, 304, 335, 447, 451, 548, 555, 558
St. Margaret, vessel, 53
St. Mary's City, 6, 47, 50, 52, 53, 55-7, 59, 60, 66-8, 81, 82, 89, 96, 99, 113, 125, 131, 134, 139, 142, 146, 147, 150, 172, 193, 195, 313, 435
St. Mary's College, 310
St. Mary's County, 6, 64, 65, 97, 102, 105, 110, 111, 285, 286, 331, 332, 409, 413, 420, 466, 546, 569, 570, 601
St. Mary's River, (St. George's River), 46, 56, 79, 244
St. Michael's Hundred, 60
Salem, N.J., 120
Salisbury, 4, 15, 388, 474, 486, 543, 580, 592
Sandy Hook, 440
Sandy Spring, 9
Sandys, Sir Edwin, 31
Savage, John, 12
Savage River, 13, 363, 367, 369, 370
Sawyer, Sir Robert, 126
Scarborough, Colonel Edmond, 116
Scharf, J. Thomas, 450
Scheib, Heinrich, 544
Schenck, General Robert C., 457, 458
Schlatter, The Reverend Michael, 208
Scott, Gustavus, 276
Scott, Sir Walter, 7
Scott, General Winfield, 444, 445, 447
Secession. See States' Rights.
Secretary, 15
Seneca Creek, 11, 372, 455
Seton, Elizabeth Ann Bayley, 310
Seven Years War. See French and Indian War
Severn River, 65, 95, 97, 100, 110, 132, 311, 569
Severn River Naval Command, 569
Sewall, Henry, 15, 108
Seymour, John, Gov. of Md., 154, 159, 163, 164
Shapiro, Karl J., 571
Sharpe, Horatio, Gov. of Md., 198, 200, 212-21, 224-27, 230-33, 235
Shays' Rebellion, 283
Shenandoah Valley, Va., 12, 13, 20, 295, 296, 363, 380, 384
Shepherdstown, W. Va., 455

Index

Sherman, Roger, 284
Shirley, William, Gov. of Mass., 216, 220, 225
Sideling Creek, 13
Sideling Hill, 12
Silver Spring, 15, 16, 565
Simpson, Wallis Warfield, 581
Sinclair, Upton Beall, 555
Sinepuxent Bay, 3
Skinner, John Stuart, 313, 335
Slavery. See Negroes.
Sluyter, Peter, 117-19, 278
Smallwood, William, Gov. of Md., 263, 285, 287
Smith, Captain John, 21, 23, 29, 30, 41
Smith, John Walter, Gov. of Md., 518-20
Smith, Robert, 304, 328, 329
Smith, Major General Samuel, 263, 324, 329, 333, 336, 356, 430
Smith, Thomas, 53-5
Smith, Dr. William, 302, 303
Smithsonian Institution, 11
Smith's Point, 1
Snow Hill, 65, 145, 408
Snow, Justinian, 57
Society of Jesus. See Maryland, Jesuits in.
Solomon's Island, 498, 502, 555, 569
Somerset County, 15, 111, 144, 145, 160, 227, 286, 331, 357, 395, 408, 412, 413, 579
Sousa, Mathias da, 42, 57
South Mountain, 222
South River Club, 195, 556
Spain, 7, 24, 25, 27, 28, 30, 34, 45, 52, 154, 402
Sparrows Point, 500-03, 511, 569, 591
Spates, Alfred, 455
Speagle, ship, 79, 80
Sprigg, Samuel, Gov. of Md., 344
Stagg, Thomas, 98
Stamp Act, 1765, 225-31, 237, 241, 255, 312
Star Chamber, Court of, 74
States' rights, 417, 424, 439, 442, 447, 449-51, 458, 470, 473, 480, 527, 534-36, 538, 539
Stevens, Samuel, Gov. of Md., 344
Stewart, Anthony, 244, 245
Stewart, Dr. David, 293
Stewart, George, 240, 251
Stewart, John, 263

Stoddart, Benjamin, 323
Stoever, John Caspar, 208
Stone, John H., Gov. of Md., 294
Stone, Thomas, 7, 253, 255, 276, 282
Stone, William, Gov. of Md., 85-7, 95-7, 99-101, 103
Strawbridge, The Reverend Robert, 306
Stricker, Brigadier General John, 331, 336
Strong, Leonard, 103
Stuyvesant, Peter, 118, 121, 122
Sugar Act (1764), 225, 226
Suitland, 566
Sunpapers, 312, 313, 443, 450, 457, 468, 507, 515, 520, 543, 552, 571, 598
Surratt, Mary E., 467
Surrattsville (Clinton), 467
Susquehanna Fort, 123
Susquehanna River, 3, 9, 15, 20, 55, 64, 125, 147, 198, 203, 205, 280, 292, 295, 368, 375, 387, 390, 446
Susquehanna River Basin Commission, 574
Susquehannock Indians, 20, 21, 46-8, 54, 55, 62-5, 68, 132, 133
Sutro, Otto, 556
Sutton, John, 100
Swann, Thomas, Gov. of Md., 383, 422, 423, 466, 469-72
Swansecute's Creek, 117
Swedes, 64, 65

Talbot, Colonel George, 125, 126
Talbot, William, 132
Talbot County, 111, 116, 150, 202, 238, 243, 286, 314, 331, 344, 348, 408, 436, 494, 579
Taney, Michael, 139, 325, 344
Taney, Roger Brooke, 305, 336, 344, 347, 349, 356, 379, 438, 449, 490, 585
Tangier Sound, 1, 264, 388
Tasker, Benjamin, Jr., 183, 194, 205, 214
Tawes, J. Millard, Gov. of Md., 582
"Taxation without representation," 178
Tea Act (1765), 243
Telegraph, 359, 385
Tennessee River, 20
Thirty Years' War, 34, 43
Thomas, Evan, 379

Thomas, Mary Whitall (Mrs. J.C. Thomas), 486
Thomas, Philip Evan, 375-77
Thomas, Philip Francis, Gov. of Md., 359, 408, 472
Thornton, William, 293
Thurmont, 567
Thurston, Thomas, 115
Tilghman, Edward, 227, 241
Tilghman, Matthew, 253, 257, 266
Tilghman, Tench, 264
Timonium, 344
Tindall, Thomas, 37
Tobacco, 6, 30, 60, 129, 131, 133, 136, 137, 140, 142, 143, 146, 155-64, 169, 170, 178-80, 182-89, 193, 197-99, 201, 212, 225, 226, 228, 229, 239-42, 256, 284, 294, 323, 400, 402, 415, 436, 494, 498, 499, 502, 507, 594 .
Toleration Act, 1689. See Act concerning Religion.
Tonoloway Creek, 220
Tonoloway Ridge, 12
Totness, ship, 245
Town Hill, 12
Townsend, George Alfred, 554
Townshend Acts, 231, 237, 238, 243
Towson, 543, 550
Towson State College, 580
Trent, Captain William, 214
Trenton, N.J., 291, 292
Tri-County Council for Southern Maryland, 601
Tri-County Council for Western Maryland, 601
Trueman, Thomas, 108, 132, 133
Tubman, Harriet, 430
Turkey Foot, 215
Turner, Nat, 428, 430
Tydings, Millard, 539, 549, 574, 603
Tyler, John, Pres. of the U.S., 315
Tyson, Isaac, Jr., 402

Underground Railroad, 430
Union Party (Unconditional Union Party), 451, 453, 457-59, 462, 466-69
Unitarianism, 311, 315
Unitas, Johnny, 558
United States Army Map Service, 566

United States Constitution, 258, 283-87, 394
 Thirteenth Amendment, 466, 474
 Fourteenth Amendment, 476, 577
 Fifteenth Amendment, 477
 Seventeenth Amendment, 575
 Eighteenth Amendment, 534, 536, 574, 575
 Nineteenth Amendment, 528, 575
 Twenty-first Amendment, 575
United States Naval Academy. See Naval Academy.
University of Maryland, 303-05, 312, 390, 450, 479, 519, 528, 529, 542, 543, 548-50, 558, 564, 565, 582, 590
Upper Marlboro, 145, 332, 335, 356, 508, 566, 570
Utie, Colonel Nathaniel, 106, 121

Van Bokkelen, Dr. Libertus, 542, 548
Vásquez, de Ayllón, Lucas, 24
Veazey, Thomas, W., Gov. of Md., 352, 356, 357
Venango, Fort, 212
Verrazano, Giovanni da, 24
Vickers, George, 472
Virginia, Colony and State, 6, 7, 9, 11-3, 23, 26-31, 36-46, 51-5, 58, 60, 62, 63, 65, 78, 81, 83-5, 94-6, 98-103, 107, 112, 115-17, 120, 124, 125, 130, 132-35, 137, 146, 147, 149, 150, 153-56, 162, 163, 173, 178, 179, 185, 186, 188, 195, 197, 198, 202, 204, 213, 214, 217, 218, 220-22, 225, 238, 246, 250, 253, 258, 263, 267, 268, 271-74, 276, 277, 279-82, 284-87, 290, 292-97, 299, 306, 312, 320, 321, 323, 324, 332, 362, 363, 365-69, 372-74, 377, 382, 384, 386, 401, 403, 406, 415, 421, 425, 426, 428, 440, 443, 445-47, 449, 455, 456, 460, 461, 477, 494, 495, 504, 519, 561, 563, 569, 573, 574, 601
Virginia, Council, 41, 51-3, 55, 79
Virginia, House of Burgesses, 31, 41, 238
Vonderhorst, Harry, 557

Wagner, Jacob, 329, 330
Waldron, Resolved, 121

Index

Wallace, George, Gov. of Ala., 577
Wallace, General Lew, 455, 458
Wallis, Severn Teackle, 446, 450, 515, 554
Walters, Henry, 506
Walters, William T., 457, 552
Ward, The Reverend James Thomas, 549
Warfield, Edwin, Gov. of Md., 520
Warner, Daniel Bashiel, 431
Warren, Lieutenant Ratcliffe, 53
Warrior Mountain, 12
Warwick, Robert Rich, Earl of, 76
Washington, Brandywine and Point Lookout Railroad, 569
Washington College, 302-04, 548
Washington County, 11, 12, 257, 275, 286, 350, 353, 357, 408, 412, 556, 566, 601
Washington, D.C., 7, 11, 14, 17, 22, 23, 67, 193, 293, 294, 332, 333, 335-37, 347, 359, 366-68, 371, 372, 374, 385, 386, 392, 394, 395, 421, 426, 429, 430, 439, 444-46, 448, 449, 453, 455, 467, 473, 480, 487, 507, 526, 550-52, 561, 563, 566, 571, 574, 578, 595, 598-600, 603, 604
Washington, George, 7, 213, 214, 221, 226, 247, 262, 264, 265, 269, 276, 277, 282, 286, 292-94, 296, 298, 302, 309, 319-21, 323, 326, 360, 362, 363, 367, 418, 489, 564
Washington, Colonel John, 132
Watkin's Point, 38, 116
Watson, Mark S., 571
Wednesday Club, 556
Weems, Mason Locke ("Parson"), 309
Welch, William H., 551
Wellington, George L., 515, 516, 518
Wentworth, Thomas, Earl of Strafford, 74
Wesley, John, 306-08
West, Captain John, Gov. of Va., 53
West, Stephen, 189
Western Maryland College, 549, 550
Western Maryland Railway Company, 8, 386, 505, 561, 568, 591
Westernport, 13, 384
Westminster, 15, 386, 408, 549, 550
Westminster Theological Seminary, 550
Weston, Thomas, 51
West Virginia, 11, 12, 14, 205, 561, 574, 601

Weverton, 12
Wheeler, Dr. Charles, 204
Wheeling, Va., and W. Va., 364, 380, 382-84, 502
Whig Party, 347-53, 356, 358-60, 385, 407-09, 413-15, 417, 419, 420-22
Whisky Rebellion, 320
Whitbourne, Captain Richard, 36
White, Father Andrew, S.J., 22, 23, 42, 44-6, 50, 56, 66-8, 70, 71, 80
White, Jerome, 108
White, John, 27
Whittingham, William R., 466
Whyte, William Pinkney, Gov. of Md., 480, 488, 544
Wicomico County, 474
Wicomico Indians, 20, 47
Wicomico River, 15, 47, 110, 116, 145, 592
Wilkinson, The Reverend Christopher, 174
William and Mary, sovereigns of England, 137-39, 142, 143, 152, 154, 163, 177
William and Mary College, 149, 173
Williams, Colonel Otho Holland, 263
Williams, Eli, 366
Williams, Roger, 43, 89
Williamsburg, Va., 154, 216
Williamsport, 205, 292, 372-74, 386, 392
Wills Creek, 13, 213, 215-18, 370, 374
Wills Mountain, 12
Wilmington (Altona), Del., 120
Wilson, James, 284
Winchester, Va., 221
Winder, Levin, Gov. of Md., 331, 343, 586
Winder, General William Henry, 332
Winston's Island. See Kent Island.
Winthrop, John, Gov. of Mass., 31, 51, 94
Wintour, Frederick, 52
Wintour, Robert, 56, 57
Wirt, William, 305, 348, 349, 393, 450
Women's Christian Temperance Union, 486
Women's Suffrage, 527, 528
Woodstock, 11
Woodstock College, 310
Worcester County, 15, 227, 286, 331, 357, 395, 408, 409, 412, 428, 518, 580
Workingmen's Party, 484
Workmen's Compensation Laws, 522-25, 539

World War II, 6, 538, 561-72, 581, 591, 603
Worthington Valley, 557, 581, 595
Wye, River, 111
Wythe, George, 282

Yaocomico Indians, 20, 46, 48, 63, 65
Yeardley, George, Gov. of Va., 40
Yeo, The Reverend John, 114

York, Pa., 205, 291, 295
York River, Va., 30
Youghiogheny River, 13, 276, 362, 370
Young, Dr. Hugh, 551
Young, Captain Thomas, 52
Yvon, Pierre, 117

Zenger, John Peter, 152, 168
Zinzendorf, Count Nicholas Ludwig von, 208, 209